Third Edition

HOMELAND SECURITY

An Introduction to Principles and Practice

Third Edition

HOMELAND SECURITY

An Introduction to Principles and Practice

Charles P. Nemeth

CRC Press
Taylor & Francis Group
Boca Raton London New York

CRC Press is an imprint of the
Taylor & Francis Group, an **informa** business

CRC Press
Taylor & Francis Group
6000 Broken Sound Parkway NW, Suite 300
Boca Raton, FL 33487-2742

© 2017 by Taylor & Francis Group, LLC
CRC Press is an imprint of Taylor & Francis Group, an Informa business

No claim to original U.S. Government works

Printed on acid-free paper
Version Date: 20160823

International Standard Book Number-13: 978-1-4987-4909-1 (Hardback)

Library of Congress Cataloging-in-Publication Data

Names: Nemeth, Charles P., 1951- author.
Title: Homeland security : an introduction to principles and practice / by
Charles P. Nemeth.
Description: 3rd ed. | New York : Routledge, 2017. | Includes bibliographical
references and index.
Identifiers: LCCN 2016019574| ISBN 9781498749091 (cloth : alk. paper) | ISBN
9781498749107 (ebook)
Subjects: LCSH: United States. Department of Homeland Security. | National
security--United States. | Terrorism--United States--Prevention.
Classification: LCC HV6432.4 .N46 2017 | DDC 363.340973--dc23
LC record available at https://lccn.loc.gov/2016019574

**Visit the Taylor & Francis Web site at
http://www.taylorandfrancis.com**

**and the CRC Press Web site at
http://www.crcpress.com**

Printed and bound in the United States of America by Sheridan Books, Inc. (a Sheridan Group Company).

To Lt. Stephen Charles Nemeth, a Marine and a gentleman—the type of man who protects the nation and its homeland and the type of son and man who impresses each and every day.

To St. Thomas Aquinas who remarked:

Nothing hinders one act from having two effects, only one of which is intended, while the other is beside the intention. Now moral acts take their species according to what is intended, and not according to what is beside the intention, since this is accidental as explained above.

Accordingly the act of self-defense may have two effects, one is the saving of one's life, the other is the slaying of the aggressor. Therefore this act, since one's intention is to save one's own life, is not unlawful, seeing that it is natural to everything to keep itself in "being," as far as possible.

Summa Theologica II-II, Question 64, Article 7

Contents

Preface

This is a book about the very complex and highly bureaucratic world of Homeland Security. It is a humble attempt to give order to a mighty colossus of agencies and personnel dedicated to the protection of the homeland. At the commencement of this project, I never envisioned the "bigness" of the undertaking—the interweaving and entangling roles of people and departments and the sweep of the endeavor. Homeland Security, by any measure, is a massive enterprise that gets larger by the moment. Much of the growth arises from our understanding of things—what was once mostly a TSA/aircraft threat evolved into a multidimensional operation. While surely aircraft and passengers remain, the book makes plain that just about everything in life has a homeland quality to it. Whether it is food or water, military or private sector justice, or the border on land or sea, the task of protecting the homeland is a work in progress. Homeland Security extends its influence to all sectors of the economy, the business and corporate world, law enforcement and military branches, as well as communities, towns, and cities.

Chapter 1 provides a foundational look at how our present system emerged by looking at the history of security threats in the American experience. In particular, the chapter considers how the Cold War period shaped our present policy on the homeland front and, just as importantly, how domestic forms of terrorism edify the Department of Homeland Security (DHS) mindset and mentality. The protesters of the 1970s tell us much about the motive and method of terrorists, as does the KKK Klansman, the spy engaged in espionage, and the anti-government zealot seeking to topple the established order. This pre-9/11 perspective is critical to any contemporary understanding of the homeland system.

Chapter 2 sees the world in the prism of events leading up to 9/11 and the subsequent evolution of policy and practice after these cataclysmic events. It is clear that a security outlook existed before 9/11, although that vision would be forever altered after the attack on the Twin Towers. Soon after these horrid events, the reaction of government and policymakers was to erect an agency and systematic response to these types of tragedies. The chapter zeroes in on the original version of the DHS and its subsequent evolution and change. The DHS of 2002 was subject to many forces as leaders continuously sought more effective means of domestic protection. From 2003 onward, diverse governmental entities were swept into the environs of DHS, from the Coast Guard to the Secret Service. Exactly how those adjustments and alterations came about and how these actions impacted the safety of our nation are closely scrutinized.

Chapter 3 stresses the legal basis and foundation for DHS. Exactly what laws, executive orders, and rulemaking made DHS possible? What is the primary legislation that enabled DHS? What other acts or laws govern homeland practice? Specific coverage includes the Patriot Act and the Homeland Security Act as well as specialized promulgations that deal with identity, chemical facilities, and safety practice. The chapter also highlights the budgetary commitment of lawmakers entrusted with the defense of a nation. From 2001 to 2009, budgets reflect the urgency of policymakers and the central mission of DHS. The genealogy of the budget is keenly reviewed since the DHS's emphasis will shift and move dependent on new threats or a better understanding of earlier homeland principles.

The nature of risk and threat is fully examined in Chapter 4. What is risk? What is a threat? How is risk defined and calculated? What types of risk and threat exist—merely nuclear, biological, and chemical? Other coverage includes risk measuring systems such as CARVER. The chapter expends considerable energy evaluating and distinguishing the world of threats and risk. Threats take many forms, including man-made and natural varieties. Special attention is given to biological and chemical threats, including plague, ricin, nerve agents, and dirty bombs. Finally, the chapter highlights how computer breaches are a new form of security risk in the world of Homeland Security and how US-CERT and the National Cyber Security Division address these issues.

Chapter 5 introduces the reader to the world of training and preparatory exercises for the homeland professional. Within DHS resides a major infrastructure of offices dedicated to the funding and actual training for Homeland Security eventualities. Offices such as the Grants and Training, the Homeland Security Exercise and Evaluation Program (HSEEP), the Emergency Management Institute (EMI), and the Center for Domestic Preparedness are fully examined. Past security practices are evaluated within the DHS Lessons Learned program, which stores experiences and results from homeland protection policy and practice. The chapter ends with a comprehensive look at the National Incident Management System (NIMS), which provides guidance and an operational methodology for hospitals, educational institutions, and other entities seeking to prevent threats.

Chapter 6 assesses the operational demands evident in the world of Homeland Security. More specifically, the chapter gauges how states and localities, which are considered the frontline of Homeland Security, can work compatibly with federal policymakers. A highly successful example of this cooperative mentality can be discovered in the funding mechanism for homeland grants and training allotments as well as the regional Fusion Centers that feed state and local information to the larger federal system. In addition, the chapter evaluates the fine line between civilian homeland function and that historically and contemporaneously assumed by the nation's military infrastructure. How do the various offices of intelligence in the military model share with DHS? Are the agencies and functions properly aligned? The chapter ends with a look at specialized entities and agencies that support the role and work of states and localities as these governmental authorities seek to advance the mission of DHS.

Chapter 7 targets the Federal Emergency Management Agency (FEMA) in both the pre- and post-9/11 world. Of all the agencies undergoing a transformation in mission and purpose since 9/11, none has been as dramatic as FEMA. FEMA has transformed itself from an agency dedicated to natural disaster to one concerned with the functions and tactics of response and recovery. The chapter examines the National Response Framework that provides protocol steps in the event of natural or man-made disasters and poses many examples of the agency's educational and mitigation function that prevents the full effect of disasters.

Chapter 8 delves into the world of intelligence. Aside from its definition and methodology, the stress is on the agencies and entities entrusted with intelligence analysis. Special attention is given to the FBI and its Joint Terrorism Task Forces and the CIA, whose various Directorates aid DHS in its overall mission. The CIA's Directorates on Intelligence, Clandestine Activities, Science and Technology, and Support make major contributions to intelligence practice in the world of Homeland Security. On top of this, the chapter provides a summary review of the Defense Intelligence Agency and its intelligence functions and the role of the Office of the Director of National Intelligence, which seeks to be a central repository for intelligence gathering across all government agencies.

The subject of border security, immigration, and U.S. citizenship makes up the bulk of Chapter 9. At the border, there are many challenges and corresponding methodologies to control access. Way beyond fencing alone, the newly developed Customs and Border Patrol (CBP) tackles myriad tasks involving violations of our border integrity. By air and boat, by foot and vehicle, the CBP tracks and traces encroachments. The CBP's involvement with cargo and containers is featured. The last portion of the chapter deals with citizenship and immigration issues, including an assessment of Project Shield, the US-VISIT program, and the Cornerstone Initiative.

The vast expanse of homeland practice in the airline industry comprises a major portion of Chapter 10. In immediate reaction to the Twin Towers attack, DHS set about to establish a series of programs and protocols involving both personnel and equipment. The Transportation Security Agency (TSA) is the center of the activities. Added to their functions would be the federal air marshals, armed officers aboard flights, and the federal flight deck officer program. Using specialized equipment, such as trace portals and biometrics, TSA has been advancing technology across its many duties and responsibilities. How Homeland Security practices play out in the maritime world receives considerable attention. From emergency to safety practice, from cargo to ports, the chapter deals with the diverse functions of the U.S. Coast Guard—a crucial player in the world of maritime security. Lastly, the chapter covers how real and mass transit systems must be attentive to homeland demands and features national, regional, and local rail systems.

The interplay between public health and Homeland Security is the chief focus of Chapter 11. Terrorists' threats are meaningful to the world's food and water supply. So, too, are the potential harms that can arise from contaminated livestock and poultry. Second, infectious diseases pose an extraordinary threat to the community from a security perspective. How DHS stores antidotes and other medical remedies receives serious attention. A close examination of the National Pharmaceutical Stockpile is part of the chapter's approach, and how a pandemic might impact both individuals and the collective is fully critiqued. Planning documents that address pandemic threats are provided.

The final chapter of the book summarizes a few of the challenges inherent in the task and the natural bureaucracy that emerges in the war on terror. DHS clearly is a work in progress and already has a lively history of change. Some examples of this critical inquiry are: Does DHS grow rationally? Does the mission of DHS match its organizational structure? Has DHS become overly bureaucratic, politically correct, and out of touch? Are the practices of DHS too centralized? Has technology been effectively integrated into the practices of DHS? Are policymakers in DHS too entrenched to think creatively, or is there a need to think outside normal channels? In the end, I have tried to capture the structure and intent of DHS. The question of what DHS really is may be more metaphysical than we think. All of us can concur on its intent—to make the nation safe. But although we are sure of its intent, it may take a generation or two before we really understand how to shape and construct DHS. Indeed, DHS is an idea on not only a righteous path but also the beginnings of a solid foundation.

Acknowledgments

The sheer volume of DHS material and content makes this a project that heavily depends on others. To be sure, I could not have authored this alone. Instead, I was heavily dependent on the skill and acumen of colleagues.

To Hope Haywood, my thanks again. I cannot envision being ever able to coordinate this maze of concepts and ideas. In this edition, and all the others, her orchestration of details really leaves me breathless and fully cognizant that these projects would not come to fruition without people like Hope. She is a master Editor.

To CRC Press, I appreciate the opportunity. Editor Mark Listewnik continues his accessible approach and displays a partnership mentality more than one who merely critiques. Always open to suggestions and forever knowledgeable about our academic discipline and the industry and constituencies we serve, Mark's editorial approach is unrivaled.

As I enter my 5th year of service at John Jay College, I am forever mindful of my good fortune to labor with academic-scholars and practitioners who engage the system in ways most colleges can only imagine. In addition, I am blessed with excellent departmental colleagues who are supportive and collegial. Lastly, I am continually thankful that John Jay provides resources for scholarship, and this prioritization is largely the result of the leadership of our Provost Dr. Jane Bowers and our President Jeremy Travis.

Part of the John Jay support system relates to the ease in which graduate students are encouraged to work closely with faculty on these types of projects. HS 3rd was blessed to engage Jennifer Bencivenga as a research assistant as she completes her master's studies. Jennifer's talents were evident from my first day of engagement. With a precise eye and a dedication to doing things with the highest professionalism, Jennifer's contribution to this textbook can only be described as significant. I am deeply appreciative.

At home, my blessings simply cannot be counted, for it is family who drives most of what I do. If I leave any legacy to my spouse and closest friend, Jean Marie, and my seven children, it is that their father loved them.

Charles P. Nemeth, JD, PhD, LLM
Chair and Professor, Security, Fire and Emergency

Author

Charles P. Nemeth, chair and professor of security, fire and emergency management at John Jay College, New York, has spent the vast majority of his professional life in the study and practice of law and justice, the role of private sector justice in a free society, and the ethical demands on justice professionals. A recognized expert on ethics and the legal system, appellate legal practice, and private-sector justice, he also is a prolific writer, having published numerous texts and articles on law and justice throughout his impressive career. His most recent works include these titles: *Private Security and the Investigative Process 3rd* (CRC Press, 2010), *Private Security and the Law*, 4th Edition (Elsevier, 2012), with a 5th edition (CRC Press, 2017), *Cicero and Aquinas: A Comparative Analysis of Nature and the Natural Law* (Bloomsbury Press, 2017), *Aquinas and King: A Discourse on Civil Disobedience* (Carolina Academic Press, 2010), *Aquinas and Crime* (St. Augustine's Press, 2009), *Criminal Law* (Prentice Hall, 2003; CRC Press, 2011), *Law & Evidence: A Primer for Criminal Justice, Criminology, Law, and Legal Studies* (Prentice Hall, 2001; Jones and Bartlett, 2010), *Aquinas in the Courtroom* (Greenwood and Praeger Publishing, 2001), *Private Sector and Public Safety: A Community Based Approach* (Prentice Hall, 2005), *The Prevention Agency* (California University of Pennsylvania Press—Institute for Law and Public Policy, 2005), and *The Paralegal Resource Manual* (McGraw-Hill, 2008).

An educator for more than 35 years, Dr. Nemeth's distinctive career is a blend of both practice and theory. A member of the Pennsylvania, New York, and North Carolina bars, Dr. Nemeth has extensive experience in all aspects of criminal and civil practice.

His previous academic appointments include Niagara University (1977–1980), the University of Baltimore (1980–1981), Glassboro State College (1981–1986), Waynesburg College (1988–1998), the State University of New York at Brockport (1998–2003), and California University of Pennsylvania (2000–2012). He is a much sought-after legal consultant for security companies on the trend of privatization, and he is a recognized scholar on issues involving law and morality and how ethics relates to the professions.

Introduction

The term "Homeland Security" is of recent invention. For the bulk of this nation's glorious history, the view that security was inexorably and inevitably tied to the homeland itself was a foreign notion. Surely, the nation always had a continuous interest in the protection of its borders from invasion, and just as assuredly, the nation and its states were perpetually concerned with the protection of the citizenry from natural disasters. To be certain, the idea that government has an obligation to protect and safeguard the citizenry is nothing new under the sun. Yet despite this penchant for safeguarding the general population, protection of the homeland took on a very different meaning in the year 2001. The world changed in more ways than we could have ever envisioned as the attacks on the Twin Towers and the Pentagon unfolded. From September 11, 2001 onward, the world will perceive the idea, the notion of security, and the homeland in a unique and very different way. Homeland Security will be referred to as a "New National Calling."[1] In *Securing the Homeland: Strengthening the Nation*, President George W. Bush exhorts the citizenry to remember this new vocation:

> The higher priority we all now attach to homeland security has already begun to ripple through the land. The Government of the United States has no more important mission than fighting terrorism overseas and securing the homeland from future terrorist attacks. This effort will involve major new programs and significant reforms by the Federal government. But it will also involve new or expanded efforts by State and local governments, private industry, non-governmental organizations, and citizens. By working together we will make our homeland more secure.[2]

Before 9/11, terrorism was surely one of many variables considered in the planning and implementation of national security. After 9/11 it became the predominant and preeminent criteria in the war on terror and a national fixation in most facets of the public domain.

Notes

1. President George W. Bush, *Securing the Homeland: Strengthening the Nation* (Washington, DC: U.S. Government Printing Office, 2002), 3.
2. Bush, *Securing the Homeland*, 3

Chapter 1

The Idea and Origin of Homeland Security

Objectives

1. To identify major twentieth- and twenty-first-century events, both domestic and international, that formed the United States' current policy position on homeland security
2. To comprehend that war, by its very nature, its military tactics and strategies, and governmental policies, relies on forms of terror to meet its goals
3. To analyze the effect the Cold War had on shaping Americans' notions of terror and to understand the evolution of the government's policy responses
4. To describe the domestic events of the turbulent 1960s and 1970s to shed light on the country's response to domestic terrorism as well as gain an understanding of the unique motivations of the domestic terrorist
5. To differentiate the motives of the international terrorist from the domestic terrorist and comprehend that although the methods may be the same, the motivations differ
6. To explain the unique motivations of the jihadist by exploring attacks against U.S. military targets and discover the motivations leading up to the events of 9/11
7. To evaluate specific international terror incidents against U.S. installations prior to 9/11 to gain an understanding of the jihadist mentality that led up to the terror attacks against the Twin Towers and the Pentagon
8. To identify specific domestic terror attacks, such as those perpetuated by Timothy McVeigh and Ted Kaczynski, in light of the effect these types of attacks have on national security policy

1.1 Introduction

The concept of a threat to the homeland has historically taken many shapes. Terror and the terrorist are not new phenomena—they are a construction of the ages, seen throughout history in various guises. In recent years, the country has focused on domestic security and preventing acts of terrorism. Couple this perspective with a predictable national desire to protect one's homeland, and nothing here is unexpected. What is of greater utility in the discussion of security of the homeland will be how we arrived at our current position. Specifically, what did we do before the jihadist? What types of terror attacks did America experience? What motivated the terrorist? For example, the Ku Klux Klansman is hardly a jihadist, although his methods may be just as dastardly. How do we reconcile that difference? What of the military dictator, the tyrant, the leader who leads his country to ruin and grounds his enterprise on hate, such as the leader of the Third Reich? This too is terror by any reasonable definition. Terror is nothing new.

The acts of the terrorist have been with us since the dawn of recorded history. It is important to keep this in context in our interpretation of history. This chapter traces a whole host of acts and movements in the twentieth century that preceded the events of 9/11. All of the examples covered illuminate how and why terrorists do what they do. All of these illustrations, from the military machine that oppresses people and states to the Weathermen who sabotage government installations, help to bring perspective to the discussion. When one scrutinizes the diversity of these acts and approaches, one can better understand the landscape of modern terrorism in a post-9/11 world.

1.2 Threats to the Homeland: Twentieth-Century Military Movements

While much can be written about the nature of threat and violence throughout U.S. history, it would appear that the best place to start in order to understand modern-day terrorism is the twentieth century—a century with complex conflicts and territorial challenges. From World War I (WWI) to World War II (WWII), the concept of threats to the homeland was largely the result of country-to-country conquests, political disagreements, and imperial empire building. For example, the Third Reich's move across the Polish frontier, in the name of the reclamation of Aryan races under the thumb of the Polish authorities, is a land grab with a eugenic flavor. This is a very different kind of threat from that currently considered by the Department of Homeland Security. Yet, these wars and conflicts serve as an appropriate backdrop for the way any nation seeks to maintain its territorial integrity. In a sense, the planes attacking the World Trade Center buildings were an assault on the country's sovereignty not unlike the way the German troops crossed into the Sudetenland (Figure 1.1).

The means and motivation are clearly different, though the net effect is not completely dissimilar. The Nazi onslaught of WWII was, in a sense, the largest whole-scale terror campaign ever inflicted on a continent (Figure 1.2).

Aside from this illegal and unjustified sweep of countries, Germany culminated its terror by implementing its Final Solution, its programs of extermination of Jews and all forms

FIGURE 1.1 German troops goose step through Warsaw, Poland, during the 1939 invasion that saw Poland fall within three weeks. The invasion caused Britain and France to declare war on Germany. (From: National Archives, image 200-SFF-52.)

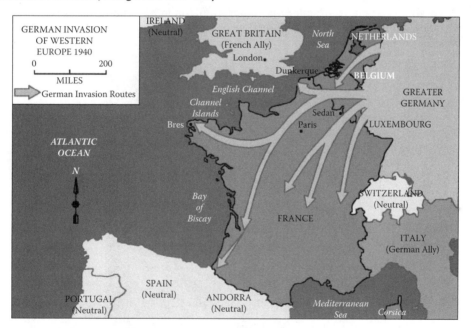

FIGURE 1.2 From Poland to Stalingrad, from Holland to Northern Africa, the propaganda of the Third Reich was a campaign that terrorized the entire civilized world. (Courtesy of the U.S. Holocaust Museum, Washington, DC.)

of resisters, of the mentally disabled, the old and infirm, of Catholic priests and Lutheran ministers. More than six million human beings perished under the crush of an evil state (Figure 1.3).

That the Nazi regime engaged in deliberate, intentional threats against whole races, ethnic types, and classifications of citizens is a self-evident conclusion when the historical record is scratched just a little. The systematic extermination program was the subject of endless meetings and conferences, though admittedly the Nazi leaders were quite effective in removing the paper trail. In 1942, at what was billed as the Wannsee Conference, the

FIGURE 1.3 A survivor stokes smoldering human remains in a crematorium oven that is still lit, Dachau, Germany, April 29–May 1, 1945. (Courtesy of the U.S. Holocaust Museum, Washington, DC.)

FIGURE 1.4 Reinhard Heydrich, chief of the SD (Security Service) and Nazi governor of Bohemia and Moravia. Place uncertain, 1942. (From: National Archives and Records Administration, College Park, MD.)

leadership of the Schutzstaffel (SS) and the Nazi and other aligned government entities met to discuss the efficacy and corresponding efficiencies of mass extermination. Leading the charge calling for the physical extermination of millions was SS officer Reinhard Heydrich (Figure 1.4).

The bureaucratic apparatus was coupled with legions of resources, from transportation to the building of crematoria. The task of moving millions of people to their own deaths

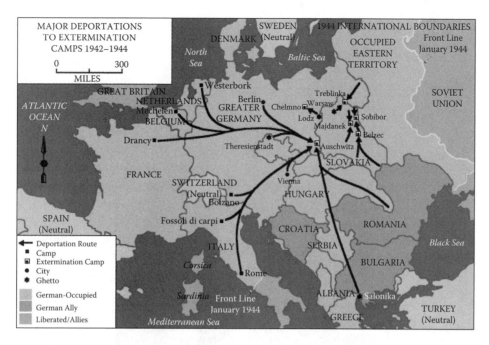

FIGURE 1.5   The Germans attempted to disguise their intentions, referring to deportations as "resettlement to the east." The victims were told they were to be taken to labor camps, but in reality, from 1942 onward, deportation for most Jews meant transit to killing centers and then death. (Courtesy of the U.S Holocaust Museum, Washington, DC.)

required extraordinary efforts by the captains of industry. Consider the complexities of rail movement alone as portrayed in Figure 1.5.

Similar arguments about Japanese imperialism can be posited, and for good reason. The Japanese intent was to dominate and rule the world using means far outside the mainstream of modern warfare. The survivors of the Japanese occupation of the Philippines or of Japan's own concentration camps tell a story of brutality and degradation that seems inexplicable when one considers the modern democratic state of Japan. The notorious Unit 731 on the Japanese mainland witnessed forced sterilization, castration, live burial, vivisection, mutilation, and mass experimentation (Figure 1.6).

Internet Exercise: Visit the National Archives collection, which catalogs Japanese war crimes in WWII at http://www.archives.gov/iwg/japanese-war-crimes/select-documents.pdf.

None of these atrocities can be adequately covered in a text on homeland security, although it is critical that the reader understands that war, by its very nature, depends on terror to some extent. Whether it is the summary execution of civilians and prisoners of war or the indiscriminate bombing of wholesale populations, terror is both an end and a by-product of war. Much of what we witness in the terror battlefield today connects its heritage to the makings and doings of war. By way of illustration, Saddam Hussein thought Joseph Stalin—one of history's most remarkable figures—was to be envied and copied in his approach. In this way, a look at twentieth-century conflicts can illuminate the rationale behind the tactics used by terrorists.

FIGURE 1.6 Camp 731 beheading an American POW. (Courtesy of the University of Minnesota, Center for the Study of Holocaust and Genocide Studies.)

1.3 Threats to the Homeland: The Cold War Experience

At the end of the conflagration known as WWII, another conflict of a very different sort emerged—the Cold War. As the victors of WWII set out to fashion a new Europe and continental framework, the Allies saw the world in distinct and sometimes incompatible ways. For sure, Britain and the United States shared the core values of freedom and democratic, republican principles. By contrast was the starkly divisive approach of our Russian ally, whose Trotskyite–Leninist revolutionary mind-set was fundamentally at odds with Western ideals. The Russian mind-set struck directly at the heart of free societies. At the end of the war, during the Potsdam Convention, Russia's expansionist desires clearly won the day (Figure 1.7).

Dividing up countries such as Germany and replacing the system in free democratic or monarchical countries such as Poland and Hungary with a Soviet-style socialist model, the Russian Bear flexed extraordinary muscle immediately after the end of the conflict. Concession after concession was made to the Soviet demand, much to the distress of Winston Churchill.

In response, Churchill ultimately sounded a clarion call for halting the expansion of the Soviet empire in one of his finest speeches.[1]

FIGURE 1.7 **Churchill, Truman, and Stalin during the Potsdam Convention. (Courtesy of the Truman Library.)**

I have a strong admiration and regard for the valiant Russian people and for my wartime comrade, Marshal Stalin. There is deep sympathy and goodwill in Britain—and I doubt not here also—toward the peoples of all the Russias and a resolve to persevere through many differences and rebuffs in establishing lasting friendships.

It is my duty, however, to place before you certain facts about the present position in Europe.

From Stettin in the Baltic to Trieste in the Adriatic an iron curtain has descended across the Continent. Behind that line lie all the capitals of the ancient states of Central and Eastern Europe. Warsaw, Berlin, Prague, Vienna, Budapest, Belgrade, Bucharest and Sofia; all these famous cities and the populations around them lie in what I must call the Soviet sphere, and all are subject, in one form or another, not only to Soviet influence but to a very high and in some cases increasing measure of control from Moscow.

Internet Exercise: To read Churchill's entire speech, titled "The Sinews of Peace," visit http://www.nato.int/docu/speech/1946/S460305a_e.htm.

By 1946, Churchill knew full well that a geopolitical shift was underway. In appealing to the United States, he urged its government to consider its many sacrifices of men and material and to envision a world where an "iron curtain" would split the free from the oppressed. He argued that the legacy of the sacrifice must amount to more than an iron wall between the totalitarian and the democratic. But this is exactly what was unfolding and with frightening speed—a new world order divided in two and directly at odds with one another. Hence, a new war emerged—one not fought on the battlefield but in the sphere of territorial conquest and subliminal and direct attempts to destroy either side. This is the stuff of the Cold War, and it escalated very quickly. The United States quickly recognized these expansionist motivations. And this sort of expansionist mentality is nothing new nor has it evaporated from the current terror scene. The Islamic State of Iraq and Syria (ISIS), the contemporary Islamic state group, also known as the Islamic State of Iraq and the Levant (ISIL), operates on the basis of a similar mentality.[2]

Internet Exercise: Read President Harry Truman's Secretary of State Keenan's letter to General George C. Marshall for his prescient commentary on an upcoming Cold War at www.trumanlibrary.org. Click on *Documents* in the main menu, then on *Cold War* under "Online Documents," then on *Documents*. Locate the January 29, 1946, telegram from George Kennan to James Byrnes.

The Cold War is not an illusory war by any means but one with significant military and political consequences. By 1947, the Soviet Union commenced the construction of the Berlin Wall—separating the East from the West and trapping East Berlin in a dark, communist world. Ever the expansionist, the Soviet Union boldly expanded its sphere of influence into countries such as Iran.

In the wake of these actions, President Harry Truman discerned a meaningful and bona fide threat to free peoples. As a result, he made plain that the United States would not sit idly by while Soviet aggression spread throughout the world. In 1947, Truman enunciated what is now known as the Truman doctrine. With the Truman doctrine, President Truman established that the United States would provide political, military, and economic assistance to all democratic nations under threat from external or internal authoritarian forces. The Truman doctrine effectively reoriented U.S. foreign policy, guiding it away from the usual stance of withdrawal from regional conflicts not directly involving the United States to one of possible intervention in faraway conflicts.

Internet Exercise: Read President Truman's diary, written in 1947, to get some sense of the threat the country was experiencing at the time: http://www.trumanlibrary.org/diary/index.html. In light of the Soviet Union's development of an atomic bomb in 1949, the doctrine was never more important to fend off threats to our national security. See Figure 1.8 for a time line of the Cold War to the point of Soviet nuclear power.

1945–1946: Creation of Eastern European People's Republics
1946: George Kennan's Long Telegram and the Policy of Containment
1946: Churchill's Iron Curtain Speech
1946: Soviet Troops in Iran
1947: Truman Doctrine
1947: U.S. Efforts to Control Atomic Energy
1947: Marshall's Offer of Economic Assistance
1948–1949: Berlin Airlift
1949: North Atlantic Treaty Organization
1949: Creation of the two Germanys
1949: Soviet Atomic Bomb

FIGURE 1.8 Time line of the Cold War: 1945–1949.

FIGURE 1.9 Berlin Airlift at Templehof Airport. (Courtesy of the Truman Library.)

With the emergence of the Cold War, relations between the Western nations and the Soviet Union spiraled in a downward fashion for years afterward. The first major test of this tension was manifest in the Berlin Airlift of 1948–1949, when supplies for beleaguered Germans were dropped daily, over objections from Soviet officials who had set up blockades to thwart delivery of much needed supplies. The Soviets also closed roads and forbade movement from one sector of the city of Berlin to the other. The western edge of Berlin largely remained in American/British hands, while the smaller northeastern portion of Germany remained Soviet. The Soviets were figuratively choking the people of Berlin. U.S. C-47s began a mass supply line to overcome this obstacle. The planes flew in three major corridors toward the city (Figure 1.9).

When the Soviet Union entered into a treaty with China, the geopolitical framework of the world stood on its historic head. As Soviet expansionism marched onward, the United States felt obliged to "save" free peoples or, when the nations were not all that free, to keep the flow of communism to a bare minimum.

Throughout the 1950s, the problems associated with the Cold War worsened. Nuclear proliferation, uprisings in Soviet-dominated countries, human rights violations without precedent, and a host of other evils heaped on unwilling populations—all signify the tragedy and the worst elements of communism in practice. The major events of the Cold War during the 1950s are outlined in Figure 1.10.

Of course, the Truman doctrine was cited in the Korean War, the Cuban Missile Crisis, and the Vietnam War. When President Kennedy confronted the Soviet government for its dispatch of long-range missiles to Cuba (Figure 1.11), the justification was the containment theory, the right of the Western hemisphere to be safe from this corrupt hegemony, and the insistence of Harry Truman that free peoples need not tolerate this political oppression.

Each of these unofficial wars was, at least in a legislative sense, an effort to contain the "threat" of communist takeover. Throughout the 1960s and 1970s and into the early 1980s, the two opposing giants in the Soviet and American systems remained entrenched. Nuclear proliferation continued unabated. A lack of trust and cooperation remained standard

1950: Sino-Soviet Treaty
1950: NSC-68
1950–1953: Korean War
1952: U.S. Hydrogen Bomb
1953: Stalin's Death
1953: Soviet Hydrogen Bomb
1954: Atomic Energy Act
1955: Creation of the Warsaw Pact
1955: Austrian State Treaty
1955: Big Four Geneva Summit
1956: Twentieth Congress of Soviet Communist Party
1956: Polish Uprising
1956: Suez Crisis
1956: Hungarian Uprising
1957–1958: Sputnik and the Space Race
1958: Suspension of Nuclear Tests
1958: Khrushchev's Berlin Demands
1959: Khrushchev Visits the United States
1959: Khrushchev-Eisenhower Meeting at Camp David
1959: Antarctic Treaty

FIGURE 1.10 The Timeline of The Cold War: 1950–1959.

FIGURE 1.11   U-2 reconnaissance photo showing concrete evidence of missile assembly in Cuba. Shown here are missile transporters and missile-ready tents where fueling and maintenance took place. (Courtesy of the CIA.)

operating procedures. Spy agencies, such as the Central Intelligence Agency (CIA) and the Soviet Committee for State Security, the KGB, spent most of their energy engaged in the activities and efforts of the Cold War.

When President Richard Nixon visited China in 1972 (Figure 1.12), a tectonic shift occurred in the Cold War. Nixon had brilliantly undercut the Sino-Soviet cooperation that had appeared impenetrable for so many generations. Nixon made possible a new vision of cooperation on missile deployment, cultural exchange, and foreign relations.

From this point onward, the Soviet system would be isolated and suffered internally from decades of misplaced investment in the military model over any other benefit for its people.

FIGURE 1.12   President and Mrs. Nixon visit the Great Wall of China and the Ming tombs, February 24, 1972. (Courtesy of the National Archives.)

The Soviet system was crumbling from within. By the time of President Ronald Reagan, the time was ripe for an end to the intolerable Cold War (Figure 1.13).

Reagan was an unabashed believer in the American way of life. He showed diplomacy in the background of negotiations and protocol, but publically there was no greater critic of the Soviet system. On March 8, 1983, when he labeled the Soviet state an "evil empire," critics charged him with sensationalism. Those who supported Reagan felt that he was defending the notion of freedom, believing that any government that dominated and oppressed its people was unjust in the eyes of history and its people. He was a strong proponent for the elimination of communism and, in particular, the Soviet-style system.

Prescient in his position on Soviet-style communism and his belief that it would ultimately fall, he remarked:

In the 1950s, Khrushchev predicted: "We will bury you." But in the West today, we see a free world that has achieved a level of prosperity and well-being unprecedented in all human history. In the Communist world, we see failure, technological backwardness, declining standards of health, even want of the most basic kind—too little food. Even today, the Soviet Union still cannot feed itself. After these four decades, then, there stands before the entire world one great and inescapable conclusion: Freedom leads to prosperity. Freedom replaces the ancient hatreds among the nations with comity and peace. Freedom is the victor.

And now the Soviets themselves may, in a limited way, be coming to understand the importance of freedom. We hear much from Moscow about a new policy of reform and openness.

FIGURE 1.13 Ronald Reagan at the Brandenburg Gate, Berlin, Germany, June 12, 1987. (Courtesy of the Ronald Reagan Library.)

Some political prisoners have been released. Certain foreign news broadcasts are no longer being jammed. Some economic enterprises have been permitted to operate with greater freedom from state control.[3]

Reagan was often labeled a dreamer, an idealist lacking common sense, and worst of all, an "actor." However, while no administration is perfect, he was consistent in his approach. Ultimately, it was his interpersonal skill and relationship with Mikhail Gorbachev that set the stage for much that followed—among other things, the fall of the Berlin Wall and, subsequently, an end to the Cold War. The threats that had generated so much fear were replaced with cautious friendship. There is something to be learned from this episode in history. Just as the Russians were deemed the ultimate threat to the United States, so too is the terrorist extremist currently considered the most immediate threat.

To be sure, both have been at the forefront of our national security over the years. What we do know is that enemies are not permanent stations. They are subject to change. Experts at the time would never have imagined the United States and Russia having closer ties and working together. Yet, the two countries have taken many diplomatic strides, though it is too early to tell with the current political leaders in Russia with the re-emergence of Vladimir Putin. Putin is often referred to as Russia's strongman, and he works arduously to develop this caricature among his countrymen.[4] Putin has been vocal and transparent in many of his efforts to consolidate power, although Russia is not the nation once ruled by the KGB but a populace that has tasted some aspects of a free society. The mass demonstrations of December 2011 say much about a Russian political system evolving (Figure 1.14).

While only time will tell in the matter of Russian political processes, it is a safe bet that once the citizenry experiences a bit of freedom, there will be no going back. It seems the prospect of improved Russian-U.S. relations appears on hold at present. There is Russia's

FIGURE 1.14 Demonstrators hold Russian opposition flags during a rally protesting against election fraud in Moscow, Saturday, December 24, 2011. (From: Massive Russian protest poses growing challenge to Putin. James Brooke, Voice of America website http://www.voanews.com/content/article---new-anti-election-fraud-protests-begin-in-moscow----136180068/149907.html)

military intervention in the Ukraine. Current foreign policy decisions regarding the Middle East, especially in regard to Syria, were once thought to be a door opener for better relations.[5] Unfortunately, in Syria, U.S. hesitancy to get involved coupled with Russian intervention has triggered the possibility of a new cold era. The Iran nuclear agreement and the Russian–Iranian partnership have also fueled tension, along with rising distrust. Other Middle Eastern countries, such as Egypt and Jordan, may provide better avenues for reconciliation, but there is little doubt that the U.S. brand has suffered setbacks in some corners of the Middle East in recent years under the Obama administration.[6]

1.4 Threats to the Homeland: Revolution, Riot, and Rightful Demonstration

There is little doubt that the concept of terror resounded across the American landscape from the nineteenth century onward.[7] From the Black Panthers to the Ku Klux Klan (KKK), from the Workers Party to communist agitators, from Students for a Democratic Society (SDS) to the Weathermen of the Vietnam era, the concept of terror against governing authority was entrenched in the political and social fabric of these organizations (Figure 1.15).

The internal urban violence of the 1960s, triggered and prompted by generations of inequality and injustice, caused law enforcement not only to challenge its historic reactions to public protest but also to see that "enemies" or antagonists of the government may actually be operating from a higher moral plane. The protests could also not be universally condemned because some were plainly justified. Certainly, the entire movement sparked by Dr. Martin Luther King Jr. challenged the status quo of police power and the remediation

FIGURE 1.15 Public protest against the Vietnam War (From: U.S. Marshal's Service, Pentagon Riot of October 21, 1967.)

of injustice. Then too, those operating without moral advantage—groups such as the KKK or the SDS—posed real and meaningful threats against the internal security of the country by their egregious actions. In a sense, both lawful and unlawful protests shaped how the justice model reacted to protest and terror.

For example, during the Nixon era, ordinary citizens were perceived as troublemakers and seditionists for any protest to the policies of the president. Much has been written about the insular and almost paranoid perceptions of Nixon insiders as that government sought to squelch public protest concerning the war in Vietnam.[8]

Enemies of the state came in many shapes and sizes, some deserving of that name and others not. In the midst of this era, the FBI posted its list of groups that were allegedly anti-American in design.[9] During this exceptionally turbulent time, politicians, government officials, and law-enforcement professionals perceived events as a threat to our democratic process.

Internet Exercise: Read about the Weathermen, a subversive antiwar, antigovernment, and anticapitalist entity active all through the late 1960s–1980s at http://www.pbs.org/independentlens/weatherunderground/movement.html.

Throughout the centuries, even up to the present day, we can see that terror has been a tool for those wishing to maintain the status quo as well as those wishing revolution. Hence, it is imperative to remember that the American justice policy has had an historic understanding and relationship with terror throughout most of its history. These acts of terror can be broken down into two essential categories: international and domestic.

Since the early 1960s, the threat of terror has sought to disrupt world economies, overthrow political structures, annihilate religious competitors, and assault value systems considered antagonistic to a perverted worldview. For most of the past 60 years, terror has been

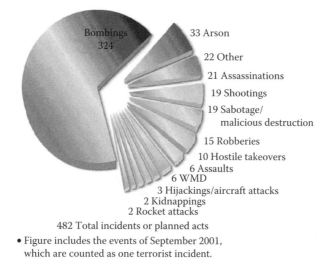

Bombings
324

33 Arson

22 Other

21 Assassinations

19 Shootings

19 Sabotage/
malicious destruction

15 Robberies

10 Hostile takeovers
6 Assaults
6 WMD
3 Hijackings/aircraft attacks
2 Kidnappings
2 Rocket attacks

482 Total incidents or planned acts

• Figure includes the events of September 2001,
which are counted as one terrorist incident.

FIGURE 1.16   Amount of terroristic activities by type of event, 1980–2001.

on the radar screen. Figure 1.16[10] lays out the full scope of terror activities, from bombings to the use of weapons of mass destruction.

1.4.1 Domestic Terrorism: Pre-9/11

Domestic terrorism is considered that which is perpetrated by U.S. nationals and not the product of fringe Islamic extremists or jihadists. Terrorists can equally come from disenfranchised citizens, hate groups, or other extreme wings within the country. There have been some consistent players in terror activities across the American landscape, and surely the KKK fits the bill of consistency. Political upheaval and radical social change by any means whatsoever appropriately describe the KKK's agenda. For the KKK, terror was central to the mission of the rabid segregationist and promoter of inequality. Historic harassment and lynchings have been replaced by slick media and membership campaigns. Their official website, the "Official Knights Party of the KKK,"[11] chastises those who see cross burnings as acts of terror and refers to the burnings as a theological exhortation. Regardless of the terrorist's mind-set or rationale, history makes clear the motivation behind the tactics.

Information on the Christian cross lighting ceremony is available from the Ku Klux Klan's website at: http://www.kkk.bz/cross.htm.

Domestic terror before the events of 9/11 occurred in a somewhat narrower or localized model, in that the motive for attack was often not on a global scale. Just as the Klansman cares little for what is beyond his or her myopic racism, the student radical, wishing the overthrow of the military complex, cannot see things in global terms. The student radical concludes that a group or a few assembled might wish to publicize their claims in every imaginable way—violence being among its approaches. This was the stuff of the

FIGURE 1.17   Weather Underground leaders John Jacobs (center) and Terry Robbins (right) at the Days of Rage protest march, Chicago, October 1969.

Weathermen—they found banks a legitimate and moral target for destruction in order that a war might end (Figure 1.17).

These operatives see the world in more myopic terms since it is the foundation of their movement that unites them and drives their relationship. In no sense does one justify the actions of the Black Panthers or the Weathermen. This merely demonstrates that a differing worldview exists when compared with the jihadist who ultimately desires the radical reconstruction of the entire planet, and the creation of a caliphate, while imposing a particular religious ideology and zealotry.

1975 TERRORISM FLASHBACK: STATE DEPARTMENT BOMBING

01/29/04

Twenty-nine years ago Thursday, an explosion rocked the headquarters of the U.S. State Department in Washington, D.C. No one was hurt, but the damage was extensive, impacting 20 offices on three separate floors. Hours later, another bomb was found at a military induction center in Oakland, California, and safely detonated. A domestic terrorist group called the Weather Underground claimed responsibility. Remember them?

Who were these extremists? The Weather Underground—originally called the Weathermen, taken from a line in a Bob Dylan song—was a small, violent offshoot of the SDS, created in the turbulent 1960s to promote social change.

When the SDS collapsed in 1969, the Weather Underground stepped forward, inspired by communist ideologies and embracing violence and crime as a way to protest the Vietnam War, racism, and other left-wing aims. "Our intention is to disrupt the empire … to incapacitate it, to put pressure on the cracks," claimed the group's 1974 manifesto, *Prairie Fire*. By the next year, the group had claimed credit for 25 bombings and would be involved in many more over the next several years.

The Chase. The Federal Bureau of Investigation (FBI) doggedly pursued these terrorists as their attacks mounted. Many members were soon identified, but their small numbers and guerilla tactics helped them hide under assumed identities. In 1978, however, the bureau arrested five members who were plotting to bomb a politician's office. More were arrested when an accident destroyed the group's bomb factory in Hoboken, New Jersey. Others were identified after two policemen and a Brinks driver were murdered in a botched armored car robbery in Nanuet, New York.

Success for the FBI/New York Police Department (NYPD) Task Force. Key to disrupting the group for good was the newly created FBI–New York City Police Anti-Terrorist Task Force. It brought together the strengths of both organizations and focused them on these domestic terrorists. The task force and others like it paved the way for today's Joint Terrorism Task Forces—created by the bureau in each of its field offices to fuse federal, state, and local law enforcement and intelligence resources to combat today's terrorist threats.

By the mid-1980s, the Weather Underground was essentially history. Still, several of these fugitives were able to successfully hide themselves for decades, emerging only in recent years to answer for their crimes. Once again, it shows that grit and partnerships can and will defeat shadowy, resilient terrorist groups.

One of the more notable domestic terror attacks against the United States was the 1993 attack on New York City's World Trade Center (Figure 1.18).

The boldness of the World Trade Center bombing shocked the Intelligence Community. The sophistication of the plan, the potential for extreme damage and destruction, and the symbolism of the target itself attested to the determination of the terrorist movement long before 9/11.[12]

Presently, terror finds root in the ideology of religious fanaticism and the jihad. The statistical reality is that jihadi motivation and Islamic extremism is a growing phenomenon

FIGURE 1.18   **Investigators going through the rubble following the 1993 bombing of the World Trade Center.**

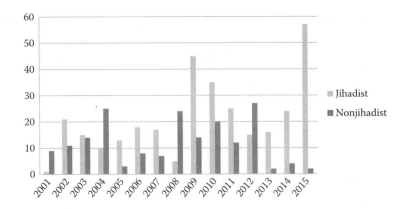

FIGURE 1.19   Number of extremists indicted or killed from 2001 through 2015. (Courtesy of International Security Data Site at http://securitydata.newamerica.net/extremists/analysis.html.)

and increasing global threat. Figure 1.19 paints an unnerving picture of this undeniable escalation.

Previously, terror was grounded in the ideology of politics and social movements. When the Communist Workers Party clamored for change, its advocacy dealt with the evils of excessive capitalism and the real need for collectivism in the distribution of goods and services. When the Black Panther Party took violent action, it did so with a political revolution in mind and aiming for the whole-scale redress and payback for injustice based on race. Neither of these arguments can justify the violence that these groups offer up, but both groups attest to their dramatically different mind-set when compared with that of the extreme and very radical Islamic fundamentalists who flew planes into the Twin Towers or the rationale for the Boston Marathon bombing, whose perpetrators used jihad and Islamic radicalism as a warped rationale for the senseless killing of completely innocent people.[13] See Figure 1.20.

Terrorism on the domestic front can be driven by diverse motivations. Race hatred, white supremacy, protests against governmental policy, and an inordinate desire to subvert and undermine the nature of the democratic state are just a few of the rationales employed. Timothy McVeigh's bombing of the federal building in Oklahoma City manifests the disproportionate dislike and distrust of government in any sense and the extreme alienation and isolation that certain terrorists seem to experience in light of the democratic process. That government may or may not be too intrusive cannot provide sufficient justification for murder, but the level of distrust and flat-out antagonism toward government is a growing phenomenon in select quarters.

Ted Kaczynski (aka the Unabomber) also reflects this loner, antigovernment tradition of the terrorist. In his "manifesto," Kaczynski railed against most aspects of modern life, industrialization, the loss of freedom, and the invasiveness of government. Kaczynski's arrest, one of the FBI's most successful apprehensions, was celebrated and recollected in 2008.[14]

WANTED
BY THE FBI

Suspect in Boston Marathon Bombings

DZHOKHAR TSARNAEV

Captured   Captured

DESCRIPTION

Date(s) of Birth Used: July 22, 1993
Age: 19 years old
Height: 5'9"

Sex: Male
Race: White

CAUTION

The Federal Bureau of Investigation (FBI) is seeking the location of, and information about, Dzhokhar Tsarnaev, a suspect in the bombings at the Boston Marathon on April 15, 2013. These bombings resulted in the deaths of three victims and the injuries of more than 170 people.

SHOULD BE CONSIDERED ARMED AND EXTREMELY DANGEROUS

If you have any information concerning this person, please call 1-800-CALL-FBI, 911, or submit information at https://bostonmarathontips.fbi.gov/. You may also contact your local FBI office or the nearest American Embassy or Consulate.

FIGURE 1.20 Dzhokhar Tsarnaev's FBI "Wanted" poster (https://www.fbi.gov/wanted/alert/dzhokhar-tsarnaev).

FBI 100: THE UNABOMBER

04/24/08

Part 4 of our history series commemorating the FBI's 100th anniversary in 2008

How do you catch a twisted genius who aspires to be the perfect, anonymous killer—who builds untraceable bombs and delivers them to random targets, who leaves false clues to throw off authorities, who lives like a recluse in the mountains of Montana and tells no one of his secret crimes?

That was the challenge facing the FBI and its investigative partners, who spent nearly two decades hunting down this ultimate lone wolf bomber.

The man that the world would eventually know as Theodore Kaczynski came to our attention in 1978 with the explosion of his first, primitive homemade bomb at a Chicago university. Over the next 17 years, he mailed or hand delivered a series of increasingly sophisticated bombs that killed three Americans and injured 24 more. Along the way, he sowed fear and panic, even threatening to blow up airliners in flight.

In 1979, an FBI-led task force that included the ATF and U.S. Postal Inspection Service was formed to investigate the "UNABOM" case, code-named for the University and Airline Bombing targets involved. The task force would grow to more than 150 full-time investigators, analysts, and others. In search of clues, the team made every possible forensic examination of recovered bomb components and studied the lives of victims in minute detail. These efforts proved of little use in identifying the bomber, who took pains to leave no forensic evidence, building his bombs essentially from "scrap" materials available almost anywhere. And the victims, investigators later learned, were chosen randomly from library research.

We felt confident that the Unabomber had been raised in Chicago and later lived in the Salt Lake City and San Francisco areas. This turned out to be true. His occupation proved more elusive, with theories ranging from aircraft mechanic to scientist. Even the gender was not certain: although investigators believed the bomber was most likely male, they also investigated several female suspects.

The big break in the case came in 1995. The Unabomber sent us a 35,000 word essay claiming to explain his motives and views of the ills of modern society. After much debate about the wisdom of "giving in to terrorists," FBI Director Louis Freeh and Attorney General Janet Reno approved the task force's recommendation to publish the essay in hopes that a reader could identify the author.

After the manifesto appeared in *The Washington Post* and *The New York Times*, thousands of people suggested possible suspects. One stood out: David Kaczynski described his troubled brother Ted, who had grown up in Chicago, taught at the University of California at Berkeley (where two of the bombs had been placed), then lived for a time in Salt Lake City before settling permanently into the primitive 10′ × 14′ cabin that the brothers had constructed near Lincoln, Montana (Figure 1.21).

Most importantly, David provided letters and documents written by his brother. Our linguistic analysis determined that the author of those papers and the manifesto were almost certainly the same. When combined with facts gleaned from the bombings and Kaczynski's life, that analysis provided the basis for a search warrant.

FIGURE 1.21   Ted Kaczynski's cabin in the mountains of Montana.

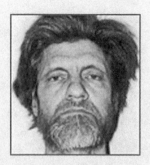

FIGURE 1.22   Ted Kaczynski, aka the Unabomber.

On April 3, 1996—a dozen years ago this month—investigators arrested Kaczynski and combed his cabin (Figure 1.22). There, they found a wealth of bomb components; 40,000 handwritten journal pages that included bomb-making experiments and descriptions of Unabomber crimes; and one live bomb, ready for mailing.

Kaczynski's reign of terror was over. His new home, following his guilty plea in January 1998: an isolated cell in a "Supermax" prison in Colorado.[15]

The array of terror groups include those advocating radical change involving racist ideologies, economic overthrow of existing governmental structures, and ideologies relating to the environment and animal rights. These groups are capable of inflicting extraordinary damage on the country, and they must remain on the radar screen of those entrusted with the security of the United States and its citizens.

1.4.2 International Terrorism: Pre-9/11

Just as in the United States, the international community had experienced a series of attacks from various constituencies. One of the more notable overseas terror attacks against the United States was at the Marine base in Beirut, Lebanon, in 1983, where 241 servicemen lost their lives (Figure 1.23).

The attack in Lebanon, in a secure military environment, made plain the tenacity of the terrorist and the willingness of this enemy to tackle any target, no matter how formidable. This attack sent a vivid reminder to the government and military that terrorism was a growing and very dangerous reality.

During the 1980s, organized terrorist groups that we have come to know only too well—al-Qaeda, Hamas, and Hezbollah—gained foundational and organizational support from many quarters in both a political and an economic sense. By the 1990s, Osama bin Laden had developed a network of terrorists eager to carry out attacks.

In Yemen and Somalia, Bin Laden funded, planned, and orchestrated acts that killed and injured a number of U.S. soldiers. Eighteen Special Forces members were attacked and killed in Somalia in 1993. In 1996, Bin Laden set out to attack the Khobar Towers in Saudi Arabia, where 19 American airmen died. In August 1998, Bin Laden and al-Qaeda bombed the embassies of Kenya and Tanzania, which resulted in the death and injury of thousands

FIGURE 1.23 The aftermath of the attack on the Marine base in Lebanon. (From: Department of Defense.)

FIGURE 1.24 The USS *Cole* suffered the loss of 17 crewmen, representing the first attack against a naval vessel of the United States in nearly 25 years. (From: Department of Defense by Sgt. Don L. Maes, U.S. Marine Corps.)

of innocents. Al-Qaeda and Bin Laden were getting even bolder as time progressed, carrying out a direct attack on a U.S. warship—the USS *Cole*—in Yemen in 2000 (Figure 1.24). Using a small boat as a suicide projectile, al-Qaeda operatives displayed unparalleled methods in carrying out their attack.

None of these events occurred in a vacuum but rather as a progressive series of events that eventually culminated in the single largest attack by a foreign enemy on American soil. Each attack displayed an evolving aggressiveness toward America, each attack employed a variety of tactics to keep the defenders off guard, and each attack manifested an increasing fanaticism in the Islamic extremist world. Succinctly, 9/11 did not occur out of the blue. Terror has a progressive history.

1.5 Conclusion

The concepts of terror and the terrorist have a long and perpetual history on both the domestic and international fronts. Terrorists have always been with us in one way or another. In this short survey, the reader learns the events and conditions that led up to our present definition of terror. The chapter commences with a look at how war, military tactics and strategy, and aligned governmental policy frequently employ terror tactics. Then, the reader is exposed to how the Cold War mentality shaped our perceptions about terror and subterfuge and weighed and evaluated how government policy can be influenced by events and conditions that can make once repressive regimes into more open societies. The chapter then shifts to terrorism as it existed before 9/11. The American experience has long had vestiges of terror in its social fabric. Special attention is given to the KKK, the Weathermen, the Black Panthers, and the SDS, as well as newly developing and ever-evolving groups espousing hatred. Terrorism, pre-9/11, was rooted in differing motivations ranging from racism to a desire for change and revolution.

By the 1990s, the face of terrorism adopted a virulent form of antigovernment sentiment, evidenced by the likes of Ted Kaczynski and Timothy McVeigh. Each had more than an ax to grind and sought to destroy what he perceived as a corrupt culture and government. In addition, pre-9/11, there was the rise of Islamic jihadists who carried out a number of international attacks, most coordinated by Osama bin Laden and others who followed him.

Hijackings, terror in the skies, embassy bombings, the kidnapping of American personnel, and attacks on naval targets became commonplace events of terror. All of this culminated in the catastrophe of 9/11—events and circumstances that are still overwhelmingly shocking and tragic. More particularly, the chapter looks at the attacks on the USS *Cole* and the Marine post in Lebanon.

As a direct result of 9/11, the missions of multiple U.S. agencies would undergo exceptional reorientation. In addition, these same agencies would become part of the newly constructed agency—the Department of Homeland Security.

Keywords

Al-Qaeda	Harry S. Truman
Allies	Hezbollah
Berlin Wall	Homeland security
Black Panthers	Human rights
Cold War	Imperialism
Communism	Iron Curtain
Communist Workers Party	ISIS/ISIL
Cuban missile crisis	Islamic fundamentalism
Domestic terrorism	Jihad
Dzhokhar Tsarnaev	Joseph Stalin
Final Solution	Korean War
Hamas	Ku Klux Klan

Mikhail Gorbachev	Students for a Democratic Society
Nikita Khrushchev	Ted Kaczynski
Nuclear proliferation	Terror
Osama bin Laden	Terrorist
Potsdam Convention	Third Reich
Religious fanaticism	Timothy McVeigh
Richard Nixon	Truman Doctrine
Ronald Reagan	Vietnam War
Saddam Hussein	Weathermen
Sino-Soviet	Winston Churchill
Soviet Communist Party	

Discussion Questions

1. When one evaluates the past 50 years of terrorist activities, what threats or trends can be discovered? Is there a commonality of purpose or type?
2. Why do terrorists so often choose embassies as targets?
3. In what way are Timothy McVeigh and Osama bin Laden the same?
4. Compare and contrast domestic and international terrorism. Point out the differences.
5. What are the motivations of terrorists groups in the pre-9/11 world compared with the post-9/11 world?
6. How can war be an instrument of terror?
7. Is it fair to argue that the United States engaged in terror during any of its war campaigns?
8. What does the Cold War teach us about the transient nature of the terror threat?
9. Was the Cold War threat different from the USS *Cole* threat?
10. Is the aim of the Unabomber similar to that of Osama bin Laden?
11. Some argue that political correctness impacts our capacity to fight terrorism. Can this argument be sensibly defended? Provide examples.

Practical Exercises

1. Find out whether or not a revolutionary group such as the Aryan Brotherhood or the KKK still operates in your area.
2. Are you aware of any paramilitary organizations that train in your region?
3. What type of terror prevention programs does your area have to root out domestic terrorists?
4. Contact your local police chief. Ask whether or not he or she sees any real threats from local groups that might engage in terrorist activity.
5. Visit the Truman or Reagan Library online for a virtual tour.
6. Determine whether your community engages in religious or ecumenical dialogue, and public engagement on the nature of terrorism. Are all religious sects involved or are some silent?

Notes

1. North American Treaty Organization, W. S. Churchill, *The Sinews of Peace*, http://www.nato.int/docu/speech/1946/S460305a_e.htm (accessed September 21, 2015).
2. T. Lister, ISIS: The first terror group to build an Islamic state? CNN.com, http://www.cnn.com/2014/06/12/world/meast/who-is-the-isis/index.html, (accessed December 27, 2015); *Business Insider*, These maps show the progression of ISIS control in Iraq and Syria, http://www.businessinsider.com/these-maps-show-the-progression-of-isis-control-in-iraq-and-syria-2015-8, (accessed December 27, 2015).
3. The Ronald Reagan Presidential Foundation & Library, President R. L. Reagan, Remarks on East–West Relations at the Brandenburg Gate in West Berlin, June 12, 1987, http://www.reaganfoundation.org (accessed December 27, 2015).
4. E. D. Johnson, Putin and Putinism, *The Slavonic and East European Review*, 89(3) (2011): 788–790.
5. M. R. Gordon, U.S. begins military talks with Russia on Syria, *The New York Times Online*, September 18, 2015, at http://www.nytimes.com/2015/09/19/world/europe/us-to-begin-military-talks-with-russia-on-syria.html?_r=1 (accessed December 27, 2015); A. Tilghman, U.S., Russia resume military relations to "deconflict" in Syria, *Military Times*, September 18, 2015, available at http://www.military-times.com/story/military/pentagon/2015/09/18/russia-mil-to-mil/72395558/ (accessed December 27, 2015).
6. M. R. Gordon, U.S. begins military talks with Russia on Syria, *The New York Times Online*, September 18, 2015, at http://www.nytimes.com/2015/09/19/world/europe/us-to-begin-military-talks-with-russia-on-syria.html?_r=1 (accessed December 27, 2015).
7. For an interesting analysis of the Ku Klux Klan as it rationalized its hatred with the fervor of false patriotism, see P. D. Brister, Patriotic enemies of the state: A cross comparison of the Christian Patriot Movement and the 1920's Ku Klux Klan, *The Homeland Security Review*, 4 (2010): 173.
8. R. Perlstein, *Nixonland: America's Second Civil War and the Divisive Legacy of Richard Nixon, 1965–1972* (New York: Simon & Schuster, 2008).
9. G. R. Stone, review of *Spying on Americans: Political Surveillance from Hoover to the Huston Plan*, by Athan Theoharis, *Reviews in American History*, 8(1) (March 1980): 134–138. For a full analysis of how the Weathermen worked, see Federal Bureau of Investigation, Weathermen Underground Summary, dated 8/20/76, https://vault.fbi.gov/Weather%20Underground%20(Weathermen).
10. Federal Bureau of Investigation, *Terrorism 2000–2001*, Publication 0308 (Washington, DC: U.S. Government Printing Office, 2004), 16.
11. Official website of the Knights Party, United States, http://www.kkk.bz.
12. U.S. Fire Administration, *The World Trade Center Bombing: Report and Analysis*, ed. W. Manning (Washington, DC: U.S. Government Printing Office, 1993), 15. For a comparison of the 1993 emergency reaction with that of 2001, see R. F. Fahy and G. Proulx, *A Comparison of the 1993 and 2001 Evacuation of the World Trade Center, Proceedings of the 2002 Fire Risk & Hazard Assessment Research Application Symposium* (Fire Protection Research Foundation, Quincy, MA), 111–117. For a close look at how the World Trade Center bombings caused extraordinary upheaval from a social, behavioral, and health perspective, see R. E. Adams, J. A. Boscarino, and S. Galea, Social and psychological resources and health outcomes after the World Trade Center disaster, *Social Science & Medicine*, 62 (2006): 176–188, http://www.sciencedirect.com/science/article/pii/S027795360500239X.
13. Reuters Boston Marathon Bombing archive at www.reuters.com.
14. Federal Bureau of Investigation, Headline archives, The Unabomber, https://www.fbi.gov/news/stories/2008/april/unabomber_042408.
15. Ibid.

Chapter 2

Terror, Threat, and Disaster Post 9/11
A New Paradigm of Homeland Security

Objectives

1. To analyze the events of 9/11 and understand the effect they had on the American population's psyche in relation to domestic security
2. To identify and assess post-9/11 threats with an emphasis on lessons learned
3. To appraise the effectiveness of the immediate response by government agencies to the events of 9/11
4. To describe the shortcomings of the lack of information exchange between various government agencies prior to 9/11 and analyze the influence the lack of communication had on the day's events
5. To outline the new strategies and tactics that the safety community developed for the mitigation and prevention of terrorism immediately following 9/11
6. To describe the initial formation of the Department of Homeland Security (DHS), its structure, and policy approach, mission, and goals
7. To explain the structural changes that have taken place in DHS since its inception
8. To summarize DHS's hierarchy, major players, and various advisory committees
9. To list the various directorates and offices of DHS and discuss their mission and responsibilities

2.1 Introduction

To say the world changed on September 11, 2001, is an extraordinary understatement. As the air assault on the Twin Towers and the Pentagon unfolded, both government agencies and the general populace watched in stunned silence. Even today, it is difficult to fathom the full and sweeping implications of such an attack. Dual plane attacks on the Twin Towers of the World Trade Center are almost impossible to fathom. Yet, this is exactly what occurred. Radical Islamic extremists perpetrated the most deadly attack carried out on U.S. soil (Figure 2.1).[1]

The damage to New York's financial district was catastrophic. Not only was the loss of life at staggering proportions, but the economic impact on the New York metropolitan area and the country was significant (Figures 2.2 through 2.4).

Notions of security would be forever challenged and altered. Ideas of safety within America's borders would now be doubted.

2.2 Genesis of DHS

Confidence in our ability to withstand or detect attacks was severely undermined by the events of 9/11. The attacks on American soil were sweeping in scope and left the public safety and law enforcement communities stunned. How could planes be hijacked and crashed into the financial district of one of the largest American cities? How could the walls of the Pentagon be breached? How could a plane crash in rural Pennsylvania represent a thwarted bid to attack the White House (Figure 2.5)?

The complexity of the undertaking manifests a well-prepared and very determined enemy. The time line of the attacks says much about the complexity of these events (see Figure 2.6).[2]

It is impossible to measure the complete impact that these events had upon the American psyche, the former invincibility of our home soil, and the pronounced reexamination of our entire approach to law enforcement and the overall security of a nation (Figure 2.7).[3]

As one illustration, the Federal Bureau of Investigation (FBI), while historically concerned about the potential random acts of terrorists, had to shift into a more intense scrutiny of the terrorist impact on our way of life. The National Commission on 9/11 was attuned to this strategic shift when it wrote:

> Collection of useful intelligence from human sources was limited. By the mid-1990s senior FBI managers became concerned that the bureau's statistically driven performance system had resulted in a roster of mediocre sources. The FBI did not have a formal mechanism for validating source reporting, nor did it have a system for adequately tracking and sharing such reporting, either internally or externally. The "wall" between criminal and intelligence investigations apparently caused agents to be less aggressive than they might otherwise have been in pursuing Foreign Intelligence Surveillance Act (FISA) surveillance powers in counterterrorism investigations. Moreover, the FISA approval process involved multiple levels of review, which also discouraged agents from using such surveillance. Many agents also told us that the process for getting FISA packages approved at FBI headquarters and the Department of Justice was incredibly lengthy and inefficient. Several FBI agents added that, prior to

American Airlines #11 - Boeing 767
7:45 a.m. Departed Boston for Los Angeles - 8:45 a.m. Crashed into North Tower of World Trade Center

| Waleed M. Alshehri | Wail M. Alshehri | Satam M.A.Al Suqami | Mohamed Atta | Abdulaziz Alomari |

American Airlines #77 - Boeing 757
8:10 a.m. Departed Dulles for Los Angeles - 9:39 a.m. Crashed into Pentagon

| Khalid Almihdhar | Majed Moqed | Nawaf Alhazmi | Salem Alhazmi | Hani Hanjour |

United Airlines #93 - Boeing 757
8:42 a.m. Departed Newark for San Francisco - 10:03 a.m. Crashed in Stony Creek Township

| Saeed Alghamdi | Ahmad Ibrahim A. Al Haznawi | Ahmed Alnami | Ziad Samir Jarrah |

United Airlines #175 - Boeing 767
7:58 a.m. Departed Boston for Los Angeles - 9:05 a.m. Crashed into South Tower of World Trade Center

| Marwan Al-Shehhi | Fayez Rashid Ahmed Hassan Al Qadi Banihammad | Ahmed Alghamdi | Hamza Alghamdi | Mohand Alshehri |

FIGURE 2.1   Terrorists aboard the four highjacked flights on September 11, 2001. (Courtesy of the Federal Bureau of Investigation, Washington, D.C.)

FIGURE 2.2 Twin Towers rubble after the collapse. (www.whitehouse.gov.)

FIGURE 2.3 National Guard members at the Twin Towers disaster site. (www.fema.gov.)

FIGURE 2.4   The Pentagon after the fires were extinguished. (www.fema.gov.)

FIGURE 2.5   United Flight 93 in Shanksville, Pennsylvania. (www.fema.gov.)

9/11, FISA-derived intelligence information was not fully exploited but was collected primarily to justify continuing the surveillance. The FBI did not dedicate sufficient resources to the surveillance or translation needs of counterterrorism agents. The FBI's surveillance personnel were more focused on counterintelligence and drug cases. In fact, many field offices did not have surveillance squads prior to 9/11. Similarly, the FBI did not have a sufficient number of translators proficient in Arabic and other languages useful in counterterrorism investigations, resulting in a significant backlog of untranslated FISA intercepts by early 2001. FBI agents received very little formalized training in the counterterrorism discipline. Only 3 days of the 16-week new agent's course were devoted to national security matters, including counterterrorism and counterintelligence, and most subsequent counterterrorism training was received on an *ad hoc* basis or "on the job." Additionally, the career path for agents necessitated rotations between headquarters and the field in a variety of work areas, making it difficult for agents to develop expertise in any particular area, especially counterterrorism and counterintelligence. We were told that very few FBI field managers had any

8:00 a.m.—American Airlines Flight 11, Boeing 767 with 92 people on board, takes off from Boston's Logan International Airport for Los Angeles.

8:14 a.m.—United Airlines Flight 175, Boeing 767 with 65 people on board, takes off from Boston's Logan airport for Los Angeles.

8:21 a.m.—American Airlines Flight 77, Boeing 757 with 64 people on board, takes off from Washington Dulles International Airport for Los Angeles.

8:40 a.m.—Federal Aviation Administration notifies North American Aerospace Defense Command's Northeast Air Defense Sector about suspected hijacking of American Flight 11.

8:41 a.m.—United Airlines Flight 93, Boeing 757 with 44 people on board, takes off from Newark International Airport for San Francisco.

8:43 a.m.—FAA notifies NORAD's Northeast Air Defense Sector about suspected hijacking of United Flight 175.

8:46 a.m.—American Flight 11 crashes into north tower of the World Trade Center.

9:03 a.m.—United Flight 175 crashes into south tower of the World Trade Center.

9:08 a.m.—FAA bans all takeoffs nationwide for flights going to or through New York airspace.

9:17 a.m.—FAA closes down all New York City-area airports.

9:21 a.m.—All bridges and tunnels into Manhattan closed.

9:24 a.m.—FAA notifies the NORAD's Northeast Air Defense Sector about suspected hijacking of American Flight 77.

9:26 a.m.—FAA bans takeoffs of all civilian aircraft.

9:31 a.m.—In Sarasota, Fla., President Bush calls crashes an "apparent terrorist attack on our country."

9:40 a.m. (approx.)—American Flight 77 crashes into the Pentagon.

9:45 a.m.—FAA orders all aircraft to land at nearest airport as soon as practical. More than 4,500 aircraft in the air at the time. This is the first time in U.S. history that nationwide air traffic is suspended.

9:48 a.m.—U.S. Capitol and White House's West Wing evacuated.

9:57 a.m.—President Bush leaves Florida.

9:59 a.m.—South tower of World Trade Center collapses.

10:07 a.m. (approx.)—United Flight 93 crashes in a field in Shanksville, Pa., southeast of Pittsburgh.

10:28 a.m.—North tower of World Trade Center collapses.

10:50 a.m.—New York's primary elections, scheduled for Sept. 11, are postponed.

10:56 a.m.—Palestinian leader Yasser Arafat speaks in Gaza: "First of all, I am offering my condolences, the condolences of the Palestinian people, to their American President, President Bush, to his government, to the American people, for this terrible time. We are completely shocked, completely shocked. Unbelievable."

11:00 a.m.—New York City Mayor Rudolph W. Giuliani orders the evacuation of lower Manhattan south of Canal Street.

11:04 a.m.—The United Nations is fully evacuated.

12:04 p.m.—Los Angeles International Airport, the destination of three of the hijacked airplanes, is closed and evacuated.

12:15 p.m.—San Francisco International Airport, the destination of United Airlines Flight 93, which crashed in Pennsylvania, is closed and evacuated.

12:30 p.m.—The FAA says 50 flights are in U.S. airspace, but none are reporting any problems.

1:04 p.m.—From Barksdale Air Force base in Louisiana, Bush announces U.S. military on high-alert worldwide: "Make no mistake: The United States will hunt down and punish those responsible for these cowardly acts."

1:37 p.m.—Bush leaves Barksdale for Offutt Air Force Base, near Omaha, Neb.

2:51 p.m.—Navy dispatches missile destroyers to New York and Washington D.C.

3:07 p.m.—Bush arrives at U.S. Strategic Command at Offutt Air Force Base in Nebraska.

4:36 p.m.—Bush leaves Offutt Air Force Base aboard Air Force One to return to Washington D.C.

5:25 p.m.—The empty, 47-story Seven World Trade Center collapses.

7:00 p.m.—Bush arrives at the White House.

8:30 p.m.—Bush addresses nation and vows to "find those responsible and bring them to justice."

FIGURE 2.6 Chronology of the key events of September 11, 2001 (all times Eastern).

counterterrorism experience, and thus either were not focused on the issue or did not have the expertise to run an effective program.[4]

Aside from a lack of coordination and interagency cooperation, the events of 9/11 make plain that an actual wall did exist between the varied agencies of government. The Central Intelligence Agency (CIA) did not share with the FBI, state and local police did not communicate readily, and jurisdictional and turf issues often influenced policy making in the pre-9/11

FIGURE 2.7 Workers in the rubble of the Twin Towers. (www.fema.gov.)

world. "The absence of coordination and collaboration in the area of information and intelligence sharing contributed to the surprise of the attack."[5] After 9/11, it was blatantly obvious that walls had to be torn down and new infrastructures and agencies created based on a cooperative mentality. In general, law enforcement and emergency management authorities have to see the world in a post-9/11 prism, fully recognizing that what once was effective is now ineffectual in cases of mass terror. "There are significant changes not only in the daily lives of the American people but also in the function of the country's emergency management system."[6] In matters of command, communication, deployment, planning, and dispatch, traditional agencies were challenged in ways never before envisioned. Nothing in the status quo could have operationally prepared these professionals for a post-9/11 world. And in a sense, that is exactly what the emergency, military, and law enforcement community has been doing since 9/11—searching out the best approach and adapting to the new reality. As law enforcement and fire personnel perished in the rubble of the Twin Towers and civilians in the airplanes plummeted to their deaths, the knowledge base of traditional safety was turned on its head.

Soon after 9/11, law enforcement and intelligence agencies developed and learned new strategies and tactics for prevention and mitigation. Soon after, the safety community began to reevaluate long-established practices in light of this tragedy. From September 11, 2001, an extraordinary series of new approaches was implemented, many of which were implemented by a new DHS. Right from the start, state, local, and federal services rattled the cages of ordinary bureaucratic practices. Getting to the implementation of DHS did not happen overnight but evolved from a series of policy steps. From that tragic day until the following year, government moved at lightning speed, as evidenced by the actions during the month of September in the chart in Figure 2.8.[7]

Not only was a new department erected but so too a new policy and definitional approach. The term *homeland security* encompasses much of the emergency, military, and law enforcement sector once dedicated to a variety of relevant responsibilities involved in the defense of a nation. DHS makes every effort to unify the diverse functions of responsibilities of a homeland in need of protection. DHS is one department chosen over myriad others because DHS is

September 11
- America attacked
- Department of Defense begins combat air patrols over U.S. cities
- Department of Transportation grounds all U.S. private aircraft
- FEMA activates Federal Response Plan
- U.S. Customs goes to Level 1 alert at all border ports of entry
- HHS activates (for the first time ever) the National Disaster Medical System, dispatching more than 300 medical and mortuary personnel to the New York and Washington, D.C. areas, dispatching one of eight 12-hour emergency "push packages" of medical supplies, and putting 80 Disaster Medical Assistance Teams nationwide and 7,000 private sector medical professionals on deployment alert.
- Nuclear Regulatory Commission advises all nuclear power plants, non-power reactors, nuclear fuel facilities and gaseous diffusion plants go to the highest level of security. All complied.
- President orders federal disaster funding for New York
- FEMA deploys National Urban Search and Rescue Response team
- FEMA deploys US Army Corp of Engineers to assist debris removal

September 12
- FEMA deploys emergency medical and mortuary teams to NY and Washington
- FAA allows limited reopening of the nation's commercial airspace system to allow flights that were diverted on September 11 to continue to their original destinations

September 13
- President orders federal aid for Virginia
- Departments of Justice and Treasury deploy Marshals, Border Patrol, and Customs officials to provide a larger police presence at airports as they reopen

September 14
- President proclaims a national emergency (Proc. 7463)
- President orders ready reserves of armed forces to active duty
- FBI Releases list of nineteen suspected terrorists

September 17: Attorney General directs the establishment of 94 Anti-Terrorism Task Forces, one for each United States Attorney Office
September 18
- President signs authorization for Use of Military Force bill
- President authorizes additional disaster funding for New York

September 20: President addresses Congress, announces creation of the Office of Homeland Security and appointment of Governor Tom Ridge as Director
September 21: HHS announces that more than $126 million (part of $5 billion the President released for disaster relief) is being provided immediately to support health services provided in the wake of the attacks.
September 22: President signs airline transportation legislation, providing tools to assure the safety and immediate stability of our Nation's commercial airline system, and establish a process for compensating victims of the terrorist attacks.
September 25: The first of approximately 7,200 National Guard troops begin augmenting security at 444 airports
September 27: The FBI releases photographs of 19 individuals believed to be the 9/11 hijackers

FIGURE 2.8 Administration Homeland Security action during September 2001.

- One department whose primary mission is to protect the American homeland
- One department to secure our borders, transportation sector, ports, and critical infrastructure
- One department to synthesize and analyze homeland security intelligence from multiple sources
- One department to coordinate communications with state and local governments, private industry, and the American people about threats and preparedness
- One department to coordinate our efforts to protect the American people against bioterrorism and other weapons of mass destruction

- One department to help train and equip first responders
- One department to manage federal emergency response activities
- More security officers in the field working to stop terrorists and fewer resources in Washington managing duplicative and redundant activities that drain critical homeland security resources[8]

2.3 DHS: 2001–2003

Any conception of a government agency dedicated to the protection of the homeland takes time to develop and implement. The evolution of a governmental structure, responsible for maintaining homeland safety and security, is both complex and ever changing. Since 2001, the face and internal bureaucratic attributes of DHS have undergone birth and rebirth, change and reincarnation. The DHS of 2001 was a very different animal from the DHS of today. There have been growing pains in the development of the agency, its mission, and its structure. Despite these challenges, DHS has maintained a unique and surprising adaptability in its changing programs, mission, and structure in its short existence.

MISSION

We will lead the unified national effort to secure America. We will prevent and deter terrorist attacks and protect against and respond to threats and hazards to the nation. We will secure our national borders while welcoming lawful immigrants, visitors, and trade (U.S. Department of Homeland Security One Team, One Mission, Securing Our Homeland—U.S. DHS Strategic Plan [2008]).

Strategic Goals

Awareness—Identify and understand threats, assess vulnerabilities, determine the potential impact, and disseminate timely information to our homeland security partners and the American public.

- Prevention: Detect, deter, and mitigate threats to our homeland.
- Protection: Safeguard our people and their freedoms, critical infrastructure, property, and the economy of our nation from acts of terrorism, natural disasters, or other emergencies.
- Response: Lead, manage, and coordinate the national response to acts of terrorism, natural disasters, or other emergencies.
- Recovery: Lead national, state, local, and private sector efforts to restore services and rebuild communities after acts of terrorism, natural disasters, or other emergencies.
- Service: Serve the public effectively by facilitating lawful trade, travel, and immigration.
- Organizational Excellence: Value our most important resource, our people. Create a culture that promotes a common identity, innovation, mutual respect, accountability, and teamwork to achieve efficiencies, effectiveness, and operational synergies—U.S. Department of Homeland Security, Securing Our Homeland: U.S. DHS Strategic Plan (2004).

2.3.1 Evolution and Change in DHS

While safety and security issues are permanent national concerns, the examination of how to predict and prevent threats to the national homeland took on added importance after 9/11. On the front burner was how to take existing governmental agencies and deploy them in the fight against terrorism. On the side burner was the nagging question of whether or not the front burner was competent enough to generate the necessary heat and intensity to be successful in this new undertaking. In choosing to erect a new government agency in DHS, both President George W. Bush and Congress agreed that the "changing nature of the threats facing America requires a new government structure against the invisible enemies that can strike with a wide variety of weapons."[9] Creating a new agency could be argued as being strictly political—giving the general public a sense of action and aggressive posturing against America's enemies, although this characterization would be unfair. The previous patchwork of aligned and even competing government agencies was obvious. Even the 9/11 Commission critiqued the lack of information sharing and turf games between competing agencies.

> The agencies cooperated, some of the time. But even such cooperation as there was is not the same thing as joint action. When agencies cooperate, one defines the problem and seeks help with it. When they act jointly, the problem and options for action are defined differently from the start. Individuals from different backgrounds come together in analyzing a case and planning how to manage it.
>
> In our hearings we regularly asked witnesses: Who is the quarterback? The other players are in their positions, doing their jobs. But who is calling the play that assigns roles to help them execute as a team?[10]

The drive toward a new agency was rooted in a host of compelling rationales. Unity of purpose and mission was surely at the forefront. The "one" agency mind-set represented a significant change of ethos for the intelligence community. No longer would the CIA, FBI, National Security Agency (NSA), and North American Aerospace Defense Command (NORAD) see themselves as individual players in the fight against terrorism but instead as part of the collective and simultaneously unified effort to detect and prevent harm to the homeland. DHS refers to these shifts in operational mentality as an "evolution of the paradigm"[11]—a movement away from the decentralized toward a totally centralized approach in the management of threat. DHS would be the centerpiece of these efforts.

Not long after 9/11, Congress and the president, working swiftly and in concert, moved passage of the *Homeland Security Act of 2002*.[12] The act seeks to minimize the threat of another 9/11 and poses its mission in broad terms. Part of the act lays out the mission of DHS.

The primary mission of the department is to

- Prevent terrorist attacks within the United States
- Reduce the vulnerability of the United States to terrorism
- Minimize the damage, and assist in the recovery, from terrorist attacks that do occur within the United States

- Carry out all functions of entities transferred to the department, including by acting as a focal point regarding natural and man-made crises and emergency planning
- Ensure that the functions of the agencies and subdivisions within the department that are not related directly to securing the homeland are not diminished or neglected except by a specific explicit act of Congress
- Ensure that the overall economic security of the United States is not diminished by efforts, activities, and programs aimed at securing the homeland
- Monitor connections between illegal drug trafficking and terrorism, coordinate efforts to sever such connections, and otherwise contribute to efforts to interdict illegal drug trafficking[13]

The act further compartmentalizes the agency into four main areas of responsibility, namely, border and transportation; emergency preparedness and response; chemical, biological, radiological, and nuclear countermeasures; and information analysis and infrastructure protection. The organization chart of DHS in 2008,[14] shown in Figure 2.9, portrays those with crucial responsibility for DHS.

The significance of these categories cannot be overemphasized. In border and transportation, DHS assumed control over security services relating to our borders, territorial waters, and transportation systems. Immigration and naturalization, customs, the coast guard, and animal protection issues are now DHS functions.

In emergency preparedness and response there was a complete merger of Federal Emergency Management Agency (FEMA) operations into DHS. FEMA, as will be discussed in Chapter 7, became an organization dedicated not only to natural disaster but also to man-made events. Federal interagency emergency programs were subsumed into DHS, as were critical response units relating to nuclear and pharmaceutical events.

In matters involving the prevention of chemical, radiological, and nuclear terror, DHS plays a central, coordinating role. Efforts here would be one of centralization and coordination of diverse department activities across the spectrum of government agencies. Guidelines regarding weapons of mass destruction were rapidly promulgated.

In the area of intelligence and threat analysis, DHS acts as a central repository for information pertaining to threats to the homeland. Data from traditional intelligence organizations such as the CIA, FBI, NSA, the Immigration and Naturalization Service (INS), and the Drug Enforcement Administration (DEA) are catalogued and disseminated as needed. DHS now works closely with the FBI's Office of Intelligence.

As for infrastructure, DHS is responsible for the evaluation and protection of the country's primary infrastructure, including food and water systems; health and emergency services; telecommunications; energy; chemical and defense industries; and common carrier transportation. Issues of infrastructure continue to be pressed by both the executive and legislative branch.

Finally, DHS as of 2003 extended its program reach to state, local, and private sector justice agencies. One of the hallmarks of DHS is the cultivation of governmental inter- and intra-agency cooperation. DHS saw the essential need for mutual trust and respect between

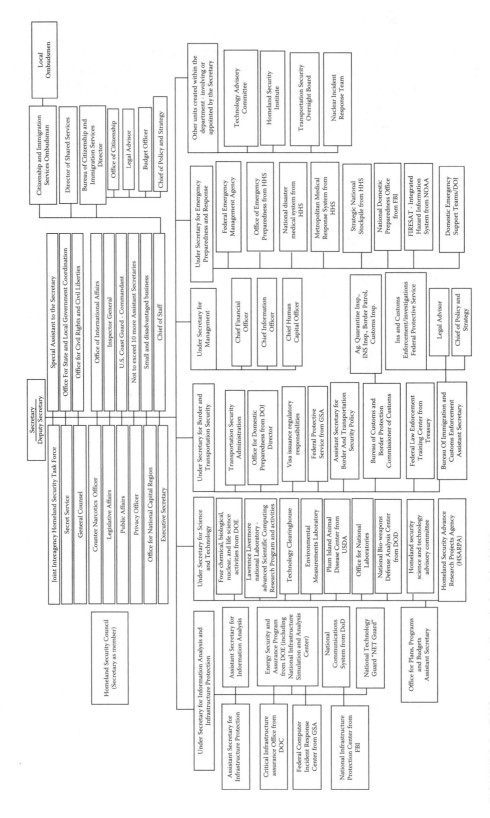

FIGURE 2.9 DHS organizational chart in 2008.

competing agencies so that the mission of DHS might be implemented. DHS erected an "intergovernmental affairs office" to coordinate the numerous initiatives emanating from the agency. Figure 6.3 in Chapter 6 contains contact information for state offices dedicated to the affairs of homeland security.

In time, these external constituencies will take on added importance for DHS. Structurally, DHS will have to adapt and evolve to serve these varied interests.

The Homeland Security Act of 2002 also mandated:

Not later than 60 days after enactment, of a reorganization plan regarding two categories of information concerning plans for DHS ("the Department" or "DHS"):

- The transfer of agencies, personnel, assets, and obligations to the Department pursuant to this Act.
- Any consolidation, reorganization, or streamlining of agencies transferred to the Department pursuant to this Act.[15]

Internet Resource: For the complete text of the Homeland Security Act of 2002, see http://www.dhs.gov/xlibrary/assets/hr_5005_enr.pdf.

2.4 Reorganization and Evolution of DHS: 2003–2015

In accordance with the act, DHS looks internally and externally for structural changes within the agency and the merger of agencies from outside. The task of DHS is to foster the unified culture of prevention and information sharing so needed in the fight against terrorism. DHS is many things to many entities, and, in the final analysis, it is a clearinghouse as well as an operational center for policy on homeland safety and security. DHS minimally

- Prevents terrorist attacks within the United States
- Reduces America's vulnerability to terrorism
- Minimizes the damage and oversees the recovery from attacks that do occur[16]

The current structure of DHS, unchanged since 2012, is charted in Figure 2.10.

Over its short life span, DHS has evolved vigorously, at least in a programmatic sense, but it has taken to a slow mode of structural change. From 2008 to the present, the structure of DHS displays only minor internal and administrative differences.

For example, the National Cyber Security Center no longer stands side by side with the Federal Law Enforcement Center and Domestic Nuclear Detection Office but has been merged into the DHS Directorate on Science and Technology. Replacing the National Cyber Security Center, as a stand-alone office, is Intergovernmental Affairs. For the remainder, the 2008 version of DHS is identical to that promulgated in 2001. Given the previous "sweeps" of agencies and personnel, it is likely the prudent course, which ensures stability. Even so, there are many legislators and policymakers who have urged some significant consolidation and merger of task and function at DHS and budget realities may force that issue in the very near future.[17]

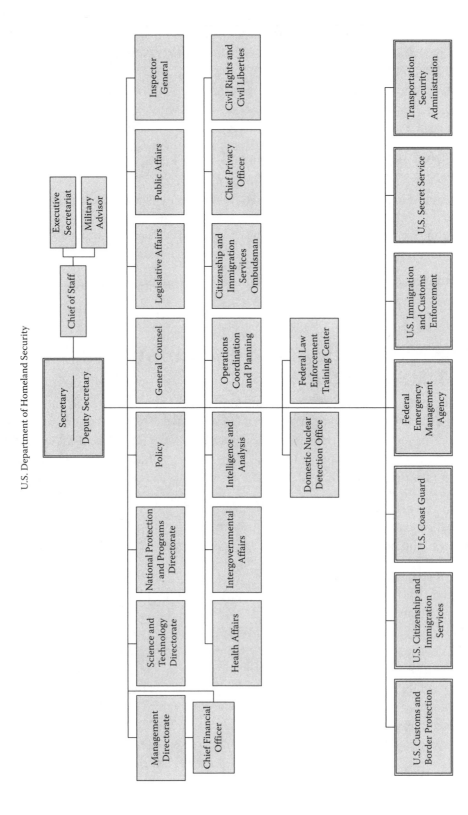

FIGURE 2.10 DHS organizational chart as of August 25, 2015. (https://www.dhs.gov/sites/default/files/publications/dhs-orgchart.pdf.)

2.4.1 Office of the Secretary of DHS

Within DHS, the organizational structure of the Office of the Secretary was altered under the provisions of the act. The secretary of homeland security oversees and provides leadership in all facets of homeland defense and protection.

During its early history, the secretary was Thomas Ridge former Pennsylvania governor (Figure 2.11).

Secretary Ridge is largely lauded for his skill and demeanor during the turbulent initial days of DHS. His reputation for integrity, consensus building, and political skill is well deserved.

After Secretary Ridge, leadership of DHS was provided by former prosecutor and judge Michael Chertoff (Figure 2.12).

Secretary Chertoff was a tireless advocate for his department. His six-point agenda for DHS, developed and announced in July 2005, ensures that the department's policies, operations, and structures are aligned in the best way to address the potential threats—both present and future—that face the United States. The agenda for DHS includes these tenets:

- Increase overall preparedness, particularly for catastrophic events
- Create better transportation security systems to move people and cargo more securely and efficiently
- Strengthen border security and interior enforcement and reform immigration processes

FIGURE 2.11   Tom Ridge, the first Secretary of the Department of Homeland Security. (From: Department of Homeland Security, Washington, D.C.)

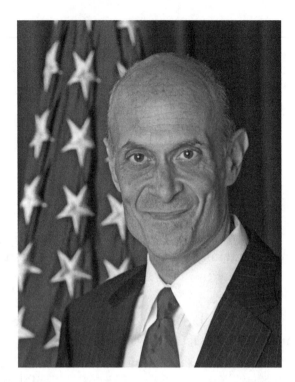

FIGURE 2.12 Michael Chertoff, Homeland Security Secretary 2005–2009. (From: Department of Homeland Security, Washington, D.C.)

- Enhance information sharing with our partners
- Improve DHS financial management, human resource development, procurement, and information technology
- Realign the DHS organization to maximize mission performance

With the election and swearing in of Barack Obama, the 44th president of the United States, a new homeland security secretary was confirmed and appointed. Janet Napolitano (Figure 2.13) was sworn in on January 21, 2009, as the third secretary of DHS.

Napolitano's homeland security background was extensive. As U.S. attorney, she helped lead the domestic terrorism investigation into the Oklahoma City bombing. As Arizona attorney general, she helped write the law to break up human smuggling rings. As governor of Arizona, she implemented one of the first state homeland security strategies in the country, opened the first state counterterrorism center, and spearheaded efforts to transform immigration enforcement. She has also been a pioneer in coordinating federal, state, local, and binational homeland security efforts, and presided over large-scale disaster relief efforts and readiness exercises to ensure well-crafted and functional emergency plans.

As the first woman to head up the new agency, the DHS chief's tenure was marked by such notable events as the Christmas Day bombing on December 25, 2009; the shooting attack and assassination attempt on House Representative Gabrielle Giffords and others in Arizona on January 8, 2011; the shooting in a movie theater in Aurora, Colorado, on July 20, 2012; the Sandy Hook Elementary School shooting in Newtown, Connecticut,

FIGURE 2.13   Janet Napolitano, the third Secretary of Homeland Security. (From: Department of Homeland Security, Washington, D.C.)

on December 14, 2012; as well as the Occupy Movement and the tragedy caused by the Boston Marathon bombing on April 15, 2013 (Figure 2.14).

These are in addition to numerous domestic terrorist plots in various stages that had been thwarted by U.S. intelligence agencies within DHS. These events and phenomena, as well as the various plots, obviously influenced the focus of the agency. The secretary's platform emphasized an increased need for utilities security, including supervisory control and data acquisition (SCADA) systems that control utilities, and the need for increased vigilance and expertise in the area of cybersecurity across both the public and private sectors.

Napolitano's tenure as DHS chief was not without controversy. This included various reports of wasteful spending by DHS, certainly something that many government agencies are not immune to. In addition, civil liberties groups decried the continued use of Transportation Security Administration (TSA) pat downs and imaging technologies—which some argue are too invasive—in airport security screening[18] (see Figure 2.15).

In the wake of the Christmas Day bombing in 2009, the secretary had to backtrack on statements that "the system worked" to concede that the system, in fact, did not work. This is because Umar Farouk Abdulmutallab was allowed to board a plane with explosives and make it all the way to Detroit before his underwear bombing device failed to detonate properly. Reports also indicate that the United States had received intelligence, prior

FIGURE 2.14 Boston, MA, April 15, 2013: Medical teams assist those injured from the bombings at the Boston Marathon. (From: FEMA News Photo, Washington, D.C.)

FIGURE 2.15 Advanced imaging technology (AIT) in use by TSA.

to the attack attempt, in reference to a Nigerian national based in Yemen planning a possible attack.

Another notable event, no fault of Secretary Napolitano's, was the disclosure of the failed "Fast and Furious" operation, conducted from 2006 to 2011, in which over 1600 firearms that were sold to dealers ultimately made their way into the hands of Mexican traffickers. The intent was to track the weapons and reveal key figures in the Mexican cartel hierarchy.

The operation, however, was a failure in that not only did authorities not track the movement of guns, according to reports, but those guns have been directly linked to over 200 deaths in Mexico. While this originated under the watch of Attorney General Eric Holder—out of the Bureau of Alcohol, Tobacco, and Firearms (ATF) and not DHS—it was perceived as a black-eye moment for the Obama administration, one that tested the public's trust of government operations in the name of security, not to mention an increasingly tense relationship with Mexico. If anything, the operation emphasized the importance of border security in the south and the need to stem the increasing threat of violence spilling over the border from Mexico, albeit not in a wholly positive way.

Despite these controversies and the increasing range of threats and challenges, Secretary Napolitano ably led the department on a range of new initiatives.

DHS is presently under the supervisory leadership of its newest secretary, Jeh Charles Johnson, a leader strong on legal preparation and analysis but with limited actual homeland security experience (see Figure 2.16). Johnson was sworn in on December 23, 2013.

While political appointments frequently reflect political realities more than experiential resumes, Jeh Johnson has been at times a polarizing and complex figurehead for DHS. For example, Secretary Johnson has shown general reticence to label terrorist acts as terrorist acts or to use nomenclature such as "jihad" or "Islamic Terrorism." This has led to a debate on political correctness and whether the avoidance of using such valid terminology ignores

FIGURE 2.16 **Fourth Director of Homeland Security, Jeh Charles Johnson. (From: Department of Homeland Security, Washington, D.C.)**

the issues and undercuts the operational integrity of what DHS must encounter each and every day.

Secretary Johnson has also called for increased and liberal discretion in the use of resources to deport or detain illegal aliens on American soil. Citing that DHS has only so many resources, his office rescinded a host of previous practices dealing with the apprehension, detention, and deportation of illegal aliens and replaced those policies with a priority system, whereby only certain groups would be subject to prosecution and deportation. His "Priority 1" grouping is as follows:

Aliens described in this priority represent the highest priority to which enforcement resources should be directed:

1. Aliens engaged in or suspected of terrorism or espionage, or who otherwise pose a danger to national security
2. Aliens apprehended at the border or ports of entry while attempting to unlawfully enter the United States
3. Aliens convicted of an offense for which an element was active participation in a criminal street gang, as defined in 18 U.S.C. § 52 l(a), or aliens not younger than 16 years of age who intentionally participated in an organized criminal gang to further the illegal activity of the gang
4. Aliens convicted of an offense classified as a felony in the convicting jurisdiction, other than a state or local offense for which an essential element was the alien's immigration status
5. Aliens convicted of an "aggravated felony," as that term is defined in section 101(a) (43) of the Immigration and Nationality Act at the time of the conviction[19]

After this priority, the DHS mandate becomes far more lenient in matters of enforcement. And when families and children are involved, Johnson has increasingly liberalized processes to ensure the least amount of detention possible. In fact, he recently concluded that "In short, once a family has established eligibility for asylum or other relief under our laws, long-term detention is an inefficient use of our resources and should be discontinued."[20]

Finally, Johnson has drawn criticism for advancing a theory of racial profiling at border enforcement relative to drug enforcement, especially at the Mexican border.

Despite some controversies, which go with the territory, Secretary Johnson successfully oversaw the establishment of policy, procedure, and protocols in the summer and fall of 2014, to identify travelers for screening in response to the Ebola crisis in West Africa. Overall, the department has undergone some significant changes in the several years under his watch.

Internet Exercise: Read Secretary Jeh Johnson's 2015 progress report on DHS at https:// www.dhs.gov/DHSin2015.

Within DHS, no matter who the secretary is, he or she orchestrates a complex bureaucracy, like most entities in federal and state service. Many DHS functions are operational and legal in design. Currently, the following departments directly answer to the secretary of DHS:

- Privacy Office: Balances and implements privacy laws relevant to DHS action
- Office of the Inspector General: Audits, investigates, and inspects practices and protocols of DHS
- Office of Civil Rights and Civil Liberties: Delivers legal and policy advice to management at DHS as to practice and constitutional implications
- Citizenship and Immigration Services Ombudsman: Resolves individual and employer disputes regarding immigration practices
- Office of Legislative Affairs: Liaison with congressional leaders, staff, and the executive branch
- Office of General Counsel: Staff of 1700 lawyers working in the Office of the Secretary as well as the various departments and divisions of DHS

Other offices include Public Affairs, Military Advisor's Office, Counter Narcotics Enforcement, and the Executive Secretariat. Of recent interest is the September 28, 2015, announcement of a new Office of Community Partnerships. The office targets the increasing caseload of domestically generated violent extremism, hoping to build bridges between DHS and community groups aware of domestic terror plots but fully in opposition to those approaches. This office will be dedicated to the mission of countering violent extremism and developing community partnerships that will combat and ferret out these threats.[21]

2.4.2 DHS Directorates

In the reorganization phase, DHS clearly articulated its internal structure by establishing various departments within the department. At various stages in 2005 until the present, directorates were implemented and then, in some cases, were later abolished. To say that DHS is a dynamic bureaucracy is an understatement. At face value, the directorates reflect the stress of the agency—what it wishes to primarily focus on. Before 2005, during reorganization, directorates were established in

- Border and transportation security
- Emergency preparedness and response
- Information analysis and infrastructure protection

By 2007, each of these directorates was abolished and the respective obligations and duties transferred to other departments within DHS. Currently, there are three directorates at DHS.

2.4.2.1 Directorate for National Protection and Programs

The Directorate for National Protection and Programs deals with risk and physical and virtual threats and dedicates itself to the analysis, identification, and elimination of risk, whether man-made or natural in design. The directorate covers risk from a definitional, operational, and personnel perspective and stresses best practices to protect infrastructure and human capital.

The directorate oversees the activities of the Federal Protective Service (FPS), which is a law enforcement entity dedicated to safety and risk reduction at federal installations (see Figure 2.17).

With more than 2000 officers and in coordination with a host of contract security firms, the FPS provides security at courthouses, federal buildings, and installations as well as conducting facility assessments and special events protection. The FPS will conduct criminal investigations if required.

Internet Resource: Find out about the many careers in the FPS service at http://www.dhs.gov/xabout/careers/gc_1271345939265.shtm.

The directorate's Office of Cybersecurity and Communications is entrusted with ensuring the integrity of governmental and private communications system in order that these systems are free from cyber vulnerabilities. The directorate is broken down into three major sectors:

1. National Communications Systems
2. National Cyber Security Division
3. Office of Emergency Communication

The directorate plays a crucial role in training and simulation for governmental and private officers entrusted with communication and cyber responsibilities. Its *Cyber Storm* exercise provides a biannual opportunity to test and confirm the integrity of communication and cyber designs (see Figure 2.18).

Cyber Storm participants perform the following activities:

* Examine organizations' capability to prepare for, protect from, and respond to cyber attacks' potential effects

FIGURE 2.17 Federal Protective Service logo.

FIGURE 2.18   DHS Cyber Storm participants, September 2010. (www.dhs.gov.)

- Exercise strategic decision-making and interagency coordination of incident response(s) in accordance with national-level policy and procedures
- Validate information-sharing relationships and communications paths for collecting and disseminating cyber-incident situational awareness, response, and recovery information.
- Examine means and processes through which to share sensitive information across boundaries and sectors without compromising proprietary or national security interests

Central to the directorate's overall mission is the protection of the infrastructure that includes but is not limited to the power grid, food and water supplies, national monuments, transportation systems, and chemical facilities.

Infrastructure sectors include

- Agriculture and food
- Banking and finance
- Chemical
- Commercial facilities
- Critical manufacturing
- Dams
- Defense industrial base
- Drinking water and water-treatment systems
- Emergency services
- Energy
- Government facilities
- Information technology
- National monuments and icons
- Nuclear reactors, materials, and waste
- Postal and shipping
- Public health and health care
- Telecommunications
- Transportation systems

The National Protection and Programs Directorate needs to analyze these critical forms of infrastructure to determine potential threats and vulnerability, management and mitigation of identified risks to same and be just as adept in the coordination of agency response in the event of threat. Covered later in this chapter will be the protocol and methodology of infrastructure analysis. Much of what state, local, and federal authorities do in response to infrastructure threat is derived from the directorate's research results and recommended best practices.

A myriad of other functions are assumed by the National Protection and Programs Directorate and will be encountered throughout the remainder of this chapter. Special offices deal precisely with matters of risk analysis, assessment, and management as well as the emerging statistical and quantitative discipline of risk analytics. The directorate oversees the US-VISIT program, which will be covered in a later section.

2.4.2.2 Directorate for Science and Technology

The role of science and technology in the world of homeland security is patently obvious. As government agencies and localities deal with shrinking budgets, the efficiency and efficacy of their practices take on added importance. The Science and Technology Directorate plays a key role in the development of all forms of technology useful to homeland defense. It serves a variety of broader functions, such as being a clearinghouse for technology practices and equipment, especially as to design and engineering; it tests and evaluates the compatibility and interoperability of diverse technologies used across the various states and weighs and assesses the primary needs of the nation's first-responder requirements for technology.

The directorate encompasses nearly a dozen divisions, including

- Borders and Maritime Security
- Chemical and Biological
- Command Control and Interoperability
- Explosives
- Human Factors/Behavioral Sciences
- Infrastructure
- Geophysical[22]

The directorate also engages technology in specific situations such as border and maritime, chemical and biological defense, explosive mitigation, and the cybersecurity threats. Among many other activities, the directorate plays a key role in science and technology development at the college and university level and coordinates a wide array of research and disseminates funds for technological and scientific innovation.

Internet Resource: Discover the many activities of the Office of University Programs at http://www.dhs.gov/xabout/structure/editorial_0555.shtm.

2.4.2.3 Directorate for Management

The Directorate for Management is the administrative arm of DHS where traditional functions of personnel, finance, and capital and procurement requirements are dealt with as well as the acquisition and maintenance of DHS properties. The directorate is responsible for budget development and oversight. With more than 200,000 employees in DHS, the management directorate takes on a major undertaking in the matter of human and physical capital. See Figure 2.19 for the organizational chart of the directorate.

2.4.3 DHS Offices

At the office level, DHS further differentiates task and function by the following:

- Office of Policy: Formulates and coordinates DHS policy and program.
- Office of Health Affairs: Deals with medically related incidents.
- Office of Intelligence and Analysis: Assesses and analyzes information and data regarding threat.
- Office of Operations Coordination: Monitors and coordinates homeland security activities and programs in the 50 states in 50 major urban areas, in conjunction with law enforcement partners.

2.4.4 Agencies Swept into DHS

After 2003, a host of external agencies were also swept into DHS during the reorganization phase:

- Federal Law Enforcement Training Center (FLETC): The premier center for professional law enforcement training, located in Glencoe, Georgia
- U.S. Customs and Border Protection (CBP): The agency primarily responsible for the security of our borders
- U.S. Citizenship and Immigration Services: Administers the immigration and naturalization adjudication
- U.S. Immigration and Customs Enforcement (ICE): The investigative arm of DHS that identifies and classifies threats at the borders
- U.S. Coast Guard (USCG): Protection of the nation's ports and waterways
- FEMA: Manages hazards and threats and responds thereto
- U.S. Secret Service: Protection of the president, vice president, and other high-level officials; investigates financial crimes
- Transportation Security Administration (TSA): Protects nation's transportation systems
- Domestic Nuclear Detection Office: Coordinates threat response related to nuclear materials

The intent was to combine, blend, and synthesize appropriate agency functions with the appropriate office. For the most part, DHS has remained largely intact since these radical days of reorganization in 2003–2004. It was not only an administrative sweep that took place when these agencies moved from familiar locale to the DHS setting. For both DHS and the incoming agency, a change of outlook and culture was required. By change, one means that a new prioritization of agency function had to occur; the former agency had to

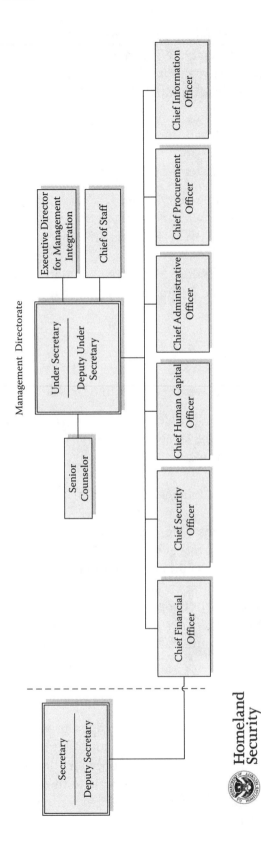

FIGURE 2.19   Management directorate organizational chart.

inculcate, acclimate, and become part of a new mission and mind-set. In a governmental life span, this is a difficult order to fulfill. Even so, it appears that DHS has done a fairly good job integrating so much in such an expeditious fashion.

To truly appreciate these cultural and administrative shifts, one need only look to the moves from one agency to another (Table 2.1).

In DHS, these moves are simply unrivaled in the history of the government—the movement can only be termed radical in scope. Sweeping moves, from so many governmental agencies, are not the stuff of government personality, whether it is local, state, or federal.

In the final analysis, such shifts and mergers were essential to any notion of a "single roof" for homeland security. While many of these former agencies and offices will be covered in other sections of this chapter, this section will highlight four significant structural shifts into DHS.

2.4.4.1 U.S. Coast Guard

The placement of the USCG within DHS was considered a radical shift by many, but on close inspection, it makes perfect sense. Historically, the coast guard's dedication to safety and security in our waterways and coastline makes the agency the perfect complement to DHS (Figure 2.20).

The mission of the USCG is

- *Maritime safety*: To eliminate deaths, injuries, and property damage associated with maritime transportation, fishing, and recreational boating
- *Maritime security*: To protect America's maritime borders from all intrusions by (a) halting the flow of illegal drugs, aliens, and contraband into the United States through maritime routes; (b) preventing illegal fishing; and (c) suppressing violations of federal law in the maritime arena
- *Maritime mobility*: To facilitate maritime commerce and eliminate interruptions and impediments to the efficient and economical movement of goods and people, while maximizing recreational access to and enjoyment of the water
- *National defense*: To defend the country as one of the five U.S. armed services; to enhance regional stability in support of the National Security Strategy, utilizing the coast guard's unique and relevant maritime capabilities
- *Maritime Stewardship Council*: To eliminate environmental damage and the degradation of natural resources associated with maritime transportation, fishing, and recreational boating (Figure 2.21)[23]

Long considered a military operation, as one of the five traditional branches in the military complex, the USCG increasingly evolved into a safety and law enforcement organization as well as a military command. How the USCG contributes to the defense of the country is quite evident in its homeland security functions, which include

- Protecting ports, the flow of commerce, and the marine transportation system from terrorism
- Maintaining maritime border security against illegal drugs, illegal aliens, firearms, and weapons of mass destruction

TABLE 2.1 Agency Relocations within DHS

Original Agency (Department)	Current Agency/Office
The U.S. Customs Service (Treasury)	U.S. Customs and Border Protection—inspection, border, and ports of entry responsibilities U.S. Immigration and Customs Enforcement—customs law enforcement responsibilities
The Immigration and Naturalization Service (Justice)	U.S. Customs and Border Protection—inspection functions and the U.S. Border Patrol U.S. Immigration and Customs Enforcement—immigration law enforcement: Detention and removal, intelligence, and investigations U.S. Citizenship and Immigration Services—adjudications and benefits programs
The Federal Protective Service	U.S. Immigration and Customs Enforcement
The Transportation Security Administration (Transportation)	Transportation Security Administration
Federal Law Enforcement Training Center (Treasury)	Federal Law Enforcement Training Center
Animal and Plant Health Inspection Service (part) (Agriculture)	U.S. Customs and Border Protection—agricultural imports and entry inspections
Office for Domestic Preparedness (Justice)	Responsibilities distributed within FEMA
The Federal Emergency Management Agency (FEMA)	Federal Emergency Management Agency
Strategic National Stockpile and the National Disaster Medical System (HHS)	Returned to Health and Human Services, July, 2004
Nuclear Incident Response Team (Energy)	Responsibilities distributed within FEMA
Domestic Emergency Support Teams (Justice)	Responsibilities distributed within FEMA
National Domestic Preparedness Office (FBI)	Responsibilities distributed within FEMA
CBRN Countermeasures Programs (Energy)	Science & Technology Directorate
Environmental Measurements Laboratory (Energy)	Science & Technology Directorate
National BW Defense Analysis Center (Defense)	Science & Technology Directorate
Plum Island Animal Disease Center (Agriculture)	Science & Technology Directorate
Federal Computer Incident Response Center (GSA)	US-CERT, Office of Cybersecurity and Communications in the National Programs and Preparedness Directorate
National Communications System (Defense)	Office of Cybersecurity and Communications in the National Programs and Preparedness Directorate
National Infrastructure Protection Center (FBI)	Dispersed throughout the department, including Office of Operations Coordination and Office of Infrastructure Protection
Energy Security and Assurance Program (Energy)	Integrated into the Office of Infrastructure Protection
U.S. Coast Guard	U.S. Coast Guard
U.S. Secret Service	U.S. Secret Service

FIGURE 2.20   U.S. Coast Guard approaching a cargo ship.

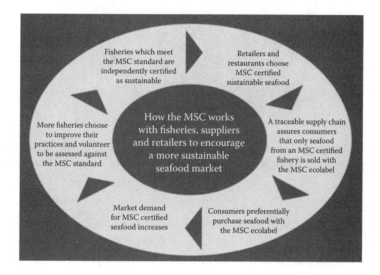

FIGURE 2.21   Fishing as a sustainable product is part of the USCG's mission.

- Ensuring that we can rapidly deploy and resupply our military assets, both by keeping coast guard units at a high state of readiness and by keeping marine transportation open for the transit assets and personnel from other branches of the armed forces
- Protecting against illegal fishing and indiscriminate destruction of living marine resources, and preventing and responding to oil and hazardous material spills—both accidental and intentional
- Coordinating efforts and intelligence with federal, state, and local agencies[24]

With its extraordinary infrastructure of maritime resources, its skill in the detection and prevention of crime on the seas and waterways, and its technical superiority in a host of operations, the USCG has been called on to be a major player in the fight against terrorism (see Figure 2.22).

Its flexibility of vision is what makes it a key component of a national strategy. Former Vice Admiral Vivien Crea of the USCG rightfully argues:

FIGURE 2.22 New York (September 11, 2001): A Coast Guard patrol boat secures New York Harbor as smoke rises from where the World Trade Center buildings once stood. (From: PA2 Tom Sperduto.)

The need to protect the homeland in the context of the "long war" against terrorism has been a key force for change in the Coast Guard. Although our initial response to this new terrorism threat temporarily drained resources from other mission areas, we have worked to restore the maritime safety and security mission balance. Congress and the administration have provided critical funding support. New and more capable assets have been added, and all of our resources present a multi-mission capability that can instantly and flexibly surge from search and rescue, to restoration of our ports and waterways, to response to avert threat to our homeland security.[25]

The transition, of course, has not been without its share of challenges. The USCG has a variety of masters to answer to. The sheer volume of coverage, in both task and geography, is daunting. "With 95,000 miles of coastline and close to 360 ports of entry, the United States is challenged daily with monitoring maritime safety, securing national borders and the global supply chain, and protecting natural resources,"[26] the USCG labors under heavy demands. It has undergone a "fundamental reordering,"[27] which requires it to be an "instrument of national security."[28]

2.4.4.2 U.S. Secret Service

Given how threat and attack targets are often high-profile political figures, the decision to move the Secret Service under the roof of DHS is mission consistent.

The Secret Service is entrusted with the protection of the following figures:

- The president, the vice president (or other individuals next in order of succession to the Office of the President), the president-elect, and the vice president-elect.
- The immediate families of the above individuals.
- Former presidents and their spouses for their lifetimes, except when the spouse remarries. In 1997, congressional legislation became effective limiting Secret Service protection to former presidents for a period of not more than 10 years from the date the former president leaves office.
- Children of former presidents until age 16.
- Visiting heads of foreign states or governments and their spouses traveling with them, other distinguished foreign visitors to the United States, and official representatives of the United States performing special missions abroad.
- Major presidential and vice presidential candidates, and their spouses, within 120 days of a general presidential election.
- Other individuals as designated per executive order of the president.
- National Special Security Events, when designated as such by the secretary of DHS (Figure 2.23).

The Secret Service also deals with counterfeiting and select federal crimes not aligned to homeland security issues. Its investigations unit deals with identity crimes such as access device fraud, identity theft, false identification fraud, bank and check fraud, telemarketing fraud, telecommunications fraud (cellular and hard wire), computer fraud, fraud targeting automated payment systems and teller machines, direct deposit fraud, and investigations of forgery. For homeland purposes, the protection unit assumes a central role.

Two areas where the Secret Service orchestrates protective services are in major events and threat assessment. In the first instance, major events, the Secret Service coordinates

FIGURE 2.23 Pope Francis on his September 15, 2015 visit with Secret Service protection. (http://www.secretservice.gov/press/gallery.)

agencies and their respective resources when a significant public event, involving protected persons, takes place. In this case, the secretary of DHS designates the event as a National Special Security Event (NSSE). The Secret Service assumes its mandated role as the lead agency for the design and implementation of the operational security plan. The NSSE is coordinated in cooperation with its established partnerships with law enforcement and public safety officials at the local, state, and federal levels.

A second integral contribution of the service is the development and operational oversight of the National Threat Assessment Center. The center focuses its research and activities on the protection of public figures, the creation and implementation of best practices in the protection thereof, and recommendations on how best to serve potential targets of threat. The center directs its attention chiefly to

- Research on threat assessment and various types of targeted violence
- Training on threat assessment and targeted violence to law enforcement officials and others with protective and public safety responsibilities
- Information sharing among agencies with protective or public safety responsibilities
- Programs to promote the standardization of federal, state, and local threat assessment and investigations involving threats

Internet Resource: While the Secret Service generally has had an impeccable and unassailable reputation, certain allegations emerged regarding improper behavior in Cartagena, Colombia, in 2013 and other failures to protect the White House perimeter in 2014–2015. The reports by the inspector general (IG) regarding these investigations are heavily redacted. See the Office of the Inspector General (OIG) website at http://www.oig.dhs.gov; click on the Freedom of Information Act (FOIA) Reading Room link and review the records concerning the U.S. Secret Service.

2.4.4.3 Federal Protective Service

Once a part of the General Service Administration, the FPS is the law enforcement and security force that protects federal buildings and installations. In the reorganization of DHS, the agency was moved to Immigration and Customs Enforcement (ICE). ICE is under the supervision of DHS. The FPS provides security services to all federal buildings, including office buildings, courthouses, border stations, and warehouses. FPS services include but are not limited to

- Providing a visible uniformed presence in our major federal buildings
- Responding to criminal incidents and other emergencies
- Installing and monitoring security devices and systems
- Investigating criminal incidents
- Conducting physical security surveys
- Coordinating a comprehensive program for occupants' emergency plans
- Presenting formal crime prevention and security awareness programs

- Providing police emergency and special security services during natural disasters such as earthquakes, hurricanes, and major civil disturbances—as well as during man-made disasters, such as bomb explosions and riots

The FPS also takes a lead role in the assurance that federal buildings and installations are rid of security problems and that the design, operation, and layout of facilities are as conducive as possible to safe security practices. In each facility, the FPS sets up a Building Security Committee, which conducts a vulnerability assessment of each facility.

The FPS administers a program for lost and missing children in federal installations called Code Adam Alert (see Figure 2.24).

Internet Resource: For a copy of the FPS brochure *Making Buildings Safe*, see http://www.cdc.gov/niosh/topics/emres/pdfs/FedBuildSafe.pdf.

FIGURE 2.24 Code Adam Alert Flyer. U.S. General Services Administration. (http://www.gsa.gov/graphics/pbs/Code_Adam_Poster.pdf.)

2.4.4.4 Federal Law Enforcement Training Center

Just as it was wise to relocate the USCG and the Secret Service to DHS, it makes eminent sense to move the federal government's premier training agency under the same roof (Figure 2.25).

FLETC has assumed a central role in the training of law enforcement professionals across the United States. From every jurisdiction, justice professionals benefit from expertise and cutting-edge subject matter relevant to homeland security (Figure 2.26).

FLETC is located in Glynco, Georgia, with satellite facilities in Washington, DC; Jacksonville, Florida; Charleston, South Carolina; Artesia, New Mexico; and Cheltenham, Maryland. The strategic goals of FLETC are to

- Provide training that enables our partners to accomplish their missions
- Foster a high-performing workforce
- Provide mission-responsive infrastructure
- Optimize business practices

See Figure 2.27 for an organization chart of the FLETC hierarchy.

Each facility provides a wide array of training opportunities. Those more appropriately applicable to homeland security are

- Antiterrorism Intelligence Awareness Training Program (AIATP)
- Commercial Vehicle Counterterrorism Training Program (CVCTP)
- Computer Network Investigations Training Program (CNITP)
- Covert Electronic Surveillance Program (CESP)
- Covert Electronic Tracking Program (CETP)
- Crisis Management Training Program (CMTP)
- Critical Incident Response Training Program (CIRTP)
- Critical Infrastructure Key Resource Protection Qualification Training Program (CIKRTP)

FIGURE 2.25 Federal Law Enforcement Training Center in Glynco, Georgia. (National Parks Service website at www.nps.gov.)

FIGURE 2.26   On any given day, there are roughly 7000 personnel at the Federal Law Enforcement Training Centers (FLETC) facilities across the nation. (From: Department of Homeland Security.)

- Critical Infrastructure Protection Training Program (CIPTP)
- Cyber Counterterrorism Investigations Training Program (CCITP)
- Domestic Terrorism and Hate Crimes Training Program (DTHCTP)
- Intelligence Analyst Training Program (IATP)
- Intelligence Awareness for Law Enforcement Executives Training Program (IALEETP)
- International Banking and Money Laundering Training Program (IBMLTP)
- Internet Investigations Training Program (IITP)
- Internet Protocol Camera Program (IPCP)
- Introductory Intelligence Analyst Training Program (IIATP)
- Operations Security for Public Safety Agencies Counterterrorism Training Program (OPSACTP)
- Seaport Security Antiterrorism Training Program (SSATP)
- Suicide Bomber Mitigation Training Program (SBMTP)
- Vehicle Ambush Countermeasures Training Program (VACTP)
- Weapons of Mass Destruction Training Program (Level I) (WMDTP L1—Operations—Core NFPA 472.5)
- Weapons of Mass Destruction Training Program (Level II) (WMDTP L2—Technician)

FLETC dedicates a large portion of its training to terrorism and counterterrorism. An entire certification program exists for those seeking this specialized knowledge. FLETC delivers state-of-the-art training in advanced topics relevant to homeland security, including

- Cyber-terrorism training
- Critical infrastructure training
- Antiterrorism intelligence

Internet Resource: For a full catalog of courses, see http://www.fletc.gov/training-catalog.

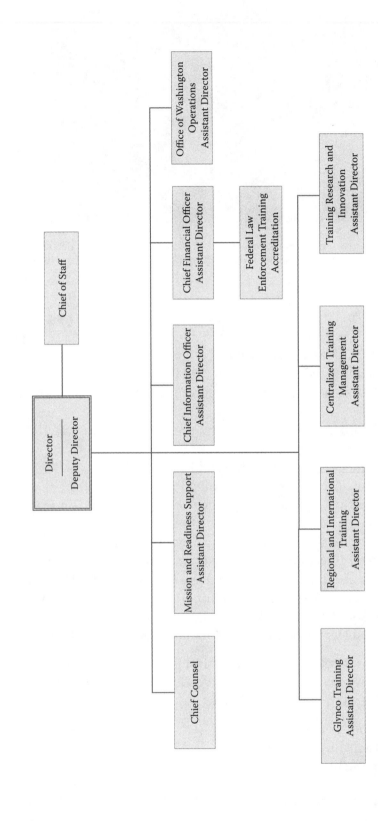

FIGURE 2.27 Federal Law Enforcement Training Center hierarchy, July 12, 2015. (http://www.fletc.gov/fletc-organization-chart-ppt.)

2.4.5 Advisory Panels and Committees

One of the recurring themes in DHS operations is the agency's willingness to work with external authority—both public and private. The council is more than a mere formality but an essential contributor to the integrity of the homeland effort. So integral is the council considered to the mission of DHS that the body is statutorily required to report its recommendations every 4 years. Reports from May 27, 2010, urge the agency to "define and operationalize the strategic framework; to delineate roles and responsibilities" with a keener eye and to measure DHS mission with "measurable outcomes...and targets to drive alignment of the Department's priorities, structures, systems and resources."[29]

That operational outlook was further confirmed in the IG's management and performance review of the agency in February 2015. This report, as well as other recent studies, urges DHS to be far more efficient in resources, to keep open to external partnerships, and to take the needed steps to ensure a safe border.[30]

In 2015, DHS was to center its attention on nine areas of performance:

- DHS operations integration
- Acquisition management
- Financial management
- IT management and privacy issues
- Transportation security
- Border security and immigration enforcement
- Grants management
- Employee accountability and integrity
- Infrastructure protection, cybersecurity, and insider threat[31]

These reports serve as a critique of DHS using the combined wisdom of the committee as outside, objective observers. The aim is for the council to turn a critical and pragmatic eye on DHS programs and offer recommendations for improvement and to curtail initiatives that may be redundant or not properly vetted, to avoid unnecessary bureaucracy within the department.

The council wisely calls for the aggressive integration and melding of state and local governmental authorities, working side by side with federal entities in law enforcement and the intelligence community; the agency also seeks input and professional participation by other suitable means. One avenue erects and establishes a body of government leaders, scholars, and practitioners that give advice to DHS. Some of the more prominent panels are

- Homeland Security Advisory Council (HSAC): Advice and recommendations on homeland practices
- National Infrastructure Advisory Council: Advice on information systems for both the public and private sector
- Homeland Security Science and Tech Advisory Committee: Independent scientific advice for planning purposes within DHS
- Critical Infrastructure Partnership Advisory Council: Coordinates state, local, tribal, and federal reporting on critical infrastructure protection

- Interagency Coordinating Council on Emergency Preparedness and Individuals with Disabilities: Group that reviews DHS practices and recommendations in light of disability
- Task Force on New Americans: Supports immigrants in the learning of language and American culture

Current members of the Homeland Security Advisory Council are a who's who of distinguished citizens.

- William Webster (chair) retired partner, Milbank, Tweed, Hadley & McCloy LLP
- Bill Bratton (vice-chair) police commissioner, City of New York
- Art Acevedo, chief of police, Austin Police Department, Texas
- Stephen Adegbite, chief information security officer, E*Trade Financial Corporation
- John Allen, General (ret.), U.S. Marine Corps
- Thad Allen, executive vice president, Booz| Allen| Hamilton Inc.
- Norman Augustine, retired chairman and CEO, Lockheed Martin Corporation
- Ron Barber, former congressman Arizona 2nd district, 112/113th Congress
- Chuck Canterbury, national president, Fraternal Order of Police
- Richard Danzig, chairman of the board of directors of the Center for a New American Security
- Elaine C. Duke, principal of Elaine Duke & Associates, LLC
- Marshall Fitz, managing director of immigration, Emerson collective and senior fellow at the Center for American Progress
- Paul Goldenberg, president and CEO, Cardinal Point Strategies, LLC
- Lee Hamilton, director, Center on Congress, Indiana University
- Jane Harman, president and director, Woodrow Wilson Center
- Elizabeth "Liz" Holtzman, cochair, Herrick's Government Relations Practice
- Jim Jones, chairman/CEO, ManattJones Global Strategies, LLC
- Juliette Kayyem, founder of Juliette Kayyem Solutions, LLC
- Gary Kelly, chairman/CEO, Southwest Airlines
- Carie Lemack, cofounder, Global Survivors Network and Families of September 11
- Wilson "Bill" Livingood, president and partner, Livingood Advisors, LLC
- Jane Holl Lute, president/CEO, Cyber Security Council
- John Magaw, consultant, Domestic and International Security
- David A. Martin, professor of law at the University of Virginia (UVA)
- Walter McNeil, past president, International Association of Chiefs of Police
- Jeffrey "Jeff" Miller, senior vice president and chief security officer, National Football League
- Jeff Moss, founder of Black Hat and DEF CON Conferences
- Ned Norris Jr., former chairman of the Tohono O'odham Nation
- Matthew Olsen, former director of the National Counterterrorism Center
- Farah Pandith, adjunct senior fellow, Council on Foreign Relations
- Annise D. Parker, mayor, City of Houston, TX
- John Pistole, president, Anderson University

- Chuck Ramsey, commissioner, Philadelphia Police Department
- Robert Rose, senior advisor to the chairman and founder, Bridgewater Associates
- Harold Schaitberger, general president, International Association of Fire Fighters
- Ali Soufan, chairman and chief executive officer, The Soufan Group LLC
- Paul Stockton, managing director, Sonecon LLC
- Lydia Thomas, retired president and CEO, Noblis Inc.

For the charter that established the HSAC, see Appendix A.

DHS also relies on specialized committees that deal with topics of significant interest to the agency. Presently, these committees are designated as senior advisory committees, an example referenced later in this chapter.

Other areas of expertise are solicited in private sector justice, secure borders, state and local officials, and the academe. These committees issue reports and recommendations to the secretary as needed.

Internet Resource: For an example of a committee report dealing with secure borders, visit http://www.dhs.gov/xlibrary/assets/hsac_SBODACreport508-compliant_version2.pdf.

Since 2011, under the leadership of President Barack Obama, the Advisory Council has been asked to erect a Task Force on Secure Communities. The initiative gives special attention to the problem of illegal immigration and how it impacts community safety.

Internet Resource: Visit the task force's draft recommendations on how to secure border towns directly suffering from the problems and challenges of illegal immigration at http://www.dhs.gov/xlibrary/assets/hsac-task-force-on-secure-communities.pdf.

2.5 Conclusion

Chapter 2 began with a review of the events of September 11, 2001, as well subsequent examples of this nation's perpetual challenge against threats coupled with a discussion of the immediate responses of governmental agencies. The lack of coordination, cooperation, and information sharing between federal agencies was discussed as a contributing factor to the attacks. The strategies and tactics developed as a result, namely, the creation of DHS and its many directorates and committees, were next introduced.

DHS was created to be a flexible entity, one that can change to reflect national security needs at any given time. This is apparent in the fluctuation in the organization's structure in its first 8 years of existence. The text next turned to the initial formation of the department from 2001 to 2003, its strategic goals and mission, and its initial policy formulation. The *Homeland Security Act of 2002* established the department itself and outlined its powers, main areas of responsibility, and authority. Its early evolution and early department mergers were presented.

As with any bureaucratic entity, change is inevitable, and this was never more apparent than in the major reorganization of DHS between 2003 and 2008. The text next highlighted the first four secretaries of DHS and the agency's various directorates and offices and their corresponding responsibilities. During this major reorganization phase, many government agencies were swept under DHS's mantle and partially or, in some cases, completely reorganized. The four major agency reorganizations, the USCG, the Secret Service, FPS, and FLETC, were analyzed in depth. Finally, DHS's advisory panel and committee structure were explained.

Keywords

Agency culture
Border security
Bureaucracy
Central Intelligence Agency
Coast Guard
Counterterrorism
Critical infrastructure
Customs and Border Protection
Department of Homeland Security
Directorate
Domestic Nuclear Detection Office
Drug Enforcement Administration
Emergency management
Federal Aviation Administration
Federal Bureau of Investigation
Federal Emergency Management Agency
FLETC
Hijack
Homeland Security Act of 2002
Illegal aliens
Immigration and Customs Enforcement
Infrastructure
Intelligence
Intelligence sharing

Interagency cooperation
Law enforcement
Maritime security
Mitigation
National Commission on 9/11
National defense
National Security Agency
National Threat Assessment Center
Natural disaster
NORAD
Pentagon
Prevention
Protective services
Public safety
Secret Service
Security survey
Targeted violence
Threat analysis
Threat assessment
Transportation Security Administration
U.S. Citizenship and Immigration
    Services
Vulnerability assessment
Weapons of mass destruction

Discussion Questions

1. How would you rate the federal government response to 9/11 as compared with more recent disasters such as Hurricane Katrina and Hurricane Sandy?

2. Why did an agency for homeland security evolve?

3. What alternatives to DHS are possible?

4. What is the most striking difference between DHS 2003 and DHS today?

5. Does DHS have a political edge? Does DHS reflect who is in power?

6. Which agencies might be arguably misplaced in DHS?

7. How do lay people and lay organizations impact DHS?

Practical Exercises

1. Visit DHS's website and access the pages regarding the three directorates. List the programs and offices that each directorate supervises.

2. Review the list of agencies that were swept into DHS during the reorganization. Can you think of a better plan or reorganization? Does the current organization make sense from an operational perspective?

3. Visit the USCG website. Find out about maritime security (MARSEC) levels.

4. Visit the U.S. Secret Service's website and locate information on the National Threat Assessment Center. Find out about their current major research projects.

5. Visit the FPS section of the ICE website. Locate current job vacancies and familiarize yourself with the requirements for hire by the FPS.

Notes

1. Federal Bureau of Investigation, Famous cases and criminals, 9/11 Investigation (PENTTBOM), https://www.fbi.gov/about-us/history/famous-cases/9-11-investigation (accessed December 27, 2015).
2. FOXNews.com, News Archive, Timeline: Sept. 11, 2001, http://www.foxnews.com/story/0,2933,62184,00.html.
3. For an interesting look into the cultural shifts in the intelligence community as it evaluated terrorism, see T. A. Gilly, Deconstructing terrorism: Counter-terrorism's trajectory for the 21st century, *The Homeland Security Review*, 5 (2011): 5.
4. National Commission on Terrorist Attacks upon the United States, Tenth Public Hearing, Law Enforcement, Counterterrorism, and Intelligence Collection in the United States prior to 9/11, Staff Statement No. 9, April 13, 2004, 8, http://govinfo.library.unt.edu/911/staff_statements/staff_statement_9.pdf.
5. R. Ward et al., *Homeland Security: An Introduction* (Cincinnati, OH: Anderson Publishing Co., 2006), 57.
6. Bullock, Homeland Security, 23.
7. President G. W. Bush, *The Department of Homeland Security* (Washington, DC: U.S. Government Printing Office), June 19–23, 2002, http://www.dhs.gov/xlibrary/assets/book.pdf.
8. Bush, Department Homeland Security, 1, http://www.dhs.gov/xlibrary/assets/book.pdf.
9. Ibid.
10. *The 9/11 Commission Report: Final Report of the National Commission on Terrorist Attacks upon the United States*, Official Government Edition (Washington, DC: U.S. Government Printing Office, July 22, 2004), 400.
11. Homeland Security Council, National Strategy for Homeland Security (October 2007), 3, https://www.dhs.gov/national-strategy-homeland-security-october-2007.
12. Homeland Security Act of 2002, U.S. Code 6 (2002), § 101.

13. Ibid, § 101 (b).

14. S. S. Gressle, CRS Report for Congress, Department of Homeland Security Organization Chart, Order Code RS21366 (Jan. 14, 2004), available at https://www.hsdl.org/?view&did=451595 (accessed December 27, 2015).

15. Homeland Security Act of 2002, U.S. Code 6 (2002), § 1502.

16. Office of Homeland Security, The National Strategy for Homeland Security (June 16, 2002), vii, http://www.dhs.gov/xlibrary/assets/nat_strat_homelandsecurity_2007.pdf.

17. The Federal News Radio reports that support for consolidation is growing in the U.S. Senate. See http://www.federalnewsradio.com/?nid=108&sid=2545915.

18. See B. Forer, TSA Full-Body Scanners: No More Naked Images, ABCnew.com, July 21, 2011, at http://abcnews.go.com/Travel/Travel/tsa-full-body-scanners-naked-images/story?id=14125474.

19. J. C. Johnson, *Memorandum on Policies for the Apprehension, Detention and Removal of Undocumented Immigrants* (Nov. 20, 2014), https://www.dhs.gov/sites/default/files/publications/14_1120_memo_prosecutorial_discretion.pdf.

20. C. Carcamo, U.S. policy change may enable speedy release of detained immigrant families, LA Times Online (June 24, 2015), http://www.latimes.com/nation/la-na-immigration-family-detention-20150624-story.html.

21. Statement by Secretary Jeh C. Johnson on DHS's New Office for Community Partnerships (Sept. 28, 2015), https://www.dhs.gov/news/2015/09/28/statement-secretary-jeh-c-johnson-dhs%E2%80%99s-new-office-community-partnerships.

22. See Department of Homeland Security website, Science and Technology Resources, at https://www.dhs.gov/science-and-technology.

23. United States Coast Guard, "Missions," at http://www.uscg.mil/top/missions (accessed January 2, 2016).

24. United States Coast Guard at http://www.uscg.mil (accessed January 2, 2016).

25. V. Crea, The U.S. coast guard: A flexible force for national security, *Naval War College Review*, 60 (Winter 2007): 15–23.

26. T. Allen, New threats, new challenges: The coast guard's new strategy, *Proceedings*, 133 (March 2007): 74.

27. B. B. Stubbs, U.S. coast guard annual review, *Proceedings*, 133 (May 2007): 84.

28. Stubbs, *Proceedings*, 84; see also *The US Coast Guard of the 21st Century*, www.uscg.mil/history/articles/21stcentury.pdf.

29. Department of Homeland Security, Homeland Security Advisory Council, Quadrennial Review Advisory Committee: Final Report 8–9 (May 27, 2010).

30. Office of the Inspector General, *Major Management and Performance Challenges Facing the Department of Homeland Security* (Revised), (Feb. 23, 2015) https://www.oig.dhs.gov/assets/Mgmt/2015/OIG_15-09_Feb15.pdf.

31. Office of the Inspector General, *Major Management and Performance Challenges Facing the Department of Homeland Security* (Revised), 1 (Feb. 23, 2015) https://www.oig.dhs.gov/assets/Mgmt/2015/OIG_15-09_Feb15.pdf.

Chapter 3

Homeland Security Law, Regulations, and Budgeting

Objectives

1. To identify the major laws, regulations, and executive orders that form and govern the Department of Homeland Security (DHS)
2. To analyze Executive Order 13228, which created DHS; and Executive Order 12231, which focuses on the national infrastructure and its protection
3. To summarize the provisions of the Homeland Security Act of 2002
4. To describe the USA Patriot Act, its provisions, and its authority
5. To comprehend the various specialized laws that govern certain operations within DHS, such as the REAL ID program, Office of Biometric Identity Management, the SAFETY Act, and the like
6. To explain the reasoning behind budgeting priorities in DHS and why the priorities fluctuate from year to year
7. To compare the changes in allotments and priorities in DHS budgets from the agency's inception to the present
8. To predict where future allotments in DHS budgets may change and why

3.1 Introduction

Exactly how the affairs of DHS are managed is an ongoing and very vibrant topic. The power of DHS emanates from the legal authority that initiated its existence. Laws, regulations, and executive orders enable the agency to carry out its aim and purpose. Many laws touch on the functions of homeland defense, such as in matters of privacy, arrest, search, and wiretap, while other laws establish centers of research, operational funds for new initiatives, or primers for a new directive. Funding for DHS is just as important. Without money, the agency would have no life whatsoever. How Congress and the president eventually agree to fund DHS is an annual responsibility. From another management perspective, DHS needs to evaluate how it interacts with other governmental authorities—namely, state and local entities; this is a perpetual policy concern and consideration for DHS. If anything is certain, it is that DHS needs to collaborate at every governmental level. Just as importantly, DHS will need to work closely and cooperatively with private-sector justice as well, since private-sector justice is the country's fastest-growing arm in the criminal justice body. Privatization is a reality that must be factored in as DHS manages its affairs.

3.2 Homeland Security Law, Regulations, and Executive Orders

The power of DHS is derived from its legal authority. Soon after the September 11, 2001, attacks, President George W. Bush sought to establish an agency dedicated to the protection of the homeland. The speed with which these promulgations occurred not only impressed but also manifested the urgency of these tragic events.

3.2.1 Executive Order 13228: Origin of DHS

By executive order dated October 11, 2001, the president calls for the establishment of DHS, lays out its mission, categorizes its purpose and aim, and sets an early tone for how this agency will develop (see Figure 3.1).

3.2.2 Executive Order 12231: Protection of Infrastructure

Shortly thereafter, President Bush issued another executive order that focused on the nation's infrastructure. Given the recent events, the president, as well as Congress, was rightfully concerned about the country's infrastructure of transportation, water, energy and power plants, and other essential components of the American way of life. At the time, there were serious, very legitimate concerns about these facilities. Executive Order 12231 (Figure 3.2), signed October 16, 2001, dealt directly with infrastructure.

Internet Resource: For final administrative rules on the protection of infrastructure, see https://www.dhs.gov/sites/default/files/publications/pcii_final_rule_federal_register9-1-06-2_508.pdf.

The executive branch's view of infrastructure has been heightened over the term of President Barack Obama. In matters of funding and operational priorities, President Obama has repeatedly emphasized the interconnectedness of our infrastructure assets and urges agencies to prioritize the protection of our infrastructure in a more holistic way.

EXECUTIVE ORDER: ESTABLISHING THE OFFICE OF HOMELAND SECURITY AND THE HOMELAND SECURITY COUNCIL

By the authority vested in me as President by the Constitution and the laws of the United States of America, it is hereby ordered as follows:

Section 1. Establishment. I hereby establish within the Executive Office of the President an Office of Homeland Security (the "Office") to be headed by the Assistant to the President for Homeland Security.

Sec. 2. Mission. The mission of the Office shall be to develop and coordinate the implementation of a comprehensive national strategy to secure the United States from terrorist threats or attacks. The Office shall perform the functions necessary to carry out this mission, including the functions specified in section 3 of this order.

Sec. 3. Functions. The functions of the Office shall be to coordinate the executive branch's efforts to detect, prepare for, prevent, protect against, respond to, and recover from terrorist attacks within the United States.

a. National Strategy. The Office shall work with executive departments and agencies, State and local governments, and private entities to ensure the adequacy of the national strategy for detecting, preparing for, preventing, protecting against, responding to, and recovering from terrorist threats or attacks within the United States and shall periodically review and coordinate revisions to that strategy as necessary.

b. Detection. The Office shall identify priorities and coordinate efforts for collection and analysis of information within the United States regarding threats of terrorism against the United States and activities of terrorists or terrorist groups within the United States. The Office also shall identify, in coordination with the Assistant to the President for National Security Affairs, priorities for collection of intelligence outside the United States regarding threats of terrorism within the United States.

　　i. In performing these functions, the Office shall work with Federal, State, and local agencies, as appropriate, to:

　　　　A. Facilitate collection from State and local governments and private entities of information pertaining to terrorist threats or activities within the United States;

　　　　B. Coordinate and prioritize the requirements for foreign intelligence relating to terrorism within the United States of executive departments and agencies responsible for homeland security and provide these requirements and priorities to the Director of Central Intelligence and other agencies responsible collection of foreign intelligence;

　　　　C. Coordinate efforts to ensure that all executive departments and agencies that have intelligence collection responsibilities have sufficient technological capabilities and resources to collect intelligence and data relating to terrorist activities or possible terrorist acts within the United States, working with the Assistant to the President for National Security Affairs, as appropriate;

　　　　D. Coordinate development of monitoring protocols and equipment for use in detecting the release of biological, chemical, and radiological hazards; and

　　　　E. Ensure that, to the extent permitted by law, all appropriate and necessary intelligence and law enforcement information relating to homeland security is disseminated to and exchanged among appropriate executive departments and agencies responsible for homeland security and, where appropriate for reasons of homeland security, promote exchange of such information with and among State and local governments and private entities.

　　ii. Executive departments and agencies shall, to the extent permitted by law, make available to the Office all information relating to terrorist threats and activities within the United States.

c. Preparedness. The Office of Homeland Security shall coordinate national efforts to prepare for and mitigate the consequences of terrorist threats or attacks within the United States. In performing this function, the Office shall work with Federal, State, and local agencies, and private entities, as appropriate, to:

　　i. Review and assess the adequacy of the portions of all Federal emergency response plans that pertain to terrorist threats or attacks within the United States;

　　ii. Coordinate domestic exercises and simulations designed to assess and practice systems that would be called upon to respond to a terrorist threat or attack within the United States and coordinate programs and activities for training Federal, State, and local employees who would be called upon to respond to such a threat or attack;

　　iii. Coordinate national efforts to ensure public health preparedness for a terrorist attack, including reviewing vaccination policies and reviewing the adequacy of and, if necessary, increasing vaccine and pharmaceutical stockpiles and hospital capacity;

FIGURE 3.1   Executive order establishing the Department of Homeland Security.

iv. Coordinate Federal assistance to State and local authorities and nongovernmental organizations to prepare for and respond to terrorist threats or attacks within the United States;

v. Ensure that national preparedness programs and activities for terrorist threats or attacks are developed and are regularly evaluated under appropriate standards and that resources are allocated to improving and sustaining preparedness based on such evaluations; and

vi. Ensure the readiness and coordinated deployment of Federal response teams to respond to terrorist threats or attacks, working with the Assistant to the President for National Security Affairs, when appropriate.

d. Prevention. The Office shall coordinate efforts to prevent terrorist attacks within the United States. In performing this function, the Office shall work with Federal, State, and local agencies, and private entities, as appropriate, to:

i. Facilitate the exchange of information among such agencies relating to immigration and visa matters and shipments of cargo; and, working with the Assistant to the President for National Security Affairs, ensure coordination among such agencies to prevent the entry of terrorists and terrorist materials and supplies into the United States and facilitate removal of such terrorists from the United States, when appropriate;

ii. Coordinate efforts to investigate terrorist threats and attacks within the United States; and

iii. Coordinate efforts to improve the security of United States borders, territorial waters, and airspace in order to prevent acts of terrorism within the United States, working with the Assistant to the President for National Security Affairs, when appropriate.

e. Protection. The Office shall coordinate efforts to protect the United States and its critical infrastructure from the consequences of terrorist attacks. In performing this function, the Office shall work with Federal, State, and local agencies, and private entities, as appropriate, to:

i. Strengthen measures for protecting energy production, transmission, and distribution services and critical facilities; other utilities; telecommunications; facilities that produce, use, store, or dispose of nuclear material; and other critical infrastructure services and critical facilities within the United States from terrorist attack;

ii. Coordinate efforts to protect critical public and privately owned information systems within the United States from terrorist attack;

iii. Develop criteria for reviewing whether appropriate security measures are in place at major public and privately owned facilities within the United States;

iv. Coordinate domestic efforts to ensure that special events determined by appropriate senior officials to have national significance are protected from terrorist attack;

v. Coordinate efforts to protect transportation systems within the United States, including railways, highways, shipping, ports and waterways, and airports and civilian aircraft, from terrorist attack;

vi. Coordinate efforts to protect United States livestock, agriculture, and systems for the provision of water and food for human use and consumption from terrorist attack; and

vii. Coordinate efforts to prevent unauthorized access to, development of, and unlawful importation into the United States of, chemical, biological, radiological, nuclear, explosive, or other related materials that have the potential to be used in terrorist attacks.

f. Response and Recovery. The Office shall coordinate efforts to respond to and promote recovery from terrorist threats or attacks within the United States. In performing this function, the Office shall work with Federal, State, and local agencies, and private entities, as appropriate, to:

i. Coordinate efforts to ensure rapid restoration of transportation systems, energy production, transmission, and distribution systems; telecommunications; other utilities; and other critical infrastructure facilities after disruption by a terrorist threat or attack;

ii. Coordinate efforts to ensure rapid restoration of public and private critical information systems after disruption by a terrorist threat or attack;

iii. Work with the National Economic Council to coordinate efforts to stabilize United States financial markets after a terrorist threat or attack and manage the immediate economic and financial consequences of the incident;

iv. Coordinate Federal plans and programs to provide medical, financial, and other assistance to victims of terrorist attacks and their families; and

v. Coordinate containment and removal of biological, chemical, radiological, explosive, or other hazardous materials in the event of a terrorist threat or attack involving such hazards and coordinate efforts to mitigate the effects of such an attack.

FIGURE 3.1 (Continued)

g. Incident Management. The Assistant to the President for Homeland Security shall be the individual primarily responsible for coordinating the domestic response efforts of all departments and agencies in the event of an imminent terrorist threat and during and in the immediate aftermath of a terrorist attack within the United States and shall be the principal point of contact for and to the President with respect to coordination of such efforts. The Assistant to the President for Homeland Security shall coordinate with the Assistant to the President for National Security Affairs, as appropriate.

h. Continuity of Government. The Assistant to the President for Homeland Security, in coordination with the Assistant to the President for National Security Affairs, shall review plans and preparations for ensuring the continuity of the Federal Government in the event of a terrorist attack that threatens the safety and security of the United States Government or its leadership.

i. Public Affairs. The Office, subject to the direction of the White House Office of Communications, shall coordinate the strategy of the executive branch for communicating with the public in the event of a terrorist threat or attack within the United States. The Office also shall coordinate the development of programs for educating the public about the nature of terrorist threats and appropriate precautions and responses.

j. Cooperation with State and Local Governments and Private Entities. The Office shall encourage and invite the participation of State and local governments and private entities, as appropriate, in carrying out the Office's functions.

k. Review of Legal Authorities and Development of Legislative Proposals. The Office shall coordinate a periodic review and assessment of the legal authorities available to executive departments and agencies to permit them to perform the functions described in this order. When the Office determines that such legal authorities are inadequate, the Office shall develop, in consultation with executive departments and agencies, proposals for presidential action and legislative proposals for submission to the Office of Management and Budget to enhance the ability of executive departments and agencies to perform those functions. The Office shall work with State and local governments in assessing the adequacy of their legal authorities to permit them to detect, prepare for, prevent, protect against, and recover from terrorist threats and attacks.

l. Budget Review. The Assistant to the President for Homeland Security, in consultation with the Director of the Office of Management and Budget (the "Director") and the heads of executive departments and agencies, shall identify programs that contribute to the Administration's strategy for homeland security and, in the development of the President's annual budget submission, shall review and provide advice to the heads of departments and agencies for such programs. The Assistant to the President for Homeland Security shall provide advice to the Director on the level and use of funding in departments and agencies for homeland security-related activities and, prior to the Director's forwarding of the proposed annual budget submission to the President for transmittal to the Congress, shall certify to the Director the funding levels that the Assistant to the President for Homeland Security believes are necessary and appropriate for the homeland security-related activities of the executive branch.

GEORGE W. BUSH
THE WHITE HOUSE,
October 8, 2001.

FIGURE 3.1 (Continued)

By Presidential Proclamation 8607, President Obama declared that December 2010 was "Critical Infrastructure Protection Month" and noted that infrastructure is "essential to the security, economic welfare, public health and safety of the United States."[1] In 2012, the proclamation was renamed "Critical Infrastructure and Resilience Month."[2] A year later, President Obama continued his rightful emphasis on the protection of infrastructure by adding a "cybersecurity" dimension to previous decrees[3] (see Figure 3.3).

3.2.3 Executive Order 13493 of January 22, 2009

Soon after his inauguration as president, Barack Obama reiterated his long-held view that the Guantanamo facility and its interrogation practices should be ended. In early 2009, he

By the authority vested in me as President by the Constitution and the laws of the United States of America, and in order to ensure protection of information systems for critical infrastructure, including emergency preparedness communications, and the physical assets that support such systems, in the information age, it is hereby ordered as follows:

Section 1. Policy.
a. The information technology revolution has changed the way business is transacted, government operates, and national defense is conducted. Those three functions now depend on an interdependent network of critical information infrastructures. The protection program authorized by this order shall consist of continuous efforts to secure information systems for critical infrastructure, including emergency preparedness communications, and the physical assets that support such systems. Protection of these systems is essential to the telecommunications, energy, financial services, manufacturing, water, transportation, health care, and emergency services sectors.
b. It is the policy of the United States to protect against disruption of the operation of information systems for critical infrastructure and thereby help to protect the people, economy, essential human and government services, and national security of the United States, and to ensure that any disruptions that occur are infrequent, of minimal duration, and manageable, and cause the least damage possible. The implementation of this policy shall include a voluntary public-private partnership, involving corporate and nongovernmental organizations.

Sec. 2. Scope. To achieve this policy, there shall be a senior executive branch board to coordinate and have cognizance of Federal efforts and programs that relate to protection of information systems and involve:
a. Cooperation with and protection of private sector critical infrastructure, State and local governments, critical infrastructure, and supporting programs in corporate and academic organizations;
b. Protection of Federal departments, and agencies, critical infrastructure; and
c. Related national security programs.

Sec. 3. Establishment. I hereby establish the "President's Critical Infrastructure Protection Board" (the "Board").

FIGURE 3.2 Executive order on critical infrastructure protection.

issued an order setting up a commission to end the status quo and seek transfer and other disposition of those residing in the facility. This promise was quite controversial. The order posed in part:

Review of Detention Policy Options

By the authority vested in me as President by the Constitution and the laws of the United States of America, in order to develop policies for the detention, trial, transfer, release, or other disposition of individuals captured or apprehended in connection with armed conflicts and counterterrorism operations that are consistent with the national security and foreign policy interests of the United States and the interests of justice, I hereby order as follows:

Section 1. Special Interagency Task Force on Detainee Disposition.

(a) Establishment of Special Interagency Task Force. There shall be established a Special Task Force on Detainee Disposition (Special Task Force) to identify lawful options for the disposition of individuals captured or apprehended in connection with armed conflicts and counterterrorism operations.[4]

The sum and substance of this decree was to find ways to end Guantanamo operations. However, while the president promised this policy during his first presidential campaign and in the early days of his administration, the decree has not been realized. By 2011, his position on Guantanamo was reversed. In January of that year, he signed the Defense Authorization Bill, essentially restricting the transfer of Guantanamo prisoners to

EXECUTIVE ORDER: IMPROVING CRITICAL INFRASTRUCTURE CYBERSECURITY

By the authority vested in me as President by the Constitution and the laws of the United States of America, it is hereby ordered as follows:

Section 1. Policy. Repeated cyber intrusions into critical infrastructure demonstrate the need for improved cybersecurity. The cyber threat to critical infrastructure continues to grow and represents one of the most serious national security challenges we must confront. The national and economic security of the United States depends on the reliable functioning of the Nation's critical infrastructure in the face of such threats. It is the policy of the United States to enhance the security and resilience of the Nation's critical infrastructure and to maintain a cyber environment that encourages efficiency, innovation, and economic prosperity while promoting safety, security, business confidentiality, privacy, and civil liberties. We can achieve these goals through a partnership with the owners and operators of critical infrastructure to improve cybersecurity information sharing and collaboratively develop and implement risk-based standards.

Sec. 2. Critical Infrastructure. As used in this order, the term critical infrastructure means systems and assets, whether physical or virtual, so vital to the United States that the incapacity or destruction of such systems and assets would have a debilitating impact on security, national economic security, national public health or safety, or any combination of those matters.

Sec. 3. Policy Coordination. Policy coordination, guidance, dispute resolution, and periodic in-progress reviews for the functions and programs described and assigned herein shall be provided through the interagency process established in Presidential Policy Directive-1 of February 13, 2009 (Organization of the National Security Council System), or any successor.

Sec. 4. Cybersecurity Information Sharing. (a) It is the policy of the United States Government to increase the volume, timeliness, and quality of cyber threat information shared with U.S. private sector entities so that these entities may better protect and defend themselves against cyber threats. Within 120 days of the date of this order, the Attorney General, the Secretary of Homeland Security (the "Secretary"), and the Director of National Intelligence shall each issue instructions consistent with their authorities and with the requirements of section 12(c) of this order to ensure the timely production of unclassified reports of cyber threats to the U.S. homeland that identify a specific targeted entity. The instructions shall address the need to protect intelligence and law enforcement sources, methods, operations, and investigations.

b. The Secretary and the Attorney General, in coordination with the Director of National Intelligence, shall establish a process that rapidly disseminates the reports produced pursuant to section 4(a) of this order to the targeted entity. Such process shall also, consistent with the need to protect national security information, include the dissemination of classified reports to critical infrastructure entities authorized to receive them. The Secretary and the Attorney General, in coordination with the Director of National Intelligence, shall establish a system for tracking the production, dissemination, and disposition of these reports.

c. To assist the owners and operators of critical infrastructure in protecting their systems from unauthorized access, exploitation, or harm, the Secretary, consistent with 6 U.S.C. 143 and in collaboration with the Secretary of Defense, shall, within 120 days of the date of this order, establish procedures to expand the Enhanced Cybersecurity Services program to all critical infrastructure sectors. This voluntary information sharing program will provide classified cyber threat and technical information from the Government to eligible critical infrastructure companies or commercial service providers that offer security services to critical infrastructure.

d. The Secretary, as the Executive Agent for the Classified National Security Information Program created under Executive Order 13549 of August 18, 2010 (Classified National Security Information Program for State, Local, Tribal, and Private Sector Entities), shall expedite the processing of security clearances to appropriate personnel employed by critical infrastructure owners and operators, prioritizing the critical infrastructure identified in section 9 of this order.

e. In order to maximize the utility of cyber threat information sharing with the private sector, the Secretary shall expand the use of programs that bring private sector subject-matter experts into Federal service on a temporary basis. These subject matter experts should provide advice regarding the content, structure, and types of information most useful to critical infrastructure owners and operators in reducing and mitigating cyber risks.

Sec. 5. Privacy and Civil Liberties Protections. (a) Agencies shall coordinate their activities under this order with their senior agency officials for privacy and civil liberties and ensure that privacy and civil liberties protections are incorporated into such activities. Such protections shall be based upon the Fair Information Practice Principles and other privacy and civil liberties policies, principles, and frameworks as they apply to each agency's activities.

FIGURE 3.3 2013 Presidential proclamation.

    b. The Chief Privacy Officer and the Officer for Civil Rights and Civil Liberties of the Department of Homeland Security (DHS) shall assess the privacy and civil liberties risks of the functions and programs undertaken by DHS as called for in this order and shall recommend to the Secretary ways to minimize or mitigate such risks, in a publicly available report, to be released within 1 year of the date of this order. Senior agency privacy and civil liberties officials for other agencies engaged in activities under this order shall conduct assessments of their agency activities and provide those assessments to DHS for consideration and inclusion in the report. The report shall be reviewed on an annual basis and revised as necessary. The report may contain a classified annex if necessary. Assessments shall include evaluation of activities against the Fair Information Practice Principles and other applicable privacy and civil liberties policies, principles, and frameworks. Agencies shall consider the assessments and recommendations of the report in implementing privacy and civil liberties protections for agency activities.

    c. In producing the report required under subsection (b) of this section, the Chief Privacy Officer and the Officer for Civil Rights and Civil Liberties of DHS shall consult with the Privacy and Civil Liberties Oversight Board and coordinate with the Office of Management and Budget (OMB).

    d. Information submitted voluntarily in accordance with 6 U.S.C. 133 by private entities under this order shall be protected from disclosure to the fullest extent permitted by law.

Sec. 6. Consultative Process. The Secretary shall establish a consultative process to coordinate improvements to the cybersecurity of critical infrastructure. As part of the consultative process, the Secretary shall engage and consider the advice, on matters set forth in this order, of the Critical Infrastructure Partnership Advisory Council; Sector Coordinating Councils; critical infrastructure owners and operators; Sector-Specific Agencies; other relevant agencies; independent regulatory agencies; State, local, territorial, and tribal governments; universities; and outside experts.

Sec. 7. Baseline Framework to Reduce Cyber Risk to Critical Infrastructure. (a) The Secretary of Commerce shall direct the Director of the National Institute of Standards and Technology (the "Director") to lead the development of a framework to reduce cyber risks to critical infrastructure (the "Cybersecurity Framework"). The Cybersecurity Framework shall include a set of standards, methodologies, procedures, and processes that align policy, business, and technological approaches to address cyber risks. The Cybersecurity Framework shall incorporate voluntary consensus standards and industry best practices to the fullest extent possible. The Cybersecurity Framework shall be consistent with voluntary international standards when such international standards will advance the objectives of this order, and shall meet the requirements of the National Institute of Standards and Technology Act, as amended (15 U.S.C. 271 et seq.), the National Technology Transfer and Advancement Act of 1995 (Public Law 104-113), and OMB Circular A-119, as revised.

    b. The Cybersecurity Framework shall provide a prioritized, flexible, repeatable, performance-based, and cost-effective approach, including information security measures and controls, to help owners and operators of critical infrastructure identify, assess, and manage cyber risk. The Cybersecurity Framework shall focus on identifying cross-sector security standards and guidelines applicable to critical infrastructure. The Cybersecurity Framework will also identify areas for improvement that should be addressed through future collaboration with particular sectors and standards-developing organizations. To enable technical innovation and account for organizational differences, the Cybersecurity Framework will provide guidance that is technology neutral and that enables critical infrastructure sectors to benefit from a competitive market for products and services that meet the standards, methodologies, procedures, and processes developed to address cyber risks. The Cybersecurity Framework shall include guidance for measuring the performance of an entity in implementing the Cybersecurity Framework.

    c. The Cybersecurity Framework shall include methodologies to identify and mitigate impacts of the Cybersecurity Framework and associated information security measures or controls on business confidentiality, and to protect individual privacy and civil liberties.

    d. In developing the Cybersecurity Framework, the Director shall engage in an open public review and comment process. The Director shall also consult with the Secretary, the National Security Agency, Sector-Specific Agencies and other interested agencies including OMB, owners and operators of critical infrastructure, and other stakeholders through the consultative process established in section 6 of this order. The Secretary, the Director of National Intelligence, and the heads of other relevant agencies shall provide threat and vulnerability information and technical expertise to inform the development of the Cybersecurity Framework. The Secretary shall provide performance goals for the Cybersecurity Framework informed by work under section 9 of this order.

    e. Within 240 days of the date of this order, the Director shall publish a preliminary version of the Cybersecurity Framework (the "preliminary Framework"). Within 1 year of the date of this order, and after coordination with the Secretary to ensure suitability under section 8 of this order, the Director shall publish a final version of the Cybersecurity Framework (the "final Framework").

FIGURE 3.3 (Continued)

f. Consistent with statutory responsibilities, the Director will ensure the Cybersecurity Framework and related guidance is reviewed and updated as necessary, taking into consideration technological changes, changes in cyber risks, operational feedback from owners and operators of critical infrastructure, experience from the implementation of section 8 of this order, and any other relevant factors.

Sec. 8. Voluntary Critical Infrastructure Cybersecurity Program. (a) The Secretary, in coordination with Sector-Specific Agencies, shall establish a voluntary program to support the adoption of the Cybersecurity Framework by owners and operators of critical infrastructure and any other interested entities (the "Program").

b. Sector-Specific Agencies, in consultation with the Secretary and other interested agencies, shall coordinate with the Sector Coordinating Councils to review the Cybersecurity Framework and, if necessary, develop implementation guidance or supplemental materials to address sector-specific risks and operating environments.

c. Sector-Specific Agencies shall report annually to the President, through the Secretary, on the extent to which owners and operators notified under section 9 of this order are participating in the Program.

d. The Secretary shall coordinate establishment of a set of incentives designed to promote participation in the Program. Within 120 days of the date of this order, the Secretary and the Secretaries of the Treasury and Commerce each shall make recommendations separately to the President, through the Assistant to the President for Homeland Security and Counterterrorism and the Assistant to the President for Economic Affairs, that shall include analysis of the benefits and relative effectiveness of such incentives, and whether the incentives would require legislation or can be provided under existing law and authorities to participants in the Program.

e. Within 120 days of the date of this order, the Secretary of Defense and the Administrator of General Services, in consultation with the Secretary and the Federal Acquisition Regulatory Council, shall make recommendations to the President, through the Assistant to the President for Homeland Security and Counterterrorism and the Assistant to the President for Economic Affairs, on the feasibility, security benefits, and relative merits of incorporating security standards into acquisition planning and contract administration. The report shall address what steps can be taken to harmonize and make consistent existing procurement requirements related to cybersecurity.

Sec. 9. Identification of Critical Infrastructure at Greatest Risk. (a) Within 150 days of the date of this order, the Secretary shall use a risk-based approach to identify critical infrastructure where a cybersecurity incident could reasonably result in catastrophic regional or national effects on public health or safety, economic security, or national security. In identifying critical infrastructure for this purpose, the Secretary shall use the consultative process established in section 6 of this order and draw upon the expertise of Sector-Specific Agencies. The Secretary shall apply consistent, objective criteria in identifying such critical infrastructure. The Secretary shall not identify any commercial information technology products or consumer information technology services under this section. The Secretary shall review and update the list of identified critical infrastructure under this section on an annual basis, and provide such list to the President, through the Assistant to the President for Homeland Security and Counterterrorism and the Assistant to the President for Economic Affairs.

b. Heads of Sector-Specific Agencies and other relevant agencies shall provide the Secretary with information necessary to carry out the responsibilities under this section. The Secretary shall develop a process for other relevant stakeholders to submit information to assist in making the identifications required in subsection (a) of this section.

c. The Secretary, in coordination with Sector-Specific Agencies, shall confidentially notify owners and operators of critical infrastructure identified under subsection (a) of this section that they have been so identified, and ensure identified owners and operators are provided the basis for the determination. The Secretary shall establish a process through which owners and operators of critical infrastructure may submit relevant information and request reconsideration of identifications under subsection (a) of this section.

Sec. 10. Adoption of Framework. (a) Agencies with responsibility for regulating the security of critical infrastructure shall engage in a consultative process with DHS, OMB, and the National Security Staff to review the preliminary Cybersecurity Framework and determine if current cybersecurity regulatory requirements are sufficient given current and projected risks. In making such determination, these agencies shall consider the identification of critical infrastructure required under section 9 of this order. Within 90 days of the publication of the preliminary Framework, these agencies shall submit a report to the President, through the Assistant to the President for Homeland Security and Counterterrorism, the Director of OMB, and the Assistant to the President for Economic Affairs, that states whether or not the agency has clear authority to establish requirements based upon the Cybersecurity Framework to sufficiently address current and projected cyber risks to critical infrastructure, the existing authorities identified, and any additional authority required.

b. If current regulatory requirements are deemed to be insufficient, within 90 days of publication of the final Framework, agencies identified in subsection (a) of this section shall propose prioritized, risk-based, efficient, and coordinated actions, consistent with Executive Order 12866 of September 30, 1993 (Regulatory Planning and Review), Executive Order 13563 of January 18, 2011 (Improving Regulation and Regulatory Review), and Executive Order 13609 of May 1, 2012 (Promoting International Regulatory Cooperation), to mitigate cyber risk.

FIGURE 3.3   (Continued)

c. Within 2 years after publication of the final Framework, consistent with Executive Order 13563 and Executive Order 13610 of May 10, 2012 (Identifying and Reducing Regulatory Burdens), agencies identified in subsection (a) of this section shall, in consultation with owners and operators of critical infrastructure, report to OMB on any critical infrastructure subject to ineffective, conflicting, or excessively burdensome cybersecurity requirements. This report shall describe efforts made by agencies, and make recommendations for further actions, to minimize or eliminate such requirements.

d. The Secretary shall coordinate the provision of technical assistance to agencies identified in subsection (a) of this section on the development of their cybersecurity workforce and programs.

e. Independent regulatory agencies with responsibility for regulating the security of critical infrastructure are encouraged to engage in a consultative process with the Secretary, relevant Sector-Specific Agencies, and other affected parties to consider prioritized actions to mitigate cyber risks for critical infrastructure consistent with their authorities.

Sec. 11. Definitions. (a) "Agency" means any authority of the United States that is an "agency" under 44 U.S.C. 3502(1), other than those considered to be independent regulatory agencies, as defined in 44 U.S.C. 3502(5).

b. "Critical Infrastructure Partnership Advisory Council" means the council established by DHS under 6 U.S.C. 451 to facilitate effective interaction and coordination of critical infrastructure protection activities among the Federal Government; the private sector; and State, local, territorial, and tribal governments.

c. "Fair Information Practice Principles" means the eight principles set forth in Appendix A of the National Strategy for Trusted Identities in Cyberspace.

d. "Independent regulatory agency" has the meaning given the term in 44 U.S.C. 3502(5).

e. "Sector Coordinating Council" means a private sector coordinating council composed of representatives of owners and operators within a particular sector of critical infrastructure established by the National Infrastructure Protection Plan or any successor.

f. "Sector-Specific Agency" has the meaning given the term in Presidential Policy Directive-21 of February 12, 2013 (Critical Infrastructure Security and Resilience), or any successor.

Sec. 12. General Provisions. (a) This order shall be implemented consistent with applicable law and subject to the availability of appropriations. Nothing in this order shall be construed to provide an agency with authority for regulating the security of critical infrastructure in addition to or to a greater extent than the authority the agency has under existing law. Nothing in this order shall be construed to alter or limit any authority or responsibility of an agency under existing law.

b. Nothing in this order shall be construed to impair or otherwise affect the functions of the Director of OMB relating to budgetary, administrative, or legislative proposals.

c. All actions taken pursuant to this order shall be consistent with requirements and authorities to protect intelligence and law enforcement sources and methods. Nothing in this order shall be interpreted to supersede measures established under authority of law to protect the security and integrity of specific activities and associations that are in direct support of intelligence and law enforcement operations.

d. This order shall be implemented consistent with U.S. international obligations.

e. This order is not intended to, and does not, create any right or benefit, substantive or procedural, enforceable at law or in equity by any party against the United States, its departments, agencies, or entities, its officers, employees, or agents, or any other person.

BARACK OBAMA

FIGURE 3.3   (Continued)

other countries and the U.S. mainland. President Obama further clarified his position on Guantanamo in March 2011, when he signed Executive Order 13567.

3.2.4 Executive Order 13567 of March 7, 2011

Disposing of some of the world's most suspect figures in the underbelly of terrorism can be quite a challenge. President Obama, after over two years in office, essentially reverses his position on the closure of Guantanamo Bay by an order calling for periodic review and assessment of the prison's inhabitants.

The more pertinent part of the order declares:

Section 1. Scope and Purpose.
a. The periodic review described in Section 3 of this order applies only to those detainees held at Guantanamo on the date of this order, whom the interagency review established by Executive Order 13492 has (i) designated for continued law of war detention; or (ii) referred for prosecution, except for those detainees against whom charges are pending or a judgment of conviction has been entered.
b. This order is intended solely to establish, as a discretionary matter, a process to review on a periodic basis the executive branch's continued, discretionary exercise of existing detention authority in individual cases. It does not create any additional or separate source of detention authority, and it does not affect the scope of detention authority under existing law. Detainees at Guantanamo have the constitutional privilege of the writ of habeas corpus, and nothing in this order is intended to affect the jurisdiction of Federal courts to determine the legality of their detention.
c. In the event detainees covered by this order are transferred from Guantanamo to another U.S. detention facility where they remain in law of war detention, this order shall continue to apply to them.
Section 2. Standard for Continued Detention. Continued law of war detention is warranted for a detainee subject to the periodic review in Section 3 of this order if it is necessary.[5]

At Section 2 of the order, the president makes plain that continued detention is within the discretionary authority of the United States under the law of war principles. President Obama has been severely critiqued for essentially maintaining the policy of former George Bush. "The American Civil Liberties Union has been less than kind about the determination holding the decree shameful."[6]

3.2.5 Homeland Security Act of 2002

At the congressional level, there was nothing but cooperation during the early stages of homeland security policy. By November 2002, Congress had passed the Homeland Security Act of 2002. The act was a comprehensive response to terror threats at every level. A summary of the act's provisions is outlined in its table of contents (Figure 3.4).

The act lays out a national blueprint for homeland security and delineates the areas of vital national interest: borders; information and infrastructure; chemical, biological, and nuclear threats; and emergency preparedness and response. The act has been subject to various revisions over the last 13 years regarding critical infrastructure and financial reporting and accountability problems, as well as various privacy clarifications. The act is a work in progress by any measure.

3.2.5.1 Homeland Security Act and Posse Comitatus

An often overlooked section of the Homeland Security Act makes reference to the *Posse Comitatus Act* of 1878. The Posse Comitatus Act, passed June 18, 1878, essentially outlines

TITLE I — DEPARTMENT OF HOMELAND SECURITY		
	Sec. 101.	Executive department; mission.
	Sec. 102.	Secretary; functions.
	Sec. 103.	Other officers.
TITLE II — INFORMATION ANALYSIS AND INFRASTRUCTURE PROTECTION		
	Sec. 201.	Under Secretary for Information Analysis and Infrastructure Protection.
	Sec. 202.	Functions transferred.
	Sec. 203.	Access to information.
	Sec. 204.	Information voluntarily provided.
TITLE III — CHEMICAL, BIOLOGICAL, RADIOLOGICAL, AND NUCLEAR COUNTERMEASURES		
	Sec. 301.	Under Secretary for Chemical, Biological, Radiological, and Nuclear Countermeasures.
	Sec. 302.	Functions transferred.
	Sec. 303.	Conduct of certain public health-related activities.
	Sec. 304.	Military activities.
TITLE IV — BORDER AND TRANSPORTATION SECURITY		
	Sec. 401.	Under Secretary for Border and Transportation Security.
	Sec. 402.	Functions transferred.
	Sec. 403.	Visa issuance.
TITLE V — EMERGENCY PREPAREDNESS AND RESPONSE		
	Sec. 501.	Under Secretary for Emergency Preparedness and Response.
	Sec. 502.	Functions transferred.
	Sec. 503.	Nuclear incident response.
	Sec. 504.	Definition.
	Sec. 505.	Conduct of certain public health-related activities.
TITLE VI — MANAGEMENT		
	Sec. 601.	Under Secretary for Management.
	Sec. 602.	Chief Financial Officer.
	Sec. 603.	Chief Information Officer.
TITLE VII — COORDINATION WITH NON-FEDERAL ENTITIES; INSPECTOR GENERAL; UNITED STATES SECRET SERVICE; GENERAL PROVISIONS		
Subtitle A — Coordination with Non-Federal Entities		
	Sec. 701.	Responsibilities.
Subtitle B — Inspector General		
	Sec. 710.	Authority of the Secretary.
Subtitle C — United States Secret Service		
	Sec. 720.	Functions transferred.
Subtitle D — General Provisions		
	Sec. 730.	Establishment of human resources management system.
	Sec. 731.	Advisory committees.
	Sec. 732.	Acquisitions; property.
	Sec. 733.	Reorganization; transfer.
	Sec. 734.	Miscellaneous provisions.
	Sec. 735.	Authorization of appropriations.
TITLE VIII — TRANSITION		
	Sec. 801.	Definitions.
	Sec. 802.	Transfer of agencies.
	Sec. 803.	Transitional authorities.
	Sec. 804.	Savings provisions.

FIGURE 3.4 Table of contents of the *Homeland Security Act of 2002.*

Sec. 805.	Terminations.
Sec. 806.	Incidental transfers.
TITLE IX — CONFORMING AND TECHNICAL AMENDMENTS	
Sec. 901.	Inspector General Act.
Sec. 902.	Executive Schedule.
Sec. 903.	United States Secret Service.
Sec. 904.	Coast Guard.
Sec. 905.	Strategic National Stockpile and smallpox vaccine development.
Sec. 906.	Select agent registration.
Sec. 907.	National Bio-Weapons Defense Analysis Center.

FIGURE 3.4   (Continued)

limits on the federal government's use of military force for the purposes of law enforcement. Section 886 of the Homeland Security Act refers to Posse Comitatus:

> SEC 886(b) SENSE OF CONGRESS.—Congress reaffirms the continued importance of section 1385 of title 18, United States Code, and it is the sense of Congress that nothing in this Act should be construed to alter the applicability of such section to any use of the Armed Forces as a posse comitatus to execute the laws.[7]

Section 1385 of title 18 is the reference to Posse Comitatus and, per November 11, 2002 remarks of then-President George W. Bush, essentially the Homeland Security Act and Section 886(b) "does not purport to alter, modify, or otherwise affect the Posse Comitatus Act or judicial interpretations of that Act, and the executive branch shall construe this provision accordingly."[8]

This becomes relevant and creates an interesting debate, however, as on October 1, 2002, just past the one-year anniversary of 9/11, United States Northern Command (USNORTHCOM, or simply, NORTHCOM) was created.[9] A Unified Combatant Command (UCC) of the U.S. military, meaning it has multiple branches of the military under a single command, its purpose is to provide command and control of Department of Defense (DoD) homeland defense efforts and to coordinate defense support of civil authorities. In recent years, there has been a growing debate among politicians and government policymakers and scholars over what role, if any, the U.S. military should take in domestic operations. Though not exempt when deployed under federal service, the National Guard is exempt during peacetime or when specifically called on by state governors during crisis and disaster situations. The U.S. Coast Guard (USCG) is likewise exempt from Posse Comitatus.

Since its creation, NORTHCOM has aided in counter-drug operations as well as in response to Hurricane Katrina and multiple California and Colorado wildfires, as well as other similar regional domestic natural disaster events. Most recently, NORTHCOM provided logistical support during Hurricane Sandy when mid-Atlantic states like New York and New Jersey were devastated by severe coastal erosion and water and wind damage[10] (see Figure 3.5).

It remains to be seen what the ultimate policy on and role of NORTHCOM will be in responding to natural disasters or mass civil disturbances in the future.

FIGURE 3.5 Hurricane Sandy—Rockaway, New York. (Courtesy of FEMA.)

3.2.6 USA Patriot Act: USA Freedom Act of 2015

One of the most controversial pieces of legislation that arose from the turbulent post-9/11 period was the Patriot Act.[11] The Patriot Act was developed out of the belief that our intelligence had been very poor prior to the attacks. It sought to remediate the perceived failures in intelligence and ensure such an attack would never occur again. Patriot Act proposals, swiftly drafted, were just as quickly signed and executed by President Bush on October 26, 2001. Given the intensity of the times, it is not surprising that a bill of this import found formal approval in so short a time span. The times influenced the aggressive nature of the bill. A thumbnail sketch of the act displays this inclination to expand or alter historic restrictions:

- Information sharing—The act liberalizes the sharing of intelligence information and removes most historical barriers to said sharing. Critics argue that the data will be used by other agencies for unrelated purposes or improper reasons.
- Roving wiretaps—The act permits the jurisdictional grant of one wiretap order that works or roves in multiple jurisdictions. Given the transiency of terrorists and the difficulties of dealing with diverse jurisdictions, the policy makes sense. Critics claim it will lead to an open-ended form of electronic surveillance.
- Foreign intelligence and wiretaps—The act liberalizes the grant and extent of this activity. New standards for use have been enacted. Critics claim this will lead to abuse.
- Sneak and peek warrants—In criminal parlance, "exigent" circumstances have always permitted law enforcement to search a house without a warrant. The act permits quick searches, without notification, of a suspected terrorist place of abode under an "any crime" provision. Critics note that the historic standard of these types of searches relates to loss of evidence or other exigency.
- Material support—The act expands the definition of support to include advice and counsel. Historically, "material" support related to economic or planning support

that was central to the plot and plan. The idea of how one can support has been expanded. Critics claim this violates free speech.

The Patriot Act was reauthorized in 2006 despite significant controversy[12] (see Figure 3.6). One of the act's most formidable allies was DHS. DHS publicly advocated for the passage of the reauthorization since it had amassed concrete examples of how effective the act had been in the apprehension of terrorists and the prevention of terror. In December 2005, DHS exhorted Congress to finish up its business relative to the act by noting

> The Department of Homeland Security (DHS) benefits significantly from the USA Patriot Act and urges the United States Congress to reauthorize this proven tool in the global war on terror. The Patriot Act breaks down barriers to information sharing, enabling law enforcement and intelligence personnel to share information that is needed to help connect the dots and disrupt potential terror and criminal activity before they can carry out their plots. The broad information sharing provisions better enables U.S. Customs and Border Protection to screen international visitors and determine whether an apprehended alien presents a threat to security or public safety.[13]

Internet Resource: To see the more important changes in the reauthorization bill, go to http://www.govtrack.us/congress/bill.xpd?bill=h109-3199&tab=summary.

During 2010–2011, the Patriot Act was reauthorized, although the debate was spirited and highly contentious on both sides of the aisle. The dissent even crossed party lines as liberals construed the broad sweep of police powers as being too unchecked, while conservatives concerned about the constitutional implications reached similar conclusions.[14] In particular, the "roving wiretaps" provision, whereby investigators seek court orders that allow changing phone-number follow-ups without court scrutiny, was a stumbling block. Concerns also emerged regarding the sweeping data collection powers and the warrantless

FIGURE 3.6 President George W. Bush is joined by House and Senate representatives as he signs H.R. 3199, USA Patriot Improvement and Reauthorization Act of 2005, Thursday, March 9, 2006, in the East Room of the White House. (White House photo by Eric Draper.)

scrutiny of metadata and other communication information that the act seemed to allow without legal oversight. The act reiterated its three-part requirement when seeking the court order:

- Establishing probable cause that the target of the surveillance is a foreign power or agent of a foreign power
- Establishing probable cause that the device is being used or about to be used by a foreign power or agent of a foreign power
- Establishing that the actions of the target may have the effect of blocking their identification[15]

The reauthorized act also retained the more liberal and flexible standard when seizing the business records of a suspected terrorist, and instead of the historic "specific and articulable facts" requirement, a court could issue an order based on a "relevancy standard."[16]

By 2015, and with the media explosion caused by the Edward Snowden defection to Russia and his release of documents exposing the powers exerted by the National Security Agency (NSA), the Central Intelligence Agency (CIA), and law enforcement under this act, Congress revised and retitled the act the "Freedom Act of 2015."[17] The act's primary aim was

> To reform the authorities of the Federal Government to require the production of certain business records, conduct electronic surveillance, use pen registers and trap and trace devices, and use other forms of information gathering for foreign intelligence, counterterrorism, and criminal purposes, and for other purposes.[18]

Internet Exercise: Review the Edward Snowden interview and time line at http://www. nbcnews.com/feature/edward-snowden-interview/edward-snowden-timeline-n114871.

The provisions of the act now restrict broad, sweeping review of various forms of data without prior judicial approval from either traditional or specialized courts set up for said review.

Internet Exercise: For the full text of the U.S. Freedom Act, visit https://www.congress.gov/bill/114th-congress/house-bill/2048.

3.2.7 Specialized Laws

Aside from the broader legislation and regulations covering the world of homeland security, there are myriad other laws and rules promulgated on behalf of or by administrative agencies and departments entrusted with functions in homeland protection.

3.2.7.1 REAL ID Program

Concerns over the legitimacy and integrity of driver's licenses resulted in the promulgation of a new DHS program—REAL ID.[19] The program sets minimum standards for the issuance of driver's licenses, including

- Information and security features that must be incorporated into each card
- Proof of identity and U.S. citizenship or legal status of an applicant
- Verification of the source documents provided by an applicant
- Security standards for the offices that issue licenses and identification cards

Eventually, there will be an integration of other identification (ID) triggers such as social security and birth certificates; however, at this stage, the driver's license has yet to be systematically governed. Critics of the act claim that it devises a national identity card program, but this criticism seems somewhat inaccurate. The provisions of the act reaffirm the preeminence of state governments in the matter of issuance and oversight. DHS posts a Q&A piece that deals with common misconceptions regarding REAL ID, shown in Figure 3.7.

Even DHS fosters an ambivalent and less than supportive view of the program due to costs and implementation challenges. In its Inspector General (IG) report, DHS remarked:

> Potentially high costs pose a significant challenge to states in their efforts to implement REAL ID. Specifically, state officials considered REAL ID implementation costs prohibitive because of requirements such as the reenrollment of all current driver's license and identification card holders and the new verification processes. Further, state officials in 17 of the 19 states we contacted indicated they needed more timely guidance from DHS to estimate the full cost of implementing REAL ID. State officials also said that REAL ID grants did not sufficiently mitigate the costs, and they viewed communication of grant information by DHS as ineffective.[20]

With nearly a decade of legislative life, the REAL ID program has yet to fully materialize on a state-by-state level. Implementation results have been dramatically mixed. By 2011, only 11 states had completely implemented the program.[21]

Pace and commitment still differ among the states, but there is a noteworthy reduction in discussion as states are finding out that implementation, on the whole, is not as expensive as they thought and is achievable. States such as Maryland and Delaware, once committed, have completed the implementation of the 18 benchmarks needed to fulfill material compliance with the law within a year for only twice the grant monies provided by the federal government. Extrapolated out, that puts the total costs for implementing these key 18 REAL ID benchmarks in the range from $350 million to $750 million, an order of magnitude less than estimated previously. And with metrics in place, the story of REAL ID's value in securing against fraud is beginning to take shape not simply as theory but as reality.[22]

The card design requirements are estimated at $1.1 billion.[23]

While compliance dates have been extended twice now, it appears unlikely that most states will ever be compliant with the diverse requirements of the act.[24]

DHS continues to issues extension to a great many states that have yet to comply and presently only designates American Samoa and Minnesota as fully noncompliant. Critics have also called into question the constitutionality of this sort of federalized oversight in the matter of national identity.[25]

Myth: REAL ID creates a national identification (ID) card

Fact: REAL ID simply sets minimum standards so that the public can have confidence in the security and integrity of driver's licenses and identification cards issued by all participating states and jurisdictions.

States and jurisdictions will maintain their ability to design and issue their own unique driver's licenses and identification cards. Each state and jurisdiction will continue to have flexibility with regard to the design and security features used on the card. Where REAL ID details the minimum data elements that must be included on the face of the card, most states and jurisdictions already include all or almost all of these data elements on their cards.

REAL ID identification documents will not be the only form of documentation accepted by the federal government or any other entity. You can still present another form of acceptable identification such as a U.S. passport, military ID, or government identification badge. If you do not have another form of acceptable documentation, however, you may experience delays at the airport due to the requirement for additional security screening.

Myth: REAL ID creates a national database of personal information

Fact: REAL ID requires that authorized DMV officials have the capability to verify that an applicant holds only one valid REAL ID. REAL ID does not grant the Federal Government or law enforcement greater access to DMV data, nor does it create a national database.

States will continue to manage and operate databases for driver's license and identification card issuance.

REAL ID does not create a national database or require additional personal information on your driver's license than is already required by most states. It simply verifies the documents an applicant presents at the DMV to confirm the individual's identity and ensure that each individual has only one valid REAL ID.

Personally identifiable information, beyond the minimum information necessary to appropriately route verification queries, will not be stored.

Myth: REAL ID will diminish privacy

Fact: The REAL ID final rule calls on states to protect personal identity information. It requires each state to develop a security plan and lists a number of privacy and security elements that must be included in the plan.

The DHS Privacy Office has also issued Best Practices for the Protection of Personally Identifiable Information Associated with State Implementation of the Real ID Act, which provides useful guidance to states on how to address the privacy and security of information related to REAL ID.

The REAL ID Act will not allow motor vehicle driver's data to be made available in a manner that does not conform to the Driver's Privacy Protection Act. Furthermore, with

REAL ID, DMV employees will be subject to background checks, a necessary step to protect against insider fraud, just one of the vulnerabilities to a secure licensing system. These steps raise the bar for state DMVs beyond what was previously required.

DHS recognizes the importance of protecting privacy and ensuring the security of the personal information associated with implementation of the REAL ID Act.

Myth: DHS is creating a "hub" in order to gain access to Department of Motor Vehicle (DMV) information

Fact: An electronic verification hub will be designed to facilitate connectivity between the states and data owners to ensure that people applying for a REAL ID are who they say they are. The Federal Government will not gain greater access to DMV information as a result. Only authorized DMV officials and law enforcement will have access to DMV records.

REAL ID requires state DMVs to verify an applicant's identity document, date of birth, Social Security Number, residence and lawful status, as well as ensure that each individual has only one valid REAL ID. For example, the electronic verification hub will facilitate the statetostate exchange of information to check for duplicate registrations in multiple states, therefore limiting the ability for persons to obtain multiple licenses for fraudulent purposes.

While DHS has pledged to fund the development and deployment of the hub, states will continue to manage and operate databases for driver's license and identification card issuance. DHS and the states will work together to ensure that security measures are in place to prevent unauthorized access or use of the information. Personally identifiable information, beyond the minimum information necessary to appropriately route verification queries, will not be stored.

Myth: REAL ID is an unfunded mandate

Fact: To date, approximately $90 million in dedicated grant funds have been offered by DHS to assist states with REAL ID implementation. This includes approximately $40 million in Fiscal Year (FY) 2006 and $50 million in FY 2008. An additional 20% of State Homeland Security Grant funds are discretionary and can be used for this purpose as well.

The President's Fiscal Year 2009 budget request includes up to $150 million in grants for states to implement REAL ID (up to $110 million from National Security and Terrorism Prevention Grants and again, 20% of the State Homeland Security Grants).

DHS requested $50 million in Fiscal Year 2009 appropriated funds for the establishment of a stateowned and operated verification system. Furthermore, DHS cut the total costs to states by more than $10 billion from an original estimate of $14.6 billion to approximately $3.9 billion, a 73% reduction. States will continue to have discretionary authority to use up to 20% of their Homeland Security Grant funds for REAL ID implementation.

In order to focus the first phase of enrollment on those persons who may present the highest risk, DHS outlined an agebased enrollment approach to REAL ID allowing other individuals to be phasedin later. Phasedin enrollment eases the burden on states to reenroll their entire driver's license and identification card population by providing additional time to accommodate the reenrollment process.

FIGURE 3.7   REAL ID myths and facts.

3.2.7.2 *Office of Biometric Identity Management;*
Formerly Office of US-VISIT

The Office of Biometric Identity Management (OIBM), formerly known as U.S. Visitor and Immigrant Status Indicator Technology (US-VISIT), resides in DHS and under the National Protection and Programs Directorate and was established to track the entry and exit of travelers to the United States by biometric means—digital fingerprints and photographs. The guiding principles of OIBM are to

- Enhance the security of our citizens and visitors
- Facilitate legitimate travel and trade
- Ensure the integrity of the immigration system
- Protect the privacy of our visitors

The use of biometrics represents the cutting edge of identity assurance. By using unique physical characteristics, the agency can zero in on identity in a highly dependable way. OIBM uses biometric information to

- Check a person's biometrics against a watch list of known or suspected terrorists, criminals, and immigration violators
- Check against the entire database of all of the fingerprints DHS has collected since US-VISIT began to determine if a person is using an alias and attempting to use fraudulent identification
- Check a person's biometrics against those associated with the identification document presented to ensure that the document belongs to the person presenting it and not to someone else

Presently, the office is proposing a series of protocols for visitation. Upon a person's entry into the United States, a Customs and Border Protection officer (CBPO) uses inkless, digital finger scanners to scan both the left and right index finger of the person. The officer also takes a digital photograph.

OBIM's Biometric Support Center (BSC) provides DHS biometric verification services. Its primary mission is to provide expert fingerprint identification services to support DHS components along with federal, state, and local law enforcement agencies; intelligence agencies; and foreign partners.[26]

To support this diverse customer base, OBIM employs contractor resources of highly skilled 10-print and latent fingerprint examiners operating 24 hours per day, 7 days per week to support critical immigration and border management missions, investigations, and identifications of potential persons of interest and unknown individuals. Specifically, the BSC supports OBIM's biometric verification capabilities by providing

- 10-print verification services to supplement IDENT's automated matching capabilities
- Latent print services involving the comparison and verification of known fingerprints with previously unidentified latent fingerprints

- Supplemental biometric services including IDENT biometric watchlist enrollments and biometric searches of IDENT for non-DHS stakeholders, including unknown deceased individuals, and biometric record maintenance[27]

Internet Resource: See the DHS instructional guidance for visitors at http://www.dhs.gov/ xlibrary/assets/usvisit/US-VISIT_Updated_Entry_StepxStep.pdf.

3.2.7.3 Chemical Facilities

DHS has been actively involved in the oversight of chemical facilities due to their capacity to inflict widespread damage. Antiterrorism standards must be integrated in the design, plan, and operational security of designated chemical facilities. Congress, in passage of the 2007 Homeland Security reauthorization,[28] applies these standards because of the inherent risk to these facilities. DHS defines the risk as

- The consequence of a successful attack on a facility (consequence)
- The likelihood that an attack on a facility will be successful (vulnerability)
- The intent and capability of an adversary in respect of attacking a facility (threat)

DHS establishes risk-based performance standards for the security of the country's chemical facilities. Covered chemical facilities are required to

- Prepare security vulnerability assessments, which identify facility security vulnerabilities
- Develop and implement site security plans, which include measures that satisfy the identified risk-based performance standards

Internet Resource: Review the anti-terrorism standards for chemical plants at http://www. dhs.gov/cfats-risk-based-performance-standards.

DHS publishes a list of chemical products of significant interest to the country and a list of assessment tools to ensure compliance.[29] Chemical facilities are construed as infrastructure.

3.2.7.4 Invention and Technology: The SAFETY Act

One of the best-kept secrets of the Homeland Security Act of 2002 was its desire to promote innovation in antiterrorism efforts. Innovation in technology is always a risky business. When the potential legal liabilities are added to the process of invention, such as being open to a lawsuit, the inventor is less aggressive. The *Support Antiterrorism by Fostering Effective Technologies Act of 2002 (SAFETY Act)*[30] provides a safe harbor for the inventor and the product developer.

Internet Resource: For a complete review of the Safety Act's many facets, see https://www. safetyact.gov/pages/homepages/Home.do.

It also provides a certification process whereby DHS approves a product for use in the fight against terrorism (see Figure 3.8).

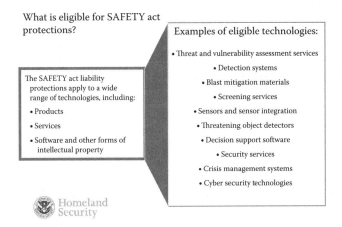

FIGURE 3.8   Technologies protected by the SAFETY Act.

As of 2015, hundreds of products and services have been approved. Some recent examples are shown in Figure 3.9.

To be an approved seller or certified developer of antiterrorism technology, the party has to register. The process commences in a fairly simple way (see the registration document in Figure 3.10).

Internet Resources: For numerous guides and instructions, visit the Safety Act website at https://www.safetyact.gov and access their "printer friendly materials" list.

3.3 Budgeting, Finance, and Funding in Homeland Security

Allocation of funds for operations depends on a multiplicity of factors. The age and history of a department influence funding; so too do the level of political importance and the social and cultural demand for a particular service or program. Priorities in budgeting are guided by many forces.[31] In the very short life of DHS, we have witnessed a radical evolution and an equally radical budgetary maturation. In less than 12 years, DHS has grown exponentially in matters of budget. In each of those years, while its numbers grew, it decided on a new and hopefully improved allocation formula. From 2003 on, Congress and the executive branch looked closely at how best to allocate these precious funds. What has been patently obvious is that the investment in homeland security has not been cheap.

3.3.1 Budget Year: 2003

Since budgets are prepared a year in advance, the events of 9/11, happening close to the end of 2001, made any 2002 budget a factual impossibility. At best, the funds earmarked for homeland security in early 2002 would be strictly supplemental in design. Add to this the fact that DHS had yet to become a complete department with cabinet status, and the budget

FIGURE 3.9 Safety Act approved technologies listings. (https://www.safetyact.gov.)

for the financial year (FY) 2002 was nothing more than a hodgepodge of supplemental additions to existing agencies. By March 2003, the initial allocations were targeted at

- Supporting first responders
- Defending against bioterrorism
- Securing America's borders
- Using twenty-first-century technology to secure the country (see Figure 3.11).

The lack of a centralized cabinet-level agency was obvious as money was distributed during this budget cycle. Departments such as the Federal Emergency Management Agency (FEMA) and the departments of justice, health and human services, and energy all shared some portion of these homeland funds. In the 2003 budget cycle, the diversity of agencies participating foreshadowed the natural growing pains of an agency soon to be at the forefront (see Figure 3.12).

3.3.2 Budget Year: 2004

By mid-2003, the idea of a cabinet-level agency for homeland security had come to fruition. Like any new agency of government, special allotments—as start-up costs, so to speak—were

The initial step in applying for the liability protections available under the SAFETY Act or for requesting a Pre-Application Consultation is to register with OSAI. Registration can be done electronically at the SAFETY Act website (http://www.safetyact.gov). You can also register by mail, using the forms included in this kit, or you can download an electronic copy of the form, complete it, and mail in the electronic document on a compact disc. Mailed registrations (hard copy or CD) should be sent to:

U.S. Department of Homeland Security
ATTN: Office of SAFETY Act
Implementation
245 Murray Lane, Building 410
Washington, DC 20528

Remember that physical mail sent to DHS is screened and processed, which may delay the Department's response to your submission. Registering with OSAI does not commit you to any further actions. The purpose of Registration is to establish an official point of contact for the Department to use in its interactions with you concerning your Technology and to create a unique identification number for you as a potential seller. This identifier will help the Department track and maintain your application. The SAFETY Act application process is designed to be flexible and to involve ongoing dialogue with the Applicant. Appropriate "points of contact" will facilitate this dialogue. The Applicant's point of contact may be any person you desire to coordinate your application and may include counsel, a representative of management, a technical expert or any other person you consider appropriate for this purpose.

(Registration Form on following page)

REGISTRATION AS A SELLER
OF ANTITERRORISM TECHNOLOGY

ACTION

R1. Purpose of Registration *(choose one)*:
　　Initial Registration
　　Updated or Corrected Registration Information

REGISTRATION DATA

R2. Seller Name:
R3. Data Universal Numbering System (DUNS) Number (if available):

_____

R4. North American Industry Classification System (NAICS) Code (if available):

POINT-OF-CONTACT INFORMATION

R5. Primary Point of Contact:
　　Name: _____
　　Address: _____
　　State/Province: _____ Country: _____ ZIP/Mail Code: _____
　　Telephone No.: _____ Fax No.: _____ E-mail: _____
　　E-mail Communication Authorized?　Yes　No

R6. Secondary Point of Contact (*optional*):
　　Name: _____
　　Address: _____
　　State/Province:_____ Country:_____ ZIP/Mail Code: _____
　　Telephone No.:_____ Fax No.:_____ E-mail:_____
　　E-mail Communication Authorized?　Yes　No

FIGURE 3.10　Registration as a seller of antiterrorism technology.

Instructions for Completing Registration Form:

ACTION

Item R1. Purpose of Registration

If your company or business unit has not previously registered with OSAI, check "Initial registration." A company may file more than one registration; certain companies may wish to file multiple registrations if it has multiple business units selling dissimilar types of Technologies. As a rule, the entity that sells the Technology is the entity that should register.

If you are updating or correcting previous registration information, check "Updated or Corrected Registration Information." OSAI strongly encourages you to keep your registration information up to date. In particular, be sure to notify OSAI of any changes in contact information.

REGISTRATION DATA

Item R2. Seller Name

Enter the legal name of your organization. If there will be business affiliates who will also be "sellers" of the Technology, please enter their legal names.

Item R3. Data Universal Numbering System (DUNS) Number

If your company has a nine-digit DUNS number, enter it here. If your company does not have a DUNS number, you do not need to provide one.

Item R4. North American Industry Classification System (NAICS) Code

NAICS Codes can be found in the official 2002 US NAICS Manual North American Industry Classification System—United States, 2002, available from the National Technical Information Service, (800) 553-6847 or (703) 605-6000, or directly from http://www.census.gov/epcd/www/naics.html.

POINT-OF-CONTACT INFORMATION

Item R5. Primary Point of Contact

Enter the name of the individual who will serve as the primary point of contact for interactions between your organization and OSAI. Provide a business address and telephone information for this person. OSAI prefers not to use personal or home contact information unless no other contact information is available. Include area codes and any non-U.S. country codes in telephone and fax numbers. If you wish to permit OSAI to correspond with this individual by e-mail, enter a valid e-mail address in the space provided.

The Applicant's point of contact may be any person you desire to coordinate your application and may include counsel, a representative of management, a technical expert or any other person you consider appropriate for this purpose.

Item R6. Secondary Point of Contact

Enter the name and contact information for an alternate point of contact in your organization. OSAI will attempt to contact this person only if it is unable to reach the primary point of contact identified in item R5.

FIGURE 3.10 (Continued)

issued. In addition, during the reorganization phase of 2003, a host of agencies and departments, such as the USCG and Secret Service, were merged into DHS. Hence, operational budgets had to reflect these costs of operation. By late 2003 and into 2004, a cabinet mentality was emerging in matters of homeland security. Yet, despite this developing culture, there were a series of adjustments, both structurally and fiscally, that DHS had to go through.

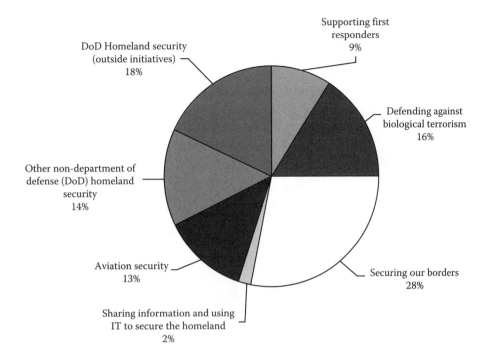

FIGURE 3.11   Homeland security distribution for FY 2003 by activity. (George W. Bush, *Securing Our Homeland: Strengthening our Future* [June 2003].)

Homeland security distribution of FY 2003 request by agency

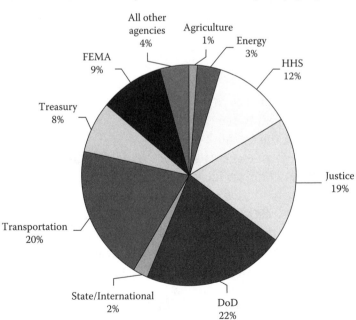

FIGURE 3.12   Homeland security budget distribution for FY 2003. (George W. Bush, *Securing Our Homeland: Strengthening our Future* [June 2003].)

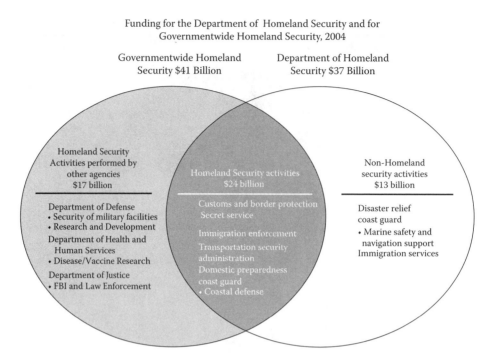

Funding for the Department of Homeland Security and for
Governmentwide Homeland Security, 2004

FIGURE 3.13   DHS funding and aligned governmental agency funding.

The Office of Management and Budget charted this truncated approach by displaying how agencies and their functions often mix and merge together (see Figure 3.13).[32]

Here, we witness how historic governmental entities, such as the Department of Defense (DoD), FEMA, the Federal Bureau of Investigation (FBI), and the USCG, would continue historic contributions to the protection of the homeland. In time, more and more of these bifurcated functions coalesced into DHS. By 2004, DHS had centered its attention on four areas of responsibility:

- Border and transportation security—encompasses airline security and inspection of cargo at points of entry into the United States to prevent unwanted individuals or weapons from entering the country.
- Domestic counterterrorism—consists largely of federal law enforcement and investigative activities that center on identifying and apprehending terrorists. Primary responsibility for those activities rests with the Department of Justice's FBI.
- Protection of critical infrastructure and key assets—includes ensuring the physical security of national landmarks and critical infrastructure (e.g., bridges and power plants) as well as the physical security of federal buildings and installations. The DoD receives the largest share of funding for this purpose.
- Defense against catastrophic threats—entails efforts to prevent terrorists from obtaining weapons of mass destruction (WMD: chemical, biological, or nuclear) and activities to mitigate the effects of such weapons if they are used. The Department of Health and Human Services (HHS) carries out most of those tasks.

FIGURE 3.14   U.S. Coast Guard's Deepwater logo.

With full department status, 2004 saw an extraordinary operational infusion. At the same time, the department stressed certain core values in its mission. Budgetary allotments mirrored these values, which were

- Securing the nation's borders and transportation systems
- Securing the nation's ports and ensuring safety in our waters
- Improving information analysis and infrastructure protection
- Advancing and harnessing science and technology
- Preparing for and responding to national emergencies
- Improving immigration services
- Other DHS activities and support

As for border and transportation, DHS doubled the budget from the previous year, which largely reflected the cache of new employees—approximately 60,000 individuals were hired. Many of these employees were sent directly to the nation's airports to carry on the business of the Transportation Security Agency (TSA). Training funds were also widely disseminated to ensure a "same page" mentality among all agencies and departments, as well as state and local contributors responsible for homeland security.

As for ports and waterways, the emphasis was the same—to launch and support DHS initiatives. New maritime safety and security teams were developed; seed money for a maritime 911 was provided and multimillions given to the USCG to shore up and increase its aging fleet (see Figure 3.14).

In the area of emergency response, the 2004 budget initiated the merger of FEMA and DHS, expanding and redefining the nature of disaster. From this budgetary cycle forward, DHS would see terror and hurricane from an identical prism. Billions were made available to develop a national stockpile for drugs, vaccines, and other medical supplies.

DETAILED INFORMATION ABOUT THE STOCKPILE: HELPING STATE AND LOCAL JURISDICTIONS PREPARE FOR A NATIONAL EMERGENCY

An act of terrorism (or a large-scale natural disaster) targeting the U.S. civilian population will require rapid access to large quantities of pharmaceuticals and medical supplies. Such quantities may not be readily available unless special stockpiles are created. No one can anticipate exactly where a terrorist will strike, and few state or local governments have the resources to create sufficient stockpiles on their own. Therefore, a national stockpile has been created as a resource for all.

FIGURE 3.15 A national repository of life-saving pharmaceuticals and medical material.

In 1999, Congress charged the HHS and the Centers for Disease Control and Prevention (CDC) with the establishment of the National Pharmaceutical Stockpile (NPS). The mission was to provide a resupply of large quantities of essential medical material to states and communities during an emergency within 12 hours of the federal decision to deploy.

The Homeland Security Act of 2002 tasked DHS with defining the goals and performance requirements of the Strategic National Stockpile (SNS) program as well as managing the actual deployment of assets. Effective on March 1, 2003, the NPS became the SNS program managed jointly by DHS and HHS. With the signing of the BioShield legislation, the SNS program was returned to HHS for oversight and guidance. The SNS program works with governmental and nongovernmental partners to upgrade the nation's public health capacity to respond to a national emergency. Critical to the success of this initiative is ensuring capacity is developed at federal, state, and local levels to receive, stage, and dispense SNS assets (see Figure 3.15).

The SNS is a national repository of antibiotics, chemical antidotes, antitoxins, life-support medications, IV administration, airway maintenance supplies, and medical/surgical items. The SNS is designed to supplement and resupply state and local public health agencies in the event of a national emergency anywhere and at any time within the United States or its territories.

The SNS is organized for flexible response. The first line of support lies within the immediate response 12-hour Push Packages. These are caches of pharmaceuticals, antidotes, and medical supplies designed to provide rapid delivery of a broad spectrum of assets for an ill-defined threat in the early hours of an event. These Push Packages are positioned in strategically located, secure warehouses ready for immediate deployment to a designated site within 12 hours of the federal decision to deploy SNS assets.

If the incident requires additional pharmaceuticals and/or medical supplies, follow-on vendor managed inventory (VMI) supplies will be shipped to arrive within 24–36 hours. If the agent is well defined, VMI can be tailored to provide pharmaceuticals, supplies, and/or products specific to the suspected or confirmed agent(s). In this case, the VMI could act as the first option for immediate response from the SNS program.

To advance the use of science and technology in the fight against terrorism, the 2004 budget proposed a sevenfold increase over the previous year. The key emphasis was on the detection of radiological, chemical, nuclear, and biological threats. A total of $137 million was earmarked for detection systems at points of entry and within the transportation infrastructure, and $365 million was allotted for the detection and prevention of biological attacks and the implementation of a new department exclusively dedicated to these tasks—the National Biodefense Analysis and Countermeasures Center (NBACC) (see Figure 3.16).

FIGURE 3.16 National Biodefense Analysis and Countermeasures Center.

Internet Resource: Read a recent report on the progress, successes, and struggles in the development of the NBACC at http://www.fas.org/sgp/crs/homesec/RL32891.pdf.

ABOUT NATIONAL BIODEFENSE ANALYSIS AND COUNTERMEASURES CENTER

National Biodefense Analysis and Countermeasures Center

The gross space, or entire footprint of the facility, is expected to be about 160,000 square feet. This includes administrative areas, BSL-2, 3, and 4 laboratory spaces, air-handling equipment space, security controls, and other supporting features. NBACC expects to employ 120 researchers and support staff.

NBACC Interim Capability

An interim capability for the NBFAC has been established in partnership with the FBI and the U.S. Army at the U.S. Army Medical Research Institute of Infectious Diseases (USAMRIID). The BTCC supports risk assessment and threat characterization research in other established government and nongovernmental laboratories, including USAMRIID.

   The permanent NBACC facility will be located at Fort Detrick, Maryland, once construction is completed in 2008.

Safety Measures

The NBFAC will employ state-of-the-art biosafety procedures and equipment to prevent biological material from escaping into the environment. Rigorous safeguards protect those who work in the laboratory and the surrounding community.

   Once construction is complete, the NBACC facility will feature proven safeguards, applying time-tested rigorous design standards, special safety equipment, and exacting operating procedures to govern all research.

   These standards, equipment, and procedures have been demonstrated to provide the highest level of safety in existing laboratories elsewhere at Fort Detrick and throughout the United States.

> The security of the NBACC facility will be safeguarded through strict control access at all times for those working in the laboratory facility. To gain access to select agents, individuals must complete an in-depth background investigation and demonstrate competency in safety and security equipment and procedures in accordance with both Department of Homeland Security regulations and federal law.
>
> By locating the NBACC facility at Fort Detrick, the Department leverages the security provided by the U.S. Army military garrison with biocontainment-specific capabilities to create a controlled, secure environment.

In the area of information sharing and analysis and infrastructure protection, the DHS budget of 2004 funded shared databases, provided essential mechanisms for shared intelligence, and erected a 24/7 intelligence and warning system. The 2004 budget delivered funds to states and localities to develop partnerships and information-sharing systems as well as finances to establish compatible communication systems. The budget provided the necessary funds to create the Homeland Security Advisory Warning System (see Figure 3.17).

Finally, the 2004 budget recognized the dramatic need for improved immigration services. In particular, the budget fully recognized the negative impacts caused by chronic and continuous backlogs.

By 2011, however, the National Advisory System, the color-coded version, had been scrapped in favor of the National Terrorism Advisory System (NTAS) (see Figure 3.18).

This new system provides timely, detailed information to the public, government agencies, first responders, airports and other transportation hubs, and the private sector about terrorist threats. See Figure 3.19[33] for a sample alert format.

Finally, the 2004 budget recognized the dramatic need for improved immigration services. In particular, the budget fully recognized the negative impacts caused by chronic and continuous backlogs.

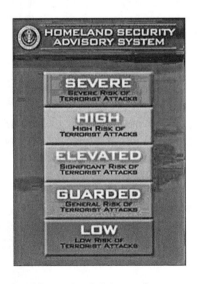

FIGURE 3.17   Levels of the Homeland Security Advisory System.

FIGURE 3.18 The Homeland Security Advisory Warning System was replaced by the National Terrorism Advisory System (NTAS).

Internet Resource: For the documentary side of the immigration application, see http://www.uscis.gov/forms.

3.3.3 Budget Year: 2005

Expenditures for homeland defense reflected the growth and priorities of the agency. Now in its second full year of operation, DHS, aside from support for the agency and its structure, targeted specific activities and honed its purpose. What is undeniably certain is that growth in the budget continued unabated[34] (see Figure 3.20).

As each year passes, the department searches for best practices and discerns where the threat is most imminent. By 2005, DHS stressed ports and maritime security, streamlined preparedness models, and enhanced biodefense practices through the increased use of science and technology, as well as providing sufficient funding for the training of first responders at the state and local levels.

Maritime concerns clearly took center stage in 2005 with the budget addressing numerous initiatives associated with port and shipping safety and security. Some examples worth noting are

- The Container Security Initiative (CSI), which focuses on prescreening cargo before it reaches our shores. The first phase of CSI focused on implementing the program at the top 20 foreign ports, which ship approximately two-thirds of the containers to the United States. Phase II expands the program to additional ports based on volume, location, and strategic concerns. Phase III further increases security at the highest-risk ports. The three core elements of CSI are to
  - Identify high-risk containers. Automated targeting tools are used to identify containers that pose a potential risk for terrorism, based on advance information and strategic intelligence.
  - Prescreen and evaluate containers before they are shipped. Containers are screened as early as possible in the supply chain, generally at the port of departure.
  - Use technology to prescreen high-risk containers to ensure that screening can be done rapidly without slowing down the movement of trade. This technology includes large-scale x-ray and gamma-ray machines and radiation detection devices.
- The Customs-trade Partnership Against Terrorism (C-TPAT), which began in November 2001, is another essential cargo security effort. C-TPAT focuses on

National Terrorism Advisory System

Alert

www.dhs.gov/alerts

DATE & TIME ISSUED: XXXX

SUMMARY

The Secretary of Homeland Security informs the public and relevant government and private sector partners about a potential or actual threat with this alert, indicating whether there is an "imminent" or "elevated" threat.

DURATION

An individual threat alert is issued for a specific time period and then automatically expires. It may be extended if new information becomes available or the threat evolves.

DETAILS

• This section provides more detail about the threat and what the public and sectors need to know.

• It may include specific information, if available, about the nature and credibility of the threat, including the critical infrastructure sector(s) or location(s) that may be affected.

• It includes as much information as can be released publicly about actions being taken or planned by authorities to ensure public safety, such as increased protective actions and what the public may expect to see.

AFFECTED AREAS

▪ This section includes visual depictions (such as maps or other graphics) showing the affected location(s), sector(s), or other illustrative detail about the threat itself.

HOW YOU CAN HELP

• This section provides information on ways the public can help authorities (e.g. camera phone pictures taken at the site of an explosion), and reinforces the importance of reporting suspicious activity.

• It may ask the public or certain sectors to be alert for a particular item, situation, person, activity or developing trend.

STAY PREPARED

• This section emphasizes the importance of the public planning and preparing for emergencies before they happen, including specific steps individuals, families and businesses can take to ready themselves and their communities.

• It provides additional preparedness information that may be relevant based on this threat.

STAY INFORMED

• This section notifies the public about where to get more information.

• It encourages citizens to stay informed about updates from local public safety and community leaders.

• It includes a link to the DHS NTAS website http://www.dhs.gov/alerts and http://twitter.com/NTASAlerts

If You See Something, Say Something™. Report suspicious activity to local law enforcement or call 911.

The National Terrorism Advisory System provides Americans with alert information on homeland security threats. It is distributed by the Department of Homeland Security. More information is available at: **www.dhs.gov/alerts.** To receive mobile updates: **www.twitter.com/NTASAlerts**
If You See Something Say Something™ used with permission of the NY Metropolitan Transportation Authority.

FIGURE 3.19 Sample DHS National Terrorism Advisory System alert.

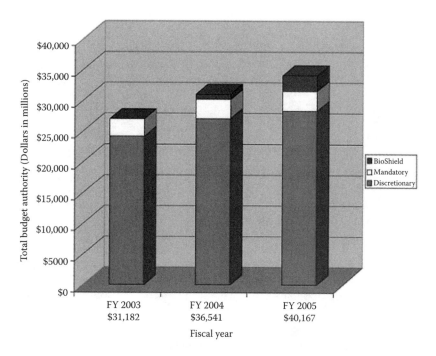

FIGURE 3.20   DHS funding 2003–2005.

partnerships all along the entire supply chain, from the factory floor, to foreign vendors, to land borders and seaports.

- Customs and border protection targeting systems aid in identifying high-risk cargo and passengers. The budget included an increase of $20.6 million for staffing and technology acquisition to support the National Targeting Center (NTC), trend analysis, and the automated targeting systems (ATS) (Figure 3.21).
- The US-VISIT program's first phase is being deployed at 115 airports and 14 seaports. US-VISIT expedites the arrival and departure of legitimate travelers, while making it more difficult for those intending to do us harm to enter our nation.
- Radiation detection monitors screen passengers and cargo coming into the United States. The budget includes $50 million for the next generation of screening devices (Figure 3.22).
- Aerial surveillance and sensor technology increases the effectiveness of the more than 12,000 Border Patrol agents deployed along the northern and southern borders, and it also supports other missions, such as drug interdiction (Figure 3.23).

On the biodefense front, DHS advanced a mix of technology with proven practices in the fight against terrorism. Project BioShield purchased and collected essential vaccines and medications for use in the event of a biological attack. Particular emphasis was given to vaccines for smallpox and anthrax exposure. In addition, just as in the nuclear theater, DHS expended millions developing and installing monitoring equipment that detects biological threats (Figure 3.24).

FIGURE 3.21 President George W. Bush tours the National Targeting Center (NTC) in Reston, Virginia, February 6, 2004. The NTC is part of Homeland Security's Bureau of Customs and Border Protection, and the center provides analytical research support for counterterrorism efforts.

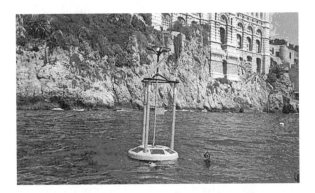

FIGURE 3.22 A radiation monitor at the entrance of a port. (Courtesy of International Atomic Energy Agency.)

FIGURE 3.23 Cargo ship at sea.

FIGURE 3.24 Example of a monitoring system installed at a port where cargo containers are unloaded. (www.whitehouse.gov.)

In the area of preparedness, the 2005 budget developed and implemented the National Incident Management System (NIMS) program and corresponding systems (Figure 3.25). NIMS is a program for all critical infrastructures and provides agencies, hospitals, and justice facilities with a plan of action that protects the facility and prevents attacks. In most jurisdictions, legislation now requires that staff and managers be educated in NIMS practices. NIMS trains and certifies both the personnel and agency.

In the areas of information and infrastructure protection, the budget reflected increased concerns over cyberterrorism (Figure 3.26). Expending nearly $68 million on the National Cyber Security Division—a center that identifies and analyzes cyber vulnerability—the 2005 budget appreciated the extraordinary implications of threats in the virtual world.

Cybersecurity threats generally fall into the following categories:

- Attempts (either failed or successful) to gain unauthorized access to a system or its data, including personally identifiable information (PII)-related incidents
- Unwanted disruption or denial of service
- Unauthorized use of a system for processing or storing data
- Changes to system hardware, firmware, or software characteristics without the owner's knowledge, instruction, or consent

The budget also delivered funding to develop threat assessment tools for infrastructure protection. Strategic assessments of threats to the country's critical infrastructures and key assets, including 168,000 public water systems, 300,000 oil and natural gas production facilities, 4,000 offshore platforms, 278,000 miles of natural gas pipelines, 361 seaports, 104 nuclear power plants, 80,000 dams, and tens of thousands of other potentially critical targets across 14 diverse critical infrastructure sectors, are a central aim of the budget.

The 2005 budget contributed more than just funding to the vision and plan of homeland security. Just as critically, the budget tied budgetary practices to general principles

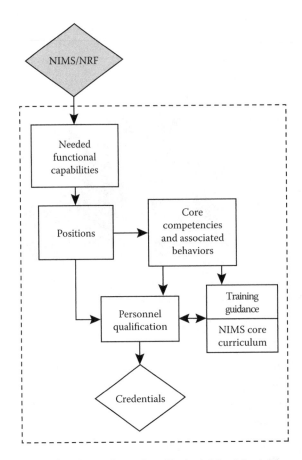

FIGURE 3.25 Department of Homeland Security, National Incident Management System (NIMS): Five-year NIMS training plan: National Integration Center (NIC), Incident Management Systems Integration (IMSI) Division, 4.

FIGURE 3.26 October is National Cyber Security Awareness Month.

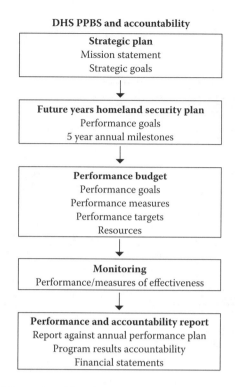

DHS PPBS and accountability

Strategic plan
Mission statement
Strategic goals

Future years homeland security plan
Performance goals
5 year annual milestones

Performance budget
Performance goals
Performance measures
Performance targets
Resources

Monitoring
Performance/measures of effectiveness

Performance and accountability report
Report against annual performance plan
Program results accountability
Financial statements

FIGURE 3.27   **Department of Homeland Security: Performance budget overview FY 2005, page 3.**

of accountability and assessment. In other words, the budget evaluated the efficacy of the disbursement in light of present strategic directions, future ambition of the departments, and overall accountability. As such, the budget became performance driven. Referring to a loop, the 2005 budget seeks to tie disbursement to effectiveness, as charted in Figure 3.27.

The goals and mission of DHS are evaluated in light of budgetary disbursement,[35] an example of which is shown in Figure 3.28.

3.3.4 Budget Year: 2006

Expenditures for homeland security continue an upward trek in 2006. When compared with 2005, the amount allotted for homeland protection is up 7%[36] (see Figure 3.29).

As each year passes, DHS expends more and more of its energy measuring and evaluating the effectiveness of its programs. In addition, it assesses all of its practices in light of changing demands and new detectable threats. To illustrate, the budget established the Domestic Nuclear Detection Office (DNDO), which seeks to detect and report efforts to acquire and deploy nuclear materials. The strategic objectives of the DNDO are to

- Develop the global nuclear detection and reporting architecture
- Develop, acquire, and support the domestic nuclear detection and reporting system
- Fully characterize detector system performance before deployment
- Facilitate situational awareness through information sharing and analysis

Performance Goal: Establish a fully capable Command, Control, Operations, and Information Exchange System.

Measure: Percentage increase in time efficiency of issuance of information and warning advisories.	Fiscal Year	FY 2003	FY 2004	FY 2005
	Target	None	Baseline	Increase by 10%
	Actual	None	t.b.d.	t.b.d.
Program: Homeland Security Operations Center	$ Thousands	None	$20,878	$36,212
Lead Organization: Information Analysis and Infrastructure Protection Directorate	FTE	None	None	8

Performance Goal: Increase time efficiency of issuance of information and warnings advisories by fifty percent.

Measure: Time efficiency of issuance of information and warning advisories	Fiscal Year	FY 2003	FY 2004	FY 2005
	Target	None	Baseline	Increase by 10%
	Actual	None	t.b.d.	t.b.d.
Program: Information & Warning Advisories	$ Thousands	None	$79,314	$93,056
Lead Organization: Information Analysis and Infrastructure Protection Directorate	FTE	None	None	202

Performance Goal: Reduction of "general" warnings as compared to "at risk" warnings by sixty percent from 2003 levels.

Measure: Reduction of general warnings, as compared to "at risk" warnings	Fiscal Year	FY 2003	FY 2004	FY 2005
	Target	None	Baseline	20%
	Actual	None	t.b.d.	t.b.d.
Program: Infrastructure Vulnerability & Risk Assessment	$ Thousands	None	$95,173	$85,033
Lead Organization: Information Analysis and Infrastructure Protection Directorate	FTE	None	None	85

FIGURE 3.28   Performance goals for DHS.

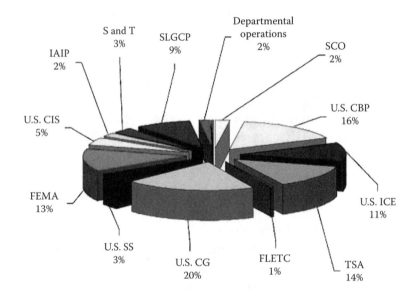

FIGURE 3.29   DHS budgetary lines—FY 2006.

- Establish operation protocols to ensure detection leads to effective response
- Conduct a transformational research and development program
- Provide centralized planning, integration, and advancement of U.S. government nuclear forensics programs

The budget additionally consolidated a host of research, development, and testing offices into the Science and Technology Directorate. In the area of border security, the line items recognize the increasing importance of safety and security at the country's geographic borders. Substantial funding for WMD detection equipment became available, as well as the institution of America's Shield Initiative, which employs electronic surveillance equipment at our borders. Long-range radar technology, which detects and intercepts aircraft illegally entering the United States, also received support.

The 2006 budget is generous in the area of law enforcement by supporting a host of initiatives, including

- The Armed Helicopter for Homeland Security Project—a project to provide the USCG with more firepower
- Federal Air Marshal Service—$689 million for increased safety in the air
- Response boats, cutters—increased budgeting for USCG upgrades (Figure 3.30)
- Flight deck and crew training in self-defense

The budget recognized the need for assistance to first responders by erecting the Office of State and Local Government Coordination and Preparedness (SLGCP). In the area of communications and first response, the Office of Interoperability and Compatibility will fund emergency systems to ensure compatible communication systems. As unbelievable as it may seem, emergency responders often cannot talk to some parts of their own agencies—let alone communicate with agencies in neighboring cities, counties, or states. DHS instituted the SAFECOM program, which plans and implements interoperability solutions for data and voice communications.

Internet Exercise: View the Introduction to SAFECOM Presentation accessible from SAFECOM's website at http://www.dhs.gov/safecom/about-safecom.

FIGURE 3.30   U.S. Coast Guard at work. (U.S. Navy photo by Kelly Newlin.)

Interoperability will succeed when the following five elements are achieved:

- Gain leadership commitment from all disciplines (e.g., emergency medical services [EMS], fire rescue response, and law enforcement)
- Foster collaboration across disciplines through leadership support
- Interface with policymakers to gain leadership commitment and resource support
- Use interoperability solutions regularly
- Plan and budget for ongoing updates to systems, procedures, and documentation

Communication upgrades are in store for the USCG. Rescue 21 will replace aging and often cumbersome equipment for coast guard service (see Figure 3.31).

How it works:

- A call for help is sent.
- Direction finding (DF) equipment from one or more high sites computes the direction from which the signal originated or the line of bearing (LOB).
- Distress audio and the LOB are sent to the closest ground center(s).
- Appropriate resources are dispatched to respond immediately—even across regional boundaries.[37]

Other programs emphasized in the 2006 budget include internal funding for more efficient DHS operation, including human resources, information sharing, electronic data capability, high-speed operational connectivity, and sufficient funding to operate the Homeland Security Operations Center (HSOC) (Figure 3.32).

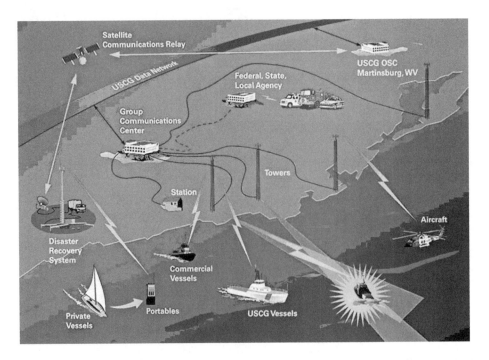

FIGURE 3.31   Rescue 21.

FIGURE 3.32   The Homeland Security Operations Center. (www.whitehouse.gov.)

Internet Resource: To evaluate the 2006 budget in light of performance, visit http://www.dhs.gov/xlibrary/assets/Budget_PBO_FY2006.pdf.

3.3.5 Budget Year: 2007

As DHS entered its fourth year of department status, it was clear that it continued to strive for efficiency in both an internal and an external sense. DHS is well aware that being prepared has much to do with prevention and mitigation of disaster in any form. To anticipate terror or plan for natural disasters, the department is forced to target its resources and focus its efforts on what is yet to happen. In this sense, the department is becoming a proactive, rather than a strictly reactionary, entity.

In the world of preparedness, the 2007 budget expended a good deal of investment. Millions were directed to the National Preparedness Integration program, a historic FEMA responsibility involving catastrophic planning, emergency communication improvements, and command and control alignment. FEMA received $29 million to reinforce its readiness, mitigation, response, recovery, and national security programs under the initiative Strengthen Operational Capability. Upgrades to the Emergency Alert System (EAS) were also provided. EAS is an integral part of the public alert and warning system in the United States. It provides the president and other authorized federal, state, and local officials with the capability to transmit an emergency message to the public during disasters or crises. The national EAS, regulated by the Federal Communications Commission (FCC), is administered by DHS through FEMA.

Internet Resource: For a comprehensive critique of the EAS system, see http://www.gao.gov/new.items/d07411.pdf.

FIGURE 3.33 An HH65 Coast Guard helicopter passes by the Washington Monument during a National Capital Region Air Defense training mission. (U.S. Coast Guard news photo.)

The Coast Guard received $60 million to enhance its National Capital Region Air Defense program (Figure 3.33).[38]

Border security and reform of the immigration process continued to see substantial support in the budgetary process up to and including 2007. Cutting-edge technology was employed across the borders using electronic surveillance. Coupled with technology and surveillance was an infusion of funds, some $459 million, to hire and train 3000 new border agents (Figure 3.34).

Additional fencing, detention beds, and work location and employment verification programs were also included in the 2007 budget.

Maritime and cargo continued to be a forefront concern in the budgetary process in matters of homeland security in the year 2007. The use of technology continued to be heavily supported when it came to the detection of explosives, nuclear materials, and WMD (Figure 3.35).

At America's ports, the threat that may emerge from cargo is a story likely to be told in the future. Law enforcement cannot inspect all of the cargo that enters our ports, since manual inspection would be ludicrous given the sheer volume of incoming goods.

FIGURE 3.34   U.S. Border Patrol on duty. Department of Homeland Security, Washington, D.C.

FIGURE 3.35   Explosive detection system. Department of Homeland Security, Washington, D.C.

FIGURE 3.36   Radiographic image of a truck.

Advanced radiography is considered a sensible solution to inspecting the millions of cargo containers that reach the American shores each and every year. The 2007 budget funds Cargo Advanced Automated Radiography Systems[39] (see Figure 3.36).

Information sharing takes a preeminent position in the 2007 budget. In the world of IT infrastructure, DHS stressed the common and reliable e-mail systems, the centralization of data centers, the modernization of desktops and workstations, and the update of voice, video, and wireless infrastructure. Nearly $50 million was geared to the Office of Intelligence and Analysis and the Operations Directorate, where threat information is analyzed and disseminated and other information pertinent to homeland threat is sent to all partners and governmental entities. Of particular interest in 2007 was the Secure Border Initiative. The goals of the initiative are

- More agents to patrol our borders, secure our ports of entry, and enforce immigration laws
- Expanded detention and removal capabilities to eliminate "catch and release" once and for all
- A comprehensive and systemic upgrading of the technology used in controlling the border, including increased manned aerial assets, expanded use of unmanned aerial vehicles (UAVs), and next-generation detection technology
- Increased investment in infrastructure improvements at the border—providing additional physical security to sharply reduce illegal border crossings
- Greatly increased interior enforcement of our immigration laws—including more robust work site enforcement

The initiative's focus on fencing is quite a challenge; from autos and trucks to pedestrians, the erection of a border fence across the continental United States is a project in the making[40] (Figure 3.37).

Finally, DHS will continue to infuse funds into its own internal operations in order that it might be an agency for the twenty-first century. Special disbursements for human services and procurements were made.

3.3.6 Budget Year: 2008

In its fifth year of operation, DHS had had sufficient time to examine its practices, to weigh and assess the effectiveness of its plan and operation, and to act and react to existing and novel challenges. What is plain is that budgets continue to rise and threats manifest an uncanny capacity to evolve. DHS needs to stay sharp and always on the offense to fend off a very dangerous world. Congress and the president seem to appreciate the financing demand that DHS naturally entails. Since its inception, the budget has matured[41] (see Figure 3.38).

The mission of DHS stays firm and resolute in this budgetary process—first and foremost, to protect the country from danger and threat. Another 3000 Border Patrol agents were added during this cycle. The Transportation Security Administration saw increased funding for explosives detection, document processes, and the new identification programs.

Border protection received strong support in the 2008 budget. SBInet, a program instituted under the Secure Border Initiative, was slated to provide form and structure to the 6000 miles of border in need of protection. The goal of this program, by technology, infrastructure, staffing, and response resource, was the integration of border protection into a single comprehensive border security suite for the department. U.S. CBP was to serve as executive agent for the department's SBInet program (Figure 3.39). The program was cancelled in January 2011.[42]

Vehicle 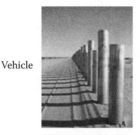 Used in more remote areas that can be reached by vehicle

Pedestrian  Used in areas where many people cross illegally

Technology  Mixes tower-based integrated cameras and sensors, ground-based radar, mobile surveillance systems, and unmanned aerial systems with traditional border patrols

Natural barrier  Rivers, mountain ranges, and other geographic features can provide a natural barrier to illegal entry

FIGURE 3.37   DHS barrier and border techniques. (www.dhs.gov.)

Foreign visitors will be subject, depending on location of entry, to biometric screening or other advanced fingerprint imprint analysis (Figure 3.40).

Included in the budget were funds to launch the Secure Flight system. Secure Flight will match limited passenger information against government watch lists to identify known and suspected terrorists, prevent known and suspected terrorists from boarding an aircraft, facilitate legitimate passenger air travel, and protect individual privacy. Secure Flight will

- Identify known and suspected terrorists
- Prevent individuals on the No Fly List from boarding an aircraft
- Identify individuals for enhanced screening
- Facilitate passenger air travel by providing a fair, equitable, and consistent matching process across all aircraft operators

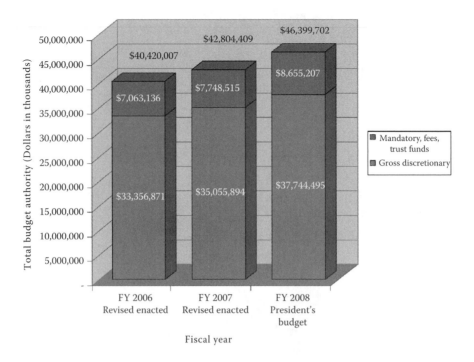

FIGURE 3.38 Budget growth: 2006–2008.

FIGURE 3.39 U.S.-Mexico Border. Mexico is on the right. (www.cpg.gov.)

"In addition to Secure Flight's efforts to improve the efficiency and effectiveness of passenger prescreening, TSA, in conjunction with Secure Flight, has developed the Joint Analysis Center. This center is colocated within the SOC and uses encounter match data to perform broader aviation security analysis. Analysts located at Secure Flight work jointly with TTAC [Transportation Threat Assessment and Credentialing] and TSA OI [Office of Intelligence] analysts to use passenger vetting results from Secure Flight and other programs to identify trends and patterns in aviation security."[43] At our commercial ports and points of entry, the 2008 budget demonstrated innovation at the technological level. Advanced spectroscopic

FIGURE 3.40   A biometric fingerprint device. (Courtesy of CRT Computers.)

portal systems will scan and screen 98% of incoming containers at the end of the budget cycle. Raytheon delivered the first prototype and portal for commercial use in 2006 (see Figure 3.41).

The Secure Freight program (Figure 3.42) received its start-up costs of $15 million in the 2008 budget. Secure Freight screens foreign containers bound for U.S. ports for radiological and nuclear risk. Containers are screened before leaving a foreign port. DHS and the Department of Energy will partner with international terminal operators, ocean carriers, and host governments.

Containers arriving at participating seaports overseas will be scanned with both nonintrusive radiographic imaging and passive radiation detection equipment placed at terminal arrival gates. Sensor and image data gathered regarding containers inbound to the United States will be encrypted and transmitted near real time to the NTC operated by DHS's Customs and Border Protection.

As for infrastructure, the 2008 budget heartily supported a continuation of the Domestic Nuclear Detection Office and established an Office of Innovation in the Directorate of Science and Technology (S&T). The S&T directorate is the intellectual arm of DHS and a place of innovation and invention. Partnering with the private sector, national laboratories, universities, and other government agencies, the office promotes the use of high technology in support of homeland security.

The budget allotted a significant increase for chemical site security programs.

Internet Resource: Find out about the registration process for chemical facilities at http://www.dhs.gov/chemical-security-laws-and-regulations.

From the vantage point of emergency preparedness, DHS works hard to finalize the acculturation of FEMA. FEMA has been an agency under siege since the days of Katrina, and it has taken heartfelt introspection and diligence to reset the agency moorings. The consolidation of FEMA into DHS caused further consternation for personnel. As a result,

Raytheon

Advanced Spectroscopic Portal (ASP)

The Advanced Spectroscopic Portal (ASP) is an advanced nuclear screening portal system designed to identify and interdict the illegal entry of nuclear devices and materials into the United States.

Benefits

Critical defense tool for the Department of Homeland Security (DHS) and the Domestic Nuclear Detection Office (DNDO)

Senses nuclear materials at various points of entry into the United States, as well as other locations such as domestic checkpoints and rail lines

Capable of screening cars, trucks, cargo containers and mail

Modular architecture allows system to be mounted in several configurations

Multiple detector types ensure high gamma and neutron sensitivity over full range of usage conditions

Designed to minimize false alarms that would unnecessarily impede the flow of border traffic and commerce

System incorporates advanced threat identification algorithms

Designed to Counter Nuclear Threat

Covert nuclear attack is the foremost threat facing the United States today. The safety of the nation depends upon its ability to design and field systems to detect and interdict smuggled nuclear weapons and materials. For this reason, the ASP is a high-priority program within DHS and a key component of DNDO and other federal national nuclear detection initiatives to meet homeland security needs. By enhancing the country's early detection capabilities, ASP detectors address the threat of radiological dispersal devices, improvised nuclear devices or a nuclear weapon being used by terrorists inside the United States.

Upgrade Over Current Detector Portals

Since Sept. 11, 2001, the Bureau of Customs and Border Protection has deployed nearly 600 first-generation Radiation Portal Monitors at manned ports of entry, international mail and express consignment courier facilities, land border crossings, airports and seaports. As a point of reference, DHS reports that 360,000 vehicles, 5,100 trucks and containers, 2,600 aircraft, and 600 vessels cross into the United States at more than 600 points of entry every day.

Built with available technology, these first-generation Radiation Portal Monitors are unable to distinguish between legitimate naturally occurring radioactive materials such as fertilizer and bananas that are not harmful, and illicit materials that pose a threat. These situations necessitate secondary screening, which is manpower intensive and slows the flow of commerce. Therefore, a more discriminating primary screening system — the ASP — is needed.

FIGURE 3.41 Raytheon's advanced spectroscopic portal.

FEMA revisited its vision and overall mission and, on completion, was given an additional $100 million to carry out these adjusted aims. FEMA will zero in on these activities:

- Incident management
- Hazard mitigation
- Operational planning
- Disaster logistics
- Service to disaster victims
- Public disaster communication
- Continuity programs

FIGURE 3.42   Secure freight initiative in Hamburg, Germany.

More than $3.2 billion was made available for state and local preparedness training. A total of $3.2 billion was allotted for state and local preparedness expenditures as well as assistance to firefighters. The Homeland Security Grants, Infrastructure Protection, Assistance to Firefighters, and Public Safety Interoperable Communications (PSIC) grant programs fund activities necessary to support the National Preparedness Goal and related national doctrine, such as the NIMS, National Response Plan (NRP), and the National Infrastructure Protection Plan (NIPP). Funds requested through these programs will (1) provide critical assistance to state and local homeland security efforts, (2) support resources available through other federal assistance programs that center on first-responder terrorism preparedness activities, and (3) deliver support to all state and local first-responder organizations (Figure 3.43).

Finally, the 2008 budget financed internal operations with the hope of improved efficiency at DHS. Funds were directed to internal oversight of personnel, further consolidation of duplicate functions and offices, a permanent Office of Chief Procurement, and increased funding for oversight and audit provided by the Office of the Inspector General (OIG).

3.3.7 Budget Years: 2009–2010

Not surprisingly, increased allocations for DHS activities continue their upward march. While it is not difficult to anticipate increasing expenditures for homeland security, it is not as simple to predict where portions of money will go for innovation or changed focus. To be sure, DHS will always have an operational side. Then too, DHS will most likely continue the bulk of its initiatives. Government can change, but the likelihood of radical change or whole-scale change is very remote. For 2009 and 2010, DHS stayed true to its basic mission. Some of the proposed highlights were

- Aggressive increase in Border Patrol—2200 new agents and further funding for Secure Flight (Figure 3.44)

FIGURE 3.43   CBRN response drill.

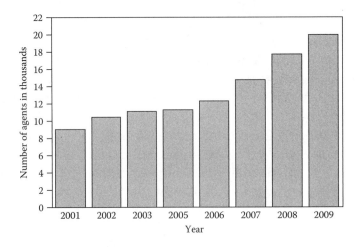

FIGURE 3.44   Border patrol staffing, 2001–2009. (www.white.gov/omb/budget/fy2009/homeland. html.)

- TSA funds for ID programs and crew vetting as well as a new program that tracks international students
- An automated, electronic system of worker verification, E-Verify (see Figure 3.45)
- $10 million in increased funding for the Federal Law Enforcement Training Center (FLETC) relating to border enforcement
- Increased funding for the U.S. Secret Service for equipment that detects WMD and other attacks
- Improvised explosive device (IED) research

FIGURE 3.45   E-Verify logo.

3.3.8 Budget Years: 2011–2012

Two forces were at work in the budgets posed by DHS officials and adopted or under legislative consideration. First, for the first time in its administrative life, there is actually discussion of better efficiencies and trimmed funding for DHS.[44] Across the governmental horizon, there is bleeding in federal overspending, and each agency is being asked to cull where it can. For example, DHS is required to conduct due diligence on its payments to vendors to ensure proper amounts and reduce duplication in payments.[45] DHS is required to make public and publish incorrect payments. A few examples of high-dollar overpayments are charted in Figure 3.46.[46]

DHS continues its high-level emphasis on technology as a tool of efficiency. At the same time, despite the technological advances, the agency continues to splurge on employees and increased staff across various departments. What is clear is that budgets are moving across a relative flat-line—at least in a governmental sense. From 2010 to 2011, the department's funds dipped $118,000,000, though the proposed 2012 budget seeks an increase of those losses. See Figure 3.47[47] for a 3-year comparison.

Over the same 3-year period, one can glean some targeted spending as well as some deemphasis. The proposed 2012 budget reduces funding to the following categories:

- Citizenship and Immigration Services
- FEMA grant programs
- FLETC
- Domestic Nuclear Detection Office

While the reductions are not fantastic, these cuts reflect support for ICE activities in the present administration as well as the law enforcement sector in its training activities. FEMA is likely just tapped out given the disaster calendar.

All other remaining functions and offices retain their upward trend in budgetary allocation (see Figure 3.48).[48]

For the 2011 budget year, there is ample support for technological innovation, including but not limited to

- Advanced imaging technology
- Portable explosive trace detection
- Radiological/nuclear detection equipment
- E-Verify increase
- Cyber-network funds
- Modernization of flood mapping
- Sensor technology
- Safecon cargo scanners

Department of Homeland Security

Current Status of Outstanding High-Dollar Overpayments Reported on the Previous Secretary's High-Dollar Overpayments Report

for the Quarter Ending December 31, 2011

Debts Sent to the Treasury Offset Program for Collection

	A	B	C	D	E	F	G	H	I	J	K	L
	Component	Recipient Type	City and State	Program(s) Responsible	Recovery Actions Taken or Planned	Payment Date	High $ Overpayment Date Identified	Amount Paid	Correct Amount	Recovered Amount	Outstanding Balance	Days Outstanding as of December 31, 2011
	FEMA	INDIVIDUAL	Seabrook, TX	Individuals and Households Payments	Recoupment package sent to individual. Debt later sent to the Treasury Offset Program for collection.	November 11, 2008	September 30, 2010	$19,239.54	$0.00	$0.00	$19,239.54	457
	USCG	ENTITY	Miami, FL	Air Station Miami	Contacted vendor who confirmed overpayment. Vendor added to USCG "Do Not Pay List" with automatic offset of overpayment on next invoice. Debt sent to Treasury Offset Program for collection.	September 25, 2010	January 10, 2011	$76,740.37	$38,177.37	$0.00	$38,563.00	355
							Totals	$95,979.91	$38,177.37	$0.00	$57,802.54	

Debts Under Collection by DHS

	A	B	C	D	E	F	G	H	I	J	K	L
	Component	Recipient Type	City and State	Program(s) Responsible	Recovery Actions Taken or Planned	Payment Date	High $ Overpayment Date Identified	Amount Paid	Correct Amount	Recovered Amount	Outstanding Balance	Days Outstanding as of December 31, 2011
	FEMA	ENTITY	Carson City, NV	Homeland Security Grant Program	Additional supporting documentation received from grantee. FEMA reviewing for sufficiency with resolution expected by January 2012. DHS senior management to elevate this issue to FEMA senior management to ensure timely resolution. State is appealing improper payment.	September 30, 2009	August 5, 2010	$27,609.10	$0.00	$0.00	$27,609.10	513
	FEMA	ENTITY	District of Columbia, DC	Homeland Security Grant Program	Program office completed a review of recipient provided documentation and fully discussed results with grant recipient. Proper support was found for an additional $1,348,108.50 of the original payment. A collection bill for the remaining $643,115.65 was sent.	August 19, 2009	July 28, 2010	$3,133,009.25	$2,489,893.60	$0.00	$643,115.65	521
	USCG	INDIVIDUAL	Seattle, WA	Coast Guard Pay & Personnel Center/Direct Access	Notice of Overpayment sent to member and copy to Servicing Personnel Office. Collection by payroll deductions begun.	November 11, 2008	June 15, 2011	$8,903.21	$1,051.71	$1,023.96	$6,827.54	199
							Totals	$3,169,521.56	$2,490,945.31	$1,023.96	$677,552.29	
							Grand Totals	$3,265,501.47	$2,529,122.68	$1,023.96	$735,354.83	

FIGURE 3.46 High-dollar overpayments still in the collection process.

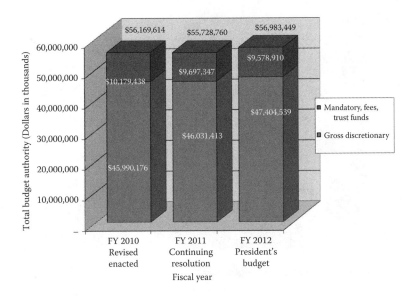

FIGURE 3.47 U.S. Department of Homeland Security, total budget authority.

TOTAL BUDGET AUTHORITY BY ORGANIZATION
Gross Discretionary, Mandatory, Fees, and Trust Funds

	FY 2010 Revised Enacted[1]	FY 2011 Continuing Resolution[2]	FY 2012 President's Budget	FY 2012 +/- FY 2011	FY 2012 +/- FY 2011
	$000	$000	$000	$000	%
Departmental Operations[3]	$ 809,531	$ 800,931	$ 947,231	$ 146,300	18%
Analysis and Operations (A&O)	333,030	335,030	355,368	20,338	6%
Office of the Inspector General (OIG)	113,874	129,874	144,318	14,444	11%
U.S. Customs & Border Protection (CBP)	11,540,501	11,544,660	11,845,678	301,018	3%
U.S. Immigration & Customs Enforcement (ICE)	5,741,752	5,748,339	5,822,576	74,237	1%
Transportation Security Administration(TSA)	7,656,066	7,649,666	8,115,259	465,593	6%
U.S. Coast Guard (USCG)	10,789,076	10,151,543	10,338,545	187,002	2%
U.S. Secret Service (USSS)	1,710,344	1,722,644	1,943,531	220,887	13%
National Protection and Programs Directorate (NPPD)	2,429,455	2,432,756	2,555,449	122,693	5%
Office of Health Affairs (OHA)	136,850	139,250	160,949	21,699	16%
Federal Emergency Management Agency (FEMA)	6,200,618	6,181,718	6,218,433	36,715	1%
FEMA: Grant Programs	4,165,200	4,165,200	3,844,663	(320,537)	-8%
U.S. Citizenship & Immigration Services (USCIS)	2,870,997	3,054,829	2,906,866	(147,963)	-5%
Federal Law Enforcement Training Center (FLETC)	282,812	282,812	276,413	(6,399)	-2%
Science &Technology Directorate (S&T)	1,006,471	1,006,471	1,176,432	169,961	17%
Domestic Nuclear Detection Office (DNDO)	383,037	383,037	331,738	(51,299)	-13%
TOTAL BUDGET AUTHORITY:	$ 56,169,614	$ 55,728,760	$ 56,983,449	$ 1,254,689	2.25%
Mandatory, Fee, and Trust Funds	(10,179,438)	$ (9,697,347)	$ (9,578,910)	$ 118,437	-1.22%
Discretionary Offsetting Fees	(3,533,561)	(3,442,780)	(4,180,357)	(737,577)	21%
NET DISC. BUDGET AUTHORITY:	$ 42,456,615	$ 42,588,633	$ 43,224,182	$ 635,549	-
Less Rescission of Prior-Year Carryover - Regular Appropriations:[4]	(151,582)	(40,474)	(41,942)	-	0%
ADJUSTED NET DISC. BUDGET AUTHORITY:	$ 42,305,033	$ 42,548,159	$ 43,182,240	$ 634,081	1%
SUPPLEMENTAL: [5]	$ 5,865,603	-	-	-	-

FIGURE 3.48 U.S. Department of Homeland Security, total budget authority by organization.

FIGURE 3.49 A TSA VIPR member. (www.tsa.gov.)

In addition to these innovations, DHS allotted a plethora of funds to new positions in canine departments, behavioral detection teams, detachment units, federal air marshals, and intelligence analysts.

The 2012 budget requests include a host of ambitious projects. True to its general trend, DHS mixes personnel with emerging technologies in hopes of fielding the most efficient practices. On the personnel front, the agency increases the use of behavior detection officers in both airports and other settings. The budget simultaneously seeks funding for 37 visual intermodal prevention and response teams (VIPR) whose task is to identify terrorists by behavior, security screening, and other methods of targeting (see Figure 3.49).

Internet Resource: Find out about VIPR teams at https://www.youtube.com/watch?v=T_Y93bin2b0.

The 2012 budget seeks funds to bolster ranks in the historically understaffed USCG, and at the same time increase funding for marine safety programs and environmental protection and response as well as patrol vigilance in American fishing zones. The USCG will also receive funds for its severely depleted capital fleet and facilities. The budget requests increases for various technological innovations, including

- Federal network protection and the deployment of Einstein 3-Computer Protection
- BioWatch 2–3 Detection Systems
- Southwest and northern border technology

Finally, the 2012 budget appears most dedicated to workplace enforcement in the matter of immigration violations. For many years, critics of ICE urged more emphasis on businesses that employ illegals. DHS officials seem inclined to go in that direction with increased funding requests for

- Workplace enforcement
- E-Verify
- VISA security program
- Detention reform
- Funding for beds
- Secure communities

3.3.9 Budget Year: 2013

During the short history of DHS, it has been rare to discern or discover any cuts or reductions in the DHS budget. 2013 is a rare exception to that rule, though in the grand scheme of things, the reductions are minor. Figure 3.50[49] lays out the impact.

Part of the reason for reduction relates to mandatory cuts posed under various budgetary restrictions imposed by Congress, but it is fair to say that the unbridled growth of DHS has not gone unnoticed. Spending has been escalating with little restraint, and DHS has learned that money alone is not the sole solution to the security problem. For the budget year 2013, the emphasis has been, allegedly, on greater efficiencies on how funds are expended. With a $59,000,000,000 billion budget, it is a reasonable line of scrutiny (see Figure 3.51).[50]

In this budgetary cycle, the emphasis will include a reinforcement of traditional models of homeland defense as well as some significant innovation, including but not limited to these crucial missions:

- Preventing terrorism and enhancing security
- Securing and managing our borders
- Enforcing and administering our immigration laws
- Safeguarding and securing cyberspace
- Ensuring resilience to disasters[51]

A host of new programmatic designs and initiatives were launched and supported during this budget year. In the transportation sector, especially in relation to air travel, the TSA PreCheck program was expanded and assessed in order that more travelers might avoid the headaches of long security lines (see Figure 3.52).

Based on the Israeli model, TSA has been increasing its human observation program of ferreting out suspected terrorists by observational techniques by and through its Screening of Passengers through Observation Techniques (SPOT) program. Some signs worth noting are shown in Figure 3.53.

Like many TSA programs, the intentions do not always lead to desired, or acceptable, results. After spending nearly $1 billion on the program, the General Accounting Office, by audit, indicates the results are mixed and that further investment may be unwise.[52]

Other highlights of the budget year include these undertakings:

- Implementation of the National Terrorism Advisory System to replace the historic color-coded model
- Increased funding for fusion centers and joint terrorism task forces

	FY 2011 Enacted [1]		FY 2012 Enacted [2]	FY 2013 Pres. Budget	FY 2013 +/- FY 2012
	$000		$000	$000	$000
Net Discretionary:	$	42,206,179	46,248,145	$ 44,942,110	$ (1,306,035)
Discretionary Fees:		3,442,780	3,547,405	3,756,720	209,315
Less rescission of prior year funds: [3]		*(524,185)*	*(200,736)*	-	*200,736*
Gross Discretionary		**45,124,774**	**49,594,814**	**48,698,830**	**(895,984)**
Mandatory, Fee, Trust Funds:		9,682,503	10,118,541	10,333,516	214,975
Total Budget Authority:	$	54,807,277	59,713,355	$ 59,032,346	$ (681,009)
Supplemental: [4]	$	-	-	$ -	$ -
Less rescission of prior year supplemental funds:	$	-	-	$ -	$ -

FIGURE 3.50 Fiscal year 2013 overview.

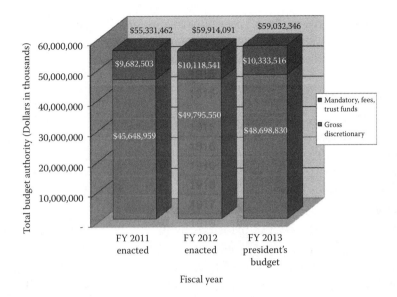

FIGURE 3.51   Total budget authority in thousands of dollars.

FIGURE 3.52   TSA PreCheck program logo.

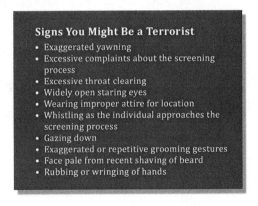

FIGURE 3.53   Signs of a possible security risk.

- Enhanced cargo security screening programs
- Increased Border Patrol personnel
- Launched E-Verify Self-Check program to allow easier decision-making on the part of foreign workers to enter the country or not

The 2013 budget year also witnessed increased recognition of cyber threats and cyber-crime as a means or methods of terror as well as the need to enhance border security. In the latter case, the funding has shown little effectiveness in limiting the unceasing wave of illegals crossing the American frontier.

3.3.10 Budget Year: 2014

For the 2014 budgetary cycle, the amount allotted to DHS again remains somewhat static, though the sum could not ever be construed as paltry. While there is a small decline in the overall budget of nearly $60,000,000,000 billion, that portion has little impact on the day-to-day operations of this agency. The question is not whether the department has sufficient funding but whether its funding is being used wisely and intelligently. Part of that determination is how the pie is sliced from the original budget granted—for in evaluating where the money goes, one discerns DHS's priorities by its trail of expenditures and spending. In 2014, the funds were parsed up by various percentages as is evident in Figure 3.54.[53]

Stresses on efficiency and wise use of taxpayer funding continues in this budget year. DHS willingly indicates a desire to remove duplicative processes; to sell and alienate real property that does not advance the mission of the agency; and to find "commonalities" in the various processes it undertakes such as in investigations, travel and conferences, vetting and screening techniques, and hiring and staffing practices. DHS also concludes that its impact, aside from security, is economic by the many services provided and constituencies served.

In general terms, the department continues its mission orientation in light of the budget and how those mission goals and objectives are achieved by the disbursement of those special funds. In this budget year, certain priorities emerge especially as relates to the cyber world and its global impact. Other highlights in the cycle include

- Preboard aviation vetting program that identifies and prevents known threat parties from ever boarding a plane
- Increased funding for VIPR teams working in public transit
- Development and strategic placement of equipment and technology that targets radiological threats

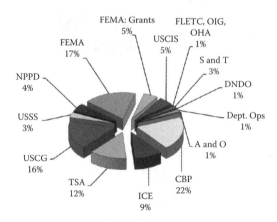

FIGURE 3.54 Total budget authority by organization.

FIGURE 3.55   National Bio and Agro-Defense Facility, Manhattan, Kansas.

- Funding for a National Bio and Agro-Defense Facility in the state of Kansas (see Figure 3.55).
- Increased aircraft resource for customs and border patrol
- Recapitalization of the aging USCG fleet
- Substantial funding to U.S. computer emergency readiness teams
- Consolidation of diverse grant programs into a central office

The 2014 DHS budget confronts, willingly or not, the turmoil and tumult caused by a porous and insecure border. Admitting that its immigration system "is broken and outdated,"[54] DHS has clearly failed to allay the natural fears of a nation on edge from an unchecked influx of illegals. And while there is a more liberal tolerance for not checking admittees to this country, nor dealing with those here illegally for political reasons, the citizenry clearly pays a price in matters of security and domestic tranquility. Undeniably, the immigration system mirrors the chaos of our current political climate. DHS has committed express funds, in substantial numbers, to deal with the immigration issue. Some examples are

- *Law enforcement officers*—The FY 2014 budget supports 21,370 CBP Border Patrol agents and a record 25,252 CBPOs who work with federal, state, and local law enforcement.
- *Increase to CBPO staffing level*: $210.1M—CBP requests an increase of $210.1 million to fund 1600 additional CBPOs, to include 70 canine teams at ports of entry (POEs) and 245 mission and operational support positions, equating to 1845 positions.
- *Trusted Traveler programs (composed of NEXUS, SENTRI, FAST, and Global Entry)*— The Trusted Traveler programs continue to expand and included more than 1.5 million members in FY 2012.
- *Integrated fixed towers*: $77.4M (0 FTE)—An increase of $77.4 million is requested to support the deployment of proven, effective surveillance technology along the highest trafficked areas of the southwest border in Arizona.
- *King Air (KA)-350CER multi-role enforcement aircraft (MEA)*: $43.0M (0 FTE)—The budget requests an increase of $43 million for two KA-350CER MEA.

- *Tactical communication (TACCOM)*: $40.0M (0 FTE)—The FY 2014 request includes $40 million for development and deployment of CBP's land mobile radio TACCOM systems.
- *Tethered Aerostat Radar System (TARS)*: $37.4M (0 FTE)—The TARS program is a multimission capability that supports the counter-narcotics, air surveillance, and U.S. air sovereignty missions.
- *Targeting systems*: $31.6M (0 FTE)—The requested increase of $31.6 million will support enhancements to targeting systems by updating rules in real time and providing CBP with 24/7 targeting capability.
- *ATS operations and maintenance (O&M)*: $31.1M (0 FTE)—The request of $31.1 million maintains current service levels and ensures sustained operations and performance of ATS and subsystems, addresses resource requirements that will support the maintenance of and enhancements and improvements to ATS, and support the overall O&M of the six modules that comprise ATS.
- *P-3 Service Life Extension program (SLEP)*: $24.0M (0 FTE)—The budget requests $24 million for the P-3 SLEP.
- *Consolidation of the NTC*: $13.2M (0 FTE)—The requested $13.2 million will fund the initial cost of consolidating CBP's NTCs for passengers and cargo into one location.
- *CBP Mobile program*: $10.8M (0 FTE)—CBP requests an increase of $10.8 million for 1500 additional mobile devices, which include electronic link mobile operations (ELMO) devices, handheld license plate/document readers (MC75A), and secure electronic enrollment kits (SEEK).
- *Integrated traveler processing*: $8.0M (0 FTE)—CBP requests an increase of $8 million for investing in technology to improve processing at air and land POEs through the acquisition of 60 kiosks at airports and at eight high-volume pedestrian crossings.
- *NTC—enhanced targeting*: $7.8M (0 FTE)—The requested increase of $7.8 million will allow CBP to continue to support significant workload increases and program expansion.
- *Sensor upgrades for tactical aircraft*: $3.5M (0 FTE)—The budget requests $3.5 million for tactical aircraft sensor upgrades.
- *Marine vessels*: $3.5M (0 FTE)—The budget requests $3.5 million for marine vessels.
- *Single Transaction Bond Centralization*: $3.3M (0 FTE)—The request includes $3.3 million for the Single Transaction Bond Centralization initiative.[55]

Internet Exercise: For the full text of the appropriations act, which authorizes funds for DHS, see https://www.congress.gov/bill/113th-congress/house-bill/2217.

3.3.11 Budget Year: 2015

Funding for the 2015 budget cycle is slightly higher than the previous three years of allotments, but this increase has only been in small sums when compared with the rate of government growth and expenditure (see Figure 3.56).[56]

Gross Discretionary, Mandatory, Fees, and Trust Funds

	FY 2013 Revised Enacted[1]	FY 2014 Enacted[2]	FY 2015 Pres. Budget[3]	FY 2015 +/− FY 2014	FY 2015 +/− FY 2014
	$000	$000	$000	$000	%
Departmental Operations[4]	$ 708,695	$ 728,269	$ 748,024	$ 19,755	2.7%
Analysis and Operations (A&O)	301,853	300,490	302,268	1,778	0.6%
Office of the Inspector General (OIG)	137,910	139,437	145,457	6,020	4.3%
U.S. Customs & Border Protection (CBP)	11,736,990	12,445,616	12,764,835	319,219	2.6%
U.S. Immigration & Customs Enforcement (ICE)	5,627,660	5,614,361	5,359,065	(255,296)	−4.5%
Transportation Security Administration (TSA)	7,193,757	7,364,510	7,305,098	(59,412)	−0.8%
U.S. Coast Guard (USCG)	9,972,425	10,214,999	9,796,995	(418,004)	−4.1%
U.S. Secret Service (USSS)	1,808,313	1,840,272	1,895,905	55,633	3.0%
National Protection and Programs Directorate (NPPD)	2,638,634	2,813,213	2,857,666	44,453	1.6%
Office of Health Affairs (OHA)	126,324	126,763	125,767	(996)	−0.8%
Federal Emergency Management Agency (FEMA)	11,865,196	11,553,899	12,496,517	942,618	8.2%
FEMA: Grant Programs	2,373,540	2,530,000	2,225,469	(304,531)	−12.0%
U.S. Citizenship & Immigration Services (USCIS)	3,378,348	3,219,142	3,259,885	40,743	1.3%
Federal Law Enforcement Training Center (FLETC)	243,111	258,730	259,595	865	0.3%
Science &Technology Directorate (S&T)	794,227	1,220,212	1,071,818	(148,394)	−12.2%
Domestic Nuclear Detection Office (DNDO)	302,981	285,255	304,423	19,168	6.7%
TOTAL BUDGET AUTHORITY:	$ 59,209,964	$ 60,655,168	$ 60,918,787	$ 263,619	0.4%
Less: Mandatory, Fee, and Trust Funds:	(11,308,307)	(11,526,210)	(11,890,496)	(364,286)	3.2%
GROSS DISC. BUDGET AUTHORITY:	47,901,657	49,128,958	49,028,291	(100,667)	−0.2%
Less: Discretionary Offsetting Fees:	(3,553,282)	(3,733,428)	(4,414,798)	(681,370)	18.3%
NET DISC. BUDGET AUTHORITY:	$ 44,348,375	$ 45,395,530	$ 44,613,493	$ (782,037)	−1.7%
Less: FEMA Disaster Relief - Major Disasters Cap Adjustment:	$ (6,075,554)	$ (5,626,386)	$ (6,437,793)	$ (811,407)	14.4%
Less: Rescission of Prior-Year Carryover - Regular Appropriations:[5]	(151,463)	(543,968)	-	543,968	−100.0%
ADJUSTED NET DISC. BUDGET AUTHORITY:	$ 38,121,358	$ 39,225,176	$ 38,175,700	$(1,049,476)	−2.7%
Supplemental:[6]	$ 11,483,313	-	-	-	-

FIGURE 3.56 Total budget authority by organization.

DHS Secretary, Jeh Johnson, refers to the amount as "historic" when it comes to the investment in people needed to carry out the diverse functions of the department.[57] More interestingly, the budgetary analysis displays a new and heightened sensitivity concerning the relationship of effective practice and expenditure—this being a matter of first instance in the budgetary process. In other words, DHS is now not simply demanding funds for its endless array of responsibilities but is also asking whether or not the funds have been intelligently and effectively expended in light of specific results. The 2015 budget begins that new approach with a look at TSA—an agency that has brought significant negative press, and embarrassment, to DHS. TSA agents have been caught stealing property during searches, taking and selling imagery from full body scans, and even been indicted on charges of using their positions to smuggle drugs. This in addition to subjecting children and the elderly—apart from the general population—to what have been argued are over-the-top screening practices. Despite recent relaxing of some screening policies, and as a result of past improprieties, the 2015 budget manifests a novel mentality of questioning whether or not there is a better way to conduct business—not only for TSA but for other arms of DHS as well. Thus, when DHS indicates that it must align "passenger screening resources based on risk,"[58] the conclusion demonstrates a desire to correlate expenditure with sensible practices—a philosophical outlook long overdue at the agency. As a result, TSA is now investing more in

- TSA PreCheck, which eliminates a portion of those known to be safe bets from the screening process
- Increasing preflight watch list analysis in its Secure Flight program, which targets those more likely to be security problems
- Expending more funds on the screening of bags for explosives, ensuring 100% compliance since mechanical processes are always more efficient than human interaction

The 2015 budget also witnesses increased funding for both capital and operations for the USCG—likely the most efficient and well run agency in the entire DHS. Aside from updating its cutter fleet and replacing old and aging equipment, the USCG continues to receive funding based on exceptional performance. Some examples include

- Increased funding for aircraft and air vessels dedicated to first-responder activity
- Enhanced funding for offshore boarding and interdiction for ships before port entry
- Funding for additional vessel board and search teams (VBSTs)

Other evidence that DHS is trying to correlate expenditures with efficient operations include

- ICE's determination that paper-based worker verifications system can be replaced with electronic methods
- Creation of an E-Verify Self-Check system, which is computer based at lower cost
- Priority funding for computer-based cybersecurity capable of tracking cybercrime and other offenses, which ICE can employ to discover patterns of identity theft and other computer-based frauds
- Increased cybersecurity funding for the U.S. Secret Service, who must be vigilant in both physical and cyberspace

Finally, the 2015 budget delivered a new category of funding, designated "opportunity funding."[59] At this level of budget, DHS identifies "climate change" as being a variable that is crucial to FEMA planners and first responders. While some may argue the science is settled as to climate change, it is a fair conclusion that the agreement on what to do about climate change is anything but universal.

Over the last decade, the inevitable march of bureaucratic growth and budgetary increase unfolds. While there may be less funding, temporarily, to go around, DHS maintains its bureaucratic perpetuity by the myriad of functions and tasks that have been entrusted to it. The only forces that appear to chink its armor has been budgetary restrictions, which Congress bemoans but lacks the will and tenacity to enforce; and the increased role of private-sector partners, who have demonstrated greater efficiencies and dedication to consumer and customer service.

3.4 Conclusion

Exactly how DHS was established, shaped, and foundationally organized receives significant attention in this chapter. DHS arises from both political and security influences, though it could not be erected until a legal framework had been established. The various executive orders and legislative enactments that lead to DHS are fully analyzed. In addition, aligned legislation that impacts how DHS conducts its business, such as the USA Patriot Act, presently the U.S. Freedom Act of 2015, is fully covered. Specialized subject matter legislation is given a broad overview, including the REAL ID program, the US-VISIT, now the Office of Biometric Identity Management, regulations and the entity renamed the Office of Biometric Identity Management, the SAFETY Act, and the laws governing registration of select industries.

The chapter also delves into the budget and finance aspects of DHS. In particular, the chapter traces the budgetary history of DHS and correlates budgetary allotments to mission decisions. Hence, budget years 2002–2015 evidence both consistency and adaptability in how budgets are calculated. Basic homeland functions remain a constant in every budget, though the rise of technology funds in the delivery of homeland services has surely seen growth. The budgetary analysis also features new initiatives that require an infusion of funds, especially as to cybersecurity, border patrol, and physical assets dedicated to such, and capital investments in the long neglected USCG fleet. While the budget history of DHS has many constants and predictable line items, change is often driven by new technologies, innovative software and hardware programs dedicated to particular industries as well as by the endless array of new security challenges that have become part of the American landscape.

Keywords

Allotments
Best practices
Biometrics
Budgeting
Cabinet
CBP targeting systems
Container Security Initiative
Core values
Customs-Trade Partnership Against Terrorism
Cybersecurity
Domestic Nuclear Detection Office
Emergency Alert System
Executive branch
Executive order
Exigent circumstances

Federal Communications Commission
Finance
Jurisdiction
Laws
Legal authority
Legislation
National Biodefense Analysis and Countermeasure Center
National Incident Management System
National Preparedness Integration program
Office of Management and Budget
Passive radiation detection
Posse Comitatus Act
Private sector justice
Privatization

Project BioShield	SBInet
Radiation detection monitors	Secure Border Initiative
Radiography	Secure Flight system
REAL ID program	Spectroscopic portal
Regulations	USA Patriot Act
Rescue 21	USNORTHCOM or NORTHCOM
SAFETY Act	US-VISIT

Discussion Questions

1. Explain how the DHS of today differs from the DHS of 2003.

2. Critics of the early acts and executive orders relating to the establishment of DHS often say that these promulgations suffered from a lack of vision and thinking. Can you make this argument in any meaningful way?

3. The USA Patriot Act has received blistering critiques from civil libertarians. Why? Do you concur?

4. Why do early executive orders and legislation so firmly emphasize the role of infrastructure?

5. In the assessment of budget histories, point out two trends over the life of DHS.

6. In the assessment of the DHS budget, are there any shortcomings or oversights? Lay out precise examples.

7. Discuss two recent initiatives involving global trade and DHS.

8. If you had to predict, will future budgets of DHS be increased or decreased in the next decade?

Practical Exercises

1. Visit www.whitehouse.gov. Find and summarize three recent executive orders relating to homeland security.

2. Assess and evaluate recent amendments to the Homeland Security Act of 2002. List four major categories of adaptation and adjustment in the act since 2002.

3. Compare and contrast the original USA Patriot Act with the provisions enacted in 2008. Some have argued that the later act lacks teeth and rigor. Is there any truth to this assertion? Provide proof by the language of the acts.

4. Prepare a form file for the Office of Biometric Identity Management program.

5. Review the budgetary cycle of DHS over the period 2003–2015. Identify four major trends in the allotment of funds. Evaluate whether budgetary cycles are influenced by trends and pressures to target specialized activities.

Notes

1. Federal Register, Friday, December 3, 2010, 75(232), Proclamation 8607, 75613.
2. Executive Order, Improving Critical Infrastructure Cybersecurity, February 12, 2013.
3. Presidential Proclamation, Critical Infrastructure Security and Resilience Month, 2015, October 29, 2015.
4. Federal Register, Tuesday, January 27, 2009, Executive Order 13493, 74 FR 4901, available at https://federalregister.gov/a/E9-1895.
5. Federal Register, Thursday, March 10, 2011, Executive Order 13567, 76 FR 13277, available at http://www.gpo.gov/fdsys/pkg/FR-2011-03-10/pdf/2011-5728.pdf.
6. American Civil Liberties Union, President Obama issues executive order institutionalizing indefinite detention, March 7, 2011, available at http://www.aclu.org/national-security/president-obama-issues-executive-order-institutionalizing-indefinite-detention.
7. Homeland Security Act of 2002. Public Law 107-296, November 25, 2002, available at http://www.dhs.gov/xlibrary/assets/hr_5005_enr.pdf.
8. President's Remarks at Homeland Security Bill Signing. Department of Homeland Security Official Home Page. November 25, 2002, available at http://www.presidency.ucsb.edu/youtubeclip.php?clipid=63129&admin=43.
9. J. David, The defense of North America: NORAD & NORTHCOM, *Canada-United States Law Journal*, 29 (2003): 261.
10. NORAD and USNORTHCOM Public Affairs, USNORTHCOM Hurricane Sandy Response Support, November 7, 2012, available at http://www.northcom.mil/Newsroom/tabid/3104/Article/563649/usnorthcom-hurricane-sandy-response-support-nov-7.aspx.
11. C. Khalil, Thinking intelligently about intelligence: A model global framework protecting privacy, *George Washington International Law Review*, 47 (2015): 919; A. Deeks, An international legal framework for surveillance, *Virginia Journal of International Law*, 55 (2015).
12. See K. L. Hermann, Reviewing Bush-era counter-terrorism policy after 9/11: Reconciling ethical and practical considerations, *Homeland Security Review*, 4 (2010): 139; See also C. L. Richardson, The creation of judicial compromise: Prosecuting detainees in a National Security Court System in Guantanamo Bay, Cuba, *Homeland Security Review*, 4 (2010): 119.
13. U.S. Department of Homeland Security, *Fact Sheet: The USA Patriot Act—A Proven Homeland Security Tool* (12/14/050).
14. C. Savage, Deal reached on extension of Patriot Act, *New York Times*, May 19, 2011.
15. Republican Study Committee, *Legislative Bulletin*, May 26, 2011.
16. See U.S. Patriot Act, section 215 (2011).
17. USA Freedom Act of 2015, Public Law No: 114-23, June 2, 2015.
18. Ibid.
19. REAL ID Act of 2005, P.L. 109-13, *U.S. Statutes at Large*, 119 (2005): 231, http://www.govtrack.us/congress/bill.xpd?tab=summary&bill=h109-418.
20. Department of Homeland Security, Office of Inspector General, Potentially high costs and insufficient grant funds pose a challenge to REAL ID implementation, 1 (OIG-09-36) (March 2009).
21. Center for Immigration Studies, REAL ID implementation: Less expensive, doable, and helpful in reducing fraud (January 2011), available at http://cis.org/real-id.

22. Center for Immigration Studies, REAL ID implementation: Less expensive, doable, and helpful in reducing fraud (January 2011), available at http://cis.org/real-id; J. Hatch, Requiring a nexus to national security: Immigration, "terrorist activities," and statutory reform," *Brigham Young University Law Review*, 2014 (2014): 697, available at http://digitalcommons.law.byu.edu/lawreview/vol2014/iss3/10.

23. Department of Homeland Security, Office of Inspector General, Potentially high costs and insufficient grant funds pose a challenge to REAL ID implementation, 6 (OIG-09-36) (March 2009).

24. J. Hatch, Requiring a nexus to national security: Immigration, "terrorist activities," and statutory reform, *Brigham Young University Law Review*, 2014 (2014): 697, available at http://digitalcommons.law.byu.edu/lawreview/vol2014/iss3/10; G. D. Kravitz, REAL ID: The devil you don't know, *Harvard Law and Policy Review*, 3 (2009): 431.

25. J. Harper, Florida's implementation of the federal Real ID Act of 2005 (February 24, 2011), available at http://www.cato.org/pub_display.php?pub_id=12818.

26. Office of Biometric Identity Management Expenditure Plan, Fiscal Year 2015 Report to Congress (June 11, 2015).

27. Ibid., 14–16.

28. Homeland Security Appropriations Act of 2007, P.L. 109-295, Section 550, *U.S. Statutes at Large*, 120 (2006): 1355.

29. For a complete list of chemicals subject to the administrative regulations, see Code of Federal Regulations, title 6, part 27 (2007), https://www.dhs.gov/xlibrary/assets/chemsec_appendixafinalrule.pdf.

30. Code of Federal Regulations, title 6, sec. 25.7(j) (2004).

31. M. Paddock, Homeland Security funding since 9/11, *Homeland Security Today* (September 2011): 9.

32. Congressional Budget Office, Economic and issue brief: Federal funding for Homeland Security (April 30, 2004): 5, http://www.cbo.gov/ftpdocs/54xx/doc5414/homeland_security.pdf.

33. U.S. Department of Homeland Security, *Sample National Terrorism Advisory System Alert*, available at http://www.dhs.gov/sites/default/files/publications/ntas-sample-alert_0_0.pdf.

34. Department of Homeland Security, *Budget in Brief: Fiscal Year 2005* (Washington, DC: U.S. Government Printing Office, 2005), 12, http://www.dhs.gov/sites/default/files/publications/FY_2005_BIB_4.pdf.

35. Department of Homeland Security, *Performance Budget Overview FY 2005* (Washington, DC: U.S. Government Printing Office, 2005), 8, http://www.dhs.gov/xlibrary/assets/2004PBO_FINAL_29_JAN_04.pdf.

36. Department of Homeland Security, *Budget-in-Brief: Fiscal Year 2006* (Washington, DC: U.S. Government Printing Office, 2006), 16, http://www.dhs.gov/xlibrary/assets/Budget_BIB-FY2006.pdf.

37. General Dynamics, *Rescue 21: Saving Lives for the 21st Century*, C4 Systems, http://gacc.nifc.gov/eacc/dispatch_centers/ILC/Mobilizaton_Guide/Chapter%2020%202011.pdf at Section 21.1.

38. J. Edwards, U.S. Coast Guard taking a Coast Guard mission to new heights, Military.com, February 23, 2007, http://www.military.com/features/0,15240,126499,00.html.

39. For a full analysis of various detection systems, see A. Glaser, *Detection of Special Nuclear Materials* (Princeton University, April 16, 2007), http://www.princeton.edu/~aglaser/lecture2007_detection.pdf.

40. S. Rosière and R. Jones, Teichopolitics: Re-thinking globalization through the role of walls and fences, *Geopolitics*, 17 (2012): 217; C. Amuedo-Dorantes and S. Pozo, On the intended and unintended consequences of enhanced U.S. border and interior immigration enforcement: Evidence from Mexican deportees, *Demography*, 51 (2014): 2255.

41. Department of Homeland Security, *Budget-in-Brief: FY 2008* (Washington, DC: U.S. Government Printing Office, 2008), 15, http://www.dhs.gov/xlibrary/assets/budget_bib-fy2008.pdf.

42. The USA's SBInet Border Security Project, *Defense Industry Daily* at http://www.defenseindustry-daily.com/21b-sbinet-border-security-contract-goes-to-team-boeing-02648/; A. Lipowicz, Boeing's SBInet contract gets the axe (January 14, 2011), available at https://washingtontechnology.com/articles/2011/01/14/dhs-cancels-rest-of-sbinet-and-plans-mix-of-new-technologies-at-border.aspx.

43. Implementation and Coordination of TSA's Secure Flight Program (July 2012) https://www.oig.dhs.gov/assets/Mgmt/2012/OIGr_12-94_Jul12.pdf.

44. M. Paddock, Cuts affect more than just the bottom line, *Homeland Security Today*, June (2011): 9.

45. See Executive Order: Reducing Improper Payments and Eliminating Waste in Federal Programs, November 23, 2009.

46. Memorandum from DHS Secretary Janet Napolitano to C. K. Edwards Acting Inspector General, Council of Inspectors General on Integrity and Efficiency, *Quarterly High-Dollar Overpayments Report for the period October to December 2011*, February 22, 2012, available at http://www.dhs.gov/xlibrary/assets/mgmt/cfo-high-dollar-overpayments-october-december-2011.pdf.

47. U.S. Department of Homeland Security, *Budget-in-Brief, Fiscal Year 2012*, 17 (2011).

48. Ibid., 21.

49. Department of Homeland Security, *2013 Budget in Brief*, 3 (2013), available at http://www.dhs.gov/xlibrary/assets/mgmt/dhs-budget-in-brief-fy2013.pdf.

50. Ibid., 21.

51. Ibid., 8–9.

52. GAO Report, *TSA Should Limit Future Funding for Behavior Detection Activities* GAO-14-159 (November 2013), available at http://www.gao.gov/assets/660/658923.pdf.

53. Department of Homeland Security, *2014 Budget in Brief*, 5 (2014), available at https://www.dhs.gov/sites/default/files/publications/MGMT/FY%202014%20BIB%20-%20FINAL%20-508%20Formatted%20(4).pdf.

54. Ibid., 8.

55. Ibid., 114–117.

56. Department of Homeland Security, *2015 Budget in Brief*, 7 (2015), available at http://www.dhs.gov/publication/fy-2015-budget-brief.

57. Ibid., 9.

58. Ibid., 10.

59. Ibid., 14.

Chapter **4**

Risk Management, Threats, and Hazards

Objectives

1. To define the standard and best practices used in risk management in the world of homeland security
2. To describe the process of basic risk assessment and the CARVER+Shock assessment tool
3. To distinguish between threats and hazards and describe how they are analyzed and rated in risk assessment
4. To define the various categories of weapons of mass destruction (WMD), including nuclear, chemical, biological, and nerve agents
5. To differentiate between specific nuclear and radiological WMD and biological and chemical agents, such as anthrax, sarin, and ricin; their delivery methods; and their effects
6. To comprehend the importance of the country's information infrastructure and its vulnerability to an attack and identify the steps taken to secure it
7. To recognize the various government agencies involved in the cybersecurity of the United States and outline their mission and responsibilities
8. To illustrate the various public–private partnerships in homeland security and analyze their effectiveness

4.1 Introduction

The fundamental thrust of homeland security, dealing with risk, threats, and hazards, and how to prepare, respond, and recover from their effects, encompasses this chapter. In other words, how does government operate in the world of risk and threat and simultaneously provide for a secure homeland? What means and methods for prediction, mitigation, and recovery in the matter of risk are the most suitable? What types of plans and planning seem to work best in the world of homeland security? How does the governmental entity prepare and train for such events? This chapter delves into standard as well as best practices in the defense of a nation. First, it will consider the idea of threat, its scope and definition, its types and categories, and the distinction between the natural and man-made varieties. Second, the coverage will include an analysis of risk theory—that body of thought that teaches operatives how to identify risk, how to assess its impact, and how to track its influence. In addition to risk and threat, the chapter will evaluate the most efficacious means of planning and preparedness. It could be no truer than an ounce of prevention is worth a pound of cure in the world of homeland security. How one prepares for tragedy has much to do with success or failure in response and recovery. How one trains and educates the homeland security professional can be just as telling. Finally, this section will evaluate how agencies and their operatives need to communicate so that homeland security protocol achieves its ultimate end—that of safety and security for the community.

4.2 Risk Management

The work of homeland security delves into the nature of risk, whether at airports or busways, public courthouses, or national monuments. Risk constitutes what might happen or what is likely to happen given a certain set of circumstances. Risk is what can go wrong. A risk is what the stay-behind homeowner takes when he or she fails to get out of the path of a hurricane. Risk is what air travelers are willing to tolerate in an air system that lacks security checkpoints. Risk is what the country will tolerate when no mechanisms exist to check visitors at the border. In a word, risk is something each person lives with each day, from driving in a car to cycling across the hinterlands. Yet, some risks are more preventable and less serious than others. In evaluating risk, one must look to not only the nature of any risk but also to its consequences in both an individual and collective sense. Some refer to this formula in an equational sense[1]—as a series of risk constituents. The risk is calculated relative to the harm the hazard causes and the level and magnitude of exposure to the said harm. The formula might look like this:

$$Risk = Hazard \times Exposure$$

Hazard is the mechanism that causes the harm, and exposure is the extent, depth, and breadth of the risk as influenced by the nature of the hazard. Thus, if anthrax is plugged into the risk equation, it is a small chore to conclude that anthrax constitutes the type of risk the individual and the collective should avoid. In a policy context, therefore, it makes perfect sense for governments to marshal resources to attack this risk—more so than an avalanche of candy bars from an upended truck. Herein lies the rub—to weigh and factor the risk in light of harm and its scope. Some risks are high and others lower, and some "risks" pose no risk at all. To be sure, terrorism is high up on the list of potential harm that homeland specialists must prepare for. "Terrorism has many faces and countless are the possibilities of implementing an attack against American interests under the umbrella of terrorism."[2] The risk manager must anticipate every imaginable version of terrorist act to properly prepare for it.

Looked at from a different perch, risk relies on probability analysis.

4.2.1 The Nature of Risk

Risk is not an easy concept to fully define for it has both actual and anticipatory qualities.[3] On the one hand, all one can do is predict or anticipate what might happen yet on the other, experience dictates the reality of risk. For example, will the risk injure a human? Is it likely that this risk will be in the form of a weapon? Is there a correlation between some religious practice and an act of terror? Is there a particular day, holiday, or anniversary—such as the September 11, 2012, Benghazi consulate attack—where terrorist events are more apt to occur? If a chemical industry fails to secure a certain substance, what are the health ramifications? One could endlessly go on about the nature of risk and its various types. To be sure, the concept is forever evolving. The Federal Emergency Management Agency (FEMA) makes a valiant effort to quantify the process. FEMA employs probability theory when making judgments about risk. In short, risk is the probability that something will occur with an evaluation of consequence[4] (see Figure 4.1.)

The Department of Homeland Security (DHS) defines the nature of risk by three principal variables: *threat*, or the likelihood of a type of attack that might be attempted; *vulnerability*, or the likelihood that an attacker would succeed with a particular attack method; and *consequence*, or the potential impact, individually or collectively, of a particular attack. In this context, one deals in generalities rather than specifics. Sound risk reasoning demands that a measure or modality of quantification be employed when making policy about risk. In other words, can risk be quantified in some way? FEMA thinks so by evaluating some specific variable relative to the nature of the risk[5] (see Figure 4.2).

Here, the evaluator of risk moves beyond the definition seeking to formalize the precise nature and attributes of risk. What is this risk worth? How much, in terms of assets will

Risk is a combination of:

- The probability that an event will occur
- The consequences of its occurrence

	Low risk	Medium risk	High risk
Risk factors total	1–60	61–175	≥176

Risk = Asset value × threat rating × vulnerability rating

FIGURE 4.1 Definition of risk table.

> *Risk assessment*
>
> Determine asset value
> Determine threat rating value
> Determine vulnerability rating value
> Determine relative risk for each threat against each asset

FIGURE 4.2 Quantifying risk.

TABLE 4.1 Critical Infrastructure

Infrastructure	Cyber Attack	Armed Attack (Single Gunman)	Vehicle Bomb	CBR Attack
Site	48	80	108	72
Asset value	4	4	4	4
Threat rating	4	4	3	2
Vulnerability	3	5	9	9
Structural Systems	48	128	192	144
Asset value	8	8	8	8
Threat rating	3	4	3	2
Vulnerability rating	2	4	8	9

it destroy? What level, in a global sense, of seriousness does this risk pose? How much is at stake? When, compared with other assets, is it worth our dedication to thwart all risks? For homeland security, the thrust will be toward quantification—using distinct variables with assigned point values to type the risk. The DHS risk formula would look something like this:

$$\text{Risk} = \text{Asset value} \times \text{threat rating} \times \text{vulnerability rating}$$

The severity of a risk will be assessed in light of its value, the nature of the threat itself, and the potential for harm and injury. So, as is evident in Table 4.1, infrastructure damage is heavily weighted yet variably dependent on the method employed to inflict the damage and harm.[6]

So this leads to the matter of risk assessment in particular terms. How do our homeland professionals and policy makers decide that this risk is worth more than another? Can they devise a meaningful system of quantification that reliably measures the effect and consequence of a risk gone wrong?

4.2.2 Risk Assessment

There are diverse ways in which risk can be measured. The Rand Organization suggests three methodologies of risk assessment[7]:

- *Analytic*: An analytic process must address all three factors that determine terrorism risk—threat, vulnerability, and consequences.
- *Deliberative*: A deliberative process is necessary because the notion of a cold, actuarial terrorism risk assessment is unrealistic. Values and judgment are part and parcel of the process and require transparency and a comprehensive public discussion of outcomes.
- *Practical*: Finally, risk assessment must be practical, which means that data collection and management requirements must be technically and economically feasible.

If DHS has any preference, it would be the analytic, though it would be shortsighted to avoid the other modalities. DHS posits new interesting variables into its risk assessment formula primarily in two ways: the value of asset and the impact on geography. In both instances, the more value, the more coverage; and the greater the impact on the populace, the higher the event will place in tabulations. At first glance, it may seem arbitrary, although nothing in the soft sciences can ever lay claim to the certitude of the hard sciences. What is so strikingly evident is that DHS is willing to place a value on these two things. In a sense, it is about as good as it can be in the imperfect world of risk assessment.

As for value, the DHS risk assessment model highlights the most notable of the targets a terrorist might choose—chemical plants, stadiums, and commercial airports. DHS then analyzes the vulnerability of each asset type relative to each attack method and the plausibility of the chosen attack method.

Additionally, DHS computes the consequential costs of a successful attack and its impact on the value of assets, the health of the collective, our economic system, and the military, and its overall psychological impact on the national psyche. This analysis yields a relative risk estimate for each asset type, applied to a given geographic area and based on the number of each asset type present within that area. DHS lists those assets that carry higher values in its equation in Figure 4.3.[8]

- Chemical manufacturing facilities
- City road bridges
- Colleges and universities
- Commercial airports
- Commercial overnight shipping facilities
- Convention centers
- Dams
- Electricity generation facilities
- Electricity substations
- Enclosed shopping malls
- Ferry terminals–buildings
- Financial facilities
- Hospitals
- Hotel casinos
- Levees
- Liquefied natural gas (LNG) terminals
- Maritime port facilities
- Mass transit commuter rail and subway stations
- National health stockpile sites
- National monuments and icons
- Natural gas compressor stations
- Non-power nuclear reactors
- Nuclear power plants
- Nuclear research labs
- Petroleum pumping stations
- Petroleum refineries
- Petroleum storage tanks
- Potable water treatment facilities
- Primary and secondary schools
- Railroad bridges
- Railroad passenger stations
- Railroad tunnels
- Road commuter tunnels
- Road interstate bridges
- Road interstate tunnels
- Stadiums
- Tall commercial buildings
- Telcomm-telephone hotels
- Theme parks
- Trans-oceanic cable landings

FIGURE 4.3 High value assets as determined by DHS.

- Defense industrial base facilities
- Federal Bureau of Investigation (FBI) basic and special cases
- Gross domestic product (GDP)
- I–94 visitors from countries of interest
- Intelligence community credible and less credible threat reports
- Immigration and customs enforcement (ICE) basic and special cases
- Miles of international border
- Military bases
- Nuclear waste isolation pilot plan (WIPP) transportation routes
- Population

- Population density
- Port of entry/border crossings (people from countries of interest and annual throughput)
- Ratio of law enforcement to population
- Special events
- State international export trade

- State total agriculture sales

- Sum of population density of urban areas in state
- Sum of population of urban areas in state
- Suspicious incidents (credible and less credible)

FIGURE 4.4   High value geographic target regions.

The risk assessment formula is then tested geographically. The geographically based approach weighs the value of assets in that particular region. Geographic regions are weighted in accordance with their area listings[9] (see Figure 4.4).

In light of this valuation, DHS computes the threat level and police and law enforcement activity relative to threats, as well as intelligence from customs and immigration and other suspicious incident data. Then, DHS considers vulnerability factors for each geographic area, such as the area's proximity to international borders and the potential for international incident. Lastly, DHS estimates the potential consequences of an attack on that area, including human health, size of population, economic conditions, military complex, and overall business and industry. DHS charts its methodology in Figure 4.5.[10]

On a narrower front, the task of risk assessment can be departmentally and programmatically driven. For example, risk for FEMA may be distinctively different from the risks of concern to immigration and citizenship. Each agency and department needs to perceive risk in light of its overall mission. One of the more telling illustrations can be discovered in the workings of the Federal Protective Service (FPS), which is entrusted with the protection of nearly 9000 federal facilities. Risk assessment is central to its overall task and mission.

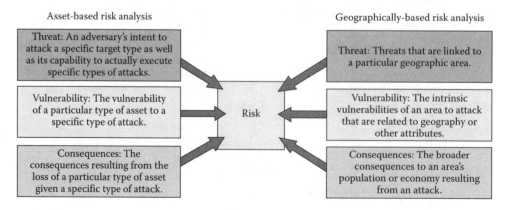

FIGURE 4.5   Asset-based risk analysis vs. geographically based risk analysis methodology comparison.

Therefore, the FPS has developed a Risk Assessment and Management Program (RAMP), which aids FPS officers carrying out facility assessment plans.

RAMP is a risk assessment tool that is multitasked and multivariate in approach. RAMP's intent is to

- Assess and analyze the risk posed to federal facilities from terrorism, crime, natural hazards, and other serious incidents
- Centrally store, access, and report risk assessment findings, including historical information from previous assessments and other documentation
- Manage all aspects of the formal safety assessment (FSA) process
- Manage security post inspections, contracts, and individual guard certification compliance
- Recommend and track the implementation of countermeasures throughout their life cycle
- Perform inventory-wide analysis of the risks posed to federal facilities and the means of reducing them
- Automate and track countermeasure recommendations, implementation status, and life-cycle replacement schedules
- Track financial information for countermeasures throughout their life cycle
- Provide Occupancy Emergency Plan information, call-back lists, and so on
- Provide security access to tools and information, including a comprehensive help file
- Generate and route letters, reports, presentations and statistical analyses and perform other administrative functions
- Provide a comprehensive comparison across the entire general services administration (GSA) inventory that FPS protects

RAMP has taken serious recent critiques over its lack of efficiency, corruption in the ranks, and an overall programmatic ineptitude that has been critiqued by the political establishment. So troublesome was the performance and cost overruns that Congress asked the inspector general (IG) to review the program. The IG essentially confirmed what Congress and select officials had already concluded: that RAMP has yet to meet its stated goals and suffers structurally from poor management and corrupt oversight. Hence, RAMP continues to remain on hold as a DHS initiative.

Internet Exercise: Read the IG report on RAMP at https://www.oig.dhs.gov/assets/Mgmt/2012/OIG_12-67_Aug12.pdf.

Whatever approach is taken with risk assessment, it is critical to gather information, anticipate events and incidents, understand the value of assets and potential harm, and weigh and contrast the functionality and importance of geographic territory. FEMA lists the potential incidents, and plugging into the formula is what is required in Table 4.2.

Internet Exercise: The Homeland Infrastructure Threat and Risk Analysis Center (HITRAC) contains both region- and sector-specific analysts and manages the advanced

TABLE 4.2 Possible Hazards and Emergencies Risk Abatement

Possible Hazards and Emergencies	Hazards		
	Risk Level (None, Low, Moderate, or High)	How can I Reduce my Risk?	
Natural Hazards			
1. Floods			
2. Hurricanes			
3. Thunderstorms and Lightning			
4. Tornadoes			
5. Winter Storms and Extreme Cold			
6. Extreme Heat			
7. Earthquakes			
8. Volcanoes			
9. Landslides and Debris Flow			
10. Tsunamis			
11. Fires			
12. Wildfires			
Technological Hazards			
1. Hazardous Materials Incidents			
2. Nuclear Power Plants			
Terrorism			
1. Explosions			
2. Biological Threats			
3. Chemical Threats			
4. Nuclear Blasts			
5. Radiological Dispersion Device (RDD)			

modeling, simulation, and analysis efforts of the National Infrastructure Simulation and Analysis Center (NISAC). Become familiar with HITRAC—a risk-informed analytic tool that deals with infrastructure—at http://www.dhs.gov/xabout/structure/gc_1257526699957.shtm#1.

We should not ignore the capability to mitigate potential harm. Every event can be influenced in some way, whether it is the movement of people or the protection of property. Every risk can be addressed in some fashion. Government has choices in the matter to some extent. Hazard mitigation planning is the process of determining how to reduce or eliminate the loss of life and property damage resulting from natural and human-caused hazards. Figure 4.6[11] charts the four-step process of mitigation.

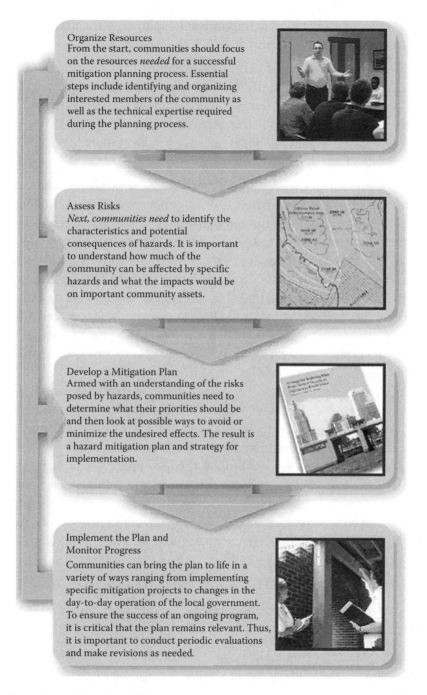

Organize Resources
From the start, communities should focus on the resources *needed* for a successful mitigation planning process. Essential steps include identifying and organizing interested members of the community as well as the technical expertise required during the planning process.

Assess Risks
Next, communities need to identify the characteristics and potential consequences of hazards. It is important to understand how much of the community can be affected by specific hazards and what the impacts would be on important community assets.

Develop a Mitigation Plan
Armed with an understanding of the risks posed by hazards, communities need to determine what their priorities should be and then look at possible ways to avoid or minimize the undesired effects. The result is a hazard mitigation plan and strategy for implementation.

Implement the Plan and Monitor Progress
Communities can bring the plan to life in a variety of ways ranging from implementing specific mitigation projects to changes in the day-to-day operation of the local government. To ensure the success of an ongoing program, it is critical that the plan remains relevant. Thus, it is important to conduct periodic evaluations and make revisions as needed.

FIGURE 4.6 Four-step mitigation process.

4.2.3 CARVER+Shock Assessment Tool

How assessments are carried out invariably depends on the subject matter. In the area of food supply, water, and consumables, risk evaluators have come to depend on the CARVER+Shock assessment methodology. The CARVER system employs various criteria labeled as CARVER; CARVER is an acronym for the following six attributes used to evaluate the attractiveness of a target for attack:

- Criticality—Measure of public health and economic impacts of an attack
- Accessibility—Ability to physically access and egress from target
- Recuperability—Ability of system to recover from an attack
- Vulnerability—Ease of accomplishing attack
- Effect—Amount of direct loss from an attack as measured by loss in production
- Recognizability—Ease of identifying target

In addition, the modified CARVER tool evaluates a seventh attribute, the combined health, economic and psychological impacts of an attack, or the shock attributes of a target.

The CARVER system attempts to quantify risk by assigning specific numbers for specific conditions. It looks to products and food, facilities, and manufacturing processes. So valued is its methodology that the U.S. Food and Drug Administration (FDA) has developed and disseminated software that is downloadable on the web. CARVER+Shock software requires the user to build a process flow diagram for the system to be evaluated and to answer a series of questions for each of the seven CARVER+Shock attributes for each process flow diagram node. Flow processes can be shaped and designed in a host of applications. The CARVER program employs an icon system that correlates to a particular industry or business application. Table 4.3 is a sample listing of the flow process possibilities.[12]

Each question has an associated score. Based on the answers given, the software calculates a score for each CARVER+Shock attribute and sums them to produce a total score for each node. Analogous to a face-to-face session, total scores range from 1 to 10 for each CARVER+Shock attribute and therefore from 7 to 70 for each node.

The interview questions seek to corroborate the flow process according to the variables under the CARVER acronym. Then, once the results are tabulated, a scoring system is linked to each of these variables. Table 4.4 displays the scoring criteria for accessibility.

This process relies on a comprehensive interview schema in order that calculations have reliability. In Figure 4.7, a sample interview page, published by the software, is provided.

CARVER+SHOCK DEFINITIONS

Criticality—A target is critical when the introduction of threat agents into food at this location would cause significant sickness, death, or economic impact.

Accessibility—A target is accessible when an attacker can reach the target, conduct the attack, and leave the target undetected.

Recognizability—A target's recognizability is the degree to which it can be identified by an attacker without confusion.

Vulnerability—Given a successful attack, vulnerability is the likelihood that the contaminant will achieve the attacker's purpose. It considers both processing steps and analytical steps at and downstream of the point of attack.

Effect—Effect is a measure of the percentage of system productivity damaged by an attack at a single facility. Thus, effect is inversely related to the total number of facilities producing the same product.

Recuperability—A target's recuperability is measured in the time it will take for the specific system to recover productivity.

Shock—Shock is the combined measure of the psychological and collateral national economic impacts of a successful attack on the target system. Shock is considered on a national level. The psychological impact will be increased if the target has historical, cultural, religious, or other symbolic significance. Mass casualties are not required to achieve widespread economic loss or psychological damage. Collateral economic damage includes such items as decreased national economic activity, increased unemployment in collateral industries, and so on. Psychological impact will be increased if victims are members of sensitive subpopulations, such as children or the elderly.

Internet Resource: Visit, download, and survey the CARVER software at http://www.fda.gov/Food/FoodDefense/ToolsEducationalMaterials/ucm295900.htm.

4.3 Threats and Hazards

4.3.1 Concept of Threat and Hazard

Threats come in many forms, and if anything is true about the last decade, it would be the evolution in the definition of threat. Some might argue that threats are those things emanating from military sources alone—in the form of armies or weaponry. Of even more compelling recent interest has been the emergence of the homegrown, domestic terrorist threat where our enemies reside among the populace, waiting to carry out the deed. This is part of what Secretary Janet Napolitano called the "New Threat Picture."[13] Others might claim that a threat is driven by natural disaster or events that are unpredictable, such as a typhoon or hurricane. And still another conception deals with the threats of nuclear, chemical, and biological incidents. Threats and hazards are often distinguished by their motive and purpose. Hazards are generally construed as acts of nature; unintentional events without political motive or purpose. Threats, on the other hand, are usually bound to some improper aim or end, such as the political destruction of a government or the radical altering of leadership. Hurricanes and floods are events lacking any animus and, as such, are relegated to the hazard category.

What can be agreed on is that the United States daily remains subject to a host of threats and hazards from every imaginable direction. Professor Daniel Dunai, of Hungary's National Defence University, graphically charts the onslaught in Figure 4.8.[14]

Natural hazards fall into these categories:

- Hurricanes
- Tornadoes
- Floods
- Winter storms
- Heat-related emergencies
- Droughts

TABLE 4.3 CARVER+Shock Flow Process Possibilities (United States Food and Drug Administration, *CARVER+Shock Users' Manual* Version 1.0, 2007 Appendix B: Alphabetical Icons with Descriptions).

Icon	Category	Subcategory	Description
Acid	Materials	Processed ingredients	A water-soluble chemical compound with a pH of less than 7 when dissolved; has a sour taste
Air dryer	Processing	Drying	Device that dries product by direct contact with heated air
Aircraft	Transportation/ distribution		Using an aircraft for the transportation of materials from one location to another
Aseptic packager	Packaging		Equipment that places and seals product in a sterile container/package
Auger tank	Processing	Processing tanks	Enclosure for a large mechanical screw that mixes and moves material/product
Bags	Packaging	Packaging materials	A container of flexible material (paper, plastic, etc.) used for packaging
Bakery	Retail food service		Location where products such as bread, cake, and pastries are baked
Balance tank	Processing	Processing tanks	Used to balance the pH of a discharge so it is within certain parameters
Barge	Transportation/ distribution		Transportation of materials along a body of water from one location to another
Batch tank	Storage	Storage tanks	A mixing/storage tank large enough for a single batch of product
Batterer	Processing	Other processing	A machine used to mix or beat a material
Bin/tub	Storage	Other storage	A large open storage vessel
Blancher	Processing	Cooking	Equipment that uses water or steam to parboil or scald material/product to remove skin or stop enzymatic action
Blast freezer	Processing	Chilling	Device that quickly freezes materials or products as they move along a conveyor using a controlled stream of cold air; generally used when small pieces need to be kept separate as they freeze, such as cut-up vegetables
Blend tank	Processing	Processing tanks	A tank used to blend/mix materials
Blender	Processing	Mixing	Mechanical mixer for chopping, mixing, or liquefying materials
Blower	Conveyance		A machine, such as a fan, that produces an air current to move materials
Bottle cleaner	Cleaning/ washing		A process to clean, wash, and sterilize bottles
Bottle hopper	Packaging		Provides continuous flow of containers to be loaded on a conveyer
Bottler	Packaging		Automated equipment for filling bottles

TABLE 4.3 (CONTINUED) CARVER+Shock Flow Process Possibilities (United States Food and Drug Administration, *CARVER+Shock Users' Manual* Version 1.0, 2007 Appendix B: Alphabetical Icons with Descriptions).

Icon	Category	Subcategory	Description
Bottles	Packaging	Packaging materials	Containers with a narrow neck and no handles that can be plugged, corked, or capped
Boxes	Packaging	Packaging materials	Container with four sides and a lid or cover used for storage or transport
Breader	Processing	Other processing	Equipment used to coat meat/fish/poultry with a crumb coating
Briner	Processing	Other processing	Process to preserve food using a concentrated salt solution
Browner	Processing	Cooking	Equipment used to sear the outside surface of meats
Bulk storage	Storage	Other storage	Storage for a large amount of ingredient/product in a single container
Butcher	Processing	Meat processing	To cut up meat or poultry
Cans	Packaging	Packaging materials	Cylindrical metal container
Capper	Packaging		Applies caps to containers
Car	Storage	Other storage	Storage for a material waiting to be shipped
Caser	Packaging		Sorts and places product into cases
Centrifuge	Processing	Separation/ extraction	Machine that uses centrifugal force to separate substances with different densities
Check weigher	Control checks		A scale to check the weight of product
Chemicals	Materials	Processing materials	Cleaning chemicals
Chilled distribution	Transportation/ distribution		Refrigerated transport of product

- Wildfires
- Thunderstorms
- Geologic events

Government agencies and policy makers frequently underestimate the full impact of these natural disasters, at least as to the homeland defense mind-set. These events wreak extraordinary havoc. The death toll alone is a distressingly impressive count (see Figure 4.9).[15]

More than seven billion people worldwide have been negatively impacted by natural disasters in the last century—a statistic that lays out a permanent obligation for homeland personnel (see Figure 4.10).[16]

Threats fall into these typologies:

- Crimes
- Terrorism

TABLE 4.4 CARVER+SHOCK SCORING CRITERIA

Accessibility Criteria	Scale
Easily accessible (e.g., target is outside building and no perimeter fence). Limited physical or human barriers or observation. Attacker has relatively unlimited access to the target. Attack can be carried out using medium or large volumes of contaminant without undue concern of detection. Multiple sources of information concerning the facility and the target are easily available.	9–10
Accessible (e.g., target is inside building, but in unsecured part of facility). Human observation and physical barriers limited. Attacker has access to the target for an hour or less. Attack can be carried out with moderate to large volumes of contaminant, but requires the use of stealth. Only limited specific information is available on the facility and the target.	7–8
Partially accessible (e.g., inside building, in a relatively unsecured, but busy, part of facility). Under constant possible human observation. Some physical barriers may be present. Contaminant must be disguised, and time limitations are significant. Only general, nonspecific information is available on the facility and the target.	5–6
Hardly accessible (e.g., inside building in a secured part of facility). Human observation and physical barriers with an established means of detection. Access generally restricted to operators or authorized persons. Contaminant must be disguised and time limitations are extreme. Limited general information available on the facility and the target.	3–4
Not accessible. Physical barriers, alarms, and human observation. Defined means of intervention in place. Attacker can access target for less than 5 min with all equipment carried in pockets. No useful publicly available information concerning the target.	1–2

- Unintentional events
- Blackouts
- Radiological events
- Hazmat incidents
- Fires

Threats arising from terrorism signify a malicious intent to intentionally threaten lives and property. These acts may range from a single person on a shooting rampage, to a cyber attack that harms computer systems, to the organized use of WMD. WMD events could involve chemical, biological, explosive, or radioactive weapons. Acts of terrorism include threats of terrorism, assassinations, kidnappings, hijackings, bomb scares, and bombings. High-risk targets for acts of terrorism include military and civilian government facilities, international airports, large cities, and high-profile landmarks. Terrorists might also target large public gatherings, water and food supplies, utilities, and corporate centers. The recent events in France manifest this tendency to choose targets for maximum effect. In Paris, the choice of a soccer stadium, a concert hall, and public restaurants all achieve the underlying goal of the terrorist, which is to inflict maximum terror with maximum results. In Nice, it was one driver targeting crowds celebrating Bastille Day.

ABC
Criticality category interview report

What is the serving size for the product? (If the product is used as an ingredient, how much of the product is used in each serving?)

What is the distribution unit (package size sold to the consumer)?

How many retail outlets typically receive units from one batch?
- O   1
- O   2–3
- O   3–20
- O   >10

What percentage of each batch is sold...

–	Within one day of purchase?
–	Within first three days after purchase?
–	Within first two weeks after purchase?
–	Within first month after purchase?
–	During the first two months?

What percentage of the product is typically consumed ...

–	Within one day of purchase?
–	Within the first three days after purchase?
–	Within the first week after purchase?
–	Within two weeks after purchase?
–	Within first month after purchase?
–	Within first two months after purchase?

On average, how many individuals eat from the same distribution unit?

Does the company have a published support line for end consumers with concerns or questions?
- O   Yes
- O   No

Is there a formal company procedure for communicating information on a contamination incident to the public?
- O   Yes
- O   No

Does your company or facility have a mechanism in place to effectively implement a recall and withdraw product from the marketplace?
- O   Yes
- O   No

Does your company conduct mock product recalls?
- O   Yes
- O   No

How well can you trace your product to the distribution centers (D.C.s) and retail outlets?
- O   Cannot trace at all.
- O   Can identify independent D.C.s and entire distribution chains to major distributors that may have received units from one batch.
- O   Can trace specific pallets to independent D.C.s and entire distribution chains to major distributors such as Wal-Mart.
- O   Can identify all retail outlets that received units from a batch.
- O   Can trace specific pallets to each retail outlet that received it.

Is this product an uncoded product or uncoded raw ingredient?
- O   Yes
- O   No

Are you aware of large-scale counterfeiting or diversion for this product?
- O   Yes
- O   No

FIGURE 4.7   CARVER+Shock sample interview page.

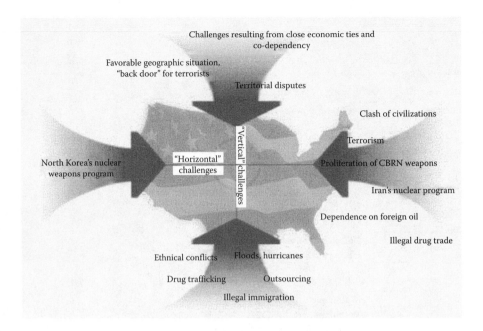

FIGURE 4.8 A convenient scheme for categorizing different threats and challenges.

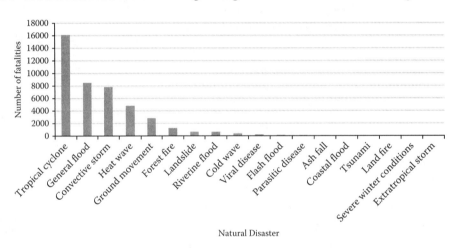

FIGURE 4.9 Fatalities from natural disasters in the United States from 1900 to 2015.

Internet Exercise: Visit CNN's website and explore the videos on the Paris attacks: http://www.cnn.com/2015/11/13/europe/paris-attacks-francois-hollande.

Infrastructure of every variety needs constant vigilance in the matter of threat, from its original construction phase to its maintenance. Building design must anticipate threat even in terms of the materials used so that the structure might withstand natural disasters, blast, projectiles, and fire.[17]

Identifying, anticipating, and defending against such a broad band of threats can only be described as daunting. For if homeland policy makers have learned anything over the last

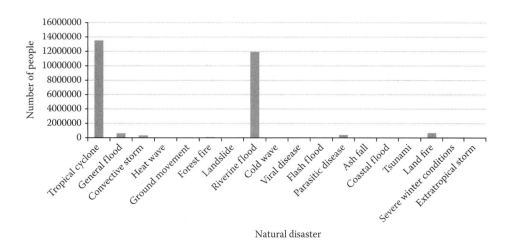

FIGURE 4.10 **People affected by natural disasters in the United States from 1900 to 2015.**

decade, it is that these concepts, like threat and disaster, have an evolutionary quality. In short, both the ideas and the means of execution change whether we admit it or not. Those entrusted must stay "in the box" as well as be capable of jumping "out of the box." In other words, past history tells us much about these events, although these same events may not evolve in just the way predicted. Alain Bauer's insights on this dilemma are most helpful, for he urges the policy maker to find the commonality in all forms of terror. He argues that no matter what the group, what the religious sect, what the purpose or aim, all terrorists

- Have common harmonies
- Frequent common lands and territories
- Have a common (submerged) economy
- Offer real opportunities for symbiosis[18]

Agencies and communities can chart potential threats by using the checklist in Table 4.5.

Of course, hazards can arise through human negligence and carelessness, which gives rise to a man-made catastrophe.

4.3.2 Weapons of Mass Destruction

No ambition is more glorifying for the terrorist than the successful delivery of a WMD. The terror associated with WMD is well founded and not to be addressed cavalierly. The stuff of WMD can only be described as frightful and has the capacity to inflict global injury. There are four generally accepted categories of WMD, covered in the following subsections.

4.3.2.1 Nuclear

Some terrorist organizations, such as al Qaeda, openly declare their desire to acquire and use nuclear weapons. Even the complexities of devising a nuclear delivery mechanism are amply documented. The complete production of a nuclear weapon largely depends on the terrorist group's access to nuclear material and a high level of scientific expertise.

TABLE 4.5 Local Threats and Hazards

Type of Hazard	Likelihood of Occurrence	Potentially Devastating Impact on People	Potentially Devastating Impact on Structures
Natural Hazards			
Floods			
Winter storms			
Tornadoes			
Thunderstorm			
Hurricanes			
Extreme heat/cold			
Viral epidemics			
Human-Induced Hazards			
Hazardous materials incidents			
Transportation accidents			
Infrastructure disruptions			
Workplace violence			
Civil disorder/disobedience			
Terrorist Hazards			
Conventional weapons			
Incendiary devices			
Biological and chemical agents			
Radiological			
Cyber-terrorism			
Weapons of mass destruction			

Source: Hazard Analysis and Vulnerability Study, done under contract to DC Emergency Management Agency, May 2002.

Black-market materials can be utilized, though the crudeness of the enterprise is dangerous in and of itself (Figure 4.11).

DHS, by and through its Office of Domestic Nuclear Detection, is entrusted with the detection and prevention of nuclear terrorist threats. The basic objectives of the office are

- To develop the global nuclear detection and reporting architecture
- To develop, acquire, and support the domestic nuclear detection and reporting system
- To fully characterize detector system performance before deployment
- To establish situational awareness through information sharing and analysis
- To establish operation protocols to ensure detection leads to effective response
- To conduct a transformational research and development program

FIGURE 4.11   Nuclear power plant.

- To establish the National Technical Nuclear Forensics Center to provide planning, integration, and improvements to the U.S. government (USG) nuclear forensics capabilities.

The demands and complexities of nuclear threat call for constant and continuous assessment. Aside from perimeter concerns and access issues, the typical nuclear power facility not only utilizes physical materials capable of mass destruction but also must find ways to store and treat the by-products of nuclear power and production. Hence, DHS has recently tried to regularize practices in the nuclear industry regarding data storage and collection, physical security plans, and disposal.[19] The organization of the Domestic Nuclear Detection Office is illustrated in Figure 4.12.

Physical security at nuclear power plants is provided by well-armed and well-trained security personnel who remain ready to respond to an attack 24 hours a day, 7 days a week. The sites are protected by sensitive intrusion detection equipment, fences, and barriers and are monitored by cameras and security patrols (Figure 4.13).

DHS has realized that the department cannot function in an isolated fashion when it comes to nuclear threat and that interagency cooperation is central to its mission. "Federal, state, local and private sector partners regularly and actively assess the risk environment in the Nuclear Sector in light of changes or potential changes to threats, vulnerabilities and consequences."[20] In 2002, the Nuclear Regulatory Commission (NRC) announced the creation of the Office of Nuclear Security and Incident Response (NSIR) to improve NRC effectiveness in ensuring protection of public health and safety from security threats at licensed facilities. On January 20, 2004, the commission announced the creation of the Emergency Preparedness Project Office (EPPO) to improve NRC's effectiveness. On June 13, 2004, EPPO was integrated within NSIR, creating the Emergency Preparedness Directorate (EPD) and aligned the NRC's preparedness, security, and incident response missions.

Nuclear terrorism can also be carried out at nuclear facilities. Each nuclear facility has high-level security responsibilities and must take seriously its charge to thwart any attempts on the facility. Nuclear facilities are required to have layers of security systems in place to

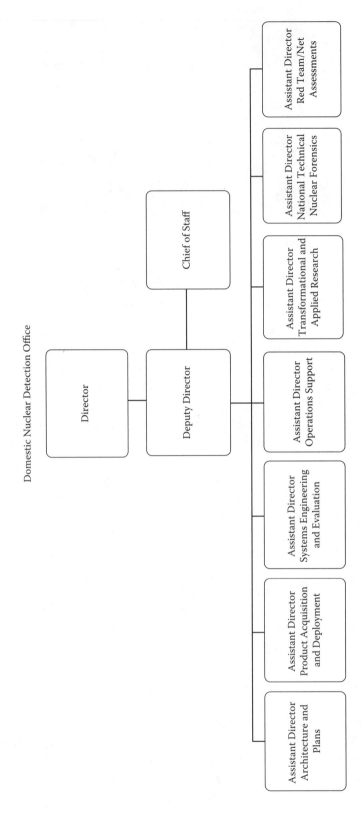

FIGURE 4.12 Organization chart of the office of Domestic Nuclear Detection Office.

FIGURE 4.13 Protection officer at a nuclear facility.

prevent intrusion, contamination, the release of materials, or the loss or theft of radioactive and plutonium materials. In the most general terms, a security program for nuclear facilities minimally includes

- A well-trained security force
- Robust physical barriers
- Intrusion detection systems
- Surveillance systems
- Plant access controls

In addition, nuclear facilities are required to conduct threat assessments regularly and are subject to regular and continuous security visitations by the NRC.

Internet Resource: Visit the NRC web location for the results of security visits and requirements at plants throughout the United States at http://www.nrc.gov/reading-rm/doc-collections/insp-manual/manual-chapter/mc0320.pdf.

Training is rigorous and continuous. So concerned are the operators of nuclear reactors that extensive training, labeled *force on force* (FOF) training, anticipates an assault on the facility itself. Two sets of security officers—the first for maintenance of the actual facility and the other being the attack force—will engage one another in mock battle. The FOF exercise is highly realistic and essential to a preventive security program (see Figure 4.14).

NRC's FOF security exercises realistically test security forces' capability and security programs at nuclear power plants.

The NRC requires nuclear power plant operators to defend the plant against attackers seeking to cause damage to the reactor core or spent fuel, resulting in a release of radiation.

During FOF exercises, a number of commando-style attacks are carried out against a plant's security forces, looking for deficiencies in the plant operator's defensive strategy.

Any significant problems are promptly identified, reviewed, and fixed.

Each nuclear power plant site will have at least one FOF exercise every three years.

The NRC and plant operator ensure the safety of plant employees and the security of the plant during FOF exercises.

FIGURE 4.14   NRC Force on force training.

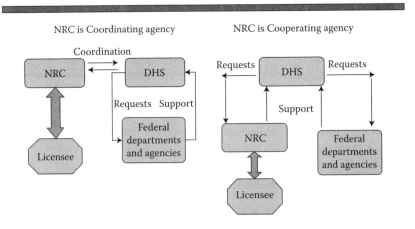

FIGURE 4.15   NRC interface with Department of Homeland Security.

The NRC requires nuclear power plant operators to defend the plant against attackers seeking to cause damage to the reactor core or spent fuel to prevent the release of radiation. Postassessment highlights any deficiencies in training and security protocol and is an important part of the day-to-day security plan at the facility.

As in all aspects of nuclear security, there must be clear lines of authority and agency cooperation at every level of government. In the event of a nuclear breach, the line between the NRC and DHS is precisely drawn, as shown in Figure 4.15.[21]

Finally, in terms of response and advance mitigation, FEMA is entrusted with dealing with the effects and aftereffects of a nuclear blast. The extent of that participation will depend on a host of variables, including the size of the nuclear device, its detonation height, the nature of the ground surface, and existing meteorological conditions. FEMA will not only encounter the damage resulting from blast and explosion but also the long-term effects of fallout.

Practitioners are now lucky enough to be able to conduct measurements for present and future harm regarding nuclear and radiological threats and consequences by modeling and software programs. The Radiological Assessment System for Consequence Analysis (RASCAL) is considered the industry's best example of this sort of measuring tool.

Internet Exercise: To gain an overview of how RASCAL works, visit pbadupws nrc.gov/docs/ML1008/ML100810144.pdf.

4.3.2.2 Radiological

Some terrorists seek to acquire radioactive materials for use in a radiological dispersal device (RDD) or "dirty bomb." In conjunction with the NRC, the Domestic Nuclear Detection Office is always on the hunt for individuals or groups intent on delivering nuclear WMD (Figure 4.16).

FIGURE 4.16   Nuclear specialist at Nellis Air Force Base.

The most referenced threat in this sector is the use of a dirty bomb. The dirty bomb combines a conventional explosive, such as dynamite, with radioactive material. Upon detonation, aside from the immediate injuries inflicted, there will be severe collateral damage from the nuclear material itself.

The extent of local contamination will depend on a number of factors, including the size of the explosive, the amount and type of radioactive material used, the means of dispersal, and the weather conditions. The effects of radiation exposure is determined by

- Amount of radiation absorbed by the body
- Type of radiation (gamma, beta, or alpha)
- Distance from the radiation to an individual
- Means of exposure—external or internal (absorbed by the skin, inhaled, or ingested)
- Length of time exposed

See the graphic from the NRC in Figure 4.17 representing the various modes of exposure.

Most radioactive materials lack sufficient strength to present a significant public health risk once dispersed, and the materials posing the greatest hazard would likely infect the

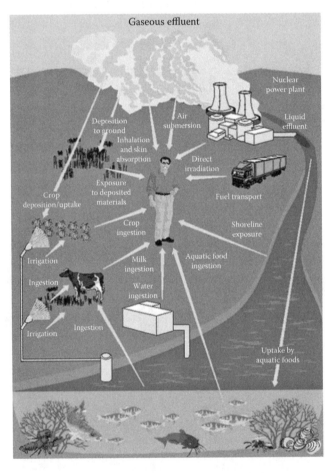

FIGURE 4.17 Radiation released in the environment will result in the exposure of general members of the public. The diagram shows some of the pathways that may lead to exposure.

terrorists themselves.[22] The secondary and cultural effects of a dirty bomb would be quite acute since fear and panic would naturally be expected. The availability of radiological source material is more extensive than most know since this product is used widely in industrial, medical, and research applications; cancer therapy; food and blood irradiation techniques; and radiography.

Internet Resource: To learn about survival steps in the event of a nuclear attack by a dirty bomb or other method, read the instructions issued by the Centers for Disease Control and Prevention (CDC) at http://emergency.cdc.gov/radiation/dirtybombs.asp.

Law enforcement takes the dirty bomb seriously, and agencies throughout the country regularly engage in tabletop or field exercises anticipating the dynamics of the event. In May 2003, DHS hosted a large, multiagency, and international exercise dealing with a dirty bomb in Seattle and a covert biological attack in Chicago. In all, 25 federal agencies, as well as the American Red Cross, were involved in the 5-day exercise, as well as partner agencies from the Canadian government. Overall, DHS continues its emphasis on exercises to give realism to its constituencies. In 2011, DHS announced a more formal "National Exercise Program," which lays out a strategic vision of how tabletop and other realistic programs can be used to prepare and mitigate security threats.[23]

Aside from these broader exercises, DHS stressed particularized training to ensure the best possible response. The trend continues with regularly scheduled dirty bomb and disaster drills at federal, state, and local levels (Figure 4.18).

Internet Resource: For an NRC fact sheet on dirty bombs, see http://www.nrc.gov/reading-rm/doc-collections/fact-sheets/fs-dirty-bombs.html.

FIGURE 4.18   KINGSTON, NY—Soldiers from the 222nd Chemical Company in full hazardous material gear assist civilian participants during the decontamination phase of a joint force first-responders exercise in reaction to a radioactive attack. New York National Army and Airmen Guardsmen collaborate with local authorities to help train for the response to a radioactive terrorist attack, November 6, 2011. (Courtesy of Spc. Brian Godette, New York Army National Guard, 138th PAD.)

4.3.2.3 Biological

Bioterrorism, another deadly threat and one discussed widely throughout this chapter, is the deliberate dispersal of pathogens through food, air, water, or living organisms in order to cause disease and other harm to the public. Biological agents can kill on a massive scale and have the potential to move quickly through large populations, leaving high rates of mortality.[24] Biological agents are, for the most part, tasteless, odorless, and invisible. The havoc occurs quickly and without much warning. Biological agents can be introduced by air, water, or in the food supply. FEMA categorizes agents by application, duration, extent of effects, and mitigation, as shown in Figure 4.19.

DHS has played an increasing role in this sort of detection. Through its Science and Technology Directorate, a series of programs that identify and detect biological agents have been implemented. Of recent interest is BioWatch—a program that measures air samples in 30 urban areas across the United States. Using BioWatch sensors, the technology monitors specific locations as well as events of national significance such as the Olympics or the Superbowl.[25] Figure 4.20 illustrates the latest generation in BioWatch technology, though there have been technical difficulties with version 3.[26]

When compared with nuclear technology, this is a much easier scientific row to hoe, and anyone with some level of biological training and access to common laboratory equipment can develop terror tools that emerge from biological products. Biological agents, as the anthrax cases of the last decade demonstrate, foment high rates of fear in the general public (Figure 4.21).

The CDC assumes the preeminent position when it comes to the identification and mitigation of, the response to, and the recovery from a biological attack. It classifies biological agents into three major categories:

Category A diseases/agents: The U.S. public health system and primary health-care providers must be prepared to address various biological agents, including pathogens that are rarely seen in the United States. High-priority agents include organisms that pose a risk to national security because they

- Can be easily disseminated or transmitted from person to person
- Result in high mortality rates and have the potential for major public health impact
- Might cause public panic and social disruption
- Require special action for public health preparedness

Category B diseases/agents: Second highest priority agents include those that

- Are moderately easy to disseminate
- Result in moderate morbidity rates and low mortality rates
- Require specific enhancements of the CDC's diagnostic capacity and enhanced disease surveillance

Category C diseases/agents: Third highest priority agents include emerging pathogens that could be engineered for mass dissemination in the future because of

Agent Type	Disease/Condition *Causative Agent/ Pathogen*	Description of Agent	Transmissible Person to Person	Infectivity/ Lethality	Incubation Period	Duration of Illness	Persistence/ Stability	Vaccination/ Toxoids	Rate of Action	Symptoms	Treatment	Possible Means of Delivery
BACTERIA	Anthrax (inhalation) *Bacillus anthracis*	Rod-shaped, gram-positive, aerobic sporulating micro-organism, individual spores ~(1–1.2)x(3–5)μ	No	Moderate/ High	1–7 days	3–5 days	Spores are highly stable	Yes	Symptoms in 2–3 days; Shock and death occurs with 24–36 hrs after symptoms	Fever, malaise, fatigue, cough and mild chest discomfort, followed by severe respiratory distress with dyspnea, diaphoresis, stridor, and cyanosis	Usually not effective after symptoms are present, high dose antibiotic treatment with penicillin, ciprofloxacin, or doxycycline should be undertaken. Supportive therapy may be necessary.	Aerosol.
	Brucellosis *Brucella suis, melitensis & abortus*	All non-motile, non-sporulating, gram negative, aerobic bacterium; ~(0.5-1)x(1-2)μ	No	High/Low	Days to months	Weeks to months	Organisms are stable for several weeks in wet soil and food.	Yes	Highly variable, usually 6-60 days.	Chills, sweats, headache, fatigue, myalgias, arthralgias, and anorexia. Cough may occur. Complications include sacroiliitis, arthritis, vertebral osteomyelitis, epididymoorchitis, and rarely endocarditis.	Recommended treatment is doxycycline (200 mg/day) plus rifampin (900 mg/day) for 6 weeks.	Aerosol. Expected to mimic a natural disease.
	Cholera *Vibrio cholerae*	Short, curved, motile, gram-negative, non-sporulating rod. Strongly anaerobic, these organisms prefer alkaline and high salt environments.	Negl.	Low/Moderate-High	1-5 days	1 or more weeks	Unstable in aerosols and pure water, more so in polluted water.	Yes	Sudden onset after 1-5 day incubation period.	Initial vomiting and abdominal distension with little or no fever or abdominal pain. Followed rapidly by diarrhea, which may be either mild or profuse and watery, with fluid losses exceeding 5 to 10 liters or more per day. Without treatment, death may result from severe dehydration, hypovolemia, and shock.	Therapy consists of fluid and electrolyte replacement. Antibiotics will shorten the duration of diarrhea and thereby reduce fluid losses. Tetracycline, ampicillin, or trimethoprim-sulfamethoxazole are most commonly used.	1. Sabotage (food/water supply) 2. Aerosol
	Glanders *Burkholderia mallei*	Gram-negative bacillus primarily noted for producing disease in horses, mules, and donkeys	Negl.	/Moderate-High	10-14 days	N/A	N/A	No	N/A	Inhalational exposure produces fever, rigors, sweats, myalgia, headache, pleuritic chest pain, cervical adenopathy, splenomegaly, and generalized papular/pustular eruptions. Almost always fatal without treatment.	Few antibiotics have been evaluated *in vivo*. Sulfadiazine may be effective in some cases. Ciprofloxacin, doxycycline, and rifampin have *in vitro* efficacy. Extrapolating from melioidosis guidelines, a combination of TMP-SMX + ceftazidime ± gentamicin might be considered.	Aerosol.
	Plague (pneumonic, bubonic) *Yersinia pestis*	Rod-shaped, non-motile, non-sporulating, gram-negative, aerobic bacterium; ~(0.5-1)x(1-2)μ	High	High/Very High in untreated personnel, the mortality is 100%	2 to 6 days for bubonic and 3 to 4 days for pneumonic	1-2 days	Less important because of high transmissibility.	Yes	Two to three days	High fever, chills, headache, hemoptysis, and toxemia, progressing rapidly to dyspnea, sturdier, and cyanosis. Death results from respiratory failure, circulatory collapse, and a bleeding diathesis.	Early administration of antibiotics is very effective. Supportive therapy for pneumonic and septicemic forms is required.	May be delivered via contaminated vectors (fleas) causing bubonic type, or, more likely, via aerosol causing pneumonic type.
	Shigellosis *Shigella Dysenteriae*	Rod-shaped, gram-negative, non-motile, non-sporulating bacterium	Negl.	High/Low	1-7 days (usually 2-3)	N/A	Unstable in aerosols and pure water, more so in polluted water.	No	Symptoms usually within 2-3 days, however, known to demonstrate in as little as 12 hours or as long as 7 days.	Fever, nausea, vomiting, abdominal cramps, watery diarrhea, and occasionally, traces of blood in the feces. Symptoms range from mild to severe with some infected individuals not experiencing any symptoms.	The antibiotics commonly used for treatment are ampicillin, trimethoprim/sulfamethoxazole (also known as Bactrim* or Septra*), nalidixic acid, or ciprofloxacin. Persons with mild infections will usually recover quickly without antibiotic treatment. Antidiarrheal agents such as loperamide (Imodium*) or diphenoxylate with atropine (Lomotil*) are likely to make the illness worse and should be avoided.	Contaminated food or water
	Tularemia *Francisella tularensis*	Small, aerobic, non-sporulating, non-motile, gram-negative *cocco-bacillus* ~0.2x(0.2-0.7)μ	No	High/ Moderate if untreated	1-10 days	2 or more weeks	Not very stable	Yes	Three to five days	Ulceroglandular tularemia with local ulcer and regional lymphadenopathy, fever, chills, headache, and malaise. Typhoidal or septicemic tularemia presents with fever, headache, malaise, substernal discomfort, prostration, weight loss, and non-productive cough.	Administration of anitbiotics with early treatment is very effective. Streptomycin – 1 gm I. M. q. 12 hrs x 10 10-14 d. Gentamicin – 3-5 mg/kg/day x 10-14 d.	Aerosol.
	Typhoid *Salmonella typhi*	Rod-shaped, motile, non-sporulating gram-negative bacterium	Negl.	Moderate/ Moderate if untreated	6-21 days	Several weeks	Stable	Yes	One to three days	Sustained fever, severe headache, malaise, anorexia, a relative bradycardia, splenomegaly, nonproductive cough in the early stage of the illness, and constipation more commonly than diarrhea.	Chloramphenicol amoxicillin or TMP-SMX. Quilone derivatives and third generation cephalusporins and supportive therapy.	Sabotage of food and water supplies.
RICKETTSIAE	Q-Fever *Coxiella burneti*	Bacterium-like, gram-negative organism, pleomorphic 300-700 nm	No	High/Very low	10-20	2 days to 2 weeks	Stable	Yes	Onset may be sudden	Chills, retrobulbar headache, weakness, malaise and severe sweats.	Tetracycline or doxycycline are the treatment of choice and are given orally for 5 to 7 days.	May be a dust cloud either from a line source or a point source (downwind one-half mile or more).
	Typhus (classic) *Rickettsia prowazeki*	Non-motile, minute, coccoid or rod shaped rickettsiae, in pairs or chains, 300 nm	No	High/High	6-15 days	Weeks to months	Not very stable	No	Variable onset, often sudden. Terminates by rapid lysis after about 2 weeks of fever	Headache, chills, prostration, fever, and general pain. A macular eruption appears on the fifth to sixth day, initially on the upper trunk, followed by spread to the entire body, but usually not the face, palms, or soles.	Tetracyclines or chlormphenical orally in a loading dose of 2-3 g, followed by daily doses of 1-2 g/day in 4 divided doses until ind. becomes afelorite (usually 2 days) plus 1 day.	May be delivered via contaminated vectors (lice or fleas).
VIRUSES	Encephalitis	Lipid-enveloped virions of 50-60 nm dia., icosohedral nucleocapsid w. 2 glycoproteins										
	-Eastern/Western Equine Encephalitis (EEE, WEE)		Negl.	High/High	5-15 days	1-3 weeks	Relatively unstable	Yes		Inflammation of the mengies of the brain, headache, fever, dizziness, drowsiness or stupor, tremors or convulsions, muscular incoordination.	No specific treatment; supportive treatment is essential	Airborne spread possible.
	-Venezuelan Equine Encephalitis		Low	High/Low	1-5 days	Days to weeks	Relatively unstable	Yes	Sudden	Inflammation of the mengies of the brain, headache, fever, dizziness, drowsiness or stupor, tremors or convulsions, muscular incoordination.	No specific treatment; supportive treatment is essential	Airborne spread possible.
	Hemorrhagic Fever									Malaise, myalgias, headache, vomiting, and diarrhea may occur with any of the hemorrhagic fevers	No specific treatment; intensive supportive treatment is essential	Airborne spread possible.
	-Ebola Fever	Filovirus	Moderate	High/High	7-9 days	5-16 days	Relatively unstable	No		May also include a macular dermatologic eruption.		
	-Marburg	Filovirus	Moderate					No		May also include a macular dermatologic eruption.		
	-Yellow Fever	Flavivirus. Isosahedral nucleocapsid 37-50 nm diam., lipoprotein env. w/ short surface spikes	Negl.	High/High	3-6 days	1-2 weeks	Relatively unstable	Yes	Sudden			
	Variola Virus (Smallpox)	Asymmetric, brick-shaped, rounded corners: DNA virus	High	High/High	7-17 days	1-2 weeks	Stable	Yes	2-4 days	Malaise, fever, rigors, vomiting, headache, and backache. 2-3 days later lesions appear which quickly progress from macules to papules, and eventually to pustular vesicles. They are more abundant on the extremities and face, and develop synchronously.	No specific treatment; supportive treatment is essential	Airborne spread possible.
TOXIN	Botulinum Toxin	any of the seven distinct neurotoxins produced by the bacillus, *Clostridium botulinum*	No	NA/High	Variable (hours to days)	24-72 hours/Months if lethal	Stable	Yes	12-72 hours	Initial signs and symptoms include ptosis, generalized weakness, lassitude, and dizziness. Diminished salivation with extreme dryness of the mouth and throat may cause complaints of a sore throat. Urinary retention or ileus may also occur. Motor symptoms usually are present early in the disease; cranial nerves are affected first with blurred vision, diplopia, ptosis, and photophobia. Bulbar nerve dysfunction causes dysarthria, dysphonia, and dysphagia. This is followed by a symmetrical, descending, progressive weakness of the extremities along with weakness of the respiratory muscles. Development of respiratory failure may be abrupt.	(1) Respiratory failure—tracheostomy and ventilatory assistance, fatalities should be <5%. Intensive and prolonged nursing care may be required for recovery (which may take several weeks or even months). (2) Food-borne botulism and aerosol exposure—equine antitoxin is probably helpful, sometimes even after onset of signs of intoxication. Administration of antitoxin is reasonable if disease has not progressed to a stable state. Use requires pretesting for sensitivity to horse serum (and desensitization for those allergic). Disadvantages include rapid clearance by immune elimination, as well as a theoretical risk of serum sickness.	1. Sabotage (food/water supply) 2. Aerosol
	Ricin	Glycoprotein toxin (66,000 daltons) from the seed of the castor plant	No	NA/High	Hours	Days	Stable	Not effective	6-72 hours	Rapid onset of nausea, vomiting, abdominal cramps and severe diarrhea with vascular collapse; death has occurred on the third day or later. Following inhalation, one might expect nonspecific symptoms of weakness, fever, cough, and hypothermia followed by hypotension and cardiovascular collapse.	Management is supportive and should include maintenance of intravascular volume. Standard management for poison ingestion should be employed if intoxication is by the oral route.	Aerosol
	Staphylococcal enterotoxin B	One of several exotoxins produced by *Staphylococcus aureus*	No	NA/Low	Days to weeks	Days to weeks	Stable	Not effective	30 min-6 hours	Fever, chills, headache, myalgia, and nonproductive cough. In more severe cases, dyspnea and retrosternal chest pain may also be present. In many patients nausea, vomiting, and diarrhea will also occur.	Treatment is limited to supportive care. No specific antitoxin for human use is available.	1. Sabotage (food/water supply) 2. Aerosol
	Trichothecene (T-2) Mycotoxins	A diverse group of more than 40 compounds produced by fungi.	No	NA/High	Hours	Hours	Stable	Not effective	Sudden	Victims are reported to have suffered painful skin lesions, lightheadedness, dyspnea, and a rapid onset of hemorrhage, incapacitation and death. Survivors developed a radiation-like sickness including fever, nausea, vomiting, diarrhea, leukopenia, bleeding, and sepsis.	General supportive measures are used to alleviate acute T-2 toxicoses. Prompt (within 5-60 min of exposure) soap and water wash significantly reduces the development of the localized destructive, cutaneous effects of the toxin. After oral exposure management should include standard therapy for poison ingestion.	1. Sabotage 2. Aerosol

FIGURE 4.19 Selected biological agent characteristics.

FIGURE 4.20   BioWatch: Generation 3 monitoring station. DHS.

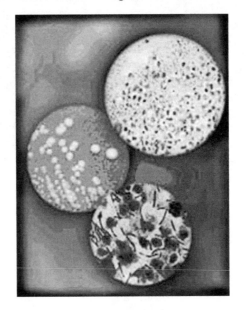

FIGURE 4.21   Biological agents under a high-powered microscope.

- Availability
- Ease of production and dissemination
- Potential for high morbidity and mortality rates and major health issues

The CDC types of all known biological agents are listed into these three categories.[27] As of 2015,[28] the list of biological agents was composed of

- Anthrax (*Bacillus anthracis*)
- Arenaviruses
- *Bacillus anthracis* (anthrax)
- Botulism (*Clostridium botulinum toxin*)
- Brucella species (*brucellosis*)
- *Brucellosis* (Brucella species)

- *Burkholderia mallei* (glanders)
- *Burkholderia pseudomallei* (melioidosis)
- *Chlamydia psittaci* (psittacosis)
- Cholera (*Vibrio cholerae*)
- *Clostridium botulinum toxin* (botulism)
- *Clostridium perfringens* (Epsilon toxin)
- *Coxiella burnetii* (Q fever)
- Ebola virus hemorrhagic fever
- E. coli O157:H7 (*Escherichia coli*)
- Emerging infectious diseases such as Nipah virus and hantavirus
- Epsilon toxin of *Clostridium perfringens*
- *Escherichia coli* O157:H7 (*E. coli*)
- Food safety threats (e.g., salmonella species, *E. coli* O157:H7, shigella)
- *Francisella tularensis* (tularemia)
- Glanders (*Burkholderia mallei*)
- Lassa fever
- Marburg virus hemorrhagic fever
- Melioidosis (*Burkholderia pseudomallei*)
- Plague (*Yersinia pestis*)
- Psittacosis (*Chlamydia psittaci*)
- Q fever (*Coxiella burnetii*)
- Ricin toxin from *Ricinus communis* (castor beans)
- *Rickettsia prowazekii* (typhus fever)
- Salmonella species (salmonellosis)
- *Salmonella typhi* (typhoid fever)
- Salmonellosis (salmonella species)
- Shigella (shigellosis)
- Shigellosis (shigella)
- Smallpox (*Variola major*)
- Staphylococcal enterotoxin B
- Tularemia (*Francisella tularensis*)
- Typhoid fever (*Salmonella typhi*)
- Typhus fever (*Rickettsia prowazekii*)
- *Variola major* (smallpox)
- *Vibrio cholerae* (cholera)
- Viral encephalitis (alphaviruses [e.g., Venezuelan equine encephalitis, eastern equine encephalitis, western equine encephalitis])
- Viral hemorrhagic fevers (filoviruses [e.g., Ebola, Marburg] and arenaviruses [e.g., Lassa, Machupo])
- Water safety threats (e.g., *Vibrio cholerae*, *Cryptosporidium parvum*)

For the present, the bulk of attention has been on four to five biological agents with the potential for severe harm. A summary analysis of these follows.

4.3.2.3.1 Anthrax

Few words evoke the terror that anthrax does. Anthrax has a long history of infecting nations and individuals, and even today it does not respond readily to medical intervention. Anthrax is caused by B. anthracis, a disease-causing bacterium that forms spores. A spore is a cell that is dormant (asleep) but over time may arise from its slumber.

Anthrax can be broken down anatomically:

- Skin (cutaneous)
- Lungs (inhalation)
- Digestive (gastrointestinal)

The diagnosis of anthrax will be evidenced by certain warning signs in the infected party and where the disease has found a home:

- *Cutaneous*: Initial symptoms are blisters that eventually turn black.
- *Gastrointestinal*: Symptoms are nausea, loss of appetite, bloody diarrhea, fever, and significant stomach pain.
- *Inhalation*: Cold or flu symptoms, including a sore throat, mild fever, and muscle aches. Later symptoms include cough, chest discomfort, shortness of breath, tiredness, and muscle aches.

The effects of anthrax on the human body are both painful and extreme (Figure 4.22). Without care, death is the ultimate fate of the infected party.

Remediation of anthrax will be dependent on its stage and the party's resistance to antibiotics. The sooner medical attention is sought, the better the cure.

Emergency providers include anthrax in their planning and preparedness model. In general, the emergency plan should include

- Response plans and procedures for anthrax
- Training and equipping emergency response teams

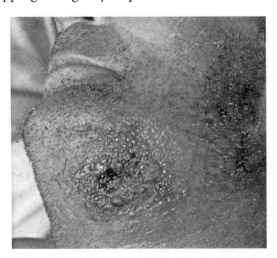

FIGURE 4.22 **Anthrax infection. (Courtesy of Anthrax Vaccine Immunization Program for Combined Services.)**

- Collaborative arrangements with health departments, veterinarians, and laboratories to watch for suspected cases of anthrax
- Sufficient laboratories for quick testing of suspected anthrax cases
- Sufficient medical supplies

The Coast Guard and the four branches of the U.S. military are so concerned that anthrax may be used in conflict against them that all military branches launched the Anthrax Vaccine Immunization Program (AVIP). See the general order implementing the AVIP program for all personnel in Figure 4.23.

4.3.2.3.2 Plague

The term plague conjures up images of the Dark Ages, when disease ravaged the countryside, killing millions over short periods of time. Yet, plague is a very real phenomenon that those concerned about biological attacks should never forget. Just as in centuries past, plague is an infectious bacteria carried by rats, flies, and fleas. Plague is an infectious airborne disease that affects others who come into contact with its strain of bacteria. Plague is normally transmitted from an infected rodent to humans by infected fleas. Bioterrorism-related outbreaks are likely to be transmitted through the dispersion of an aerosol. Person-to-person transmission of pneumonic plague is possible by a large dose of aerosol droplets. There are three kinds of plague:

- Pneumonic plague can spread from person to person through the air. Transmission can take place if someone breathes in aerosolized bacteria, which could happen in a bioterrorist attack.
- Bubonic plague is the most common form of plague. This occurs when an infected flea bites a person or when materials contaminated with *Y. pestis* enter through a break in a person's skin.
- Septicemic plague occurs when plague bacteria multiply in the blood. It can be a complication of pneumonic or bubonic plague, or it can occur by itself.

Several terrorist groups and some nations are experimenting with biological weapons programs. Plague could be used in an aerosol that would cause the pneumonic version. Once the disease is contracted, the bacteria can spread to others by close contact. Bubonic plague could be generated by releasing plague-infected fleas or animals. The *Y. pestis* bacterium occurs in nature and is also widely available in microbiology laboratories around the world. Thousands of scientists are working with plague organisms on a daily basis (see Figure 4.24).[29]

If detected early enough, antibiotics can be effective. A vaccine has yet to be developed.

Internet Resource: Watch the CDC training video on the preparation and management of plague at http://emergency.cdc.gov/agent/plague/trainingmodule/powerpoint.asp.

4.3.2.3.3 Smallpox

Smallpox has been referred to as the king of bioterrorism due to its ease of transmission and simplicity of delivery. It was the scourge of many a nation until its almost complete

DEPUTY SECRETARY OF DEFENSE
1010 DEFENSE PENTAGON
WASHINGTON, DC 20301-1010

OCT 1 2 2006

MEMORANDUM FOR SECRETARIES OF THE MILITARY DEPARTMENTS
CHAIRMAN OF THE JOINT CHIEFS OF STAFF
UNDER SECRETARIES OF DEFENSE
ASSISTANT SECRETARIES OF DEFENSE
GENERAL COUNSEL, DEPARTMENT OF DEFENSE
INSPECTOR GENERAL, DEPARTMENT OF DEFENSE
DIRECTORS OF DEFENSE AGENCIES
COMMANDANT OF THE US COAST GUARD

SUBJECT: Anthrax Vaccine Immunization Program

Based on the continuing heightened threat to some U.S. personnel of attack with anthrax spores, the Department of Defense will resume a mandatory Anthrax Vaccine Immunization Program, consistent with Food and Drug Administration guidelines and the best practice of medicine, for designated military personnel, emergency-essential and comparable Department of Defense civilian employees, and certain contractor personnel performing essential services. Vaccination is mandatory for these personnel based on geographic area of assignment or special mission roles, except as provided under applicable medical and administrative exemption policies.

As it was under the Deputy Secretary of Defense Memorandum of June 28, 2004, "Expansion of Force Health Protection Anthrax and Smallpox Immunization Programs for DoD Personnel," the scope of the mandatory Anthrax Vaccine Immunization Program shall encompass personnel assigned to or deployed for 15 or more consecutive days in higher-threat areas and certain other personnel with special mission roles. Other personnel determined by the Assistant Secretary of Defense for Health Affairs, in consultation with the Chairman of the Joint Chiefs of Staff, to be at higher risk of exposure to anthrax may also be included in the program. Vaccinations shall begin, to the extent feasible, up to 60 days prior to deployment or arrival in higher-threat areas.

Consistent with the FDA-approved guidelines for use of anthrax vaccine, all personnel who begin the six-dose vaccine series (unless excluded for medical reasons) will be offered all six doses and the annual booster as long as they remain members of the armed forces or maintain a civilian employee or contractor status covered by the program. For those no longer deployed to a higher threat area or no longer assigned designated special mission roles, these later vaccine doses will be on a voluntary basis. Individuals whose vaccine series was interrupted are not required to restart the vaccine series, but will proceed in accordance with appropriate medical practice.

OSD 15400-06

10/12/2006 4:35:12 PM

FIGURE 4.23 **General Order from the Deputy Secretary of Defense implementing the Anthrax Vaccine Immunization Program (AVIP) for all personnel.**

eradication in the 1970s. Unfortunately, the world has seen a return of this virulent disease and, just as distressingly, has heard of its potential to be a weapon of mass destruction. Smallpox is a serious, contagious, and sometimes fatal infectious disease. Smallpox comes in two varieties: V. major, the most severe and most common form of smallpox; and V. minor, a less common presentation of smallpox with medical effects.

Symptoms

Plague symptoms depend on how the patient was exposed to the plague bacteria. Plague can take different clinical forms, but the most common are bubonic, pneumonic, and septicemic.

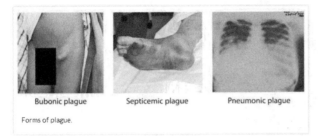

| Bubonic plague | Septicemic plague | Pneumonic plague |

Forms of plague.

Bubonic plague: Patients develop sudden onset of fever, headache, chills, and weakness and one or more swollen, tender and painful lymph nodes (called buboes). This form usually results from the bite of an infected flea. The bacteria multiply in the lymph node closest to where the bacteria entered the human body. If the patient is not treated with the appropriate antibiotics, the bacteria can spread to other parts of the body.

Septicemic plague: Patients develop fever, chills, extreme weakness, abdominal pain, shock, and possibly bleeding into the skin and other organs. Skin and other tissues may turn black and die, especially on fingers, toes, and the nose. Septicemic plague can occur as the first symptom of plague, or may develop from untreated bubonic plague. This form results from bites of infected fleas or from handling an infected animal.

Pneumonic plague: Patients develop fever, headache, weakness, and a rapidly developing pneumonia with shortness of breath, chest pain, cough, and sometimes bloody or watery mucous. Pneumonic plague may develop from inhaling infectious droplets or may develop from untreated bubonic or septicemic plague after the bacteria spread to the lungs. The pneumonia may cause respiratory failure and shock. Pneumonic plague is the most serious form of the disease and is the only form of plague that can be spread from person to person (by infectious droplets).

Plague is a serious illness. If you are experiencing symptoms like those listed here, seek immediate medical attention. Prompt treatment with the correct medications is critical to prevent complications or death.

FIGURE 4.24   CDC's web page on plague symptoms.

There is no specific treatment for smallpox, and the only prevention is vaccination. Generally, direct and fairly prolonged face-to-face contact is required to spread smallpox, usually by saliva, from one person to another. Smallpox can also be spread through direct contact with infected bodily fluids or contaminated objects (Figure 4.25).

Smallpox has the capacity to inflict horrid damage and is considered part of the arsenal for the terrorist. Containment and isolation are urgent requirements. Calming the public, the victims' families, and loved ones is another essential task. The CDC publishes protocols on how to handle the smallpox case—from the initial communications chain to isolation, vaccination, and subsequent media demands. Use the checklist in Table 4.6 to organize that sort of operation.[30]

Internet Resource: The United Nations (UN) has dedicated a good portion of its resources to the eradication of biological weapons. The UN library in Geneva is an excellent source center for data and literature on these efforts. Visit the library at http://librarycat.unog.ch.

4.3.2.4 Chemical

Chemical weapons represent another form of WMD for terrorists. Chemical weapons have seen usage in both accidental and intentional terms. For example, the release of chemical

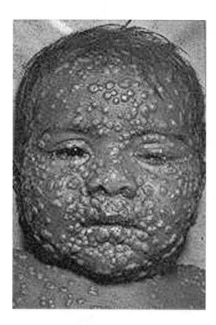

FIGURE 4.25 The rash and body lesions that result from smallpox are intense and unrivaled in epidemiology. Less than a week after an infection, the results are plain enough.

toxins in an industrial accident can wreak havoc on the public health. More maliciously, the intentional infliction of chemical toxins by a terrorist manifests their mind-set and a complete and utter disregard for human life. In World War I, soldiers on the trench fronts experienced the ferocity and terminal quality of various chemical gases. Chemical weapons can cause high levels of mortality. This conflict is often referred to as the chemist's war, and the range, depth, and breadth of usage shocks even today's hardened soldier. These agents could cause mass casualties, as demonstrated by the use of chemical weapons during World War I (see Table 4.7).

Today's terrorist threat is just as real and dangerous. As recently as 1995, the Tokyo subway was flooded with sarin gas, delivered via plastic bottles; it is miraculous that more injuries and deaths did not occur.

More recently, terrorists have concentrated on acquiring and employing chemical materials with dual uses, such as pesticides, poisons, and industrial chemicals. In the Syrian Civil War, chemical attacks—once a declared "red line" by the Obama administration—have been unfortunately far too common,[31] and all use of chemical weaponry has been largely agreed to by the community of nations.[32]

Chemical threats come in a variety of forms and delivery systems. These agents are far more common and much easier to develop and distribute than their biological and nuclear counterparts. Many household products, farm fertilizers, and other agricultural and industrial products contain the elements necessary to shape chemical terror.

The general typology of chemical agents includes

- Biotoxins—Poisons that come from plants or animals
- Blister agents/vesicants—Chemicals that severely blister the eyes, respiratory tract, and skin on contact

TABLE 4.6 Team Leader's List of Actions and Decisions to Be Considered

Action or Decision	Lead Person—State or Local HD	Lead Person—CDC Team
Identify key decision-makers and infrastructure at State and local HD		
Identify with above officials the counterparts for CDC team members		
Identify and review existing State/local emergency or BT plans		
Identify State/local chains of command for action- and decisions and communications and agree on access points		
Negotiate roles of CDC team in collaboration with State/local officials		
Identify office space, transport and facilities for team members		
Identify and clarify roles of press spokespersons		
Review smallpox response plan and priority task lists and establish plan for implementation		
Identify other State/local/federal agencies involve and their roles		
Identify serious issues (isolation policy, quality of medical care vs. isolation) for which immediate, high-level discussions and decisions are needed— note 8 areas below		
• Immediate need to determine number. composition and identify personnel for State/local 1st response team and facilities such as vaccination clinics and isolation/hospitals, assure training, vaccination, transport and other support needs		
• Surveillance/reporting—provider and public health alert system; laboratory alert system; active/ passive rash illness reporting networks; ER alert; case response plan in place; source of exposure; data compiling support		
• Contact and contacts of contact identification, tracing, vaccination, and surveillance for fever/rash, vaccine site and severe adverse events; risk prioritization for contact tracing.		
• Vaccination policy(s): Who, where, when and by whom; containment or containment and mass; fixed vaccination clinics, household/neighborhood vaccination, mobile teams; separate vaccination sites for contacts, response teams, and essential services (police, water, power, fireman, other security groups, child health services, etc; Smallpox vaccine storage, distribution and security		

(Continued)

TABLE 4.6 (CONTINUED) Team Leader's List of Actions and Decisions to Be Considered

Action or Decision	Lead Person—State or Local HD	Lead Person—CDC Team
• Decide on isolation policy(s): Home, hospital, smallpox isolation facility; transport of cases; security, enforcement and maintenance issues; level of medical care to be provided • Status of State quarantine rules/laws and who and how would they be implemented		
• Training and educational plans: Supplies of educational and training materials; facilities, trainers, schedules needed; various curricula; identifying personnel to be trained; web-based and other alternatives for training and education		
• Security arrangements for all team members; plans for controlling the population and enforcement of vaccination and isolation		
• Supplies on hand/needed such as: Bifurcated needles, forms of many types. Spox disease identification cards, vaccine take cards, VIS (languages), and so on		
Delegate assignments reflecting above needs and begin implementation with written notes of persons responsible and deadlines		
Identify political officials needed (e.g., Governor, Mayor, etc.) to reach decision quickly.		
Reach consensus and schedule daily (or more frequent) meetings with key officials		
Schedule phone briefings and meetings with team members daily		
Arrange conference calls with CDC "Smallpox central" in Atlanta		

- Blood agents—Poisons that affect the body by being absorbed into the blood
- Caustics (acids)—Chemicals that burn or corrode people's skin, eyes, and mucus membranes
- Choking/lung/pulmonary agents—Chemicals that cause severe irritation or swelling of the respiratory tract
- Incapacitating agents—Agents that can affect consciousness
- Long-acting anticoagulants—Poisons that prevent blood from clotting properly
- Metals—Agents that consist of metallic poisons
- Nerve agents—Highly poisonous chemicals that work by preventing the nervous system from working properly
- Organic solvents—Agents that damage the tissues of living things by dissolving fats and oils

TABLE 4.7 Types of Chemical Weapons Utilized in World War I

Name	First Use	Type
Chlorine	1915	Irritant/lung
Phosgene	1915	Irritant/skin and mucous membranes, corrosive, toxic
Chloromethyl chloroformate	1915	Irritant/eyes, skin, lungs
Trichloromethyl chloroformate	1916	Severe irritant, causes burns
Chloropicrin	1916	Irritant, lachrymatory, toxic
Stannic chloride	1916	Severe irritant, causes burns
a-Chlorotoluene (benzyl chloride)	1917	Irritant, lachrymatory
Bis(chloromethyl) ether (dichloromethyl ether)	1918	Irritant, can blur vision
Diphenylchloroarsine (diphenyl chlorasine)	1917	Irritant/sternutatory
Ethyldichloroarsine	1918	Vesicant
N-Ethylcarbazole	1918	Irritant
Benzyl bromide	1915	Lachrymatory
Ethyl iodoacetate	1916	Lachrymatory
Bromoacetone	1916	Lachrymatory, irritant
Bromomethyl ethyl ketone	1916	Irritant/skin, eyes
Acrolein	1916	Lachrymatory, toxic
Hydrocyanic acid	1916	Paralyzing
Hydrogen sulfide	1916	Irritant, toxic
Mustard gas	1917	Vescant (blister)

- Riot control agents/tear gas—Highly irritating agents normally used by law enforcement for crowd control
- Toxic alcohols—Poisonous alcohols that can damage the heart, kidneys, and nervous system
- Vomiting agents—Chemicals that cause nausea and vomiting

Internet Resource: Find out more about chemical threats by visiting the National Institute of Occupational Safety and Health (NIOSH) pocket guide on chemical threats at http://www.cdc.gov/niosh/npg.

The sheer volume of chemical agents makes full coverage impossible. Those agents most likely to be encountered in the world of homeland security will be part of this overview (see Figure 4.26).

4.3.2.4.1 Ricin

Ricin is a poison found naturally in castor beans. Ricin can be made from the waste material left over from processing castor beans (Figure 4.27).

Be Informed

Chemical Threat

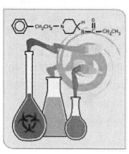

1. A chemical attack is the deliberate release of a toxic gas, liquid, or solid that can poison people and the environment.

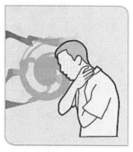

2. Watch for signs such as many people suffering from watery eyes, twitching, choking, having trouble breathing, or losing coordination.

3. Many sick or dead birds, fish, or small animals are also cause for suspicion.

4. If you see signs of a chemical attack, quickly try to define the impacted area or where the chemical is coming from, if possible.

5. Take immediate action to get away from any sign of a chemical attack.

6. If the chemical is inside a building where you are, try to get out of the building without passing through the contaminated area, if possible.

FIGURE 4.26 **Chemical threat response actions.**

FIGURE 4.27 **Castor beans. (Courtesy of Minnesota Department of Health.)**

Ricin may be produced in various forms, including powder, mist, or pellet. It can also be dissolved in water or weak acid. Castor beans are processed throughout the world to make castor oil, and its by-product, the "mash," provides the source material for the dangerous chemical.

The production is not a natural by-product but an intentional manufacture, which indicates malevolence on the part of the maker of the ricin. Ricin can be delivered in various ways, including

- *Indoor air*: Ricin can be released into indoor air as fine particles (aerosol).
- *Water*: Ricin can be used to contaminate water.
- *Food*: Ricin can be used to contaminate food.
- *Outdoor air*: Ricin can be released into outdoor air as fine particles.
- *Agricultural*: If ricin is released into the air as fine particles, it can damage and contaminate agricultural products.

Ricin can be absorbed into the body through ingestion, inhalation, or eye contact. Ricin can be absorbed through open skin or wounds but most likely not through intact skin, unless aided by a solvent. Ricin causes acute respiratory problems, impacts central organs in the human body, and can negatively affect eyes and ears. It can cause death in less than 24 hours (Figure 4.28).

Clues that indicate the presence or release of ricin include but are not limited to

- An unusual increase in the number of patients seeking care for potential chemical release–related illness
- Unexplained deaths among young or healthy persons
- Emission of unexplained odors by patients
- Clusters of illness in persons who have common characteristics, such as drinking water from the same source
- Rapid onset of symptoms after an exposure to a potentially contaminated medium
- Unexplained death of plants, fish, or animals (domestic or wild)

FIGURE 4.28   A ricin exercise conducted by the U.S. Army.

- A syndrome suggesting a disease associated commonly with a known chemical exposure (e.g., neurologic signs or pinpoint pupils in eyes of patients with a gastro-enteritis-like syndrome or acidosis in patients with altered mental status)[33]

Internet Resource: For a recent case of ricin contamination at a South Carolina postal facility, see http://www.cdc.gov/nceh/hsb/chemicals/pdfs/mmwr5246p1129.pdf.

4.3.2.4.2 Nerve Agents

Chemicals can also influence, in an extremely negative way, the central nervous system of the human body. Chemical nerve agents and gases have been around for more than a century. There are four main nerve agents: nerve agents GA (Tabun), GB (Sarin), GD (Soman), and VX are manufactured compounds. The G-type agents are clear, colorless, tasteless liquids miscible in water and most organic solvents. Sarin is odorless and is the most volatile nerve agent. Tabun has a slightly fruity odor, and Soman has a slight camphor-like odor. VX is a clear, amber-colored, odorless, oily liquid. It is miscible with water and dissolves in all solvents. VX is the least volatile nerve agent. Most nerve agents were originally produced in a search for insecticides, but because of their toxicity, they were evaluated for military use.

Sarin was produced before the commencement of World War II and was primarily used as a pesticide. However, the gas was quickly valued for its capacity for use as chemical weaponry and was tested, though not used, during World War II. It has been alleged that Saddam Hussein used sarin against the Iranians in the long and very costly war between Iraq and Iran in the 1980s and early 1990s.[34] As noted above, it was delivered into a Tokyo subway by the radical terrorist cult Aum Shinrikyo (Figure 4.29), a cell that intended to install Shoko Asahara as its new savior. Asahara, who strove "to take over Japan and then

FIGURE 4.29 Shoko Ashara, cult leader who carried out Tokyo terrorism.

the world," according to the State Department, was arrested in May 1995 for his role in the subway attack. His trial took 8 years, from 1996 to 2004, when he was sentenced to death.

Sarin gas is a preferred method for the terrorist due to its ease of delivery. Aerosol or vapor forms are the most effective for dissemination; these can be carried by sprayers or an explosive device.

Internet Resource: Chemical facilities, due to their stockpiles and ready availability of chemical substances, need to conduct vulnerability assessments of their facilities. DHS has published a vulnerability assessment guide at http://www.dhs.gov/sites/default/files/publications/csat-ssp-template-508.pdf.

Tabun is a man-made chemical warfare agent classified as a nerve agent. Nerve agents are the most toxic and rapidly acting of the known chemical warfare agents. Tabun was originally developed as a pesticide in Germany in 1936. In a plot to kill Hitler in early 1945, Reich Minister of Armaments Albert Speer made inquiries about a certain quantity to be introduced into an airshaft in Hitler's final bunker. The deed was never carried out.

As in all other forms of nerve agents and other threats, the CDC disseminates educational literature to the professional community. Known as cards, these informational pieces lay out symptoms and response regarding a particular agent. See the complete description of Tabun in Table 4.8.

VX is another recent nerve agent originally developed for industrial purposes but then construed to be an effective tool in chemical warfare. VX was originally developed in the United Kingdom in the early 1950s. VX is tasteless and slow to evaporate. Following release of VX into the air, people can be exposed through skin or eye contact or inhalation. It can also be ingested through contaminated water or food (Figure 4.30).

VX, like other nerve gases, generally causes death by asphyxiation. The symptoms include

- Blurred vision
- Runny nose
- Slurred speech
- Tightness in the chest and constriction of the pupils
- Breathing difficulties, along with vomiting, drooling, urinating, and defecating
- Areflexia (loss of reflexes)
- Ataxia (lack of muscle control)—twitching and jerking

After the victim has lost control of his or her bodily functions, suffocation and convulsive spasms cause death. Atropine is an effective antidote if given in time.

Soman also qualifies under the definition of nerve agent. Soman was originally developed as an insecticide in Germany in 1944. Soman is commonly referred to as GD. It becomes a vapor if heated. Soman is not found naturally in the environment. Soman, like other nerve agents, can be disseminated by air, touch, or contaminated food or water. The most likely method of transmission is for people to breathe air containing Soman gas or droplets, or when the liquid form of Soman comes into contact with the skin or eyes. Because Soman mixes easily with water, it has the potential to be used as a poison for food and water

TABLE 4.8 Tabun Card

Nerve Agent CAS # 77-81-6 RTECS # Counter Terrorism Card 0002	Dimethylphosphoramidocyanidic Acid, Ethyl Ester Ethyl N,N-Dimethylphosphoramidocyanidate Chemical Formula C5H11N2O2P Molecular Mass: 162.12		TABUN (GA)

Types of Hazard/ Exposure	Acute Hazards/Symptoms	Prevention	First Aid/Fire Fighting
Fire	React with steam or water to produce toxic and corrosive vapors.	Contain to prevent contamination to uncontrolled areas.	Water mist, fog, and foam, CO_2. Avoid methods that will cause splashing or spreading.
Explosion	May result in the formation of hydrogen cyanide.		
Exposure	Liquid or vapors can be fatal. Clothing releases agent for about 30 min after contact with vapor. Contaminated surfaces present long-term contact hazard.	Do not breathe fumes. Skin contact must be avoided at all times.	Seek medical attention immediately.
Inhalation	Inhalation can cause symptoms in 2–5 min. Same sequence of symptoms despite the route of exposure: MILD • Runny nose • Tightness of the chest and breathing difficulty • Eye pain, dimness of vision, and pinpointing of pupils (miosis) • Difficulty in breathing and cough MODERATE • Increased eye symptoms with blurred vision • Drooling and excessive sweating • Severe nasal congestion • Increased tightness of the chest and breathing difficulty	Hold breath until respiratory protective mask is donned. Firefighting personnel should wear full protective clothing and respiratory protection during firefighting and rescue. Positive pressure, full face piece, NIOSH-approved self-contained breathing apparatus (SCBA) will be worn.	If severe signs, immediately administer, in rapid succession, all three Nerve Agent Antidote Kit(s), Mark I injectors (or atropine if directed by a physician). If signs and symptoms are progressing, use injectors at 5–20 min intervals. (No more than three injections unless directed by medical personnel.) Maintain record of all injections given. Give artificial respiration if breathing has stopped. Use mouth-to-mouth when mask-bag or oxygen delivery systems not available. Do not use mouth-to-mouth if face is contaminated. Administer oxygen if breathing is difficult.

- Nausea, vomiting, diarrhea, and cramps
- Generalized weakness, twitching of large muscle groups
- Headache, confusion, and drowsiness

SEVERE
- Involuntary defecation and urination
- Very copious secretions
- Twitching, jerking, staggering, and convulsions
- Cessation of breathing, loss of consciousness, coma, and death

Skin	See Inhalation. Lethal doses can kill in 1–2 hours. Pupil size may range from normal to moderately reduced.	Protective Gloves: Butyl Rubber Glove M3 and M4 Norton, Chemical Protective Glove Set	The primary mode for decontamination of chemical agents is soap and water. A 0.5% hypochlorite solution can be used. There are differing guidelines for decontamination, and more research is needed to identify the optimal decontamination method. See "Personal Decontamination" and "Appendix D" in *Treatment of Chemical Agent Casualties and Conventional Military Chemical Injuries* (from the U.S. Navy Counterproliferation Office). See also the *Medical Management of Chemical Casualties Handbook* (from the U.S. Army Medical Research Institute of Chemical Defense [USAMRICD]) for a general review of the issues and more on the military decontamination powder approach.
Eyes	See Inhalation. Very rapid onset of symptoms (less than 2–3 min).	Chemical goggles and face shield.	
Ingestion	See Inhalation. Pupil size may range from normal to moderately reduced.	Do not induce vomiting. First symptoms are likely to be gastrointestinal. Immediately administer Nerve Agent Antidote Kit, Mark I.	

FIGURE 4.30 VX gas stored on pallets. (Courtesy of the U.S. Army.)

supplies. Clothing from a contaminated person can release vapors for about 30 min after exposure, thus endangering people who were not in an original area of release.

Exposure to Soman can be treated with specific antidotes—atropine and pralidoxime chloride (2-PAM)—along with supportive medical care in a hospital. These nerve agent antidotes are most effective when given within minutes of exposure.

4.3.2.5 Improvised Explosive Devices

In addition to WMD and potential weapons of mass effect, there is the threat of terrorist attack by means of an improvised explosive device (IED). IED weapons are explosive devices fashioned and deployed by means other than through conventional military operations—thus the term *improvised*. They can be created from traditional explosive devices such as bombs, warheads, grenades, or land mines or otherwise fashioned from explosive raw materials. Ball bearings, nails, metal filings, and other materials can be utilized as damage-causing projectiles.[35] Detonation can be accomplished by wired means or remotely through a rigged cell phone, handheld device, or other wireless technology. The fuel to ignite the IED can be common products such as "drain openers, sulfuric acid, and car batteries."[36] The Federal Bureau of Investigation (FBI) disseminates an IED threat card that categorizes the various products, compounds, and chemicals common to IEDs (see Figure 4.31).[37]

The methods of IED delivery will vary depending on the target as well as the IED design. The Consortium of National Academies, including Science, Engineering, Medicine and the National Research Council, charts the variety in Figure 4.32.

An inordinately high number of incidents of IED attack globally over the last several years have occurred in Iraq and Afghanistan, in addition to attacks in a number of other countries that have begun to experience increased terrorist attacks first hand. Unfortunately, there exist numerous online terrorist organization websites and sources that provide detailed instructions, including videos, on how to construct and deploy bombs. Often, new sites crop up as quickly as sites can be discovered and deactivated by the authorities.

IED attacks have given rise to other means and related classifications of attack. Multiple IEDs can be strung together to create a "daisy chain" whereupon multiple devices can be

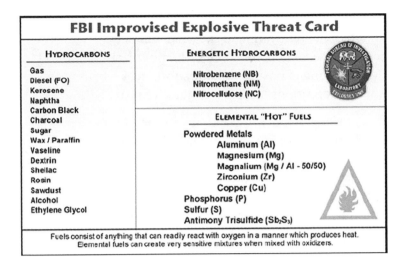

FIGURE 4.31   IE fuels.

Threat		Threat Description	Explosive Capacity	Building Evacuation Distance	Outdoor Evacuation Distance
		Small package/letter	1 lb	40 ft	900 ft
		Pipe bomb	5 lb	70 ft	1200 ft
		FedEx package	10 lb	90 ft	1080 ft
		Vest/container bombs	20 lb	110 ft	1700 ft
		Parcel package	50 lb	150 ft	1850 ft
		Compact car	500 lb	320 ft	1900 ft
		Full size car/minivan	1000 lb	400 ft	2400 ft
		Van/SUV/pickup truck	4000 lb	640 ft	3800 ft
		Delivery truck	10,000 lb	860 ft	5100 ft

FIGURE 4.32   Courtesy U.S. Technical Support Working Group (TSWG).

discharged, either at once or concurrently, with a single signal. Other means of attack include a vehicle-borne improvised explosive device (VBIED), a suicide vehicle-borne improvised explosive device (SVBIED), and a suicide pedestrian-borne improvised explosive device (SPBIED). Either way, the results are often physically devastating. Health impacts are immediate when in proximity to an IED and include

- Overpressure damage to the lungs, ears, abdomen, and other pressure-sensitive organs. Blast lung injury, a condition caused by the extreme pressure of an explosion, is the leading cause of illness and death for initial survivors of an explosion.
- Fragmentation injuries caused by projectiles thrown by the blast—material from the bomb, shrapnel, or flying debris that penetrates the body and causes damage.

- Impact injuries caused when the blast throws a victim into another object, that is, fractures, amputation, and trauma to the head and neck.
- Thermal injuries caused by burns to the skin, mouth, sinuses, and lungs.
- Other injuries including exposure to toxic substances, crush injuries, and aggravation of preexisting conditions (asthma, congestive heart failure, etc.).

Timothy McVeigh carried out a VBIED attack in the case of the Oklahoma City bombing in 1995. A waterborne SVBIED attack method was utilized in the bombing of the USS *Cole* in 2000. It can be argued that the 9/11 attacks were the largest ever SVBIED attack carried out, with the jet fuel on board the planes serving as the explosive material. A series of SBIED attacks were carried out in perpetrating the London bombings of July 7, 2005. Just as tragically, the Metrojet crashing over the Sinai in Egypt on October 31, 2015, for which Islamic State in Iraq and Syria (ISIS) takes credit, appears to have relied on inside employees of the airline sympathetic to ISIS.[38]

While generally smaller in scale than WMD attacks, the various IED attack methods pose an increasingly real and challenging threat in the United States and particularly to interests globally. In addition, the acquisition of bomb-making materials and the delivery and discharge of the weapon is generally far easier than with WMD weapons, and the effects are certainly just as deadly. The Paris attacks predominantly relied on AK-47 weaponry and yet the results were devastating.

The level of harm caused by IED attacks will also depend on its delivery location. A deserted road is a very different setting than a mass transit station. Terrorists are always looking for the maximum effect possible.

4.4 Computer Security and Information Infrastructure

The cyber world presents its own array of security challenges, and not to be forgotten is that the terrorists know that damage to the national cyber system can be devastating. Cyberspace has been defined as "the independent network of information technology infrastructures, and includes the Internet, telecommunications networks, computer systems, and embedded processors and controllers in critical Industries."[39]

From a terrorist perspective, the virtual world provides a host of avenues of attack. From their vantage point, terrorists see a world of opportunity—the disruption of essential systems, the ruination of data and protection systems, the destruction of finance and banking, and the chance to destroy and disrupt on a major scale. Security in the virtual world should not be taken lightly. In essence, the computer system is nothing less than information infrastructure—as legitimate and likely a target for the terrorist as a bridge or water-treatment center. The information infrastructure, including government, educational institutions, and research centers as well as business and industry, is rich in potential damage. Terrorists will target U.S. corporations, facilities, personnel, information, or computer, cable, satellite, or telecommunications systems—all of which are part of the information infrastructure. The possibilities are limitless and can include

- Denial or disruption of computer, cable, satellite, or telecommunications services
- Unauthorized monitoring of computer, cable, satellite, or telecommunications systems
- Unauthorized disclosure of proprietary or classified information stored within or communicated through computer, cable, satellite, or telecommunications systems
- Unauthorized modification or destruction of computer programming codes, computer network databases, stored information, or computer capabilities
- Manipulation of computer, cable, satellite, or telecommunications services resulting in fraud, financial loss, or other federal criminal violations[40]

Internet Resource: For a full listing of potential avenues of harm in the virtual world, visit the US-CERT reading room at http://www.us-cert.gov/reading_room.

So serious and continuous are the threats to our cybersecurity structure that in the early days of DHS's formation, there was a keen recognition that a unit dedicated to this protection would be necessary. The United States Computer Emergency Readiness Team (US-CERT) was designated as that unit. US-CERT is responsible for the management, defense, and mitigation of cyber attacks for the federal government. To get some sense of just how extensive and continuous these threats to the cyber world are, review the reportable, high-level threats, for 1 week, as catalogued by US-CERT.

Internet Exercise: Browse the US-CERT bulletin for the week of November 9, 2015, at https://www.us-cert.gov/ncas/bulletins/SB15-320.

Threats can be categorized as shown in Table 4.9.[41]

The US-CERT program is expected to advance information sharing among all agencies dedicated to the defense of the homeland. Its overall mission can be summarized as

- Providing support to national and international public and private sectors
- Event monitoring, predictive analysis, and aligned reporting tools
- Providing advance warnings regarding emerging threats
- Providing incident response for national agencies, malware analysis, and recovery support
- Involvement in national and international exercises

Threats of every sort and variety are vulnerabilities to both software and hardware. US-CERT defines cyber threats by using six distinct categories, as shown in Table 4.10.[42]

The National Strategy to Secure Cyberspace delineates the challenges of the cyber world in the world of terrorism. Security will depend on mastery of the following tasks:

- Establishing a public–private architecture for responding to national-level cyber incidents
- Providing for the development of tactical and strategic analysis of cyber attacks and vulnerability assessments

TABLE 4.9 Cybersecurity Threats

Threat	Description
Bot-network operators	Bot-network operators are hackers; however, instead of breaking into systems for the challenge or bragging rights, they take over multiple systems in order to coordinate attacks and to distribute phishing schemes, spam, and malware attacks. The services of these networks are sometimes made available in underground markets (e.g., purchasing a denial-of-service attack, servers to relay spam, or phishing attacks).
Criminal groups	Criminal groups seek to attack systems for monetary gain. Specifically, organized crime groups are using spam, phishing, and spyware/malware to commit identity theft and online fraud. International corporate spies and organized crime organizations also pose a threat to the United States through their ability to conduct industrial espionage and large-scale monetary theft and to hire or develop hacker talent.
Foreign intelligence services	Foreign intelligence services use cyber tools as part of their information-gathering and espionage activities. In addition, several nations are aggressively working to develop information warfare doctrine, programs, and capabilities. Such capabilities enable a single entity to have a significant and serious impact by disrupting the supply, communications, and economic infrastructures that support military power—impacts that could affect the daily lives of U.S. citizens across the country.
Hackers	Hackers break into networks for the thrill of the challenge or for bragging rights in the hacker community. While remote cracking once required a fair amount of skill or computer knowledge, hackers can now download attack scripts and protocols from the Internet and launch them against victim sites. Thus, while attack tools have become more sophisticated, they have also become easier to use. According to the CIA, the large majority of hackers do not have the requisite expertise to threaten difficult targets such as critical U.S. networks. Nevertheless, the worldwide population of hackers poses a relatively high threat of an isolated or brief disruption causing serious damage.
Insiders	The disgruntled organization insider is a principal source of computer crime. Insiders may not need a great deal of knowledge about computer intrusions because their knowledge of a target system often allows them to gain unrestricted access to cause damage to the system or to steal system data. The insider threat also includes outsourcing vendors as well as employees who accidentally introduce malware into systems.
Phishers	Individuals or small groups who execute phishing schemes in an attempt to steal identities or information for monetary gain. Phishers may also use spam and spyware/malware to accomplish their objectives.
Spammers	Individuals or organizations who distribute unsolicited e-mail with hidden or false information in order to sell products, conduct phishing schemes, distribute spyware/malware, or attack organizations (i.e., denial of service).
Spyware/malware authors	Individuals or organizations with malicious intent carry out attacks against users by producing and distributing spyware and malware. Several destructive computer viruses and worms have harmed files and hard drives, including the Melissa Macro Virus, the Explore.Zip worm, the CIH (Chernobyl) Virus, Nimda, Code Red, Slammer, and Blaster.
Terrorists	Terrorists seek to destroy, incapacitate, or exploit critical infrastructures in order to threaten national security, cause mass casualties, weaken the U.S. economy, and damage public morale and confidence. Terrorists may use phishing schemes or spyware/malware in order to generate funds or gather sensitive information.

TABLE 4.10 US-CERT Federal Agency Incident Categories

Category	Name	Description	Reporting Time Frame
CAT 0	Exercise/network defense testing	This category is used during state, federal, national, and international exercises and approved activity testing of internal/external network defenses or responses.	Not applicable; this category is for each agency's internal use during exercises.
CAT 1	Unauthorized access	In this category, an individual gains logical or physical access without permission to a federal agency network, system, application, data, or other resource.	Within 1 hour of discovery/detection.
CAT 2	Denial of service (DoS)	An attack that *successfully* prevents or impairs the normal authorized functionality of networks, systems, or applications by exhausting resources. This activity includes being the victim or participating in the DoS.	Within 2 hours of discovery/detection if the successful attack is still ongoing and the agency is unable to successfully mitigate activity.
CAT 3	Malicious code	*Successful* installation of malicious software (e.g., virus, worm, Trojan horse, or other code-based malicious entity) that infects an operating system or application. Agencies are *not* required to report malicious logic that has been *successfully quarantined* by antivirus (AV) software.	Daily note: Within 1 hour of discovery/ detection if widespread across agency.
CAT 4	Improper usage	A person violates acceptable computing use policies.	Weekly.
CAT 5	Scans/probes/ attempted access	This category includes any activity that seeks to access or identify a federal agency computer, open ports, protocols, service, or any combination for later exploit. This activity does not directly result in a compromise or denial of service.	Monthly note: If system is classified, report within 1 hour of discovery.
CAT 6	Investigation	*Unconfirmed* incidents that are potentially malicious or anomalous activity deemed by the reporting entity to warrant further review.	Not applicable; this category is for each agency's use to categorize a potential incident that is currently being investigated.

- Encouraging the development of a private sector capability to share a synoptic view of the health of cyberspace
- Expanding the Cyber Warning and Information Network to support the role of DHS in coordinating crisis management for cyberspace security
- Improving National Incident Management Systems (NIMS)

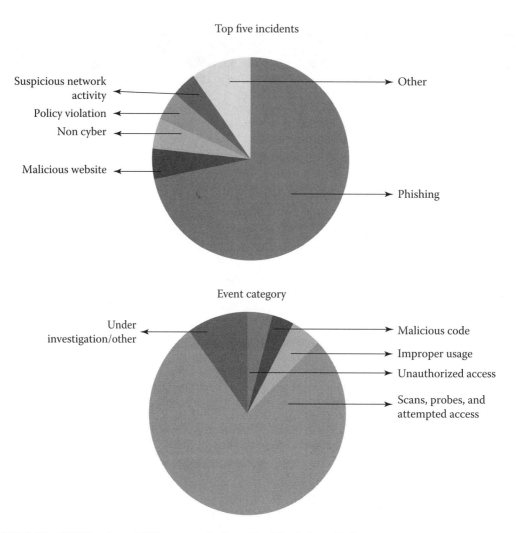

FIGURE 4.33 CERT vulnerabilities reported and incidents handled.

- Coordinating processes for voluntary participation in the development of national public–private continuity and contingency plans
- Exercising cybersecurity continuity plans for federal systems
- Improving and enhancing public–private information sharing involving cyber attacks, threats, and vulnerabilities[43]

The author of these threats is not always discernible. What is clear has been the dramatic increase in every type of vulnerability that attacks systems and software. Carnegie Mellon University operates a Computer Emergency Readiness Team (CERT), and its statistics tracking vulnerabilities show a steady and dramatic rise of these intrusions. From 1995 to 2002, the increase has been quite marked, from 1090 to over 4100[44] (see Figure 4.33).

Each cyber threat displays an uncanny knack to change and alter to avoid detection, while newer versions of similar threats make detection an impossibility. To illustrate the

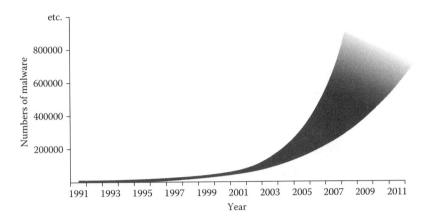

FIGURE 4.34   **Approximate growth of malware since 1991.**

trends, dramatic increases are shown in the growth of malware since the early 1990s (see Figure 4.34).[45]

4.4.1 National Cyber Security Division

DHS erected the National Cyber Security Division (NCSD) to be the chief DHS entity setting policy for cyber threats and the protection of cyber assets. The NCSD seeks to protect the critical cyber infrastructure 24 hours a day, 7 days a week. NCSD has identified these fundamental objectives:

- To build and maintain an effective national cyberspace response system
- To implement a cyber-risk management program for the protection of critical infrastructure

NCSD, in order to give operational meaning to the National Strategy to Secure Cyberspace, established the National Cyberspace Response System. The National Cyberspace Response System coordinates the cyber leadership, processes, and protocols that will determine when and what actions need to be taken as cyber incidents arise. The Cyberspace Response System tackles other projects as well, such as

- Cybersecurity preparedness and the National Cyber Alert System—an information and alert system that warns of vulnerabilities.
- US-CERT operations—US-CERT is responsible for analyzing and reducing cyber threats and vulnerabilities, disseminating cyber-threat warning information, and coordinating incident response activities.
- National Cyber Response Coordination Group—made up of 13 federal agencies, this is the principal federal agency mechanism for cyber-incident response.
- Cyber cop portal—coordination with law enforcement helps capture and convict those responsible for cyber attacks.

- Cyber risk management—assesses risk, prioritizes resources, and executes protective measures critical to securing our cyber infrastructure.
- Cyber exercises—Cyber Storm is a nationwide cybersecurity exercise series that takes place every 2 years. Cyber Storm was DHS's first cyber exercise, testing response across the private sector and public agencies.

4.4.2 US-CERT: Computer Emergency Response Team

That virtual security poses similar challenges to physical threats has not been lost on our nation's leaders in homeland security. Even in 2003, Homeland Security Presidential Directive 7 proclaimed that critical infrastructure includes much more than highways and transportation systems—that it just as rightfully includes the physical, virtual, and technological. America's open and technologically complex society includes a wide array of critical infrastructures and key resources that are potential terrorist targets. The majority of these are owned and operated by the private sector and state or local governments. These critical infrastructures and key resources are both physically and virtually based and span all sectors of the economy.[46]

In the National Strategy to Secure Cyberspace, the designation of infrastructure relating to cyberspace could not have been clearer:

Our Nation's critical infrastructures are composed of public and private institutions in the sectors of agriculture, food, water, public health, emergency services, government, defense industrial base, information and telecommunications energy, transportation, banking and finance, chemicals and hazardous materials, and postal and shipping. Cyberspace is their nervous system—the control system of our country. Cyberspace is composed of hundreds of thousands of interconnected computers, servers, routers, switches, and fiber optic cables that allow our critical infrastructures to work. Thus, the healthy functioning of cyberspace is essential to our economy and our national security.[47]

At DHS, the recognition that the virtual world was a critical component of our infrastructure was adopted head on. With the implementation of the US-CERT department, the agency made plain its prioritization in the virtual world. The US-CERT is a partnership between DHS and the public and private sectors. US-CERT is the operational arm of the NCSD at DHS (Figure 4.35).

The NCSD was established by DHS to serve as the federal government's cornerstone for cybersecurity coordination and preparedness. Established in 2003, it is charged with protecting the Internet infrastructure of the United States by coordinating defense against and response to cyber attacks. US-CERT is responsible for

- Analyzing and reducing cyber threats and vulnerabilities
- Disseminating cyber-threat warning information
- Coordinating incident response activities

FIGURE 4.35   FBI cyber agents at work. (www.fbi.gov.)

US-CERT depends on the cooperative endeavors of other federal agencies, industry, the research community, state and local governments, and premier companies such as Apple and Microsoft and regular contributors to their protection program.

US-CERT provides a reporting mechanism in the event of a threat or an assault on the computer infrastructure. The reporting should not be for technical malfunction, nor should the error or problem in hardware and software be construed as unfounded or illegal. US-CERT lays out some general parameters for what types of events may qualify for reporting:

- Attempts (either failed or successful) to gain unauthorized access to a system or its data, including personally identifiable information (PII)-related incidents
- Unwanted disruption or denial of service
- The unauthorized use of a system for processing or storing data
- Changes to system hardware, firmware, or software characteristics without the owner's knowledge, instruction, or consent

If the violation fits this schema, the intrusion should be reported (see Figure 4.36).

Internet Resource: Visit the National Vulnerability Center at http://nvd.nist.gov/.

US-CERT was expected to be the facilitator of communication between the diverse agencies of homeland security. Part of the 9/11 critique was the lack of communication between police and fire, state and local, federal, state and local, to list just a few disconnects. US-CERT has to deal with "the various network architectures" of competing and even incompatible systems.[48] In addition, intelligence agencies do not naturally and easily share sensitive data and some agencies "lack access to classified networks."[49] US-CERT is required to compile and analyze information on cybersecurity incidents and to share it with diverse constituencies. US-CERT "disseminates reasoned and actionable cybersecurity information to the public; and facilitates information sharing with state and local government, industry and international partners."[50]

Section: Reporter's Contact Information

First Name *(Required)*
Last Name *(Required)*
Email Address *(Required)*
Telephone number
(Required)

Are you reporting as part
of an Information Sharing
and Analysis Center
(ISAC)? | No, this is not an ISAC report ▼ |

What type of organization
is reporting this incident?
(Required) | Please select ▼ |

What is the impact to the
reporting organization?
(Required) | Please select ▼ | .

What type of followup
action are you requesting
at this time? *(Required)* | Please select ▼ |

Describe the current
status or resolution of this
incident. *(Required)* | Please select ▼ |

From what time zone are
you making this report?
(Required) | Please select a time zone ▼ |

What is the approx time
the incident started?
(localtime) | August ▼ | 21 ▼ | 2008 ▼ |: | 22 ▼ |:
                  | 20 ▼ |

When was this incident
detected? (localtime) | August ▼ | 21 ▼ | 2008 ▼ |, | 22 ▼ |:
                             | 20 ▼ |

Section: Incident Details

Please provide a short description of the incident and impact *(Required)*

[text area]

How many systems are
impacted by this incident?
(Leave blank if Unknown)

How many sites are
impacted by this incident?
(Leave blank if Unknown)

Was the data involved in
this incident encrypted? | N/A ▼ |

Was critical infrastructure
impacted by this incident? | N/A ▼ |

What was the primary
method used to identify
the incident | Unknown ▼ |

If available, please include 5-10 lines of time-stamped logs in plain ASCII
text. (e.g.,CSV).

[text area]

FIGURE 4.36   Cybersecurity intrusion report form.

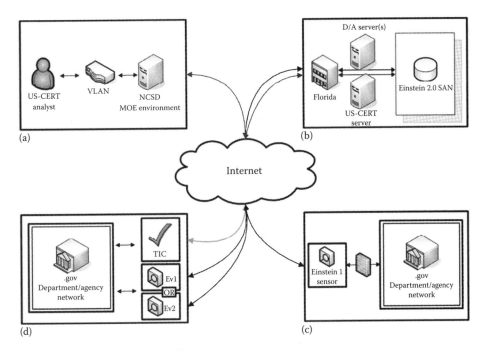

FIGURE 4.37 **Einstein data collection infrastructure and process.**

A recent Office of the Inspector General (OIG) assessment shows that US-CERT is clearly struggling to reach this mandate. The OIG is quite cognizant of the compatibility problems and other issues but makes plain that the department is really faltering on this responsibility despite earnest efforts at a sophisticated program called *Einstein*. Einstein collects network flow information and observes and identifies malicious activity in the computer network traffic. Newer versions of Einstein automatically detect intrusions and then automatically alert US-CERT to the presence of these threats. See Figure 4.37[51] for a schematic of the Einstein process and method.

The OIG notes that while on paper these software approaches seem sensible, their operational reliability is less than sterling. It is clear that the task of full integration in the world of cyber systems will be a generational undertaking.[52]

4.5 Private Sector and Homeland Security

How the private sector contributes to the fight against terrorism is a story worth telling. Since 9/11, governmental agencies have urged the participation of not only state and local governments but also the active input and involvement of the general citizenry.[53] On top of this, there has been a continuous push for private business and commercial entities to be involved and an expectation that much of the American economy would need to be active players in the fight against terrorism. For example, America's chemical, water, utility, and nuclear sectors would have to be aggressively involved in the defense of their facilities and thus of the country itself.[54] Commercial interests could not simply wait for the government to do it all but instead had to jump into the mix of deterrence and prevention of terror. Infrastructure is largely owned by private enterprise and is in need of a homeland defense plan. "Industries must plan to respond...and undertake recovery under severe conditions where much of the infrastructure of the surrounding area is unavailable and site access is limited."[55] Preparedness is an industrial and commercial concern. And it is also the private citizen that encompasses the private sector. The question of how much more prepared private homes and families are has yet to be fully measured.[56]

Each facet of the private sector needs to understand

- How communities are impacted by terrorism
- How to create a plan of response consistent with state and federal standards
- How to mitigate loss in the event of catastrophe and disaster
- How to be active partners in the development of homeland policy
- How to work closely with public agencies
- How to add new programs in traditional Neighborhood Watch programs that focus on terrorism[57]

The National Infrastructure Advisory Council, in its report on public–private sector intelligence coordination, identified 17 business and commercial sectors that need to step up in the fight against terrorism:

- Communications
- Chemical and hazardous materials
- Commercial facilities
- Dams
- Defense industrial base
- Energy
- Emergency services
- Financial services
- Food and agriculture
- Government facilities
- Information technology
- National monuments and icons
- Nuclear power plants
- Postal and shipping
- Public health and health care
- Transportation
- Water[58]

On a second front, the role of private-sector security firms and personnel can only be described as significant. The private-sector portion of criminal justice operations grows at an almost immeasurable clip.[59] According to the Homeland Security Research Corporation, by 2011, the private sector "will trail only DHS in HLS industry procurement volume. This stems from the forecasted 50% private sector procurement growth from 2007 to

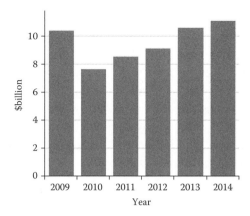

FIGURE 4.38   U.S. private sector homeland security market.

FIGURE 4.39   Private sector security personnel with Iraqi citizens.

2011, totaling an accumulated $28.5B."[60] While there have been some slight pauses in that growth, the trend for private sector and DHS partnering is onward and upward according to the Homeland Security Research Council (see Figure 4.38).[61]

The face of private-sector justice can be discovered across the DHS spectrum; from privatized forces seeking out terrorists in Iraq and Afghanistan to the protection of federal installations across the mainland, private-sector justice makes extraordinary contributions in the defense of the country (Figure 4.39).[62]

From Iraq to the local water facility, private-sector justice operatives are engaged in a host of activities once exclusively reserved for the public sector. This trend, often labeled "privatization," assumes that the private sector, with its usual efficiencies and profit motivations, will carry out its task with greater effectiveness. Unions and entrenched government bureaucracies tend to be on the defensive with those promoting privatization. Those seeking greater accountability and freedom of operation tend to the privatized.[63] On paper, the concept is attractive, and in many cases, it is clear that the private sector can do a better job than the government in ensuring safety and security.[64] It will all depend on the subject matter of that security and the corresponding costs. To illustrate, there are some who have argued that the Transportation Security Agency (TSA) should never have been invented and that these same services should be subcontracted to private business. Of course, this is the model pre-9/11. Since 9/11, there has been a continuous debate over the preferability of public or private in the delivery of security services. What can be agreed on is that both domains have essential responsibilities in combating terrorism—some exclusive, though most shared.

Internet Resource: To see how private security's premier professional association, the American Society for Industrial Security (ASIS), gets involved in the standards and practices of homeland security, see https://www.asisonline.org/Standards-Guidelines/Standards/published/Pages/default.aspx.

In this sense, private sector justice is driven by bottom-line considerations more than its governmental counterpart. It is motivated by efficiencies never weighed or evaluated in the public sector. And given this general motivation to the profit mentality, there are those who critique it as being willing to cut corners so that the bottom line will be brighter. Quality allegedly suffers. Indeed, many are suspicious of the qualifications of those entrusted with security responsibilities from the private sector. Do recent attempts to increase qualification and conduct legitimate background investigations on security officer applicants calm frayed nerves?[65] Ian Patrick McGinley, when critiquing federal legislation to ensure suitable licensure and background requirements for security officers, found that the industry is in a state of market failure.

> Nevertheless, significant problems with leaving regulation to the market make this option unfeasible. For one, despite laudable attempts, the industry's self-regulation track record has been poor. Second, profit margins in the security industry are tight because many companies view security as a necessary evil. As a result, there is a race to the bottom—in terms of pricing and salaries—in order to gain a competitive advantage relative to other firms, resulting in less qualified officers.[66]

However, this argument does not pan out in so many governmentally operated entities. What of the public school system nationally? Are these systems not in crisis? What of public transportation systems? What of roads and bridges in near collapse? It is not difficult to discern where government fails to meet its mission. Privatization is evident everywhere—prisons, policing, and courts, to name just three, are examples of fields seeing these trends.[67] As the Bureau of Justice Assistance notes in its *Engaging Private Security to Promote Homeland Security*, private-sector justice can jump in feet first.

Private security can

- Coordinate plans with the public sector regarding evacuation, transportation, and food services during emergencies
- Gain information from law enforcement regarding threats and crime trends
- Develop relationships so that private practitioners know whom to contact when they need help or want to report information
- Build law enforcement understanding of corporate needs (e.g., confidentiality)

- Boost law enforcement's respect for the security field

Working together, private security and law enforcement can realize impressive benefits:

- Creative problem-solving
- Increased training opportunities
- Information, data, and intelligence sharing
- Force multiplier opportunities
- Access to the community through private-sector communications technology
- Reduced recovery time following disasters[68]

The National Defense Industrial Association (NDIA), another premier professional group for the private sector, argues as if the task of homeland security is integral to any private security firm. It unequivocally aims

- To provide legal and ethical forums for the exchange of information, ideas, and recommendations between industry and government on homeland security issues
- To promote a vigorous, robust, and collaborative government–industry homeland security team
- To advocate for best-in-class, high-technology equipment, systems, training, and support for America's first-responder community[69]

And not only is it capable of carrying out its own mission in the world of homeland security, but it should do so with collaboration and collegiality in regard to its public partners. The worlds of public and private are not distinct or radically different; rather, these are compatible and complementary domains where a shared mission is obvious. Partnerships are what each should be looking for since the public and the private share 12 essential components:

- Common goals
- Common tasks
- Knowledge of participating agencies' capabilities and missions
- Well-defined projected outcomes
- A timetable
- Education for all involved
- A tangible purpose
- Clearly identified leaders
- Operational planning
- Agreement by all partners as to how the partnership will proceed
- Mutual commitment to providing necessary resources
- Assessment and reporting[70]

DHS formally encourages interplay and cooperation between private-sector justice entities and the public law enforcement function. Throughout DHS policy making is the perpetual recognition that it cannot go it alone and that it needs the daily cooperation of the private sector. Within its Office of Policy, DHS has erected a Private Sector Office, its chief aims being

- To engage individual businesses, trade associations, and other nongovernmental organizations in fostering dialogue with the department
- To advise the secretary on prospective policies and regulations and, in many cases, on their economic impact
- To promote public–private partnerships and best practices to improve the nation's homeland security
- To promote department policies to the private sector

The Private Sector Office focuses on two major functions: the Business Outreach Group and the Economics Group. In the first instance, DHS affirmatively connects with the business and commercial sector, fully realizing that cooperation and joint endeavors fare better than isolation or turf protection. The Outreach Group seeks input and advice from the business sector before the institution or implementation of policy. The Outreach Group

- Meets with private-sector organizations and department components to promote public–private partnerships
- Promotes departmental policies
- Gathers private-sector perspectives for use by the department

The Economics Group weighs policy in cost–benefit terms. Here, DHS is deaf to the costs of policy implementation since each new regulation or requirement does have a corresponding price tag. As a result, the group looks at the impact of policy from various directions, including

- Policy analysis—it evaluates the economic impacts of departmental policies on the private sector.
- Process analysis—it evaluates departmental processes that will allow the private sector to operate efficiently while meeting national security needs.
- Regulatory analysis—it provides a resource to the department on regulatory/economic analyses.
- Metrics—it promotes the use of metrics to identify successes and areas needing improvement.
- Benefits methodology—it actively works on the development of methodologies to quantify the benefits of homeland security investments.

The Economics Group coordinates economic roundtables and publishes white papers and other studies that highlight cost–benefit.

Finally, DHS, not long after 9/11, instituted an advisory committee on private-sector cooperation and collaboration. Members of the committee represent the full panoply of industry, corporate interests, and security firms with shared interests. From the outset of DHS, it was clear that policy making would not occur without the input of industry and commerce. It was equally evident that the skilled practitioners of private-sector justice would be crucial contributors.

The current committee includes the following:

- Richard D. Stephens (chair), senior vice president, Human Resources and Administration, The Boeing Company
- Herbert Kelleher (vice chair), founder and chairman emeritus, Southwest Airlines Co.
- Stephen M. Gross, president, BiNational Logistics, LLC
- Monica Luechtefeld, executive vice president, Business Development and IT, Office Depot, Inc.
- Maurice Sonnenberg, senior international advisor and director, JP Morgan Chase
- Jean E. Spence, executive vice president, Global Technology and Quality, Kraft Foods Inc.
- George A. Vradenburg III, president, Vradenburg Foundation
- Emily Walker, international consultant/former 9/11 commission staff
- William C. Whitmore, Jr., chief executive officer, AlliedBarton Security Services
- Houston L. Williams, principal owner, Raven Oaks Vineyards and Winery
- Jack L. Williams, former president and chief executive officer, Eos Airlines

Internet Resource: For a collaboration and partnerships course through the operational philosophy of DHS, see http://www.adcouncil.org/Our-Campaigns/Safety/(sort)/alpha.

4.6 Conclusion

Any operational notion of what homeland security is must include a look at traditional aspects of security, such as risk and threat, as well as new and emerging hazards. This chapter surveys the likely and even unlikely events that will challenge those laboring in the field of homeland security. First, how does the professional define and measure risk? What criteria and variables need to be considered when assessing risk? Are some risks worth taking and others never tolerable? Are some locations more vulnerable to risk than others? Are the costs of the risk, relative to its potential harm, worth the investment? In short, risk cannot be assessed in a vacuum but must be weighed in light of the likelihood of occurrence, costs of prevention, and the nature of the harm to be inflicted. Various systems of measurement relative to risk are also provided, including CARVER+Shock methodology.

Next, the chapter's coverage turns to the typology of threat and hazard. From natural to terrorist in design, threats and hazards must be evaluated in light of the perpetrator's motivation. In the natural world, there is no malice. In the world of terrorism, the homeland professional must anticipate how far the actor will go to achieve a particular end. Hijackings, bombs, and WMD manifest a direct intentionality, while the hurricane and flood does not.

As for threats that impact the homeland security dimension, nothing is more pressing or compelling than the world of WMD. WMD are unique in many senses, especially when one considers the nature of the harm inflicted and the potentiality for widespread destruction.[71]

The fear and dread of a nuclear event is probably the most pronounced of any form of WMD. In particular, the chapter looks at the relative ease of delivery of various WMD by a dirty bomb mechanism. In addition, particular agencies such as the NRC are highlighted regarding radiological security programs. The world of bioterrorism is just as frightening, and the accessibility and general availability of bioagents should give any homeland professional cause for concern. The chapter expends considerable energy discussing anthrax, plague, and smallpox—three biological invasions that would cause both terror and widespread injury. Also covered are the diverse means to deliver and infect by chemical substance. The use of sarin gas, used as recently as 1995, indicates the extraordinary potential for harm that these agents can inflict. Biotoxins, blister agents, blood agents, acids, and other caustics, as well as respiratory agents, are all evaluated. Special coverage of ricin, Tabun, and other specific nerve agents is included.

The next portion of this chapter deals with the need to protect computer data and secured information and the equal imperative placed on information sharing between the full array of agencies involved in the homeland response. DHS fosters this approach by operating a National Cyber Alert System, where threats to computer infrastructure are catalogued and publicly announced. DHS posts a National Strategy to Secure Cyberspace, which urges both the public and private sectors to take the necessary steps to ensure continued operation of computer functions and maintenance of data integrity. Cyber threats are just as real as any other threat. The NCSD is DHS's chief arm to ensure integrity in the system. US-CERT plays a deterrence and prevention role in cyber threats and also serves as an analysis reaction team to cyber threats.

The final section reviews the collaboration of private-sector interests with the public functionality of homeland practice. Exactly how does the private sector aid in the fight against terrorism? To illustrate, the American industrial complex of utilities, chemical facilities, and manufacturing centers that produce defense products are all relevant to homeland defense. These private entities are construed as critical infrastructure in need of both plan and protection. The National Infrastructure Advisory Council highlights the need for private interests to aggressively participate in the defense of the country. Just as significant will be the rise of private sector justice operatives fighting terrorism. In Iraq, the growth of private security firms, the recognition that private soldiers now engage or protect, and the fact that private companies and firms are better suited to the reconstruction of Iraq than governmental entities are now indisputable conclusions. DHS encourages the partnership of the public with the private by and through its Private Sector Office and its Advisory Committee on the Private Sector.

Keywords

Accessibility	Blood agent
Analytic risk assessment	CARVER+Shock assessment
Anthrax	Chemical WMD
Asset value	Civil hazard
Biological WMD	Consequence
Bioterrorism	Criticality
Biotoxin	Cyber Warning and Information Network
Blister agent	Cyberspace

Daisy chain
Deliberative risk assessment
Dirty bomb
Effect
Flow process
Force-on-force training
Harm
Hazard
IED (improvised explosive device)
Information infrastructure
National Cyber Security Division
National Cyberspace Response Team
National Vulnerability Center
Natural hazard
Nerve agent
Nuclear Regulatory Commission
Nuclear WMD
Pathogen
Plague
Practical risk assessment
Private sector
Privatization
Public health risk
Public–private partnership
Radiological dispersion device

Radiological WMD
Recognizability
Recuperability
Ricin
Risk
Risk assessment
Risk management
Sarin
Shock
Smallpox
Soman
SPBIED (suicide pedestrian-borne improvised explosive device)
SVBIED (suicide vehicle-borne improvised explosive device)
Tabun
Threat
Threat rating
US-CERT
VBIED (vehicle-borne improvised explosive device)
Vulnerability
Vulnerability rating
VX
WMD

Discussion Questions

1. In the area of risk analysis, the question of exposure is heavily emphasized. Can you envision a circumstance when a risk that lacks significant exposure would still be considered more serious than a risk with a higher exposure?

2. Can another formula for the measure of risk be formulated?

3. Relay your view of the CARVER+Shock system of risk assessment. What are its strengths and shortcomings?

4. Some have argued that DHS should not concern itself with the world of natural hazards and threats. Comment on this school of thought.

5. It has been said that the world of WMD is highly exaggerated. How so? Can you provide an example of this hyperbole?

6. Biological terrorism is probably the easiest form of WMD to construct and deliver. Explain.

7. Chemical weaponry can be produced with easy access to products and components. Discuss.

8. Chemical weapons are not always the invention of the chemist but instead can be natural in design and makeup. Discuss.

9. Discuss the role and functions of a US-CERT team.

10. Discuss how computer networks can be designated critical infrastructure.

11. Relate three common threats to a cybersystem.

12. The role of the private sector in homeland defense continues unabated. Why do you think the privatization of homeland services will march forward with very little resistance?

13. What types of industries need the highest level of concern regarding homeland security?

Practical Exercises

1. Conduct a threat and risk assessment regarding chemical facilities in your region. Respond to the following questions:
   What type of products exist?
   What potential injuries can arise from these products?
   What is the potential for mass destruction?
   What safety and security information on the company's website addresses risk in the community?

2. Create a flowchart assessment mechanism, under the CARVER+Shock method, to measure a manufacturing threat in your area.

3. Identify nuclear facilities within 100 miles of your residence. Respond to the following:
   Describe the facility.
   How many people and communities does the facility serve?
   In the event of a nuclear event, explain how the surrounding environs would be impacted.
   In what way would injury touch the largest base of people?
   Discuss the facility's evacuation policy relative to the community.

4. Contact your local office dedicated to homeland security. Gather information on your area's anthrax program. Explain in two paragraphs what that plan or program is.

5. Identify and chart transportation infrastructure in your area. Respond to the following:
   Which infrastructure has the capacity to inflict the most damage?

What steps are being taken to secure that infrastructure?

Despite these steps, how can a terrorist bypass the protections?

Point out specific vulnerabilities that you can identify.

6. The Emergency Management Institute publishes a bevy of very useful assessment tools. Complete the community and geography survey at https://training.fema.gov/hiedu/needsat.aspx.

7. Find out about FEMA's Hazus program—a risk assessment tool for natural disasters (http://www.fema.gov/hazus-software).

8. Visit the Cyber Storm web location and evaluate how your department or community might have responded. Provide a two- to three-page response and assessment.

9. Make a list and database for at least 10 private companies that design and manufacture explosive detection equipment, scanning devices, cargo and container scanners, and other novelties in the screening of commercial goods and trade.

10. List six applications of biometrics and the companies that produce the technology.

Notes

1. J. C. Chicken and T. Posner, *The Philosophy of Risk* (London: Thomas Telford, 1998).
2. D. Dunai, A framework of cardinal directions: Threats and challenges to the United States, *AARMS Security*, 10 (2011): 327–357, at 331.
3. See Appendix B for the full range of definitions and terms relevant to risk analysis.
4. Federal Emergency Management Agency, *Building Design for Homeland Security* (Washington, DC: U.S. Government Printing Office, 2004), V-5.
5. FEMA, *Building Design*, V-6.
6. Ibid., V-9.
7. H. R. Willis, *Risk Informed Resource Allocation at the Department of Homeland Security* (Santa Monica, CA: Rand Corporation, 2007), 3.
8. U.S. Department of Homeland Security, *Risk Analysis: Fact Sheet Series*, 2006.
9. USDHS, *Risk Analysis Sheet*.
10. Ibid.
11. Federal Emergency Management Agency, *Mitigation Planning How-to Guide #3: Developing the Mitigation Plan* (Washington, DC: U.S. Government Printing Office, April 2003), 1.
12. See U.S. Food and Drug Administration, *CARVER+Shock Users' Manual*, Version 1.0, 2007, Appendix B.
13. Prepared remarks by Secretary Napolitano at Harvard University's John F. Kennedy Jr. Forum, April 15, 2010, at www.dhs.gov/ynews/speeches/sp_1271366935471.shtm.
14. D. Dunai, *A Framework*, at 330.
15. Data from the Centre for Research on the Epidemiology of Disasters, 2015, www.cred.be.
16. Ibid.
17. See Department of Homeland Security, Science and Technology Directorate http://www.dhs.gov/science-and-technology/our-work; T. P. McAllister, F. Sadek, J. L. Gross, J. D. Averill, and R. G. Gann, Overview of the structural design of World Trade Center 1, 2, and 7 buildings, *Fire Technology* 49 (2013): 587; R. L. Reid, NIST: World Trade Center Building 7 is first known case of a tall building collapsing 'primarily' from fire, *Civil Engineering-ASCE* 78 (2008): 30.

18. Bauer, War on terror or policing terrorism? *Radicalization and Expansion of the Threats, Police Chief*, (2011): 46–52, 52.

19. See Department of Homeland Security, *Nuclear Reactors, Materials, and Waste Sector-Specific Plan: An Annex to the National Infrastructure Protection Plan*, 2010.

20. Department of Homeland Security, *Nuclear Sector—Specific Plan* 47, 2010.

21. U.S. Nuclear Regulatory Commission, *Office of Nuclear, Security and Incident Response* (Washington, DC: U.S. Government Printing Office, April 2005), 44.

22. D. G. Arce and K. Siqueira, Motivating operatives for suicide missions and conventional terrorist attacks, *Journal of Theoretical Politics* 26 (2014): 677; R. Braun and M. Genkin, Cultural resonance and the diffusion of suicide bombings: The role of collectivism, *Journal of Conflict Resolution* (2013).

23. FEMA, *National Exercise Program* (2001), available at http://www.fema.gov/media-library-data/20130 726-1829-25045-3774/national_exercise_program_base_plan__2011_03_18_.pdf.

24. White House Office of the Press Secretary, President Obama releases National Strategy for Countering Biological Threats, December 9, 2009, available at https://www.whitehouse.gov/the-press-office/ president-obama-releases-national-strategy-countering-biological-threats.

25. Testimony of Tara O'Toole before the House Subcommittee on Homeland Security Appropriations, on Biosurveillance, April 16, 2010, Washington, DC.

26. Observations on the cancellation of BioWatch Gen-3 and future considerations for the program, GAO-14-267T (June 10, 2014), available at http://www.gao.gov/products/GAO-14-267T.

27. See the National Institute of Health's list of pathogens and infectious materials at https://www.niaid. nih.gov/topics/biodefenserelated/biodefense/pages/cata.aspx.

28. Centers for Disease Control and Prevention, bioterrorism agents/diseases list, available at http://emergency.cdc.gov/agent/agentlist.asp.

29. Centers for Disease Control and Prevention, Division of Vector-Borne Diseases, Plague symptoms, available at http://www.cdc.gov/plague/symptoms/index.html, last updated September 14, 2015.

30. Centers for Disease Control, *Smallpox Response Plan and Guidelines* (Washington, DC: U.S. Government Printing Office, November 2002), Annex 8.

31. Ian Pannell, Syria civilians still under chemical attack, *BBC News Online*, September 10, 2015 at http://www.bbc.com/news/world-middle-east-34212324.

32. A. Üzümcü, The chemical weapons convention-disarmament, science and technology, *Analytical and Bioanalytical Chemistry* 406 (2014): 5071.

33. M. Patel, MD et al., Recognition of illness associated with exposure to chemical agents—United States, 2003, *Morbidity and Mortality Weekly Report*, 52 (October 3, 2003): 938–940, http://www.cdc.gov/mmwr/preview/mmwrhtml/mm5239a3.htm#tab.

34. The Arms Control Association makes this claim in M. Nguyen, Report confirms Iraq used Sarin in 1991, *Arms Control Today*, 36 (January/February 2006), http://www.armscontrol.org/act/2006_01-02/JANFEB-IraqSarin.

35. H. Hogan, Identifying explosives, after the fact, *Homeland Security Today Magazine* (September 2011): 18–19.

36. K. Yeager, What law enforcement needs to know about improvised explosives, *Police Chief* (September 2011): 52–55.

37. National Academies & Department of Homeland Security, *Fact Sheet: IED Attack Improvised Explosive Devices, News & Terrorism, Communicating in a Crisis*.

38. C. Smith, ISIS says soda can bomb detonated on Russian plane was intended for western passenger jet, November 19, 2015, http://bgr.com/2015/11/19/isis-soda-can-bomb-airplane-metrojet-kgl9268.

39. National Security Presidential Directive 54, *Cyber Security and Monitoring*, January 8, 2008.

40. The National Threat Center, Counterintelligence Guide: The National Security Threat List, http://www.wrc.noaa.gov/wrso/security_guide/nstl.htm.

41. Government Accountability Office (GAO), *Department of Homeland Security's (DHS's) Role in Critical Infrastructure Protection (CIP) Cybersecurity, GAO-05-434* (Washington, DC: May 2005), http://www. gao.gov/htext/d05434.html.

42. US-CERT Website, Federal Incident Reporting Guidelines, at Federal Agency Incident Categories, https://www.us-cert.gov/government-users/reporting-requirements, last accessed January 3, 2016.

43. Office of the President, *The National Strategy to Secure Cyberspace* (February 2003), x, https://www. us-cert.gov/sites/default/files/publications/cyberspace_strategy.pdf.

44. See Carnegie Mellon University, *Computer Emergency Readiness Team: Vulnerability Statistics*, https:// www.cert.org/vulnerability-analysis/publications/index.cfm. See also President, Strategy to Secure Cyberspace, 10.

45. Microsoft Security Intelligence Report, *The Evolution of Malware and the Threat Landscape—a 10-Year Review*, 20 (February 2012), available at https://www.microsoft.com/en-us/download/details. aspx?id=29046.

46. Office of the President, *Homeland Security Presidential Directive 7*, December 2003, 3.

47. President, *Strategy to Secure Cyberspace*, viii.

48. R. Skinner, Einstein presents big challenge to US-CERT. IG: US-CERT fails to adequately share critical data with agencies. *GovInfo Security*, June 22, 2010, available at www.govinfosecurity.com/p_print. php?t=a&id=2677.

49. Ibid., at 2.

50. Office of the Inspector General, Department of Homeland Security, *DHS Needs to Improve the Security Posture of its Cybersecurity Program Systems 2*, July 30, 2010.

51. Office of the Inspector General, Department of Homeland Security, *DHS Needs to Improve the Security Posture of its Cybersecurity Program Systems 5*, July 30, 2010; US-CERT Federal Incident Notification Guidelines at https://www.us-cert.gov/incident-notification-guidelines; U.S. Dept. of Homeland Security, Office of Inspector General, Implementation Status of the Enhanced Cybersecurity Services Program, OIG-14-119 (July 2014), available at https://www.oig.dhs.gov/assets/Mgmt/2014/OIG_14-119_Jul14.pdf.

52. See J. G. Schwitz, Risk-based cybersecurity policy, *American Intel Journal*, 29 (2011).

53. This approach has been repeatedly advanced by those arguing for private policing systems working side by side with public policing systems. See J. F. Pastor, Public–private policing arrangements & recommendations, *The Homeland Security Review*, 4 (2010): 71; See also C. P. Nemeth and K. C. Poulin, The Prevention Agency, 2006; C. P. Nemeth and K. C. Poulin, *Private Security and Public Safety: A Community Based Approach*, 2005; J. F. Pastor, *Terrorism and Public Safety Policing: Implications for the Obama Presidency*, 2010.

54. N. Santella and L. J. Steinberg, Accidental releases of hazardous materials and relevance, *Journal of Homeland Security and Emergency Management*, 8 (2011).

55. Santella and Steinberg, at 11.

56. M. Kano et al., Terrorism preparedness and exposure reduction since 9/11: The status of public readiness in the United States, *Journal of Homeland Security & Emergency Management*, 8 (2011).

57. J. Fleischman, Engaging the private sector in local homeland defense: The Orange County private sector terrorism response group, *Sheriff* (September/October, 2004): 33.

58. National Infrastructure Advisory Council, Public–private sector intelligence coordination: Final report and recommendations by the council, July 2006, 67.

59. C. P. Nemeth, *Private Security and the Law* (London: Elsevier, 2008), 12.

60. Homeland Security Research Corporation, Private sector to become 2nd largest homeland security industry customer by 2011, news release, April 9, 2008.

61. Homeland Security Research, *U.S. Private Sector Homeland Security Market, 2010–2014*, available at http://homelandsecurityresearch.com/2010/08/us-private-sector-homeland-security-market-2010-2014/.

62. For an examination of how these privatized practices prompt ethical concerns, see K. Carmola, *Private Security Contractors in the Age of New Wars: Risk, Law & Ethics* (New York: Routledge Press, 2008).

63. P. Starr, The meaning of privatization, *Yale Law and Policy Review,* 6 (1988): 6–41. This article also appears in Alfred K. and S. Kamerman, eds., *Privatization and the Welfare State* (Princeton, NJ: Princeton University Press, 1989).

64. F. Chen, Structuring public–private partnerships: Implications from the 'Public-Private Investment Program for Legacy Securities,' *Columbia Journal of Law and Social Problems* 46 (2013): 509.

65. Private Security Officer Employment Authorization Act of 2004, U.S. Code 28, 2004, § 534.

66. I. P. McGinley, Regulating "rent-a-cops" post 9/11: Why the Private Security Officer Employment Act fails to address homeland security concerns, *Cardozo Public Law, Policy and Ethics,* 6 (2007): 145.

67. C. P. Nemeth, *Private Security and the Investigative Process,* 2nd ed. (Boston, MA: Butterworth Heinemann, 2000), 1–4.

68. Bureau of Justice Assistance, *Engaging the Private Sector to Promote Homeland Security: Law Enforcement–Private Security Partnerships,* 2003, 11.

69. National Defense Industrial Association, www.ndia.org/Aboutus/pages/default.aspx.

70. Bureau of Justice Assistance, *Engaging the Private Sector,* 13.

71. This is why efforts at threat reduction as to nuclear arsenals are a sensible part of the homeland plan. See A. F. Woolf, Department of Defense Cooperative Threat Reduction Program, Nonproliferation and Threat Reduction Assistance: U.S. Programs in the Former Soviet Union (Congressional Research Service, March 6, 2012).

Chapter 5

Training and Exercises in Homeland Security

Objectives

1. To appraise the mission of the Department of Homeland Security's (DHS) grants and training opportunities for funding
2. To describe "Top Officials" (TOPOFF), National Exercise Program (NEP), and National Level Exercise (NLE) exercises and simulation programs and identify to whom they are offered, as well as the goals of the training program
3. To explain the mission and objectives of the Center for Domestic Preparedness (CDP) and their training programs
4. To summarize the activities of the Emergency Management Institute (EMI), including their course offerings and the constituencies they serve
5. To evaluate the usefulness and effectiveness of the Homeland Security Exercise and Evaluation Program (HSEEP), the Homeland Security Digital Library (HSDL), and the Lessons Learned Information Sharing Program (LLIS.gov)
6. To compare the seven types of exercises defined by HSEEP and identify the difference between discussion-based and operations-based exercises
7. To evaluate the usefulness and effectiveness of Community Emergency Response Teams (CERTs) across the country and explain their mission and goals
8. To outline the organization, purpose, and processes of the National Incident Management System (NIMS) and its various components

5.1 Introduction

The breadth, depth, scope, and coverage of training programs in homeland security are simply mind-boggling. Not only do agencies of government at the state, local, and federal levels devise, design, and deliver training in all the affairs of homeland, but so too do a plethora of private companies and businesses. In a nutshell, training is a fast-growing business for both the public and the private sector. In the public sense, government agencies, in seeking to carry out their mission, educate the public and the professionals who must labor each day in the justice and emergency model. DHS is the preeminent figure in the training modality and delivers programs to every imaginable sector. A partial list of the agency's more prominent programs is charted in Figure 5.1.

This section will scan some of these training systems with the full recognition that it can only touch the surface of most. DHS not only delivers a wide array of educational programs but also seeds the entire country with grants and other support so that localities and nonfederal jurisdictions can educate their constituencies with a local flavor. Billions of dollars in grants flow to every state, with most major urban areas receiving additional funding—so too with various special agencies at the federal level. As this chapter makes plain, while DHS leads the overall effort in homeland security, other agencies of government have their

FEMA Training and National Domestic Preparedness Consortium - Direct training for state and local jurisdictions to enhance capacity and preparedness

The Federal Law Enforcement Training Center - Up-to-date, low or no cost training opportunities for state and local law enforcement officers

National Preparedness Network (PREPnet) - First responder information programming schedule, all open and available to the public

The National Fire Academy - Training and educational opportunities for members of the fire, emergency services and allied professionals

Noble Training Center - Hospital-based medical training in disaster preparedness and response

The Emergency Management Institute - Training to ensure the effectiveness of organizations and individuals working together in disasters and emergencies

National Integration Center (NIC) - Incident Management Systems Division Information, guidance and resources to assist state, local, tribal and federal agencies in adopting and implementing the National Incident Management System.

National Incident Management System (NIMS) Online Training - Introduction to the purpose, principles, key components and benefits of NIMS.

Comprehensive Haz-Mat Emergency Response Capability Assessment Program (CHER-CAP) - Resource to prepare for hazardous materials incidents

National Exercise Program - Training, exercising, and collaboration among partners at all levels.

Homeland Security Exercise and Evaluation Program - Threat- and performance-based exercise activities of varying degrees of complexity and interaction

Lessons Learned Information Sharing - Best practices and lessons learned from actual terrorist events and training exercises

U.S. Fire Administration Publications - Free publications for emergency responders including manuals, reports & incident reports

FIGURE 5.1 DHS programs.

fingers in the homeland pie. Witnessed in Chapter 11 is the oversight role of the Centers for Disease Control and Prevention (CDC) in matters of bioterrorism, chemical attacks, and other weapons of mass destruction (WMD). Other agencies, such as the Department of Agriculture, the Nuclear Regulatory Commission, the Food and Drug Administration (FDA), and the military, play integral roles as well. Both funding and training spill out to the practitioners from these agencies in the same way as DHS does.

5.2 Grants and Training

Long part of its historic mission, DHS has actively supported the training of personnel at the state, federal, and local level as well as provided direct block grounds to states and localities for on-location training in various jurisdictions. DHS, since its earliest days of operation, allowed competitive grant processes to be available to both public and private-sector partners. During the formative stages of the department, there was a complete hodgepodge of various entities administering these activities. DHS, in its quest for centralization and improved efficiency, blended a host of diverse offices into the Office of Grants and Training (G&T). The *Post-Katrina Emergency Reform Act of 2006* amended the Homeland Security Act and mandated some mergers and realignments. As part of this reorganization, major national preparedness components and functions, which include the Office of G&T, the United States Fire Administration, National Capital Region Coordination, Chemical Stockpile Emergency Preparedness, and the Radiological Emergency Preparedness Program, while still operational under the DHS heading, were transferred to the Federal Emergency Management Agency (FEMA), effective April 1, 2007.

The new organization reflected the expanded scope of FEMA's departmental responsibilities. It strengthens FEMA's coordination with other DHS components as well as with agencies and departments outside of DHS. It also enhances FEMA's ability to partner with emergency management, law enforcement, preparedness organizations, and the private sector. Aside from this bureaucratic realignment, the Office of G&T makes possible a bevy of training opportunities for homeland security specialists. Its mission is multifaceted but directed primarily at those in the first-responder category, such as fire and emergency medical technicians (EMT), police, and paramedics. The agency posts a well-defined mission:

> The mission of G&T is to prepare America for acts of domestic terrorism by developing and implementing a national program to enhance the capacity of state and local agencies to respond to incidents of terrorism, particularly those involving chemical, biological, radiological, nuclear and explosive (CBRNE) incidents, through coordinated training, equipment acquisition, technical assistance, and support for Federal, state, and local exercises.[1]

Soon after these mergers, FEMA set out specific strategic goals that advance its grand vision to be the "Nation's Preeminent Emergency Management and Preparedness Agency."[2] The extensive grant programs had to be aligned with FEMA's overall strategic goals and mission. Review Figure 5.2[3] to see how it envisioned the compatibility of these goals as it carried out the mission.

GPD strategic goals	FEMA strategic goals				
	Goal 1: Lead an integrated approach that strengthens the nation's ability to address disasters, emergencies, and terrorist events	Goal 2: Deliver easily accessible and coordinated assistance for all programs	Goal 3: Provide reliable information at the right time for all users	Goal 4: FEMA invests in people and people invest in FEMA to insure mission success	Goal 5: Build public trust and confidence through performance and stewardship
Goal 1: Emphasize employee development and human capital planning				✓	
Goal 2: Team with internal and external stakeholders	✓		✓		
Goal 3: Provide accurate and timely information and services		✓	✓		
Goal 4: Build a robust and standardized data analysis capability	✓		✓		✓
Goal 5: Streamline, standardize and document key processes		✓			✓

FIGURE 5.2 Grant Programs Directorates (GPD) alignment to FEMA's strategic goals.

FEMA sees the entire picture of G&T in an agency–individual employee horizon, making a noble effort to connect the larger purposes of the agency's purpose with the roles, tasks, and functions of its employees downstream. It labels this a *cascade up* or a *cascade down*. Hence, the agency authors grant and training policies that compliment individual performance and the efficacy of the agency itself (see Figure 5.3).[4]

G&T fulfills this mission through a series of program efforts responsive to the specific requirements of state and local agencies. G&T works directly with emergency responders and conducts assessments of state and local needs and capabilities to guide the development and execution of these programs. Assistance provided by G&T is directed at a broad

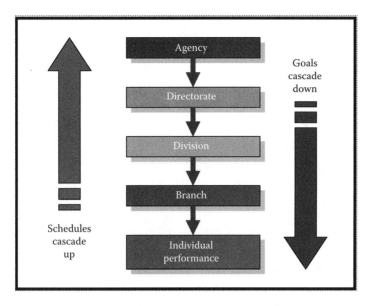

FIGURE 5.3 Strategy implementation chart.

spectrum of state and local emergency responders, including firefighters, emergency medical services (EMS), emergency management agencies, law enforcement, and public officials.

G&T attends to this mission in a variety of ways by providing grants to states and local jurisdictions, providing hands-on training through a number of residential training facilities and in-service training at the local level, funding and working with state and local jurisdictions to plan and execute exercises, and providing technical assistance on-site to state and local jurisdictions. In many respects, the office fervently addresses Homeland Security Presidential Directive 8, which encourages all agencies of government to be prepared, train their personnel, and establish a national program and a multiyear planning system to conduct homeland security preparedness–related exercises that reinforce identified training standards, provide for evaluation of readiness, and support the national preparedness goal. The establishment and maintenance of the program will be conducted in maximum collaboration with state and local governments and appropriate private sector entities.[5] For the 2011 grant cycle, the Office of G&T prioritizes the funding of the following programs:

- State Homeland Security Program (SHSP)
- Urban Areas Security Initiative (UASI)
- Tribal Homeland Security Grant Program (THSGP)
- Nonprofit Security Grant Program (NSGP)
- Regional Catastrophic Preparedness Grant Program (RCPSP)
- Emergency Operations Center Grant Program (EOC)
- Driver's License Security Grant Program (DLSGP)
- Transit Security Grant Program (TSGP)
- Freight Rail Security Grant Program (FRSGP)
- Intercity Passenger Rail (IPR-Amtrack) Program
- Intercity Bus Security Grant Program (IBSGP)

- Port Security Grant Program (PSGP)
- Emergency Management Performance Grants (EMPG)[6]

The Office of G&T supports cooperative partnerships among all relevant homeland constituencies. By and through the National Domestic Preparedness Consortium, the Office of G&T identifies, develops, tests, and delivers training to state and local emergency responders (see Figure 5.4).

The Office of G&T has also funded equipment purchases for justice and emergency agencies. An approved equipment list is published by the department. The office has supported the following equipment acquisitions:

- Personal protective equipment
- Equipment—explosive device mitigation and remediation
- CBRNE operational and search and rescue equipment
- Information technology equipment
- Cybersecurity enhancement equipment
- Interoperable communications equipment
- Detection equipment
- Decontamination equipment
- Medical equipment
- Power equipment
- CBRNE reference materials
- CBRNE incident response vehicles
- Terrorism incident prevention equipment
- Physical security enhancement equipment
- Inspection and screening systems
- Agricultural terrorism prevention, response, and mitigation equipment
- CBRNE prevention and response watercraft
- CBRNE aviation equipment

FIGURE 5.4   National Domestic Preparedness Consortium logo.

- CBRNE logistical support equipment
- Intervention equipment
- Other authorized equipment

The Office of G&T coordinated TOPOFF exercises and simulation programs. TOPOFF signifies "top officials" or those higher up in the homeland supervisory chain. Officials from state, local, and federal agencies work collaboratively on a homeland problem, assess and evaluate the homeland dilemma, and publish best practices in dealing with the security question. As of 2011, the Office of G&T had conducted four major TOPOFF exercises, as illustrated in Figure 5.5.

The TOPOFF program has been replaced by what is now designated the *National Exercise Program* (NEP). The NEP allows federal, state, and local agencies to work collaboratively on all sorts of risks and hazards. Thus far, there has been a variety of NEPs whose coverage has included

- *National Level Exercise 2012 (NLE 12)*: NLE 12 was a series of exercise events that examined the ability of the United States to execute a coordinated response to a series of significant cyber incidents. As a part of the NEP, NLE 12 emphasized the shared responsibility among all levels of government, the private sector, and the international community to secure cyber networks and coordinate response and recovery actions. The NLE 12 series was focused on examining four major themes: planning and implementation of the draft National Cyber Incident Response Plan (NCIRP), coordination among governmental entities, information sharing, and decision-making.
- *National Level Exercise 2011 (NLE 11)*: NLE 11 was an operations-based exercise centered on the scenario of a catastrophic earthquake in the New Madrid Seismic Zone, encompassing four FEMA regions (IV, V, VI, and VII) and eight Central U.S. earthquake states: Alabama, Arkansas, Kentucky, Illinois, Indiana, Mississippi, Missouri, and Tennessee. NLE 11 exercised initial incident response and recovery capabilities and tested and validated existing plans, policies, and procedures to include the New Madrid Catastrophic Plan. NLE 11 was conducted in May 2011.
- *National Level Exercise 2010 (NLE 10)*: FEMA conducted NLE 10 on May 17–18, 2010. NLE 10 engaged federal, state, and local partners in a series of events and opportunities to demonstrate and assess federal emergency preparedness capabilities pertaining to a simulated terrorist attack scenario involving an improvised nuclear device.
- *National Level Exercise 2009 (NLE 09)*: NLE 09 was designated as a Tier I NLE. Tier I exercises (formerly known as the Top Officials exercise series or TOPOFF) are conducted annually in accordance with the NEP, which serves as the nation's overarching exercise program for planning, organizing, conducting, and evaluating NLEs. The NEP was established to provide the U.S. government, at all levels, with exercise opportunities to prepare for catastrophic crises ranging from terrorism to natural disasters.[7]

TOPOFF 4: Increasing Coordination through Collaboration

Conducted in October 2007, TOPOFF 4 took place in Portland, Ore.; Phoenix, Ariz.; and for the first time, the U.S. territory of Guam as well as in Washington, D.C. for federal partners.

The exercise built on past lessons learned while adding new goals, including: an increased level of coordination with U.S. Department of Defense exercises to combat global terrorism, closer cooperation with the private sector, an expanded emphasis on prevention, a deeper focus on mass decontamination and long-term recovery and remediation issues, and strengthened coordination and communications with international allies.

More than 15,000 participants representing federal, state, territorial, and local entities, as well as the governments of Australia, Canada, and the United Kingdom, participated in the exercise.

All venues responded to a radiological RDD attack.

TOPOFF 3: Exercising National Preparedness

Conducted in April 2005, TOPOFF 3 was the first test of the National Response Plan (NRP) and National Incident Management System (NIMS).

TOPOFF 3 continued to evolve and included an increased focus on bolstering international and private sector participation, terrorism prevention activities, risk communication and public information functions, and long-term recovery and remediation issues.

Over 10,000 participants, including responders and officials from Canada and the United Kingdom, responded to a simulated chemical attack in New London, Conn., and a biological attack in the state of New Jersey.

The exercise marked the launch of a new simulated media tool – the interactive web site VNN.com.

TOPOFF 2: Assessing Homeland Security Planning

Conducted in May 2003, TOPOFF 2 was the first national exercise following the September 11, 2001 attacks and was led by the newly-formed Department of Homeland Security (DHS).

TOPOFF 2 provided the first opportunity for DHS to exercise its organizational functions and assets, including tests of the Homeland Security Advisory System (HSAS).

Participants in Seattle faced a simulated radiological dispersal device (RDD) attack, while those in the Chicago faced a biological attack.

The exercise engaged 8,500 responders and top officials from the United States and Canada – the first international partner to participate.

TOPOFF 2000: Coordinated, Strategic National Response

In May 2000, the Department of Justice, the Department of State, and the Federal Emergency Management Agency (FEMA) led the first exercise in the TOPOFF series.

The primary goal of the exercise was to improve the capability of government officials and agencies, both within the United States and abroad to provide an effective, coordinated, and strategic response to a terrorist attack.

More than 6,500 federal, state, and local personnel – including top officials – responded to a simulated biological attack in Denver, Colorado and a simulated chemical attack in Portsmouth, N.H.

The exercise introduced a new element in preparedness exercises: a simulated media outlet known as the Virtual News Network (VNN). VNN kept players up-to-date on unfolding events and forced decision-makers to face the challenge of communicating with real-world media in a crisis.

FIGURE 5.5 TOPOFF exercises through 2011.

The office reserved a portion of its grant funding exclusively for firefighters and fire administration. DHS is well aware of this pressing need since so much of what fire personnel undertake often relates to hazardous activities. Three types of grants are available: Assistance to Firefighters Grant (AFG), Fire Prevention and Safety (FP&S), and Staffing for Adequate Fire and Emergency Response (SAFER) (Figure 5.6).

FIGURE 5.6   Assistance to Firefighters Grant Program logo.

Eligible applicants for AFG are limited to fire departments and nonaffiliated EMS organizations operating in any of the 50 states plus the District of Columbia, the Commonwealth of the Northern Mariana Islands, the Virgin Islands, Guam, American Samoa, and Puerto Rico.[8]

Internet Resource: Review the various grants available through the AFG Program at https://www.fema.gov/welcome-assistance-firefighters-grant-program.

Without much fanfare, the Office of G&T was submerged into a host of other DHS offices and bureaucracies after the 2011 cycle. For various reasons, both political and economic, G&T was replaced by the DHS Preparedness Grant Program and the DHS Homeland Security Grant Program. Under this new umbrella, DHS continues to administer and fund a wide assortment of worthy endeavors and to train a myriad of partners and players in the world of homeland security. For the 2015 cycle of awards, DHS announced the following program initiatives:

- *Homeland Security Grant Program (HSGP)*: Provides more than $1 billion for states and urban areas to prevent, protect against, mitigate, respond to, and recover from acts of terrorism and other threats
- *State Homeland Security Program (SHSP)*: Provides $402 million to support the implementation of the National Preparedness System to build and strengthen preparedness capabilities at all levels
- *Urban Areas Security Initiative (UASI)*: Provides $587 million to enhance regional preparedness and capabilities in 28 high-threat, high-density areas
- *Operation Stonegarden (OPSG)*: Provides $55 million to enhance cooperation and coordination among local, tribal, territorial, state, and federal law enforcement agencies to jointly enhance security along the United States land and water borders where there are ongoing U.S. Customs and Border Protection missions

- *Emergency Management Performance Grant (EMPG) Program*: Provides over $350 million to assist local, tribal, territorial, and state governments in enhancing and sustaining all-hazards emergency management capabilities
- *Tribal Homeland Security Grant Program (THSGP)*: Provides $10 million to eligible tribal nations to implement preparedness initiatives to help strengthen the nation against risks associated with potential terrorist attacks and other hazards
- *Nonprofit Security Grant Program (NSGP)*: Provides $13 million to support target hardening and other physical security enhancements for nonprofit organizations that are at high risk of a terrorist attack and are located within one of the 28 fiscal year (FY) 2015 UASI-eligible urban areas
- *Intercity Passenger Rail—Amtrak (IPR) Program*: Provides $10 million to protect critical surface transportation infrastructure and the traveling public from acts of terrorism and increase the resilience of the Amtrak rail system
- *Port Security Grant Program (PSGP)*: Provides $100 million to help protect critical port infrastructure from terrorism, enhance maritime domain awareness, improve port-wide maritime security risk management, and maintain or reestablish maritime security mitigation protocols that support port recovery and resiliency capabilities
- *Transit Security Grant Program (TSGP)*: Provides $87 million to owners and operators of transit systems to protect critical surface transportation and the traveling public from acts of terrorism and to increase the resilience of transit infrastructure
- *Intercity Bus Security Grant Program (IBSGP)*: Provides $3 million to assist operators of fixed-route intercity and charter bus services within high-threat urban areas to protect bus systems and the traveling public from acts of terrorism, major disasters, and other emergencies

Internet Exercise: Review the various grants available and the process for applying at the Homeland Security Grant Program website at https://www.fema.gov/fiscal-year-2015-homeland-security-grant-program.

5.3 Center for Domestic Preparedness

The CDP operates within the FEMA construct and delivers key training and education in specialized fields. Located in Aniston, Alabama, the CDP is fully accredited and is a comprehensive facility that provides both resident and commuter training in highly technical areas. Its specialty training relates to WMD. At the Chemical, Ordnance, Biological, and Radiological Training Facility (COBRATF), the CDP offers the only program in the nation featuring civilian training exercises in a true toxic environment, using chemical agents. The advanced, hands-on training enables responders to effectively respond to real-world incidents involving chemical, biological, explosive, radiological, or other hazardous materials.

Internet Exercise: Visit the CDP Student Portal for Educational Program Offerings at https://cdp.dhs.gov/news-media/articles/cdps-student-portal-provides-a-single-easy-location-for-student-training-documents/.

The CDP educates homeland professionals with graduated levels of sophistication and recognizes the most highly proficient practitioners. FEMA's CDP has trained more than 93,500 local, state, and tribal responders from across the United States in preventing and responding to disasters and other terrorist threats involving CBRNE materials.

5.4 Emergency Management Institute

EMI, located in Emmittsburg, Maryland, is the lead national emergency management training, exercising, and education institution. EMI is located on a pristine campus near Mt. St. Mary's College and shares its facilities with the U.S. Fire Administration's training center (see Figure 5.7).

EMI offers a plethora of course offerings covering all aspects of emergency preparedness in conjunction with its agency partners. The scope and influence of EMI has been significant since it has served an impressive number of customers:

- 993 resident course offerings in 2010, training 24,173 individual participants.
- The EMI Independent Study (IS) Program delivered extensive online training in more than 110 courses and trained more than 1.9 million individuals.
- In 2011, 13 new and 14 revised courses were added to the curriculum.[9]

A partial listing of course offerings includes

- E0101: Foundations of Emergency Management
- E0102: Science for Disasters
- E0103: Planning

FIGURE 5.7   EMI in Emmittsburg, MD.

- E0104: Exercise Design
- E0105: Public Information and Warning
- E0110: Foundations of Emergency Management Train-the-Trainer
- E0122: Emergency Management Accreditation Program (EMAP) Training Course
- E0133: Operations-Based Exercise Design and Evaluation (MEPP Candidates *only*)
- E0141: Instructional Presentation and Evaluation Skills
- E0157: Hazard Mitigation Community Education and Outreach (CEO) Specialist Qualifying Course
- E0158: Hazard Mitigation Community Planner Specialist Qualifying Course
- E0167: Core Principles for HM HPA Specialists
- E0180: Core Principles for Hazard Mitigation Insurance Specialists
- E0197: Integrating Access and Functional Needs into Emergency Planning
- E0202: Debris Management Planning for State, Tribal, and Local Officials
- E0207: Introduction to Hazard Mitigation Field Operations
- E0272: Managing the Floodplain Post-Disaster
- E0273: Managing Floodplain Development thru the NFIP
- E0274: National Dam Safety Program Technical Seminar (NDSPTS)
- E0285: Providing Post-Disaster Substantial Damage Technical Assistance to Communities
- E0291: Community Dam Safety, Preparedness, & Mitigation
- E0296: Application of Hazus-MH for Risk Assessment
- E0313: Basic Hazus-MH
- E0337: Posting IFMIS Transactions
- E0349: Mission Assignment (MA) Processing
- E0352: Crisis Counseling Assistance and Training Program: Training State Trainers
- E0361: Multi-Hazard Emergency Planning for Schools
- E0364: Multihazard Emergency Planning for Schools
- E0426: Implementing Whole Community Resilience and Citizen Corps Programs
- E0542: Basic Mediation Skills
- E0580: Emergency Management Framework for Tribal Governments
- E0604: Emergency Manager Orientation (EMO)/FEMA Incident Workforce Academy (FIWA) Tier IV-Specialist
- E0706: Disaster Contracting
- E0726: Financial Management Concepts for Disaster Operations
- E0791: Interagency Consultation for Endangered Species
- E0827: Geospatial Information System Managers and Unit Leaders
- E0953: NIMS ICS All-Hazards Public Information Officer TTT
- E0955: NIMS ICS All-Hazards Safety Officer TTT
- E0968: NIMS ICS All-Hazards Logistics Section Chief TTT

Internet Exercise: For a complete listing of courses in 2016, visit https://training.fema.gov/emicourses/docs/fy16%20catalog.pdf.

EMI supports national and international emergency management with more than 50 countries participating in EMI's training and educational activities. EMI also enjoys close relations with several nationally recognized professional emergency management and related organizations, such as the International Association of Emergency Managers (IAEM), the National Emergency Management Association (NEMA), the Association of State Flood Plain Managers (ASFPM), the American Public Works Association (APWA), the American Society of Civil Engineers (ASCE), and the American Society of Engineering Management (ASEM). EMI is fully accredited by the International Association for Continuing Education and Training (IACET) and the American Council on Education (ACE). In the last decade, EMI has delivered hundreds of residential courses at the National Emergency Training Center (NETC) campus, training nearly 20,000 individual students. The EMI IS Program, a web-based distance learning program open to the public, has delivered extensive online training in 62 courses and has trained more than 2.8 million individuals. The EMI IS website receives from 2.5 to 3 million visitors a day.

EMI operates the Disaster Field Training Operations (DFTO) Program. The mission of the DFTO is to "Plan, develop, promote and deliver disaster performance improvement and training opportunities in coordination with the Emergency Management Institute and Regional Offices. The Disaster Field Training Operations provides training to the Federal disaster workforce in support of FEMA's mission."[10] In 2010 alone, the DFTO trained 31,834 disaster response and recovery employees at disaster sites throughout the United States[11] (Figure 5.8).

EMI conducts national-level conferences that are well received, including the National Preparedness Annual Training and Exercise Conference and the EMI Higher Education Conference. The conference collects and catalogs institutions, course materials such as syllabi and university texts, and programmatic directions in emergency management. EMI has just implemented a School Program,[12] which prepares elementary and secondary administrators for risk and threat.

Internet Resource: See the EMI compilation of college and university syllabi at https://www.training.fema.gov/hiedu/syllabi.aspx/.

FIGURE 5.8   Firefighters in training at EMI.

There are 16 critical infrastructure and key resources designated by DHS and Presidential Policy Directive/PPD-21:[13]

- Chemical sector
- Commercial facilities sector
- Communications sector
- Critical manufacturing sector
- Dams sector
- Defense industrial base sector
- Emergency services sector
- Energy sector
- Financial services sector
- Food and agriculture sector
- Government facilities sector
- Health-care and public health sector
- Information technology sector
- Nuclear reactors, materials, and waste sector
- Transportation systems sector
- Water and wastewater systems sector

5.5 Homeland Security Exercise and Evaluation Program

The HSEEP, a unit of DHS, provides a standardized methodology and terminology for exercise design, development, conduct, evaluation, and improvement planning. HSEEP develops national standards for training exercises and promulgates means and modalities of assessments and evaluation to ensure agency efficiency.[14] The key component of HSEEP is the design and implementation of exercises—simulations and reenactments of events and circumstances likely to be encountered in the world of homeland security. Exercises allow homeland security and emergency management personnel, from first responders to senior officials, to train and practice prevention, protection, response, and recovery capabilities in a realistic but risk-free environment.

The intent of HSEEP is to provide a common exercise policy and program guidance capable of constituting a national standard for all exercises. HSEEP employs consistent terminology and protocols that can be used by agencies and individuals universally. HSEEP traditionally published its recommendations in a series of volumes, all of which were consolidated in 2013. The protocol and doctrine of HSEEP is summarized in chapter format:

- Chapter 1: HSEEP Fundamentals describes the basic principles and methodology of HSEEP.
- Chapter 2: Exercise Program Management provides guidance for conducting a Training and Exercise Planning Workshop (TEPW) and developing a multiyear Training and Exercise Plan (TEP).

- Chapter 3: Exercise Design and Development describes the methodology for developing exercise objectives, conducting planning meetings, developing exercise documentation, and planning for exercise logistics, control, and evaluation.
- Chapter 4: Exercise Conduct provides guidance on setup, exercise play, and wrap-up activities.
- Chapter 5: Evaluation provides the approach to exercise evaluation planning and conduct through data collection, analysis, and development of an after-action report (AAR).
- Chapter 6: Improvement Planning (IP) addresses corrective actions identified in the exercise IP and the process of tracking corrective actions to resolution.[15]

HSEEP advises agencies on best practices and lessons learned in given scenarios. All training conducted under the HSEEP banner adheres to the training template charted in Figure 5.9.[16]

For the exercise to be educationally meaningful and realistically based, the following criteria need to be considered in the development process from concept to implementation:

- Setting the exercise foundation by reviewing elected and appointed officials' guidance, the TEP, and other factors
- Selecting participants for an exercise planning team and developing an exercise planning time line with milestones
- Developing exercise-specific objectives and identifying core capabilities based on the guidance of elected and appointed officials
- Identifying evaluation requirements
- Developing the exercise scenario
- Creating documentation
- Coordinating logistics
- Planning for exercise control and evaluation[17]

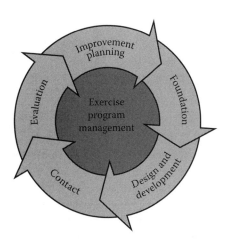

FIGURE 5.9   HSEEP exercise cycle.

There are seven types of exercises defined within HSEEP, each of which is either discussion based or operations based. Discussion-based exercises include

- *Seminar.* A seminar is an informal discussion designed to orient participants to new or updated plans, policies, or procedures.
- *Workshop.* A workshop resembles a seminar but is employed to build specific products, such as a draft plan or policy.
- *Tabletop exercise (TTX).* A TTX involves key personnel discussing simulated scenarios in an informal setting.
- *Games.* A game is a simulation of operations that often involves two or more teams, usually in a competitive environment, using rules, data, and procedures designed to depict an actual or assumed real-life situation.

Operations-based exercises include

- *Drill.* A drill is a coordinated, supervised activity usually employed to test a single specific operation or function within a single operation.
- *Functional exercise (FE).* An FE examines or validates the coordination, command, and control between various multiagency coordination centers.
- *Full-scale exercise (FSE).* An FSE is a multiagency, multijurisdictional, multidisciplinary exercise involving functional response.

For operations-based exercises, HSEEP recommends broad-based participation and the widest array of agency inclusion feasible. HSEEP publishes a recommended list of participants for the planning phase of the exercise:

- *Emergency management*
- Emergency manager
- Homeland security
- Public health
- Public works
- Transportation/transit authority
- Public affairs
- Exercise venue/site management (e.g., stadium security)

Specific	Objectives should address the five Ws- who, what, when, where, and why. The objective specifies what needs to be done with a timeline for completion .
Measurable	Objectives should include numeric or descriptive measures that define quantity, quality, cost, etc. Their focus should be on observable actions and outcomes.
Achievable	Objectives should be with in the control, influence, and resources of exercise play and participant actions.
Relevant	Objectives should be instrumental to the mission of the organization and link to its goals or strategic intent.
Time-bound	A specified and reasonable timeframe should be incorporated into all objectives.

FIGURE 5.10 SMART guidelines for exercise objectives.

- *Fire*
- Fire department
- Communications/dispatch
- Special operations (e.g., hazmat, Metropolitan Medical Response System [MMRS])
- Mutual aid fire
- *Law enforcement*
- Police
- Special operations (e.g., bomb squad, Special Weapons and Tactics [SWAT])
- Sheriff's department
- Local Federal Bureau of Investigation (FBI)
- Mutual aid law enforcement
- *Medical*
- Hospital representatives (primary trauma center or hospital association)
- Emergency medical services (i.e., public and private)
- Mutual aid
- Medical examiner/coroner

In discussion-based exercises, the participants consider the threat and security dilemma involved and then determine the necessary players. In other words, not all homeland security threats will need medical personnel, nor will law enforcement necessarily be the preeminent actor in a homeland security dilemma.

Whatever the chosen exercise, make sure the exercise leads to achievable and measurable results in terms of understanding and performance. HSEEP publishes an excellent graphic that prioritizes the exercise's overall purpose, shown in Figure 5.10.[18]

FIGURE 5.11 Factors for consideration in developing exercise program priorities.

HSEEP urges agency trainers and instructional personnel to target the purpose and end of any selected training exercise. At a minimum, make the exercise count for something; make it relevant and meaningful for the participants and players and see the entire process as one of agency improvement. Keep the factors in Figure 5.11[19] in mind when developing your exercise priorities.

Professional participation makes far more sense when those enrolled understand the nature of the training, its ultimate purpose, and how the training achieves a homeland security purpose.

5.6 Lessons Learned: Best Practices (LLIS.GOV)/Homeland Security Digital Library (HSDL)

Training, in order to be effective, must correlate to best practices and success in the field. Training that lacks the cohesion of theory and application—training that appears disconnected from a stated goal or end—lacks relevance to those laboring in homeland security. With so much at stake and so many opportunities for intellectual and practical advancement in the field, those entrusted with training must be mindful of its effectiveness. The Lessons Learned Information Sharing (LLIS) Program (Figure 5.12[20]) promotes preparedness by identifying lessons learned and innovative practices, analyzing recurring trends,

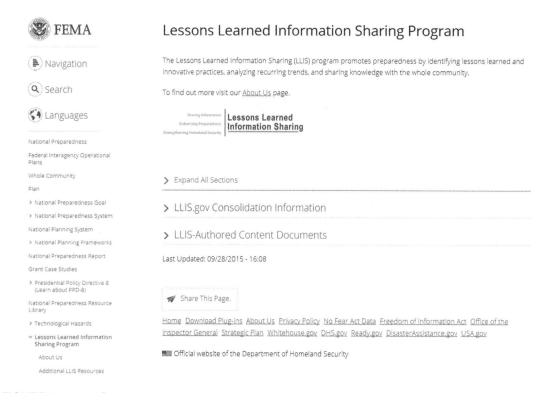

FIGURE 5.12   LLIS.gov homepage.

and sharing knowledge with the whole community. The web page and various requirements have just undergone a major overhaul. FEMA's LLIS program consolidated their content with the Naval Postgraduate School's HSDL.

Internet Exercise: You can register for full access to these reports and research data by visiting https://www.hsdl.org/?llis.

LLIS delivers the practices that work, not the initiatives that simply get played and replayed due to some mindless funding or programmatic fad. LLIS is an encrypted system that is not readily available to the general public. Terrorists, hoping to discern our security practices, would be regular visitors without the encryption. Learned and best practices are peer validated by homeland security professionals. AARs and an information clearinghouse

FIGURE 5.13   HSDL web page.

are catalogued and monitored and include the bulk of serious and significant documents for homeland security.

There are four types of LLIS.gov original research:

- *Lessons learned* are positive or negative experiences derived from actual incidents, operations, training, or exercises.
- *Best practices* are peer-validated techniques, procedures, and solutions that have demonstrated their effectiveness in operations, training, and exercises across multiple jurisdictions or organizations.
- *Practice notes* describe procedures, techniques, or methods that have been adopted by a single jurisdiction or organization.
- *Good stories* describe successful, innovative programs and initiatives developed by a jurisdiction that others may wish to emulate.

The HSDL is housed and maintained by the Naval Postgraduate School in California. It serves as a repository for all LLIS results and AARs as well as an updated list of homeland security documents from DHS and other federal, state, and local organizations, validated by subject matter experts, to capture expertise and innovation at the state and local levels.[21] See Figure 5.13[22] for the HSDL's homepage.

Internet Exercise: Visit the Naval Postgraduate School website, which serves as a clearinghouse for the HSDL, at www.hsdl.org.

5.7 Community Emergency Response Teams

Another avenue of education and training rests with CERT training and CERT teams. The CERT Program educates people about disaster preparedness, the nature of hazards, and basic disaster response skills such as fire safety, light search and rescue, team organization, and disaster medical operations. CERT teams dot the entire American landscape and serve a crucial educational function. CERT personnel train to prepare for a disaster or overwhelming events by

- Identifying and mitigating potential hazards in the home and workplace
- Initiating plans to prepare themselves and their loved ones for the hazards that they face
- Learning skills to help themselves, loved ones, and neighbors or fellow employees until professional response resources arrive
- Working cooperatively as a team within their neighborhoods or workplaces
- Maintaining a relationship with the agency that sponsors the CERT Program
- Participating in continuing education and training
- Volunteering for projects to enhance the public safety of their communities
- Understanding their capabilities and limitations when deployed

Internet Resource: See the CERT tutorial on search and rescue at http://www.fema.gov/training-materials.

Much more can be said about the critical role that training and education play in the world of homeland security. Throughout this text, there will be other references to the training mentality that is now so heavily engrained in the task of homeland security. In other portions of this text, you have already analyzed the role of the Federal Law Enforcement and Training Center (FLETC)—a place where training goes on day and night. And there are other forums in the mix, such as the U.S. Fire Administration, the National Fire Academy, and the Community Hazards Emergency Response-Capability Assurance Process (CHER-CAP). You can visit these and many locations as you discover the world of homeland security.

Internet Resource: Visit Community Hazards Emergency Response-Capability Assurance Process (CHER-CAP) at http://www.fema.gov/es/node/100051. Visit the National Fire Academy at http://www.usfa.dhs.gov/nfa. Visit the U.S. Fire Administration at http://www.usfa.dhs.gov/about.

5.8 National Incident Management System

Another approach relevant to preparedness and readiness is the NIMS.[23] NIMS is a by-product of Homeland Security Presidential Directive 5, which held that

> To prevent, prepare for, respond to, and recover from terrorist attacks, major disasters, and other emergencies, the United States Government shall establish a single, comprehensive approach to domestic incident management. The objective of the United States Government is to ensure that all levels of government across the Nation have the capability to work efficiently and effectively together, using a national approach to domestic incident management. In these efforts, with regard to domestic incidents, the United States Government treats crisis management and consequence management as a single, integrated function, rather than as two separate functions.[24]

FEMA takes the lead in the administration of the NIMS program. FEMA's National Integration Center (NIC) Incident Management Systems Integration Division was established by the secretary of Homeland Security to oversee NIMS and provide a research and evaluation arm regarding its standards and procedures (see Figure 5.14).

The NIMS mandate extends to every sector of government. Each and every agency of government has to plan and prepare for disaster—and must do so internally as well as externally by working efficiently and effectively with all other departments of government. NIMS reflects the clear and unbridled need for less turf protection by departments and more cooperation along federal, state, and local lines. NIMS expects that the following parties and entities will work to a common purpose regarding terror and disaster:

- Federal government
- States
- Territories
- Cities, counties, and townships

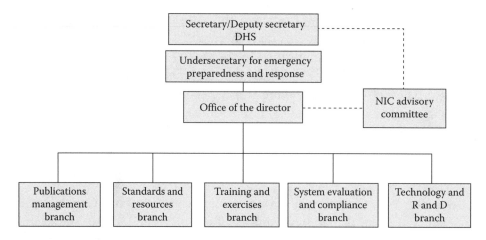

FIGURE 5.14   NIMS Integration Center (NIC) organization chart.

- Tribal officials
- First responders

NIMS extends to the private sector as well as to facilities of import, such as hospitals, power plants, and chemical and other related industrial centers, and all are expected to be on the same page. NIMS provides a systematic, proactive approach, guiding departments and agencies at all levels of government, in the private sector, and in nongovernmental organizations to work seamlessly to prepare for, prevent, respond to, recover from, and mitigate the effects of incidents, regardless of cause, size, location, or complexity, in order to reduce loss of life and property and harm to the environment. This consistency mirrors the need for uniform practices in the world of homeland security and ensures predictable and dependable protocols when dealing with terror or disaster.

Internet Resource: For a suggested NIMS plan for business and industry as to business continuity, published by FEMA, see https://www.fema.gov/media-library/assets/documents/89510.

The NIMS program is broken down into various components. First, compliance as to standards and practices in incident command and response is required. To accomplish this, the NIMS Compliance and Technical Assistance Branch relies on input from federal, state, local, tribal, multidiscipline, and private-sector stakeholders to ensure continuity and accuracy of ongoing implementation efforts. Compliance ensures that best practices are adopted and that ineffective programs and stratagems are abandoned. Each year, DHS issues compliance standards for both the public and the private sector. In 2010, by way of illustration, the NIMS compliance standards were published and can be found here for reference:

https://www.fema.gov/pdf/emergency/nims/FY2010_FederalNIMSImplementation ObjectivesMetrics.pdf

Next, the NIMS program depends on a common command and managerial structure to identify, respond to, and mitigate risk and harm. The NIMS command and management construct finds a home in the Incident Command System (ICS). ICS is a standardized on-scene incident management concept designed specifically to allow responders to adopt an integrated organizational structure equal to the complexity and demands of any single incident or multiple incidents without being hindered by jurisdictional boundaries. Before the ICS, the handling of disaster, catastrophe, or terror could only be described as non-uniform. Each incident would be tackled differently depending on the jurisdiction. The differences were starkly apparent with personnel and chain of command. Unpredictable communications systems, incompatible and not interoperable, caused a lack of interagency communication; and even language, often confusing and contradictory, was a challenge. The ICS promotes uniformity of practice, multiagency coordination, and a public information system that all constituencies can comprehend. The ICS, instead of a fractured hodgepodge of differing practices, brings to the table a common language, a common set of operating principles, and a sorely needed standardization to terror and disaster.

The ICS usually takes the form illustrated in Figure 5.15.[25]

The ICS stresses preparedness in every context of homeland protection. Preparedness involves an integrated combination of planning, training, exercises, personnel qualification and certification standards, equipment acquisition and certification standards, and publication management processes and activities.

Planning also takes center stage in the ICS model. Plans describe how personnel, equipment, and other resources are used to support incident management and emergency response activities. Plans provide mechanisms and systems for setting priorities, integrating multiple entities and functions, and ensuring that communications and other systems are available and integrated in support of a full spectrum of incident management requirements.

Other characteristics of the ICS emphasize the importance of training for personnel—not only for internal agency preparation but also multiagency coordination. NIMS training modules are professionally developed and widely available to the professional community. For a survey of NIMS classes, see Table 5.1.[26]

NIMS command staff author realistic training exercises in which organizations and personnel participate. Interoperability and other multiagency interactions are the key thrusts in these exercises. Drills and exercises are often used to test disaster and emergency response plans and to provide qualitative and quantitative measurements as to the effectiveness of the plan. Exercises that involve responders from multiple disciplines and multiple jurisdictions are the best way to measure the incorporation of NIMS principles and practices and provide a measurement criterion for NIMS compliance.

The ICS provides mechanisms for personnel, institutions, and equipment to be certified or officially endorsed. NIMS provides a checklist for compliance with its standards. NIMS is presently developing a credentialing program for particular occupations in homeland security. Called the National Emergency Responder Credentialing System, it will document minimum professional qualifications, certifications, training, and education requirements that define the standards required for specific emergency response functional positions.

Job titles under consideration for the credential program are

- Incident management
- Emergency medical services

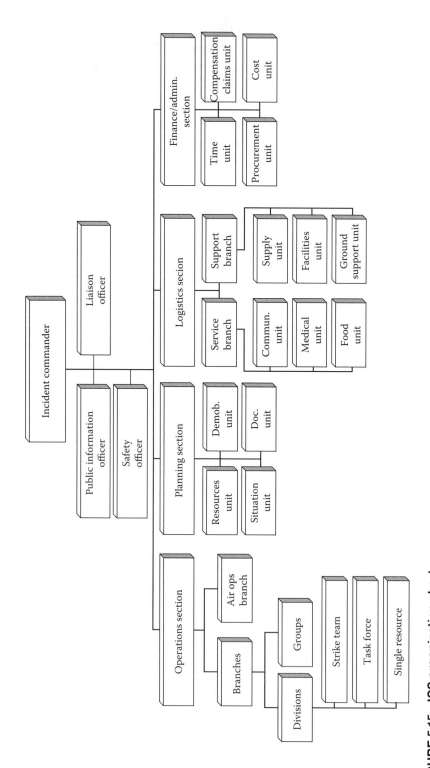

FIGURE 5.15 ICS organization chart.

TABLE 5.1 NIMS Class List

Course Code	Course Title	CEUs	College Credits
IS-1.a	Emergency Manager: An Orientation to the Position—(2/7/2013)	0.6	1.0
IS-3	Radiological Emergency Management—(10/31/2013)	1	1.0
IS-5.a	An Introduction to Hazardous Materials—(10/31/2013)	1	1.0
IS-8.a	Building for the Earthquakes of Tomorrow: Complying with Executive Order 12699—(10/31/2013)	1	1.0
IS-10.a	Animals in Disasters: Awareness and Preparedness—(10/2/2015)	0.4	1.0
IS-11.a	Animals in Disasters: Community Planning—(10/2/2015)	0.5	1.0
IS-15.b	Special Events Contingency Planning for Public Safety Agencies—(10/31/2013)	0.4	1.0
IS-18.16	FEMA EEO Employee Course 2016—(1/4/2016)	0.1	1.0
IS-19.16	FEMA EEO Supervisor Course 2016—(1/4/2016)	0.2	1.0
IS-20.15	Diversity Awareness—(1/2/2015)	0.1	1.0
IS-21.16	Civil Rights and FEMA Disaster Assistance—(1/4/2016)	0.1	1.0
IS-22	Are You Ready? An In-depth Guide to Citizen Preparedness—(10/31/2013)	1	1.0
IS-26	Guide to Points of Distribution—(8/11/2010)	0.4	1.0
IS-27	Orientation to FEMA Logistics—(10/31/2013)	0.4	1.0
IS-29	Public Information Officer Awareness—(10/31/2013)	0.2	1.0

- Fire/hazardous materials
- Law enforcement
- Medical and public health, public works
- Search and rescue

Institutions can be certified as compliant with NIMS standards and requirements (see Figure 5.16).

NIMS fosters interagency cooperation by recognizing the need for mutual aid and cooperation rather than insular turf protection. NIMS encourages governmental entities to enter into formal agreements to assist one another in the event of disaster or a terrorist event.

NIMS CERTIFICATION

Please sign and return this form with your Homeland Security Grant Program

I certify that _____ (Jurisdiction/Tribe/Agency Name) has successfully complied with the following 23 NIMS compliance requirements ("taken as a whole") as directed by the NIMS Integration Center and the U.S. Department of Homeland Security for the Homeland Security Grant Programs.

Jurisdiction Adoption and Infrastructure

- Adopted NIMS at the jurisdictional/tribal/agency level as well as promoted and encouraged jurisdiction-wide adoption.
- Established a planning process to ensure the communication and implementation of NIMS requirements across the jurisdiction. This process must provide a means for measuring progress and facilitate reporting.
- Designated a single point of contact within the jurisdictional government to serve as the principal coordinator for NIMS implementation jurisdiction-wide.
- To the extent permissible by law, ensured that federal preparedness funding to the jurisdiction/tribe/agency is linked to satisfactory progress in meeting the requirements related to FY06 NIMS implementation requirements.
- To the extent permissible by jurisdictional/tribal/agency law, audit agencies, and review organizations routinely included NIMS implementation requirements in all audits associated with federal preparedness grant funds. This process will validate the self-certification process for NIMS compliance.

Command and Management

- Incident Command System (ICS): Managed all emergency incidents and preplanned (recurring/special) events in accordance with ICS organizational structure, doctrine, and procedures, as defined in NIMS. ICS implementation must have included the consistent application of Incident Action Planning and Common Communication Plans.
- Multi-agency Coordination System: Coordinated and supported emergency incident and event management through the development and use of integrated multi-agency coordination systems.
- Public Information System: Institutionalized, within the framework of ICS, the Public Information System, comprising of the Joint Information System (JIS) and a Joint Information Center (JIC). The public Information System ensures an organized, integrated, and coordinated mechanism to perform critical emergency information, crisis communications and public affairs functions which is timely, accurate, and consistent. This includes training for designated participants from the jurisdiction/tribe/agency management and key agencies.

Preparedness: Planning

- Established the jurisdiction's NIMS baseline against the FY05 and FY06 implementation requirements.
- Coordinated and leveraged all federal preparedness funding to implement the NIMS.
- Revised and updated plans and SOPs to incorporate NIMS and National Response Plan (NRP) components, principles and policies, to include planning, training, response, exercises, equipment, evaluation, and corrective actions.
- Promoted intrastate and interagency mutual aid agreements, to include agreements with the private sector and non-governmental organizations.

Preparedness: Training

- Leveraged training facilities to coordinate and deliver NIMS training requirements in conformance with the NIMS National Standard Curriculum.
- Completed IS-700 NIMS: An Introduction

FIGURE 5.16 NIMS certification.

- Completed IS-800 NRP: An Introduction
- Completed ICS 100 and ICS 200 Training

Preparedness: Exercises

- Incorporated NIMS/ICS into all regional and jurisdictional training and exercises.
- Participated in an all-hazard exercise program based on NIMS that involves responders from multiple disciplines and multiple jurisdictions.
- Incorporated corrective actions into preparedness and response plans and procedures.

Resource Management

- Inventoried jurisdictional response assets to conform to Homeland Security resource typing standards.
- Developed state plans for the receipt and distribution of resources as outlined in the National Response Plan (NRP) Catastrophic Incident Annex and Catastrophic Incident Supplement.
- To the extent permissible by state and local law, ensured that relevant national standards and guidance to achieve equipment, communication and data interoperability are incorporated into state and local acquisition programs.

Communication and Information Management

- Applied standardized and consistent terminology, including the establishment of plain English communication standards across public safety sector.

(Name & Title of Jurisdictional Official): _____

(Name of Jurisdiction/Tribe/Agency): _____

Signature: _____ Date: _____

Exceptions to the above (please list): _____

FIGURE 5.16 (Continued)

See the sample mutual aid agreement, courtesy of the Minnesota Municipalities Utilities Association, in Figure 5.17.

The ICS plays a central role in the publication of NIMS forms and publications and educational materials. NIMS, as part of its mission, seeks out its constituencies with an educational aim.

The ICS is charged with the management of resources relating to a given incident. NIMS establishes requirements for inventory and the mobilization, dispatch, tracking, and recovery of resources over the life cycle of an incident. In addition, NIMS provides a standardized protocol for all communications and media at every level of incident management, including the sharing of information among all interested agencies, the implementation of interoperable communication systems, and the storage and management of information relating to the incident (see Figure 5.18).

Internet Resource: To access the entire NIMS guide, published by FEMA, see http://www.fema.gov/nims-doctrine-supporting-guides-tools.

MUTUAL AID AGREEMENT

In consideration of the mutual commitments given herein each of the Signatories to this Mutual Aid Agreement agrees to render aid to any of the other Signatories as follows:

1. Request for aid. The Requesting Signatory agrees to make its request in writing to the Aiding Signatory within a reasonable time after aid is needed and with reasonable specificity. The Requesting Signatory agrees to compensate the Aiding Signatory as specified in this Agreement and in other agreements that may be in ef fect between the Requesting and Aiding Signatories.

2. Discretionary rendering of aid. Rendering of aid is entirely at the discretion of the Aiding Signatory. The agreement to render aid is expressly not contingent upon a declaration of a major disaster or emergency by the federal government or upon receiving federal funds.

3. Invoice to the Requesting Signatory. Within 90 days of the return to the home work station of all labor and equipment of the Aiding Signatory, the Aiding Signatory shall submit to the Requesting Signatory an invoice of all charges related to the aid provided pursuant to this Agreement. The invoice shall contain only charges related to the aid provided pursuant to this Agreement.

4. Charges to the Requesting Signatory. Charges to the Requesting Signatory from the Aiding Signatory shall be as follows:
   a. Labor force. Charges for labor force shall be in accordance with the Aiding Signatory's standard practices.
   b. Equipment. Charges for equipment, such as bucket trucks, digger derricks, and other special equipment used by the Aiding Signatory, shall be at the reasonable and customary rates for such equipment in the Aiding Signatory's location.
   c. Transportation. The Aiding Signatory shall transport needed personnel and equipment by reasonable and customary means and shall charge reasonable and customary rates for such transportation.
   d. Meals, lodging, and other related expenses. Charges for meals, lodging, and other expenses related to the provision of aid pursuant to this Agreement shall be the reasonable and actual costs incurred by the Aiding Signatory.

5. Counterparts. The Signatories may execute this Mutual Aid Agreement in one or more counterparts, with each counterpart being deemed an original Agreement, but with all counterparts being considered one Agreement.

6. Execution. Each party hereto has read, agreed to, and executed this Mutual Aid Agreement on the date indicated.

Date _____   Entity

_____ By

Title_____

FIGURE 5.17   Mutual aid agreement.

NIMS is an ongoing process with improvements, refinements, and adjustments occurring on a regular basis. From another perspective, NIMS builds on its infrastructure year by year. NIMS, being of relatively young design, learns from both its successes and failures. In directing agencies to implement the program, it looks not only to the present requirements but also to past demands and future expectations. NIMS expects the agency to track its history and trace its evolution in the process. See Figure 5.19 for this historical approach.

Incident Radio Communications Plan		1. INCIDENT NAME	2. DATE/TIME PREPARED	3. OPERATIONAL PERIOD DATE/TIME
4. BASE RADIO CHANNEL UTILIZATION				
SYSTEM/CACHE	CHANNEL	FUNCTION	FREQUENCY/TONE	ASSIGNMENT	REMARKS
5. PREPARED BY (COMMUNICATIONS UNIT)				

FIGURE 5.18   Incident radio communications plan.

5.9 Conclusion

Identifying risk, threats, and hazards is the first piece in the homeland security puzzle. Homeland security professionals must prepare, plan for, and respond to these potential risks. Hence, the role of training and exercises that anticipate these harms is crucial in any homeland security plan. DHS stresses training for all eventualities, as evidenced through its organizational structure, budgets and grants, and core competencies. The DHS Office of G&T is the funding mechanism for training. DHS coordinates major training events, at a national scale through its TOPOFF program. The emergency side of homeland training is centered at EMI, which delivers a bevy of programs for first responders. In the world of WMD, the CDP is considered the key trainer. All training for homeland security is evaluated by HSEEP, which delivers standardized methodology and terminology for exercise design, development, and planning. HSEEP regularly promulgates best practices for the homeland security industry. Specialized training for critical infrastructure holds a prominent place in the training portion of the homeland mission. Other training modalities include the HSDL, LLIS, AARs, CERTs, and NIMS—a planning process for institutions, in both the private and the public sectors, that anticipates threat and hazard.

How homeland security professionals respond to and recover from threats and hazards is keenly dealt with in this chapter. Response is how government attends to the event in an immediate sense. The lessons learned from both Hurricane Katrina and Hurricane Sandy say much about the importance of response. DHS publishes a National Response Framework

FEMA   NIMS IMPLEMENTATION ACTIVITY SCHEDULE

The matrix below summarizes by Federal Fiscal Year (FY) all ongoing NIMS implementation activities that have been prescribed by the NIMS Integration Center in FYs 2005 and 2006, as well as the seven new activities for states and territories and six new activities for tribes and local jurisdictions required in FY 2007. State territorial, tribal, and local jurisdictions should in mind that implementation activities from previous fiscal years remain on-going commitments in the present fiscal year. Jurisdictions must continue to support all implementation activities, required or underway in order to achieve NIMS bear compliance.

Future refinement of the NIMS will evolve as policy and technical issues are further developed and clarified. As a result, the NIMS Integration Center may issue additional requirements to delineate what constitutes NIMS compliance in FY 2008 and beyond. With the completion of the FY 2007 activities, state, territorial, tribal, and local jurisdictions will have the foundational support for future NIMS implementation and compliance. The effective and consistent implementation of the NIMS nationwide will result in a strengthened national capability to prevent, prepare for, respond to and recover from any type of incident.

	NIMS IMPLEMENTATION ACTIVITY	FY 2007 STATE/TERRITORY	FY 2007 TRIBAL/LOCAL	FY 2006 STATE/TERRITORY	FY 2006 TRIBAL/LOCAL	FY 2005 STATE/TERRITORY	FY 2005 TRIBAL/LOCAL
ADOPTION	1. Support the successful adoption and implementation of the NIMS.					✓	✓
	2. Adopted NIMS for all government departments and agencies; as well as promote and encourage NIMS adoption by associations, utilities, non-governmental organizations (NGOs), and private sector incident management and response organizations.			✓	✓		
	3. Monitor formal adoption of NIMS by all tribal and local jurisdictions.			✓			
	4. Establish a planning process to ensure the communication and implementation of NIMS requirements, thereby providing a means for measuring progress and facilitate reporting.		✓	✓			
	5. Designate a single point of contact to serve as the principal coordinator for NIMS implementation.			✓			
	6. Designate a single point of contact within each of the jurisdiction's Departments and Agencies.	✓					
COMMAND & MANAGEMENT	7. To the extent permissible by law, ensure that Federal preparedness funding, including DHS Homeland Security General Program and the Urban Areas Security Initiative (UASI) support NIMS implementation at the state and local levels and incorporate NIMS into existing training programs and exercises.					✓	
	8. To the extent permissible by law, ensure that federal preparedness funding to state and territorial agencies and tribal and local jurisdictions is linked to satisfactory process in meeting FY2006 NIMS implementation requirements.			✓	✓		
	9. To the extent permissible by state and territorial law and regulations, audit agencies and review organizations routinely include NIMS implementation requirements in all audits associated with federal preparedness grant funds validating the self-certification process for NIMS compliance.			✓			
	10. Monitor and assess outreach and implementation of NIMS Requirements.	✓					
	11. Coordinate and provide technical assistance to local entities regarding NIMS institutionalized use of ICS.		✓			✓	
	12. Manage all emergency incident and pre-planned (recurring/special) events in accordance with ICS organizational structures, doctrine and procedures, as defined in NIMS. ICS implementation must include the consistent application of Incident Action Planning and Common Communications Plans.			✓	✓		
	13. Coordinate and support emergency incident and event management through the development and use of integrated multi-agency coordination systems, i.e develop and maintain connectivity capability between local Incident Command Posts (ICP) local 911 Centers, local Emergency Operations Centers (EOCs), the state EOC and regional and federal EOCs and NRP organizational elements.			✓	✓		
	14. Institutionalize, within the transmission of ICS the Public Information System (PIS), comprising the Joint Information Systems (JIS) and a Joint Information Center (JIC).			✓	✓		
	15. Establish public information system to gather, verify, coordinate, and disseminate information during an incident.	✓	✓				
	16. Establish NIMS baseline against the FY2005 and FY2006 implementation requirements.			✓	✓		
	17. Develop and implement a system to coordinate and leverage all federal preparedness funding to implement the NIMS.			✓	✓		

FIGURE 5.19   NIMS implementation activity schedule.

PREPAREDNESS PLANNING	18. Incorporate NIMS into Emergency Operation Plans (EOP).						
	19. Revise and update plans and SOPs to incorporate NIMS and National Response Plan (NRP) components, principles and polices, to include planning, training, response, exercises, equipment, evaluation, and corrective actions.			✓	✓	✓	
	20. Promote intrastate mutual aid agreements, to include agreements with private sector and non-governmental organizations.			✓	✓	✓	✓
PREPAREDNESS TRAINING	21. Participate in and promote intrastate and interagency mutual aid agreements, to include agreements with the private sector and non-governmental organizations.			✓	✓		
	22. Leverage training facilities to coordinate and deliver NIMS training requirements in conformance with the NIMS National Standard Curriculum.			✓			
	23. Complete-training—IS-700 *NIMS, An introduction, IS-800 NRP, An introduction*, ICS-100 and ICS-200.			✓	✓	✓	
	24. Complete training—ICS-300, ICS-400.	✓				✓	
	25. Incorporate NIMS/ICS into training and exercises.					✓	✓
PREPAREDNESS EXERCISES	26. Participate in an all-hazard exercise program based on NIMS that involves responders from multiple disciplines and multiple jurisdictions.			✓	✓		
	27. Incorporate corrective actions into preparedness and response plans and procedures.			✓	✓		
	28. Inventory response assets to conform to FEMA Resource Typing standards.			✓	✓		
RESOURCE MANAGEMENT	29. Develop state plans for the receipt and distribution of responses as outlined in the National Response Plan (NRP) Catastrophic incident Annex and Catastrophic incident Supplement.			✓			
	30. To the extent Permissible by state and local law, ensure that relevant national standards and guidance to achieve equipment, communication and data interoperability are incorporated into state and local acquisition programs.			✓	✓		
	31. Validate that inventory of response assets conform to FEMA Resource Typing Standards.	✓	✓	✓			
	32. Utilize response assets inventory for mutual aid requests, exercises, and actual events.	✓	✓	✓			
COMMUNICATION & INFORMATION MANAGEMENT	33. Apply standardized and consistent terminology, including the establishment of plain language communications standards across public safety sector.	✓		✓	✓		
	34. Develop systems and processes to ensure that incident managers at all levels share a common operating picture of an incident.	✓	✓	✓			

FIGURE 5.19 (Continued).

(NRF) to guide homeland and governmental agencies. The framework stresses the need to partner and work collaboratively, the necessity for layers of government to work in unity, the recognition that one command will corral these various constituencies, and that flexibility and readiness in response are central to the mission.

Keywords

After-Action Reports
Assistance to Firefighters Grant
Best practices
Center for Domestic Preparedness
Chemical, Ordnance, Biological, and Radiological Training Facility
Community Emergency Response Teams
Compliance standards
Continuing education
Credentialing
Disaster Field Training Organization
Disaster preparedness
Discussion-based exercises
Emergency Management Institute
EMI Independent Study Program
Fire Prevention and Safety Grant
Fire safety
Homeland Security Exercise and Evaluation Program

HSEEP exercises
Incident Command System
In-service training
Lessons Learned Information Sharing
National Domestic Preparedness Consortium
National Emergency Responder Credentialing System
National Incident Management System
National Integration Center
NIMS certification
Office of Grants and Training
Operations-based exercises
Residential training facility
Search and rescue
TOPOFF exercise
U.S. Fire Administration

Discussion Questions

1. Discuss the importance of training in the world of homeland security.
2. Critics of DHS frequently cite the agency's tendency to bite off more than it can chew. In the area of training, is this legitimate?
3. Explain the critical function of EMI.
4. Why did DHS design and implement HSEEP?
5. Discuss how homeland professionals train for the protection of critical infrastructure.
6. Of what import is the LLIS program? How does such a program benefit homeland leaders?
7. What are the general goals of NIMS?
8. Why is it essential that an ICS be implemented?
9. What is the value of a NIMS certification program?
10. Explain the philosophy of the NRF. In particular, comment on why shared responsibility is so important in the NRF.

Practical Exercises

1. Collect and collate a NIMS file. Prepare an index of these documents.
2. Draft a NIMS implementation plan for your place of work. Use the FEMA template for the implementation at https://www.fema.gov/planning-templates.
3. Contact your statewide DHS office. Determine whether a TOPOFF exercise will occur in your region.
4. Contact a local police department. Find out if that office has applied for DHS training funds.
5. Write to EMI for a course catalog.
6. Find out where CERTs exist in your area.

Notes

1. DHS, FEMA, Office of G&T, G&T Mission, http://ojp.gov/funding/.
2. FEMA, *Grant Programs Directorate Strategic Plan, FY 2009–2010*, October 9, 2008.
3. Ibid.
4. Ibid.
5. Office of the President, *Homeland Security Presidential Directive* 8, December 17, 2003.
6. DHS press release, DHS announces grant allocations for fiscal year (FY) 2015 preparedness grants (July 28, 2015), available at http://www.dhs.gov/news/2015/07/28/dhs-announces-grant-allocations-fiscal-year-fy-2015-preparedness-grants.
7. DHS, *Fact Sheet: National Level Exercise 2012* (June 5, 2012), available at https://www.dhs.gov/news/2012/06/05/fact-sheet-national-level-exercise-2012; *FEMA, National Level Exercise 2012 Quick Look Report* (March 2013), available at http://www.fema.gov/media-library-data/20130726-1911-25045-9856/national_level_exercise_2012_quick_look_report.pdf.
8. See M. Paddock, Get your fire grants while they last, *Homeland Security Today*, August 2011: 8.
9. FEMA, EMI, History at https://training.fema.gov/history.aspx, accessed January 10, 2016.
10. FEMA, EMI, Disaster Field Training Operations, Mission, at https://training.fema.gov/programs/dfto, accessed January 10, 2016.
11. FEMA, EMI, History at https://training.fema.gov/history.aspx, accessed January 10, 2016.
12. FEMA, EMI, EMI School Program, available at https://training.fema.gov/programs/emischool/emischool.aspx, accessed January 10, 2016; W. D. Jones, Recruiting future safety professionals, 60 *Professional Safety* 22 (2015).
13. DHS, Critical Infrastructure Sectors, available at http://www.dhs.gov/critical-infrastructure-sectors, accessed January 10, 2016; Presidential Policy Directive/PPD-21, Critical Infrastructure Security and Resilience, (February 12, 2013), available at http://www.whitehouse.gov/the-press-office/2013/02/12/presidential-policy-directive-critical-infrastructure-security-and-resil, accessed January 10, 2016.
14. Practitioners are generally favorable to the reality-based exercise. HSEEP stress that sort of training as well as scenario-based learning. See D. R. Hales and P. Race, Applying a framework of defining emergency management scenarios, *Journal of Emergency Management*, 9 2011: 15.
15. *DHS, Homeland Security Exercise and Evaluation Program (HSEEP)* Intro-2 (April 2013), available at https://hseep.preptoolkit.org/docs/HSEEP_Revision_Apr13_Final.pdf.
16. DHS, *Homeland Security Exercise and Evaluation Program (HSEEP)* Figure 1.1, at 1–2 (April 2013), available at https://hseep.preptoolkit.org/docs/HSEEP_Revision_Apr13_Final.pdf.
17. DHS, *Homeland Security Exercise and Evaluation Program (HSEEP)* 3–1 (April 2013), available at https://hseep.preptoolkit.org/docs/HSEEP_Revision_Apr13_Final.pdf.

18. DHS, *Homeland Security Exercise and Evaluation Program (HSEEP)* Table 3.1, at 3–11 (April 2013), available at https://hseep.preptoolkit.org/docs/HSEEP_Revision_Apr13_Final.pdf.

19. DHS, *Homeland Security Exercise and Evaluation Program (HSEEP)* Figure 2.1, at 2–3 (April 2013), available at https://hseep.preptoolkit.org/docs/HSEEP_Revision_Apr13_Final.pdf.

20. FEMA, LLIS program, https://www.fema.gov/lessons-learned-information-sharing-program, accessed January 10, 2016.

21. R. Kelly, 10 Years after 9/11: Lessons learned by the New York City Police Department, *Police Chief*, September 2011: 20–25.

22. Naval Postgraduate School, Center for Homeland Defense and Security, Homeland Security Digital Library, at https://www.hsdl.org/, accessed January 10, 2016.

23. A. I. Anderson, D. Compton, and T. Mason, Managing in a dangerous world: The National Incident Management system, *Engineering Management Journal* 16(3) 2004: 114.

24. Office of the President, *Homeland Security Presidential Directive* 5, February (2003): 3.

25. ICS Organization, available at https://training.fema.gov/emiweb/is/icsresource/assets/icsorganization.pdf, last accessed January 10, 2016.

26. FEMA, Emergency Management Institute, ISP Courses, available at https://training.fema.gov/is/crslist.aspx, accessed January 10, 2016.

Chapter 6

DHS Challenges
National versus State and Local, National Security versus Homeland Security

Objectives

1. To evaluate the various national, state, and local relationships relating to homeland security that exist in U.S. government agencies
2. To compare and contrast homeland security agencies at the state level, including their organization, policies, and operating parameters
3. To analyze the many types of homeland security task forces and commissions that exist at the state level
4. To describe the homeland security structures that are in place at the local level and analyze the differences that arise in major metropolitan, urban, suburban, and rural areas
5. To describe fusion centers, their purpose, staffing, and locations
6. To explain the various funding programs available from the federal government for state and local homeland security initiatives
7. To describe current military initiatives specifically relating to homeland security intelligence gathering
8. To describe current military initiatives specifically relating to specialized units dedicated to homeland security and the identification and tracking of weapons of mass destruction (WMDs)

6.1 Introduction

From its earliest conception, the authors of a national Department of Homeland Security (DHS) envisioned the widespread participation of states and localities as the programs and policies of homeland security were implemented. As early as 2004, the shift away from centralized authority had taken root in the culture of homeland security. The department's own *Report from the Task Force on State and Local Homeland Security Funding* unequivocally endorses not only local involvement but local control. In addition, it urges policymakers to author policy from the ground level up rather than it being descended from DHS itself.

> Those at the municipal, state, tribal and federal level responsible for using these funds have a better understanding of what each needs to do to achieve success. Recommendations for major changes would have only added confusion where clarity is emerging. It is our belief that these recommended actions coupled with expected maturity of the program will result in measurable progress towards making the nation safer, stronger, and better.[1]

The federal government, despite its agency status, cannot carry out the local and regional field requirements of DHS, nor would it be wise to over centralize these diverse functions. If history elucidates anything, it is that DHS and its size directly correlate to its level of effectiveness. The larger the enterprise gets, the more an unmanageable beast it becomes. At the outset of DHS, there was an unequivocal understanding concerning shared responsibilities in these matters. Early on in the life of DHS, there was full recognition of the necessity of federal, state, and local interaction. Under the DHS Office of Intelligence and Analysis, there is a structure for such reporting under the "State and Local Program Office" slot (see Figure 6.1).

The National Governors' Association has taken the lead in the statewide role, especially by and through its National Governors' Association (NGA) Center for Best Practices (Figure 6.2[2]).

Intelligence, in order to have any significant meaning in homeland defense (HD), must be naturally and continuously shared rather than protected or hidden due to bureaucratic layers of multiple agencies. Intelligence is the best and most telling example of how important the interaction between state, federal, and local authorities is and must be.[3] President Bush, when recommending the establishment of DHS, wanted to set a tone and mission for the new federal agency. He did, however, allow for states to maintain autonomy as well as have a mechanism for input. By his presidential directive, it was clear that a collaborative and integrative approach in the application of homeland security was the intended goal. Bush noted

> The Federal Government recognizes the roles and responsibilities of State and local authorities in domestic incident management. Initial responsibility for managing domestic incidents generally falls on State and local authorities. The Federal Government will assist State and local authorities when their resources are overwhelmed, or when Federal interests are involved. The Secretary will coordinate with State and local governments to ensure adequate

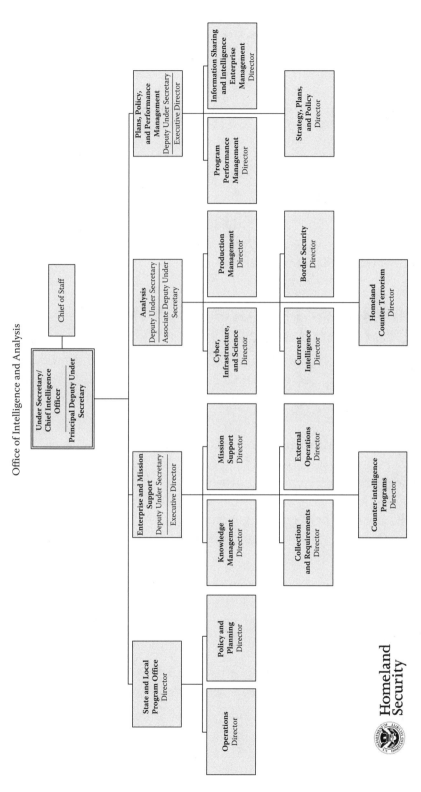

FIGURE 6.1   Department of Homeland Security, Office of Intelligence and Analysis Organizational Chart.

FIGURE 6.2 National Governors' Association Center for Best Practices logo.

planning, equipment, training, and exercise activities. The Secretary will also provide assistance to State and local governments to develop all-hazards plans and capabilities, including those of greatest importance to the security of the United States, and will ensure that State, local, and Federal plans are compatible.[4]

Internet Resource: Become familiar with the nature and structure of our 50 state centers for homeland security by visiting http://www.nga.org/files/live/sites/NGA/files/pdf/2014/HomelandStateGovernanceStructures.pdf.

6.2 Challenge of National Policy at the State and Local Levels

The department itself fully understood the necessity for fruitful and productive relationships with state and local authorities. By setting up the State, Local, Tribal, and Territorial Government Coordinating Council (SLTTGCC), DHS sought the membership of those in the state and local trenches. Membership criteria included

- A state, local, tribal, or territorial homeland security director or equivalent with relevant programmatic planning and operational responsibilities
- Accountable for the development, improvement, and maintenance of critical infrastructure protection policies or programs at the state, local, or tribal level
- Recognized among his or her peers as a leader
- Committed to acting as national representative regarding homeland practices relevant to states and localities

The council conducts much of its business through working groups, charted in Figure 6.3.

Hence, while policy making emanates from the federal system, management inevitably falls to the states and localities. How these policies are carried out, and whether they can be carried out, is a question more appropriate for the local level.

6.2.1 Structure at the State Level

Relevant departments and agencies of the federal government must take the lead in implementing this system, while state and local governments must implement and adopt homeland policies consistent with DHS policy. State homeland security entities were created to ensure that states were prepared at the frontlines for terrorist attacks. State entities provide a structural entity for a mission of state protections by coordinating the various needs

Working Groups, State, Local, Tribal and Territorial Government Coordinating Council

Working groups for the State, Local, Tribal and Territorial Government Coordinating Council, which works with the federal government and critical infrastructure/key resources owners to protect the nation's critical infrastructure.

Access Credentialing Working Group (ACWG)

The ACWG is responsible for reviewing all current national credentialing efforts including existing working groups and policies/guidelines.

The working group is responsible for providing recommendations on how to enhance the collaboration of all the existing credentialing efforts.

Automated Critical Asset Management System Working Group (ACAMSWG)

The ACAMSWG is responsible for reviewing and developing baseline training for the ACAMS program by providing the SLTT perspective in close collaboration with the Infrastructure Information Collection Division of the Department's Office of Infrastructure Protection.

This work includes, but is not limited to,

- developing user requirements,
- requesting technology to facilitate requirements, and
- performing essential outreach to the State, Local, Tribal, and Territorial (SLTT) critical infrastructure community for the ACAMS project.

Cybersecurity Working Group (CSWG)

The CSWG is responsible for developing guidance for and advocating on behalf of SLTT governments, in relation to efforts to enhance cybersecurity and resilience.

The working group also serves as the Council's point of contact for Federal requests for input on cyber initiatives and proposals.

Homeland Security Advisor Working Group (HSAWG)

The HSAWG is responsible for bridging any communication gaps that exist with the Governor's Homeland Security Advisory Council (GHSAC).

The working group is also responsible for incorporating state critical infrastructure protection managers into the SLTTGCC.

Information Sharing Working Group (ISWG)

The ISWG is responsible for monitoring and improving the critical infrastructure information sharing environment between federal, SLTT, and private sector partners as well as assisting in the development of collaborative partnerships and mechanisms to share critical infrastructure information. They also facilitate the generation and collection of feedback on SLTTGCC and DHS initiatives and coordinate with the HITRAC and works to provide SLTT feedback and input on programs such as IRAPP and Virtual USA.

IP Gateway Working Group (IPGWG)

The IP Gateway WG is an integral part of the development of system requirements for the IP Gateway suite of tools and an advocate on behalf of SLTT governments, in relation to DHS' efforts to undertake assessment tool integration and broader data sharing and analytics and implement initiatives in support of broader information sharing and data analysis.

The working group also serves as the Council's point of contact for Federal requests for input on physical security assessment tools and proposals.

Policy and Planning Working Group (PPWG)

The PPWG is responsible for reviewing and providing feedback to the Department regarding federal and SLTT guidelines regarding critical infrastructure protection.

In particular, the PPWG considers how these guidelines interact with SLTT efforts in order to help ensure the smooth implementation of actionable national critical infrastructure policies conducive to successful federal and SLTT critical infrastructure protection efforts.

FIGURE 6.3 State, Local, Tribal, and Territorial Government Coordinating Council working groups.

This mission entails detailed PPWG review of national plans and strategies such as the NIPP Sector Specific Plans (SSPs), the National Response Framework, and the National Annual CIKR Report to provide feedback and input from the SLTT perspective.

Regional Resiliency Assessment Program Working Group (RRAPWG)

The RRAPWG serves as an open line of communication between the state officials undertaking RRAPs and DHS representatives executing the program.

The working group is responsible for collaborating to devise solutions for problems with the RRAP in order to make the RRAP worthwhile for all states.

State Asset Criteria Working Group (SACWG)

The SACWG was created to help develop best practices for establishing prioritization criteria for critical infrastructure sites, facilities, and assets within an SLTT jurisdiction.

The working group's goal is to provide flexible guidelines that can apply to State and local governments in all phases of the prioritization process.

Tribal and Territorial Working Group (TTWG)

The TTWG was created to help raise awareness of issues specific to tribal nations and territories.

They are responsible for creating greater visibility of tribal and territorial viewpoints and needs within the Partnership and beyond.

FIGURE 6.3   (Continued).

of the governor's office, the homeland security director, the state emergency management office, other state agencies, local governments, the private sector, volunteer organizations, and the federal government. Every state erected an Office of Homeland Security soon after 9/11. The current compendium includes those offices shown in Figure 6.4.

How states choose to construct their Offices of Homeland Security is unique to the given jurisdiction. Most states relied on the governor to designate a person to be a homeland security director. The position is advisory panel and agency driven, as well as the office where related functions of homeland security are coordinated, such as emergency management, law enforcement, health, and related public safety functions. To see a common design, review the example from Louisiana in Figure 6.5.

Some states tackle the many demands of homeland security better than others. To be certain, New York State, due to its 9/11 connection and having an already highly trained law enforcement emergency community, represents a splendid example of skill and determination in the defense of the homeland and the active prevention of terror.[5] Aside from this traditional outlook, New York State has done a very effective job in dealing with the risk and emergency side of things. The entire state has been broken down into response regions for emergency purposes (see Figure 6.6).[6]

Other designs incorporate existing offices at the state level, such as the adjutant general, the National Guard, or specialized task forces that are composed of executive office staff and agency heads from law enforcement, fire and rescue, public health, and public works.

States are increasingly being asked to assume more under homeland security protocols. For some, the farther away from federal control the process is, the more effective. DHS itself

State Homeland Security Contacts						
Alabama	Spencer Collier	Alabama Department of Homeland Security	PO BOX 1471	Montgomery, Ala. 36130-4115	334-353-3050	www.alea.gov
	Director					
Alaska	Mike O'Hare	Alaska Division of Homeland Security & Emergency Services	P.O. Box 5750	Ft. Richardson, Alaska 99505	907-428-7062	www.ak-prepared.com/
	Director	Department of Military and Veteran Affairs	Bldg. 4900, Suite B-214			
Arizona	Gilbert M. Orrantia	Arizona Department of Homeland Security	1700 West Washington Street, #210	Phoenix, Ariz. 85007	602-364-1521	http://www.azdohs.gov/
	Director					
Arkansas	Dave Maxwell	Arkansas Department of Emergency Management	Building 9501	North Little Rock, Ark. 72119-9600	501-683-6700	www.adem.arkansas.gov
	Director		Camp Robinson			
California	Mark Ghilarducci	CAL OES Governor's Office of Emergency Services	3650 Schriever Avenue	Mather, Calif. 95655	916-845-8510	www.caloes.ca.gov
	Acting Secretary					
Colorado	Stan Hikey	Colorado Department of Public Safety	700 Kipling Street	Denver, Colo. 80215	303-239-4400	http://cdpsweb.state.co.us/
	Executive Director					
Connecticut	Bill Hackett	Department of Emergency Services and Public Protection Emergency Management & Homeland Security	25 Sigourney Street	Hartford, Conn. 06106-5042	860-256-0800	http://www.ct.gov/demhs/
	Emergency Management Director					
Delaware	James N. Mosey	Department of Safety and Homeland Security	303 Transportation Circle	Dover, Del. 19903	302-744-2680	http://dshs.delaware.gov/
	Cabinet Secretary		P.O. Box 818			
District of Columbia	Chris T. Geldhart	Homeland Security & Emergency Management Agency	2720 Martin Luther King Jr. Avenue, SE	Washington, D.C. 20032	202-727-6161	www.hsema.dc.gov
	Director					
Florida	Richard L. Swearingen	Florida Department of Law Enforcement	P.O. Box 1489	Tallahassee, Fla. 32302-1489	850-410-7000	www.fdle.state.fl.us
	Commissioner					
Georgia	Jim Butterworth	Georgia Emergency Management Agency/ Homeland Security	P.O. Box 18055	Atlanta, Ga. 30316-0055	404-635-7000	www.gema.ga.gov
	Director					
Hawaii	MG Arthur J. Logan	Hawaii Emergency Management Agency	3949 Diamond Head Rd.	Honolulu, Hawaii 96816-4495	808-733-4300	808-733-4300
	Director					

FIGURE 6.4 **List of state homeland security office contacts.**

Idaho	William B. (Brad) Richy Director	Bureau of Homeland Security	4040 West Guard Street, Bldg 600	Boise, Idaho 83705-5004	208-422-3040	www.bhs.idaho.gov
Illinois	James K. Joseph Director	Illinois Emergency Management Agency	2200 South Dirksen Parkway	Springfield, Ill. 62703	217-782-2700	www.illinois.gov/iema
Indiana	David Kane Executive Director	Indiana Department of Homeland Security	Indiana Government Center South 302 W. Washington Street, Rm. E-208	Indianapolis, Ind. 46204	317-232-3980	www.in.gov/dhs/
Iowa	Mark Schouten Director	Iowa Homeland Security and Emergency Management Division	7900 Hickman Road, Suite 500	Windsor Heights, IA 50324	515-725-3231	http://homelandsecurity.iowa.gov
Kansas	Major General Lee Tafanelli Homeland Security Advisor	Kansas Adjutant General's Department	2800 SW Topeka	Topeka, Kan. 66611-1287	785-274-1190	http://kansastag.ks.gov/kshls_default.asp
Kentucky	Gene Kiser Executive Director	Kentucky Office of Homeland Security	200 Mero Street	Frankfort, Ky. 40622	502-564-2081	http://homelandsecurity.ky.gov/
Louisiana	Kevin Davis Director	Governor's Office of Homeland Security and Emergency Preparedness	7667 Independence Blvd	Baton Rouge, La. 70806	225-925-7500	www.gohsep.la.gov
Maine	Brigadier General Gerard F. Bolduc	Department of Defense, Veterans & Emergency Management	33 State House Station, Camp Keyes	Augusta, Maine 04333-0001	207-626-4271	http://www.maine.gov/dvem/
Maryland	Thomas E. (Tim) Hutchins Homeland Security Advisor	State of Maryland Executive Department Governor's Homeland Security Office	The Jeffrey Building 16 Francis Street	Annapolis, Md. 21401	410-974-3901	www.gov.state.md.us/homelandsecurity.html
Massachusetts	Daniel Bennett Secretary	Executive Office of Public Safety and Security	1 Ashburton Place, Rm. 2133	Boston, Mass. 02108	517-332-2521	http://www.mass.gov/eopss/
Michigan	COL. Kriste Kibbey Etue Homeland Security Advisor	Michigan State Police	333 S. Grand Avenue P.O. 30634	Lansing, Mich. 48909	517-241-0401	www.michigan.gov/homeland/
Minnesota	Joe Kelly Director	Homeland Security & Emergency Management	444 Cedar Street	St. Paul, Minn. 55101	651-201-7400	https://dps.mn.gov/divisions/hsem/Pages/default.aspx
Mississippi	Everett L. (Rusty) Barnes, Jr. Executive Director	Mississippi Office of Homeland Security	P.O. Box 958	Jackson, Miss. 39205	601-346-1500	www.homelandsecurity.ms.gov

FIGURE 6.4   (Continued).

Missouri	Lane Roberts	Missouri Department of Public Safety	P.O. Box 749	Jefferson City, Mo. 65102	573-522-3007	www.dps.mo.gov/homelandsecurity/
	Director					
Montana	Steve Knecht	Disaster & Emergency Services	P.O. Box 4789 - 1956 Mt Majo Street	Fort Harrison, Mont. 59636	406-324-4777	http://dma.mt.gov/DES/default.asp
	Division Administrator	Department of Military Affairs				
Nebraska	Adjutant General, Major General Daryl Bohac	Nebraska Emergency Management Agency	2433 N.W. 24th Street	Lincoln, Neb. 68524-1801	402-471-7421	http://www.nema.ne.gov/preparedness/homeland-security-home.html
	Director					
Nevada	Christopher Smith	Department of Public Safety	2478 Fairview Drive	Carson City, Nev. 89701	775-687-0300	http://homelandsecurity.nv.gov/
	Chief of Emergency Management	Division of Emergency Management - Homeland Security				
New Hampshire	Perry Plummer	Division of Homeland Security and Emergency Management	33 Hazen Drive	Concord, N.H. 03305	800-735-2964	http://www.nh.gov/safety/divisions/hsem/index.html
	Director					
New Jersey	Dr. Chris Rodriquez	New Jersey Office of Homeland Security and Preparedness	P.O. Box 091	Trenton, N.J. 08625	609-584-4000	www.njhomelandsecurity.gov
	Director					
New Mexico	M. Jay Mitchell	New Mexico Deptartment of Homeland Security & Emergency Management	13 Bataan Blvd.	Santa Fe, N.M. 87508	505-476-9600	http://nmdhsem.org
	Secretary					
New York	James Sherry	Homeland Security and Emergency Services	1220 Washington Avenue	Albany, N.Y. 12242	518-242-5000	http://www.dhses.ny.gov/oct/
	Acting Commissioner & Director		State Office Campus- Building 7A Suite 710			
North Carolina	Frank Perry	Department of Public Safety	4201 Mail Service Center	Raleigh, N.C. 27699	919-733-2126	www.nccrimecontrol.org
	Secretary					
North Dakota	Greg Wilz	Homeland Security Division	P.O. Box 5511	Bismarck, N.D. 58506	701-328-8100	www.nd.gov/des/
	Director	Department of Emergency Services				
Ohio	Richard L. Zwayer II	Ohio Homeland Security	1970 W. Broad Street	Columbus, Ohio 43223-1102	614-387-6171	www.homelandsecurity.ohio.gov
	Executive Director					
Oklahoma	Kim Edd Carter	Oklahoma Office of Homeland Security	P.O. Box 11415	Oklahoma City, Okla. 73136-0415	405-425-7296	www.homelandsecurity.ok.gov/
	Director					
Oregon	Brigadier General Michael E. Stencel	Oregon Military Department	P.O. Box 14350	Salem, Ore. 97309-5047	503-584-3991	http://www.oregon.gov/OMD/
	Homeland Security Advisor					

FIGURE 6.4   (Continued).

Pennsylvania	Tyree Blocker	Pennsylvania State Police	1800 Elmerton Avenue	Harrisburg, Penn. 17110	717-783-5599	http://www.psp.state.pa.us
	Commissioner,					
Puerto Rico	Ramón Rosario Cortes		P.O. Box 9066597	San Juan, P.R. 00906-6597	787-721-0435	
	Homeland Security Advisor					
Rhode Island	Major Lester King	Joint Force Headquarters	645 New London Ave.	Cranston, R.I. 02920	401-275-4100	http://ri.ng.mil/army/jfhq/SitePages/Home.aspx
	Homeland Security Advisor					
South Carolina	Trevor Jones	Department of Public Safety	4400 Broad River Run Road.	Columbia, S.C. 29210	605-773-3178	http://www.sled.sc.gov/HSOfficeHome.aspx?MenuID=HSOffice
	Department Secretary					
South Dakota	James Carpenter	Office of Homeland Security	118 West Capitol Avenue	Pierre, S.D. 57501	605-773-3450	http://dps.sd.gov/homeland_security/default.aspx
	Director					
Tennessee	Bill Gibbons	Tennessee Department of Safety and Homeland Security	1150 Foster Avenue	Nashville, Tenn. 37243	615-251-5166	http://www.tn.gov/homelandsecurity
	Assistant Commissioner					
Texas	Steve McCraw	Texas Department of Public Safety	P.O. Box 4087	Austin, Texas 78773-0001	512-424-2000	https://www.txdps.state.tx.us
	Director					
Utah	Keith D. Squires	Department of Public Safety	4501 South 2700 West	Salt Lake City, Utah 84114-1775	801-965-4461	http://publicsafety.utah.gov
	Deputy Commissioner					
Vermont	Keith Flynn	Department of Public Safety	45 State Drive	Waterbury, Vt. 05671-2101	802-241-5000	http://dps.vermont.gov
	Commissioner					
Virginia	Terri Suit	Secretary of Veterans Affairs & Homeland Security	Patrick Henry Building	Richmond, Va. 23219	804-225-3826	http://www.commonwealthpreparedness.virginia.gov/
			1111 East Broad Street			
Washington	Robert Ezelle	State Military Department	Bldg 1, Camp Murray	Tacoma, WA 98430-5000	253-512-8201	http://mil.wa.gov/index.shtml
	Adjutant General and Director	Emergency Management Division				
West Virginia	Joseph Thornton	Department of Military Affairs and Public Safety	1900 Kanawha Blvd., E. Building 1, Room W-400	Charleston, W.V. 25305	304-558-2930	http://www.dmaps.wv.gov/Pages/default.aspx
	Secretary					
Wisconsin	BG Donald Dunbar	Wisconsin Homeland Security	2400 Wright Street PO Box 14587	Madison, Wisc. 53708-8111	608-242-3000	http://homelandsecurity.wi.gov
	Homeland Security Advisor					

FIGURE 6.4 (Continued).

Wyoming	Guy Cameron	Wyoming Office of Homeland Security	122 W. 25th Street	Cheyenne, Wyo. 82002-0001	307-777-4663	http://wyohomelandsecurity.state.wy.us/main.aspx
	Director		Herschler Bldg 1st Floor East			
Guam	Brigadier General, Johnny Lizama	Guam Homeland Security Office of Civil Defense	221-B Chalan Palasyo	Agana Heights, Guam 96910	671-475-9600	http://ghs.guam.gov
	Homeland Security Advisor					
Northern Mariana Islands	Marvin Seman	Special Advisor for Homeland Security	Caller Box 10007	Saipan, MP 96950	670-322-8004	http://cnmihsem.gov.mp
Virgin Islands	Mona Barnes	USVI Territorial Emergency Management Agency	8221 Estate Nisky	St. Thomas, V.I. 00803	340-774-2244	http://www.vitema.gov/index.html
	Director					
American Samoa	Mike Sala	Department of Homeland Security	American Samoa Government	Pago, Pago, AS 96799	684-633-2827	
	Director					

FIGURE 6.4   (Continued).

realizes the necessity of state and local influence and allots a sizable portion of government funding to advance this ambition. For the fiscal year 2009, the budgetary allotment increased in terms of both size and scope of operations[7] (see Table 6.1).

Tennessee, for example, has a sophisticated network of homeland programs and personnel carrying out the homeland mission. Its overall purpose is as follows:

The Tennessee Office of Homeland Security has the primary responsibility and authority for directing statewide activities pertaining to the prevention of, and protection from, terrorist-related events. This responsibility includes the development and implementation of a comprehensive and coordinated strategy to secure the state from terrorist threats and attacks. Further, the office of Homeland Security serves as a liaison between federal, state, and local agencies, and private sector on matters relating to the security of our state and citizens.

- AWARENESS: Identify and understand terrorist threats within Tennessee.
- PREVENTION: Detect, deter, and mitigate terrorist threats to Tennessee.
- PROTECTION: Safeguard our citizens, their freedoms, property, and the economy of Tennessee from acts of terrorism.
- RESPONSE: Assist in coordinating the response to terrorist-related events.
- ORGANIZATIONAL EXCELLENCE: Putting the safety of our citizens first.[8]

As in other jurisdictions, Tennessee sets out to educate its citizens and to play an instrumental role in the prevention of and protection of its citizens from terror and its threats. It also publishes and adopts protocols for the more typical threats likely to be encountered. An example, in Figure 6.7,[9] deals with cyber-safety threats.

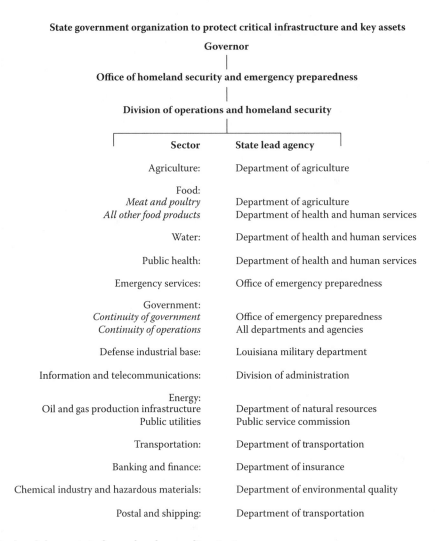

State government organization to protect critical infrastructure and key assets

Governor

Office of homeland security and emergency preparedness

Division of operations and homeland security

Sector	State lead agency
Agriculture:	Department of agriculture
Food:	
Meat and poultry	Department of agriculture
All other food products	Department of health and human services
Water:	Department of health and human services
Public health:	Department of health and human services
Emergency services:	Office of emergency preparedness
Government:	
Continuity of government	Office of emergency preparedness
Continuity of operations	All departments and agencies
Defense industrial base:	Louisiana military department
Information and telecommunications:	Division of administration
Energy:	
Oil and gas production infrastructure	Department of natural resources
Public utilities	Public service commission
Transportation:	Department of transportation
Banking and finance:	Department of insurance
Chemical industry and hazardous materials:	Department of environmental quality
Postal and shipping:	Department of transportation

FIGURE 6.5 Louisiana state homeland security strategy.

Task forces and commissions play a central role in state homeland policy since the composition of these bodies tends to include major players in law enforcement and emergency preparedness.

All 50 states have some version of an agency dedicated to the task of homeland security. As the states soon discovered, participation at even lower levels, that of the locality, is just as necessary as the federal–state nexus.

6.2.2 Structure at the Local Level

States as large as Texas or Pennsylvania came to realize that local input, local direction, and local assessment are crucial to any plan of homeland security. And in major metropolitan areas, such as New York and Los Angeles, cooperation at the state level is mandatory. What

FIGURE 6.6   New York homeland security and emergency services regions.

is inevitable is sweeping change in how things have been carried out in traditional law enforcement. Structures changed simply due to the new and corresponding demands. Some argue that the "organizational boundaries" have been changed in ways never envisioned by traditional law enforcement.[10] States such as Pennsylvania divide up its geography into distinct regions (see the map in Figure 6.8).

In each region, the pertinent agencies, for example, the Federal Bureau of Investigation (FBI), Bureau of Alcohol, Tobacco, and Firearms (ATF), Pennsylvania State Police, National Guard, Environmental Protection Agency, and health and medical entities, make up its membership. The objectives of the regional program are to

- Develop county task forces
- Develop regional counterterrorism task forces
- Integrate federal/state/county response
- Institutionalize mutual aid in the region
- Establish standing regional response groups
- Encourage regional networking

TABLE 6.1 FY2010 Enacted and FY2011 Budget Request for State and Local Programs (All Amounts in Millions of Dollars)

Programs	FY2010 Enacted	FY2011 Budget Request
State and Regional Preparedness Programs		
State Homeland Security Grant program	950	1050
Emergency Management Performance Grant program	340	345
Regional Catastrophic Preparedness program	35	35
Assistance to Firefighters program	810	610
Metropolitan Statistical Area Preparedness Programs		
Urban Area Security Initiative	887	1100
Port Security Grant program	300	300
Public Transportation Security Grant program	300	300
Over-The-Road Bus Security program	12	0
Buffer Zone Protection program	50	50
Training, Measurement, and Exercise Programs		
Continuing training grants	29	22
National Domestic Preparedness Consortium	102	52
Center for Domestic Preparedness / Noble Training Center	63	63
National Exercise program	40	42
Technical Assistance programs	13	15
Evaluations and assessments	16	18
Programs Proposed for Elimination by the Administration		
Driver's License Security program	50	0
Metropolitan Medical Response System	41	0
Citizen Corps programs	13	0
Interoperable Emergency Communications program	50	0
Emergency operations centers	60	0
Cybercrime counterterrorism training	2	0
Rural Domestic Preparedness Consortium	3	0
Total	4166	4002

Source: CRS analysis of the *FY2011 DHS Congressional Budget Justifications*, and the *FY2011 DHS Budget in Brief*.

Another example of state-to-regional design resides in the Commonwealth of Massachusetts. Reporting directly to the statewide Homeland Security Office are five geographically designed regions—the Northeast, Southeast, Central, Western, and Metro Boston—created to support strategic planning and operational coordination at the local level. Regional planning councils are responsible for developing and guiding the implementation of regional homeland security plans. The councils oversee all grant program

Cyber Safety Tips

Cyber Safety 101

Keep a Clean Machine.
- Keep software current.
- Automate software updates.
- Protect all devices that connect to the Internet.
- Scan all external mass storage devices and your machine for viruses and malware regularly.

Protect your personal information.
- Secure your accounts and take advantage of additional ways to verify your identity before you conduct business online.
- Make passwords complex. Combine capital and lowercase letters with numbers and symbols.
- Separate passwords for every account.
- Write it down and keep it safe.
- Own your online presence. Set privacy and security settings on websites to your comfort level.

Connect with care.
- When in doubt, throw it out. Links in e-mail, tweets, posts and online advertising are often the way cybercriminals compromise your computer.
- Get savvy about Wi-Fi hotspots. Limit the type of business you conduct and adjust the security settings on your device to limit who can access your machine.
- Protect your money when banking and shopping. Take extra measures to help secure your information by looking for web addresses with "https://" or "shttp://".

Be web wise.
- Stay current. Keep pace with new ways to stay safe online.

FIGURE 6.7   Cyber-safety tips.

- Think before you act and be wary of communications that implores you to act immediately, offers something that sounds too good to be true, or asks for personal information.
- Back it up. Protect your valuable digital information by making an electronic copy.

Be a good online citizen.
- Safer for me more secure for all. What you do online has the potential to affect everyone. Practicing good online habits benefits the global digital community.
- Help the authorities fight cybercrime. Report stolen finances or identities and other cybercrime to the Internet Crime Complainant Center at http://www.ic3.gov and the Federal Trade Commission at http://www.onguardonline.gov/file-complaint .[1]

Cyber Security for Electronic Devices

Any piece of electronic equipment that utilizes a computerized component is vulnerable to software imperfections and vulnerabilities. This may include items such as cell phones, tablets, video games, car navigation systems etc. The risks increase if the device is connected to the internet or a network that may be accessible by a hacker. Security tips related to how to protect electronic devices can be found at http://www.us-cert.gov/ncas/tips/ST05-017 .[2]

Internet Crime Schemes & Prevention Tips

Stay current with ongoing Internet trends and schemes identified by the Internet Crime Complainant Center at http://www.ic3.gov/crimeschemes.aspx .Review preventative measures to stay informed prior to making online transactions at http://www.ic3.gov/preventiontips.aspx#item-1 .

Who to Contact if You Become a Victim of Cybercrime

Local law enforcement - Even if you have been the target of a multijurisdictional cybercrime, your local law enforcement agency (either police department or sheriff's office) has an obligation to assist you, take a formal report, and make referrals to other agencies, when appropriate. Report your situation as soon as

---

[1] DHS, Stop.Think.Connect Tip Sheet, http://stopthinkconnect.org/tips-and-advice/
[2] US-CERT, Cyber Security for Electronic Devices, http://www.us-cert.gov/ncas/tips/ST05-017

FIGURE 6.7 (Continued).

you find out about it. Some local agencies have detectives or departments that focus specifically on cybercrime.

IC3 - The Internet Crime Complaint Center (IC3) will thoroughly review and evaluate your complaint and refer it to the appropriate federal, state, local, or international law enforcement or regulatory agency that has jurisdiction over the matter. IC3 is a partnership between the Federal Bureau of Investigation and the National White Collar Crime Center (funded, in part, by the Department of Justice's Bureau of Justice Assistance). Complaints may be filed online at http://www.ic3.gov/default.aspx.

Federal Trade Commission - The FTC does not resolve individual consumer complaints, but does operate the Consumer Sentinel, a secure online database that is used by civil and criminal law enforcement authorities worldwide to detect patterns of wrong-doing, leading to investigations and prosecutions. File your complaint at https://www.ftccomplaintassistant.gov/FTC_Wizard.aspx?Lang=en. Victims of identity crime may receive additional help through the FTC hotline at 1-877-IDTHEFT (1-877-438-4388); the FTC website at www.ftc.gov/IDTheft provides resources for victims, businesses, and law enforcement.[3]

Additional information on what to do if you become a victim can be found at http://staysafeonline.org/ncsam/resources/victims-of-cybercrime-tip-sheet .

Social Networking Safety

While the popularity of social networking sites continue to increase, so do associated security risks. Although the majority of users do not pose a threat, malicious individuals may be drawn to such sites due to accessibility and the amount of personal information made available. Security tips on how to stay safe on social networking sites can be found at http://www.us-cert.gov/ncas/tips/ST06-003 .[4]

Resources for Keeping Kids Safe Online

http://kids.getnetwise.org/
http://www.netsmartz.org/Parents
http://www.microsoft.com/security/family-safety/childsafety-steps.aspx

---

[3] National Cyber Security Alliance, StaySafeOnline, http://staysafeonline.org/ncsam/resources/victims-of-cybercrime-tip-sheet
[4] US-CERT, Staying Safe on Social Network Sites, http://www.us-cert.gov/ncas/tips/ST06-003

FIGURE 6.7   (Continued).

Additional Resources

- Download tip sheets, posters, and other materials made available through the U.S. Department of Homeland Security STOP|THINK|CONNECT campaign at http://www.dhs.gov/national-cyber-security-awareness-month.

- Sign up for security alerts, tips, and other updates by subscribing to mailing lists and feeds on the US Computer Emergency Readiness Team website at http://www.us-cert.gov/mailing-lists-and-feeds .

- Educate yourself through the Multi-State Information Sharing & Analysis Center National Webcast Initiative (MS-ISAC). The National Webcast Initiative is a collaborative effort between the U.S. Department of Homeland Security's National Cyber Security Division and Multi-State Information Sharing & Analysis Center as a means to provide timely and relevant cyber security education and information to a broad audience. Webcasts are available to the public free of charge. Upcoming webcasts can be found at http://msisac.cisecurity.org/webcast/ .

FIGURE 6.7 (Continued).

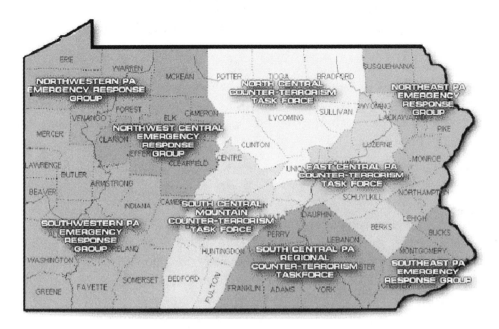

FIGURE 6.8 Map of Pennsylvania homeland security regions.

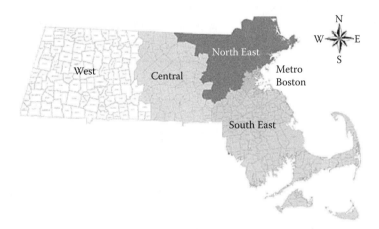

FIGURE 6.9 Map of Massachusetts homeland security regions.

expenditures. In addition, five regional homeland security advisory councils implement the strategic vision of the state Office of Homeland Security. Collaboration between the regions and the state is now commonplace (see Figure 6.9).

6.2.2.1 Fusion Centers

DHS has provided liberal funding sources for the creation of data fusion centers in a host of states and increasingly in major metropolitan areas. Fusion centers are centers for sharing information and intelligence within their jurisdictions, as well as with the federal government.[11] The crucial dynamic for the fusion center is its potentiality for sharing and dissemination. The fundamental baseline capacities for the fusion center must be and are its

- Ability to receive classified/unclassified information from federal partners
- Ability to assess local implications of threat information through formal risk assessment process
- Ability to further disseminate threat information to other state, local, tribal, and territorial (SLTT) and private-sector entities
- Ability to gather locally generated information, aggregate it, analyze it, and share it with federal partners, as appropriate[12]

Internet Exercise: Discover much more about the baseline capabilities that every fusion center should advance at http://www.dhs.gov/files/programs/gc_1296491960442.shtm.

At its center, the fusion center must become the locale for a "unified process for reporting, tracking, and accessing"[13] intelligence and information of every variety. Every state now has a fusion center. In addition, major urban or regional areas such as Orange County, California, and Boston Regional, to name two, have erected centers.[14] Major cities have constructed what DHS calls *Recognized Fusion Centers*, the most recent listing including, as of July 2015:

- Austin Regional Intelligence Center, Austin, Texas
- Boston Regional Intelligence Center, Boston, Massachusetts
- Central California Intelligence Center, Sacramento, California
- Central Florida Intelligence Exchange, Orlando, Florida
- Chicago Crime Prevention and Information Center, Chicago, Illinois
- Cincinnati/Hamilton County Regional Terrorism Early Warning Group, Cincinnati, Ohio
- Dallas Fusion Center, Dallas, Texas
- Delaware Valley Intelligence Center, Philadelphia, Pennsylvania
- Detroit and Southeast Michigan Information and Intelligence Center, Detroit, Michigan
- El Paso Multi-Agency Tactical Response Information eXchange (MATRIX), El Paso, Texas
- Houston Regional Intelligence Service Center, Houston, Texas
- Kansas City Terrorism Early Warning Fusion Center, Kansas City, Missouri
- Los Angeles Joint Regional Intelligence Center, Los Angeles, California
- Nevada Threat Analysis Center, Carson City, Nevada
- North Central Texas Fusion Center, McKinney, Texas
- Northeast Ohio Regional Fusion Center, Cleveland, Ohio
- Northern California Regional Intelligence Center, San Francisco, California
- Northern Virginia Regional Intelligence Center, Fairfax, Virginia
- Orange County Intelligence Assessment Center, Orange County, California
- San Diego Law Enforcement Coordination Center, San Diego, California
- Southeast Florida Fusion Center, Miami, Florida
- Southeastern Wisconsin Threat Analysis Center, Milwaukee, Wisconsin
- Southwest Texas Fusion Center, San Antonio, Texas

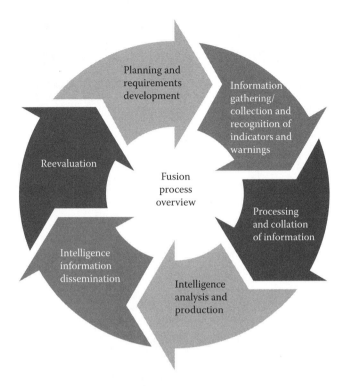

FIGURE 6.10   Figure from the U.S. government's information sharing environment depicting the fusion process as a continuous cycle in which inputs from various sources are brought together to provide state and local context to help enhance the national threat picture. Available at https:// www.ise.gov/national-network-state-and-major-urban-area-fusion-centers.

- Southwestern PA Region 13 Fusion Center, Pittsburgh, Pennsylvania
- St. Louis Fusion Center, St. Louis, Missouri

DHS's Office of Intelligence and Analysis provides personnel with operational and intelligence skills to staff the fusion centers. The centers

- Help classified and unclassified information flow
- Provide expertise
- Coordinate with local law enforcement and other agencies
- Provide local awareness and access (see Figure 6.10)

As of July 2015, there were 78 fusion centers around the country, such as the Commonwealth of Massachusetts, for example, shown in Figure 6.11.[15]

The department has deployed intelligence officers to state fusion centers in

- Arizona
- California
- Colorado
- Connecticut
- Georgia
- Florida

FIGURE 6.11 **Massachusetts Fusion Center logo.**

- Illinois
- Indiana
- Louisiana
- Maryland
- Massachusetts
- New Jersey
- New York
- Ohio
- South Carolina
- Virginia
- Washington

The department has also deployed support to fusion centers in New York City, Los Angeles, and the Dallas region.

Internet Exercise: Find out about the many facets of the fusion center at http://www.dhs.gov/files/programs/gc_1296484657738.shtm.

6.2.3 Funding and Local Initiatives

The funding and grant systems for DHS recognize the fundamental decentralization of local and state homeland security efforts. The Homeland Security Grant program funds planning, organization, equipment, training, and exercise activities in support of the National Preparedness Guidelines, as well as the National Incident Management System (NIMS), the National Response Framework (NRF), and the National Infrastructure Protection Plan (NIPP). The funds are sent directly to states for specific programs and purposes, including planning, equipment, training, and exercise activities, as well as for the implementation of new programs and initiatives. DHS additionally earmarks funds for four other sectors essential to homeland security:

Urban Area Security Initiative (UASI) Grant Program funds address the unique multidisciplinary planning, operations, equipment, training, and exercise needs of high-threat, high-density urban areas.

Law Enforcement Terrorism Prevention Program (LETPP) focuses on the prevention of terrorist attacks and provides law enforcement and public safety communities with funds to support the following activities: intelligence gathering and information sharing through

FIGURE 6.12 Citizen Corps logo.

enhancing/establishing fusion centers; hardening high-value targets; planning strategically; continuing to build interoperable communications; and collaborating with non-law-enforcement partners, other government agencies, and the private sector.

Public Safety Interoperable Communications (PSIC) Grant Program assists public safety agencies in the acquisition of, deployment of, or training for the use of interoperable communications systems that can utilize a reallocated public safety spectrum in the 700 MHz band for radio communication.

Infrastructure Protection Program (IPP) supports specific activities to protect critical infrastructure, such as ports, mass transit, highways, rail, and transportation. IPP grants fund a range of preparedness activities, including strengthening infrastructure against explosive attacks, preparedness planning, equipment purchase, training, exercises, and security management and administration costs. IPP comprises five separate grant programs: Transit Security, Port Security, Buffer Zone Protection, Trucking Security, and Intercity Bus Security.

On top of all of this, DHS, by and through the Federal Emergency Management Agency (FEMA), erects Citizen Corps Councils in nearly 2500 communities across the United States. Citizen Corps, coordinated by DHS, focuses on opportunities for people across the country to participate in a range of measures to make their families, homes, and communities safer from the threats of terrorism, crime, and disasters of all kinds. Citizen Corps also brings together a community's first responders, firefighters, emergency health-care providers, law enforcement, and emergency managers with its volunteer resources. Citizen Corps will help people across America take a more active role in crime prevention, support the emergency medical community, and be better trained in a wide range of emergency preparedness and disaster response activities (see Figure 6.12).

The focus of Citizen Corps work is at the local level. The scope of the Citizen Corps covers a wide range of activities. Citizen Corps Councils help drive local citizen participation by coordinating Citizen Corps programs, developing community action plans, assessing possible threats, and identifying local resources. Examples of corps programs are shown in Figure 6.13.

Internet Resource: Review the many organizations and associations involved in Citizen Corps at http://www.citizencorps.gov/pdf/council.pdf.

6.3 Fine Line of National and Homeland Security

It is unlikely that any firm line can be drawn between the worlds of national and homeland security. At one time, this may have been possible. Given the events of 9/11, the interconnectedness and integration of the military/defense function with that of law enforcement

The Community Emergency Response Team (CERT) Program educates people about disaster preparedness and trains them in basic disaster response skills, such as fire safety, light search and rescue, and disaster medical operations. Using their training, CERT members can assist others in their neighborhood or workplace following an event and can take a more active role in preparing their community. The program is administered by the Federal Emergency Management Agency.

The Fire Corps promotes the use of citizen advocates to enhance the capacity of resource-constrained fire and rescue departments at all levels: volunteer, combination, and career. Citizen advocates can assist local fire departments in a range of activities including fire safety outreach, youth programs, and administrative support. Fire Corps provides resources to assist fire and rescue departments in creating opportunities for citizen advocates and promotes citizen participation. Fire Corps is funded through DHS and is managed and implemented through a partnership between the National Volunteer Fire Council, the International Association of Fire Fighters, and the International Association of Fire Chiefs.

The National Neighborhood Watch Program (formerly USAonWatch), housed within the National Sheriffs' Association, has worked to unite law enforcement agencies, private organizations, and individual citizens in a nation-wide effort to reduce crime and improve local communities. In the aftermath of September 11, 2001, Neighborhood Watch programs have expanded beyond their traditional crime prevention role to help neighborhoods focus on disaster preparedness, emergency response and terrorism awareness. The Neighborhood Watch Program draws upon the compassion of average citizens, asking them to lend their neighbors a hand.

The Medical Reserve Corps (MRC) Program strengthens communities by helping medical, public health and other volunteers offer their expertise throughout the year as well as during local emergencies and other times of community need. MRC volunteers work in coordination with existing local emergency response programs and also supplement existing community public health initiatives, such as outreach and prevention, immunization programs, blood drives, case management, care planning, and other efforts. The MRC program is administered by HHS.

Volunteers in Police Service (VIPS) works to enhance the capacity of state and local law enforcement to utilize volunteers. VIPS serves as a gateway to resources and information for and about law enforcement volunteer programs. Funded by DOJ, VIPS is managed and implemented by the International Association of Chiefs of Police.

Citizen Corps is coordinated nationally by the Department of Homeland Security. DHS also works closely with the Corporation for National and Community Service (CNCS) to promote volunteer service activities that support homeland security and community safety. CNCS is a federal agency that operates nationwide service programs such as AmeriCorps, Senior Corps, and Learn and Serve America. Participants in these programs may support Citizen Corps Council activities by helping to establish training and information delivery systems for neighborhoods, schools, and businesses, and by helping with family preparedness and crime prevention initiatives in a community or across a region.

FIGURE 6.13 An assortment of Citizen Corps programs.

and security became grotesquely obvious. Indeed, the terrorists seemed to have deduced this by their mixture of targets, from the attempted White House attack, to the Twin Towers and the distressing crash into the Pentagon (Figure 6.14).

In a way, it is absurd to think that these dual lines of defense do not merge in many sectors. Some might even argue that the Iraq and Afghanistan campaigns are extensions of a security and police effort to track down the perpetrators of terror. The argument has both appeal and merit. That there must be some sort of collaboration between the military complex and the arm of homeland security is now standard operating procedure.

When speaking of the military, we reference the historic four major branches of the service. The U.S. Coast Guard (USCG) has long been out of the Department of Defense (DoD) province, initially being located in the U.S. Treasury Department, while today it is housed in DHS. Hence, the mind-set of the USCG has always been in hazard and human tragedy. So too the continuous contribution of the National Guard—an agency that attends to human suffering with professionalism and skill. Shortly after the attack of 9/11, the remaining arms of the military swung into action. The entire structure of the military was reorganized into a unified command as outlined in Figure 6.15.

Five zones are apportioned the responsibility for defense against terror based on the designated geography:

U.S. Northern Command (USNORTHCOM)
U.S. Southern Command (USSOUTHCOM)
U.S. Pacific Command (USPACOM)
U.S. European Command (USEUCOM)
U.S. Central Command (USCENTCOM)

The reorientation of the military into a terror mentality has been nothing short of dramatic, but the events of 9/11 prompted the reexamination. To be sure, Americans are generally reticent about military authority, and only in cases of extreme national emergency are the armed forces called on to assist. It could be argued that part of Katrina's problem

FIGURE 6.14 The Pentagon on 9/11.

- United States Africa Command (USAFRICOM) is responsible for military relations with African nations, the African Union and African regional security organizations. It protects and defends the interests of the United States by strengthening the defense capabilities of African nations and, in cooperation with African governments, conducts military missions that increase security while deterring and defeating a variety of transnational threats.

- United States Central Command (USCENTCOM) is responsible for operations in twenty countries that fall in the "central" area of the globe: Afghanistan, Bahrain, Egypt, Iran, Iraq, Jordan, Kazakhstan, Kuwait, Kyrgyzstan, Lebanon, Oman, Pakistan, Qatar, Saudi Arabia, Syria, Tajikistan, Turkmenistan, United Arab Emirates, Uzbekistan and Yemen. United States Central Command utilizes national and international partnerships to build cooperation among nations, respond to crisis, deter and defeat threats and support development that ultimately increases stability in the region.

- United States European Command (USEUCOM) works with NATO and other partner nations to address the security and defense needs of nations in Europe and parts of the Middle East and Eurasia. EUCOM coordinates with these nations to find cooperative solutions in peace and wartime alike, to plan training missions, provide humanitarian assistance and to develop strategies for promoting peace and stability in the region.

- United States Northern Command (USNORTHCOM) operates in the area of responsibility encompassing the continental United States, Alaska, Mexico, Canada, portions of the Caribbean and surrounding waters. NORTHCOM is primarily responsible for civil support and homeland security and also oversees the North American Aerospace Defense Command (NORAD). It has few permanent forces and is instead assigned forces by the Secretary of Defense or the President whenever required for the execution of its missions.

- United States Pacific Command (USPACOM) oversees an area of responsibility stretching from the waters of the United States west coast to the western border of India, and from Antarctica to the North Pole, encompassing 36 diverse nations. USPACOM and its partners work to promote the development of the region while cooperating to enhance security, deter aggression, respond with force when necessary and to provide humanitarian assistance.

- United States Southern Command (USSOUTHCOM) oversees an area of responsibility encompassing 31 nations in Latin America south of Mexico, Central and South America, and the Caribbean Sea. USSOUTHCOM works to increase the security of the United States by engaging its partners to enhance the peacekeeping abilities of the region, to promote human rights, to deter illegal activities associated with illicit trafficking and to conduct multinational military exercises designed to strengthen partnerships while developing collective capabilities.

- The United States Special Operations Command (USSOCOM) is responsible for planning for and conducting special operations. It offers direct action in the form of short duration strikes and small-scale offensives, special reconnaissance, unconventional warfare, foreign internal defense, civil affairs operations, counterterrorism, psychological operations, information operations, counter-proliferation of weapons of mass destruction, security force assistance, counterinsurgency operations and any specific activities directed by the President or the Secretary of Defense.

- The United States Strategic Command (USSTRATCOM) is headquartered at Offutt Air Force Base in Omaha, Nebraska. It conducts global operations in partnership with other Combatant Commands, services and U.S. government agencies to deter and detect strategic attacks against the United States. USSTRATCOM is responsible for command of U.S. nuclear capabilities, space operations, global surveillance and reconnaissance, intelligence, communications, computers, global missile defense and combatting weapons of mass destruction.

- The United States Transportation Command (USTRANSCOM) provides the Department of Defense with an aggregate of transportation capabilities and assets. Together with commercial partnerships, USTRANSCOM enables a diverse array of joint mobility missions.

FIGURE 6.15   A world map and explanation of military commanders' areas of responsibility.

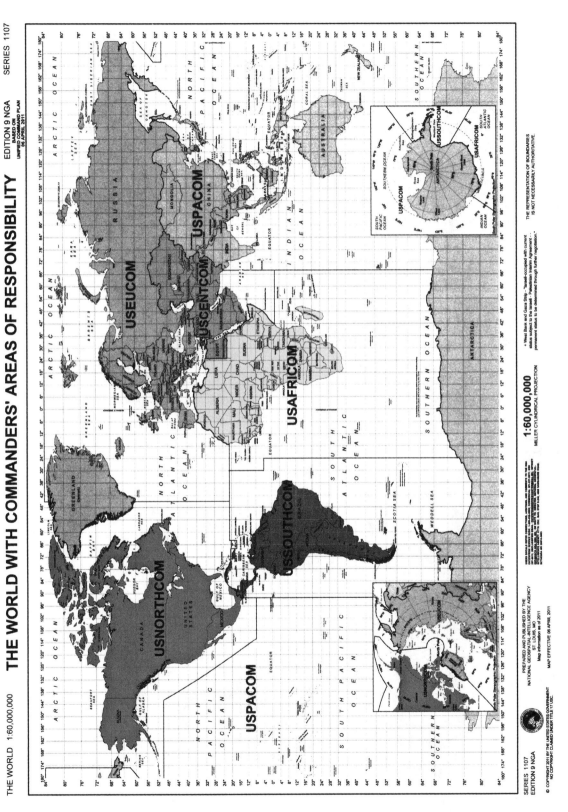

FIGURE 6.15   (Continued).

related to this hesitancy. As we gazed at the television sets, how many of us wondered aloud, "Where is the military assistance?" By any measure, it was slow in coming (Figure 6.16).

Other questions regarding the dominance of federal authority as a natural hindrance to state involvement as to the National Guard have also been raised by the Rand Commission.[16] Rand severely critiqued the command and control functionality during these crises and suggested alternative structures where the state authority takes the lead in the emergency response—even as to military resources. An example of this novel approach is evident in the suggested dual command structure for response shown in Figure 6.17.[17]

Exactly how the military assists in the homeland arena is both complicated and innovative when compared with past practices. Aside from the defense of the soil from foreign armies and attackers, the military is being asked to be partners in the fight against terrorism—tackling nontraditional enemies. Common examples of civil cooperation are

- Immediate response (any form of immediate action taken to save lives, prevent human suffering, or mitigate property damage under imminently serious conditions)
- Military support to civilian law enforcement agencies (loans of equipment, facilities, or personnel to law enforcement)
- Military assistance for civil disturbances
- Support for domestic counterterrorism operations
- Sensitive support operations
- Counterdrug operational support
- Terrorism consequence management (to include chemical, biological, radiological, nuclear, and high-yield explosive consequence management)
- Military support to civil authorities
- Support for civil disasters—natural or man-made (other than terrorism)
- Military cooperation with civil agencies

FIGURE 6.16 Air National Guard over New York City area.

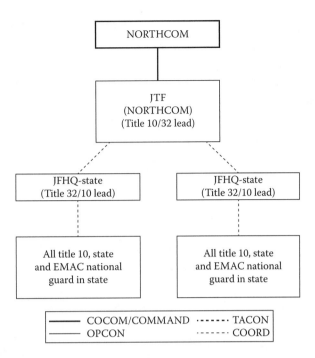

FIGURE 6.17   Dual-STATUS COMMAND.

- Response under other authorities
- Oil or hazardous material spills
- Radiological emergencies/incidents
- Emergency water requirements
- Response to flooding
- Forest fire emergencies
- Mass immigration
- Transportation support[18]

While this section cannot possibly cover each and every aspect of military cooperation, it will seek to address the most notable.

6.3.1 Department of Defense and Homeland Security

The defense of a nation fundamentally relies on its military infrastructure. Yet, in the affairs of homeland security, especially in a free society, the military sector cannot tackle the internal affairs of law enforcement and safety. That is not the military's integral mission. Nor is it the province of the military to meddle in the duties of state, local, or federal law enforcement—these being distinct and, for the most part, civilian counterparts and colleagues of the military. It is a delicate balance, with the DoD assuming primary control of the military confrontation that arises from foreign enemies and DHS and its aligned agencies and departments handling the internal affairs. The joint chiefs of staff for the military lay out the respective obligations.

DoD is the lead, supported by other agencies, in defending against traditional external threats/aggression (e.g., air and missile attack). However, against internal asymmetric, nontraditional threats (e.g., terrorism), the DoD may be in support of DHS. When ordered to conduct HD operations within U.S. territory, the DoD will coordinate closely with other federal agencies or departments. Consistent with laws and policy, the services will provide capabilities to support combatant command requirements against a variety of air, land, maritime, space, and cyber incursions that can threaten national security. These include invasion, computer network attack, and air and missile attacks.

The purpose of HD is to protect against and mitigate the impact of incursions or attacks on sovereign territory, the domestic population, and defense critical infrastructure.[19]

A graphic portrayal of this series of interrelationships is shown in Figure 6.18.[20]

These are distinct though very complementary missions. Since 9/11, those entrusted with military affairs have had to reconsider these traditional lines. Organizations like the DoD are by nature bureaucratically entrenched and slow to change. Moving away from the historic mission will not occur readily, although in administrative agency time, the DoD has sprinted to this new vision—the view that the military plays a central role in the fight against terrorism. It is now safe to say that the DoD has blended the homeland function into the military model. In a recent study by the joint chiefs of staff, the merger is blatantly apparent[21] (see Figure 6.19).

In Iraq and Afghanistan, the military has assumed a major role in the provision of safety and security for these populations. It is not just the military tactic at play here but something dramatically larger—that of the safety and security of nation-states. At no place is this

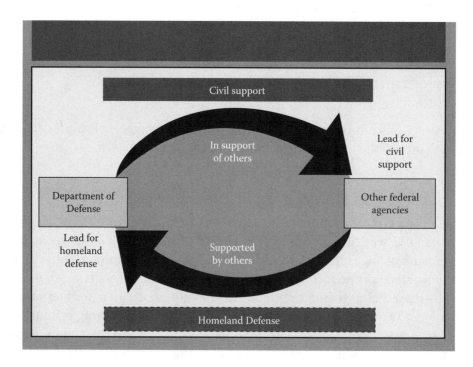

FIGURE 6.18 Lead federal agency and DoD relationships.

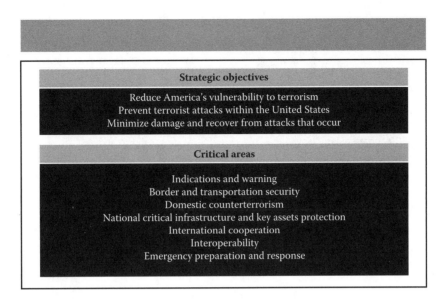

FIGURE 6.19 **National strategy for homeland security strategic objectives and critical areas of concern.**

more obvious than in the reporting of deaths in Iraq, where the task of minimizing human harm and tragedy weighs heavily on military commanders and boots on the ground. At some stages of the Iraq campaign, the casualty rates were absolutely distressing, and public outcry raged over these losses. Before the U.S. military left Iraq in 2012–2013, leaving only a small noncombatant force, the situation had dramatically improved, and with military adjustments, in both size and strategy, the unceasing and unmitigated levels of violence seemed to have halted.[22] However, in the vacuum left behind by U.S. military absence, the void was filled by forces known as the Islamic state of Iraq and Syria (ISIS). In Syria alone, nearly 200,000 people have perished in a horrible civil war with poor prospects for near-term peace.[23] Whatever peace and tranquility existed in Iraq was surely replaced by the brutality and viciousness of ISIS evil (see Figure 6.20[24]).

Internet Exercise: To update the figures on civilian deaths, visit https://www.iraqbody-count.org/analysis/numbers/2014/

In general, the DoD now thinks in terms of terror and a new war on nontraditional combatants. The DoD reported its numerous activities in the fight against terrorism in its Defend America program. Defend America has since been merged into the DoD general operations. However, DoD policy and pronouncement never strays far from the analysis of terror as it covers the Iraq, Syria, and Afghanistan campaigns. As the United States continues its slow but steady withdrawal from this region, the challenges of terror simply escalate. Even President Obama, who is severely resistant to any military involvement in the region, now recognizes that these threats know no boundaries. With the Paris attacks in the fall of 2015 and San Bernardino attack in December 2015, it can be seen that ISIS seeks

Islamic State of Iraq and the Levant's (ISIL) frontlines in much of northern and central Iraq have been pushed back since August 2014. ISIL can no longer operate freely in roughly 25 to 30 percent of populated areas of Iraqi territory where it once could. These areas translate into approximately 13,000 to 17,000 square kilometers (or 5,000 to 6,500 square miles). However, because of the dynamic nature of the conflict in Iraq and Syria, this estimate could increase or decrease depending on daily fluctuations in the battle lines. ISIL's area of influence in Syria remains largely unchanged, with its gains in As Suwayda', Damascus Countryside, and Homs Provinces offset by losses in Halab and Al Hasakah Provinces.

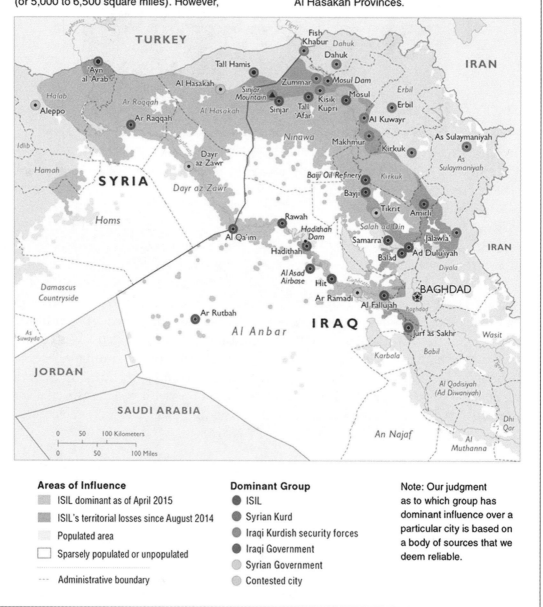

FIGURE 6.20   ISIS's reduced operating areas as of April 2015.

OPERATION INHERENT RESOLVE
TARGETS DAMAGED/DESTROYED*

Tanks	**129**
HMMWV's	**356**
Staging Areas	**676**
Buildings	**4,517**
Fighting Positions	**4,942**
Oil Infrastructure	**260**
Other Targets	**5,195**
TOTAL	**16,075**

*Numbers may fluctuate based on battle damage assessments
Current as of 13 November 2015   Source: CENTCOM CCCI

FIGURE 6.21   Targets damaged/destroyed as of December 9, 2015.

to aggressively recruit followers online and respects no nation or any geographic boundary. A recently announced defense response, Operation Inherent Resolve, lists ISIS targets destroyed by means of airstrikes alone (see Figure 6.21[25]).

The integration of the DoD into the affairs of terror and global threat can be gleaned from its own organizational changes. The DoD has erected a wide array of offices dedicated to this new war, designated and delineated its responsibility in specific instances of attack, and erected a new bureaucratic structure under the auspices of an assistant secretary of defense for homeland defense and global security—all of which targets terror and threat[26] (see Figure 6.22).

6.3.2 Intelligence Gathering and Sharing

All sectors of the military are now gathering, as well as sharing, intelligence information. Each of the four major branches has an intelligence arm that focuses its attention on threat and attack.

Internet Resource: For an excellent overview of how the military commands train for and anticipate counterterrorism, see http://www.dtic.mil/doctrine/new_pubs/jp3_26.pdf.

Since 9/11, each sector has redirected part of its approach to the prevention of terrorism. A short sketch of each follows.

6.3.2.1 Office of Naval Intelligence

The Office of Naval Intelligence (ONI) deals with both historic and new challenges. Today, ONI's mission includes providing intelligence on the capabilities of foreign naval powers, providing global maritime intelligence integration supporting the global fight against terrorism, and enabling maritime domain awareness for HD. ONI's Civil Maritime Intelligence

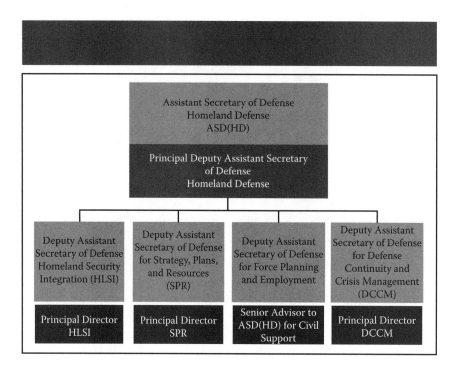

FIGURE 6.22 Organization chart of the Office of the Assistant Secretary of Defense for Homeland Defense and Global Security.

Division supports the disruption of maritime smuggling operations and the enforcement of international trade sanctions to deny terrorists use of the sea as a means of attack. Naval Intelligence—with Marine Corps Intelligence, the USCG, the Drug Enforcement Agency, and U.S. Customs—has also devoted an increased effort to nontraditional maritime intelligence missions.

6.3.2.2 Air Force Intelligence

While there has been some heated debate over the role of the air force in matters of HD, it appears that this branch of the service is crucial to success. Terrorism is now part of the air dorce mission. Dealing with this threat rests on many fronts, though none more essential than the work of the North American Aerospace Defense Command (NORAD), a binational U.S. and Canadian organization charged with providing aerospace warning and control for North America (Figures 6.23 and 6.24).

To accomplish this mission, NORAD uses a network of ground-based radars and fighters to detect, intercept, and, if necessary, engage any probable threat to the continent (see Figure 6.25).

The air force also operates a newly restructured intelligence center—the Air Force Intelligence, Surveillance, and Reconnaissance Agency. The Air Force Intelligence, Surveillance, and Reconnaissance Agency's headquarters is at Lackland Air Force Base, Texas, although the agency's 12,000 people serve at approximately 72 locations around the world. The agency's mission is to organize, train, equip, and present assigned forces and

FIGURE 6.23   NORAD Command Center.

FIGURE 6.24   NORAD mission.

capabilities to conduct intelligence, surveillance, and reconnaissance for combatant commanders and the country.

One tool of intelligence gathering has been the Predator drone, used by the navy in great quantity. Recently, the air force has been prompted to increase its production and capability in this area (Figure 6.26).

Drones, while excellent intelligence tools, have caused a good deal of consternation among critics of the Obama administration. It is no secret that the administration used drones more aggressively than any other has. Even though the fact that human costs are light, yet the devastation caused by the machines is quite substantial, the Obama White House prefers the mechanical means to not only intelligence but also the use of drones as a means of eliminating terrorists. Al-Qaeda, Taliban, and ISIS leaders have all been on the receiving end of the drone strike, but so have U.S. citizens working with the same groups

FIGURE 6.25   Map of NORAD geographic regions.

FIGURE 6.26   The Air Force MQ-1B Predator.

who met early ends. Critics argue that the drone replaces due process for those Americans who are simply executed in the theater of war.[27]

6.3.2.3 U.S. Marine Corps

While the U.S. Marine Corps (USMC) is under the operational control of the navy, it has constructed a plethora of intelligence organizations and operational programs relevant to the fight against terrorism. At its marine base in Quantico resides its intelligence headquarters, with its primary functions being to

- Discharge Marine Corps responsibilities for intelligence estimates, plans, reports, and studies
- Review, analyze, and coordinate joint papers that pertain to Marine Corps intelligence matters
- Recommend positions for approval and use by the Commandant of the Marine Corps (CMC) and the Headquarters of the Marine Corps (HQMC) staff
- Develop plans, policies, operational concepts, doctrine, and techniques in the fields of intelligence, counterintelligence, and cryptologic/signals intelligence in coordination with staff agencies
- Coordinate with the HQMC staff to develop plans and policies

The Marine Corps developed a cultural studies program for its professional and enlisted class as it seeks to understand and converse with both friendly citizens and the combatant enemy. The commandant of the Marine Corps, in his Vision and Strategy for 2025, states that the corps "will go to great lengths to understand enemies and the range of cultural, societal and political factors affecting all people Marines interact with."[28]

The USMC Center for Advanced Operational Culture Learning (CAOCL) promotes a grasp of culture and language as regular, mainstream components of the operating environment—the human terrain—throughout the full spectrum of military operations, and is the corps's one-stop clearinghouse for operational culture and language training. CAOCL is now fully integrated into the Marine Corps University[29] (see Figure 6.27).

The Marine Corps Regional, Cultural, and Language Familiarization (RCLF) program ensures that marines are equipped with operationally relevant regional, cultural, and language knowledge to allow them to plan and operate successfully in the joint and combined expeditionary environment

FIGURE 6.27   USMC Center for Advanced Operational Culture Learning (CAOCL).

- In any region of the world
- In current and potential operating conditions
- Targeting persistent and emerging threats and opportunities

The Marine Corps employs distance education techniques in its portal, Marine.net. A recent sampling of courses pertinent to homeland security include

- Cultural Awareness and Terrorism
- Risk Management: Organization Risk and Safety and Health Legislation
- Joint Anti-Terrorism Level 1
- Threat Levels and Force Protection Conditions
- Terrorism Awareness
- Stability and Support Operations
- Physical Security Specialist
- Physical Security Chief
- National and International Security Studies

6.3.2.4 U.S. Army

The U.S. Army established its own security command—the U.S. Army Intelligence and Security Command (INSCOM). INSCOM conducts intelligence, security, and information operations for military commanders and national decision makers. Headquartered at Fort Belvoir, Virginia, INSCOM is a global command with 10 major subordinate commands and a variety of smaller units with personnel dispersed over 180 locations worldwide. The subordinate commands are

1st Information Operations (IO) Command: The 1st IO Command is the only army full-spectrum IO organization engaged from information operations theory development and training to operational application across the range of military operations.

66th Military Intelligence (MI) Brigade: The 66th MI Brigade conducts theater-level multidiscipline intelligence and security operations and, when directed, deploys prepared forces to conduct joint/combined expeditionary and contingency operations in support of U.S. Army Europe and U.S. European Command.

116th Military Intelligence Brigade: The 116th MI Brigade conducts 24/7 tasking, collection, processing, exploitation, dissemination, and feedback of multiple organic and joint intelligence aerial-intelligence surveillance and reconnaissance (A-ISR) missions collected in overseas contingency areas of operation.

300th Military Intelligence Brigade: The 300th MI Brigade provides trained and ready linguist and military intelligence soldiers to commanders from brigade through army level.

470th Military Intelligence Brigade: The 470th MI Brigade provides timely and fused multidiscipline intelligence in support of U.S. Army South, U.S. Southern Command, and other national intelligence agencies.

500th Military Intelligence Brigade: The 500th MI Brigade, located at Schofield Barracks, Hawai'i, provides multidisciplinary intelligence support for joint and coalition warfighters in the U.S. Army Pacific area of responsibility.

501st Military Intelligence Brigade: The 501st MI Brigade conducts theater-level multidiscipline intelligence for joint and combined warfighters from the Republic of Korea.

513th Military Intelligence Brigade: The 513th MI Brigade deploys in strength or in tailored elements to conduct multidiscipline intelligence and security operations in support of army components of U.S. Central Command, and theater army commanders.

704th Military Intelligence Brigade: The 704th MI Brigade conducts synchronized full-spectrum signals intelligence, computer network, and information assurance operations directly and through the National Security Agency to satisfy national, joint, combined, and army information superiority requirements.

706th Military Intelligence Group: The 706th MI Group, located at Fort Gordon, Georgia, provides personnel, intelligence assets, and technical support to conduct signals intelligence operations within the National Security Agency/Central Security Service Georgia (NSA/CSS Georgia) and worldwide.

780th Military Intelligence Brigade: The 780th MI Brigade, located at Fort George G. Meade, Maryland, conducts signals intelligence and computer network operations and enables dynamic computer network defense operations of army and defense networks.

902d Military Intelligence Group: The 902d MI Group provides direct and general counterintelligence support to army activities and major commands.

Army Cryptologic Operations (ACO): ACO serves as the Army G2 and Service Cryptologic Component (SCC) representative to provide expert cryptologic leadership, support, guidance, and advice to U.S. Army warfighters and intelligence leaders. It leads the army's cryptologic effort to satisfy Signals Intelligence (SIGINT) requirements by leveraging NSA Extended Enterprise, Intelligence Community, Sister Services, and Service Laboratories. It ensures timely and effective support to operations by providing optimized capabilities, training, and resources.

Army Field Support Center (AFSC): AFSC provides specialized operational, administrative, and personnel management support to the Department of the Army and other DoD services and agencies as directed.

Army Operations Group (AOG): AOG conducts human intelligence operations and provides expertise in support of ground component priority intelligence requirements using a full spectrum of human intelligence collection methods.

Joint Surveillance Target Attack Radar System (JSTARS): Army JSTARS provides army aircrew members aboard JSTARS aircraft to support surveillance and targeting operations of army land component and joint or combined task force commanders worldwide.

National Ground Intelligence Center (NGIC): NGIC is the DoD's primary producer of ground forces intelligence.

Internet Resource: Visit the INSCOM web location for a full view of the Army Intelligence Service.

6.3.3 Specialized Military/Defense Units Dedicated to Homeland Security

There are simply too many military entities and groups to enumerate that relate to the world of homeland security. Each branch of the service dedicates some portion of its resources to the fight against terrorism, and each lends its expertise to particular tasks and challenges. This section will cover representative examples of these military contributions.

6.3.3.1 National Maritime Intelligence-Integration Office (NMIO)

Primarily a center for naval intelligence, the NMIO's resources and information are available to all branches of the military and the USCG. The NMIO is home to the ONI and is the central location for maritime intelligence (Figure 6.28).

NMIO displays a narrow intelligence interest though it has a global vision and approach. Threats are assessed and evaluated in the maritime environment rather than the whole framework in which threats occurs. Hence, NMIO targets threats in these basic categories:

Asymmetric: Terrorism, WMD proliferation, cyber attack, global supply chain disruption, and so on

Criminal/Illicit Activities: Maritime piracy, narcotics and contraband smuggling, human trafficking, illegal exploitation of marine resources, and so on

Environmental Destruction: Toxic waste, illegal dumping, overfishing, and so on[30]

Located in Washington, DC, NMIO supports joint operational commanders with a worldwide organization and an integrated workforce of active duty, reserve, and civilian personnel. NMIO supports the navy's acquisition activities by providing scientific and technical analysis of naval weapons systems.

6.3.3.2 National Reconnaissance Office

Coordinating reconnaissance activities is the DoD's National Reconnaissance Office (NRO). The NRO designs, builds, and operates the country's reconnaissance satellites. NRO products, provided to an expanding list of customers such as the Central Intelligence Agency (CIA) and the DoD, can warn of potential trouble spots around the world, help plan military operations, and monitor the environment. A DoD agency, the NRO is staffed by DoD

FIGURE 6.28 National Maritime Intelligence-Integration Office.

FIGURE 6.29   National Reconnaissance program, part of the National Foreign Intelligence program.

and CIA personnel. It is funded through the National Reconnaissance program, part of the National Foreign Intelligence program (see Figure 6.29).

6.3.3.3 *Weapons of Mass Destruction Civil Support Teams*

The U.S. Army and the National Guard play a central role in the WMD protocol. Civil Support Teams (CSTs) aid civilian authorities with military expertise regarding chemical, biological, radiological, and nuclear materials (Figure 6.30).

The CST was designed to augment local and regional terrorism response capabilities in events known or suspected to involve use of chemical, biological, or radiological agents.

FIGURE 6.30   Civil Support Team.

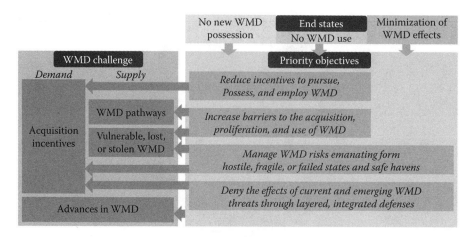

FIGURE 6.31   End states, priority objectives and the WMD challenge.

The team can be en route within 3 hours to support civil authorities in the event or suspicion of a WMD attack. Specifically, the CST deploys to an area of operations to

- Support civil authorities to identify chemical, biological, radiological, and nuclear agents/substances
- Assess current and projected consequences
- Advise on response measures
- Assist with mitigation and additional support

The role of the U.S. military in the matter of WMD has been essential. The sharing and collaboration between civil authorities seems almost natural and without equivocation. Given the seriousness of the subject matter, both the army and public authorities share a similar vision regarding WMD. The DoD, working in unison with nonmilitary authorities, seeks to minimize WMD at every level, from pure prevention to total eradication. In Figure 6.31,[31] the goals of its overall efforts are charted as *End States*.

The U.S. Army lays out its operational approach, which is clearly collaborative[32] (see Figure 6.32).

6.3.3.4 *Defense Threat Reduction Agency and USSTRATCOM Center for Combating WMD and Standing Joint Force Headquarters Elimination*

Initially located in the U.S. Strategic Command, the center has been aligned with the Defense Threat Reduction Agency (DTRA). The center provides recommendations to dissuade, deter, and prevent the acquisition, development, or use of WMD and associated technology. Through collaboration with the United States and allied organizations, the center provides situational awareness of worldwide WMD and related activities, as well as providing day-to-day and operational crisis support via the operations center. Among its responsibilities are

1. U.S. Armed Forces, in concert with other elements of U.S. national power, deter WMD use.

2. U.S. Armed Forces are prepared to defeat an adversary threatening to use WMD and prepare to deter follow-on use.

3. Existing worldwide WMD is secure and the U.S. Armed Forces contribute as appropriate to secure, reduce, reverse or eliminate it.

4. Current or potential adversaries are dissuaded from producing WMD.

5. Current or potential adversaries' WMD is detected and characterized and elimination sought.

6. Proliferation of WMD and related materials to current and/or potential adversaries is dissuaded, prevented, defeated or reversed.

7. If WMD is used against the United States or its interests, U.S. Armed Forces are capable of minimizing the effects in order to continue operations in a WMD environment and assist United States civil authorities, allies and partners.

8. U.S. Armed Forces assist in attributing the source of attack, respond decisively, and/or deter future attacks.

9. Allies and U.S. civilian agencies are capable partners in combating WMD.

FIGURE 6.32   U.S. Armed Forces WMD strategy.

- Partnering: Using our unique expertise, we are developing and strengthening the CWMD capabilities of our allies, partner nations, the military, and other federal, state, and local government agencies.

- Verifying: Treaties, conventions, documents on WMD—our WMD experts travel the globe to inspect, assess, and verify that these international agreements on WMD are being upheld.

- Researching: WMD threats are constantly changing, evolving—and new threats emerge unexpectedly. Our dedicated R&D efforts are combating today's WMD—and developing solutions to future threats.

- Responding: Whether dealing with intentional WMD use, or a natural or accidental chemical, biological, radiological, and nuclear (CBRN) incident, someone needs to be prepared to deal with a worst-case scenario—and that someone is us.

- Defending: Our adversaries fall into two categories: those who have WMD, and those who want them. We must be able to defend the warfighter, our country, and our allies from WMD—here and abroad.

- Preparing: There is no second chance to stop WMD—which is why we are constantly training, testing, and planning. We take this approach with ourselves, our military, and our international partners.

- Nuclear support: Safe. Secure. Effective. The United States' nuclear arsenal needs to be all three—and we are responsible for ensuring that these three conditions are met, every day, around the world.

The Defense Threat Reduction Agency (DTRA) is a combat support agency of the U.S. DoD (Figure 6.33).

Founded in 1998, the agency headquarters is located in Fort Belvoir, Virginia. DTRA employs over 2000 men and women, both military and civilian, at more than 14 locations around the world.

Internet Exercise: Discover where DTRA is located globally. Do you see logic in these locations? Visit http://www.dtra.mil/About/Locations.aspx.

The DTRA safeguards America and its allies from WMDs (CBRN and high explosives) by providing capabilities to reduce, eliminate, and counter the threat and to mitigate its effects. It is sometimes designated as the strategic command of WMD.

The DTRA expends a considerable portion of its time and energy on conducting basic scientific research regarding WMD. It uses "science to secure WMD." All of DRTA's research encompasses five basic lines of inquiry:

- Basic and applied science
- Chemical/biological technologies
- Counter-WMD technologies
- Nuclear technologies
- Information sciences and applications

DTRA's research seeks

- To improve scientific knowledge that supports verification of treaties, safeguards, and nonproliferation
- To safely handle, transport, secure, or eliminate WMD components and weapons; and use novel means that lead to physical or other methods to monitor compliance and reduce illegal proliferation pathways

FIGURE 6.33 DTRA symbol at headquarters entrance.

- To advance capabilities for safe and verifiable control of materials, systems, and facilities that underpin greater confidence for entering, exiting, or sustaining multinational WMD-related agreements[33]

6.4 Conclusion

The chapter scrutinizes how homeland functions need governmental collaboration.[34] DHS alone cannot carry out the multitude of homeland functions. The chapter urges practitioners to see wisdom in the mutual support of local, state, and federal agencies in the fight against terrorism. On top of this, from its earliest days of inception, DHS fostered an environment of decentralization over centralization—concluding that local officials understood the demands and dynamics of their constituencies better than removed bureaucrats. The political and structural intermix and interdependency of homeland security is the chief emphasis of this chapter. Not exclusively a federal obligation, the content lays out the mandatory and absolute need for state and local cooperation. The various state departments are highlighted, with some of the better examples of state homeland offices being fully covered. How states and localities structure the homeland mission and carry out the aligned tasks of homeland is a crucial topic. Special emphasis on the use of task forces and coordinating committees is provided in the chapter, as well as discussion of the novel innovation known as the fusion center. In addition, the reader will encounter the growing local role in homeland security. In a continuous move to decentralization, the locality, whether county or city, is increasingly called upon to deliver services to the homeland quarter. Fusion centers are covered too, where intelligence is disseminated at regional levels throughout the United States. Presently, there are 58 fusion centers in the United States. Other programs that foster the collaboration of governmental entities include Citizen Corps, Community Emergency Response Teams (CERTs), the Fire Corps, and Volunteers in Public Service.

The chapter distinguishes the differing yet complementary roles of our national security mission, the military intelligence complex, and DHS. How the branches of our military complex serve the country is narrowly covered in light of the terrorist threat. Since military commands throughout the world deal with a host of homeland issues, the line between the two forces tends to merge rather than remain separate. The military itself divides up its responsibility to now include combatant zones with HD considerations. Homeland personnel rely on air force equipment and mission activity to secure the borders. FEMA regularly depends on military capacity to serve those victimized by natural disaster. The entire DoD has integrated homeland functions into its mission and purpose. Some even argue that the present campaigns in Iraq and Afghanistan are merely extensions of the HD strategy. Surely the missions are complementary, though not identical. Both DHS and the military are concerned with intelligence and information gathering. The chapter highlights the more prominent programs of the major military branches dedicated to homeland questions. Coverage also includes a quick look at emergent departments and entities dedicated to the mix of the military and the homeland, such as the National Maritime Intelligence Center, the NRO, and the Center for Combating Weapons of Mass Destruction.

Keywords

Adjutant General
Center for Advanced Operational Culture Learning
Citizen Corps Council
Civil Support Teams
Combatant zone
Cultural Studies program
Decentralization
Defend America
Defense Threat Reduction Agency
Fusion Center
Ground-based radar
Infrastructure Protection program
Intelligence and Security Command
Intelligence officer
Intelligence Surveillance and Reconnaissance Agency
Joint chiefs of staff
Law Enforcement Terrorism Prevention program
Metropolitan area
Military incursion
Military tactic
National Foreign Intelligence program
National Guard
National Infrastructure Protection Plan
National Maritime Intelligence Center
National Preparedness Guidelines
National Reconnaissance Office
North American Aerospace Defense Command
Office of Intelligence and Analysis
Office of Naval Intelligence
Predator drone
Public Safety Interoperable Communications Grant program
Public works
Regional planning council
Sovereign territory
State homeland security director
State, Local, Tribal, and Territorial Government Coordinating Council
Task force
U.S. Strategic Command
Unified command
Urban Area Security Initiative Grant program
Working group

Discussion Questions

1. What is the purpose and aim of the fusion center?
2. How do DHS funding and grants manifest the department's preference for local input and implementation?
3. Describe three DHS program initiatives that signify the importance of local control and involvement.
4. When does the line between military command and services become muddled with the services of DHS?
5. Discuss the diverse ways in which the military commands make contributions to the fight against terrorism.
6. Explain how the typical state might garner funding for homeland security and deliver its services.
7. Relay two major challenges to the idea of state, local, and federal cooperation in the world of homeland security.

8. Is it a fair conclusion to hold that DHS prefers decentralization over centralization of services?

9. What is the best argument for local initiative in the delivery of homeland services?

10. Give three examples of DHS programs or policies that encourage intergovernmental cooperation.

Practical Exercises

1. Contact your regional or state Office of Homeland Security. List five initiatives of this office.

2. Discover whether Citizen Corps works in your community. If so, explain its current endeavors.

3. Interview a state DHS official. Try to discern how positive this office's relation to and with DHS is.

4. Discover at least two differing funding sources for local implementation of homeland security activities.

Notes

1. Department of Homeland Security, Homeland Security Advisory Council, *Report from the Task Force on State and Local Homeland Security Funding 15*, June 2004.

2. National Governors Association at http://www.nga.org/cms/center/hsps.

3. R. E. Brooks, *Improving Criminal Intelligence Sharing: How the Criminal Intelligence Coordinating Council Support Law Enforcement and Homeland Security 34*, February 2011.

4. Office of the President, *Homeland Security Presidential Directive 5*, February 2003, 6.

5. New York State, *Homeland Security Strategy 2014–2016*, available at http://www.dhses.ny.gov/media/documents/NYS-Homeland-Security-Strategy.pdf, accessed January 10, 2016.

6. New York State, *Homeland Security Strategy 2014–2016*, 48 available at http://www.dhses.ny.gov/media/documents/NYS-Homeland-Security-Strategy.pdf, accessed January 10, 2016.

7. CRS Report to Congress, *FY 2009 Appropriations for State and Local Homeland Security*, February 7, 2008, http://fpc.state.gov/documents/organization/101807.pdf, accessed February 29, 2009. See also CRS Report for Congress, *Fiscal Year 2011 Department of Homeland Security Assistance to States and Localities*, April 26, 2010, http://www.fas.org/sgp/crs/homesec/R41105.pdf, accessed April 12, 2012.

8. State of Tennessee, *Office of Homeland Security*, https://www.tn.gov/safety/section/homelandsecurity, accessed January 10, 2016.

9. Tennessee Fusion Center, Tactical Report, Cyber safety tips, available at https://www.tn.gov/assets/entities/safety/attachments/Cyber_Safety_Tips_14_OCT_13.pdf, accessed January 10, 2016.

10. D. E. Marks and I. Y. Sun, The impact of 9/11 on organizational development among state and local law enforcement agencies, *Journal of Contemporary Criminal Justice*, 23 2007: 159–173.

11. B. R. Johnson, Fusion centers: Strengthening the nation's homeland security enterprise, *Police Chief*, February 2011: 62.

12. DHS, 2010 baseline capabilities assessment of fusion centers and critical operational capabilities gap mitigation strategy, available at http://www.dhs.gov/2010-baseline-capabilities-assessment-fusion-centers.

13. D. Keyer, Nationwide SAR initiative delivers value to fusion centers, *Police Chief*, February 2011: 40.

14. See Fusion Center Locations and Contact Information at http://www.dhs.gov/fusion-center-locations-and-contact-information.

15. Commonwealth of Massachusetts, *State Homeland Security Strategy*, September 2007, 10.

16. L. E. Davis, J. Rough, G. Cecchine, A. G. Schaefer, and L.-L. Zeman, *Hurricane Katrina: Lessons for Army Planning and Operations*, RAND Corporation (2007), available at http://www.rand.org/content/dam/rand/pubs/monographs/2007/RAND_MG603.pdf, accessed January 10, 2016.

17. Ibid.

18. S. J. Tomisek, Homeland security: New role for defense, *Strategic Forum (Institute for National Strategic Studies)*, 189, February 2002.

19. Department of Defense: Joint Chiefs of Staff, *Joint Publication 3–26: Homeland Security*, August 2005, viii, http://www.fas.org/irp/doddir/dod/jp3_26.pdf.

20. Joint Chiefs, *Homeland Security*, II–17.

21. Joint Chiefs, *Homeland Security*, I–2.

22. Department of Defense, *Measuring Stability and Security in Iraq: Report to Congress in Accordance with the Department of Defense Appropriations Act 2008*, June 28, 21.

23. Suleiman Al-Khalidi, Syria death toll now exceeds 210,000: rights group, Raissa Kasolowsky, ed. *Reuters* (Feb. 7, 2015), available at http://www.reuters.com/article/us-mideast-crisis-toll-idUSKBN-0LB0DY20150207, accessed January 10, 2016.

24. U.S. D0D, Operation Inherent Resolve, http://www.defense.gov/News/Special-Reports/0814_Inherent-Resolve.

25. U.S. D0D, Operation Inherent Resolve, http://www.defense.gov/News/Special-Reports/0814_Inherent-Resolve.

26. Joint Chiefs, *Homeland Security*, II–6.

27. Michelle Sohn, Drone strikes and due process: The role of the separation of powers in Lethal action against U.S. citizens outside traditional battlefields, *Jolt Digest* http://jolt.law.harvard.edu/digest/digest-note/drone-strikes-and-due-process (Mar. 6, 2013), accessed January 10, 2016; see also William Funk, Deadly drones, due process, and the fourth amendment, 22 *Wm & Mary Bill of Rights* (2013).

28. Cpl. G. Gonzalez, *CAOCL Helps Marines Navigate through 'Cultural Terrain,'*; go to http://www.mcu.usmc.mil/caocl/SitePages/index.aspx and search "caocl helps marines" (accessed April 12, 2012).

29. For more information on CAOCL, visit www.tecom.usmc.mil/caocl.

30. National Maritime Intelligence-Integration Office, About NMIO, http://nmio.ise.gov/About-NMIO, accessed January 10, 2016.

31. DOD, *Department of Defense Strategy for Countering Weapons of Mass Destruction* 7 (2014), available at http://archive.defense.gov/pubs/DoD_Strategy_for_Countering_Weapons_of_Mass_Destruction_dated_June_2014.pdf, accessed January 10, 2016.

32. Chairman of the Joint Chiefs of Staff, *National Military Strategy to Combat Weapons of Mass Destruction*, February 4, 2006; DoD, *Department of Defense Strategy for Countering Weapons of Mass Destruction* 7 (2014), available at http://archive.defense.gov/pubs/DoD_Strategy_for_Countering_Weapons_of_Mass_Destruction_dated_June_2014.pdf, accessed January 10, 2016.

33. DTRA, *Basic Research for Countering Weapons of Mass Destruction*, 2010.

34. Erica Chenoweth & Susan E. Clarke, All terrorism is local: Resources, nested institutions, and governance for urban homeland security in the American federal system, 63 *Political Res. Q.* 495 (2010).

Chapter **7**

FEMA, Response, and Recovery

Objectives

1. To describe the early twentieth-century history of the Federal Emergency Management Agency (FEMA)
2. To outline the changes that FEMA underwent, both structural and policy oriented, between 1980 and 2015
3. To define the structural and policy changes that FEMA initiated as a result of the events of 9/11
4. To recognize the concept of preparedness and describe FEMA's philosophy, and the programs and policies that relate to it
5. To distinguish the various types of emergencies that exist—that is, natural disasters versus terrorist incidents and routine events versus catastrophic events—and their relative response differences
6. To comprehend the principle of mitigation in preparedness and outline the various FEMA programs that address mitigation
7. To understand the importance of postassessment reports in preparedness, mitigation, response, and recovery planning
8. To distinguish the concepts of response and recovery and list the various initiatives undertaken by FEMA to make response more timely and effective

7.1 Historical Foundation for FEMA

The pre-9/11 world was quite comfortable with the language of the protocol for disaster and its mitigation. From the 1930s onward, there were structural mechanisms to deal with disaster in the American landscape. The Reconstruction Finance Corporation provided loans for the repair and reconstruction of certain public facilities following disasters. The Bureau of Public Roads had the authority to fund the repairs of highways and bridges damaged by floods, earthquakes, and other disasters. In addition, the U.S. Army Corps of Engineers played an increasingly active role in the design of floodplains, levees, dams, and other edifices. In addition to the predictability of terror, and its use for pressing social and political change, it is expected that the federal government responds in times of emergency and disaster. It is a reasonable expectation that was sorely lacking in the Katrina debacle.

By the 1960s, it was evident that historic agencies were incapable of handling the larger natural disasters that plagued the country. It was clear that a major federal response and recovery agency was essential to serve those victimized by natural disaster. The Federal Disaster Assistance Administration, housed in Housing and Urban Development, was established. The National Flood Insurance program was set up in 1968, and executive orders and other presidential authority became a normative part of the disaster environment.

7.1.1 Federal Emergency Management Agency: Pre-9/11

In 1979, President Jimmy Carter, by executive order, merged a multitude of disaster agencies into FEMA. FEMA was to author an integrated emergency management system (IEMS) that covered "small isolated events to the ultimate emergency—war." FEMA struggled to corral competing agency and bureaucratic interests and readily discovered the complexities of managing large- and small-scale disasters. Early in its operation, FEMA had to contend with

- Love Canal chemical disaster in Niagara Falls, New York
- Cuban boat refugee crisis
- Three Mile Island, Pennsylvania, nuclear plant crisis
- Hurricane Andrew
- Loma Prieta, California, earthquake

That FEMA adjusted its mission based on natural disasters and other environmental pressures is undeniable. FEMA was also continually reorganized in hopes that a centralized service would be a better brand of government response. For example, Reorganization Plan #3, adopted in 1978, integrated the National Fire Prevention Control Office, the Federal Broadcast System, the Defense Civil Preparedness Agency, the Federal Disaster Assistance Administration, and the Federal Preparedness Agency. Other inclusions in the latter part of the twentieth century were agencies that monitored earthquakes, dam safety, nuclear warning systems, and severe weather policy. In general, FEMA sought to implement an IEMS. In the early 1990s, FEMA's capacity to respond to hurricanes and other natural disasters was severely tested, and "FEMA seemed incapable of carrying out the essential government function of emergency management."[1]

In its early life, FEMA's philosophy of operation was narrower—in that it stressed the disaster side of emergency.

Internet Exercise: Read closely and consider the foundational laws that give FEMA legal authority for its many actions at: http://www.fema.gov/about-agency.

That traditional definition, which includes flood, wind, earthquake, fire, and other natural disaster, tends to be distinctly different from the notion of terror. FEMA would eventually have to encompass terror—that intentionally inflicted disaster driven by an assortment of motivations. The Oklahoma City bombing of 1995 catapulted FEMA into the world of terrorist activity. Yet, the culture of FEMA, bound to the natural-disaster mentality, struggled to fit into the world of terror. At first, FEMA expended considerable energy urging communities to become disaster resistant and to erect mitigation policies that would prevent disasters of all sorts. Implementing *Project Impact: Building Disaster Resistant Communities* was the chief programmatic aim of FEMA in the late 1990s. In Project Impact, communities were to examine their communities in light of risk and adopt corresponding measures to mitigate the harm. FEMA's central contribution during this period was to refocus communities, leaders, and the citizenry into the world of risk—natural or otherwise.

7.1.2 Federal Emergency Management Agency: Post-9/11

After the horrid events of 9/11, the mission of FEMA, its operational philosophy, and its ability to carry out its command were put to the test.[2] After 9/11, FEMA had to reorganize in two ways: first, it had to continue its historic mission to deal with and respond to disaster; and second, it had to integrate a threat mentality as part of its obligation in serving the Department of Homeland Security (DHS). While natural disasters continue to be a crucial responsibility for FEMA, the world of terrorism increasingly dominates its outlook and mission. Hence, FEMA's mission is more encompassing than its historic expectation.

> FEMA's mission is to support our citizens and first responders to ensure that as a nation we work together to build, sustain and improve our capability to prepare for, protect against, respond to, recover from and mitigate all hazards.[3]

Internet Exercise: Learn all about FEMA by reviewing the YouTube profile of the agency at https://www.fema.gov/media-library/assets/videos/80684.

FEMA's merger has policy implications that it must adapt to. Figure 7.1 charts the current structure of FEMA.

FEMA is led by an administrator and a whole host of deputy directors and administrators. FEMA also depends on the input and advice of its National Advisory Council, whose membership includes experts from both the public and the private sector. The National

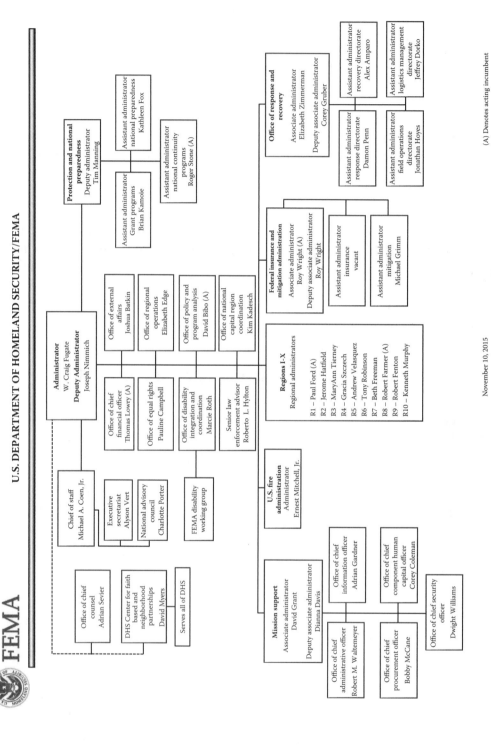

FIGURE 7.1 FEMA organization chart.

Advisory Council's input has been quite laudatory and more than pro forma comment. Since 2007, the council has directly dealt with many challenges but also with many success stories. The latest recommendations, from their September 2015 meeting, include

Recommendation 1: FEMA should advance training and professional conduct for the NFIP through the following actions:

- Explore current best practices used in the insurance industry to train, assist, and evaluate adjusters and consider implementing these best practices when and where appropriate;
- Develop and require ongoing professional education for adjusters and engineers who support the claims adjusting process, develop "Just in Time" training aids, and disseminate "best practice updates" to adjusters and engineers in the field; and
- Develop a method to track the performance of adjusters and field engineers. This could be similar to the performance metrics used to measure cadre staff.

Recommendation 2: FEMA should provide consistent, accurate guidance documents regarding the NFIP for state/local/tribal partners through the following actions:

- Develop clear, written guidance for policy coverage and claims adjustments. While there may be a need for oral guidance on occasion, FEMA should develop a process that rapidly reviews and formalizes oral guidance in a written format and disseminate this written guidance to all participants.
- Hire cadre staff focused on Quality Assurance/Quality Control to rapidly identify and correct errors, and recognize event specific trends such as wind versus flood damage (e.g., Hurricane Katrina) or foundation issues (e.g., Superstorm Sandy).

Recommendation 3: FEMA should institutionalize best practices for the NFIP. Before Superstorm Sandy, FEMA pre-authorized "partial payments of up to $30,000 to cover building systems and related repairs when prompt action was necessary …, extended the time a survivor could submit a claim, and instituted a rapid claims process." FEMA should analyze the benefits and challenges of these proactive financial options and consider formalizing and implementing them for future events. FEMA has effectively used an ad hoc appeals process for Hurricanes Katrina and Isabel and Superstorm Sandy. FEMA should formalize the ad hoc appeals process into a standing task force for appeals.[4]

Internet Exercise: Check out the membership roster of the current NAC at https://www.fema.gov/national-advisory-council and then click on "Membership."

Geographically, FEMA is further broken down into 10 distinct regions to allow for greater local input and participation (see Figure 7.2).

Finally, FEMA targets its subject matter by decentralizing into various *directorates*. These divisions provide the core, coordinated federal, operational, and logistical capability needed to save and sustain lives, minimize suffering, and protect property in a timely and effective manner in communities that become overwhelmed by natural disasters, acts of terrorism, or other emergencies. From assistance to mitigation, from logistics to the continuity programs, FEMA depends on its subject-matter specialists to deliver these services. The current directorates are

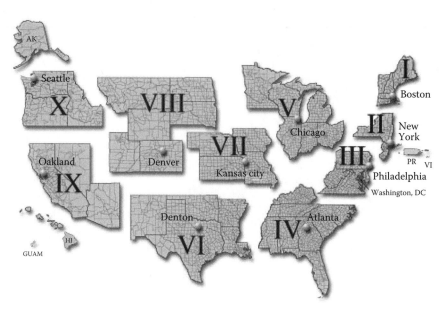

FIGURE 7.2 FEMA regions.

- Logistics management
- Response
- Recovery
- Field operations
- National continuity programs
- National preparedness
- Grant Programs

Internet Exercise: Read FEMA's strategic plan for the years 2008–2013 at https://www.fema.gov/fema-strategic-plan.

There has been some debate recently as to what FEMA's role is during and in the wake of man-made and natural disasters, particularly in the area of recovery spending. Disasters present unique challenges according to the Center for Disaster Philanthropy:

> The challenge…is that regardless of the size of the disaster, some affected individuals do not meet eligibility requirements for government disaster aid—and still others will have unmet needs even after receiving federal and/or state assistance. As FEMA Administrator Craig Fugate has said, "There's no way government can solve the challenges of a disaster with a government-centric approach. It takes the whole team. And the private sector provides the bulk of the services every day in the community."[5]

So the questions arise: Where should the money for response and recovery come from? What criteria do disaster victims need to meet to be eligible for funds? Should taxpayers bear the cost of such funding? Is this a federal obligation or should it be a state and local issue? What role should the private sector play? Should those who pay for flood or hazard insurance be somehow rewarded for their advance planning while others are penalized?

Professor William Shughart II of the University of Mississippi sees those who have taken proper precautions—those who purchased insurance prior to the disaster event and understood the risks—as the party worthy of our protection and admiration. His argument is that this is good public policy that leads to a better, independent citizenry rather than individuals who are waiting for, and are dependent solely on, government assistance. According to Schugart:

> People who voluntarily put themselves in harm's way, taking on the additional risks of living and working in disaster-prone areas, adequately insuring their lives and property against wind and flood—and paying actuarially fair premiums that reflect the greater risk—have every right to expect prompt reimbursement for the damages they sustained and every right to rebuild if they wish.[6]

As major disasters increase in scope, frequency, and damage costs—as has been the trend the last few decades—this debate as to who bears the cost of rebuilding and when to rebuild or not will certainly continue.

7.2 FEMA and Preparedness

Any effective response, recovery, or other answer to a threat or catastrophe heavily depends on preparedness. By preparedness, one means that the agency, community, and constituency affected, as well as public and private partners, stand ready to deal with the threat in an effective manner.

Questions regarding the country's preparedness rose to the front and center after Katrina. Various amendments to the *Homeland Security Act of 2002* established the National Preparedness Directorate (NPD). The directorate tackles many tasks in the area of preparedness, including

- Strategy, policy, and planning guidance to build prevention, protection, response, and recovery capabilities
- Training courses, exercises, and technical assistance to ensure capabilities are standardized
- Coordination of FEMA regions as well as emergency management personnel at the federal, state, and local levels
- Coordination with other FEMA offices and directorates to produce a unified approach to emergency management

Running things at a national level is never an easy undertaking, and this challenge always adds to the difficulties. The Early Warning System—originally in color-coded formula—did not even have consensus as to what the colors meant nor did the colors really represent anything objectively accurate.[7] So subjective was the interpretation of the color-coded warning mode that emergency planners scrapped the system in 2013. In its place, emergency planners have come to depend on Emergency Alert System (EAS) participants who naturally communicate with others in the relevant geographic area. The EAS sends warnings via broadcast, cable, satellite, and wireline pathways. EAS participants, who consist of broadcast, cable, satellite, and wireline providers, are the stewards of this important public service in close partnership with alerting officials at all levels of government.

The EAS system is now labeled the Integrated Early Warning System (IPAWS), and under this system, officials at every level of government communicate with aligned agencies, other reporting authorities, and the public at large about impending harm or catastrophe.

Internet Exercise: See the IPAWS video on how it works at https://www.fema.gov/media-library/assets/videos/77356.

Only approved public authorities may participate in the redesigned alert system used by FEMA. As of January 2016, over 700 agencies were designated approved for purposes of alert. Current lists, which are regularly updated, can be found on the IPAWS website at http://www.fema.gov/integrated-public-alert-warning-system-authorities.

Preparedness encompasses a whole range of operational and policy concerns for the homeland professional. Preparedness models envelop the capacity to plan, organize, train, equip, exercise, evaluate, and improve. FEMA charts the cycle of preparedness in Figure 7.3.[8]

The catalogue of FEMA resources regarding preparedness is quite extensive. Already discussed in the text has been the citizen portal titled *Ready.gov* as well as the many functions and activities of the Citizen Corps. In addition to these resources, FEMA publishes a digital library—a searchable web-based collection of all publicly accessible FEMA information resources, including CDs, DVDs, VHS tapes, audio tapes, disability resources, posters and display items, brochures, publications, guidance and policy papers, program regulations and guidelines, forms, slide presentations, and other documents. The library is catalogued and organized in accordance with the hazard forms in Figure 7.4.

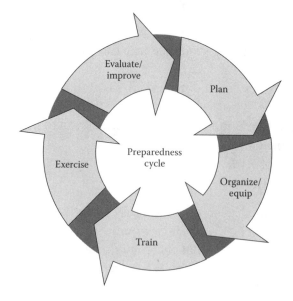

FIGURE 7.3 Preparedness cycle.

Hazard Type Associations
Use this guide if you are unable to find what you are looking for in the list of hazard type selections provided.

If you are looking for:	Consider using:
Aftershock	Earthquake
Ash Fall	Volcano
Avalanche	Mudslide/Landslide, Winter Storm
Blizzard	Severe Storm, Winter Storm
Brush Fire	Wildfire
Cold	Extreme Temperatures, Winter Storm
Cyclone	Hurricane/Tropical Storm, Typhoon
Dust Storm	Drought, Extreme Temperatures, Severe Storm
Erosion	Coastal Storm, Hurricane/Tropical Storm, Typhoon
Explosion	Chemical/Biological, Fire, Nuclear, Technological, Terrorism
Flood, Flash Flood	Dam/Levee Break, Flooding
Forest Fire	Wildfire
Freeze	Extreme Temperatures, Winter Storm
Freezing Rain	Severe Storm, Winter Storm
Funnel Cloud	Tornado
Ground Saturation	Flooding
Hail	Severe Storm, Winter Storm
Heat	Extreme Temperatures
High Surf	Coastal Storm, Hurricane/Tropical Storm, Tsunami, Typhoon
Ice	Extreme Temperatures, Winter Storm
Ice Jam	Flooding
Lava/Debris Flow	Volcano
Mold	Flooding
Power Outage	Technological, Terrorism
Radiological	Chemical/Biological, Nuclear, Terrorism
Rain	Flooding, Hurricane/Tropical Storm, Severe Storm, Typhoon, Winter Storm
Rock Slide	Mudslide/Landslide
Seismic Wave	Earthquake
Snow	Winter Storm
Snow Melt	Flooding
Storm Surge	Hurricane/Tropical Storm, Typhoon
Thunderstorm	Severe Storm
Tropical Depression	Hurricane/Tropical Storm, Severe Storm
Tidal Wave	Tsunami
Virus	Chemical/Biological, Terrorism
Wind	Coastal Storm, Hurricane/Tropical Storm, Severe Storm, Typhoon, Winter Storm
Waterspout	Tornado

FIGURE 7.4 FEMA hazard forms cross-references.

FEMA orchestrates a narrower portal dedicated to natural disasters aptly titled *DisasterAssistance.gov*. The portal's primary aim is to assist those already harmed by natural disasters (see Figure 7.5).

Being prepared for radiological fallout from nuclear contamination is another FEMA responsibility. FEMA's Radiological Emergency Preparedness Program prepares for harm that may emerge in nuclear accidents and educates the public about this unique harm.[9] Just as critically, FEMA plays a central preparedness role in the care, protection, and mitigation of chemical stockpiles across the continental United States. FEMA works in partnership with the United States Army to not only protect the stockpile but also to ensure the integrity of the same for the public at large. While stockpiles are slowly but assuredly being eliminated in the United States, there are nine locales across the nation for the storage of the same (see Figure 7.6 for current locations).

Internet Exercise: Even individuals and families must be prepared for all eventualities. See the preparedness guide for chemical stockpile emergencies at https://www.cseppportal.net/SitePages/index.html.

FIGURE 7.5 Before and after Hurricane Sandy: Georgia Avenue, Long Beach, NY, July 26, 2013. In November 2012, debris filled the streets as residents started to recover from the devastation of Hurricane Sandy (www.dhs.gov).

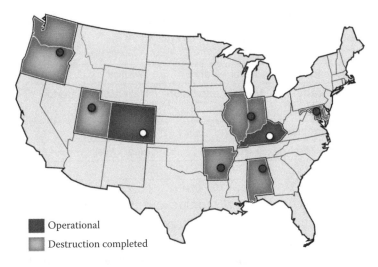

FIGURE 7.6   **National chemical stockpile. The white dots indicate the last two operational stockpiles. The black dots are stockpiles that have been destroyed.**

Preparing the citizenry for hazard, disaster, and threat is a core mission of FEMA. Being ready—understanding the risk and taking preventive and mitigatory steps to minimize the damage—are the essential FEMA principles.[10]

How one goes about these functions largely depends on the type of threat or hazard under review.[11] Floods and hurricanes are very different animals from nuclear leaks or sarin gas inhalation. The types of emergencies that occur on a daily basis, such as car accidents, road spills, or house fires, are routine events. Catastrophic events, such as tornadoes, terrorist attacks, superstorms such as Hurricane Sandy, or floods, tend to cover a larger area, impact a greater number of citizens, cost more to recover from, and occur less frequently.[12] See the table in Figure 7.7[13] for event duration estimates.

	Routine		Catastrophic	
Classification	**Local**	**Regional**	**State**	**National**
Examples	• Minor traffic incidents • Minor load spills • Vehicle fires • Minor train/bus accidents • Accidents with injuries but no fatalities	• Train derailment • Major bus/rail transit accidents • Major truck accidents • Multi-vehicle crashes • HazMat spills • Accidents with injuries and fatalities	• Train crashes • Airplane crashes • HazMat incidents • Multi-vehicle accidents • Tunnel fires • Multiple injuries and fatalities • Port/airport incidents • Large building fire or explosion • Industrial incidents • Major tunnel/bridge closure	• Terrorist attack/ WMD • Floods, blizzards, tornadoes • Transportation infrastructure collapse • Extended power/ water outages • Riots • Mass casualties
Expected event duration	**0–2 Hours**	**2–24 Hours**	**Day**	**Weeks**

FIGURE 7.7   **Duration estimates for catastrophic and routine emergency events.**

The homeland specialist must first identify the risk and then take the necessary steps compatible with that risk. Some of the usual events are

Dam failure	Fire or wildfire	Wildfire
Hurricane	Nuclear explosion	Hazardous material
Tornado	Volcano	Thunderstorm
Earthquake	Flood	Winter storm
Landslide	Terrorism	Heat
Tsunami		

FEMA uses high-level technology to estimate and predict damage and potential harm. It has developed comprehensive software programs that are crucial to predicting the outcomes of particular events (Figure 7.8).

Hazus is a product that uses current scientific and engineering knowledge, coupled with the latest geographic information systems (GIS) technology, to produce estimates of hazard-related damage before, or after, a disaster occurs. Depending on the threat or harm, Hazus will evaluate and estimate losses after inputting criteria. The Hazus software program assesses risk in a five-step process, as outlined in Figure 7.9.[14]

Hence, preparedness steps will largely depend on the threat. While Hazus works in natural disasters, its effectiveness in terror is less predictable and useful.[15] To close the knowledge gap on the national level, FEMA sponsors annual Hazus conferences, which have included specialized training in flood mitigation, cost–benefit analysis, storm surge, and other coastal threats.

Internet Exercise: Discover Hazus success stories at https://www.fema.gov/hazus.

FIGURE 7.8 The Hazus-MH data extractor is a tool for extracting data from Hazus-MH data sources.

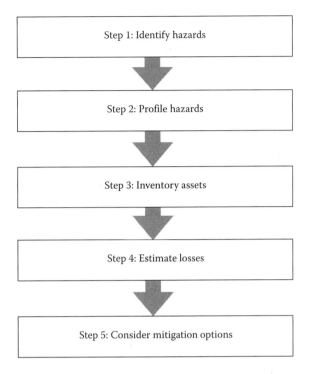

FIGURE 7.9   Hazus process flowchart.

Be mindful that software updates are going to be regular occurrences in the Hazus market. FEMA just released Hazus 3.0, and another edition can be expected in another year or so.[16]

Since Katrina, FEMA has evolved in mostly beneficial ways for many of its responses. Katrina was a wakeup call about the concept of preparedness—being able to respond with professionalism and efficacy. Since Katrina, the agency has been bombarded with a legion of natural disasters and can mostly hold its head high in its handling of these many events. "FEMA gets high marks from disaster experts for inserting field staff into the disaster zone quickly and opening up communication with local and state officials."[17] Some have even argued that during the last decade, especially since Katrina, the agency is now in the "groove."[18] The advance warning notification and response, in large part, to Hurricane Sandy is a direct reflection of some of the positive changes, particularly under Administrator Craig Fugate, who has headed up FEMA since 2009.

7.2.1 Role of Mitigation in the Preparedness Model

Once the threat has been identified and the inventory or potential costs calculated, the homeland professional seeks ways to mitigate the harm. The term *mitigation* implies an intervention before the threat or catastrophe takes place. Mitigation is the effort to reduce loss of life and property by lessening the impact of disasters. Effective mitigation measures can break the cycle of disaster damage, reconstruction, and repeated damage. While it cannot work in all homeland threats, the idea of mitigation works particularly well in the case of natural disasters, fire, and other catastrophes. For example, in the event of a hurricane or flood or even a nuclear attack, there are mitigation steps that may prevent the level of expected destruction. Building design, for instance, goes a long way to mitigate the impact of either the earthquake or the flood. Hence, FEMA encourages a variety of mitigation programs to minimize and limit damage and threat. Particular attention is given to the mitigation of buildings against terrorist threat and the security and safety of schools, hospitals, and government installations (see Figure 7.10).[19]

Congress has repeatedly increased the funding for mitigation programs, since it is now self-evident that mitigation is quantifiably demonstrable. Mitigation programs have "demonstrated cost reductions following disasters due earlier mitigation investments."[20] What is just as deducible is that mitigation plans lack a universality and national design with states and localities treating some portion of the total variable relevant in a mitigation program. For example, the premitigation analysis must consider evacuation as a legitimate part of the mitigation program. If one does not account for the means, the methods, or the alternatives

What is the Risk Management Series?

The Risk Management Series (RMS) is a new FEMA series directed at providing design guidance for mitigating multihazard events. The objective of the series is to reduce physical damage to structural and nonstructural components of buildings and related infrastructure, and to reduce resultant casualties during natural and manmade disasters.

The RMS is intended to minimize conflicts that may arise from a multihazard design approach. A multihazard approach requires a complex series of tradeoffs. Security concerns need to be balanced with requirements in terms of earthquakes, floods, high speed winds, accessibility, fire protection, and aesthetics, among others. Designing to mitigate natural hazards should avoid considering manmade hazards as an afterthought, but rather as a critical concern to be studied early during the project cycle. Natural hazards are the largest single contributor to catastrophic or repetitive damage to communities nationwide. Manmade hazards can be categorized as rare events with a potential high impact and very difficult to predict.

Risk Management Series

Minimizing the Effects of Natural Disasters and Potential Terrorist Attacks on Large Buildings

FEMA

FIGURE 7.10 FEMA's risk management series.

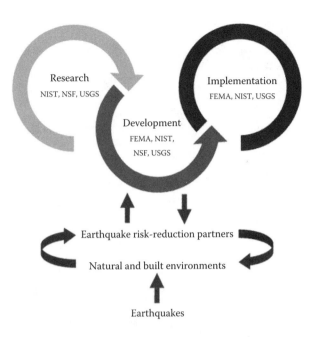

FIGURE 7.11   **National Earthquake Hazards Reduction Plan process chart.**

in evacuation, aside from being caught flat-footed, the expense of failing to plan will surely be higher than the expense of being organized. Drs. Olornilua and Ibitaya surprisingly conclude that this lack of uniformity directly undermines our planned efficiencies and that every mitigation plan must prepare for "multihazard" situations. The lack of uniformity is portrayed as "dismal."[21]

In the area of earthquakes, FEMA sponsors the National Earthquake Hazards Reduction Plan (NEHRP) (Figure 7.11).

Its primary goals are to

- Develop effective practices and policies for earthquake loss reduction and to accelerate implementation
- Improve techniques to reduce seismic vulnerability of facilities and systems
- Improve seismic hazards identification and risk assessment methods
- Improve the understanding of earthquakes

In earthquake design, the building must be capable of withstanding the move and sway caused by the earthquake. The recent completion of the Paramount, a high-rise office complex in San Francisco, an earthquake-prone area, manifests the role of engineering design in building plans. In the Paramount, precast concrete is utilized as well as the Precast Hybrid Movement Resistant Frame (PHMRF) system (Figure 7.12).

Internet Exercise: Review the construction of Donald J. Trump's tower in Chicago, which captures this sort of earthquake anticipation: https ://www.youtube.com/watch?v= pXM1UdmULPk.

FIGURE 7.12   The Paramount building in San Francisco (courtesy of FEMA).

These same mitigation principles apply to a host of other settings, including dams and waterways. FEMA's National Dam Safety Program (NDSP) identifies, develops, and enhances technology to track the condition of the dam infrastructure. FEMA hosts the following initiatives:

- National Inventory of Dams: A computerized database of U.S. dams.
- National Dam Safety Program management tools: An information collection and management system used by federal and state dam safety program managers.
- National Performance of Dams Program: A national effort headquartered at Stanford University that tracks dam performance.

Internet Exercise: Read the biennial report of the National Dam Safety Program at https://www.fema.gov/media-library/assets/documents/16240.

The preparedness and mitigation stress continues into the world of hurricanes. FEMA, in collaboration with a host of other agencies, such as the National Oceanic and Atmospheric Association, National Weather Service, U.S. Department of Transportation, and U.S. Army Corps of Engineers, is deeply involved in the preparation and planning for and the mitigation of hurricanes. Some activities include

- Planning for safe and effective evacuations
- National Hurricane Program (NHP) training
- Response and recovery

- Poststorm assessments
- Mitigation as to hurricane losses

Established in 1985, the NHP conducts assessments and provides tools and technical assistance to assist state and local agencies in developing hurricane evacuation plans. Aside from planning, preparedness, and mitigation, FEMA, by and through the NHP, relies on a Hurricane Liaison Team (HLT) that coordinates the various levels of government response as well as private-sector players. HLT members provide critical storm information to government agency decision makers at all levels to help them prepare for their response operations, which may include evacuations, sheltering, and mobilizing equipment. The HLT works closely with states and localities.[22]

FEMA also relies on Mitigation Assessment Teams (MATs), which it assigns to vulnerable areas. MATs see the real and meaningful impact of natural disasters and the steps that could have eliminated some of the losses. The MAT will

- Assess the vulnerability of buildings
- Increase building resistance to damage caused by hazard events

MATs look closely at building codes and standards, designs, methods, and materials used for new construction and post-disaster repair and recovery.

Internet Exercise: Find out about careers in MATs and the current recruitment efforts by FEMA at https://www.fema.gov/mitigation-assessment-team-program.

Flood threats are a continual concern for the FEMA mission and its operational personnel. The last decade has witnessed a wave of flood events caused by anything from heavy rains to hurricanes. This includes areas that are regularly prone to reoccurrences of disaster-level flooding. Critics, and even the independent government Congressional Research Service, have questioned the efficacy of the National Flood Insurance Program (NFIP), originally established in 1968 as a measure to "address the nation's flood exposure and challenges inherent in financing and managing flood risks in the private sector."[23]

DHS even publishes a list of repeat and very expensive performers in the world of floods (see Table 7.1).

Homebuilders are now required to anticipate the reality of flood when designing residential and commercial buildings. Gone are the days when design could disregard the elements.

FEMA publishes how-to guides for construction companies so that damage may be mitigated. Figure 7.13[24] portrays the need for a stainless-steel house wrap that minimizes water damage.

Internet Exercise: Read the FEMA construction advice on building in flood-prone areas at http://www.fema.gov/library/viewRecord.do?id=1645.

So important is the minimization of flood damage before the flood occurs that FEMA has erected a subagency—the Federal Insurance and Mitigation Administration (FIMA)—solely dedicated to flood mitigation (Figure 7.14).

TABLE 7.1 Top 15 Significant Flood Events Covered by the National Flood Insurance Program

(1978–December 31, 2010; $ nominal)

Rank	Event	Date	Number of Paid Losses	Amount Paid	Average Paid Loss
1	Hurricane Katrina	August 2005	167,979	$16,317,643,777	$97,141
2	Superstorm Sandy	October 2012	129,657	$8,085,487,407	$62,361
3	Hurricane Ike	September 2008	46,595	$2,689,915,498	$57,730
4	Hurricane Ivan	September 2004	28,297	$1,612,109,924	$56,971
5	Hurricane Irene	August 2011	44,260	$1,339,095,780	$30,255
6	Tropical Storm Allison	June 1989	30,786	$1,107,001,078	$35,958
7	Louisiana flooding	May 1995	31,343	$585,071,593	$18,667
8	Tropical Storm Isaac	August 2012	11,999	$550,373,725	$45,868
9	Hurricane Isabel	September 2003	19,938	$500,265,018	$25,091
10	Hurricane Rita	September 2005	9,528	$474,688,462	$49,820
11	Hurricane Floyd	September 1999	20,439	$462,326,389	$22,620
12	Tropical Storm Lee	September 2011	9,880	$459,813,102	$46,540
13	Texas flooding	May 2015	6,472	$412,590,049	$63,750
14	Hurricane Opal	October 1995	10,343	$405,527,543	$39,208
15	Hurricane Hugo	September 1989	12,840	$376,433,739	$29,317

Source: U.S. Department of Homeland Security, Federal Emergency Management Agency.

FIMA deals with

- Complying with or exceeding NFIP floodplain management regulations
- Enforcing stringent building codes, flood-proofing requirements, seismic design standards, and wind-bracing requirements for new construction or repairing existing buildings
- Adopting zoning ordinances that steer development away from areas subject to flooding, storm surge, or coastal erosion
- Retrofitting public buildings to withstand hurricane-strength winds or ground shaking
- Acquiring damaged homes or businesses in flood-prone areas, relocating the structures, and returning the property to open space, wetlands, or recreational uses

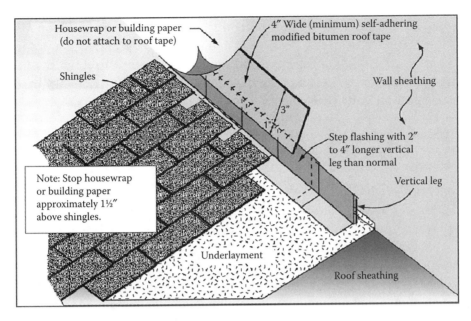

FIGURE 7.13 **FEMA construction guidelines to help mitigate roof damage.**

FIGURE 7.14 **Kelso, Washington. As a result of the heavy rainfall in Washington, earth broke loose from a hill and rammed into this home. The owner applied for assistance from FEMA and received a grant to cover reconstruction costs (courtesy of Savannah Brehmer/FEMA).**

- Building community shelters and tornado safe rooms to help protect people in their homes, public buildings, and schools in hurricane- and tornado-prone areas

In the area of risk assessment, FEMA has instituted a wide array of programs, including

- Flood hazard mapping
- Hazus-MH—the software program for disasters
- Mitigation planning—the full body of steps to minimize damage

In mapping, FEMA has made its greatest contribution. In the FEMA Flood Map Service Center, professionals can scan and assess just about every geographic area prone to flooding. FEMA's new MAP MOD program is an ambitious attempt to draw the flood-prone areas. Using the latest mapping technology, including but not limited to GIS-based format, flood maps are now digitally produced.

Internet Exercise: Find out your neighborhood's flood potential by visiting the FEMA map center at http://msc.fema.gov/portal.

Risk reduction weighs on FEMA policymakers daily, for if there is any truism about floods and other natural disasters, it is that these events will reoccur. FEMA expends significant energy educating the public about floods and how to prepare.[25] For example, FEMA's FloodSmart program delineates some excellent suggestions on how to minimize the damage in an upcoming flood event[26] (see Figure 7.15).[27]

Aside from its educational role, FEMA promotes a host of other risk reductions, including its National Flood Insurance Program, its flood map center, and its software programs for both individual and commercial interests. Additionally, FEMA has devised a repetitive loss program according to which flood-prone areas must implement mitigation steps to thwart the ensuing damages. See Figure 7.16 for the cover page relating to repetitive loss.

FEMA provides grants and other financial support to implement mitigation plans. To spend money now to avoid future catastrophic costs evidences sound policy. Just as compellingly, FEMA serves as a depository for best practices in the world of catastrophic mitigation. By best practices, we mean a collection of what in fact works in the event of flood or other hazard or threat. FEMA labels the most effective mitigation practices as either superior or commendable. FEMA publishes a compendium of exemplary or best practices in the area of mitigation and preparedness. It asks practitioners in the homeland security field to submit programs that they consider not only workable but on the cutting edge of innovation in mitigation. FEMA defines an exemplary program as

> an exemplary practice in emergency management is any practice, project, program, technique, or method that works in one place and is worthy of copying and can be copied elsewhere. It includes initiatives such as inventive coordination among organizations, volunteer projects and resource sharing, and other innovative and highly effective emergency management activities.[28]

Finally, FEMA relies on agencies to conduct postassessment reports after the hurricane has passed. Postassessment reports are essential for FEMA's future operations since these documents provide lessons learned from past storms; measures of hurricane and coastal flooding preparedness; the need for reform in public policy, building performance, and hurricane mitigation; the assessment of growth and the efficacy of evacuation shelter selection guidelines; and other contingency planning. FEMA also needs to determine where it can be more efficient and cost conscious. With rising economic challenges, the agency must

Before A Flood
After getting flood insurance, there are several things you can do to minimize losses in your home and ensure your family's safety.
EDUCATE YOURSELF
After getting flood insurance, there are several things you can do to minimize losses in your home and ensure your family's safety.

1. Safeguard your possessions.

- Create a personal flood file containing information about all your possessions and keep it in a secure place, such as a safe deposit box or waterproof container. This file should have:
- A copy of your insurance policies with your agents contact information.
- A household inventory: For insurance purposes, be sure to keep a written and visual (i.e., videotaped or photographed) record of all major household items and valuables, even those stored in basements, attics or garages. Create files that include serial numbers and store receipts for major appliances and electronics. Have jewelry and artwork appraised. These documents are critically important when filing insurance claims. For more information visit www.knowyourstuff.org.
- Copies of all other critical documents, including finance records or receipts of major purchases.

2. Prepare your house.

- First make sure your sump pump is working and then install a battery-operated backup, in case of a power failure. Installing a water alarm will also let you know if water is accumulating in your basement.
- Clear debris from gutters and downspouts.
- Anchor any fuel tanks.
- Raise your electrical components (switches, sockets, circuit breakers, and wiring) at least 12 inches above your home's projected flood elevation.
- Place the furnace, water heater, washer, and dryer on cement blocks at least 12 inches above the projected flood elevation.
- Move furniture, valuables, and important documents to a safe place.

3. Develop a family emergency plan.

- Create a safety kit with drinking water, canned food, first aid, blankets, a radio, and a flashlight.
- Post emergency telephone numbers by the phone and teach your children how to dial 911.
- Plan and practice a flood evacuation route with your family. Know safe routes from home, work, and school that are on higher ground.
- Ask an out-of-state relative or friend to be your emergency family contact.
- Have a plan to protect your pets.

For more information on emergency preparation, talk to your insurance agent or visit Ready.gov.

FIGURE 7.15   FEMA's FloodSmart Program—Educate Yourself.

carry out its functions with fewer funds and fewer people. In the age of smartphones and mobile communications, the agency must incorporate more innovative technology when communicating with its constituencies.[29] As a result, FEMA must aggressively employ all forms of social media to get the warning and alerts communicated across many strata. Mobile apps are an economical and highly efficient method of communication (Figure 7.17).

Mitigation teams play a crucial role in this stage of the natural or catastrophic event. At postassessment, the team can determine the efficacy of risk reduction methods and simultaneously recommend protocols for improvement. Postassessment is central to homeland policy making since it looks to

Federal Emergency Management Agency
National Flood Insurance Program

OMB 1660-0022 EXPIRES August 31, 2010

NFIP REPETITIVE LOSS (RL) UPDATE WORKSHEET (AW-501)

NOTE: SEE REVERSE SIDE FOR MITIGATION ACTION CODES AND PAPERWORK BURDEN STATEMENT

Printed On: THE INFORMATION ON THIS FORM IS BASED ON CLAIMS ON OR BEFORE:

REPETITIVE LOSS NUMBER:

Internal use only ☐ **A**   ☐ **N/A**   ☐ **FRR**

CURRENT NFIP COMMUNITY NAME:	
COMMUNITY ID # :	
CURRENT PROPERTY ADDRESS	**PREVIOUS PROPERTY ADDRESS/COMMUNITY ID #**
LAST CLAIMANT:	
INSURED: NAMED INSURED:	
DATES OF LOSSES	TOTAL NUMBER OF LOSSES FOR PROPERTY:

REQUESTED UPDATES
MARK ALL UPDATES BELOW THAT APPLY (IMPORTANT – READ THE INSTRUCTIONS)

1. ☐ INFORMATION PROVIDED NOT SUFFICIENT TO IDENTIFY PROPERTY.
     Choose this update if all attempts to locate the property fail. Please describe the steps you took to locate the property in the comments section below.

2. ☐ COSMETIC CHANGES REQUIRED TO THE ADDRESS:
     Use this update to correct or update the property address shown above.
     Only change the address not the name.

3. ☐ PROPERTY NOT IN OUR COMMUNITY OR JURISDICTION:
     Choose this update if you have positively determined that the property shown is not located in your community. Please provide the correct community name and if known the NFIP Community ID Number. If available, please attach a map showing the property location.

     ASSIGN TO COMMUNITY NAME: _____ NFIP COMMUNITY ID # _____

4. ☐ FLOOD PROTECTION PROVIDED.
     Choose this update if some type of structural intervention has occurred to the building, property or the source of flooding that protects the building from future events similar to those that occurred in the past. The correction must be supported by documentation such as an Elevation Certificate and the Mitigation information below must be provided.

     Mitigation Action 1.) ☐   **Source of Mitigation Funding 3.)** ☐   **See the back of this form for the appropriate codes.**

5. ☐ NO BUILDING ON PROPERTY.
     Choose this update only if the property in question can be positively identified as the site of the previously flooded building and documentation is available to support that an insurable building no longer exists at this site. The correction must be supported by documentation such as a Demolition or Relocation Permit and the Mitigation information below must be provided.

     Mitigation Action 2.) ☐   **Source of Mitigation Funding 3.)** ☐   **See the back of this form for the appropriate codes.**

6. ☐ DUPLICATE LISTING WITH RL NUMBER: _____ COMBINE AS ONE LISTING.
     Choose this update to identify two or more separate listings that are for the same building. List all other RL numbers that are duplicates to this property. Please indicate which address shown is the correct address to use.

7. ☐ HISTORIC BUILDING: Check this box if you know the building is listed on a State or National Historic Registry.

ADDITIONAL COMMENTS: _____

_____

_____

A SIGNED RL TRANSMITTAL SHEET MUST ACCOMPANY THIS FORM FOR APPOVAL OF THE UPDATE!

SEE PRIVACY ACT STATEMENT ON THE BACK

FIGURE 7.16   Repetitive loss update worksheet.

MITIGATION ACTION CODES

1.) If you checked the box that says "FLOOD PROTECTION PROVIDED," please enter the letter below (a –f) that best describes the situation:

   a. The building was elevated to or above the Base Flood Elevation (BFE).
   b. The building was elevated but not to the BFE.
   c. The building (non-residential) was floodproofed to the BFE.
   d. The building was partially floodproofed (but, not to the BFE).
   e. The building was protected by a flood control/stormwater management project.
   f. The building was replaced by a new elevated/floodproofed building.

2.) If you checked the box that says "NO BUILDING ON PROPERTY," please enter the letter below (g – i) that best describes the situation.

   g. The building was demolished, but not acquired through any program.
   h. The building was acquired and demolished as part of a program.
   i. The building was relocated out of the floodplain.

MITIGATION FUNDING CODES

3.) Please choose from the following (j – y) to identify the primary and secondary funding sources for the mitigation action described by a – i above.

FEMA PROGRAMS	NON FEMA FUNDING SOURCES
j. Hazard Mitigation Grant Program (HMGP). k. Flood Mitigation Assistance Program (FMA). l. Pre-Disaster Mitigation Grant Program (PDM). m. Repetitive Flood Claims (RFC) n. Severe Repetitive Loss Program (SRL) o. Section 1362 Acquisition Program. p. Other FEMA Programs	q. Increased Cost of Compliance (ICC) coverage. r. U.S. Housing & Urban Development (HUD) Community Development Block Grant (CDBG). s. U.S. Army Corps of Engineers or Natural Resources Conservation Service (NRCS) Project. t. Other Federal Program. u. State Program. v. Local Program. w. Property Owner x. Natural Disaster or Fire. y. Unknown

FIGURE 7.16 (Continued).

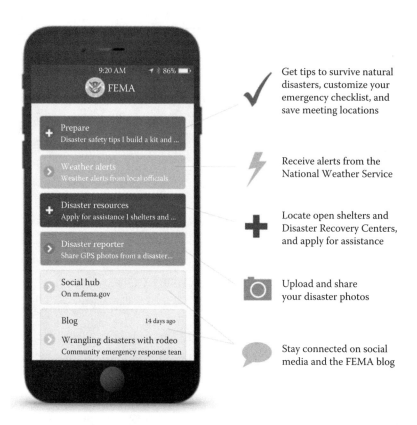

FIGURE 7.17 FEMA mobile App http://www.fema.gov/mobile-app.

- Assess factors that contributed to disaster effects
- Identify risk reduction opportunities
- Educate the public and local government officials in methods to reduce future risks
- Promote hazard mitigation community planning and project development that will result in sustainable community development
- Provide grants to fund hazard mitigation projects
- Assist communities in marketing the NFIP
- Provide technical assistance to state, tribal, and local governments to utilize rebuilding as an opportunity for enhanced local codes and ordinances

7.3 FEMA Response and Recovery

How a nation responds to terror and disaster says much about its makeup and capacity to protect its citizens. The term *response* connotes many things, including immediate actions to save lives, protect property and the environment, and meet basic human needs.[30] Response also includes the execution of emergency plans and actions to support short-term recovery. The level of response will depend on the circumstances and conditions at specific locations.[31]

The turmoil and anguish caused by the event is burdensome enough. When government fails to respond or does so in an unprofessional way, it simply adds to the pain and suffering of the general public. Nothing could have seared the national psyche more than the glaring ineptitude of state, local, and federal officials in the matter of Katrina.[32] The level of incompetence roused up even the most jaded of bureaucrats, and the toll from Katrina mounted and rose like the waters swirling about the New Orleans region.[33]

When one looks back on these events, it is almost incomprehensible that government could function so miserably. In this sense, response and recovery are just as critical to the homeland professional as planning and preparation. In many ways, response and recovery need to be embedded in any concept of planning and preparedness. These actions are not divisible but united in purpose and practice. If there is any lesson from Katrina, it is that these two worlds cannot remain disjointed but must be intimately interconnected (Figure 7.18).

It is not enough to say that Katrina was a gargantuan storm—for that was self-evident. What is equally telling is the collapse of basic services while in a disaster. Things as simple as transportation assets, such as buses, which could have been utilized to ferry people away, were left to wallow in the water by the hundreds. Mayor Ray Nagin has been rightfully faulted for his malfeasance in this matter (Figures 7.19 and 7.20).[34]

It was painfully obvious that a response and recovery protocol had completely escaped those entrusted with the disaster. As a result, DHS and FEMA authored an essential component of the homeland security model—the National Response Framework.[35]

7.3.1 National Response Framework

The framework is a guide for a national, all-hazards response—from the smallest incident to the largest catastrophe.[36] The framework identifies the key response principles, as well as the roles and structures that organize national response. How communities, states, the federal government, the private sector, and nongovernmental partners apply these principles for a coordinated, effective national response is the chief aim of the National Response Framework.[37]

FIGURE 7.18 Thousands of people sought refuge in the New Orleans Convention Center, which was lacking in basic necessities and security as nightmarish stories of crime were told and retold.

FIGURE 7.19   Buses in New Orleans during Hurricane Katrina.

FIGURE 7.20   Cameron, Louisiana, May 20, 2006. Before (left) and after photographs of FEMA-funded debris removal. The situation five years later in Louisiana demonstrates the slow pace (right) (courtesy of FEMA).

Internet Exercise: Familiarize yourself with the many resources relevant to a response plan by visiting the National Response Framework resource center at http://www.fema.gov/national-response-framework.

The framework systematically incorporates public sector agencies at all levels, the private sector, and nongovernmental organizations. The framework also emphasizes the importance of personal preparedness by individuals and households. FEMA lays out the key principles of a functional and effective response plan in Figure 7.21.

The framework operates from very distinct and enlightened premises. Its ideology is primarily one of decentralization. Both FEMA and DHS appear to agree that the best understanding of any problem resides in those experiencing it. Local, decentralized response is usually more responsive than waiting in line for the federals to show up. Here again, we saw clearly how New Orleans acted without decisiveness since it had been, at least in some ways, trained to await the federal invasion before taking action itself. On top of this, the federal

---

Engaged Partnership with the Whole Community

Engaging the whole community is critical to successfully achieving a secure and resilient Nation, and individual and community preparedness is a key component. An effective partnership relies on engaging all elements of the whole community and, when appropriate, international partners. Engaged partnership and coalition building includes clear, consistent, effective, and culturally appropriate communication and shared situational awareness. Participation within these partnerships should include advocates for all elements of the whole community. The most effective partnerships within a community capitalize on all available resources—identifying, developing, fostering, and strengthening new and existing coordinating structures to create a unity of effort.

Scalability, Flexibility, and Adaptability in Implementation

Core capabilities should be scalable, flexible, and adaptable and executed as needed to address the full range of threats and hazards as they evolve. Scalable, flexible, and adaptable coordinating structures are essential in aligning the key roles and responsibilities to deliver the core capabilities. The flexibility of such structures helps ensure that communities across the country can organize efforts to address a variety of risks based on their unique needs, capabilities, demographics, governing structures, and non-traditional partners.

Integration Among the Frameworks

The five mission areas aid in organizing national preparedness activities. Core capabilities are highly interdependent and applicable to any threat or hazard. All five mission areas integrate with each other through interdependencies, shared assets, and overlapping objectives.

Three core capabilities span all five mission areas: Planning; Public Information and Warning; and Operational Coordination. The common core capabilities serve to unify the mission areas, promote unity of effort, and are essential foundations for the success of the remaining core capabilities.

In addition to the three common core capabilities, a number of other core capabilities involve more than one mission area (e.g., Protection and Prevention share a number of common elements and rely on many of the same core capabilities). Integration among mission area resources and processes is important to maximize core capabilities and minimize risk. Many of the core capabilities can be linked across mission areas through shared assets and services. For example, functionality provided through geospatial services that build situational awareness can be applied across multiple Response core capabilities, as well as core capabilities in the other four mission areas.

FIGURE 7.21   Response doctrine key themes.

bureaucracy of FEMA and aligned agencies are part of a lumbering giant that has no conception of its own limitations. Government is by nature a self-perpetuating, self-propagating entity that mutates into forms never imagined. When this occurs, the responsiveness that the ordinary citizen rightfully hopes for simply evaporates into a sea of paperwork and indecision. Hence, the response must first and foremost be a local one. As even FEMA points out,

> Incidents begin and end locally, and most are wholly managed at the local level. Many incidents require unified response from local agencies, NGOs, and the private sector, and some require additional support from neighboring jurisdictions or the State. A small number require Federal support.[38]

In a comparative sense, the Twin Towers experience edified the power and preeminence of local control. Few would argue that the City of New York, its police and fire departments, as well as its agencies from port authorities and neighboring states, did a superlative job during this challenging period (Figure 7.22).

FIGURE 7.22 **New York City police department at Ground Zero. (Courtesy of the NYPD Police Benevolent Association).**

New York City Mayor Rudy Giuliani led the city from ashes and became the stuff of legend. His leadership skills were on display throughout the 9/11 period, while in New Orleans, during Katrina, leadership was utterly missing. New Orleans Mayor Ray Nagin, now an indicted and convicted felon, and Governor Kathleen Blanco, the clueless governor of Louisiana, became targets of constant derision in their handling of Katrina. Aside from not being prepared, the inadequacy of the response in these extreme circumstances was self-evident at every level of emergency response.

In a nutshell, the comparison illustrates the dynamism known as response. As a result, a National Response Framework advances a partner-based model—fully recognizing that the locality can and will do a better job in response. Incidents must be managed at the lowest possible jurisdictional level and supported by additional capabilities at a higher level if and when needed.

On the other hand, it is crucial that a chain of command and leadership be part of any response and recovery program. While DHS and FEMA both exhort local and state authorities to be major players in every form of threat and disaster, the scope and magnitude of these events sometimes make the federal authorities the dominant force (Figure 7.23). Congress has tried to lay out standard protocols in the matter of jurisdiction and leadership, although resources often dictate the actions of the decision maker. Even so, federal agencies can and do shine when the lower level of government, the street level where the tragedy intimately unfolds, are equal partners rather than mere bystanders awaiting instructions.

Another feature of the National Response Framework is its inherent flexibility. Instead of a one-size-fits-all mentality, the framework urges emergency professionals to apply a response that fits the event. Incidents come in many shapes and sizes, and their complexity or simplicity will affect the nature of the response. As the framework recommends,

As incidents change in size, scope, and complexity, the response must adapt to meet requirements. The number, type, and sources of resources must be able to expand rapidly to meet needs associated with a given incident. The Framework's disciplined and coordinated process can provide for a rapid surge of resources from all levels of government, appropriately scaled

Watch: President Obama Delivers a Statement in Baton Rouge

PRESIDENT OBAMA DELIVERS A STATEMENT TO THE PRESS
BATON ROUGE, LA
AUGUST 23, 2016

FIGURE 7.23   Screen capture from White House video of President Obama visiting sites of Louisiana flooding, August 2016 (www.whitehouse.gov).

to need. Execution must be flexible and adapted to fit each individual incident. For the duration of a response, and as needs grow and change, responders must remain nimble and adaptable. Equally, the overall response should be flexible as it transitions from the response effort to recovery.[39]

The response framework recommends a unified command structure in the mold and type as advanced in NIMS. Calling on responders to image the Incident Command System (ICS), the framework steadily encourages competing agencies to work in a unified way—without battles over territory or responsibility. The framework rightfully advances unity in command as

indispensable to response activities and requires a clear understanding of the roles and responsibilities of each participating organization. Success requires unity of effort, which respects the chain of command of each participating organization while harnessing seamless coordination across jurisdictions in support of common objectives. Use of the Incident Command System (ICS) is an important element across multi-jurisdictional or multi-agency incident management activities. It provides a structure to enable agencies with different legal, jurisdictional, and functional responsibilities to coordinate, plan, and interact effectively on scene. As a team effort, unified command allows all agencies with jurisdictional authority and/or functional responsibility for the incident to provide joint support through mutually developed incident objectives and strategies established at the command level. Each participating agency maintains its own authority, responsibility, and accountability.[40]

Finally, the framework advances the perpetual concept of readiness in the design of any response plan. Agencies must be prepared and ready to carry out the response mission. Agencies must understand the dilemma, have mastered the problem, and present themselves as being capable of a prepared and ready response.[41] Agencies must not victimize

---

Emergency Support Function #I –Transportation Annex

ESF Coordinator:

    Department of Transportation

Primary Agency:

    Department of Transportation

Support Agencies:

    Department of Agriculture
    Department of Commerce
    Department of Defense
    Department of Energy
    Department of Homeland Security
    Department of the Interior
    Department of Justice
    Department of State
    General Services Administration
    U.S. Postal Service

INTRODUCTION

Purpose

Emergency Support Function (ESF) #1 - Transportation provides support to the Department of Homeland Security (DHS) by assisting Federal, State, tribal, and local governmental entities, voluntary organizations, nongovernmental organizations, and the private sector in the management of transportation systems and infrastructure during domestic threats or in response to incidents. ESF # 1 also participates in prevention, preparedness, response, recovery, and mitigation activities. ESF #1 carries out the Department of Transportation (DOT)'s statutory responsibilities, including regulation of transportation, management of the Nation's airspace, and ensuring the safety and security of the national transportation system.

Scope

ESF #1 embodies considerable intermodal expertise and public and private sector transportation stakeholder relationships. DOT, with the assistance of the ESF #1 support agencies, provides transportation assistance in domestic incident management, including the following activities:

- Monitor and report status of and damage to the transportation system and infrastructure as a result of the incident.
- Identify temporary alternative transportation solutions that can be implemented by others when systems or infrastructure are damaged, unavailable, or overwhelmed.
- Perform activities conducted under the direct authority of DOT elements as these relate to aviation, maritime, surface, railroad, and pipeline transportation.
- Coordinate the restoration and recovery of the transportation systems and infrastructure.
- Coordinate and support prevention, preparedness, response, recovery, and mitigation activities among transportation stakeholders within the authorities and resource limitations of ESF #1 agencies.

FIGURE 7.24   Response plan sample page.

those harmed by delay in their operations or responsibilities. Agencies must move quickly in response and avoid the cumbersome delays that always emerge from a lack of preparation and readiness.[42] Not only must emergency and justice professionals know the risk that is to be dealt with, but just as compellingly, they need to place a high priority on the timeliness of response:

Acting swiftly and effectively requires clear, focused communication and the processes to support it. Without effective communication, a bias toward action will be ineffectual at best, likely perilous. An effective national response relies on disciplined processes, procedures, and systems to communicate timely, accurate, and accessible information on the incident's cause, size, and current situation to the public, responders, and others. Well-developed public information, education strategies, and communication plans help to ensure that lifesaving measures, evacuation routes, threat and alert systems, and other public safety information are coordinated and communicated to numerous diverse audiences in a consistent, accessible, and timely manner.[43]

Internet Exercise: Visit the Nation Incident Management System website at https://www.fema.gov/national-incident-management-system.

Depending on the subject matter, the critical infrastructure in question, and the event itself, any response will need to be tailored to it. For example, the National Response Framework resource location provides response protocols for industries and businesses, critical infrastructure, and other likely targets in need of response. An excellent illustration of this response plan can be seen in transportation. Figure 7.24 is a sample page from the response plan.

For a complete look at a response plan for a biological attack, review the annex published by the National Response Framework at Appendix III.

7.4 Conclusion

The chapter delivers essential information on the role of FEMA. FEMA, once independent of DHS, was the country's agency of natural disaster. Floods, hurricanes, fires, and earthquakes consumed its planning and response mentality. Slowly but surely, and with extraordinary reservation, the FEMA model came to accept that the regimens and protocols for natural as well as man-made disasters in the form of terrorism are really the same. While this may be conceptually true, the fit of FEMA into DHS has been tougher than anticipated. Every imaginable type of threat and hazard receives some scrutiny in this chapter, though the emphasis is on planning and preparation—rather than on response and recovery.

This chapter covers the historic role of FEMA as well as its contemporary structure and organizational design under DHS. In addition, the chapter emphasizes the role of preparedness in the FEMA mission, the importance of mitigation in the control and containment of disasters, and techniques of response and recovery.

Keywords

All-hazards response

Army Corps of Engineers

Catastrophic event

Decentralization

Disaster

Exemplary practice

Federal Broadcast System

Federal Disaster Assistance

Administration

Flood hazard mapping

FloodSmart
Geographic information system
Hazus-MH
Hurricane Liaison Team
Integrated emergency-management
system
MAP MOD
Mitigation
Mitigation Assessment Team
Mitigation planning
National Dam Safety Program
National Earthquake Hazards Reduction
Plan

National Fire Prevention Control Office
National Flood Insurance Program
National Hurricane Program
National Preparedness Directorate
Postassessment report
Preparedness
Project impact
Protocol
Reconstruction Finance Corporation
Response and recovery
Routine emergency

Discussion Questions

1. Discuss the mission of FEMA prior to 9/11. Since 9/11, how has that mission been modified?
2. Why have there been growing pains for the new FEMA since incorporation into DHS?
3. Why is planning so critical to effective homeland policy?
4. Why does mitigation have a pre- and postrole in homeland defense?
5. Discuss areas where hazards are likely events in your community.
6. What type of mitigation plan would work well once a hazard has been identified?
7. Why do response and recovery involve important public relations issues?
8. What is the general thrust of agency cooperation between federal, state, and local entities?
9. In what region of FEMA does your jurisdiction lie?
10. If a hazard or disaster took place in your region, what agency would likely be the lead player in response and recovery?
11. Compare the preparedness and response exhibited in Hurricane Katrina versus Hurricane Sandy.

Practical Exercises

1. Enroll and take the training of FEMA regarding the reading and interpretation of flood maps at http://www.fema.gov/online-tutorials.
2. Visit FEMA's software tool for mitigation at https://www.fema.gov/flood-mapping-products.
3. Discover best practices of interest to your community. Visit the FEMA database of best practices at http://www.fema.gov/mitigation-best-practices-portfolio.
4. Take a tour of the National Response Framework at http://www.fema.gov/national-response-framework.

Notes

1. J. A. Bullock et al., *Introduction to Homeland Security* (New York: Elsevier, 2005), 6.

2. R. T. Stafford, *Disaster Relief and Emergency Assistance Act, P.L. 100-707,* signed into law November 23, 1988; amended the Disaster Relief Act of 1974, P.L. 93-288. This act constitutes the statutory authority for most federal disaster response activities, especially as they pertain to FEMA and FEMA programs.

3. FEMA, About the agency, at http://www.fema.gov/about-agency, accessed January 16, 2016.

4. FEMA, NAC recommendations from September 2015 NAC meeting, available at https://www.fema.gov/media-library/assets/documents/110848, accessed January 16, 2016.

5. Center for Disaster Philanthropy, The role of FEMA in disasters, http://disasterphilanthropy.org/where/issue-insights/the-role-of-fema-in-disasters (accessed January 3, 2013).

6. W. F. Shughart II, Disaster relief as bad public policy, *The Independent Review,* 15(4) (Spring 2011): 530.

7. R. Wimberly, *First-Ever National EAS Test Will Come from the White House, Emergency Management,* at http://www.emergencymgmt.com/safety/National-Test-EAS-032111.html, March 21, 2011.

8. Department of Homeland Security, *National Response Framework,* January, 2008: 27.

9. Department of Homeland Security, *FEMA: Radiological Emergency Preparedness Program Manual and Supplement,* 2011.

10. For an overview of *Preparedness for the Citizen and the Community,* see http://www.fema.gov/pdf/areyouready/basic_preparedness.pdf. See also FEMA's website for many guides and plans; go to www.fema.gov/media-library and search "family communication plan."

11. For a general series of considerations on planning and preparation, see R. W. Perry and M. K. Lindell, Preparedness for emergency response: Guideline for the emergency planning process, *Disasters,* 27, 2003: 336–350.

12. Department of Homeland Security, *Safe Rooms and Shelters—Protecting People against Terrorist Attacks National Geospatial Preparedness Needs Assessment,* May 2006, Figure 4.3.

13. Department of Homeland Security, *Safe Rooms and Shelters,* Figure 4.1.

14. Department of Homeland Security, *Using HAZUS-MH for Risk Assessment: How-to Guide,* August 2004.

15. For a look at disaster preparedness, see National Fire Protection Association, Implementing NFPA 1600: National Preparedness Standards, ed. D. Schmidt (Quincy, MA: National Fire Protection Association, 2008).

16. FEMA, Hazus software, at https://www.fema.gov/hazus-software, accessed January 16, 2016.

17. K. Vlahos, A season of wild wind, *Wind & Water, Homeland Security Today,* August, 2011: 34.

18. K. Vlahos, A season of wild wind, *Wind & Water, Homeland Security Today,* August, 2011: 34.

19. FEMA, Risk Management Series at https://www.fema.gov/security-risk-management-series-publications, accessed August 30, 2009.

20. Congressional Research Service, FEMA's Pre-Disaster Mitigation Program: Overview and Issues 21 (Washington, DC: Congressional Research Service, 2009).

21. O. O. Olonilua and O. Ibitayo, Toward multihazard mitigation: An evaluation of FEMA-approved hazard mitigation plans under the Disaster Mitigation Act of 2000, *Journal of Emergency Management,* 9 (January/February 2011): 37–49, 48.

22. FEMA, Guide for all-hazard emergency operations planning, Chapter 4, 1996, at www.fema.gov/pdf/plan/4-ch.pdf.

23. Congressional Research Service, *National Flood Insurance Program: Background, Challenges, and Financial Status,* (Washington, DC: Congressional Research Service, 2011).

24. FEMA P-55, *Coastal Construction Manual: Principles and Practices of Planning, Siting, Designing, Constructing, and Maintaining Residential Buildings in Coastal Areas,* 4th Edition (2011).

25. For an excellent resource on flood and wind damage, see *Catalog of FEMA Flood and Wind Publications, and Training Courses,* http://www.fema.gov/library/viewRecord.do?id=3184, accessed March 9, 2009.

26. FEMA, FloodSmart.Gov, http://www.floodsmart.gov/floodsmart/pages/preparation_recovery/before_a_flood.jsp, accessed March 7, 2009.

27. FEMA, FloodSmart.Gov, http://www.floodsmart.gov/floodsmart/pages/preparation_recovery/before_a_flood.jsp, accessed January 17, 2016.

28. Federal Emergency Management Agency, *PARTNERSHIPS IN PREPAREDNESS: A Compendium of Exemplary Practices in Emergency Management, Volume II*, May 1997, http://www.fema.gov/media-library-data/20130726-1447-20490-3555/exp_v2_1_.txt.

29. Congressional Research Service, *Social Media and Disasters: Current Uses, Future Options, and Policy Considerations*, (Washington, DC: Congressional Research Service, 2011).

30. R. McCreight, Establishing a national emergency response and disaster assistance corps, *Homeland Defense Journal*, 10, September 2007; C. Hines, Disaster management, *Law & Order*, 58, August 2006: 54.

31. For an example of how distinctly and very differently FEMA would act in the case of a Dirty Bomb, see Congressional Research Service, *"Dirty Bombs": Technical Background, Attack Prevention and Response, Issues for Congress*, 2011, http://www.fas.org/sgp/crs/nuke/R41890.pdf.

32. See J. Flynn, Review of disasters and the law: Katrina and beyond, *Journal of Homeland Security and Emergency Management*, 1, 2007: 4.

33. There is little question that FEMA was rightfully criticized. One benefit from the criticism was an avalanche of new research in the area, such as R. McCreight, Aspects of emergency management, *Homeland Defense Journal*, 5, May 2007: 22–28; J. Dowle, Prepare for homeland security, *Law & Order*, 5, May 2007: 55; H. Stone, Emergencies and action plans, *Security*, 62, October 2006: 43; R. Elliott, State of readiness, *Security Management*, 50, December 2006: 51–57; and C. Perrow, *The Next Catastrophe: Reducing Our Vulnerabilities to Natural, Industrial and Terrorist Disasters* (Princeton, NJ: Princeton University Press, 2007).

34. If we did this poorly at Katrina, how would we handle a tsunami? See A. Kimery, Next tsunami, *Homeland Security Today*, July, 2011: 34.

35. For a list of authorities that permit federal, state, and local authorities to engage in homeland defense and intervention, see http://www.fema.gov/pdf/emergency/nrf/nrf-authorities.pdf.

36. See Department of Homeland Security, *National Response Framework Fact Sheet*, at http://www.fema.gov/pdf/emergency/nrf/NRFOnePageFactSheet.pdf.

37. A. Bitto, Say what? Who? Me? Right here in the trenches? Collaborate or what? Seeking common ground in regional all-hazards preparedness training, *Journal of Environmental Health*, 69, January/February 2007: 28–33.

38. Department of Homeland Security, *National Response Framework*, January 2008, 9. Despite this preference, national exercises are still in vogue at FEMA. DHS still sponsors National Level Exercise programs. See E. Pitman, National response, *Emergency Management*, March/April, 2011: 30.

39. Department of Homeland Security, *The National Response Framework* (Washington, DC: U.S. Government Printing Office, January 2008), 10, http://www.fema.gov/pdf/emergency/nrf/nrf-core.pdf.

40. Department of Homeland Security, *National Response Framework*, 10.

41. Department of Homeland Security, *National Response Framework*, 27.

42. See R. Humphress, Building an emergency response competency system: Optimizing emergency personnel mobilization, *Journal of Homeland Security and Emergency Management*, 1 (2007): 4; D. Barbee, Disaster response and recovery: Strategies and tactics for resilience, *Journal of Homeland Security and Emergency Management*, 1, 2007: 4; D. Philpott, Emergency preparedness communications, *Homeland Defense Journal*, 44, June 2007.

43. Department of Homeland Security, *National Response Framework*, 10–11.

Intelligence

Objectives

1. To comprehend the nature of the intelligence cycle
2. To outline the Department of Homeland Security's (DHS) intelligence-gathering approach in the aftermath of 9/11
3. To define the mission of the Federal Bureau of Investigation (FBI) as it relates to intelligence gathering and sharing
4. To list the various new policies, programs, and initiatives of the FBI since 9/11
5. To define the mission of the Central Intelligence Agency (CIA) as it relates to intelligence gathering and sharing
6. To list the various new policies, programs, and initiatives of the CIA since 9/11
7. To list the mission, policies, programs, and initiatives of the new Office of the Director of National Intelligence (ODNI)
8. To list the mission, policies, programs, and initiatives of the Defense Intelligence Agency (DIA) since 9/11

8.1 Introduction

Much is expected of those entrusted with homeland protection. At a minimum, there is the expectation of basic security and safety—the notion that the homeland will be safe from attack from both domestic and foreign enemies. As already noted, exactly what the functionaries of homeland security should tackle is an evolutionary project. Today's threat may be tomorrow's less worrisome problem. However, there are certain core competencies that the professional class of employees in homeland security need to master. These are the nonnegotiable skill sets that the homeland system must demonstrate competence in. These are the essential underpinnings of what makes the homeland system work in any context. These competencies include

- Intelligence
- Border security
- Immigration
- Transportation security
- Public health

8.2 Intelligence

The task of intelligence gathering and analysis could be considered an overreaching competence, for just about everything in homeland security is guided by what we do, or should, or must know. Intelligence, in a sense, is the lifeblood of operations. Sometimes practitioners witness the mindlessness, the almost unintelligence, that policymakers impose. In other words, the bureaucratic mind-set, in some cases, simply acts without intelligence because it acts or has been acting in a particular way for so long. Intelligence is more than mindless motion.[1] The idea of intelligence can be discerned in a host of contexts—domestic and international, military and covert, criminal and civil—as well as homeland security. Intelligence is, at its base, nothing more than information assessment. One way of describing it might be as follows:

> The intelligence cycle is an iterative process in which collection requirements based on national security threats are developed, and intelligence is collected, analyzed, and disseminated to a broad range of consumers. Consumers sometimes provide feedback on the finished intelligence products, which can be used to refine any part of the intelligence cycle to ensure that consumers are getting the intelligence they need to make informed decisions and/or take appropriate actions.[2]

Intelligence activities largely reflect the agency mission and overall purpose of the task at hand. In some circles, intelligence is broken down into various disciplines. "Three major intelligence disciplines or 'INTs'—signals intelligence (*sigint*), imagery intelligence (*imint*), and human intelligence (*humint*)—provide the most important information for analysts and absorb the bulk of the intelligence budget."[3]

Some might argue that homeland intelligence is a unique animal invented in the last 15 years. Others claim that intelligence is an interconnected dynamic—that homeland information can only come about in a holistic context, and that homeland security is impossible without the larger Intelligence Community inputting information. Homeland security is no better or worse than its aligned agencies of intelligence gathering. Figure 8.1 portrays this interdependence.[4]

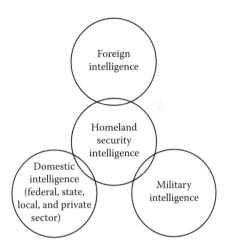

FIGURE 8.1   Intelligence-gathering matrix. From: CRS, *Homeland Security Intelligence* (Washington, DC: Library of Congress, 2006), 5.

DHS tends to favor this integrative approach and for good reason. If there was any persistent critique of government in the aftermath of 9/11, it was the failure of intelligence. But even more compellingly, the critics and commissions repeatedly castigated the Intelligence Community for its failure to share, to disseminate, and to work collaboratively with sister and brother agencies. Intelligence was boxed in prior to 9/11; it was departmentalized and compartmentalized rather than scrutinized in the national, integrative framework. Former secretary of DHS Michael Chertoff eloquently described this dilemma:

> Intelligence, as you know, is not only about spies and satellites. Intelligence is about the thousands and thousands of routine, everyday observations and activities. Surveillance, interactions—each of which may be taken in isolation as not a particularly meaningful piece of information, but when fused together, gives us a sense of the patterns and the flow that really is at the core of what intelligence analysis is all about. ... We [DHS] actually generate a lot of intelligence ... we have many interactions every day, every hour at the border, on airplanes, and with the Coast Guard.[5]

In this sense, intelligence is merely information shared that might give meaning. It is the patterns and connections that analysts are looking for. It is the overall fit of the information into particular facts and circumstances that the intelligence analyst seeks. And when intelligence works, it prevents the harm and terror from gaining a foothold. Recent killings by jihadis in San Bernardino seem to have escaped the Intelligence Community over a nearly four-year cycle of indoctrination and terrorist formation.

Just as crucially, the idea of intelligence has become fixated on things beyond basic knowledge, and in a sense, tends toward technology and gadgets over the basic acquisition of information. Many professionals in the Intelligence Community remind us that intelligence is first and foremost knowledge—something gathered and then disseminated. Mark M. Lowenthal, president of the Security and Intelligence Academy, has long been a critic of

FIGURE 8.2   TTIC logo.

our tendency to forget about the "basics" in intelligence gathering, and he urges us to "get back to the 'knowledge building' business."[6]

From the outset of the agency, DHS looked squarely and keenly into the world of intelligence and saw the necessity for integration and cohesion among all governmental agencies. Indeed, in early 2002, so did Congress by enacting the Homeland Security Act, which not only contained the administrative underpinnings of DHS, but set the professional parameters of intelligence.[7] The act precisely mandates and lays out expectations regarding the gathering of information and intelligence. It forces government as a whole to collaborate rather than insulate, and contains provisions for information analysis and intelligence within DHS. The act does not transfer to DHS existing government intelligence and law enforcement agencies but envisions an analytical office utilizing the products of other agencies—both unevaluated information and finished reports—to provide warning of terrorist attacks, assessments of vulnerability, and recommendations for remedial actions at federal, state, and local levels, and by the private sector. In 2003, DHS set up the Terrorist Threat Integration Center (TTIC), an entity directed to assess threats, but then just as commandingly ordered the sharing and collaborative interchange of said intelligence (Figure 8.2).

The TTIC was established to

- Optimize the use of terrorist threat–related information, expertise, and capabilities to conduct threat analysis and inform collection strategies
- Create a structure that ensures information sharing across agency lines
- Integrate terrorist-related information collected domestically and abroad in order to form the most comprehensive possible threat picture
- Be responsible and accountable for providing terrorist threat assessments for our national leadership

The TTIC was subsequently merged and renamed the National Counterterrorism Center, under the control and supervision of the U.S. director of national intelligence.[8]

8.3 Terror, Threats, Disaster, and Intelligence Agencies

The array of federal agencies dedicated to the task of intelligence is simply mind-boggling. Long before 9/11, the governmental and military complex was incessantly in need of intelligence. Governments cannot be run without intelligence, nor can wars be fought or borders secured. Nor is intelligence gathering a system without restraint nor counterbalanced by competing legal traditions that honor privacy. The American experiment seeks to balance these demands.[9]

Intelligence has been part of our national fabric since the days of the American Revolution. In another portion of this chapter, we examine intelligence and defense of the homeland from the post–Civil War period, to the Cold War, to the riots of the 1960s, and end in the present. In each time frame, those who labor to protect the country need intelligence. After 9/11, these agencies had to adjust and redefine traditional definitions and outlooks on exactly what intelligence is effective. Added to the agency demands was the world of terror—an evolving terror erected by the jihadists and those who hate the American experience. It changed the way the intelligence business is carried out. To be sure, even DHS sees intelligence as a core function of its purpose and operational philosophy. DHS's Office of Intelligence and Analysis has four strategic goals:

- Promote understanding of threats through intelligence analysis
- Collect information and intelligence pertinent to homeland security
- Share information necessary for action
- Manage intelligence for the homeland security enterprise

Its structure reflects the multivariate nature of intelligence, with special sections dedicated to counterintelligence (CI) and counterterrorism as well as border and intelligence management (see Figure 8.3).

Terror is not a new reality since 9/11 for federal and state justice agencies. While the attacks of 9/11 surely enhanced the nature of global terrorism in the domestic sphere, law enforcement leadership could not have been surprised by the possibility or actuality of any attack on American soil. The U.S. Intelligence Community generally comprises these agencies:

- Office of the Director of National Intelligence
- Office of the National Counterintelligence Executive
- Information-Sharing Environment
- National Counterterrorism Center
- National Intelligence Council
- Central Intelligence Agency
- Drug Enforcement Agency
- Defense Intelligence Agency
- Federal Bureau of Investigation
- Information Sharing Environment

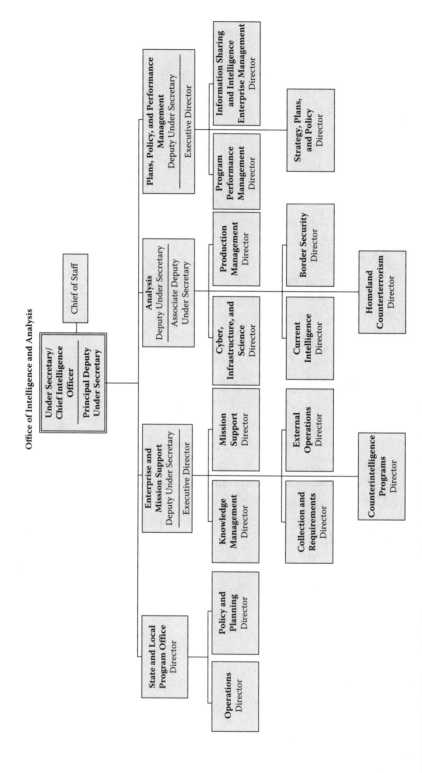

FIGURE 8.3   Office of Intelligence and Analysis organization chart.

FIGURE 8.4   DEA Intelligence Center, El Paso, Texas.

- Marine Corps Intelligence
- National Cybersecurity and Communications Integration Center
- National Geospatial Intelligence Agency
- National Reconnaissance Office
- National Security Agency
- Office of Naval Intelligence
- U.S. Air Force Office of Special Investigations
- U.S. Army Intelligence and Security Command
- U.S. Coast Guard
- U.S. Department of Energy
- U.S. Department of Homeland Security
- U.S. Department of State
- U.S. Treasury Department

Throughout this book, the reader has been exposed to many members of the homeland security community. It is impossible to cover it all due to its sheer size and scope. What follows is a cursory look at the historic and emerging agencies entrusted with diverse intelligence responsibilities (Figure 8.4).

8.3.1 Federal Bureau of Investigation

The FBI has held jurisdictional authority in matters involving terrorism since 1986. Indeed, the FBI had been busy with all sorts of terrorist activity since the early 1980s. In its long and distinguished history, the FBI has been called on in a wide array of law enforcement initiatives, from rackets and organized crime to public corruption, from attacks on U.S. embassies to terror plots against the United States.

The FBI has long been an agency capable of adaptation and mission adjustment—a characteristic referred to as *change of mandate*. This is one of its greatest strengths—that it is capable of addressing new and emerging threats to the country (Figure 8.5).

WHAT WE INVESTIGATE

Spies. Terrorists. Hackers. Pedophiles. Mobsters. Gang leaders and serial killers. We investigate them all, and many more besides.

The very heart of FBI operations lies in our investigations—which serve, as our mission states, "to protect and defend the United States against terrorist and foreign intelligence threats and to enforce the criminal laws of the United States." We currently have jurisdiction over violations of more than 200 categories of federal law, and you can find the major ones in the following table, grouped within our national security and criminal priorities. Also visit our Intelligence program site, which underpins and informs all our investigative programs.

Terrorism	White-Collar Crime
• International Terrorism	• Corporate Fraud
• Domestic Terrorism	• Financial Institution/Mortgage Fraud
Counterintelligence	• Health Care Fraud
• Counterespionage	• Identity Theft
• Counterproliferation	• Money Laundering
• Economic Espionage	• Intellectual Property Theft/Piracy
Cyber Crime	• Securities & Commodities Fraud
• Computer Intrusions	
• Internet Fraud	
Weapons of Mass Destruction	
• Key Programs	
Public Corruption	
• Border Corruption Election Crimes	
• International Corruption	
• Prison Corruption	
Civil Rights	**Violent Crime and Major Thefts**
• Hate Crimes	• Art Theft
• Human Trafficking	• Bank Robbery
• Color of Law Violations	• Cargo Theft
• Freedom of Access to Clinics	• Gangs
• International Human Rights	• Indian Country Crime
Organized Crime	• Jewelry and Gem Theft
• Italian Mafia/LCN	• Online Predators
• Eurasian	• Retail Theft
• Balkan	• Vehicle Theft
• Middle Eastern	• Violent Crimes Against Children
• Asian	• More
• African	
• Western Hemisphere Organized Crime	

From: FBI, What we investigate, http://www.fbi.gov/about-us/investigate/what_we_investigate.

FIGURE 8.5   A member of the FBI's Hostage Rescue Team practices rappelling from a helicopter during a training exercise.

Internet Resource: For the history of the FBI, see https://www.fbi.gov/about-us/history/brief-history.

The FBI has extensive experience in the world of intelligence and espionage, but these skills were largely shaped after World War II and the emergence of the Cold War. For nearly 40 years, the FBI's main thrust in the world of international activity coalesced around Cold War enemies rather than modern-day jihadists wishing the end of America and its allies. While the skill set may be complementary in both worlds, there is little question that the FBI realized that its world and the world around was changing. In the late 1980s and throughout the 1990s, the soil of the United States was stained with domestic terrorism. Both the Oklahoma City bombing and the World Trade Center attacks triggered a new approach at the FBI. The shift largely dwelled on the impact of terrorism, both domestically and internationally. After 9/11, the FBI was increasingly asked to adjust and adapt its mission to contend with terror threats. At this time, Director Robert S. Mueller III called for a reengineering of the FBI structure and operations to closely focus the bureau on the prevention of terrorist attacks, on countering foreign intelligence operations against the United States, and on addressing cybercrime-based attacks and other high-technology crimes (Figure 8.6).

From 2001 onward, the FBI has continuously designed new programs and initiatives as well as fine-tuned existing programs to reflect the never-ending challenges of terror.

8.3.1.1 Joint Terrorism Task Forces

The FBI reinforced the importance and operational role of the joint terrorism task forces (JTTFs), an amalgam of state, federal, and local law enforcement in major American cities such as New York. There are more than 100 JTTFs presently operating, 56 of which are

FIGURE 8.6   Robert S. Mueller III.

housed in local FBI headquarters. At the federal level, full-time membership in the JTTF is granted automatically to the following entities:

- FBI
- U.S. Marshals Service
- Bureau of Alcohol, Tobacco, and Firearms
- U.S. Secret Service
- U.S. State Department/Diplomatic Security Service
- Immigration and Customs Enforcement
- U.S. Border Patrol
- Postal Inspection Service
- Treasury Inspector General for Tax Administration
- Internal Revenue Service
- U.S. Park Police
- Federal Protective Service
- Department of Interior's Bureau of Land Management
- Defense Criminal Investigative Service
- Air Force Office of Special Investigations
- U.S. Army
- Naval Criminal Investigative Service
- Central Intelligence Agency
- State and Local Law Enforcement

JOINT TERRORISM TASK FORCES

They are our nation's front line on terrorism: small cells of highly trained, locally based, passionately committed investigators, analysts, linguists, SWAT experts, and other specialists from dozens of U.S. law enforcement and intelligence agencies.

When it comes to investigating terrorism, they do it all: chase down leads, gather evidence, make arrests, provide security for special events, conduct training, collect and share intelligence, and respond to threats and incidents at a moment's notice.

They are the FBI's Joint Terrorism Task Forces, or JTTFs.

Where are they based? In 100 cities nationwide, including at least one in each of our 56 field offices. Sixty-five of these JTTFs were created after 9/11/01.

How many members? 3,723 nationwide—more than four times the pre-9/11 total—including 2,196 Special Agents, 838 state/local law enforcement officers, and 689 professionals from other government agencies (the Department of Homeland Security, the CIA, and the Transportation Security Administration, to name a few).

The first JTTF? New York City, established way back in 1980.

The newest? Actually, there are 16 of them: in Montgomery, Alabama; Fayetteville, Arkansas; Fresno, California; Colorado Springs, Colorado; West Palm Beach, Florida; Bloomington, Indiana; Covington, Kentucky; Portland, Maine; Grand Rapids, Michigan; Helena, Montana; Erie, Pennsylvania; Providence, Rhode Island; Midland, Lubbock, and Plano, Texas; and Everett, Washington.

Their contributions? More than we could possibly capture here, but JTTFs have been instrumental in breaking up cells like the "Portland Seven," the "Lackawanna Six," and the Northern Virginia jihad. They've traced sources of terrorist funding, responded to anthrax threats, halted the use of fake IDs, and quickly arrested suspicious characters with all kinds of deadly weapons and explosives. Chances are if you hear about a counterterrorism investigation, JTTFs are playing an active and often decisive role.

How do these JTTFs coordinate their efforts? Largely through the interagency National Joint Terrorism Task Force, working out of FBI Headquarters, which makes sure that information and intelligence flows freely among the local JTTFs.

And here's the final—and most important—thing you should know about these JTTFs: They are working 24/7/365 to protect you, your families, and your communities from terrorist attack.

From: FBI, What We Investigate, Terrorism-Joint Terrorism Task Forces, https://www.fbi.gov/about-us/investigate/terrorism/terrorism_jttfs.

In nearly 60 major American centers, JTTFs were operating before the Twin Towers or the Pentagon were ever struck. After the attack, increased emphasis on the role of intelligence was evident in the sheer increase of JTTF entities, with 104 distinct organizations established since 9/11.[10] For a representative example of a JTTF, review the organization and structure of Albany, New York. The Albany JTTF combines federal, state, and local police forces, the U.S. Postal Service, as well as geographically aligned agencies that work in close proximity to the task force (see Figure 8.7).

Of recent interest has been the nationwide collaboration and cooperation between JTTFs and fusion centers. No two entities could better prove the advantages of information sharing

Albany, New York, JTTF

The JTTF is responsible for all domestic and international terrorism matters in the two-state territory. The JTTF's mission is to prevent acts of terrorism before they occur, and to effectively and swiftly respond to any actual criminal terrorist act by identifying and prosecuting those responsible. The following agencies participate in the JTTF on a full-time or part-time basis:

- Central Intelligence Agency
- U.S. Bureau of Alcohol, Tobacco, Firearms and Explosives
- U.S. Immigration and Customs Enforcement
- U.S. Internal Revenue Service
- U.S. Department of State (Bureau of Diplomatic Security)
- U.S. Marshals Service
- U.S. Postal Inspection Service
- New York State Office of the Inspector General
- New York State Police and Vermont State Police
- Albany, New York, Police Department
- Schenectady, New York, Police Department
- Troy, New York, Police Department

FIGURE 8.7 About the Albany, New York, Joint Terrorism Task Force, https://www.fbi.gov/history/field-office-histories/albany.

FIGURE 8.8 Faisal Shazhad: Homegrown terrorist attempt in Times Square.

than these entities. While JTTF's get their information from a variety of sources, fusion centers also aid in the sharing of intelligence and assist by providing information gathered through combining the knowledge, expertise, and information resident within law enforcement and homeland security agencies operating throughout the nation.[11]

In the recent attempt of a car bomber in Times Square, New York, the cooperation of the JTTF and the fusion center model was obvious to those investigating the case (Figure 8.8).

8.3.1.2 National Security Branch

The National Security Branch (NSB), established on September 12, 2005, combines the missions, capabilities, and resources of the counterterrorism (CT), CI, and intelligence elements of the FBI under the leadership of a senior FBI official. The NSB reflects the new focus of the FBI by assigning a significant portion of its manpower and resources to the detection, elimination, and prevention of terrorist activity (Figure 8.9).

FIGURE 8.9   FBI National Security Branch logo.

The mission and vision of the NSB are as follows:

NSB Mission Statement

The FBI's national security mission is to lead and coordinate intelligence efforts that drive actions to protect the United States.

Our goal is to develop a comprehensive understanding of the threats and penetrate national and transnational networks that have a desire and capability to harm us. Such networks include: terrorist organizations, foreign intelligence services, those that seek to proliferate weapons of mass destruction, and criminal enterprises.

In order to be successful, we must understand the threat, continue to integrate our intelligence and law enforcement capabilities in every FBI operational program, and continue to expand our contribution to the Intelligence Community knowledge base.

Because national security and criminal threats are often intertwined, our ability to integrate intelligence and investigations makes us uniquely situated to address our nation's threats and vulnerabilities.

NSB Vision Statement

To the extent authorized under the law, build a national awareness that permits recognition of a national security threat, sufficiently early to permit its disruption. This will be a discerning process that promotes the collection of relevant information and minimizes the accumulation of extraneous data that unnecessarily distract from the analytical process (https://www.fbi.gov/about/mission).

The NSB focuses on four major initiatives within the bureau: counterterrorism, CI, intelligence, and weapons of mass destruction (WMDs). An organizational chart is shown in Figure 8.10.

The counterterrorism unit tracks known and suspected terrorists in its Terrorist Screening Center (TSC). The TSC now provides "one-stop shopping" so that every government screener is using the same terrorist watch list—whether it is an airport screener, an embassy official issuing visas overseas, or a state or local law enforcement officer on the street. The TSC allows government agencies to run name checks against the same

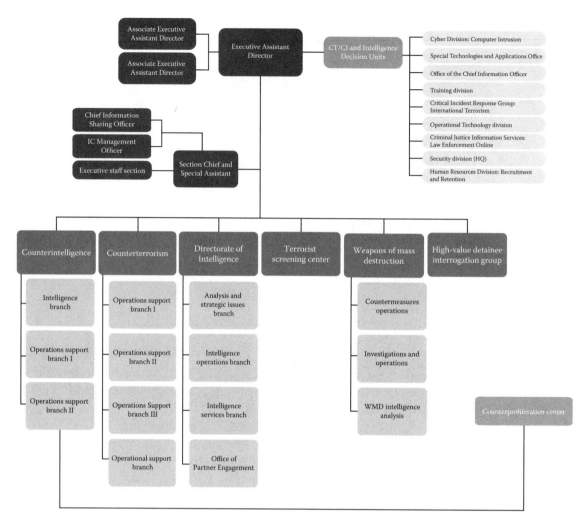

FIGURE 8.10 **FBI National Security Branch organizational chart.**

comprehensive list with the most accurate, up-to-date information about known and suspected terrorists (Figure 8.11).

In the area of intelligence gathering, the FBI extends its efforts across the world by using diverse approaches in the gathering of pertinent information. The general approaches are as follows:

- Human intelligence (HUMINT) is the collection of information from human sources. The collection may be done openly, as when FBI agents interview witnesses or suspects, or it may be done through clandestine or covert means (espionage).
- Signals intelligence (SIGINT) refers to electronic transmissions that can be collected by ships, planes, ground sites, or satellites.
- Imagery intelligence (IMINT) is sometimes also referred to as photo intelligence (PHOTINT).

FIGURE 8.11   Seal of the Terrorist Screening Center.

- Measurement and signatures intelligence (MASINT) is a relatively little-known collection discipline that concerns weapons capabilities and industrial activities. MASINT includes the advanced processing and use of data gathered from overhead and airborne IMINT and SIGINT collection systems.
- The DIA's Central MASINT Office (CMO) is the principal user of MASINT data. Measurement and signatures intelligence has become increasingly important due to growing concern about the existence and spread of WMDs.
- Open-source intelligence (OSINT) refers to a broad array of information and sources that are generally available, including information obtained from the media.

8.3.1.3 Analysis of Intelligence

In July 2006, the WMD Directorate was created within the NSB to integrate WMD components previously spread throughout the FBI (Figure 8.12).

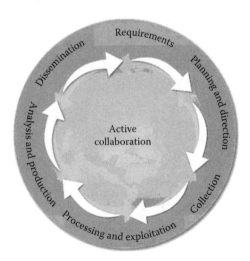

FIGURE 8.12   A graphic representation of the benefits of active collaboration between departments and agencies.

A WMD is defined as

1. Any explosive (see the following list), incendiary, or poison gas
   a. Bomb
   b. Grenade
   c. Rocket having an explosive or incendiary charge of more than 4 ounces
   d. Missile having an explosive or incendiary charge of more than 1/4 ounces
   e. Mine
   f. Device similar to any of the devices just described
2. Any weapon that is designed or intended to cause death or serious bodily injury through the release, dissemination, or impact of toxic or poisonous chemicals, or their precursors
3. Any weapon involving a disease organism
4. Any weapon that is designed to release radiation or radioactivity at a level dangerous to human life

The FBI provides support nationally to agencies of government at the state, local, and federal levels in the prevention, containment, and detection of WMDs. The mission of the WMD Directorate is essentially fourfold:

- Preparedness: The WMD Preparedness subprogram incorporates elements of planning, training, and exercises to ensure that the FBI and its U.S. government partners are ready to respond to WMD threats when they emerge.
- Countermeasures: The WMD Countermeasures subprogram consists of outreach activities and more specialized coordination called *tripwires*.
- Investigations and operations: The FBI has multiple entities and programs in place around the world for the investigative, intelligence, CI, and overall law enforcement response to a terrorist threat or incident in the United States.
- Intelligence: The basis for the FBI's proactive approach to the countermeasures, investigations, and operations is timely, relevant, and actionable intelligence analysis (Figure 8.13).

Education is an increasingly important function of the FBI in all matters relating to homeland security. In the area of WMDs, the FBI takes a special interest. See the mock exercise on a dirty bomb in Figure 8.14.

Internet Resource: Watch the training video produced by the NSB for local and state law enforcement at http://www.fbi.gov/hq/nsb/nsb_video.htm.

8.3.2 Central Intelligence Agency

Since 1947, the CIA has been a central figure in the collection and assessment of data and intelligence (Figure 8.15).

Spawned during the era of the Cold War, the agency, like so many of its fellow agencies, has had to apply its skill and knowledge in the intelligence sector, but carrying out its mission

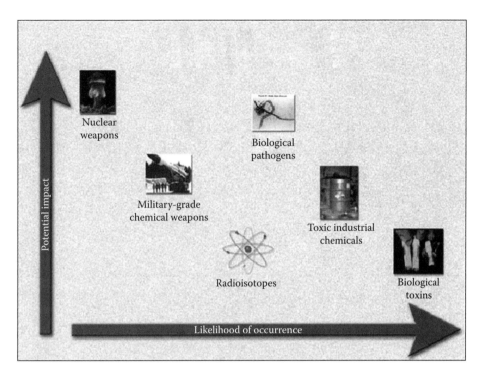

FIGURE 8.13   Scale of the threat: Likelihood vs. potential impact.

in light of terror and threats to the homeland. In 2004, President George W. Bush restructured the CIA by including a new Office of the Director of the CIA and a Director of National Intelligence—an office that oversees intelligence nationally and coordinates the activities of the National Counterintelligence Office.[12] The mission and core values of the agency are as follows:

Vision

CIA's information, insights, and actions consistently provide tactical and strategic advantage for the United States.

Mission

Preempt threats and further US national security objectives by collecting intelligence that matters, producing objective all-source analysis, conducting effective covert action as directed by the President, and safeguarding the secrets that help keep our Nation safe.

Ethos

The officers of the CIA are guided by a professional ethos that is the sum of our abiding principles, core values, and highest aspirations. This ethos holds us on course as we exercise the extraordinary influence and authorities with which we have been entrusted to protect the Nation and advance its interests. CIA's ethos has many dimensions, including

- Service: We put Nation first, Agency before unit, and mission before self. We take pride in being agile, responsive, and consequential.

A. PREPARING FOR DISASTER

An FBI SWAT team member is checked for possible radiological contamination. The event was part of a staged drill at the Orange Bowl in Miami to show the basics of how we'd respond to a threat involving a weapon of mass destruction. See more images below.

An FBI SWAT team prepares to assault the warehouse.

FBI and Miami Police SWAT teams use paintball weapons to clear the warehouse and capture the terrorist suspects. In the process, they find a mock "dirty bomb" or radiological dispersal device.

If terrorists ever do try to attack our country with a nuke or dirty bomb, the FBI and its partners must be ready.

And we are. On Wednesday, we staged a mock drill at the Orange Bowl in Miami to show the basics of how we'd respond to a threat involving a weapon of mass destruction.

In the scenario, a terrorist cell was in the process of constructing a dirty bomb in a mock warehouse set up on the field at the Orange Bowl. Two Special Weapons and Tactics (SWAT) teams—one from the FBI and one from the Miami Police—descended on the scene, cleared the warehouse, and discovered an improvised explosive device in one room and radiological material in another room. A Department of Energy Radiological Assistance Program Team used sensors to help determine the presence of radiation, and, with the help of the Miami Fire Department, a robot later destroyed the device. Then, an FBI Hazmat team in full protective gear collected radiological evidence at the scene.

The drill came on day three of the FBI's week-long event, the "Global Initiative to Combat Nuclear Terrorism Law Enforcement Conference." Delegates from 28 countries observed the demonstration from the press boxes and later saw equipment and displays showing the WMD capabilities of 15 local, state, and federal agencies.

A member of the FBI Hazardous Materials Response Team uses a long pole to safely collect evidence related to the dirty bomb.

A Miami police robot like this one destroyed an improvised explosive device with streams of water during the exercise.

FIGURE 8.14 How to respond to a dirty bomb.

FIGURE 8.15 Seal of the Central Intelligence Agency.

- Integrity: We uphold the highest standards of lawful conduct. We are truthful and forthright, and we provide information and analysis without institutional or political bias. We maintain the Nation's trust through accountability and oversight.
- Excellence: We bring the best of who we are to everything we do. We are self-aware, reflecting on our performance and learning from it. We strive to give our officers the tools, experiences, and leadership they need to excel.
- Courage: We accomplish difficult, high-stakes, often dangerous tasks. In executing mission, we carefully manage risk but we do not shy away from it. We value sacrifice and honor our fallen.
- Teamwork: We stand by and behind one another. Collaboration, both internal and external, underpins our best outcomes. Diversity and inclusion are mission imperatives.
- Stewardship: We preserve our ability to obtain secrets by protecting sources and methods from the moment we enter on duty until our last breath (https://www.cia.gov/about-cia/cia-vision-mission-values).

In recent years, the agency has undergone a mission reexamination, primarily prompted by new political leadership and priorities. Under President Obama, the vision of every agency has changed. The tendency to seek less confrontation and more conciliation with our former and present enemies has resulted in agencies, such as the CIA, stressing an altered mission that is less aggressive and more collaborative with the world community. This is evident in the revised mission.

The CIA is primarily a covert intelligence community. Its methods and means are distinct from traditional law enforcement, yet despite these differences, the need for collaboration and meaningful lines of communication became quite clear on September 11, 2001. The 9/11 Commission Report caustically critiqued the lack of communication lines between the CIA and FBI.[13]

The CIA is organizationally arranged into seven parts:

Directorate of Analysis
Directorate of Operations

Directorate of Science and Technology
Directorate of Digital Innovation
Directorate of SupportMission Centers
Offices of the Director

8.3.2.1 Directorate of Analysis

In the intelligence section, the bulk of what the CIA has refined and honed in matters of data collection and interpretation finds a home. Officers in the CIA's Directorate of Analysis anticipate and quickly assess rapidly evolving international developments and their impact, both positive and negative, on U.S. policy concerns. The intelligence support and findings are disseminated to a specific audience in need of those findings. The President's Daily Brief and the World Intelligence Review (WIRe) are examples of this intelligence reporting.

The Directorate of Analysis contains myriad officers and offices dedicated to the collection, assessment, and dissemination of intelligence.

- The CIA Crime and Narcotics Center collects and analyzes information on international narcotics trafficking and organized crime for policymakers and the law enforcement community.
- The CIA Weapons, Intelligence, Nonproliferation, and Arms Control Center provides intelligence support aimed at doing all it can to protect America from the strategic threat of foreign weapons.
- The Counterintelligence Center Analysis Group identifies, monitors, and analyzes the efforts of foreign intelligence entities against U.S. persons, activities, and interests.
- The Information Operations Center Analysis Group evaluates foreign threats to U.S. computer systems, particularly those that support critical infrastructures.
- The Office of Asian Pacific, Latin American, and African Analysis studies the political, economic, leadership, societal, and military developments in Asia, Latin America, and Sub-Saharan Africa.
- The Office of Collection Strategies and Analysis provides comprehensive intelligence collection expertise to the DI, a wide range of senior agency and intelligence community officials, and key national policymakers.
- The Office of Corporate Resources oversees support to the directorate on a wide variety of issues, including budget, contracts, diversity programs, equal employment opportunity, facilities management, human resources, and resource planning.
- The Office of Iraq Analysis provides multidisciplinary intelligence analysis on Iraq to the president and his top advisors.
- The Office of Near Eastern and South Asian Analysis provides policymakers with comprehensive analytic support on Middle Eastern and North African countries, as well as on the South Asian nations of India, Pakistan, and Afghanistan.
- The Office of Policy Support customizes DI analysis and presents it to a wide variety of policy, law enforcement, military, and foreign liaison recipients.

- The Office of Russian and European Analysis provides intelligence support on a large number of countries that have long been of crucial importance to the United States as allies or as adversaries and are likely to continue to occupy a key place in U.S. national security policy.
- The Office of Terrorism Analysis is the analytic component of the CIA Counterterrorism Center.
- The Office of Transnational Issues applies unique functional expertise to assess existing and emerging threats to U.S. national security and provides the most senior U.S. policymakers, military planners, and law enforcement with analysis, warning, and crisis support.

8.3.2.2 Office of Clandestine Services

Clandestine operations connote many images—some forbidden, others unapproved or denied upon discovery. That is a fair assessment, since to be clandestine is, minimally, to be secretive. That the United States has engaged in clandestine operations is really no secret at all. From the failed Bay of Pigs invasion to operating secret prisons for terrorists, the CIA has been a prime player in these covert activities. The agency and its supporters make no apologies for it either. Secret operations are not only essential in the protection of a country, but mandatory. Complex targets such as terrorism prompt complicated responses. Operating within the CIA is the National Clandestine Service (NCS), which conducts specialized operations for the purpose of gathering intelligence and ensuring U.S. security. The CIA references the NCS as a body that collects "information not obtainable through other means."

Internet Resource: For once-classified operations now unclassified regarding covert, clandestine operations of the CIA, see https://www.cia.gov/library/center-for-the-study-of-intelligence/csi-publications/csi-studies/index.html.

8.3.2.3 Directorate of Science and Technology

The Directorate of Science and Technology supports the CIA's mission by its expertise in technological and scientific applications. Intelligence requires the highest levels of equipment and protocol. Clandestine operations require cutting-edge equipment and technology. The mission of the directorate is to fashion and invent tradecraft that aids the operatives of the CIA and to create and develop technical collection systems, and to apply enabling technologies to the collection, processing, and analysis of information. The Directorate of Science and Technology includes the men and women of the CIA who apply their expertise and training in pure science—applied engineering, master craftsmanship, operational tradecraft, and linguistics—to provide U.S. decision makers with critically important intelligence on the world (Figure 8.16).

8.3.2.4 Directorate of Digital Innovation

The Directorate of Digital Innovation (DDI) is the CIA's office dedicated to the protection of the nation's IT structure and what it terms *cyber tradecraft*. Realizing that threats are both real and virtual, the directorate advances the most sophisticated technology and

FIGURE 8.16 CIA's Directorate of Science and Technology.

protocols to thwart cyber threats that are very real and very meaningful. In this directorate, the CIA looks for evidence of threat and terror by scanning the remnants and shadows of illegal activity capturable in the digital realm. This same office shall be the center for a CIA too long laden with old and insecure equipment across its many offices.

In addition to its overall mission to expand digital and cyber capabilities across the CIA, the new DDI will create a strategic framework to manage the CIA's digital architecture and talent, enhancing the capabilities of the agency's existing directorates and new Mission Centers. The DDI will encourage CIA leadership to aggressively implement innovation in the digital realm and oversee the career development of the agency's digital and cyber experts.

8.3.2.5 *Directorate of Support*

The Support to Mission team provides mission-focused support to the CIA through a full range of services. The office is responsible for building and operating facilities; providing robust, secure communications over multiple networks, connecting officers sitting in dispersed locations; and acquiring and shipping a full range of critical equipment. The Directorate of Support also helps hire, train, and assign CIA officers for every directorate, as well as manage the "businesses" within the CIA—contracts and acquisitions, financial services, administrative support, and even the CIA's own phone company. The Directorate of Support does everything it can to ensure that CIA officers serving around the world are safe, secure, and healthy.

8.3.2.6 *Mission Centers*

As part of its overall reorganization and updating, the CIA has erected, aside from some mission tinkering, new mission centers that stress and emphasize particular works and ambitions for the CIA. The mission centers comprise four primary functions for CIA operations and six specifically designated geographic territories.

- Mission Center for Africa
- Mission Center for Counterintelligence
- Mission Center for Counterterrorism

- Mission Center for East Asia and Pacific
- Mission Center for Europe and Eurasia
- Mission Center for Global Issues
- Mission Center for Near East
- Mission Center for South and Central Asia
- Mission Center for Weapons and Counterproliferation
- Mission Center for Western Hemisphere

Couple this realignment with the agency's stress on modernization and cyber and digital capacity, and it is clear that the CIA has undergone significant transformation during the second term of President Obama. The changes are fully charted in Figure 8.17.

8.3.3 Offices of the Director

What was painfully obvious to intelligence specialists was the lack of coordination among so many distinct bureaucracies of intelligence.[14] By 2006, it was clear that there were too many cooks in the intelligence kitchen. As a result, President Bush created the ODNI; in some circles this position is labeled "executive" or "czar." When Congress authorized the creation of the ODNI, it charged the department with diverse authorities and duties, including the following:

- Ensure that timely and objective national intelligence is provided to the president, the heads of departments, and agencies of the executive branch; the chairman of the Joint Chiefs of Staff and senior military commanders; and Congress.
- Establish objectives and priorities for the collection, analysis, production, and dissemination of national intelligence.
- Ensure maximum availability of and access to intelligence information within the Intelligence Community.
- Develop and ensure the execution of an annual budget for the National Intelligence Program (NIP) based on budget proposals provided by intelligence community (IC) component organizations.
- Oversee the coordination of relationships with the intelligence or security services of foreign governments and international organizations.
- Ensure the most accurate analysis of intelligence is derived from all sources to support national security needs.
- Develop personnel policies and programs to enhance the capacity for joint operations and to facilitate staffing of community management functions.
- Oversee the development and implementation of a program management plan for the acquisition of major systems, doing so jointly with the secretary of defense for Department of Defense (DoD) programs, that includes cost, schedule, and performance goals and program milestone criteria.

The idea was to pool all the intelligence resources, or to funnel these myriad sources through a central office with a central director. This way, one agency could not fail, either inadvertently or intentionally, to withhold intelligence from sister agencies. John

FIGURE 8.17 CIA offices organization chart (https://www.cia.gov/about-cia/leadership/cia-organization-chart.html).

Negroponte, a seasoned diplomat and security guru, was the first appointee to this position. Negroponte, by all accounts, skillfully coordinated these diverse constituencies and left the office in high esteem. After President Obama assumed office, Dennis Blair, a former Navy Commander of the Pacific Fleet, whose background includes impeccable experiential and educational preparation, was appointed to the role and served for 2 years. Blair set clear goals for the position, which include the following:

- To serve as the principal intelligence advisor to the president and his national security team. We will continue to enhance the quality of our analysis and the depth and range of collection that supports it. We will integrate contributions from all IC partners, call it as we see it and lay out the alternatives with clear statements of our level of confidence in our judgments.
- To make the whole of the Intelligence Community greater than the sum of its parts. All 17 intelligence organizations can expect clear mission direction. Common areas such as personnel, intra-IC communications, clearances, and classification deserve special emphasis, as do missions that require the capabilities of more than one agency for success. All of us are then accountable for mission success.
- To assess mission and resources and then provide resources adequate to meet assigned responsibilities and build future capabilities.[15]

His recent replacement is James R. Clapper, a retired military officer with significant intelligence experience (Figure 8.18).

The mission of the ODNI is multifaceted, but its central aim is the coordination of intelligence information across a host of agencies and operatives (Figure 8.19).

In its strategic statement, the ODNI lists the constituencies that it serves. Turf battles give way to collective cooperation and sound homeland policy. The ODNI holds that intelligence will integrate foreign, military, and domestic intelligence capabilities through policy, personnel, and technology actions to provide decisional advantage to policymakers, warfighters, homeland security officials, and law enforcement personnel.

FIGURE 8.18   **James R. Clapper, Director of National Intelligence.**

FIGURE 8.19   Seal of the Office of the Director of National Intelligence.

This ambition can only be termed a lofty one, for it properly hopes for the type of sharing and intelligence cooperation that government historically resists. The ODNI has many tools at its disposal. A summary look follows.

Internet Exercise: Visit the ODNI's Electronic Reading Room for a sample of its many findings and reports at http://www.dni.gov/index.php/intelligence-community/ic-policies-reports.

8.3.3.1 National Counterterrorism Center

The National Counterterrorism Center (NCTC) was created to be a central clearinghouse for integrating and analyzing terrorism information. The NCTC comprises people from its many partner agencies and is a center based on cooperation, collaboration, and partnership. The NCTC seal symbolizes this and, like the design of the great seal of the United States, represents a united center engaged in the global fight against terrorism (Figure 8.20).

A special emphasis of the NCTC is the detection and prediction of domestic activities that threaten the homeland. The NCTC has come under some withering criticism for its failure to share intelligence on Major Hasan, the mass murderer at Fort Hood (Figure 8.21).[16]

FIGURE 8.20   Seal of the National Counterterrorism Center.

FIGURE 8.21   Major Nidal Malik Hasan, the shooter at Fort Hood.

Congressional hearings confirmed that the structural difficulties of intelligence sharing and the "wall" between "law enforcement and intelligence"[17] still existed nearly a decade later. And this persistent shortfall may be "inevitable"[18] given the complexities of the intelligence function. However, it seems a necessary ambition to improve the methods and means by which the NCTC shares its information, as well as how all other intelligence agencies share their knowledge base.

8.3.3.2 National Counterintelligence and Security Center

The Office of the National Counterintelligence Executive (ONCIX) was part of the ODNI and staffed by CI and other specialists. The ONCIX developed, coordinated, and produced

- Foreign intelligence threat assessments and other analytic CI products
- CI strategy for the U.S. government
- CI policy on collection, investigations, and operations
- CI program budgets and evaluations
- Espionage damage assessments
- CI awareness, outreach, and training standards policies (Figure 8.22)

This office developed the National Intelligence Strategy,[19] which lays out broad policies on intelligence and produces recommendations on how to undermine terrorists and terrorism and protect intelligence capabilities.[20] The office has merged two previous sectors—namely, the Special Security Center and the Center for Security Evaluation, effective 2010. In 2014, the office was reorganized and renamed the National Counterintelligence and Security Center (NCSC) and operates under the full supervision of the ODNI (Figure 8.23).

The business of the NCSC primarily consists of the following duties:

- National Threat Identification and Prioritization Assessment (NTIPA) program and other analytic CI products
- Development of the National Counterintelligence Strategy of the United States

FIGURE 8.22 The ONCIX poster "Espionage Is No Sure Bet" serves as a reminder that there are no winners in the espionage game.

FIGURE 8.23 Seal of the NCSC.

- Counterintelligence collection, investigations, and operations
- Espionage damage assessments
- Counterintelligence awareness, outreach, and training standards

Internet Exercise: Read the NCSC's 2016 National Counterintelligence Strategy at: http://www.dni.gov/files/documents/ncsc/National%20CI%20Strategy%202016_Unclassified_Final.pdf.

8.3.3.3 *National Intelligence Council*

The National Intelligence Council (NIC) provides an intellectual and policymaking center for the director of national intelligence. Its core missions are to

- Promote exemplary use of analytic tradecraft and standards, including alternative analysis, new analytic tools and techniques, and wider collaboration within the IC
- Provide senior policymakers with coordinated views of the entire Intelligence Community, including National Intelligence Estimates
- Prepare IC principals and represent the IC at National Security Council principals and Deputies Committee meetings
- Tap non-U.S. government (USG) experts in academia and the private sector to broaden the IC's knowledge and perspectives

The NIC expends a good portion of its energy and time on projections—that is, what it expects the future holds. For terror prevention, the policymaker and homeland professional need to always stay a step or two ahead to succeed. The NIC's projections are short term and long term in design. Its projections to the year 2030 portray a world with the types of problems presently witnessed and a bold projection of emergent issues likely to be encountered.[21] A sample of these projections is reproduced in Figure 8.24.

The NIC authors the influential National Intelligence Estimates, which comprise the coordinated judgments of the Intelligence Community regarding the likely course of future events. The NIC makes every attempt to stay apolitical in its advice to politicians and policymakers, although the content of the estimate is often used for political reasons The NIC estimates have been fodder for those opposing the wars in Iraq and Afghanistan, since the pictures drawn in the estimates have not always been complementary to decisions relating to these campaigns. The estimates can ruffle feathers, but at their foundation is the desire of the NIC to deliver objective information on tough security problems.

The NIC depends on a cadre of national intelligence officers (NIOs), who engage the security questions in an applied sense and gather intelligence both nationally and internationally. Some of the common functions for NIOs are to

- Advise the DNI.
- Interact regularly with senior intelligence consumers.
- Produce top-quality estimates.
- Engage with the outside.
- Help assess the capabilities and needs of IC analytic producers.
- Promote collaboration among IC analytic producers on strategic warnings, advanced analytic tools, and methodologies.
- Articulate substantive priorities to guide intelligence collection, evaluation, and procurement.

NIO is among the more lucrative career posts in federal service. Figure 8.25 contains a recent recruitment announcement for a senior position.

Megatrends	
Individual empowerment	Individual empowerment will accelerate owing to poverty reduction, growth of the global middle class, greater educational attainment, widespread use of new communications and manufacturing technologies, and health-care advances.
Diffusion of power	There will not be any hegemonic power. Power will shift to networks and coalitions in a multipolar world.
Demographic patterns	The demographic arc of instability will narrow. Economic growth might decline in "aging" countries. Sixty percent of the world's population will live in urbanized areas; migration will increase.
Food, water, energy nexus	Demand for these resources will grow substantially owing to an increase in the global population. Tackling problems pertaining to one commodity will be linked to supply and demand for the others.
Game-changers	
Crisis-prone global economy	Will global volatility and imbalances among players with different economic interests result in collapse? Or will greater multipolarity lead to increased resiliency in the global economic order?
Governance gap	Will governments and institutions be able to adapt fast enough to harness change instead of being overwhelmed by it?
Potential for increased conflict	Will rapid changes and shifts in power lead to more intrastate and interstate conflicts?
Wider scope of regional instability	Will regional instability, especially in t he Middle East and South Asia, spill over and create global insecurity?
Impact of new technologies	Will technological breakthroughs be developed in time to boost economic productivity and solve the problems caused by a growing world population, rapid urbanization, and climate change?
Role of the United States	Will the United States be able to work with new partners to reinvent the international system?
Potential worlds	
Stalled engines	In the most plausible worst-case scenario, the risks of interstate conflict increase. The US draws inward and globalization stalls.
Fusion	In the most plausible best-case outcome, China and the US collaborate on a range of issues, leading to broader global cooperation.
Gini-out-of-the bottle	Inequalities explode as some countries become big winners and others fail. Inequalities within countries increase social tensions. Without completely disengaging, the US is no longer the "global policeman."
Nonstate world	Driven by new technologies, nonstate actors take the lead in confronting global challenges.

FIGURE 8.24 **An overview of global trends by 2030. From: NIC,** *Global Trends 2030* **(Washington, DC: NIC, December 2012), http://www.dni.gov/index.php/about/organization/global-trends-2030. Accessed August 16, 2016.**

Agency: Office of the Director of National Intelligence
Job Announcement Number: 22438
Team lead/Senior Intelligence Officer
Salary Range: 120,830.00–153,200.00 USD per year
Open Period:
Series & Grade: GS-0132-15/15
Position Information: Full-Time Permanent
Duty Locations: 1 vacancy – Washington, DC, Metro Area, DC
Who May Be Considered:
Applications will be accepted from United States citizens and nationals.
Job Summary:
The National Counterintelligence Executive (NCIX) serves as the head of national counterintelligence (CI) for the United States Government and is directly responsible to the Director of National Intelligence. NCIX facilitates and enhances US counterintelligence efforts and awareness by enabling the CI community to better identify, assess, prioritize, and counter intelligence threats from foreign powers, terrorist groups, and other non-state entities. NCIX operates the Community Acquisition Risk Section (CARS) to address the threat from foreign subversions of Intelligence Community (IC) acquisitions. As international companies and foreign individuals play a greater role in information technology and other critical industries, the risk of persistent, stealthy subversion is raised, particularly by foreign intelligence and military services, as well as international terrorists and criminal elements.
CARS evaluates the risk to the IC posed by commercial entities conducting business with the individual components of the IC.

FIGURE 8.25   National Intelligence Officer recruitment announcement.

Internet Exercise: Find out about the many careers in this arm of the Intelligence Community at http://diajobs.dia.mil/.

8.3.4 Defense Intelligence Agency

The DIA, founded on October 1, 1961, was, for a large part of its history, a combat support agency. The DIA collects and produces foreign military intelligence for the DoD and aligned intelligence agencies. The DIA reports to the defense agencies as well as the national security staff of the president, members of Congress, and military commanders. The DIA directs itself to six main areas: "all-source analysis, human intelligence, CI, a worldwide secure information technology backbone measurements and signatures intelligence."[22] The DIA also operates a fully accredited university, the Defense Intelligence University, which offers undergraduate and graduate programs.

The DIA serves as lead agency for the intelligence needs of the DoD.

Internet Exercise: To find out more about the DIA college, visit http://ni-u.edu/wp.

The DIA summarizes its mission, vision, and values as follows:

Mission

Provide intelligence on foreign militaries and operating environments that delivers decision advantage to prevent and decisively win wars.

Vision

Be the indispensable source of defense intelligence expertise.

Values

We are committed to

- Teamwork: Partnering at all levels and across organizational boundaries for mission accomplishment.
- Integrity: Adherence to the highest legal and ethical principles in our responsibilities.
- Excellence: Unrivaled defense intelligence expertise.
- Service: Putting the welfare of the Nation and commitment to our mission before oneself (http://www.dia.mil/About/Leadership/).

With nearly 17,000 employees, the DIA is a major player in the world of intelligence. DIA intelligence covers a broad spectrum of topical coverage and includes but is not limited to

- Foreign military and paramilitary forces
- Proliferation of WMDs
- International terrorism
- International narcotics trafficking
- Information operations
- Defense-related foreign political, economic, industrial, geographic, and medical and health issues

DIA is headquartered at the Joint Base Anacostia–Bolling in Washington, DC, with major operational activities at the Defense Intelligence Analysis Center, the National Center for Medical Intelligence in Frederick, Maryland, and the Missile and Space Intelligence Center in Huntsville, Alabama (Figure 8.26).

A major component of the agency, the Defense HUMINT Service, meaning human intelligence, gathers information by traditional face-to-face interaction rather than technical services. The DIA also manages the Defense Attaché System, which has military attachés assigned to more than 135 embassies overseas. In addition to these functions, the DIA operates and coordinates the functions of the Joint Intelligence Task Force for Combating Terrorism (JITF-CT).

FIGURE 8.26   Seal of the DIA at Joint Base Anacostia–Bolling.

Internet Exercise: For a time line and historical perspective on the DIA, see http://fas.org/irp/dia/dia_history.pdf.

8.4 Conclusion

The idea and concept known as intelligence is the chapter's chief aim, and how intelligence becomes part of the homeland security mission is a secondary purpose. In intelligence, the homeland professional recognizes that information is the lifeblood of any meaningful operation or policy. Acting quickly upon intelligence led to the successful raid on Osama bin Laden in his Abbottabad, Pakistan compound in the early hours of May 2nd, 2011 (Figure 8.27). Without information, and shared distribution of the same, the homeland operative works in the dark in a literal and figurative sense. Intelligence takes the guesswork out of homeland task and function. DHS promotes the integrative approach to intelligence, whereby information is gathered by the various arms of government—namely, the military, federal, state, local, and private sector justice agencies—and friendly information from foreign allies is weighed and evaluated. DHS encourages cooperation among historic competitors in the bureaucratic sense. It calls on agencies of government to shun the traditional turf systems and parochial protection mechanisms that hardly promote a policy of sharing. There are a host of structural obstacles to the sharing of intelligence. DHS devises the TTIC to serve as a central repository for relevant terrorist intelligence.

Additionally, the chapter paints the picture of intelligence agencies that have been part of the historic and contemporary landscape. Predictably, the CIA and its various branches dedicated to intelligence are featured. Special attention is given to the FBI, whose international thrust and historic responsibility for crimes of terror and espionage provide early expertise in the fight against terrorism. Terrorism would eventually sweep up the agency

FIGURE 8.27 President Obama, Vice President Biden, and then Secretary of State Hilary Clinton with members of the national security team, receive an update on Operation Neptune's Spear, a mission against Osama bin Laden, in one of the conference rooms of the Situation Room of the White House, May 1, 2011. They are watching live feed from drones operating over the bin Laden complex.

and consume it in ways it had never originally envisioned. The FBI developed advanced CI systems, the capacity to trace, detect, and prevent attacks by WMDs, and devised and erected the TSC. The FBI is on the forefront of information sharing. The educational role of the FBI in matters of terrorism is also being evaluated. With the FBI working closely with the CIA, the traditional turf protection systems that thwarted the sharing of information will end. Eventually, all agencies will contribute to the NCTC—a clearinghouse of information on threats.

Special attention is given to new agencies that have arisen since the tragedy of 9/11 as well as the reorientation of existing agencies that have had to revise operational missions to contend with the terrorist threat. In particular, the chapter scrutinizes efforts to centralize and coordinate the massive volume of intelligence across a plethora of federal agencies. Here, the ODNI will play a central role. Known as the Office of the Intelligence Czar, the ODNI has become a focal point for intelligence systems. The director oversees a host of intelligence operations and functions, including the NCTC, the ONCIX, and the NIC. Each of these entities carries out critical work in the world of intelligence. Finally, the chapter ends its coverage of the intelligence sector by reviewing the work of the DIA—that crucial collaboration of military and civilian intelligence gathering and sharing. The DIA's more essential contributions to the intelligence theater are highlighted.

Keywords

Change of mandate	Joint Terrorism Task Force
Clandestine operations	National Clandestine Service
Counterintelligence	National Counterintelligence Executive
Counterterrorism	National Counterterrorism Center
Covert intelligence community	National Espionage Estimates
Defense Attaché System	National Intelligence Council
Defense Intelligence Agency	National intelligence officers
Director of National Intelligence	National Intelligence Strategy
Directorate of Science and Technology	National Security Branch
Espionage	Office of Support
Federal Bureau of Investigation	President's Daily Brief
Global terrorism	Terrorist Screening Center
HUMINT	Terrorist Threat Integration Center
Intelligence Community	World Intelligence Review
Intelligence	

Discussion Questions

1. Explain how the FBI had to change its outlook and mission after 9/11. How significant was this reorientation?

2. Previous to 9/11, the FBI stressed what tasks and duties when compared with terrorism?

3. JTTFs assimilate many agencies into the mix. How does this assist in their outlook and work?

4. Evaluate and comment on the CIA's Directorate of Science and Technology. What is its purpose and aim?

5. Discuss the ramifications of an intelligence practice based on a nonshared environment. Why do some argue that 9/11 would never have occurred if information sharing had been commonplace?

6. Explain why cooperation between the military complex and federal intelligence agencies is so important in the fight against terrorism.

7. What types of projections make sense in the intelligence arena? What is a projection worth making?

8. Does it make sense to create an ODNI? Are there alternatives to this design?

9. What do you envision is the greatest challenge for the director of national intelligence?

10. How has the mission of the DIA changed in the last 50 years?

Practical Exercises

1. Find and locate a JTTF in your area. Respond to the following:
   a. What geographic area does the task force cover?
   b. Whom or what is eligible to join?

2. Describe at least three initiatives the JTTF is presently undertaking.

3. Watch any training video prepared by the FBI relating to terrorism. State four major findings agreed to after reviewing the media.

4. Search the DIA for career opportunities. Create a form file for these career tracks.

5. Find out about career opportunities for intelligence officers in today's military branches.

6. Visit any of the centers mentioned in this chapter.

7. Visit the CIA's Office of Clandestine Services. Analyze, assess, and critique a current operation relating to homeland security.

8. Prove whether the FBI is correct in concluding that ecoterrorists are a mighty dangerous lot.

9. Identify and create a job file for the following occupations in homeland security:
   a. Federal Protective Service
   b. Secret Service
   c. Border Patrol
   d. Customs officer
   e. FBI agent
   f. CIA officer

10. Determine where the closest intelligence center is relative to your residence. Check to determine whether any of the following apply:

a. Military base

b. Fusion center

c. JTTF

d. Regional Office of State Homeland Security

e. Special operations unit

Notes

1. See D. Khan, An historical theory of intelligence, *Intelligence and National Security 16* (Autumn 2001): 87–88; P. Gorman, *Hearings before Select Committee on Intelligence of the United States Senate, S. 2198 and S. 421, 102nd Congress* (Washington, DC: Library of Congress, 1992), 262.

2. Congressional Research Service (CRS), T. Masse, ed., *Homeland Security Intelligence: Perceptions, Statutory Definitions, and Approaches* (Washington, DC: Library of Congress, 2006), 2, http://www.fas.org/sgp/crs/intel/RL33616.pdf.

3. CRS, R. A. Best, Jr., ed., *Intelligence Issues for Congress* (Washington, DC: Library of Congress, 2011), 5, http://www.fas.org/sgp/crs/intel/RL33539.pdf.

4. See also C. G. Pernin, L. R. Moore, and K. Comanor, *The Knowledge Matrix Approach to Intelligence Fusion* (Santa Monica, CA: Rand Corporation, 2007).

5. See M. Chertoff, Current and Planned Information Sharing Initiatives, Keynote presentation, SEARCH Symposium on Justice and Public Safety Information Sharing (Washington, DC, 2006).

6. M. Lowenthal, Transforming intelligence, *American Intelligence Journal*, 29, 2011: 10.

7. Homeland Security Act of 2002, P.L. 107–296, *U.S. Statutes at Large*, 116, 2002: 2135.

8. The Intelligence Reform and Terrorism Prevention Act of 2004 (IRTPA), P.L. 108–458, *U.S. Statutes at Large*, 118, 2004: 3638.

9. E. Berman, Regulating domestic intelligence collection, 71 *Wash. & Lee L. Rev*, 3, 2014.

10. FBI, National Joint Terrorism Task Force, https://www.fbi.gov/about-us/investigate/terrorism/national-joint-terrorism-task-force, accessed January 18, 2016.

11. DHS, *Fusion Centers and Joint Terrorism Task Forces*, at https://www.dhs.gov/fusion-centers-and-joint-terrorism-task-forces.

12. CRS, R. A. Best, Jr., ed., *Intelligence Issues for Congress* (Washington, DC: Library of Congress, 2011), 20, http://www.fas.org/sgp/crs/intel/RL33539.pdf.

13. P. S. Roberts, How security agencies control change: Executive power and the quest for autonomy in the FBI and CIA, *Public Organization Review*, 9, 2009: 169–198.

14. See ODNI, ODNI fact sheet, October 2011, https://www.dni.gov/files/documents/ODNI%20Fact%20Sheet_2011.pdf.

15. ODNI, Letter of Dennis C. Blair to employees, January 30, 2009, http://www.governmentattic.org/14docs/ODNIcongCorres_2009–2010.pdf; accessed August 16, 2016.

16. CRS, R. A. Best, Jr., ed., *The National Counterterrorism Center (NCTC): Responsibilities and Potential Congressional Concerns* (Washington, DC: Library of Congress, 2011), 8–9, http://www.fas.org/sgp/crs/intel/R41022.pdf.

17. CRS, R. A. Best, Jr., ed., *The National Counterterrorism Center (NCTC): Responsibilities and Potential Congressional Concerns* (Washington, DC: Library of Congress, 2011), 9, http://www.fas.org/sgp/crs/intel/R41022.pdf.

18. CRS, R. A. Best, Jr., ed., *The National Counterterrorism Center (NCTC): Responsibilities and Potential Congressional Concerns* (Washington, DC: Library of Congress, 2011), 10, http://www.fas.org/sgp/crs/intel/R41022.pdf.

19. See ONCIX, *The National Counterintelligence Strategy of the United States*, 2009.

20. Finding out exactly who the enemy may be is always a challenge, even in the case of Al Qaeda. See M. L. Hummel, Who is running Al Qaeda?, *The Homeland Security Review*, 5, 2011: 1.

21. NIC, *Global Trends 2025: A Transformed World* (Washington, DC: U.S. Government Printing Office, November 2008), iv, https://www.dni.gov/files/documents/Newsroom/Reports%20and%20Pubs/2025_Global_Trends_Final_Report.pdf; accessed August 16, 2016.

22. R. C. Ackerman, Honing defense intelligence, *Signal*, October 2011: 47.

Chapter 9

Border Security, U.S. Citizenship, and Immigration Services

Objectives

1. To identify the various government agencies and their offices that are responsible for securing America's borders
2. To outline the history of what is now Customs and Border Protection (CBP)
3. To explain the various programs of CBP for securing our borders from the illegal entry of immigrants
4. To summarize the programs that CBP has initiated to facilitate the efficient processing and securing of cargo in ports across the globe
5. To outline the history of what is now the U.S. Citizenship and Immigration Services (USCIS)
6. To summarize the various policies and law that has been enacted relative to immigration since the 1920s
7. To explain the mission, policies, and procedures of USCIS as they relate to illegal immigration and terrorism
8. To summarize the programs that USCIS has developed in response to the threat of terrorism

FIGURE 9.1 A portal observation tower that is gaining popularity on the border.

9.1 Introduction

The task of protecting the nation's borders constitutes a major core competency for those involved in homeland security. It is an astounding responsibility with coverage areas that are almost impossible to compute. The sheer size of American geography makes the task overwhelming, though with increasing usage of technology and aircraft tools, our borders are dramatically improving (Figure 9.1).

9.2 U.S. Customs and Border Protection

Since 1924, a Border Patrol office has been responsible for making our territorial lines secure, but much has changed since the early days of border protection. In the 1980s, Americans became very familiar with the wave after wave of illegal immigrants coming across the porous lines of defense. Millions of Mexican and Third World immigrants trekked across without much resistance.

In recent years, the Border Patrol has become correctly occupied with another type of immigrant, one of the terrorist sort. The Border Patrol, as a result of the events of 9/11, was merged into the Department of Homeland Security (DHS) and then further aligned with its historic partner, Customs.[1] Customs has an even longer history than the Border Patrol. Originally established as a revenue collector with the founding of the United States in

1776, Customs evolved into much more than the revenue machine it continues to be today. Customs has primary oversight on questions of cargo, duties, and revenue enforcement; trade and environmental law questions; imports and exports; and cargo and port issues. The range and breadth of responsibilities simply impresses. On a typical day in 2014, CBP

- Processed
  - 1,026,234 passengers and pedestrians
  - 70,334 truck, rail, and sea containers
  - 307,680 incoming privately owned vehicles
- Conducted 1333 apprehensions between U.S. ports of entry
- Arrested 21 wanted criminals at U.S. ports of entry
- Refused 241 inadmissible persons at U.S. ports of entry
- Discovered 425 pests at U.S. ports of entry and 4447 materials for quarantine: plants, meat, animal by-products, and soil
- Seized
  - 10,327 pounds of drugs
  - $650,117 in undeclared or illicit currency
  - $3.4 million worth of products with intellectual property rights violations
- Identified 548 individuals with suspected national security concerns
- Intercepted 76 fraudulent documents
- Employed 59,544 CBP employees, including
  - 22,274 CBP officers
  - 2368 CBP agriculture specialists
  - 20,824 Border Patrol agents
  - 729 air interdiction agents (pilots)
  - 329 marine interdiction agents
  - 133 aviation enforcement officers
- Deployed more than 1463 canine teams and 300 horse patrols
- Flew 213 hours of enforcement missions over the United States
- Conducted operations at
  - 328 ports of entry within 20 field offices
  - 136 Border Patrol stations and five substations within 20 sectors, with 35 permanent checkpoints
  - 21 air and marine branches, six national security operations, and one air and marine operations center[2]

Today, DHS delegates the integrity of our land border to a newly formed entity within DHS—the U.S. CBP program. CBP is responsible for guarding 7000 miles of land border the United States shares with Canada and Mexico and 2000 miles of coastal waters surrounding the Florida peninsula and the coast of Southern California. The agency also protects 95,000 miles of maritime border in partnership with the U.S. Coast Guard (Figure 9.2).

The structure of CBP can be seen in Figure 9.3.

The various departments of CBP manifest the overall mission of the agency—to approach homeland security from two distinct directions. In the first instance, CBP concerns itself

FIGURE 9.2   The U.S. Coast Guard on border patrol.

with the threat of terrorism and the paths of entry the terrorist may follow into the American landscape, as well as the influx of illegal immigration. In the second instance, CBP, due to its responsibility for cargo, port, commerce and revenue collection, constantly concerns itself with the intricacies of travel and trade. The agency knows its police role keenly and, at the same time, realizes that it plays a critical role in the movement of goods and services. A closer look at these two missions of CBP follows.

9.2.1 Border Protection

With nearly 7000 miles of American border, CBP has a serious problem when it comes to ensuring the integrity of our borders. Few issues rile up public debate more than the growing issue of illegal aliens crossing into American territory, even though the illegals seeking work and a better life are not the stuff of al-Qaeda. Terrorism cannot be held to be a primary motivation for the illegal, yet one fully comprehends that illegal border crossing is a more likely means of entry for the terrorist. Terrorists are now less likely to use commercial aircraft as was done during 9/11. Hence, it is a fact that CBP must concern itself with border protection more than it has historically done. Indeed, since 2004, CBP has reoriented its mission in radical ways, and produced some very radical results (Table 9.1).

CBP represents the best in adaptation and operational flexibility in government service. At every level of its operation CBP has targeted its attention on the border while simultaneously honing in on the terrorist. CBP established the National Targeting Center—Passenger (NTC-P) as the centralized coordination point for all of CBP's antiterrorism efforts (Figure 9.4).

NTC-P also coordinates with other federal agencies, such as the U.S. Coast Guard, Federal Air Marshals, Federal Bureau of Investigation (FBI), Transportation Security Administration, and Departments of Energy and Agriculture.

Immigration and Customs Enforcement (ICE)'s National Security Investigations Division undertakes a wide variety of programs relating to terrorism and defense of the homeland.

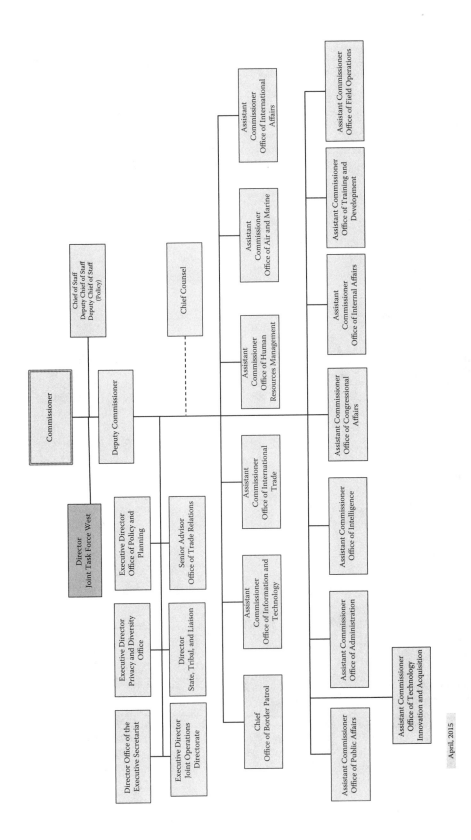

FIGURE 9.3 CBP organization chart.

TABLE 9.1 CBP Statistical Highlights FY 2011–2014

	FY 2011	FY 2012	FY 2013	FY 2014
Total employees	59,820	60,668	59,969	59,544
Total revenue	$37.2 billion	$39.4 billion	$40.9 billion	$43.5 billion
Total assets	$16.2 billion	$15.9 billion	$15.5 billion	$16.2 billion
Total net position	$9.7 billion	$9.7 billion	$9.4 billion	$9.5 billion
Total net cost of operations	$12.0 billion	$12.3 billion	$12.6 billion	$12.9 billion
Total budgetary resources	$17.0 billion	$17.2 billion	$16.2 billion	$17.3 billion
Ports of entry	329	329	328	328
Preclearance locations	15	15	15	16
Border patrol sectors	20	20	20	20
Air units	46	46	43	41
Marine units	71	71	71	71
Trade entries processed	$29.5 million	$30.4 million	$30.4 million	$31.6 million
Illegal narcotics seized	3.1 million pounds	2.8 million pounds	2.8 million pounds	2.5 million pounds
Illegal alien apprehensions between ports of entry	340,252	364,768	420,789	486,651
Inadmissible aliens interdicted at ports of entry	211,483	195,865	204,905	223,712
Pedestrians and passengers processed	$340 million	$351 million	$362 million	$375 million
Conveyances processed	$104 million	$107 million	$110 million	$113 million
Aircraft passengers processed	$94 million	$98 million	$102 million	$107 million
Prohibited plant and animal materials seized at ports of entry	1,682,881	1,576,343	1,603,944	1,623,294
Agricultural plants and pests intercepted at ports of entry	177,299	170,967	161,050	155,247

Source: CBP, *Performance and Accountability Report: Fiscal Year 2014* (2014), 8, https://www.cbp.gov/sites/default/files/documents/CBP_DHS_2014%20PAR_508C.PDF (accessed January 23, 2016).

FIGURE 9.4 CBP's National Targeting Center.

Given that borders are a pathway to the homeland, the inescapable reality is that these distinct worlds often collide. Some of the division's more notable sectors of involvement are as follows:

- *Counter-Proliferation Investigations Program*: The Counter-Proliferation Investigations Program oversees a broad range of investigations related to preventing terrorist groups from obtaining U.S. military technology, weapons of mass destruction, or chemical, biological, radiological, and nuclear materials.
- *Export Enforcement Coordination Center*: The Export Enforcement Coordination Center serves as the primary force within the federal government to coordinate U.S. export control enforcement efforts. The center was created by Executive Order 13558.
- *Counterterrorism and Criminal Exploitation Unit*: The Counterterrorism and Criminal Exploitation Unit investigates nonimmigrant visa holders who violate their immigration status. The unit places the highest priority on monitoring the activities of suspected terrorists and combating criminal exploitation of the nation's student visa system.
- *Human Rights Violators and War Crimes Unit*: The Human Rights Violators and War Crimes Unit pursues foreign war criminals, persecutors, and human rights abusers who seek shelter from justice in the United States.
- *National Security Integration Center*: The National Security Integration Center focuses on federal and interagency partner coordination through its three sections. The center's Interagency Strategic Coordination Section works with the Department of Defense to provide operational, technical, and intelligence support.
- *National Security Unit*: The National Security Unit combines the Homeland Security Investigations (HSI)'s national security and counterterrorism efforts into a single force. The unit has oversight of all counterterrorism investigations within ICE and works directly with the National Security Council and ICE senior leadership to carry out interagency policy.

- *Overstay Analysis Unit*: The Overstay Analysis Unit identifies visitors who violate their immigration status by overstaying their authorized period of admission. The unit also researches violator records from the Arrival and Departure Information System.
- *National Security Liaisons*: National Security Liaisons are senior HSI personnel who coordinate investigative activity under assignments to various federal agencies and departments. As part of the National Security Investigations Division, liaisons are essential to establishing partnerships and developing close and cooperative working relationships with HSI's partner agencies.
- *Student and Exchange Visitor Program*: The Student and Exchange Visitor Program manages information on foreign students and exchange visitors in the United States. The program uses the Student and Exchange Visitor Information System to monitor schools, active nonimmigrant students, exchange visitors, and dependents approved to participate in the U.S. education system.

Despite all these advances, CBP cannot forget its fundamental mission of securing the border—in both a physical and an intelligence sense.[3] In other sections within this chapter, programs of border protection are featured. The more prominent initiatives of CBP will be briefly covered.

9.2.1.1 Secure Border Initiative: Its Creation and Demise

The Secure Border Initiative (SBI) is a comprehensive multiyear plan to secure America's borders and reduce illegal migration. When first announced in 2005, SBI was thought to be only a few years away from full implementation.[4] The goals of SBI included, but were not limited to

- More agents to patrol our borders, secure our ports of entry, and enforce immigration laws
- Expanded detention and removal capabilities to eliminate "catch and release"
- A comprehensive and systemic upgrading of the technology used in controlling the border, including increased manned aerial assets, expanded use of unmanned aerial vehicles (UAVs) (Figure 9.5), and next-generation detection technology
- Increased investment in infrastructure improvements at the border, providing additional physical security to sharply reduce illegal border crossings
- Increased interior enforcement of our immigration laws, including more robust worksite enforcement

As the last few years have shown, these dynamic ambitions were at best naive and utterly corrupted by political and special interests working overtime, especially when the overall issue of immigration itself has yet to be fully tackled: "SBI was meant to be the enforcement component to some sort of substantive immigration reform, which has yet to take place."[5] SBI was driven by various interests: first, the very real danger of illegal entry by terrorists, and second, the increase in illegal immigrants, the latter of which results in significant social impacts, including strains on health, education, and other systems.

FIGURE 9.5   Predator B UAV.

Despite SBI's intentions, the prime aim to erect a fence worthy of defense has been nothing more than a pipedream. Probably nothing contributes to this incompetency more than our political leaders posturing and arguing about the sensibility of a virtual fence or other barrier in the first place. In Democrat quarters, a select group of political leaders call for no fences or walls, virtual or otherwise, while their counterparts advocate a virtual and physical fence that cannot be scaled. Across this chasm, SBI simply flounders and becomes ripe for the misallocation of resources so common to its overall mission. SBI, despite all good intentions, was cancelled in 2012 due to technological issues. However, SBI suffers from the current dysfunction so evident in our political infrastructure.

Illegal immigration represents a significant challenge for law enforcement too. To put the issue into perspective, the Pew Research Center estimated that the number of illegal immigrants in the United States in 2014 was 11.3 million individuals (Figure 9.6).[6]

The sheer volume of illegal immigrants over the last three decades has caused operational consternation and frustration at the highest levels of ICE, CBP, and Border Patrol. At its center, SBI, by use of technology and other tactics that employ virtual means, has sought to minimize illegal immigration by new initiatives and technology.[7] The use of surveillance and remote equipment has been greatly enhanced over the last 10 years, yet neither these technologies nor the physical fence itself have been able to stem the influx of illegal crossings completely—though the volume has slightly abated over the last few years (Figure 9.7).

Internet Resource: Visit CBP's border security mission page for an overview on their operations: http://www.cbp.gov/border-security/air-sea/operations/oam-mission.

While the clamor to clamp down on this unimpeded foe goes on with predictable regularity, the full resolution of this longstanding problem continues to elude the policymakers. On any given day, large portions of the border infrastructure are under upgrade, with existing facilities being renovated and fence and border barriers constantly under construction or repair across the continental United States. But the results, the General Accounting

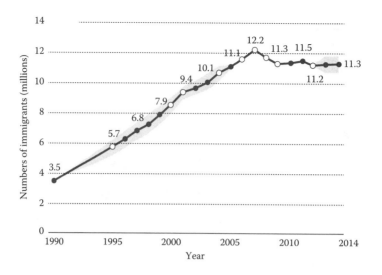

FIGURE 9.6 Unauthorized immigration into the United States has leveled off. Shading surrounding the line indicates low and high points of the estimated 90% confidence interval. White data markers indicate the change from the previous year is statistically significant (for 1995, change is significant from 1990). Data labels are for 1990, odd years from 1995–2011, 2012, 2014. Pew Research Centre estimates are based on residual methodology applied to March supplements to the Current Population Survey (1995–2004, 2013–2014) and American Community Survey (2005–2012). Estimates for 1990 from Warren and Warren (2013). From: Pew Research Center, Unauthorized immigrant population stable for half a decade, http://www.pewresearch.org/fact-tank/2015/07/22/unauthorized-immigrant-population-stable-for-half-a-decade/ft_15-07-23_unauthimmigrants (accessed January 23, 2016).

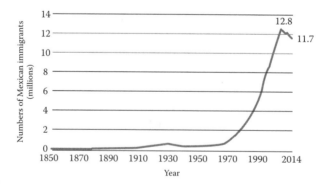

FIGURE 9.7 Decline in U.S. Mexican immigrant population. Adapted from: for 1850–1980: Campbell Gibson and Kay Jung, Historical census statistics on the foreign-born population of the United States: 1850–2000, U.S. Census Bureau, Population Division, Working Paper no. 81, 2006; for 1980 and 1990: Integrated Public Use Microdata Series (IPUMS-USA); for 2005–2012: Pew Research Center estimates based on augmented American Community Surveys; for 1995–2000 and 2013–2014: Pew Research Center estimates based on augmented March supplements to the Current Population Survey and 2000 Decennial Census.

FIGURE 9.8 **Higher Normandy fencing keeps out intruders.**

Office reports, are only partially successful.[8] The Southwest region of the United States has long been in dire need of perimeter and barrier protection. More than 670 miles of new fence have been installed and a wide array of natural barriers employed to halt the influx of illegal immigrants entering the country. While physical fencing is still heavily relied on, the nature of barriers continues to evolve. Aside from fence, CBP uses

- Vehicle bollards similar to those found around federal buildings
- "Post on rail" steel set in concrete with a mesh option
- Steel picket-style fence set in concrete
- Concrete jersey walls with steel mesh
- Normandy vehicle fence consisting of steel beams to thwart vehicular attacks (Figure 9.8)

Internet Resource: To find out more on the Southwest border fence, visit http://www.cbp.gov/newsroom/photo-gallery/gallery/2013/11/southwest-border-fence-construction-progress.

Border protection also employs natural barriers such as rivers, streams, ravines, mountains, cliffs, and other natural artifices to deliver security. Rivers make exceptional barriers, though illegal aliens have long mastered the art of crossing them.

Aside from physical fencing, border protection now relies on the virtual world of fence and barrier. With the rise of technology and the sophistication of surveillance equipment, it is now possible to detect a border crossing and then detach border units within seconds even in the absence of physical fencing. The use of canines has significantly increased as well and with particular success in matters of drug interdiction.[9] The rise in personnel at the border has been astronomical in the last decade (Figures 9.9 and 9.10).

FIGURE 9.9   CBP agent searching the shore near San Diego.

FIGURE 9.10   CBP officer monitoring surveillance cameras.

Since 2004, the amount of Border Patrol officers has risen 85%, with nearly 20,000 officers on the ground. See Figure 9.11 for a graphical representation.

Despite this dramatic investment, any plan of securing our border must consider practices and policies above and beyond traditional law enforcement. It has been the historic mission of the Border Patrol to identify, detect, and detain illegal immigrants. Accepting this as a continuing responsibility of any plan of homeland security is not debatable. However, change and innovation need to take the forefront in the homeland defense, and law enforcement alone will not be able to carry out this basic task. Congress and DHS fully understood that law enforcement, in an exclusive sense, would be incapable of securing our borders. Hence, with the merger of Customs and Border, and with the decision to integrate these functions into DHS, CBP looks at the border in an eclectic way—far beyond a traditional policing function.

Yet border protection must constantly and carefully weigh the threat of the terrorist before issuing any policy. "Terrorists also know that large segments of both the northern

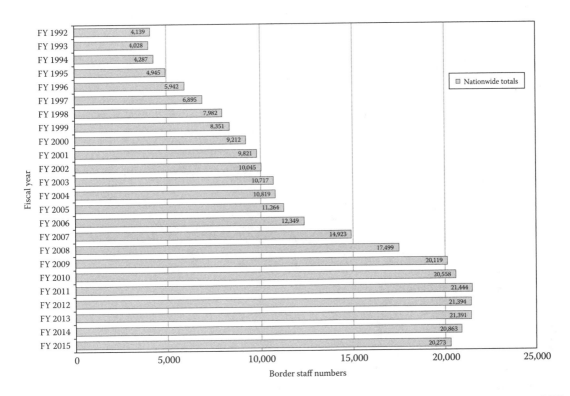

FIGURE 9.11   Border Patrol agent staffing by fiscal year (as of September 19, 2015). From: CBP, Staffing charts 1992–2014, https://www.cbp.gov/newsroom/media-resources/stats (accessed January 23, 2016).

and southern border remain relatively unsecured."[10] Hence, every CBP policy needs to anticipate these dual threats when issuing policy.

9.2.1.2 CBP Air and Marine

While CBP expends most of its energies on illegal immigrants coming into America, its mission now rightfully includes the identification, detection, and apprehension of the terrorist, as well as the interdiction of contraband. With the merger of Customs into DHS, its historic mission has shifted to other protection efforts. Realizing this, CBP developed an air and marine (A&M)-based program. The mission of A&M is as follows:

- *Interdiction* encompasses our efforts to intercept, apprehend, or disrupt threats in the land, sea, and air domains as they move toward or across the United States borders.
- AMO leverages the expertise of our agents in the air and marine domains to conduct *investigations* to defeat criminal networks.
- *Domain Awareness* is the effective understanding of the environment and information associated with the various domains (air, land, and maritime) that could affect

FIGURE 9.12   CBP patrol boat.

safety, security, the economy, or the environment. AMO employs advance systems to contribute to domain awareness.

- AMO performs a range of aviation and maritime *contingency operations and national tasking missions,* including Disaster Relief, Contingency of Operations, Humanitarian Operations, Enforcement Relocation, Search and Rescue, and National Special Security Events (https://www.cbp.gov/border-security/air-sea/missions).

With nearly 267 aircraft and 283 boat and support vessels,[11] CBP is now a major player relative to marine security seeking out illegals and potential terrorists at sea (Figure 9.12).[12] CBP has developed a law enforcement position, the marine interdiction agent, who is on the front line in the fight against terrorism.

Internet Resource: To find job announcements for the marine interdiction agent, visit http://www.usajobs.gov and search "marine interdiction agent."

In the air, CBP is just as impressive. To accomplish this mission, CBP A&M utilizes more than 700 pilots and 267 aircraft, including the use of unmanned aircraft systems (UASs). The use of unmanned drones is a critical tool in the fight against terrorism, the interception of drugs, and other illegal activity. The range and breadth of aircraft indicates the seriousness of the CBP purpose in the air. From small-propeller to Sikorsky helicopters, CBP marshals extraordinary hardware to carry out its mission.

Internet Resource: For a thoughtful look at the promise and recurring doubts about drones, see https://www.oig.dhs.gov/assets/pr/2015/oigpr_010615.pdf.

The CBP A&M program greatly increases the productivity and coverage area involved in its mission (Figure 9.13).

FIGURE 9.13   CBP patrol plane.

The A&M program delivers many services, including

- Aiding and implementing CBP antiterrorism programs
- Utilizing both manned and unmanned aircraft
- Delivering advanced technology by detection systems
- Providing unrivaled capacity to interdict aircraft, boats, vehicles, and personnel
- Fostering collaborative relationships with law enforcement and the military
- Providing secure airspace

9.2.2 CBP and the Facilitation of Trade and Commerce

Along with its partners in the Coast Guard, other military arms, and state and federal law enforcement, CBP assumes essential control and oversight of trade into the American economy—across land, sea, and air. It is not always an easy task, for the policymaker must balance safety and security with the swift and efficient movement of goods. "This becomes a growing challenge in a global economy where consumers, just-in-time processes, and integrated supply chains demand reliability, accuracy and speed."[13]

The goals of CBP in matters of trade policy are essential to the lifeblood of the American economy.

- Goal 1: Facilitate legitimate trade into the United States and ensure compliance
- Goal 2: Enforce U.S. trade laws and collect accurate revenue
- Goal 3: Advance national and economic security
- Goal 4: Intensify modernization of CBP's trade processes

Internet Exercise: Find out about this nation's many ports by using the referenced interactive map at http://www.cbp.gov/trade.

The CBP methodology on trade and commerce weighs impacts at three stages or layers: pre-entry, entry, and postentry. The layered ideal hopes and seeks to mitigate and, more importantly, to have sufficient time to communicate and work cooperatively with aligned defenders of the homeland (Figure 9.14).

9.2.2.1 Cargo

CBP tracks cargo at various points of entry in the United States. The rules and protocols are quite legalistic, and the agency realizes that the layers of bureaucratic requirements do impact the flow of goods and services on the world market. In a global economy, it is critical that goods and services move expeditiously while at the same time safely and securely. CBP, in conjunction with DHS and other agencies, has implemented some innovative programs relative to cargo. A sketch of the more notable programs follows.

9.2.2.1.1 Secure Freight Initiative

The Secure Freight Initiative (SFI) evaluates capabilities for large-scale radiation scanning of cargo before it ever reaches the United States. Presently, the SFI program is operating at less than a dozen foreign ports with a goal to fully scan all inbound cargo. The stress of the SFI is the nuclear and radiological material that might be employed as WMDs. Port security relies on a multilayered approach to security, best illustrated by Figure 9.15.

Relying on radiographic equipment, funded by the Department of Energy (DOE)'s National Nuclear Security Administration (NNSA), the SFI uses both active and passive detection systems to scan cargo in large quantities. Passive radiation detection technology includes radiation portal monitors. As the cargo and its hold pass through the system, the equipment generates various images by spectrograph, bar graph, infrared, or thermograph reading, as well as traditional x-ray imagery. Radiography uses x-rays or gamma rays to penetrate a container (Figure 9.16).

The SFI tends to favor what are known as *megaports*—that is, locations with huge volumes of cargo. This first phase of the SFI partners with Pakistan, Honduras, the United Kingdom, Oman, Singapore, and Korea, and it will provide these governments with a greater window into potentially dangerous shipments moving across their territory. In Port Qasim, Puerto Cortes, and Southampton, the deployed scanning equipment will capture data on all containers bound to the United States, fulfilling the pilot requirements set out by Congress in the SAFE Port Act (Figure 9.17).[14]

DHS, NNSA, and the DOE have launched a joint screening program that targets megaports using the SFI and the Container Security Initiative (CSI) discussed in the upcoming section, which hopes to identify radiological threats (Figure 9.18).

The SFI program also operates in selected foreign ports to scan outgoing cargo before leaving port. At the same time, the SFI integrates new data into U.S. government screening and targeting systems, including the proposed new U.S. CBP security filing, as well as the

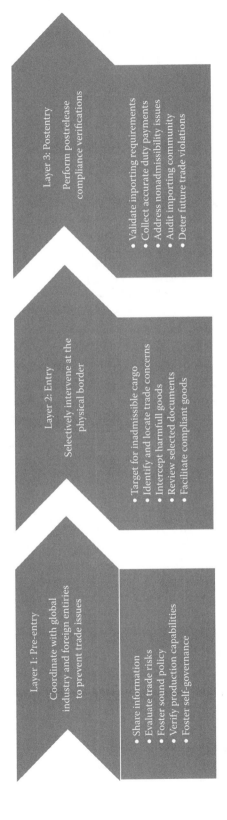

FIGURE 9.14   CBP trade strategy. From: CBP, *CBP Trade Strategy 2009–2013* (Washington, DC: CBP, 2009), 5.

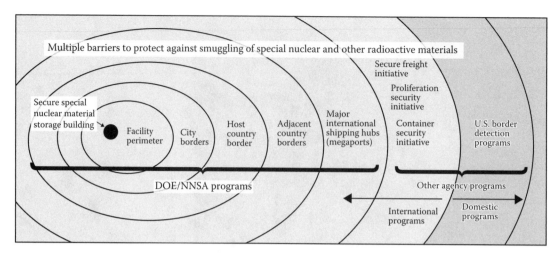

FIGURE 9.15 **DOE/NNSA program combine with DHS and other U.S. and intergovernmental efforts to protect the U.S. homeland against threats from illicit movement of special nuclear and other radioactive materials. From: NNSA,** *Megaports Initiative* **(September 2010), https://nnsa.energy.gov/ sites/default/files/nnsa/inlinefiles/singlepages_9-15-2010.pdf (accessed August 16, 2016).**

FIGURE 9.16 **X-ray image at an SFI location.**

FIGURE 9.17 **SFI scan.**

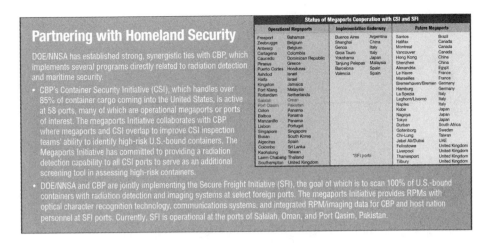

FIGURE 9.18 **Megaport cooperation with CSI and SFI implementation. From: NNSA,** *Megaports Initiative 2010* **(Washington, DC: NNSA, September 2010), http://nnsa.energy.gov/sites/default/files/nnsa/inlinefiles/singlepages_9-15-2010.pdf (accessed January 23, 2016).**

creation of a proposed private sector–operated Global Trade Exchange (GTX). The SFI is testing the feasibility of scanning 100% of U.S.-bound cargo.

9.2.2.1.2 Container Security Initiative

Beginning in January 2002, CBP proposed the CSI, which inspects cargo units rather than the entire freight load and pushes U.S. port security back into the supply chain at its port of origin. The CSI prescreens and evaluates containers before they are shipped. Under the CSI program, high-risk containers receive security inspections by both x-ray and radiation scan. Containers, before being loaded on board vessels destined for the United States, are inspected at CSI ports. Upon arrival, these same containers are exempt from further inspection, and as a result, goods move through our port system with greater efficiency. The CSI is operational in 58 foreign ports, as shown in Figure 9.19.

A total of 35 customs administrations from other jurisdictions have committed to join the CSI program.

The CSI now covers 80% of all maritime containerized cargo destined to the United States.[15] CSI ports now include

In the Americas:

- Montreal, Vancouver, and Halifax, Canada
- Santos, Brazil
- Buenos Aires, Argentina
- Puerto Cortes, Honduras
- Caucedo, Dominican Republic
- Kingston, Jamaica
- Freeport, the Bahamas
- Balboa, Colon, and Manzanillo, Panama
- Cartagena, Colombia

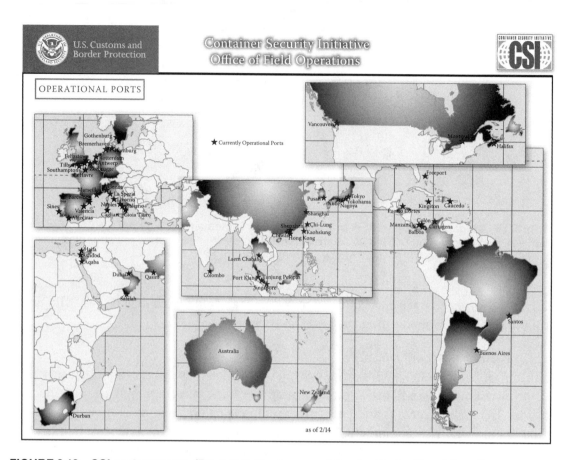

FIGURE 9.19 CSI partner ports. (From U.S. Customs and Border Protection. https://www.cbp.gov/sites/default/files/documents/CSI%20Ports%20Map%201%20page%20062614.pdf.)

In Europe:

- Rotterdam, the Netherlands
- Bremerhaven and Hamburg, Germany
- Antwerp and Zeebrugge, Belgium
- Le Havre and Marseille, France
- Gothenburg, Sweden
- Cagliari, La Spezia, Genoa, Naples, Gioia Tauro, Salerno, and Livorno, Italy
- Felixstowe, Liverpool, Thamesport, Tilbury, and Southampton, United Kingdom
- Algeciras, Barcelona, and Valencia, Spain
- Sines, Portugal

In Asia and the Middle East:

- Singapore
- Yokohama, Tokyo, Nagoya, and Kobe, Japan
- Hong Kong

- Busan (Pusan), South Korea
- Port Klang and Tanjung Pelepas, Malaysia
- Laem Chabang, Thailand
- Dubai, United Arab Emirates (UAE)
- Shenzhen and Shanghai, China
- Kaohsiung and Chi-Lung, Taiwan
- Colombo, Sri Lanka
- Port Salalah, Oman
- Port Qasim, Pakistan
- Ashdod and Haifa, Israel
- Alexandria, Egypt

In Africa:

- Durban, South Africa

9.2.2.1.3 Customs–Trade Partnership against Terrorism

CBP realizes the essential role that private cargo carriers play in the safety and security of goods flowing through ports and harbors. The Customs–Trade Partnership against Terrorism (C-TPAT) is a voluntary government–business initiative that works closely with the prime players in international cargo—namely, importers, carriers, consolidators, licensed customs brokers, and manufacturers. C-TPAT asks business to ensure the integrity of their security practices and communicate and verify the security guidelines of their business partners within the supply chain. The goals of C-TPAT are to

- Ensure that C-TPAT partners improve the security of their supply chains pursuant to C-TPAT security criteria
- Provide incentives and benefits to include expedited processing of C-TPAT shipments to C-TPAT partners
- Internationalize the core principles of C-TPAT through cooperation and coordination with the international community
- Support other CBP security and facilitation initiatives
- Improve the administration of the C-TPAT program

The general theme of C-TPAT is to promote efficiency in the cargo processes and to provide a forum for private–public cooperation in matters of cargo movement. The benefits of C-TPAT are numerous and streamline various inspection processes for cargo and container carriers.

- A reduced number of inspections and reduced border wait times.
- A C-TPAT supply chain specialist to serve as the CBP liaison for validations, security issues, procedural updates, communication, and training.
- Access to the C-TPAT members through the Status Verification Interface.
- Self-policing and self-monitoring of security activities.
- In the Automated Commercial System (ACS), C-TPAT-certified importers receive a reduced selection rate for compliance measurement examinations and exclusion from certain trade-related local and national criteria.

- C-TPAT-certified importers receive targeting benefits by receiving a credit via the CBP targeting system.
- Certified C-TPAT importers are eligible for access to the FAST lanes on the Canadian and Mexican borders.
- Certified C-TPAT importers are eligible for the Office of Strategic Trade (OST)'s Importer Self-Assessment (ISA) program and have been given priority access to participate in the Automated Commercial Environment (ACE) program.
- C-TPAT-certified highway carriers on the Canadian and Mexican borders benefit from their access to the expedited cargo processing at designated FAST lanes. These carriers are eligible to receive more favorable mitigation relief from monetary penalties.
- C-TPAT-certified Mexican manufacturers benefit from their access to the expedited cargo processing on the designated FAST lanes.
- All certified C-TPAT companies are eligible to attend CBP-sponsored C-TPAT supply chain security training seminars.

Internet Resource: For an application regarding C-TPAT membership, see http://www.cbp.gov/border-security/ports-entry/cargo-security/c-tpat-customs-trade-partnership-against-terrorism/apply#.

9.2.2.1.4 Automated Commercial Environment

Modernizing the free flow of goods takes much more than mere personnel and novel policies. The sheer volume of material flowing in and out of the global marketplace demands the highest systems of technology. CBP is upgrading and electronically manifesting the flow of goods through its ACE program. ACE is part of a multiyear CBP modernization effort that is not yet fully operational and is being deployed in phases (Figure 9.20).

ACE seeks to

- Allow trade participants access to and management of their trade information via reports.
- Expedite legitimate trade by providing CBP with tools to efficiently process imports/exports and move goods quickly across the border.
- Improve communication, collaboration, and compliance efforts between CBP and the trade community.

FIGURE 9.20 ACE program logo.

- Facilitate efficient collection, processing, and analysis of commercial import and export data.
- Provide an information-sharing platform for trade data throughout government agencies.

For example, in trucking, relative to cargo and container, the ACE electronic truck manifest capabilities are now available at all 99 U.S. land border ports of entry. Truckers electronically author e-manifests, which provide CBP with cargo information, such as crew, conveyance, equipment as applicable, and shipment details. In ports of entry, there are now mechanisms to file reports and paperwork electronically. As of late 2007, the ACE program was making significant inroads into the cargo and container fabric of America with mandatory e-manifests, the processing of 200,000 trucks per week, faster processing times for e-manifests, the establishment of 14,000 ACE secure data portal accounts, and the collection of nearly 38% of dues and fees computed through electronic periodic reports. In 2015–2016, the ACE program shall impose mandatory usage and participation dates for the program. By the end of the 2016 cargo season, nearly all cargo moving through the American marketplace shall be subject to the ACE electronic requirements. See the timelines charted in Figure 9.21.

The benefits to the ACE program are well documented and include

- Financial savings with the periodic monthly payment capability
- Reduced processing time at the border with features such as e-manifests
- Ability to view shipment status and store data via the ACE secure data portal
- Capabilities to develop over 100 customized reports

See Figure 9.22 for a graphic explanation on the ACE basics.

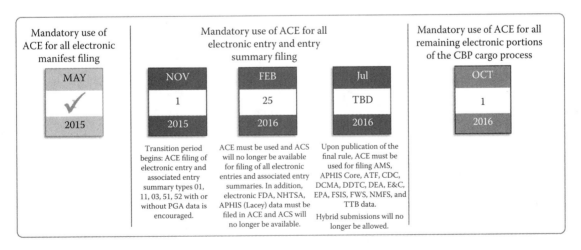

FIGURE 9.21 Mandatory use of ACE for all electronic manifest filing. From: CBP, ACE mandatory use dates, http://www.cbp.gov/trade/automated/ace-mandatory-use-dates (accessed January 23, 2016).

THE ACE BASICS

HOW TO GET STARTED WITH CBP'S AUTOMATED COMMERCIAL ENVIRONMENT

HOW IT WORKS

ACE offers the trade community a simplified process for submitting data and interacting with CBP and Partner Government Agencies (PGAs). The graphic below provides a snapshot of how to file and access data in ACE.

Transmit

1 Trade community files data directly to ACE

View

Use reports to query data in the ACE Portal

TRADE

Use to file:
- ☑ ISF Data
- ☑ Import Ocean, Rail, or Truck Manifests
- ☑ Entries
- ☑ Entry Summaries
- ☑ Export commodity data
- ☑ Supporting documentation

EDI INTERFACES

Use to file:
- ☑ ISF Data
- ☑ Import Truck Manifests
- ☑ Responses to forms 28, 29, 4647

☑ Status Notifications Sent to Trade

EDI INTERFACES

3

ACE sends responses to trade as needed

Log into the ACE Portal to:
- ☑ Run reports
- ☑ Manage account and Periodic Montly Statement info
- ☑ Create blanket declarations
- ☑ Arrive/Export In-Bonds

2 ACE processes and stores data received

ACE

ACE interacts with PGA systems to allow interagency processing

HOW TO GET STARTED

New to electronic filing?

Set up an EDI connection:
1. Send a Letter of Intent (LOI) to letterofintent@cbp.dhs.gov to begin the process.
2. You will be a assigned a client representative who will guide you through EDI connection process.

Business entities that wish to communicate via EDI to CBP may 1) use an approved software provider 2) contact a service center or 3) develop software in-house

Already filing electronically and ready to transition to ACE?

Call your client representative

Need an ACE Portal account?

Fill out an application on CBP.gov to get an ACE Secure Data Portal account

For details on how to get started, visit www.cbp.gov/trade/automated/getting-started

DATES TO KNOW
The deadlines below are important to know as you transition to ACE. Don't wait...Migrate!

May 1, 2015
Mandatory use of ACE for all electronic import and export manifest filings for all modes of transportation

Nov. 1, 2015
Transition period begins: ACE filing of electronic entry and associated entry summary types 01, 11, 03, 51, 52 with or without PGA data encouraged

Feb. 28, 2016
ACE must be used and ACS will no longer be available for filing of all electronic entries and associated entry summaries. In addition, electronic FDA, NHTSA, APHIS (Lacey) data must be filed in ACE and ACS will no longer be available

Jul. 2016
Upon publication of the Final Rule, ACE must be used for filing AMS, APHIS Core, ATF, CDC, DCMA, DDTC, DEA E&C, EPA, FSIS, FWS, NMFS and TTB data. Hybrid submissions will no longer be allowed.

Oct. 1, 2016
Mandatory use of ACE for all remaining electronic portions of the CBP cargo process

 U.S. Customs and Border Protection

www.cbp.gov/ACE
CBP PUBLICATION NUMBER: 1133-0915

FIGURE 9.22   The ACE basics: How to get started with CBP's Automated Commercial Environment. From: CBP, The ACE basics, http://www.cbp.gov/sites/default/files/documents/ACE%20Basics_Update_FINAL.pdf (accessed January 23, 2016).

9.3 U.S. Citizenship and Immigration Services

Immigration has played an important role in the American experience. Immigrants have a natural home in the newly developed country pre- and post-Revolutionary War. To encourage economic development, immigration was widely supported. In its earliest days, the question of immigration was left to the states. Major ports such as New York and Philadelphia became entry points long before federal involvement. In time, by 1875, the Supreme Court would rule that immigration is a federal responsibility. By 1891, Congress had created the Immigration Service, which foretold and dealt with waves of immigrants during the Industrial Revolution. From 1900 to 1920, nearly 24 million immigrants arrived during what is known as the *Great Wave* (Figure 9.23).

At first, immigration numbers were not limited, but eventually a quota system based on past U.S. Census figures was implemented. In 1924, Congress established the U.S. Border Patrol. For the next three to four decades, the waves of immigrants subsided, but by the 1960s Congress would have to deal with two new constituencies: refugees and transient agricultural workers. Congress passed the Refugee Act of 1980, which delineated U.S. policy on refugees.

Internet Resource: To see where and when the waves took place, see http://flowingdata.com/wp-content/uploads/2008/12/21.pdf.

In 1986, Congress passed the Immigration Reform and Control Act (IRCA). This legislation had two major eligibility standards: amnesty and enforcement. IRCA provided amnesty to aliens who had completed one of two stipulations: they had resided continually in the United States since January 1982, or they had completed 90 days of agricultural work between May 1985 and May 1986. In 1996, Congress passed the Illegal Immigrant Reform and Immigrant Responsibility Act (IIRIRA). During this same period, various amnesties for illegal immigrants were promulgated. In 1994, the Section 245(i) amnesty was enacted, which pardoned 578,000 illegal aliens, who were each fined $1000. This amnesty was later renewed in 1997 and again in 2000. The Nicaraguan Adjustment and Central American

FIGURE 9.23 Ellis Island, New York.

Relief Act (NACARA) was passed in 1997 and gave legal status to approximately 1 million illegal aliens, mostly from Central America, who had lived in the United States since 1995. In 1998, the Haitian Refugee Immigration and Fairness Act (HRIFA) passed after it was argued that excluding Haitians from NACARA was discriminatory. The most recent amnesty, passed in 2000, was the Legal Immigration Family Equity (LIFE) Act.

The terrorist attacks on September 11, 2001, provoked a profound reexamination of immigration practices since the terrorists themselves were here as illegal parties. The attack exposed longstanding holes in our immigration system that included failures at visa processing, internal enforcement, and information sharing. Various commissions and other groups have issued reports and recommendations on how improvements might be forthcoming.

In December 2005, the House passed the Border Protection, Antiterrorism, and Illegal Immigration Control Act, which focused on enforcement and on both the border and the interior. Attempts to pass recent legislation granting amnesty to illegals have been widely condemned by public opinion. Various efforts from 2006 to the present regarding immigration reform have faltered.[16]

Internet Exercise: Find out about the history of immigration in the PowerPoint program developed by the Library of Congress at http://memory.loc.gov/learn/features/immig/introduction.html.

While issues of immigration frequently touch agencies such as Border Patrol and the Coast Guard, from the prism of law enforcement, there are other issues within the province of USCIS. Once referred to as the Immigration and Naturalization Service (INS), the department was merged into DHS in 2002. USCIS is the primary entity responsible for the administration of immigration status and claims, the adjudication of findings and appeals, and the promulgation of policies and practices concerning the agency. The functions of the agency include, but are not limited to

- Adjudication of immigrant visa petitions
- Adjudication of naturalization petitions
- Adjudication of asylum and refugee applications
- Adjudications performed at the service centers
- All other adjudications performed by the INS (Figure 9.24)

The agency is involved in a wide assortment of aligned activities relating to terrorism and potential harm to the United States and its citizens. By its very nature, USCIS has the capacity to be a barrier of entry or a point of forced departure for those intent on doing harm to the United States.

9.3.1 Project Shield America Initiative

Project Shield America seeks to prevent foreign adversaries, terrorists, and criminal networks from obtaining and trafficking in WMDs (Figure 9.25).

The program seeks to thwart terrorist groups from obtaining sensitive information about American technologies, commodities, munitions, and firearms. Furthermore, Project

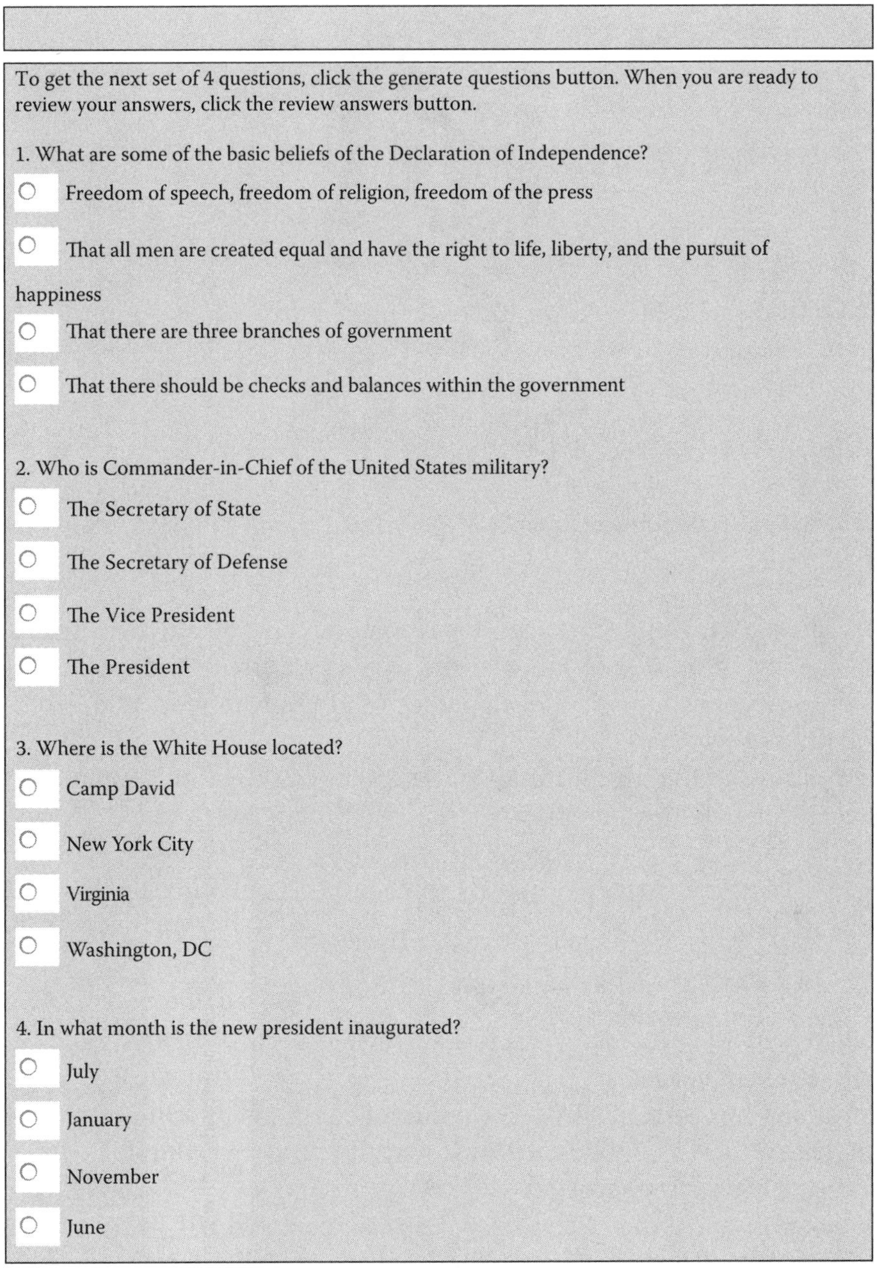

To get the next set of 4 questions, click the generate questions button. When you are ready to review your answers, click the review answers button.

1. What are some of the basic beliefs of the Declaration of Independence?

○   Freedom of speech, freedom of religion, freedom of the press

○   That all men are created equal and have the right to life, liberty, and the pursuit of happiness

○   That there are three branches of government

○   That there should be checks and balances within the government

2. Who is Commander-in-Chief of the United States military?

○   The Secretary of State

○   The Secretary of Defense

○   The Vice President

○   The President

3. Where is the White House located?

○   Camp David

○   New York City

○   Virginia

○   Washington, DC

4. In what month is the new president inaugurated?

○   July

○   January

○   November

○   June

FIGURE 9.24   Naturalization self-test.

Shield America traces financial transactions that violate U.S. sanctions or embargos. It also checks the propriety of exports to determine whether the goods shipped are legal and consistent with the laws of the United States. Most importantly, the program focuses on high-level technology that can be used against the United States in negative ways. The types of exported technology that would be subject to Project Shield America's scrutiny would encompass

FIGURE 9.25 Project Shield America logo.

- Modern manufacturing technology for the production of microelectronics, computers, digital electronic components, and signal processing systems
- Technology necessary for the development of aircraft, missile, and other tactical weapon delivery systems
- All types of advanced signal and weapons detection, tracking, and monitoring systems
- Technology and equipment used in the construction of nuclear weapons and materials
- Biological, chemical warfare agents and precursors, and associated manufacturing equipment.

Project Shield America tackles its job in three fundamental ways.

- Inspection and interdiction: Working at ports especially, both USCIS and CBP monitor potential harms.
- Investigations and outreach: USCIS conducts wide-ranging criminal investigations dealing with illegal munitions. In addition, the program educates exporters and importers on legal compliance.
- International cooperation: The agency helps support investigations by foreign law enforcement into illegal weapons and technology trafficking.

In the area of prohibited goods, illegal trafficking in goods, or other prohibited items, ICE has issues a series of *red flags* that tip the practitioner into a more suspicious mind-set of potential or actual criminal purposes. See the following list of common red flags:

Red Flags: Indications of Potential Illegal Exports
    ICE solicits the assistance of private industry to share information related to suspicious acquisitions of high technology and munitions or services relating to these items. The following are possible indicators of illegal exports or diversions.

- The customer is willing to pay cash for a high-value order rather than use a standard method of payment, which usually involves a letter of credit.
- The customer is willing to pay well in excess of market value for the commodities.
- The purchaser is reluctant to provide information on the end-use or end-user of the product.
- The end-use information provided is incompatible with the customary purpose for which the product is designed.
- The final consignee is a trading company, freight forwarder, export company or other entity with no apparent connection to the purchaser.
- The customer appears unfamiliar with the product, its application, support equipment or performance.
- The packaging requirements are inconsistent with the shipping mode or destination.
- The customer orders products or options that do not correspond with their line of business.
- The customer has little or no business background.
- Firms or individuals from foreign countries other than the country of the stated end-user place the order.
- The order is being shipped via circuitous or economically illogical routing.
- The customer declines the normal service, training, or installation contracts.
- The product is inappropriately or unprofessionally packaged (e.g., odd-sized/retaped boxes, hand lettering in lieu of printing, altered labels or labels that cover old ones).
- The size or weight of the package does not fit the product described.
- "Fragile" or other special markings on the package are inconsistent with the commodity described. (https://www.ice.gov/project-shield-america).

Internet Exercise: Read about legal cases and prosecutions of violators caught because of Project Shield America at http://www.ice.gov/news/library/factsheets/counter-proliferations.htm.

9.3.2 Fugitive Operations Program

On February 25, 2002, the National Fugitive Operations Program (NFOP) was officially established under the banner department of ICE. The primary mission of NFOP is to identify, locate, apprehend, process, and remove fugitive aliens from the United States, with the highest priority placed on those fugitives who have been convicted of crimes. Furthermore, NFOP's goal is to eliminate the backlog of fugitives and ensure that the number of aliens deported equals the number of final orders of removal issued by the immigration courts in any given year.

The NFOP fugitive operations teams strategically deployed around the country work solely on those cases identified as fugitives, and attempt to locate and apprehend those persons who will ultimately be removed from the United States. The NFOP publishes a "most wanted" list of criminals, terrorists, and other unsavory characters. A current collection includes the individuals shown in Figure 9.26.

ICE Most Wanted

Homeland Security Investigations

Antunez-Sotelo, Mario

Wanted For: Human Trafficking

Last Known Location: Tijuana, Mexico, or San Diego, California

Briand, Martin

Wanted For: Conspiracy to export cocaine

Last Known Location: Point Robert, Washington

Gula, Martin

Wanted For: Smuggling of United States Defense Articles and money laundering

Last Known Location: Slovakia

Maciel-Jaramillo, Jose Francisco

Wanted For: Alien smuggling resulting in death or serious bodily injury

Last Known Location: Encino/Falfurrias, Texas

CAPTURED

Montes Leon, Ignacio

Wanted For: Conspiracy to Possess With Intent to Distribute Cocaine

Last Known Location: Cueramaro, Guanajuato, Mexico

Pena-Pena, Luis Albeiro

Wanted For: Cocaine trafficking, money laundering and kidnapping of an ICE agent

Last Known Location: Medellin, Colombia

Sychantha, Khaophone

Wanted For: Conspiracy to Distribute a Controlled Substance and Possession with Intent to Distribute a Controlled Substance

Last Known Location: Lakeshore, Canada

Trask, Kevin

Wanted For: Distribution and Possession of Child Pornography

Last Known Location: San Diego, California

Zazueta-Perez, Clarisa

Wanted For: Conspiracy to defraud financial institutions

Last Known Location: El Paso, Texas

Zolotarev, Roman Olegovich

Wanted For: Racketeering

Last Known Location: Izhevsk, Russia

FIGURE 9.26 ICE most wanted homeland security fugitives. (From U.S. Immigration and Customs Enforcement. ICE most wanted. https://www.ice.gov/most-wanted.)

Internet Resource: For a current look at the ICE's list of foreign criminal aliens, see https://www.ice.gov/most-wanted#tab1.

The NFOP training course is conducted at the ICE Academy located at the Federal Law Enforcement Training Center (FLETC). The training stresses utilization of the Internet, databases, and other sources of information to locate where a fugitive lives, visits, and works. NFOP teams are frequent participants in joint task forces at the state and local levels.

9.3.3 Cornerstone Initiative

Terrorist and other criminal organizations need cash and finance to support illegal operations. The Cornerstone Initiative detects and closes those means to exploit the financial sector. Some of the more common targets of enforcement are

- Bulk cash smuggling
- Alternative financing mechanisms used to launder illicit proceeds
- Money service businesses, financial institutions, and international trade and transportation sectors
- Common highly profitable cross-border crimes such as commercial fraud, intellectual property rights (IPR) violations, immigration violations, identity and benefits fraud, contraband and alien smuggling, and human trafficking
- Trade-based money laundering (TBML) using the international trade system to disguise illicit proceed by altering customs and banking paperwork

The Cornerstone team looks for patterns and select indicators of behavior in the transfer of money and funds.[17] There are a host of red flags that indicate the money trail is out of mainstream financial practice. Within the Cornerstone Initiative rests the National Bulk Cash Smuggling Center, which works with diverse law enforcement agencies nationally and internationally in seeking to end the smuggle of large cash sums. Such sums are usually associated with drugs and other nefarious acts.

Internet Exercise: To learn about the complexities of this form of law enforcement visit the center's FAQ at http://www.ice.gov/bulk-cash-smuggling-center/faq/.

9.3.4 Cyber Crimes Center

Created in 1997, the Cyber Crimes Center, known as C3, brings a full range of ICE computer and forensic assets together in a single location to combat such Internet-related crimes as possession, manufacture, and distribution of child pornography; money laundering and illegal cyber banking; arms trafficking and illegal export of strategic/controlled commodities; drug trafficking; trafficking in stolen art and antiquities; and intellectual property rights violations. Cybercrimes units are not exclusively the province of CBP but exist side by side in many federal and state agencies, including the FBI and large metropolitan police departments.[18]

There are serious critics of the type of oversight and intervention evident in forensic computing and software. Civil libertarians constantly wail about privacy considerations, and policymakers need always keep their practices in check in light of these considerations.[19]

Much of what the Cyber Crimes Center undertakes relates to child pornography. The scourge of predators and their tie to cyber pornography is amply documented. ICE'S child exploitation unit, iGuardians, tackles this difficult and emotionally wrenching job (Figure 9.27).

The Virtual Global Taskforce (VGT) is made up of law enforcement agencies from around the world working together to fight child abuse online. VGT aims to build an effective,

FIGURE 9.27 Project iGuardian helps kids, teens, and parents to be smart about online safety and stay safe from online sexual predators. (From U.S. Immmigration and Customs Enforcement. www. ice.gov/guardian.)

international partnership of law enforcement agencies that helps to protect children from online child abuse. VGT strives to make the Internet a safer place, to identify, locate, and help children at risk, and to hold perpetrators accountable.

VGT comprises the Australian High Tech Crime Centre, the Child Exploitation and Online Protection Centre in the United Kingdom, the Royal Canadian Mounted Police, the U.S. DHS, the Italian Postal and Communication Police Service, and Interpol. ICE'S Operation Predator program, in collaboration with national and international partners, targets the worst of the worst in the dark world of child victimization. In addition, ICE maintains a National Child Victim Identification System.

Internet Exercise: ICE relies heavily on information relayed by the general public. The agency has created a *tipline* system. See its contents at http://www.ice.gov/exec/forms/hsi-tips/tips.asp.

FIGURE 9.28 **VGT is a group of law enforcement agencies from around the world working together to fight child pornography online. (From Virtual Global Taskforce. http://virtualglobaltaskforce. com/.)**

Since 9/11, the USCIS, through its enforcement unit, the ICE division, has used these pertinent skills in the hunt for the terrorist as well. The mission of the Cyber Crimes Center is to investigate domestic and international criminal activities occurring on or facilitated by the Internet. The Cyber Crimes Center is blessed with a state-of-the-art center that offers cybercrime training to federal, state, local, and international law enforcement agencies.

Terrorists use the Internet and find the means and methods to conduct business, transfer funds, share information, and issue instructions. ICE distinguishes itself in the area of illegal arms and money laundering. ICE's Arms and Strategic Technology division looks to prevent the proliferation of weapons, as well as the movement of terrorists and other criminals from entering the United States.

The Cyber Crimes Center has an additional competence regarding documents and related fraud. If 9/11 made plain any conclusion, it was the ease with which terrorists could fabricate documents to gain access. The threat posed by document fraud is evidenced by the ease with which seven of the 9/11 hijackers obtained identity documents in the State of Virginia.

Passports are a particular problem for USCIS since the range and design will depend on the country of issue. Figure 9.29 shows an example of a counterfeit passport card used by a terrorist who was caught before his attempted act of terror at the Los Angeles airport in 1999. He is presently serving a 22-year term in a federal penitentiary.

Documents give telltale signs of fraud, and Customs and Immigration personnel have been trained to detect it. The more common fraud indicators are

- Physically altered passports
- Passports with serial numbers that are watch listed as lost or stolen
- Handwritten documents that are easily forged or altered
- Multiple passports used by the same person with variations in the spelling/structure of the name and date of birth
- Ambiguous or contradictory information submitted to consular or border control officials

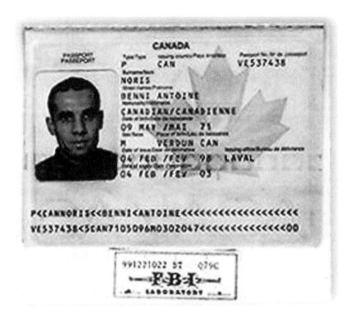

FIGURE 9.29   Counterfeit passport.

- Absence of supporting documents to corroborate passport information
- Passports with glued-in photographs
- Large gaps in travel history as reflected in stamps and visas

Internet Resource: The U.S. Department of State has authored a quick course in passport fraud at http://www.state.gov/m/ds/investigat/c10714.htm.

9.3.5 US-VISIT Program/Office of Biometric Identity Management

DHS's US-VISIT program, now renamed the Office of Biometric Identity Management (OBIM), provides visa-issuing posts and ports of entry with biometric technology that enables the U.S. government to establish and verify the identities of those who visit the United States (Figure 9.30).

Internet Exercise: Find out about the many services OBIM provides by visiting http://www.dhs.gov/obim-biometric-identification-services.

This process begins overseas at a U.S. visa-issuing post, where a traveler's biometrics—digital fingerprints and a photograph—are collected and checked. Upon arrival in the United States, these same biometrics verify the identity of that person at the port of entry.

The guiding principles of OBIM are to

- Enhance the security of our citizens and visitors.
- Facilitate legitimate travel and trade.
- Ensure the integrity of the immigration system.
- Protect the privacy of our visitors.

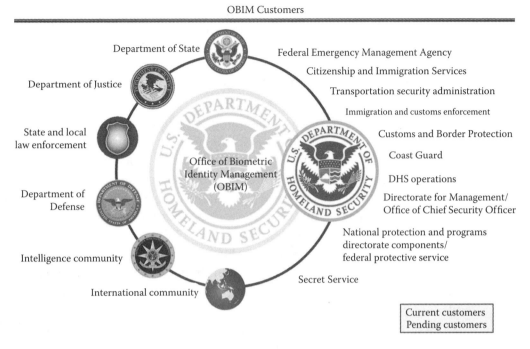

FIGURE 9.30   Many federal, state and local agencies use OBIM services. (From Homeland Security. Office of Biometric Identity Management. https://www.dhs.gov/obim.)

Even though OBIM is an additional layer of security, most travelers will not notice the difference. At an airport or seaport, travel documents such as a passport and a visa will be reviewed and a U.S. CBP officer will ask specific questions regarding the visitor's stay in the United States.

Visitors traveling on visas will have two fingerprints scanned by an inkless device and a digital photograph taken. Data and information are then used to assist the border inspector in determining whether to admit the traveler. All data obtained from the visitor are securely stored as part of the visitor's travel record. This information is made available only to authorized officials and selected law enforcement agencies on a need-to-know basis in their efforts to help protect the country against those who intend to harm American citizens or visitors to the United States.

9.4 Conclusion

Protection of the border rightfully consumes the energy of the homeland community. The idea of border extends far beyond any notions of continental geography, but includes the diverse ways in which visitors to the United States can find entry. Soon after 9/11, DHS recognized the need to subsume the functions of Border with those of Customs—erecting a new department, CBP. The work of CBP is extensive and includes encounters with millions of passengers and pedestrians, thousands of truck, rail, and sea containers and air travelers, shipments, and the computation of tariffs, duties, and other fees. More than a million illegal aliens have been apprehended since 2004. CBP has also erected targeted operations such as SBI, which increases manpower and resources across the entire national border. SBI upgrades all facets of border hardware and infrastructure, employs new technology to discover breaches in the border, and erects and maintains natural and artificial barrier systems to stem illegal entry. The rise in Border Patrol agents—some 50,000 additional needed in the next decade—proves the seriousness of the task.

CBP continually adds sophisticated equipment and technology to carry out its mission. The use of drones and other unmanned air devices is now part and parcel of the delivery system. CBP now has an A&M division that zeroes in on breach locations or unsafe entry points. Seven hundred pilots now man 267 differing types of aircraft in this challenge.

CBP assumes an integral role in the world of trade and commerce. With its cargo responsibilities, CBP scans and screens incoming cargo throughout the nation and even in foreign ports before its departure to the United States. In its SFI, radiation scanners inspect large-scale shipping holds before ever leaving worldwide ports. Usually at megaports such as England's Southampton or Singapore, the SFI not only scans vessels but registers and tracks them over the life of their journey. In the area of cargo containers, the CSI inspects incoming goods by both radiation and x-ray. The CSI is operational in foreign ports as well, covering 80% of the world's cargo destined to the United States. CBP partners with private companies in shipping and cargo through its C-TPAT program. C-TPAT promotes efficiency in cargo processes and serves as a liaison for business and industry security practices and the requirements of CBP. Electronic modernization of cargo manifests and other practices are made possible by the protocols of the ACE program.

In the area of immigration and citizenship, the DHS department of USCIS, once referred to as the INS, administers the status of immigrants, their claims, and adjudication processes, as well as promulgates protocols on naturalization, asylum, and refugee petitions and the granting or denial of visas. The Project Shield America initiative is a USCIS function that tracks illegal financial transactions, illegal munitions, and trafficking in contraband and WMDs. USCIS runs NFOP, which targets a most wanted list of illegal aliens and criminals. The USCIS administers a host of other programs relating to cybercrime and fraud, financial support for terrorists transfers, and passport forgery.

Keywords

Air and Marine	**Cornerstone Initiative**
Amnesty	**Customs**
Automated Commercial Environment	**Customs and Border Protection**
Automated Commercial System	**Customs-Trade Partnership against**
Biometrics	**Terrorism**
Border Patrol	**Cyber Crimes Center**
Citizenship and Immigration Services	**Fugitive operations team**
Common operating procedure	**Global Trade Exchange**
Container Security Initiative	**The Great Wave**
Contraband	**Illegal immigration**

Immigrant
Immigration and Naturalization Service
Immigration reform
Marine interdict officer
Megaport
National Fugitive Operations Program
National Targeting Center
Natural barriers
Naturalization
Partner ports
Ports of entry

Project Shield America
Radiation portal monitor
Refugees
Secure Border Initiative
Secure data portal account
Secure Freight Initiative
SFI scan
Transient workers
US-VISIT
Visa

Discussion Questions

1. Given the resource and expenditure investment in border security, is it fair to expect safe and secure borders? Is there a correlation between the dollars invested and success at the border?
2. Evaluate how the merger of Border, Customs, and Immigration into DHS has affected the operational outlook of these former agencies. Has it been a healthy merger?
3. Discuss how armed law enforcement aids plane and travel security. Highlight specific programs.
4. Critics of the border fencing hold that it cannot work. Why not?
5. Lay out three perennial problems in the protection of U.S. borders.
6. In what ways does CBP aid or interfere with commerce?

Practical Exercises

1. Review your geography. Where does the influx of illegal immigrants occur in your region? If not a border state, explain the social, cultural, and economic implications of an unguarded border. What is the public sentiment concerning illegal aliens?
2. Visit usajobs.gov. Create a job database of present opportunities for Border, Customs, and Immigration officers. Provide examples of each career opportunity.
3. Prepare a form file for the ACE program.
4. Customs deals with trade in diverse ways. Give four examples of how technology aids or even eliminates manpower in the moves of trade.
5. Take the naturalization test for citizenship administered by Immigration and Citizenship. Evaluate the level of ease or difficulty.

Notes

1. L. C. Frederking, A comparative study of framing immigration policy after 11 September 2001, *Policy Studies* 283(33), 2012; M. Haberfield, C. A. Lieberman, Foreign threats to national security and an alternative model to local enforcement of US immigration laws, *Police Practice & Research* 155(13), 2012.

2. CBP, Snapshot: A summary of CBP fact and figures, https://www.cbp.gov/sites/default/files/documents/cbpsnapshot-121415.pdf (accessed January 23, 2016).

3. And this is not a uniquely American experience either. See R. Nicholson, Swedish open immigration policies: Correlation with terrorism, *The Homeland Security Review*, 4, 2010: 193.

4. Walter Ewing, Looking for a quick fix: The rise and fall of the Secure Border Initiative's high-tech solution to unauthorized immigration, *Immigration Policy Center: Just the Facts*, April 15, 2010, http://www.immigrationpolicy.org/sites/default/files/docs/SBInet_-_Looking_for_a_Quick_Fix_041510.pdf (accessed January 23, 2016).

5. Walter Ewing, Looking for a quick fix, 1.

6. A. Gonzalez-Barrera, More Mexicans leaving than coming to the U.S., *Pew Research Center: Hispanic Trends*, November 19, 2015, http://www.pewhispanic.org/2015/11/19/more-mexicans-leaving-than-coming-to-the-u-s/ (accessed January 23, 2016).

7. C. Bolkcom, *Homeland Security: Unmanned Aerial Vehicles and Border Surveillance* (Washington, DC: Library of Congress, 2005), http://www.fas.org/sgp/crs/homesec/RS21698.pdf; *Border Security: Enhanced DHS Oversight and Assessment of Interagency Coordination Is Needed for the Northern Border* (2010); *Border Security: Additional Actions Needed to Better Ensure a Coordinated Federal Response to Illegal Activity on Federal Lands* (2010); *Moving Illegal Proceeds: Challenges Exist in the Federal Government's Effort to Stem Cross-Border Currency Smuggling* (2010); *Border Security: Preliminary Observations on the Status of Key Southwest Border Technology Programs* (2011); *Moving Illegal Proceeds: Opportunities Exist for Strengthening the Federal Government's Efforts to Stem Cross-Border Currency Smuggling* (2011); *Border Security: Preliminary Observations on Border Control Measures for the Southwest Border* (2011).

8. U.S. Government Accountability Office, *Border Security: DHS Progress and Challenges in Securing the U.S. Southwest and Northern Borders* (Washington, DC: U.S. Government Printing Office, 2011).

9. H. Hogan, CBP's best- and newest-friends, *Homeland Security Today*, 17, July 2011.

10. T. Steinmetz, Mitigating the exploitation of U.S. borders by jihadists and criminal organizations, *Journal of Strategic Security*, 4, 2011: 35.

11. CBP, Frequently asked questions: About air and marine, available at http://www.cbp.gov/border-security/air-sea/faq/about (accessed January 23, 2016).

12. C. Collins, Border enforcement: Migrant interdiction at sea, *Year in Homeland Security*, 2010/2011: 76.

13. CBP, *CBP Trade Strategy 2009–2013* (Washington, DC: CBP, 2009), 24.

14. Security and Accountability for Every Port Act of 2006, P.L. 109–347, *U.S. Statutes at Large*, 120, 2006: 1884.

15. CBP, CSI: Container Security Initiative, http://www.cbp.gov/border-security/ports-entry/cargo-security/csi/csi-brief (accessed January 23, 2016).

16. The White House, Streamlining legal immigration, https://www.whitehouse.gov/issues/immigration/streamlining-immigration (accessed January 23, 2016); The White House, Continuing to strengthen border security, https://www.whitehouse.gov/issues/immigration/border-security (accessed January 23, 2016); The White House, Earned citizenship, https://www.whitehouse.gov/issues/immigration/earned-citizenship (accessed January 23, 2016).

17. Homeland Security Investigations: Trade Transparency Unit, *The Cornerstone Report*, Winter 2011.

18. A. P. Gerglas, The New York FBI and the cyberthreat, *Homeland Security Today*, July 2011: 6; See also J. R. Wilson, IT & cyber security, *Year in Homeland Security*, 2010/2011: 83.

19. M. McCarter, ID Management, *Homeland Security Today*, August 2011: 48.

Chapter 10

Transportation Security

Objectives

1. To describe the mission and scope of operation of the Transportation Security Administration (TSA)
2. To explain the programs and policies created by TSA to ensure secure air transportation in the United States
3. To outline the technological advances in transportation security in use at airport screening points
4. To describe the mission and scope of operation of the U.S. Coast Guard
5. To explain the programs and policies created by the U.S. Coast Guard to ensure secure maritime transportation in the United States
6. To outline the technological advances in security in use at maritime and cargo screening points
7. To explain the programs and policies in place to ensure secure passenger rail transportation in the United States
8. To explain the programs and policies in place to ensure secure cargo rail transportation in the United States

10.1 Introduction

In the broadest context, transportation security encompasses air, rail, bus, shipping and ports, and mass transit safety. Most of these centers of movement can properly be characterized as critical infrastructure. Many agencies of government deal with transportation safety and security questions. The Department of Homeland Security (DHS) and Federal Aviation Administration (FAA) first come to mind since each regulates and promulgates administrative practices regarding these industries. The Department of Commerce involves itself in a host of travel questions, as does the Federal Highway Administration. Because of the multiagency involvement in the world of travel and transportation, it would be impossible to cover each and every aspect of the homeland question relative to the diversity of government agencies and missions. What we will try to do is highlight the most relevant for homeland security purposes, starting with TSA.

10.2 Transportation Security Administration

Of any portion of the homeland security enterprise, the one that touches the general public the most is the work of TSA. Most American citizens come face-to-face with TSA—the visible arm of airport safety in our terminals. Passenger and baggage screening are the prime tasks of TSA. Despite these responsibilities, TSA engages in a broad range of other activities. TSA is a component of DHS and not only is responsible for the security of the country's airline transportation systems, but also, with state, local, and regional partners, oversees security for the highways, railroads, buses, mass transit systems, ports, and the 450 U.S. airports. TSA employs approximately 60,000 people. TSA is a large bureaucracy that has yet to fully find its way, nor has it sucessfully captured significant public support in how it carries out its mission. In many ways, TSA antagonizes far too many constituencies, and in other ways it really has a thankless and difficult job. Controversial practices include enhanced physical pat-down searches of young children and the elderly as well as scanners that provide near-naked pictures of passengers.[1] Scandals include naked body imagery shared on the Internet, undetected contraband making it through screenings at various airports, and TSA agents indicted for corruption and drug trafficking. TSA has tried to counter the bad press with an aggressive use of social media.[2] It is well aware of how public aggravation at the screening process, increasing public distrust, and the agency's high attrition rate undercut its efforts to become a professional body.[3]

In 2010, TSA began a program with Global Corporate College—provided through regional community colleges around the country—to further educate and train TSA employees. In addition, it has recently engaged in a series of public relations campaigns to bolster its image. See Figure 10.1 for an example from a public relations campaign.[4]

The agency designates a public affairs officer line in its organizational structure (Figure 10.2).

TSA recently adopted a series of core values that stress the professionalism and integrity it aspires to. The agency indicates the need for a positive "culture" to carry out its stated mission. The core values include

FIGURE 10.1   TSA public relations campaign.

- Integrity:
  - We are a people of integrity who respect and care for others and protect the information we handle.
  - We are a people who conduct ourselves in an honest, trustworthy, and ethical manner at all times.
  - We are a people who gain strength from the diversity in our cultures.
- Innovation:
  - We are a people who embrace and stand ready for change.
  - We are a people who are courageous and willing to take on new challenges.
  - We are a people with an enterprising spirit, striving for innovations who accept the risk taking that comes with it.
- Team Spirit:
  - We are a people who are open, respectful, and dedicated to making others better.
  - We are a people who have a passion for challenge, success, and being on a winning team.
  - We are a people who will build teams around our strengths. (https://www.tsa.gov/about/tsa-mission)

The bulk of what TSA does relates to airline safety (see Figure 10.3). Indeed, if the terrorist attacks of 9/11 had occurred on a boat, the likely location for our front line of defense would have been in the harbor. Location has much to do with policy and practice. Then again, the nature of the 9/11 attacks also prompted this emphasis. Perhaps not ideal, airport safety screening surely adds a layer of safety to the culture (Figure 10.4).[5]

TSA's primary mission is transportation—all forms and all locales. It is a gargantuan responsibility. In 2014, TSA dealt with a staggering array of travelers, personnel, and issues. Consider the scope of the jurisdiction.

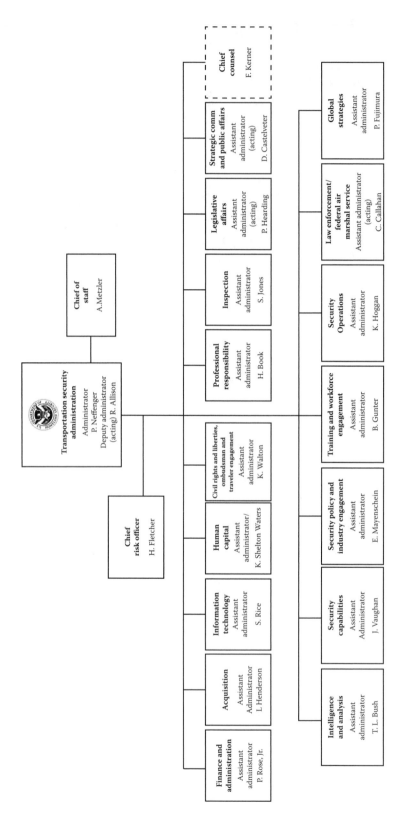

FIGURE 10.2 TSA organization chart (https://www.tsa.gov/about/tsa-leadership).

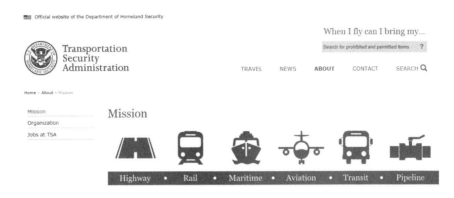

FIGURE 10.3   Redesigned TSA Web location.

FIGURE 10.4   TSA officer at a security checkpoint.

- 3.9 million miles of public roads.
- 100,000 miles of rail.
- 600,000 bridges.
- 300 tunnels and numerous seaports.
- 2 million miles of pipeline.
- 500,000 train stations.

- 500 public use airports.
- 1.2 million trucking companies operating 15.5 million trucks, including 42,000 hazmat trucks.
- 10 million licensed commercial vehicle drivers, including 2.7 million hazmat drivers.
- 2.2 million miles of hazardous liquid and natural gas pipeline.
- 120,000 miles of major railroads.
- 25,000 miles of commercial waterways.
- 361 ports.
- 9.0 million containers through 51,000 port calls.
- 11.2 million containers via Canada and Mexico.
- 19,576 general aviation airports, heliports, and landing strips.
- 459 federalized commercial airports.
- 211,450 general aviation aircraft.
- Screened 653,487,270 aviation passengers (nearly 1.8 million/day), more than 443 million checked bags and nearly 1.7 billion carry-on bags.
- Enrolled over 800,000 travelers in TSA Pre✓® in 2014.
- 2,212 firearms were discovered in carry-on bags at checkpoints across the country, averaging over six firearms per day. Of those detected, 83% were loaded.
- Processed more than 374 million travelers at air, land, and sea ports of entry in 2014.
- Installed automated passport control kiosks in 22 locations to streamline the traveler inspection process.
- An additional 1.25 million people enrolled in the agency's Trusted Traveler programs (Global Entry, SENTRI, NEXUS, and FAST) in 2014 to bring total enrollment to more than 3.3 million members.
- In January 2014, Customs and Border Protection (CBP) expanded preclearance operations to a 15th location, Abu Dhabi International Airport.
- More than 16 million travelers went through one of CBP's preclearance locations in Canada, Ireland, the Caribbean, and the United Arab Emirates in 2014, accounting for 15% of total international air travel that year.
- Collected more than $34 billion in duties in 2014, processed more than $1.6 trillion worth of U.S. exported goods, and conducted more than 23,000 seizures of goods that violated intellectual property rights.

From airports to bus stations, rail terminals to pipelines, TSA is entrusted with extraordinary responsibilities. In each of these sectors TSA must be mindful of the

- Completion of industry threat, vulnerability, and consequence assessment
- Development of baseline security standards
- Assessment of operator security status versus existing standards
- Development of plan to close gaps in security standards
- Enhancement of systems of security

FIGURE 10.5   A VIPR team at Union Station in Washington, DC.

TSA has shown little hesitation in expanding its reach into all forms of transportation.[6] For example, recent implementation of the Visible Intermodal Prevention and Response (VIPR) program—including teams of local and federal law enforcement officers, along with TSA specialists combing the subways, the ferries, and all forms of public transportation—signifies TSA's reach over the entire national transportation system (Figure 10.5).

Whatever system is reviewed, TSA's mission includes the development of various layers of security protection at the facilities it is entrusted with. By layers, we mean barriers or checkpoints for protection. The more checkpoints that exist, the greater the likelihood is that a threat is detected. In the aviation sector, the layers of security are both sophisticated and largely effective. TSA works to identify questionable passengers long before the security checkpoint, including intelligence analysis, watch lists and passenger manifests, random canine searches, and insertion of federal air marshals, flight deck officers, and crew. TSA charts these layers in Figure 10.6.

TSA also recognizes that it must rely on the public for constant vigilance and assistance in carrying out its mission. Its "If You See Something, Say Something" campaign encourages an active public partnership (Figure 10.7).

Internet Exercise: Find out about all the parameters of the "See Something, Say Something" program at http://www.dhs.gov/see-something-say-something/about-campaign.

At any given point along this detection continuum, the terrorist is vulnerable. Whether at the airport screening machine or vetted by random checks, in order to succeed, the terrorist will have to pass through a multitiered checkpoint system. The sheer volume of detection points reduces the chance for terrorist activity.

Aside from staffing airport screening lines, TSA involves itself in a diversity of programs (Figure 10.8).

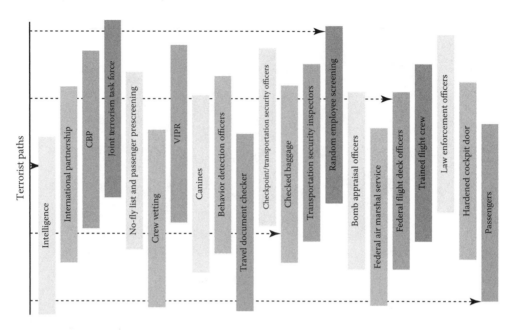

FIGURE 10.6 Layers of U.S. aviation security. (From Homeland Security. Aviation security. https://www.dhs.gov/aviation-security.)

FIGURE 10.7 DHS and its partners raise public awareness of the indicators of terrorism and terrorism-related crime through the "If You See Something, Say Something" campaign. They engage and inform the public through television and radio public service announcements (PSAs), partner print materials, transit opportunities, billboards, and other media. An example of their print media is shown here. (From Department of Homeland Security. Transportation Security Administration. If you see something, say something. https://www.tsa.gov/news/top-stories/2014/07/28/if-you-see-something-say-somethingTM.)

FIGURE 10.8 Seal of the TSA.

10.2.1 Federal Air Marshals

The federal air marshal program plants undercover law enforcement on airline flights. The program operates with specific intelligence or through random flight assignment. Federal air marshals are skilled in the use of weaponry and defense/offense tactics that involve restraint. Marshals must blend in with passengers, keeping any unsuspecting terrorist unaware of his or her presence on that plane. Marshals employ investigative techniques, criminal terrorist behavior recognition, firearms proficiency, aircraft-specific tactics, and close-quarters self-defense measures to protect the flying public (Figure 10.9).

Internet Exercise: Learn more about a career in the Federal Air Marshal Service at http://www.usmarshals.gov/careers.

10.2.2 Federal Flight Deck Officers

The Federal Flight Deck Officer (FFDO) program permits aviation pilots to be fully armed in the cockpit. TSA identifies and trains qualified officers for this position. Under this program, eligible flight crew members are authorized by the TSA Office of Law Enforcement/Federal Air Marshal Service to use firearms to defend against an act of criminal violence or air piracy that attempts to gain control of an aircraft. A flight crew member may be a pilot, flight engineer, or navigator assigned to the flight. The program is required to maintain strict confidentiality of its participants. The FFDOs are further characterized and empowered by these criteria:

- FFDOs are considered federal law enforcement officers only for the limited purposes of carrying firearms and using force, including lethal force, to defend the flight deck of an aircraft from air piracy or criminal violence.
- FFDOs are not granted or authorized to exercise other law enforcement powers, such as the power to make arrests, or seek or execute warrants for arrest, or seizure of evidence, or to otherwise act as federal law enforcement outside the jurisdiction of aircraft flight decks.

FIGURE 10.9   Federal air marshal patch.

- FFDOs are issued credentials and badges to appropriately identify themselves to law enforcement and security personnel, as required in the furtherance of their mission.
- FFDOs are issued firearms and other necessary equipment by the Federal Air Marshal Service.
- FFDOs are responsible for the readiness and daily security of their firearms, credentials, and equipment.
- FFDOs are authorized to transport secured firearms in any state for a flight on which they are flying to or from as approved by the Federal Air Marshal Service as necessary for their participation and activities in the program.

10.2.3 Law Enforcement Officers Flying Armed

TSA always oversees a program on instruction and general guidance for law enforcement officers wishing to fly while armed. The program recognizes the critical role a legitimately armed law enforcement officer might play in the event of a terrorist incident. Just as critical is the program's desire to promulgate standards for any law enforcement officer flying on official business. Transporting prisoners, tailing a suspect, or other investigative practice demands an official protocol for the use and storage of firearms. Any officer desiring to fly armed must complete a course of instruction and file the required paperwork giving notice of this intention.

Internet Resource: For a policy directive from TSA on flying armed, see https://www.tsa.gov/travel/law-enforcement.

10.2.4 TSA's Canine Explosive Detection Unit

Given the broadening responsibilities of TSA, moving beyond the airports and venturing into seaports, harbors, and train and municipal transit facilities, TSA has had to get creative in how it carries out its task.[7] The use of canines has long been a beneficial and very economical police practice. TSA uses canines to detect explosives in various quarters (Figure 10.10).

Canines are particularly effective in ports and harbor areas, where the sheer volume of coverage area can be daunting for law enforcement. TSA has developed certification standards for canine units for purposes of uniformity and quality in practice. TSA is aggressively developing units and teams throughout the United States. The agency will train and certify more than 400 explosive detection canine teams, composed of one dog and one handler, during the next 2 years. Eighty-five of these teams will be TSA employee led and will primarily search cargo bound for passenger-carrying aircraft. TSA handlers will be non-law-enforcement employees and will complement the 496 TSA-certified state and local law enforcement teams currently deployed to 70 airports and 14 mass transit systems. Currently, there are now 800 various canine teams throughout the United States (Figure 10.11).

Internet Exercise: Find out about the crucial role canines play in the defense of our nation at https://www.youtube.com/watch?v=AV4I7XNSph0.

(a)   (b)   (c)

FIGURE 10.10   Law enforcement officer (LEO), transportation security inspection (TSI), and passenger-screening canine (PSC) teams performing searches in different environments: (a) LEO team patrolling a mass transit terminal; (b) TSI team screening air cargo; (c) PSC team searching an airport terminal. From: Jennifer Grover, Explosives detection canines, GAO-14-695T, June 24, 2014, http://www.gao.gov/assets/670/664331.pdf (accessed January 24, 2016).

FIGURE 10.11   An explosive detection canine team screens cargo.

TSA operates a puppy-breeding program to fill the ranks of the future. Volunteers staff the operation and raise puppies who will work in TSA functions. During this time, volunteers provide a well-rounded, socialized, and nurturing environment. TSA delivers an orientation program for volunteers and makes technical staff available during this period of upbringing (Figure 10.12).

Internet Exercise: Find out about the retired dog adoption program that TSA recently announced at https://www.tsa.gov/news/releases/2015/11/02/tsa-seeking-people-adopt-dogs-who-have-retired-or-have-not-mastered.

FIGURE 10.12 TSA puppy-breeding program recruits.

10.2.5 Risk Management Programs

TSA has played an integral role in the development of risk assessment protocols and tools for the transportation system, though not without regular criticism.[8] Opponents of TSA argue that there is not much thinking going on when it comes to new and innovative protocols. Some have said that the agency agrees too quickly to adopting new technology. Even the General Accounting Office (GAO) found that TSA "does not routinely consider costs and benefits when acquiring new technologies."[9]

Despite this, TSA completely appreciates the interrelationship between a risk or series of risks and the critical infrastructure and assets it protects. To understand the risk is to comprehend the landscape to be protected. To comprehend the landscape to be protected surely leads to the identification and mitigation of risk. TSA also recognizes that transportation assets, such as airplanes and tunnels, are part of larger systems, such as the national aviation system or a mass transit system. Taken together, all the individual transportation systems form the national transportation system. Essentially, TSA discerns systems within systems. The behavior of transportation systems cannot be fully explained by confining observations to individual cars, vessels, and aircraft or fixed infrastructure. As a result, TSA has developed self-assessment tools for maritime, transportation, and mass transit systems.

In 2014, TSA modified its approach to risk management by adopting a new methodology: enterprise risk management (ERM) (Figure 10.13).

ERM tries to find appropriate targets rather than attempting to screen the entire universe for threats and harm. The primary goals of ERM are to

- Provide a structured, disciplined, and consistent approach to assessing risk aligned with U.S. Department of Homeland Security guidance.
- Identify strategic risks that threaten TSA's achievement of our long-term objectives and goals, and manage those risks at the enterprise level through the ERSC.
- Ensure that risks are managed in a manner that maximizes the value TSA provides to the nation consistent with defined risk appetite and risk tolerance levels.

FIGURE 10.13 ERM protocol. (From Transportation Security Administration. ERM policy manual. August 2014. https://www.aferm.org/wp-content/uploads/2015/10/TSA-ERM-Policy-Manual-August-2014.pdf.)

- Align our strategy, process, people, technology, and information to support agile risk management.
- Provide greater transparency into risk by improving our understanding of interactions and relationships between risks in support of improved risk-based decision-making.
- Establish clear accountability and ownership of risk.[10]

Internet Resource: For a full analysis of the ERM methodology, visit https://www.aferm.org/wp-content/uploads/2015/10/TSA-ERM-Policy-Manual-August-2014.pdf.

10.2.6 TSA Technology and Innovation

Cutting-edge technology is a desired end for TSA. The costs of human intelligence versus mechanical versions are always higher, and realizing the volume of TSA activities, the need for high-level technology has never been greater. The world is a very large place to screen, and the human eye is simply incapable of seeing it all. To stay ahead of the terrorist, TSA has developed and employed some incredible technology, again not without some controversy. In air, cargo holds, ports, and harbor shipping, the use of technology will permit TSA to extend its reach.[11] A thumbnail review of a few of the more exciting advances is covered in the following.

10.2.6.1 Trace Portals and Their Demise

The use of the trace portal was a highly touted technique for detection of dangerous items, such as explosives and anthrax. The portals were allegedly capable of detecting trace, minute quantities of many materials including explosives. From 2007 to 2011, the machines

FIGURE 10.14   Trace portal.

were installed at a host of airports. As passengers entered the trace portal, standing still for a few seconds, several puffs of air are released, dislodging microscopic particles from passengers that are then collected and analyzed for traces of explosives. TSA installed trace portals in Baltimore; Boston; Gulfport, Mississippi; Jacksonville, Florida; Las Vegas; Los Angeles; Miami; Newark; New York (JFK); Phoenix; Providence, Rhode Island; Rochester, New York; San Francisco; San Diego; and Tampa, Florida. See Figure 10.14 for a trace portal.

Unfortunately, the machines proved so ineffective and unpredictable that TSA slowly but surely withdrew the technology, commencing in 2011. With nearly 200 machines in place at a cost of nearly $30,000,000 million, the program represents another public relations problem for the agency.

10.2.6.2 Millimeter Wave/Advanced Imaging Technology

The new means for discerning explosives, improvised explosive devices (IEDs), and other concealed materials are the *millimeter wave device* and *advanced imaging technology* (AIT). TSA currently uses both types at 78 airports. Around 500 AIT and 300 millimeter wave machines are presently in use (Figure 10.15).

Millimeter wave imaging technology uses harmless electromagnetic waves to detect potential threats. Beams of radio frequency (RF) energy in the millimeter wave spectrum are projected over the body's surface at high speed from two antennas simultaneously rotating around the body. The RF energy reflected back from the body or other objects on the body constructs a three-dimensional image. The three-dimensional image of the body, with facial features blurred for privacy, is displayed on a remote monitor for analysis. The machine itself is innocuous. Earlier imagery lacked specificity relative to identity and hence could not be used for illicit purposes.

However, more modern AIT machines provide exquisite detail as to the physical features and, as a result, have been the subject of some passenger abuse. The resulting images are labeled *backscatter*. Backscatter technology projects an ionizing x-ray beam over the body

FIGURE 10.15   AIT machine: the millimeter wave unit.

surface at high speed. The reflection, or backscatter, of the beam is detected, digitized, and displayed on a monitor.

Both systems have generated a stir of comment and criticism. For some, the safety of the imagery and its mechanics trump the safety of the general public. If the technology utilizes waves, in whatever form, critics indicate there may be health risks. TSA has taken these critiques seriously and tried to calm the public by making comparisons. For example, the exposure to waves during a backscatter scan is like flying a plane for 2 minutes, while those experienced during a millimeter wave scan are similar to using a cell phone (Figure 10.16).

In addition, the machines cannot sensibly differentiate common medical devices that are absolutely innocent by design, such as an insulin pump monitor for diabetics, pacemakers for heart conditions, and neurostimulators for neurological problems. As such, since the machines tend to lump the common terrorist together with the sickly patient, this likewise causes a further erosion of trust regarding TSA.[12]

Internet Exercise: Read about the various health assessments that have been done on AIT at http://www.dhs.gov/sites/default/files/publications/tsa-safety-study-ait-info-memo_0.pdf

Even more common has been the privacy challenge to intrusive machinery.[13] AIT and millimeter wave machines peer deep into the private range of human operations. Balancing the rationale of safe travel with minimal intrusiveness may be less compelling than the searched bag comparison. Surely, every traveler realizes that privacy concerns are not idyllic

Millimeter wave safety

Backscatter safety

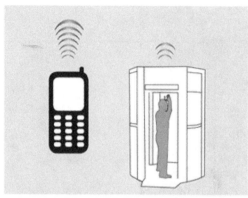

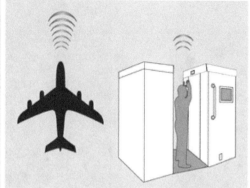

Millimeter wave technology emits thousands of times less energy than a cell phone transmission.

One backscatter technology scan produces the same exposure as two minutes of flying on an airplane.

FIGURE 10.16   AIT safety information from TSA (https://www.tsa.gov/graphics/images/approach/ait_safety_demo.jpg).

and untouchable. In a post-9/11 world, most people accept the burdens and inconveniences of security checkpoints.

Internet Exercise: See how TSA portrays its version of the imaging technology at https://www.youtube.com/watch?v=phBfsI5PlzI.

Even so, the intrusiveness has limits and this machinery may have reached the threshold where the public's patience runs out. TSA has some sensitivity to the privacy concerns.[14] It has altered the imagery to a generic format that cannot personally be identified, it has the screener in a distinct position from the officer assisting the customer, and it has assured that imagery cannot be stored, printed, transmitted, or saved.[15]

The agency has modified its software packages to show a generic figure that lacks specificity. Known as *automated target recognition*, ATR eliminates the image of the individual body while still recognizing anomalies.[16] See Figure 10.17 for an ATR image.

Granting the intrusiveness of these technologies, the price of that intrusion may be worth the results in weaponry confiscation alone; 2014 was a banner year for firearms confiscation (Figure 10.18).

10.2.6.3 Biometrics

The world of *biometrics* has clearly invaded the day-to-day life of TSA. Biometrics can be defined as follows:

- Biometrics is a general term used alternatively to describe a characteristic or a process.
- As a characteristic, a biometric is a measurable biological (anatomical and physiological) and behavioral characteristic that can be used for automated recognition.

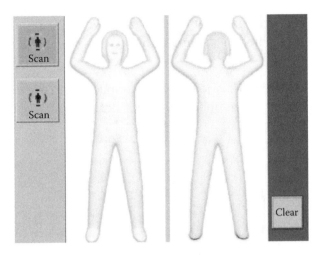

FIGURE 10.17   TSA is using software that enhances privacy by highlighting any potential threats on the same generic outline of a person for every passenger. (From Transport Security Administration. https://www.tsa.gov/.)

FIGURE 10.18   2014 TSA firearms confiscations. (From Transport Security Administration. https://www.tsa.gov/.)

- As a process, a biometric is an automated method of recognizing an individual based on measurable biological (anatomical and physiological) and behavioral characteristics.[17]

Biometrics is a means of identification using both machine and man.[18] Presently, biometrics can target various bodily components for identification, including

- Palm
- Fingerprint
- Face
- Vascular system
- Speech
- Eye

Both retinal scans and fingerprint analysis by digital means are available to the agency. Biometric fingerprint machines are becoming a common experience for both residential and international travelers (Figure 10.19).

Machines that trace and match retinal patterns are sure to grow just as quickly.

10.2.6.3.1 Biometric Application: The Registered Traveler Program

Biometric applications are becoming very common in the travel and transportation industries. The FBI has taken the lead on the various modalities relating to biometric applications by and through its biometric center of excellence (Figure 10.20).[19]

All of these new technologies hope to speed up the travel process and may or may not use biometric applications. Early on, TSA created the Registered Traveler (RT) program in an effort to speed up the traveling process for business and repeat travelers. In order to participate, passengers undergo a TSA-conducted security threat assessment (STA). It is a voluntary program with both corporate entities and individuals participating. Biometrics plays

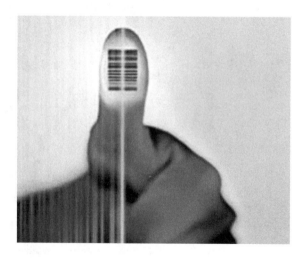

FIGURE 10.19 Biometric fingerprint scanner.

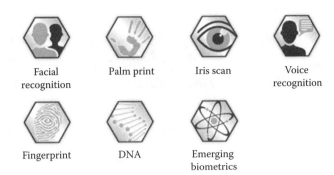

FIGURE 10.20   Various biometric modalities.

a key role in this program. To enroll, applicants voluntarily provide RT-sponsoring entities (participating airports/air carriers) and service providers with biographic and biometric data needed for TSA to conduct the STA and determine eligibility. To date, the following agencies participate in the RT program.

- Air France (operating out of Terminal 1 at JFK)
- AirTran Airways (operating out of the Central Terminal at LGA)
- Albany International Airport (ALB)
- British Airways (operating out of Terminal 7 at JFK)
- Cincinnati/Northern Kentucky International Airport (CVG)
- Denver International Airport (DEN)
- Gulfport–Biloxi International Airport (GPT)
- Indianapolis International Airport (IND)
- Jacksonville International Airport (JAX)
- Little Rock National Airport (LIT)
- Norman Mineta San Jose International Airport (SJC)
- Oakland International Airport (OAK)
- Orlando International Airport (MCO)
- Reno/Tahoe International Airport (RNO)
- Ronald Reagan Washington National Airport (DCA)
- Salt Lake City International Airport (SLC)
- San Francisco International Airport (SFO)
- Virgin Atlantic (operating out of Terminal B at EWR)
- Virgin Atlantic (operating out of Terminal 4 at JFK)
- Washington Dulles International Airport (IAD)
- Westchester County Airport (HPN)

The RT program has largely been replaced with the Trusted Traveler programs of TSA, which are: TSA PreCheck, and in conjunction with CBP, Global Entry, NEXUS, and SENTRI programs. A comparison chart of these four expedited programs is reproduced in Table 10.1 (https://www.dhs.gov/trusted-traveler-programs).

TABLE 10.1 Trusted Traveler Programs Offered by DHS

Agency	TSA	CBP		
Program	TSA Pre✓	Global Entry	NEXUS	SENTRI
Website	www.tsa.gov/tsa-precheck	www.globalentry.gov	NEXUS	SENTRI
Eligibility required	U.S. citizens and U.S. lawful permanent residents	U.S. citizens, U.S. lawful permanent residents, and citizens of certain other countries[a]	U.S. citizens, lawful permanent residents, Canadian citizens, and lawful permanent residents of Canada	Proof of citizenship and admissibility documentation
Application fee	$85.00 (5 years' membership)	$100.00 (5 years' membership)	$50.00 (5 years' membership)	$122.25 (5 years' membership)
Passport required	No	Yes, or lawful permanent resident card	No	No
Application process	Pre-enroll online, visit an enrollment center; provide fingerprints and verify ID	Pre-enroll online, visit an enrollment center for an interview; provide fingerprints and verify ID	Pre-enroll online, visit an enrollment center for an interview; provide fingerprints and verify ID	Pre-enroll online, visit an enrollment center for an interview; provide fingerprints and verify ID
Program experience	TSA Pre✓ expedited screening at participating airports	Expedited processing through CBP at airports and land borders upon arrival in the United States Includes TSA Pre✓ experience	Expedited processing at airports and land borders when entering the U.S. and Canada Includes Global Entry benefits Includes TSA Pre✓ benefits for U.S. citizens, U.S. lawful permanent residents, and Canadian citizens	Expedited processing through CBP at land borders Includes Global Entry and TSA Pre✓ benefits for U.S. citizens and U.S. lawful permanent residents

Internet Resource: The U.S. Army has produced an excellent overview of biometric applications at http://www.eis.army.mil/programs/biometrics.

10.2.6.3.2 *TSA Paperless Boarding Pass*

In an effort to streamline security processes and to assure a free flow of traffic in congested airports, TSA has implemented a paperless boarding pass program. Here, the passenger downloads the boarding pass to a cell phone

FIGURE 10.21   An example of a paperless boarding pass as it appears on a smartphone.

or other device and scans it at a designated station. Currently, 69 airports have adopted the program. Using a scan code, the TSA agent verifies the pass by a mere swipe (Figure 10.21).

The program has been favorably received by the general public, though there are the usual caveats about privacy issues and the sharing of this personal information. TSA has issued strict guidelines on privacy requirements and reigned in the technology to prevent unauthorized disclosure.[20]

There is much more that could be written concerning the activities of TSA. Throughout the remainder of this chapter, the role of TSA in other aspects involving the transportation industry will be highlighted. In fact, our coverage turns to two key areas in the transportation arena: maritime and rail.

10.3 Maritime Security

Maritime security is an interagency operation at the federal level, with the prime players being the Coast Guard, Customs and Immigration Service, and DHS. In 2011, DHS announced a more formal association of the major players in maritime security titled the Marine Operations Coordination (MOC) plan. MOC will coordinate and plan for the integration of maritime operations of the U.S. Coast Guard, CBP, and Immigration and Customs Enforcement. The MOC plan focuses on improved collaboration across five key sectors.

- Coordination
- Planning
- Information sharing
- Intelligence integration
- Response activities

DHS has also fostered interagency cooperation in maritime threat affairs by the creation of the Maritime Operational Threat Response (MOTR) program. The primary aim of the program is to coordinate all relevant agencies of government that might encounter

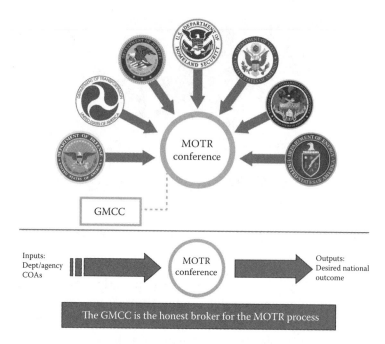

FIGURE 10.22 Maritime operational threat response process.

maritime threats and to assure the free flow of information to all interested agencies. A schematic of how all agencies report to MOTR is in Figure 10.22.

Previous to 9/11, conceptions of maritime security largely dealt with smuggling, theft, and drug trafficking.[21] Since that time, maritime security has been evaluated in more global terms. Maritime enforcement can only be described as a major undertaking that draws in all sectors of defense, including the traditional branches of the armed services.[22]

The maritime domain is defined as all areas and things of, on, under, relating to, adjacent to, or bordering on a sea, ocean, or other navigable waterway, including all maritime-related activities, infrastructure, people, cargo, and vessels, and other conveyances. The maritime domain for the United States includes the Great Lakes and all navigable inland waterways, such as the Mississippi River and the Intracoastal Waterway.

In the most general terms, maritime security seeks to accomplish the following ends:

- Prevent terrorist attacks and criminal or hostile acts
- Protect maritime-related population centers and critical infrastructures
- Minimize damage and expedite recovery
- Safeguard the ocean and its resources

The Maritime Security Transportation Act of 2002 was the initial legislative response after the attack of 9/11.[23] The act requires vessels and port facilities to conduct vulnerability assessments and develop security plans that may include passenger, vehicle, and baggage screening procedures, security patrols, establishing restricted areas, personnel identification procedures, access control measures, and installation of surveillance equipment. Developed using risk-based methodology, the security regulations focus on those sectors of maritime industry that have a higher risk of involvement in a transportation security incident, including various tank vessels, barges, large passenger vessels, cargo vessels, towing vessels, offshore oil and gas platforms, and port facilities that handle certain kinds of dangerous cargo or service these vessels.

Internet Resource: For the entire language of the act, see https://www.gpo.gov/fdsys/pkg/PLAW-107publ295/pdf/PLAW-107publ295.pdf.

10.3.1 National Strategy for Maritime Security

The complexities of maritime security arise from geography, legal issues, and a host of competing agencies and departments who have some portion of the pie—for example, defense, energy, interior, state, and DHS. Matters of territorial waters can be daunting and any effort to secure the homeland must weigh these competing interests.

In 2005, DHS published its National Strategy for Maritime Security.[24] The national strategy hones in on these fundamental objectives:

- Detect, deter, interdict, and defeat terrorist attacks, criminal acts, or hostile acts in the maritime domain, and prevent its unlawful exploitation for those purposes.
- Protect maritime-related population centers, critical infrastructure, key resources, transportation systems, borders, harbors, ports, and coastal approaches in the maritime domain.
- Define and set out the maritime domain.
- Minimize damage and expedite recovery from attacks within the maritime domain.
- Safeguard the ocean and its resources from unlawful exploitation and intentional critical damage.
- Enhance international cooperation to ensure lawful and timely enforcement actions against maritime threats.
- Embed security into commercial practices to reduce vulnerabilities and facilitate commerce.
- Deploy layered security to unify public and private security measures.
- Ensure continuity of the marine transportation system to maintain vital commerce and defense readiness.

The national strategy fully accepts that the world's waterways depend on extraordinary cooperation at both the national and international levels. Any strategy must balance commerce with defense considerations, international rights with sovereignty of the coastline, and with the full recognition that certain bodies of water are internationally accessible while others are protected. Figure 10.23 portrays all these dynamics.

Both government and commercial interests need to work together. Nations and states must coordinate response and action and adopt common definitions and parameters for what constitutes the maritime domain. The National Strategy on Maritime Security realizes the complexity of protecting the world's seas and waterways. It realizes that governmental entities and bodies need coordination. As a result, the strategy erects the Interagency Maritime Security Policy Coordinating Committee—established to serve as the primary

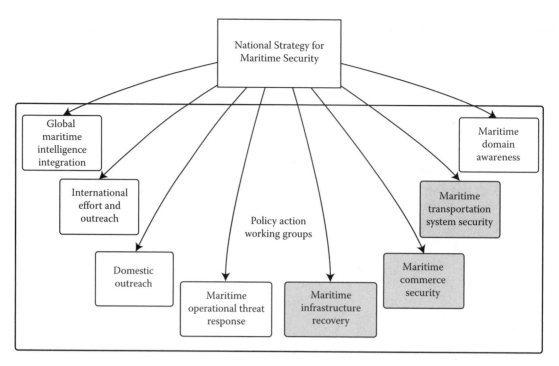

FIGURE 10.23 **National strategy for maritime security.**

forum for coordinating U.S. government maritime security policies. The committee reviews existing interagency practices, and coordination and execution of U.S. policies and strategies relating to maritime security, and recommends improvements, as necessary.

10.3.2 Other Maritime Plans

At the national level there are eight other plans or programs dedicated to the protection of the maritime domain—namely:

- The National Plan to Achieve Maritime Domain Awareness lays the foundation for an effective understanding of anything associated with the maritime domain that could impact the security, safety, economy, or environment of the United States.
- The Maritime Transportation System Security Plan responds to the president's call for recommendations to improve the national and international regulatory framework regarding the maritime domain.
- The Maritime Commerce Security Plan establishes a comprehensive plan to secure the maritime supply chain.
- The Maritime Infrastructure Recovery Plan recommends procedures and standards for the recovery of the maritime infrastructure following attack or similar disruption.
- The International Outreach and Coordination Strategy provides a framework to coordinate all maritime security initiatives undertaken with foreign governments and international organizations.

- The Global Maritime Intelligence Integration Plan uses existing capabilities to integrate all available intelligence regarding potential threats to U.S. interests in the maritime domain.
- The Maritime Operational Threat Response Plan aims for coordinated U.S. government response to threats against the United States and its interests in the maritime domain by establishing roles and responsibilities.
- The Domestic Outreach Plan engages nonfederal input to assist with the development and implementation of maritime security policies.

Space limitations prevent full coverage of each of the plans, but it shall be sufficient to cover the more prominent ideas in maritime security.

10.3.2.1 National Plan to Achieve Maritime Domain Awareness

The National Plan to Achieve Maritime Domain Awareness educates the public about the nature of a maritime domain in order that threats may be identified. Maritime domain awareness involves anything associated with the global maritime domain that could impact the United States' security, safety, economy, or environment. A range of federal departments and agencies will need to coordinate closely to identify threats as early and as distant from our shores as possible. By unifying U.S. government efforts and supporting international efforts, this plan will help achieve maritime domain awareness across the federal government, with the private sector and civil authorities within the United States, and with our allies and partners around the world.[25]

10.3.2.2 Maritime Transportation System Security Plan

The Maritime Transportation System (MTS) Security Plan seeks to improve the national and international regulatory framework regarding the maritime domain. The MTS evaluates maritime security in light of its various systems. The MTS is a network of maritime operations that interface with shore-side operations at intermodal connections as part of overall global supply chains or domestic commercial operations. The various maritime operations within the MTS operating network have components that include vessels, port facilities, waterways and waterway infrastructure, intermodal connections, and users. DHS will issue a series of continuing recommendations regarding the safety of the network and its various components.

What is undeniable is that terrorists have attempted to use terrorism in the maritime domain. Professionals from all branches of defense and law enforcement constantly watch the horizon for new means and methods of attacks.

10.3.3 DHS: Borders and Marine Division

The long-held view that cargo and port inspections were the exclusive province of the U.S. Coast Guard has been set aright since 9/11. Multiple agencies of government are now taking on active roles to assure the safety and security of what comes in and what goes out. Discussed throughout this chapter is the role of the Border Division and its many dedicated employees. DHS, by and through its Border and Marine Division takes these activities to a higher plane. Marine security does not end when the boat or ship docks, but is simply at another layer of scrutiny. Cargo, containers, cartons, and supplies stowed on these vessels are part of that secure continuum. While the Coast Guard interdicts and inspects, it cannot be stretched much thinner than its present state. Hence, the work of DHS in this critical area fills a crucial void in assuring the flow of goods and the safe environment the public expects. A thumbnail sketch of the more relevant projects follows.

The Advanced Container Security Device (ACSD) project involves developing an advanced sensor system for monitoring a container's integrity from the point of consolidation to the point of deconsolidation in the maritime supply chain. The ACSD is a small unit that attaches to the inside of a container to monitor all six sides to report any intrusion or door opening, including the presence of human cargo in the container. If the ACSD detects an intrusion, it will transmit this alarm information through the Marine Asset Tag Tracking System (MATTS) to CBP. The ACSD would also build in a standard plug-and-play interface capability so that users can easily integrate other security or commercial sensors (e.g., radiological/nuclear and chemical/biological) through the standard interface.

The CanScan project is developing a next-generation nonintrusive inspection (NII) system that will be used to detect terrorist materials, contraband items (e.g., drugs, money, illegal firearms), and stowaways at border crossings, maritime ports, and airports. These new systems may provide increases in penetration, resolution, and throughput, and will support marine containerized cargo as well as airborne break-bulk, palletized, and containerized cargo; CanScan will provide improved cargo screening.

The Container Security Device (CSD) project is developing a security device with sensors that can detect the opening of container doors from the point of consolidation to the point of deconsolidation in the maritime supply chain. The CSD will provide an interim capability to monitor the status of container doors until the ACSD is available. The CSD is a small, low-cost device mounted on or within a container that detects the opening or removal of container doors and reports its status to CBP.

The Hybrid Composite Container project is developing a next-generation International Standards Organization (ISO) composite shipping container with embedded security sensors to detect intrusions from the point of consolidation to the point of deconsolidation in the maritime supply chain. Composites are stronger than steel, 10%–15% lighter than current shipping containers, and are easier to repair. Weight savings can benefit shippers by allowing them to load more goods per container within weight limits.

The MATTS project is establishing a remote, global communications and tracking network that works with ACSD from the point of consolidation to the point of deconsolidation in the maritime supply chain. MATTS communicates security alert information globally through the use of RF, cellular, and satellite technology. In addition, the commercial shipping industry can track and monitor cargo as it moves through the supply chain.

The Secure Carton project develops technology to detect any shipping carton tamper event and transmit an alert to authorities after it leaves the point of manufacture to the point that it is delivered in the supply chains. This project provides improved supply chain visibility, chain of custody, and security. It is scalable and applicable across the various shipping modalities, including trucking, rail, maritime, and air cargo.

The Secure Wrap project provides a transparent, flexible, and tamper-indicative wrapping material to secure and monitor palletized cargo after it leaves the point of manufacture to the point of delivery in the land, maritime, and air cargo supply chains. The wrap will provide a visible and/or fluorescent tamper indication and is deployable with little or no impact to current supply chain logistics and processes. Subsequent iterations of this wrap will support increasing levels of automated monitoring, thereby reducing the manpower required to ensure cargo integrity.

10.3.4 Role of the Coast Guard in Maritime Security

At sea and on the continental shelf, in major lakes and rivers, the U.S. Coast Guard assumes the preeminent role in maritime security. With its fleet of cutters and world-class tugs and rescue vessels, high-level technology, skill in port and harbor investigations, and a professional class of officers and staff, it is difficult to find a better fit (Figure 10.24).

The Coast Guard's central mission relates to maritime activities. The Coast Guard's 11-part mission focuses on issues integral to a safe maritime environment.

- Ports, waterways, and coastal security
- Drug interdiction
- Aids to navigation
- Search and rescue
- Living marine resources
- Marine safety
- Defense readiness
- Migrant interdiction
- Marine environmental protection
- Ice operations
- Other law enforcement

FIGURE 10.24 U.S. Coast Guard patrol vehicles.

With this multifaceted mission in mind, it is no wonder that the Coast Guard so actively intervenes in the day-to-day grind of the maritime sector and it is equally not surprising that the Coast Guard is severely starved for resources to carry out the depth and breadth of these 11 mission areas. Examples of Coast Guard roles and functions in the maritime world are myriad.

10.3.4.1 Emergency Safety

The effectiveness and professionalism of the Coast Guard can always be gleaned from their role in emergency response. Coast Guard assistance in times of storms, hurricanes, floods, and other natural disasters is the stuff of legend (Figure 10.25).

Throughout its distinguished history, the Coast Guard has more than saved lives: it has also rescued whole communities. At no place was this more obvious than during Hurricane Katrina. Referred to as the only shining moment and silver lining in the debacle, Coast Guard personnel swept up person after person in the raging waters of New Orleans. The Coast Guard single-handedly saved more residents of New Orleans than any other governmental authority (Figure 10.26).

Wherever water runs, the Coast Guard is always prepared and ready to serve those in distress. From Hatteras, North Carolina, beaches to Lake Superior, maritime safety comes first for this service.

The most prominent safety unit in the Coast Guard is its search and rescue (SAR) team (Figure 10.27).

The primary goal of SAR is to minimize the loss of life to those in distress, and the Coast Guard saves more than 85% of those who call. When one evaluates the locations of these dangerous rescues, it is simply an extraordinary statistic. The Coast Guard employs a formula to account for the effectiveness in mitigating the loss of life.[26]

$$= \frac{LS}{\left(LS + \left(LLB + LLA + LUF\right)\right)}$$

where:
LS = lives saved
LLB = lives lost before notification
LLA = lives lost after notification
LUF = lives unaccounted for (or missing), as defined and input into Marine Information for Safety and Law Enforcement (MISLE)

FIGURE 10.25 The U.S. Coast Guard is instrumental in saving lives.

FIGURE 10.26   Coast Guard over New Orleans after Hurricane Katrina.

FIGURE 10.27   Search and rescue patch.

Internet Resource: Read about the SAR program in *Coast Guard* magazine at http://www. uscg.mil/hq/g-o/g-opr/SAR%20Watch%20newsletter/newsletter.htm.

The SAR program is physically demanding and recruits experience a significant attrition rate of nearly 50%. Check with your local Coast Guard recruiter on eligibility standards (Figure 10.28).

Internet Resource: To learn about the curriculum and the physical demands leading to high attrition rates, see http://www.defenselink.mil/news/-newsarticle.aspx?id=25362.

10.3.4.2 Security and Law Enforcement

Law enforcement functions constitute a major portion of Coast Guard activity. In a way, the Coast Guard polices the waters for a host of things, from smuggling to drugs, from illegal human cargo to WMDs. On the water and in the ports, one discovers the critical role of the Coast Guard. The Coast Guard is the law of the sea and waterways.

FIGURE 10.28 Coast Guard SAR team member at training.

The Coast Guard is the lead federal agency for maritime drug interdiction. In conjunction with the U.S. Customs Service, the Coast Guard combats and interdicts illegal drugs, interferes with and deters the activities of smugglers using the maritime for illegal delivery of drugs, and engages those that seek to pollute our cities and towns with contraband. Over the last decade, Coast Guard activity in the area of drug interdiction has been active (Table 10.2).

The Coast Guard has dramatically reoriented its mission to the law enforcement model. The Coast Guard law enforcement mission is statutorily outlined in these general terms:

> The Coast Guard shall enforce or assist in the enforcement of all applicable Federal laws on, under, and over the high seas and waters subject to the jurisdiction of the United States; shall engage in maritime air surveillance or interdiction to enforce or assist in the enforcement of the laws of the United States; shall administer laws and promulgate and enforce regulations for the promotion of safety of life and property on and under the high seas and waters subject to the jurisdiction of the United States covering all matters not specifically delegated by law to some other executive department; shall develop, establish, maintain, and operate, with due regard to the requirements of national defense, aids to maritime navigation, ice-breaking facilities, and rescue facilities for the promotion of safety on, under, and over the high seas and waters subject to the jurisdiction of the United States; shall, pursuant to international agreements, develop, establish, maintain, and operate icebreaking facilities on, under, and over waters other than the high seas and waters subject to the jurisdiction of the United States; shall engage in oceanographic research of the high seas and in waters subject to the jurisdiction of the United States; and shall maintain a state of readiness to function as a specialized service in the Navy in time of war, including the fulfillment of Maritime Defense Zone command responsibilities.[27]

In 2004, the Coast Guard established the Maritime Law Enforcement Academy in Charleston, South Carolina. The academy prepares Coast Guard personnel to perform as

TABLE 10.2 Coast Guard Drug Removal Statistics

Fiscal Year	Events	Vessels Seized	Detainees	Marijuana (lbs)	Cocaine (lbs)
2015	98	72	257	31,224	147,268.8
2014	164	93	344	108,534	198,636.5
2013	159	64	230	81,008	194,886.6
2012	162	70	352	124,585	236,002.5
2011	129	40	191	39,246	166,631.1
2010	122	57	237	36,739	202,438.8
2009	123	58	322	71,234.1	352,862.8
2008	85	43	209	23,485.3	367,926.1
2007	65	37	188	14,213.0	355,754.6
2006	64	23	200	9,059.3	287,035.4
2005	87	66	364	12,126.0	338,205.6
2004	104	71	326	26,014.9	293,993.0
2003	65	56	283	14,059.0	136,865.0
2002	58	40	207	40,316.0	117,780.0
2001	65	30	114	34,520.0	138,393.0
2000	92	56	204	50,463.0	132,480.0
1999	118	74	304	61,506.0	111,689.0
1998	129	75	297	31,390.0	82,623.0
1997	122	64	233	102,538.0	103,617.0
1996	36	41	112	42,063.0	44,462.0
1995	44	34	56	48,148.3	45,750.4
1994	67	28	73	90,041.7	65,254.1

Source: U.S. Coast Guard, Office of Law Enforcement (CG-531), Coast Guard drug removal statistics, April 30, 2015, http://www.uscg.mil/hq/cg5/cg531/Drugs/stats.asp., accessed August 16, 2016.

boarding officers and boarding team members; develops the maritime law enforcement skills of professionals from federal, state, and local agencies, as well as the international community; and provides assistance to law enforcement agencies (Figure 10.29).

The Coast Guard also operates an investigative service (Figure 10.30). The office concentrates on drugs and other smuggling, illegal immigration activities, and environmental violations. The following charts the competencies and skills expected for the professional investigator.

Receipt, analysis, and disposition of allegations(s)

- Obtain data from complainant or source.
- Document complaint in writing.
- Know prosecutorial or regulatory criteria.

FIGURE 10.29 **Maritime Law Enforcement Academy patch.**

FIGURE 10.30 **Seal of the U.S. Coast Guard Investigative Service.**

- Identify violations (elements of crime) or administrative standards.
- Review and identify significant information or potential evidence.
- Determine correct disposition of complaint (criminal, civil, or administrative).
- Open investigation, if appropriate, and coordinate with appropriate authorities (internally/externally).

Assessment, focus, and preparation of investigative plan

- Review available information and evidence.
- Review legal decisions and guidelines.
- Review agency programs, operational policies, and procedures.
- Determine focus and scope of investigation.
- Assess and identify required resources.
- Identify potential witnesses, suspects, relevant documents, and evidence.
- Organize and prioritize investigative activities.
- Prepare initial investigative plan.

Conduct investigation

- Maintain focus and follow investigative plan (revise as necessary).
- Prepare for anticipated investigative activities (interviews, taking statements).
- Apply knowledge of laws and regulations.
- Understand and apply techniques to ensure constitutional rights.
- Project a professional image.
- Use good oral and written communicative skills.
- Know evidentiary rules.
- Collect, analyze, and preserve evidence.
- Use appropriate specialized techniques (search warrants, forensics, consensual monitoring).
- Conduct reviews and data inquiries and promptly document such activities.
- Collect and analyze financial data.
- Assess progress and refocus when necessary.
- Coordinate progress with supervisor (prosecutors or management, as appropriate).
- Maintain appropriate liaison.
- Effectively manage the case and assist personnel and meet planned milestones.
- Obtain IG or grand jury subpoenas and testify before grand jury.

Review, organize, and evaluate investigative findings

- Review and understand the information gathered.
- Organize the information and evidence gathered.
- Correlate data, witnesses, and records.
- Consider internal/external customer needs.

Draft report, validate contents, and submit final report

- Write draft report—ensure accuracy, thoroughness, objectivity, proper format, clarity, and correct grammar.
- Review report to ensure information is correct and complete.
- Consider issues such as confidentiality, the Privacy Act, the Freedom of Information Act, and security classification.
- Include disclosure caveats where appropriate.
- Write final report.
- Distribute to appropriate entities.

Postinvestigative tasks

- Know rules of criminal and civil procedures.
- Assist with preparation for court/administrative proceedings.
- Serve witness subpoenas.
- Assist U.S. attorney/district attorney at trial.
- Testify at trial.
- Document and report results, dispositions, and outcomes.

- Obtain disposition of exhibits and evidence after trial/hearing.
- Return and document proper disposition of documents and evidence.
- Review the organization of investigative files for efficient retrieval.
- Archive investigative files.
- Ensure information management database reflects accurate and final case information.[28]

The Coast Guard tackles law enforcement from the homeland security end too. Here, the Coast Guard displays its multitasking ability and its capacity to blend safety, emergency, defense, and homeland protection into its mission. "Domestically, the Coast Guard–led Area Maritime Security Committees carry out much of the maritime security regimes effort."[29]

Counterterrorism efforts are an ongoing Coast Guard responsibility as well, with a plethora of activities including the Maritime Security Response Team (MSRT)—a first responder to terrorist activities on the seas (Figure 10.31).

In the area of homeland security, the Coast Guard assumes these responsibilities:

- Protect ports, the flow of commerce, and the marine transportation system from terrorism.
- Maintain maritime border security against illegal drugs, illegal aliens, firearms, and WMDs.
- Ensure that we can rapidly deploy and resupply our military assets, both by keeping Coast Guard units at a high state of readiness and by keeping marine transportation open for the transit assets and personnel from other branches of the armed forces.
- Protect against illegal fishing and indiscriminate destruction of living marine resources, and prevention and response to oil and hazardous material spills—both accidental and intentional.
- Coordinate efforts and intelligence with federal, state, and local agencies.

FIGURE 10.31 MSRT boat crews maneuver into formation during training on Chesapeake Bay, February 17, 2011. The mission of the MSRT is to provide a short-notice, threat-tailored, maritime response force to deter, protect against, and respond to threats of maritime terrorism and to higher-risk criminal law enforcement threats on the water or in a port. (U.S. Coast Guard photo by Petty Officer 2nd Class Michael Anderson.)

The Coast Guard also works closely with the other branches of the military to provide homeland defense and civil support to federal, state, and local agencies in the United States, and includes the increased security measures taken after the 9/11 terrorist attacks.

The Coast Guard joined the other services in making its services available to the larger law enforcement community. This program, dubbed Operation Noble Eagle, seeks to meld the missions of the military into the homeland strategy (Figure 10.32).

Career opportunities abound for those interested in military service with a safety and law enforcement approach. The Coast Guard career track delivers fascinating and challenging paths to professionalism.

10.3.4.3 Cargo and Ports

The responsibility for cargo and port protection resides primarily with the U.S. Coast Guard, though its aligned partners—DHS and the Customs and Immigration Service—aid in the endeavor. Bureaucratically, the Coast Guard administers its cargo, container, and facilities program through its Inspection and Compliance Directorate.

For the Coast Guard, as part of its overall mission of safety and security on the high seas and waterways, it would be a natural and very complementary function for this service. With billions of tons of cargo, and nearly 52,000 foreign ships visiting the United States, the job can be daunting.[30] Balance this with the entrepreneurial bent of the shipping and cargo industry—which needs to move goods and services fast, efficiently, and profitably—and you have a delicate policy problem. On the one hand, the safety and security issue runs front and center, yet on the other hand, the Coast Guard needs to be sensitive to the question of productivity and finance. Some have argued that the costs of maritime security may be too high and not worth the investment.[31] From afar, the costs associated with ensuring security are staggering and sometimes demonstrate the subservience of the maritime industry, which is "at the beck and call of a government whose legal initiatives, understandably, are

FIGURE 10.32   Operation Noble Eagle patch.

more in tune with security than economy."[32] In a global economy, with significant trade entering American ports each and every day, the imposition of security measures in a free economy requires keen balancing. Implementing "new security policies with economic and trade objective is a complicated task given the potential risks to human life should the United States under-protect its borders."[33]

Each and every day, the U.S. Coast Guard is responsible for every visitation of a foreign ship, the safety and security of America's ports, and the implementation of sweeping maritime policies. The Coast Guard's Office of Port and Facility Compliance is responsible for

- Overseeing onshore and offshore domestic commercial facilities, including deep-water ports, and cargo safety, security, and environmental protection compliance programs, including the direction of Coast Guard field activities, and industry partnerships in support of applicable laws and regulations
- Advising the Office of Investigation and Analysis regarding the notice of violation enforcement program policy as applied to cargo and commercial facilities
- Maintaining liaison and outreach with key industry, interagency, and international partners on related facility and cargo safety, security, and environmental protection activities
- Developing policy for facility security plans (FSPs) review and approval, facility alternative security programs (ASPS), and public access/waivers/exemptions
- Establishing and interpreting standards and regulations, and participating in the rule making and the legislative change process for onshore and offshore domestic commercial facilities
- Administering the standard safety and security Facility Inspection and Pollution Prevention Compliance programs
- Administering program activities for military and commercial explosives, radio-active materials, packaged hazardous materials, cargoes of particular hazard, and classified cargoes
- Maintaining a database of all U.S. waste reception
- Developing inspection, enforcement, and safety and security policy for the Coast Guard Container Inspection Program and overseeing the operation of the Container Inspection Training and Assist Team (CITAT)
- Developing regulations and policy guidance for the implementation of a biometric credential for port workers and updating access control regulations and security plan requirements to implement requirements for such a credential
- Establishing policy and policy guidance and overseeing the enforcement of international treaties, conventions, and domestic regulations for domestic onshore and offshore commercial facilities, including deep-water ports and cargoes.
- Coordinating with interdepartmental agencies and other departments on the application of a coordinated cargo safety and security legislations, regulations, standards, and rules
- Coordinating U.S. participation in international maritime groups

FIGURE 10.33   Operation Homeport inspection.

10.3.4.3.1 Operation Homeport   *Homeport* is the code name given by the Coast Guard to signify all of its port activities. The activities are extensive and this short section will only highlight a few of them (Figure 10.33).

Internet Resource: To become familiar with the diverse Homeport functions, visit http://homeport.uscg.mil/mycg/portal/ep/home.do.

10.3.4.3.1.1 Port and Harbor Facilities   Port facilities are subject to a wide array of safety and security standards. Coast Guard personnel inspect the facilities—some 3200 facilities in the United States alone. Each facility is required under the Maritime Security Act of 2002 to develop and implement a security plan. By 2005, some 9500 vessels and 3500 facilities submitted both a security assessment and a security plan. The Coast Guard was entrusted with assessing these plans and, once determining vulnerabilities, working with these parties to adjust and correct deficiencies. Coast Guard inspectors enter the facility to determine the consistency of the plan with the reality of that facility. Breaches in facilities are noted as well as deficiencies relating to record keeping and access control.

Internet Resource: For the federal regulations regarding the content of the security plan, see http://edocket.access.gpo.gov/cfr_2003/julqtr/pdf/33cfr105.305.pdf.

By 2006, the GAO, when reviewing the results of Coast Guard inspections, found patterns of deficiencies.[34] See Figure 10.34 for a chart depicting the results.

Upon the completed inspection, the Coast Guard issues a vulnerability report that the carrier will concur with or appeal (Figure 10.35).

10.3.4.3.1.2 Container Inspection   The Coast Guard deploys teams to moving and stationary vessels for inspection of cargo and containers. The Coast Guard has developed and deployed CITATs to conduct container inspections at harbors and ports.

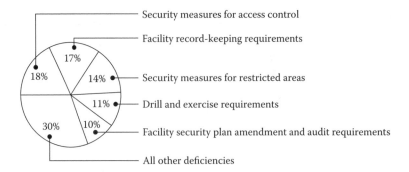

FIGURE 10.34 Types of deficiencies noted by the Coast Guard in facility inspections during 2006.

10.3.4.3.1.3 Vessel Inspection On the high seas and waterways, the Coast Guard has jurisdictional authority to board vessels for inspection purposes. This practice is one of its most crucial missions. Section 89 of Title 14 of the U.S. Code authorizes the Coast Guard to board vessels subject to the jurisdiction of the United States, any time on the high seas and on waters over which the United States has jurisdiction, to make inquiries, examinations, inspections, searches, seizures, and arrests. Even despite the statutory authority, there are multiple reasons why boarding programs exist.

First, the Coast Guard tracks and issues certificates of operation to vessel owners.

Internet Resource: Download the certification form at http://www.uscg.mil/nvdc/nvdc-forms.asp.

Second, the Coast Guard maintains a central depository of vessel records at its National Vessel Documentation Center. Records of registered vessels are fully cataloged and documented and serve as an information center in the event of accident or other calamity.

Third, the Coast Guard boards ships to conduct inspections or to carry out interdiction or intervention actions in the event of criminal activities. In the first instance, the Coast Guard may simply board under a voluntary request for ship inspection (Figure 10.36). To commence the voluntary inspection program, the applicant need only fill out the request as outlined in Figure 10.37. In the latter instance (involuntary boarding), the Coast Guard may board if legally justified. Any question regarding safety, any issue of equipment, and surely any suspicion of illegal activity make boarding, despite a lack of consent, acceptable. When compared with their civilian law enforcement counterparts, whose action generally must be supported by probable cause, the rationale for boarding is much less legally rigorous. The Coast Guard expends considerable energy preparing boarding officers and, just as attentively, refines the boarding process to ensure a professional and legally defensible protocol. The Coast Guard certifies boarding officers in training locales at its network of facilities. The designated curriculum for the boarding officer stresses a legalistic approach to training, as evidenced by the subject matter.

- Authority and jurisdiction
- Use of force

U.S. DEPARTMENT OF HOMELAND SECURITY U.S. COAST GUARD CG-6025 (05/03)	**FACILITY VULNERABILITY AND SECURITY MEASURES SUMMARY**	OMB APPROVAL NO. 1625-0077

An agency may not conduct or sponsor, and a person is not required to respond to a collection of information unless it displays a valid OMB control number.

The Coast Guard estimates that the average burden for this report is 60 minutes. You may submit any comments concerning the accuracy of this burden estimate or any suggestions for reducing the burden to: Commandant (G-MP), U.S. Coast Guard, 2100 2nd St, SW, Washington D.C. 20593-0001 or Office of Management and Budget, Paperwork Reduction Project (1625-0077), Washington, DC 20503.

FACILITY IDENTIFICATION

1. Name of Facility

2. Address of Facility

3. Latitude

4. Longitude

5. Captain of the Port Zone

6. Type of Operation (check all that apply)

☐ Break Bulk ☐ Petroleum ☐ Certain Dangerous Cargo ☐ Passengers (Subchapter H) ☐ If other, explain below:
☐ Dry Bulk ☐ Chemical ☐ Barge Fleeting ☐ Passengers (Ferries)
☐ Container ☐ LHG/LNG ☐ Offshore Support ☐ Passengers (Subchapter K)
☐ RO-RO ☐ Explosives and other dangerous cargo ☐ Military Supply

VULNERABILITY AND SECURITY MEASURES

7a. Vulnerability

7b. Vulnerability Category

☐ If other, explain

8a. Selected Security Measures (MARSEC Level 1)

8b. Security Measures Category

☐ If other, explain

9a. Selected Security Measures (MARSEC Level 2)

9b. Security Measures Category

☐ If other, explain

10a. Selected Security Measures (MARSEC Level 3)

10b. Security Measures Category

☐ If other, explain

VULNERABILITY AND SECURITY MEASURES

7a. Vulnerability

7b. Vulnerability Category

☐ If other, explain

8a. Selected Security Measures (MARSEC Level 1)

8b. Security Measures Category

☐ If other, explain

9a. Selected Security Measures (MARSEC Level 2)

9b. Security Measures Category

☐ If other, explain

10a. Selected Security Measures (MARSEC Level 3)

10b. Security Measures Category

☐ If other, explain

FIGURE 10.35   Facility security and vulnerability measures summary form. (From U.S. Department of Homeland Security.)

FIGURE 10.36 **Coast Guard officers conducting inspections.**

- Tactical procedures
- Criminal law
- Constitutional law
- Defensive tactics
- Arrest procedures
- Maritime law enforcement boarding procedures
- PWCS (ports, waterways and coastal security) boarding procedures
- Confined spaces
- Boating safety regulations
- Commercial fishing industry regulations
- Boating under the influence enforcement
- Testify in court
- Hostage situations
- Fraudulent document

The Coast Guard lays out a precise protocol for boarding a vessel. A uniformed Coast Guard boarding team gives notification of its intent to board. Generally the team is armed. At first, the team will conduct an initial safety inspection to identify any obvious safety hazards and to ensure the sea worthiness of the vessel. The boarding officer will then ask to see the vessel registration or documentation and proceed with the inspection. The scope of the vessel inspection during most boardings is limited to determining the vessel's regulatory status (e.g., commercial, recreational, passenger, cargo, or fishing vessel) and checking for compliance with U.S. civil law applicable to vessels of that status. The Coast Guard may also enforce U.S. criminal law. The boarding officer then completes a Coast Guard boarding form and notes any discrepancies (Figure 10.38).

Space limitations make impossible a full picture of how the U.S. Coast Guard lends its services in the maritime world. In many ways, it is the branch of the service most dedicated to the cause of homeland security. Every minute of its operations is about safety and security, and since 9/11, the Coast Guard has been called on to do more than it has ever

U.S. DEPARTMENT OF HOMELAND SECURITY U.S. COAST GUARD CG-3752 (Rev. 6-04)	APPLICATION FOR INSPECTION OF U.S. VESSEL	FORM APPROVED OMB NO. 1625-0002

An agency may not conduct or sponsor, and a person is not required to respond to, a collection of information unless it displays a valid OMB control number.

The Coast Guard estimates that the average burden for this report is 15 mins. You may submit any comments concerning the accuracy of this burden estimate or any suggestion reducing the burden to: Commandant (G-MOC), U.S. Coast Guard, Washington, DC 20593-0001 or Office of Management and Budget, Paperwork Reduction Project (1625-0002), Washington, DC 20503.

Address to reply to:

TO: Officer in Charge, Marine Inspection

Marine Inspection Zone _____

The undersigned applies to have the ☐ Steam Vessel ☐ Motor Vessel

TELEPHONE NUMBER:

DATE:

☐ Motorboat ☐ Barge ☐ Other *(Indicate)* _____

named _____ Official or Award No. _____

inspected under the laws of the United States; to be employed as a ☐ Passenger Vessel *(No. of Passengers _____)*

☐ Cargo Vessel ☐ Tank Vessel ☐ MODU ☐ Other *(Indicate)* _____

on the following route: *(Waters, Geographical limits)* _____

_____

Liquid cargo in bulk ☐ will ☐ will not be carried as follows:

☐ Flammable or Combustible *(Indicate grade)* _____

☐ Chemicals *(Indicate)* _____

Length of vessel _____ ft.

Hull material: ☐ Steel ☐ Other *(Indicate)* _____

Vessel will be at *(Port, Pier, etc.)* _____

The current Certificate of Inspection expires on _____ .

Inspection is desired on _____ .

Cargo Ship Safety Construction Certificate to be issued by ☐ ABS ☐ USCG.

Vessel ☐ is ☐ is not to be classed.

If classed, indicate Classification Society: ☐ ABS ☐ Other *(Indicate)* _____

I CERTIFY that previous application for this inspection ☐ has ☐ has not been made. I further certify that I have instructed

the master to present the vessel ready in all respects for the above requested inspection on the date specified. I understand that if this inspection is

to be conducted at foreign port or place the vessel owners will be billed for the costs incurred in accordance with 46 USC 385b-1.

(Signature) _____

(Title) _____

FIGURE 10.37 **Application for inspection of a U.S. vessel by the Coast Guard.**

FIGURE 10.38 Coast Guard boarding a vessel for inspection.

imagined since its inception in 1790. Of all the governmental entities called on to strike back and detect our enemies, the Coast Guard has been asked to reinvent itself. A report about the Coast Guard from the Government Accounting Office warned of this tendency to throw everything at this arm of the service.

The difficulty of meeting these challenges is compounded because the Coast Guard is not just moving to a new parent agency: it is also substantially reinventing itself because of its new security role. Basically, the agency faces a fundamental tension in balancing its many missions. It must still do the work it has been doing for years in such areas as fisheries management and search and rescue, but now its resources are deployed as well in homeland security and even in the military buildup in the Middle East. The Coast Guard's expanded role in homeland security, along with its relocation in a new agency, have changed many of its working parameters, and its adjustment to this role remains a work in process. Much work remains.[35]

If history demonstrates anything, it would be the capacity of the Coast Guard to meet any challenge assigned to it. The Coast Guard adapts to meet the mission of homeland protection and makes a mighty contribution in the fight against terrorism.

10.4 Rail and Mass Transit

The task of securing the country's rail and mass transit system is just as critical as the air industry protections. Mass transit systems carry nearly 10 billion passengers per year and the mass transportation fleet is nearly 150,000 vehicles, and the trend toward mass transit is both short term and longitudinally upward (Figure 10.39).

Amtrak carries nearly 31 million passengers on its national network.[36] The country's rail system, a series of weaving lines for both freight and passenger traffic, constitutes a major part of this country's economic life. In the world of commerce, trains deliver more cargo per mile, and more efficiently than any on-land trucking company is capable of doing. "Every day, more than one million shipments of hazardous chemicals are transported throughout

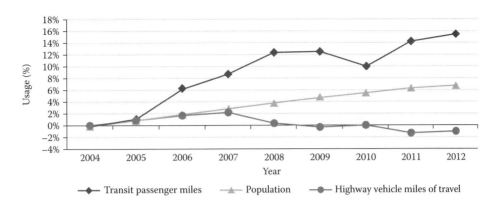

FIGURE 10.39 Since 2004, transit use has grown more than population or highway travel. From: American Public Transportation Association (APTA), *2013 Public Transportation Fact Book* **(Washington, DC: APTA, 2013), 11, http://www.apta.com/resources/statistics/Documents/ FactBook/2013-APTA-Fact-Book.pdf (accessed January 24, 2016).**

the nation's infrastructure; a large percentage of these chemicals are transported by rail and are prone to becoming airborne."[37]

The security of this commercial flow is critical to the economic health of the United States, and just the sort of target a terrorist would hope to disrupt. If terrorists seek to inflict widespread harm on the U.S. economy, they have "a number of strategies that pose serious threats to and through the rail system of the country"[38] (Figure 10.40).

The potential for both human and infrastructural destruction is easy to project and anticipate. For the terrorist, the prime aim generally relates to larger, more grandiose impacts. The act may "use the rails as a way of conveying an instrument of mass destruction on its human agents than an attack on any one point in the physical infrastructure."[39] As a result, the target of mass transit and its infrastructure is attractive due to the strength of its destructive message. A horrid picture of destruction and loss of life occurred in Madrid,

FIGURE 10.40 High-speed passenger train.

FIGURE 10.41   Destroyed railway carriages sit on the tracks after the attack on Atocha railway station in Madrid.

FIGURE 10.42   A family grieves as they stand next to a memorial to victims of the July 2005 bus bombing near Tavistock Square on July 7, 2015 in London, England. This was the 10th anniversary of the 7/7 bombings, when four suicide bombers struck the transport system in central London on Thursday, July 7, 2005, killing 52 people and injuring more than 770 in simultaneous attacks. (Peter Macdiarmid/Getty Images).

Spain, in 2004. Two hundred people lost their lives in this terrorist act (Figure 10.41).[40] In 2005, the London transit bombing is still a searing reality for so many of its victims. Here too the jihadis looked for maximum impact, where concentrations of people in crowded transit systems delivered the harm and terror sought. Londoners recently memorialized the 10th anniversary of this dreadful event (Figure 10.42).

It is extremely logical to conclude that either passenger or freight might be the means of transport, and if the human casualties are the end sought, the terrorist act may predictably occur near an urban center. In the final analysis, both rail and mass transit systems are part of the family of critical infrastructure essential to a secure America. DHS has now rightfully concluded that mass transit systems and rail lines may be the next generation of threat targets.

Internet Exercise: To assess the vulnerabilities of a mass transit system and discover proper steps to prevent terrorism, visit http://www.apta.com/resources/standards/Documents/APTA-SS-SIS-RP-012-13.pdf.

In rail and mass transit, the demands of risk assessment are more global and less contained than the security checkpoint at an airport. TSA, working closely with state, federal, and local law enforcement, must see vulnerability, threat, and risk in a much larger framework. Instead of the targeted emphasis of passengers at a point of entry, the risk analysis in transit and rail must be conducted at various headquarters and stations, as well as in the whole field of operation. The tracks are the path to follow, so to speak. In 2010, TSA published a series of recommendations about rail and mass transit, all of which are worthy of our consideration.

1. Designate a lead agency to coordinate periodic modal and cross-modal security risk analyses.
2. Implement an integrated federal approach that consolidates capabilities in a unified effort for security assessments, audits, and inspections to produce more thorough evaluations and effective follow-up actions to reduce risk, enhance security, and reduce burdens on assessed surface transportation entities.
3. Identify appropriate methodologies to evaluate and rank surface transportation systems and infrastructure that are critical to the nation.
4. Implement a multiyear, multiphase grants program based on a long-term strategy for surface transportation security.
5. Establish a measurable evaluation system to determine the effectiveness of surface transportation security grants.
6. Establish an interagency process to inventory education and training (E&T) requirements and programs; identify gaps and redundancies in surface transportation owner/operator E&T, and ensure that federal training requirements support counterterrorism and infrastructure protection.
7. Implement a unified environment for sharing transportation security information that provides all relevant threat information and improves the effectiveness of information flow.
8. Reemphasize National Infrastructure Protection Plan (NIPP) framework priorities with the Sector-Specific Agencies (SSA); surface transportation owners/operators; and state, local, tribal, and territorial (SLTT) partners in order to focus development and implementation of a relevant and representative model that enhances security of the Transportation Systems Sector partners.
9. Fully identify federal roles and responsibilities in surface transportation security, taking steps to efficiently leverage resources and ultimately lead to a budget "cross cut" that extends federal coordination to include both surface transportation safety and security.
10. Identify an interagency lead to establish a single data repository for all federally obtained security risk–related information on transportation systems and assets.

11. Coordinate data requests with the established single data repository to avoid redundant efforts, take advantage of existing data sets, and establish data access control.
12. Analyze the common features of existing analysis methods and tools, and then perform a gap analysis to identify additional characteristics that would ensure that analyses are more closely comparable and consistent with the risk assessment principles in the NIPP.
13. Define a process to assess and certify extant industry risk assessments for ranking risk remediation projects under the Transit Security Grant Program or other similar federal programs.
14. Establish a fee-based, centrally managed "clearing house" to validate new privately developed security technologies that meet federal standards.
15. Encourage the use of SECURE™ (Systems Efficacy through Commercialization, Utilization, Relevance, and Evaluation) and FutureTECH™ programs within appropriate directives.
16. Create a more efficient federal credentialing system by reducing credentialing redundancy, leveraging existing investments, and implementing the principle of "enroll once, use many" to reuse the information of individuals applying for multiple access privileges.
17. Collaborate with the SCCs to develop a proposal for security threat assessments standards.
18. Incorporate formal and informal methods for surface transportation owners/operators, as well as SCCs that represent them, to provide direct input into setting surface transportation research and development priorities.
19. Develop a formal, recurring surface transportation security grants process for meeting with surface transportation SCCs, owners/operators, and SLTT governments; collecting and adjudicating recommendations; and making final decisions.
20. Review key policy issues and questions identified by the Surface Transportation Security Priority Assessment to address unresolved policy issues and provide solutions for resolving identified security gaps.[41]

With these real threats in mind, DHS has increasingly given higher priority to train and rail over the last few years, strengthened the security of the country's freight and passenger rail systems, and reduced the risk associated with the transportation of security-sensitive materials, such as poisonous inhalation hazard (PIH) materials, certain explosive materials, and certain high-level radioactive material shipments. DHS has also formally codified the right of TSA to inspect rail facilities and equipment for these purposes. DHS works closely with a wide array of other federal agencies to carry out this purpose, including the Department of Transportation, the Federal Railroad Administration, and federal law enforcement agencies concerned about interstate crime and terrorism.[42] DHS also depends on the cooperation of the country's numerous freight carriers, such as CSX, Union Pacific, and others, to carry out its mission on the rails. DHS created a committee of both public and private entities to consult on rail policy. Its members include

- Association of American Railroads
- American Short Line and Regional Railroad Association
- Amtrak
- Anacostia and Pacific
- BNSF Railway Company
- Canadian National
- Canadian Pacific Railway
- CSX Transportation
- Genesee and Wyoming
- Iowa Interstate Railroad Ltd
- Kansas City Southern Railway Company
- Metra
- Norfolk Southern
- RailAmerica
- Union Pacific Railroad Company
- Wheeling and Lake Erie Railway

Both the public and the private sector are stakeholders in ensuring a safe and secure rail and mass transit system. More than 6000 transit service providers, commuter railroads, and long-distance trains travel daily. Nearly 600 transit systems operate in urban areas, while Amtrak provides passenger service on nearly 22,000 miles of track. The story for freight is even more positive (Figure 10.43).

With the rise of gasoline prices, the country's commuter lines are showing extraordinary growth in ridership. As a result of this growth, the security dynamics are intensifying. In November 2008, DHS promulgated rules that ensure a safer system, which include

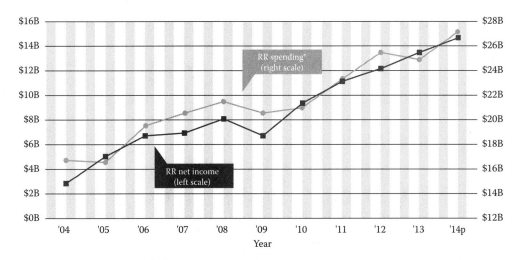

FIGURE 10.43 Net railroad income correlates to railroad spending on capital and maintenance expenditures. * Capital spending plus maintenance costs. Data are for Class I railroads. p = Preliminary. From: Association of American Railroads (AAR), *2015 Outlook* **(Washington, DC: AAR, 2015), https://www.aar.org/Documents/Outlook%202015/2015OutlookReport.pdf (accessed January 24, 2016).**

- *Secure chain of custody*: Shippers will physically inspect security-sensitive materials railcars prior to shipment. The rule is applicable to 46 key urban areas.
- *Communication*: The rule requires freight and passenger railroad carriers, rail transit systems, and certain rail hazardous materials facilities to designate a rail security coordinator (RSC). The RSC will serve as the liaison to DHS for intelligence information, security-related activities, and ongoing communications with TSA.
- *Reporting security concerns*: The rule requires freight and passenger railroads to immediately report incidents, potential threats, and significant security concerns to TSA.
- *Location tracking*: The rule requires freight railroad carriers and certain rail hazardous materials shippers and receivers, at the request of TSA, to report the location of individual railcars containing security-sensitive materials within 5 minutes, and the locations of all cars containing security-sensitive materials within 30 minutes.
- *Inspection authority*: TSA is authorized to inspect freight and passenger railroad carriers, rail transit systems, and certain facilities that ship or receive specified hazardous materials by rail.

TSA, in conjunction with the Federal Transit Administration, has published specific protective measures for mass transit systems. Review this comprehensive list of recommendations in the document from November 2006 entitled *Transit Agency Security and Emergency Management Protective Measures* found at this URL: http://www.trb.org/Main/Blurbs/158319.aspx.

10.4.1 Representative Security Programs for Rail and Transit

To illustrate the emerging homeland security demands for rail, a brief look at some representative programs is in order. Whether for freight or passenger, whether operated by public or private entities, the demand for security protocols has never been greater. Indeed, DHS concluded in 2007 that rail and mass transit operations were woefully inadequate in various areas, including information sharing, research and development, public education, training and exercises, tunnels, and underwater passages (Figure 10.44).[43]

Despite some predictable shortcomings, most rail and transit systems have made enormous strides in the world of homeland security. The GAO concluded that slow but sure

FIGURE 10.44   An engine in the depot awaiting inspection.

improvements to rail security were being made but further improvements were critical to its future as an industry.[44] The GAO also concluded that the rail industry failed to share information as seamlessly as need be in matters of security and called on the industry to make improvements in this direction.[45]

The array of new initiatives in rail and mass transit is beginning to make its mark in the world of homeland security.[46] Aside from inculcating a general theory of risk assessment and mitigation, the industry sees itself as a partner with public officials. A cursory outline of these activities follows:

1. *Layers of security*: The TSA mind-set on the various layers of security has now become part of the rail and mass transit approach.
2. *Transit inspectors through the Surface Transportation Security Program*: 100 officers now inspect the rail infrastructure.
3. *VIPR teams*: Using canines, advanced screening technology, and behavioral detection, the VIPR team can be dispatched to any rail location.
4. *Grants and funding*: The rail industry as well as the public transit systems may participate in funding programs that advance security.
5. *Mobile checkpoints*: An economical way to view containers for security breaches.
6. *Site assessments*: At any location, inspectors and TSA officers can give insight and professional advice on the security and safety of an installation.
7. *Security and Emergency Preparedness Action Items*: The top 20 steps the industry must take to prepare for security risks.
8. *Training for employees*: Security awareness and skill is essential for all employees.
9. *TSA's Land Transportation Anti-terrorism Training Program (LTATP)*: Offered at FLETC.
10. *Connecting communities*: A program that highlights the unique security and emergency issues that arise in transit situations.

10.4.1.1 Amtrak

Amtrak carries out both behind-the-scenes and frontline security measures aimed at improving passenger rail security. Depending on the locale and other factors, the security practices may be uniform or random in design. Some of the common Amtrak security protocols are

- Uniformed police officers and mobile security teams
- Random passenger and carry-on baggage screening
- K-9 units
- Checked baggage screening
- On-board security checks
- Identification checks

Amtrak has also received generous funding for the safety and security of its complex infrastructure. In the Northeast corridor, Amtrak operates in diverse environments with dramatic challenges for the security operative. In 2008, DHS awarded $25 million to Amtrak to begin the process of securing bridges, tunnels, overhangs, and other locations with target potential. That sum has either been renewed or increased until the present.[47] Preparedness grants have been regularly awarded to Amtrak and other intercity passenger rail programs since that time. In 2015, DHS provided more than $10 million to protect critical surface transportation infrastructure and the traveling public from acts of terrorism and increase the resilience of the Amtrak rail system.[48]

Amtrak now deploys specialized mobile tactical units that conduct random baggage searches and other security responsibilities. The mobile security team's squads take on many forms, including armed specialized Amtrak police, explosive-detecting K-9 units, and armed counterterrorism special agents in tactical uniforms. The mobile units were developed in conjunction with the federal, state, and private industry sectors to improve security practices. The mobile security team's procedures will not impact train schedules (Figure 10.45).

The new procedures are an enhancement to strategic security measures already in place, such as

- Uniformed police and plainclothes officers on trains and in stations
- Security cameras
- Random identification checks
- "See Something, Say Something" passenger education program to promote involvement and raise vigilance
- Investments in state-of-the-art security technology
- Security awareness training for the entire Amtrak workforce
- Behind-the-scenes activities that remain undisclosed

Amtrak is also investing in cutting-edge technologies to improve its security efforts and is presently testing intrusion detection technologies, employing explosive detection and vapor K-9 teams, conducting more passenger screenings, and actively participating in the joint terrorism task forces in its various regions. Finally, Amtrak is calling on its customer base to be active players in the security effort. Through its Partners for Amtrak Safety and Security (PASS) program, customers are asked to be active participants in the who, what, where, when, and how of criminal conduct.

Internet Exercise: Learn about the PASS program at https://pass.amtrak.com.

FIGURE 10.45   Amtrak's Mobile Tactical Unit helps secure the railways.

10.4.1.2 CSX: The Freight Line

Just as the public rail entities have core responsibilities, so too do the private rail companies. CSX is an excellent example of a progressive freight shipper with a massive route network in the eastern half of the United States. It, like all other rail concerns, has had to reconsider how it carries out its business since 9/11. As noted, shipments of hazardous and security-sensitive materials are subject to a host of regulations and other requirements.[49] Railroads also must

- Compile security data based on commodity and route type
- Identify security vulnerabilities
- Identify alternative routes
- Develop programs of safety and security
- Revisit route selections
- Communicate with state and federal officials
- Design tracking systems for sensitive material
- Work in unity with the motor carriers whose cargo the rail transports

See Figure 10.46 for a map of CSX's rail system.

CSX, just as its sister carriers, abides by a host of regulations. Of recent interest are the TSA requirements that shipments to designated urban areas be processed according to new protocols, and additionally, that the chain of custody of these shipments be tracked. The materials subject to the rules include explosives, toxic inhalation hazard (TIH) materials, PIH materials, and bulk amounts of radioactive materials, all of which are now designated rail security-sensitive materials.

TSA now insists that certain rail secure areas be the exclusive points of shipping or receiving. As of February 15, 2009, rail companies, such as CSX, are only able to accept shipments of rail security-sensitive materials from rail secure areas. In areas designated high-threat urban areas (HTUA), delivery will only be possible to a rail secure area.

Another facet of the new rules on rail shipments will involve written certifications of compliance. Shipments of rail security-sensitive materials are subject to TSA chain-of-custody requirements. The rules require (1) all consignors and (2) those consignees located in a HTUA to have personnel physically present for attended handoffs of all railcars containing rail security-sensitive materials. TSA has promulgated that it expects the personnel attending the handoff of railcars with rail security-sensitive materials to document the transfer by recording (1) each railcar's initials and number, (2) the individuals attending the transfer, (3) the location of the transfer, and (4) the date and time of the transfer. Contending with new rules of the road will be an ongoing demand for the freight industry (Figure 10.47).

Internally, CSX has established a sophisticated and impressive security and safety program. Aside from its materials training, emphasis on employee safety, and other industrial applications, CSX fully comprehends the mix of the public and private interests in its rail operation. The line shares information with governmental entities and partners, with myriad agencies dedicated to safety and security. Examples of these efforts are

CSX SYSTEM MAP

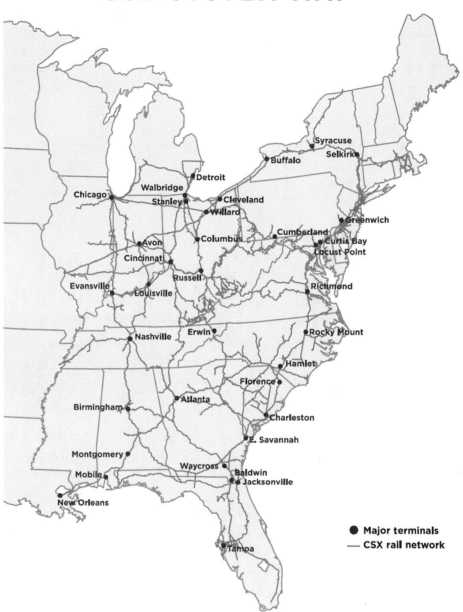

FIGURE 10.46 CSX rail system map.

- CSX Transportation's (CSXT) Network Operations Workstation (NOW): A cornerstone of this partnership is CSXT's sharing of its highly specialized secure NOW system. Key highlights of the NOW system include
  - Enhanced monitoring: Provides state homeland security and law enforcement officials with a tool to identify the status of CSXT trains and railcars in each state. Before, officials needed to call CSXT to access this information.

FIGURE 10.47   CSX freight train.

- Information sharing: Helps security officials prepare for and, if needed, respond to emergency situations.
- Targeted security: With additional information about what is carried on rails, state officials can more efficiently allocate law enforcement resources, coordinate with CSXT security officials, and integrate rail security into ongoing law enforcement operations.
- Joint law enforcement and emergency responder training: Law enforcement officials train with the CSXT Police Rapid Response Team—a group of highly skilled police officers specifically trained to respond to security incidents. Additionally, state and community emergency first responders train alongside CSXT's experts in hazardous materials and emergency response.
- Sharing of hazardous materials density studies: These data help emergency response organizations plan their resources and identify the types of emergency response training applicable to their jurisdiction.
- Closer coordination of law enforcement operations in and around CSXT yards: CSXT can provide its partners with around-the-clock access to its rail security professionals.
- Developing better rail security policies: States and CSXT continue to work with policymakers to identify important public policy issues that can impact and improve rail security.

CSX, like its counterparts in the industry, sees the world in differing terms than pre-9/11. The industry works closely with local, state, and federal authorities to secure the nation's railroads. Freight railroads remain in constant communication with the U.S. Department of Transportation security personnel, the FBI, the National Security Council, and state and local law enforcement officers.

10.4.1.3 SEPTA: Rail Mass Transit

The Southeastern Pennsylvania Transit Authority (SEPTA) is one of the nation's largest rail commuter systems. It also connects and collaborates with other carriers and is part and parcel of a very large collective of mass transit providers, including New Jersey Transit, Delaware Area Transit, and Amtrak. The system can readily and very easily hook up the rider to New York, Baltimore, and Washington, DC. In this extreme congestion, SEPTA needs to always be mindful of the security threat (Figure 10.48).

Prevention of future terrorist attacks is both a national and a local concern. SEPTA takes the threat of terrorism very seriously. Passengers are afforded maximum security and protection. Increased presence of transit police officers on the system's cars and stations have been a high priority for SEPTA management. Also present throughout the transit system, although obviously less visible, is a trained team of undercover, plainclothes SEPTA police officers who are working to ensure the security of our passengers.

SEPTA's police officers have been thoroughly trained in antiterrorism awareness. Specially trained officers have instructed additional SEPTA personnel in an antiterrorism program that includes recognition, response, and prevention techniques.

Internet Resource: Learn about careers in law enforcement in SEPTA at http://autohire. careershop.com/septajobs/default.asp?ContentID=7.

See Figure 10.49 for a route map from SEPTA.

Yet when one considers the sheer volume of passengers on this system day to day, are these general recommendations enough? Does a transit police force have the capability to trace and track every imaginable threat? Is the geography alone too much to cover? Most observers of mass transit indicate there are simply too many holes in the dike to be confident about thwarting the terrorist threat—and just as frustratingly, too many players in the overall mix. To be successful, mass transit systems will have to be better organized. Here are some suggestions:

FIGURE 10.48 SEPTA's Wilmington, Delaware station.

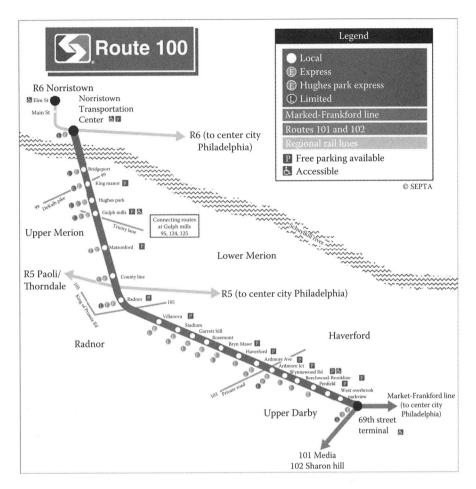

FIGURE 10.49 **Railway route map. (From Southeastern Pennsylvania Transport Authority. Maps and stations. http://www.septa.org/maps/.)**

TSA's 17 Security and Emergency Preparedness Action Items

1. Establish written System Security Programs and Emergency Management Plans.
2. Define roles and responsibilities for security and emergency management.
3. Ensure that operations and maintenance supervisors, forepersons, and managers are held accountable for security issues under their control.
4. Coordinate Security and Emergency Management Plan(s) with local and regional agencies.
5. Establish and maintain a security and emergency training program.
6. Establish plans and protocols to respond to the DHS Homeland Security Advisory System threat levels.
7. Implement and reinforce a public security and emergency awareness program.
8. Conduct table top and functional drills.
9. Establish and use a risk management process to assess and manage threats, vulnerabilities, and consequences.

10. Participate in an information-sharing process for threat and intelligence information.
11. Establish and use a reporting process for suspicious activity (internal and external).
12. Control access to security-critical facilities with identification badges for all visitors, employees, and contractors.
13. Conduct physical security inspections.
14. Conduct background investigations of employees and contractors.
15. Control access to documents of security-critical systems and facilities.
16. Implement a process for handling and access to sensitive security information.
17. Conduct security program audits.[50]

While all of the recommendations are poignant, the training side of the security and risk plan cannot be forgotten or neglected. In every facet of mass transit, the risk to passengers and employees is high. Those entrusted with transit operation must be sure to train the employees to the highest level. TSA has devised an excellent matrix of learning to assure that the essential subject matter is covered and that costs are contained (Figure 10.50).

10.5 Conclusion

Transportation runs heavily throughout the pages of this chapter. More specifically, the chapter delves into the full menu of TSA activities. The most visible of homeland departments, TSA, is now part of the fabric of travel and travel installations. Usually associated with airports, TSA has additional responsibilities involving public roads, bridges, rail, pipelines, and train stations. At its base, TSA is responsible for transportation threat assessment and vulnerability, the promulgation of standards and practices regarding safety and security, and the anticipation of novel innovations in the homeland dimension. Trace portals, millimeter wave machines, and biometrics are examples of how technology impacts TSA operations. TSA adopts a policy of layered security, whereby at various stages of security scrutiny it is unlikely that a terrorist will escape each and every level of oversight.

Other transportation initiatives highlighted in this chapter include the federal air marshal, federal flight deck officers, and law enforcement officers flying armed. Each of these programs provides an added layer of armed protection in the air travel industry. TSA employs canines in various components of its practices, especially regarding explosives.

The chapter looks intently on how homeland functions are pertinent to the world of the maritime. The prevention of terrorist attacks on maritime critical infrastructure, the safeguarding of oceans and corresponding resources, and the minimization of economic losses in the maritime domain are highly relevant homeland functions. In implementing the National Strategy for Maritime Security, DHS operatives accept the broad-based perspective on what constitutes the maritime domain and rely heavily on the maritime industry to advise as to best practices. In maritime security, government and commerce work collaboratively. Featured with rightful relevancy is the role and function of the U.S. Coast Guard, which naturally operates in the maritime. The Coast Guard, as part of its

Training description	Focus	Categories of employees to receive										Total training cost
		Front line employees	Station managers	Administrative and support staff	Maintenance workers	Mid-Level management	Senior management	Operations control center staff	Security guards	Law enforcement		
Security awareness	Enhance capability to identify, report, and react to suspicious activity and security incidents											$0
Behavior recognition	Recognize behaviors associated with terrorists' reconnaissance and planning activities, including the conduct of surveillance. Applies lessons learned from the Israeli security meeting.											$0
Immediate emergency response	Prepare passenger rail train operators to deal with explosive detonations, incendiaries, released chemical hazards, and similar threats in the confines of trains and system infrastructure.											$0
National incident management system (NIMS)	Ensure transit agency emergency preparedness and response personnel gain and retain the knowledge and skills necessary to operate under NIMS in accordance with the National Response Plan (NRP).											$0

FIGURE 10.50   Basic mass transit security training program. (From: Transportation Security Administration. www.tsa.gov.)

Training description	Focus	Categories of employees to receive									Total training cost
		Front line employees	Station managers	Administrative and support staff	Maintenance workers	Mid-Level management	Senior management	Operations control center staff	Security guards	Law enforcement	
Operations control Center readiness	Identify security vulnerabilities. Understand and exercise role of OCC personnel in preventing terrorist attacks. Distinguish characteristics of improvised explosive devices (IEDs) and weapons of mass destruction. Specify priorities during a terrorist attack and manage incident response. Apply transit agency's operational plans for response to IED and WMD scenarios, directing and coordinating activities in the system.											$0

Mass transit security follow-on courses

Training description	Focus	Front line employees	Station managers	Administrative and support staff	Maintenance workers	Mid-Level management	Senior management	Operations control center staff	Security guards	Law enforcement	Total training cost
Management of transit emergencies I (4-day course)	Ensure employees throughout the transit agency understand individual roles in emergency response and the transit system's role in emergencies or disasters in the system and the broader community.										$0

FIGURE 10.50   (Continued).

Management of transit emergencies II (1-day course)	Ensure employees throughout the transit agency understand individual roles in emergency response and the transit system's role in emergencies or disasters in the system and the broader community.								$0
Coordinated interagency emergency response	Advance interoperability of the transit agency with multiple responding entities in emergency response.				░	░	░		$0
Managing counterterrorism programs	Enable transit agency management officials to develop and manage a counterterrorism program in a transit system.	░		░			░	░	$0
Prevention and mitigation—IEDS and WMD: T4 3-day course	Enhance capabilities to identify threats from improvised explosive devices and weapons of mass destruction (chemical, biological, radiological, nuclear) to identify, report, and react to suspicious activity and security incidents				░	░			$0

FIGURE 10.50 (Continued).

Training description	Focus	Mass transit security follow-on courses									Total training cost
		Front line employees	Station managers	Administrative and support staff	Maintenance workers	Mid-Level management	Senior management	Operations control center staff	Security guards	Law enforcement	
Prevention and Mitigation—IEDS and WMD: CBRNE Incident Management 1-day course	Enhance capabilities to identify threats from improvised explosive devices and weapons of mass destruction (chemical, biological, radiological, nuclear) to identify, report, and react to suspicious activity and security incidents.										$0
Transit vehicle hijacking prevention and response	Enable employees to develop and implement plans and procedures to respond to transit vehicle hijackings and workplace violence.										$0
Integrated anti-terrorism security program	Enhance capabilities of transit agency security officials, law enforcement personnel, and others with interaction with passengers to detect, deter, and prevent acts of terrorism.										$0
Transit system security design	Expand integration of security considerations into designs of new transit systems and improvements of existing systems.										$0

FIGURE 10.50 (Continued).

Training description	Focus	Categories of employees to receive									Total training cost
		Front line employees	Station managers	Administrative nd support taff	Maintenance workers	Mid-Level management	Senior management	Operations control center staff	Security guards	Law enforcement	
Security a wareness train-the-trainer	Enhance capability to identify, report, and react to suspicious activity and security incidents.										$0
Behavior recognition train-the-trainer	Recognize behaviors associated with terrorists' reconnaissance and planning activities, including the conduct of surveillance. Applies lessons learned from the Israeli security meeting.										$0

Total training costs—all courses

FIGURE 10.50 (Continued).

core mission, provides maritime safety and security in multiple contexts. In addition, the Coast Guard needs to maintain mobility in waterways and other ports of interest, assist in the protection of natural resources, respond to emergencies and catastrophes, and is part of the U.S. national defense. In each of these categories, the Coast Guard's history displays extraordinary success. Saving thousands of lives is simply the mission, a Coastie would argue. Aside from the endless plucking of victims from water peril, the Coast Guard operates the premier SAR team—legendary in both requirements and results. The Coast Guard wears comfortably the hat of law enforcement as well, by targeting smugglers and drug traffickers, terrorists, and other undesirables. The Coast Guard operates a specialized facility to train its members in law enforcement functions—the Maritime Law Enforcement Academy in Charleston, South Carolina. The sweep of Coast Guard services is difficult to fully catalog since, aside from all these functions, the command deals with port and harbor protections, container and vessel inspection, offshore drilling facilities, cargo safety, and environmental crimes. The Coast Guard's Homeport program encompasses all of these activities.

Finally, the chapter takes a close look at the rail and mass transit industry. While rail is both publicly and privately operated, the types of mass transit make full coverage an impossibility. Hence, the stress here is on rail, due to its potential to be a medium of delivery for the terrorist, or the locus with the most potential for human loss of life. As in Spain a few years ago, the compelling and hideous impact of a terrorist on a train system has unfortunately been displayed. How Amtrak, CSX, and the SEPTA system address the many challenges of homeland security is fully assessed.

Keywords

Baggage screening
Boarding officer
Canine explosive detection unit
Cargo and Facilities Division
Certificate of operation
Container Inspection Training and
  Assistance Team
Department of Commerce
Federal air marshal
Federal Aviation Administration
Federal flight deck officer
Federal Highway Administration
Inspection and Compliance Directorate
Law enforcement officer flying armed
Maritime security
Mass transit
Millimeter wave

Mobile tactical unit
National Strategy for Maritime Security
National Vessel Documentation Center
Operation Homeport
Operation Noble Eagle
Passenger screening
Poisonous inhalation hazard
Rail secure area
Rail security-sensitive material
Rail transit system
Registered Traveler program
Search and rescue team
Security threat assessment
Toxic inhalation hazard
Trace portal
Transportation security
Transportation Security Administration

Discussion Questions

1. The Coast Guard Container Inspection Program assumes much about our trading partners. Comment.
2. In what way has trade and commerce benefited from electronic tracking and computer systems?
3. Some argue that U.S. Citizenship and Immigration Services is delving into activities best left to other historic agencies. Can you identify an example of where this criticism might be relevant?
4. TSA is often labeled a reactive agency that gives little thought to its practices. Do you think this conclusion is reasonable in any sense?
5. Why does TSA have such turnover problems in personnel?
6. Explain why the layered security practice of TSA works so effectively.
7. How should TSA be a leader in the use of technology and computer innovation in its practices?
8. How do biometric measures replace human function and task?
9. The Coast Guard is often labeled as an entity being asked to do everything and even more. How is this so? And how has this condition led to stresses in the Coast Guard?
10. Discuss some of the more recent plans and programs designed for the maritime world.
11. Discuss three programs of the Coast Guard that deal with vessels and law enforcement function.
12. Why is rail and mass transit rail such a difficult industry in which to apply uniform standards?
13. Of the three types of rail systems—namely, freight, passenger, and public mass transit—which has the greatest demands when it comes to security issues?

Practical Exercises

1. Evaluate TSA's 20 layers of security. Which could readily be eliminated and why?
2. Prepare a career file with representative positions for the following occupations:
   - Federal air marshal
   - Federal flight deck officer
   - TSA
   - TSA canine
3. Review the career options in the Coast Guard. Explain how many of the career paths deal with homeland security. Provide at least three examples.
4. Prepare a mock vessel inspection request for the U.S. Coast Guard.
5. Contact your local mass transit provider. Find out what steps the entity has taken relative to homeland security preparedness.

Notes

1. K. Vlahos, Pat-down dust-up renews screening debate, *Homeland Security Today*, June, 2011: 10–11.

2. TSA, Social media, https://www.tsa.gov/news/social_media (accessed January 23, 2016).

3. For some representative examples of TSA abuse and unprofessionalism, visit the following links: Failure rate of inspections at airport facilities: K. Pavlich, Surprise: TSA hasn't improved since failing 95 percent of security tests, Townhall, November 4, 2015, http://townhall.com/tipsheet/katiepavlich/2015/11/04/surprise-tsa-is-still-sucking-terribly-n2075370; J. Fishel, P. Thomas, M. Levine, and J. Date, Undercover DHS tests find security failures at US airports, ABC News, June 1, 2015, http://abcnews.go.com/US/exclusive-undercover-dhs-tests-find-widespread-security-failures/story?id=31434881; on the failure rate on weapons and explosives: E. Bradner and R. Marsh, Acting TSA director reassigned after screeners failed tests to detect explosives, weapons, CNN, June 2, 2015, http://www.cnn.com/2015/06/01/politics/tsa-failed-undercover-airport-screening-tests; on TSA as an institutional failure as an operating agency: M. Fox, TSA a failure at every level: Security expert, CNBC, June 9, 2015, http://www.cnbc.com/2015/06/09/tsa-a-failure-at-every-level-security-expert.html, accessed August 16, 2016.

4. E. Ashford, More than a revenue source, *Community College Daily*, September 11, 2015, http://www.ccdaily.com/Pages/Workforce-Development/Corporate-colleges-are-more-than-a-revenue-source.aspx, accessed August 16, 2016.

5. There have been increasing, unrelenting calls for the TSA to be privatized; see: C. Edwards, Privatizing the transportation security administration, *Policy Analysis*, 742, November 19, 2013, http://object.cato.org/sites/cato.org/files/pubs/pdf/pa742_web_1.pdf, accessed August 16, 2016.

6. C. J. Ciaramella, Abolish the TSA, *The Washington Post*, April 16, 2015, https://www.washingtonpost.com/posteverything/wp/2015/04/16/abolish-the-tsa/?utm_term=.bcb5d054cad8, August 16, 2016.

7. Statement of Jennifer Grover, acting director, Homeland Security and Justice, Explosives detection canines: TSA has taken steps to analyze canine team data and assess the effectiveness of passenger screening canines (Testimony before the Subcommittee on Transportation Security, Committee on Homeland Security, House of Representatives), GAO-14-695T, June 24, 2014, http://www.gao.gov/assets/670/664331.pdf (accessed January 24, 2016).

8. GAO, Aviation security: TSA has made progress, but additional efforts are needed to improve security, *GAO Highlights*, 2011.

9. A. Sternstein, Experts chide TSA for poor risk assessment of security measures, NextGov.com, September 30, 2011, http://www.nextgov.com/technology-news/2011/09/experts-chide-tsa-for-poor-risk-assessment-of-security-measures/49866, accessed August 16, 2016. See also: GAO, Aviation security: A national strategy and other actions would strengthen TSA's efforts to secure commercial airport perimeters and access controls, September 30, 2009, http://www.gao.gov/assets/300/296396.pdf, accessed August 16, 2016.

10. TSA, *Enterprise Risk Management: ERM Policy Manual* (August 2014), 8, https://www.aferm.org/wp-content/uploads/2015/10/TSA-ERM-Policy-Manual-August-2014.pdf, accessed August 16, 2016.

11. TSA, Innovation & technology, July 10, 2011, http://www.tsa.gov.

12. The TSA Blog, TSA travel tips Tuesday: Traveling with personal medical electronic devices, February 25, 2014, http://blog.tsa.gov/2014/02/tsa-travel-tips-tuesday-blog-post.html (accessed January 24, 2016).

13. Privacy problems sprinkle throughout the world of DHS and homeland defense. See B. K. Collins and H. Morrow, Using shared technology in bioterrorism planning and response: Do privacy laws affect administrative judgments? *The Homeland Security Review*, 4, 2010: 43.

14. DHS, Privacy assessment update for TSA advance imaging technology, December 18, 2015, https://www.dhs.gov/sites/default/files/publications/privacy-tsa-pia-32-d-ait.pdf (accessed January 24, 2016).

15. DHS, Privacy impact assessment update for TSA advanced imaging technology, January 25, 2011, http://www.dhs.gov/xlibrary/assets/privacy/privacy-pia-tsa-ait.pdf, accessed August 16, 2016.

16. Article—The Sky's the Limit, Article—Asking the Right Questions; DHS, Privacy impact assessment update for TSA advanced imaging technology, January 25, 2011, http://www.dhs.gov/xlibrary/assets/privacy/privacy-pia-tsa-ait.pdf, accessed January 24, 2016.

17. Biometrics.gov, Introduction to biometrics, 1, http://www.biometrics.gov/Documents/BioOverview.pdf, accessed January 24, 2016.

18. P. Wolfhope, Mobile biometric devices: What the future holds, *The Police Chief*, September, 2011: 38–40.

19. FBI, About the Biometric Center of Excellence, https://www.fbi.gov/about-us/cjis/fingerprints_biometrics/biometric-center-of-excellence/about/about-the-biometric-center-of-excellence (accessed January 24, 2016).

20. DHS, Privacy impact assessment update for the credential authentication technology/boarding pass scanning system, August 11, 2009, http://www.dhs.gov/xlibrary/assets/privacy/privacy_pia_tsa_catbpss.pdf.

21. J. Wade, Maritime security, *Risk Management*, 52, December 2005: 40.

22. A. G. Grynkewich, Maritime homeland defense, *Air and Space Power Journal*, Winter 2007: 86.

23. Maritime Transportation Security Act of 2002, P.L. 107–295, *U.S. Statutes at Large* 116, 2002: 2064.

24. Office of the President, *The National Strategy for Maritime Security* (Washington, DC: U.S. Government Printing Office, 2005), http://www.whitehouse.gov/homeland/4844-nsms.pdf (accessed January 24, 2016).

25. At present there is a good bit of discussion as to the future structure and organization of maritime domain awareness. MDA.gov, *Maritime Domain Awareness: Reconsidering Governance, Structure and Organization*, December 9, 2010, http://www.mda.gov/2010/12/09/maritime-domain-awareness-reconsidering-governance-structure-and-organization, accessed January 24, 2016.

26. U.S. Coast Guard, SAR program information, http://www.uscg.mil/hq/cg5/cg534/SAR_Program_Info.asp (accessed January 24, 2016).

27. 14 U.S. Code, section 2, 2008.

28. President's Council on Integrity and Efficiency, *Quality Standards for Investigations* (Washington, DC: U.S. Government Printing Office, 2003), 17, http://www.ignet.gov/pande/standards/invstds.pdf, accessed January 24, 2016.

29. U.S. Coast Guard, Office of Counterterrorism and Defense operations policy: Ports, waterways and coastal security, https://www.uscg.mil/hq/cg5/cg532/pwcs.asp (accessed January 24, 2016).

30. D. Philpott, Improving the security of U.S. harbors and seaports, *Homeland Defense Journal*, November 2007: 31

31. K. L. Walters III, Industry on alert: Legal and economic ramifications of homeland security act on maritime commerce, *Tulane Maritime Law Journal*, 30, 2006: 311.

32. Walters, Industry on alert, 334–35.

33. M. Florestal, Terror on the high seas: The trade and development implications of the U.S. National Security Measures, *Brooklyn Law Review*, 72, 2007: 441.

34. GAO, *Maritime Security: Coast Guard Inspections Identify and Correct Facility Deficiencies* (Washington, DC: U.S. Government Printing Office, 2008), 1, http://www.gao.gov/new.items/d0812.pdf, accessed January 24, 2016.

35. GAO, *Homeland Security: Challenges Facing the Coast Guard as It Transitions to a New Department* (Washington, DC: U.S. Government Printing Office, 2003), 1, http://www.gao.gov/new.items/d03467t.pdf, accessed January 24, 2016.

36. Amtrak, National fact sheet: FY 2014, https://www.amtrak.com/ccurl/101/724/Amtrak-National-Fact-Sheet-FY2014,0.pdf (accessed January 24, 2016).

37. R. C. Paolino, All aboard: Making the case for a comprehensive rerouting policy to reduce the vulnerability of hazardous rail-cargoes to terrorist attack, *Military Law Review*, 193, 2007: 144.

38. J. Plant, Terrorism and the railroads: Redefining security in the wake of 9/11, *Review of Policy Research*, 293, 2004: 301.

39. J. Plant, Terrorism and the railroads, 301.

40. Waiting for al-Qaeda's next bomb, *The Economist* May 3, 2007: 29; A. Loukaitou-Sideris et al., Rail transit security in an international context: Lessons from four cities, *Urban Affairs Review*, 41(6), 2006: 21; B. Johnstone, *New Strategies to Protect America: Terrorism and Mass Transit after London and Madrid* (Washington, DC: Center For American Progress, 2005), 21; M. Sanadjian, Fear, terror, and the new global economy of salvation-global excess and "suicide" bombing of London, *Social Identities*, 12(6), 2006: 701–725.

41. The White House, *Surface Transportation Security Priority Assessment*, March 2010, http://www.white-house.gov/sites/default/files/rss_viewer/STSA.pdf, accessed January 24, 2016.

42. Congressional Research Service, *Transportation Security: Issues for the 112th Congress*, February 1, 2011, http://www.fas.org/sgp/crs/homesec/RL33512.pdf, accessed January 24, 2016.

43. DHS, Transportation systems: Critical infrastructure and key resources sector specific plan as input to the National Infrastructure Protection Plan A81-81, 2007, http://www.cfr.org/us-strategy-and-politics/transportation-systems-critical-infrastructure-key-resources-sector-specific-plan-input-national-infrastructure-protection-plan/p14638, accessed January 24, 2016.

44. GAO, Rail security: TSA improved risk assessment but could further improve training and information sharing, June 14, 2011, http://www.gao.gov/assets/130/126419.html, accessed January 24, 2016.

45. GAO, *Transit Security Information Sharing: DHS Could Improve Information Sharing through Streamlining and Increased Outreach* (Washington, DC: GAO, September 2010), http://www.gao.gov/new.items/d10895.pdf, accessed January 24, 2016. See also GAO, Rail security.

46. GAO, *Positive Train Control: Additional Oversight Needed as Most Railroads Do Not Expect to Meet 2015 Implementation Deadline*, GAO-15-739 (Washington, DC: GAO, September 2015), http://www.gao.gov/assets/680/672320.pdf (accessed January 24, 2016); GAO, *Passenger Rail Security: Consistent Incident Reporting and Analysis Needed to Achieve Program Objectives*, GAO-13-20 (Washington, DC: GAO, December 2012), http://www.gao.gov/assets/660/650995.pdf (accessed January 24, 2016).

47. DHS, Office of Inspector General, *DHS Grants Used for Mitigating Risk to Amtrak Rail Stations* (Washington, DC: DHS, March 2010), http://www.documentcloud.org/documents/240714-dhs-grants-used-for-mitigating-risks-to-amtrak.html (accessed January 24, 2016).

48. DHS, DHS announces grant guidance for fiscal year (FY) 2015 preparedness grants, http://www.dhs.gov/news/2015/04/02/dhs-announces-grant-guidance-fiscal-year-fy-2015-preparedness-grants (accessed January 24, 2016).

49. J. B. Reed, Securing dangerous rail shipments, *State Legislatures*, 38 (October/November 2007).

50. DHS, Office of Inspector General, *TSA's Preparedness for Mass Transit and Passenger Rail Emergencies* (Washington, DC: DHS, March 2010), 32, https://www.oig.dhs.gov/assets/Mgmt/OIG_10-68_Mar10.pdf, accessed January 24, 2016.

Chapter 11

Homeland Security and Public Health

Objectives

1. To define the various public health concerns in the field of homeland security
2. To outline the various agencies involved in public health risks in homeland security
3. To comprehend the various methods that may be used in an attack on the public water supply
4. To describe how vulnerability assessments are used in the protection of the country's water and food supplies
5. To comprehend the various methods that may be used in an attack on the public food supply
6. To identify the programs in place to protect and test the country's food supply
7. To explain the various infectious and communicable diseases that can be used as tools of terrorism
8. To list the various pandemic threats that may be used in a terror attack

11.1 Introduction

At first glance, it seems that public health and homeland security are unrelated in scope and design. Nothing could be farther from the truth, for questions involving public health inexorably wind their way back to issues of safety and security in a host of contexts. By any reasonable intersect, health dilemmas, whether infectious, toxic, metabolic, or otherwise, and regardless of intent or national origin, can cause significant harm to both individuals and the collective. The entire world of biotoxins injures by attacking the physical integrity of the body. For example, anthrax's confrontation is not with the mind, but the body itself. Pathogens, chemical release agents, and biological and chemical substances can wreak havoc on individual chemistry, let alone the communal sense of tranquility. As has been witnessed with these types of threats, the fear of the result appears more pronounced than the possible delivery of a dirty bomb.[1] Assaults on the public health can have catastrophic consequences. The destruction of the water supply by the delivery of a toxic substance or the release of a chemical or bacteriological agent into the air impacts many. Catastrophic health events, such as a terrorist attack with a weapon of mass destruction, a naturally occurring pandemic, or a calamitous meteorological or geological event, likely would inflict death and destruction in incalculable numbers. These same events would undermine the economic and social fabric, weaken the infrastructure of defense, cause tens or hundreds of thousands of casualties or more, damage public morale and confidence, and threaten our national security. When one considers the potentiality for a public health attack, it no longer seems folly to connect its prevention to the world of homeland defense.

The Department of Homeland Security (DHS) fully connects the dots of health and security in both its mission and operations. In fact, health is one of its 16 critical areas of infrastructure (Boxes 11.1 and 11.2).[2]

Hospitals, labs, pharmaceutical companies, water and energy companies, and a host of aligned facilities all play a key role in the event of an attack on the public health.[3] DHS is not the sole agency entrusted with this sort of assessment since others need to be involved, such as HHS, the EPA, the Department of Energy, and the Departments of the Interior and Agriculture. While space cannot allow for coverage of each and every element in the health sector, this section will assess the more commonly known homeland–public health connections.

11.2 Water

It would be difficult to name a more essential component to physical life than water itself. Treatment plants have been a target of the terrorist, and in a perverse way, successful access to a treatment plant would be a dramatic victory for America's enemies. The EPA assumes the lead role in the protection of our water supply from a public health attack. As in all aspects of traditional American life, 9/11 triggered a new way of looking at water facilities. Soon after 9/11, Congress passed the Public Health Security and Bioterrorism Preparedness and Response Act of 2002 (Public Law No: 107-188), which zeroed in on the horrid possibility of water contamination as an act of terror. In Section 402 of the act it states:

> VULNERABILITY ASSESSMENTS—(1) Each community water system serving a population of greater than 3,300 persons shall conduct an assessment of the vulnerability of its system to a terrorist attack or other intentional acts intended to substantially disrupt the ability of the system to provide a safe and reliable supply of drinking water. The vulnerability assessment shall include, but not be limited to, a review of pipes and constructed conveyances, physical

11.1 VULNERABILITY ASSESSMENT FACTSHEET

What Is the Purpose of Vulnerability Assessments?

Vulnerability assessments help water systems evaluate susceptibility to potential threats and identify corrective actions that can reduce or mitigate the risk of serious consequences from adversarial actions (e.g., vandalism, insider sabotage, terrorist attack, etc.). Such an assessment for a water system takes into account the vulnerability of the water supply (both ground and surface water), transmission, treatment, and distribution systems. It also considers risks posed to the surrounding community related to attacks on the water system. An effective vulnerability assessment serves as a guide to the water utility by providing a prioritized plan for security upgrades, modifications of operational procedures, and/or policy changes to mitigate the risks and vulnerabilities to the utility's critical assets. The vulnerability assessment provides a framework for developing risk reduction options and associated costs. Water systems should review their vulnerability assessments periodically to account for changing threats or additions to the system to ensure that security objectives are being met. Preferably, a vulnerability assessment is *performance based*, meaning that it evaluates the risk to the water system based on the effectiveness (performance) of existing and planned measures to counteract adversarial actions.

What Are the Basic Elements of Vulnerability Assessments?

The following are common elements of vulnerability assessments. These elements are conceptual in nature and not intended to serve as a detailed methodology.

1. Characterization of the water system, including its mission and objectives
2. Identification and prioritization of adverse consequences to avoid
3. Determination of critical assets that might be subject to malevolent acts that could result in undesired consequences
4. Assessment of the likelihood (qualitative probability) of such malevolent acts from adversaries
5. Evaluation of existing countermeasures
6. Analysis of current risk and development of a prioritized plan for risk reduction

The vulnerability assessment process will range in complexity based on the design and operation of the water system itself. The nature and extent of the vulnerability assessment will differ among systems based on a number of factors, including system size, potential population affected, source water, treatment complexity, system infrastructure, and other factors. Security and safety evaluations also vary based on knowledge and types of threats, available security technologies, and applicable local, state and federal regulations.

barriers, water collection, pretreatment, treatment, storage and distribution facilities, electronic, computer or other automated systems which are utilized by the public water system, the use, storage, or handling of various chemicals, and the operation and maintenance of such system. The Administrator, not later than August 1, 2002, after consultation with appropriate departments and agencies of the Federal Government and with State and local governments, shall provide baseline information to community water systems required to conduct

11.2 CRITICAL INFRASTRUCTURE SECTORS

There are 16 critical infrastructure sectors whose assets, systems, and networks, whether physical or virtual, are considered so vital to the United States that their incapacitation or destruction would have a debilitating effect on security, national economic security, national public health or safety, or any combination thereof.

Presidential Policy Directive 21 (PPD-21): Critical Infrastructure Security and Resilience advances a national policy to strengthen and maintain secure, functioning, and resilient critical infrastructure. This directive supersedes Homeland Security Presidential Directive 7.

PPD-21 identifies 16 critical infrastructure sectors:

Chemical Sector
DHS is designated as the sector-specific agency for the chemical sector.

Commercial Facilities Sector
DHS is designated as the sector-specific agency for the commercial facilities sector.

Communications Sector
The communications sector is an integral component of the U.S. economy, underlying the operations of all businesses, public safety organizations, and government.

Critical Manufacturing Sector
DHS is designated as the sector-specific agency for the critical manufacturing sector.

Dams Sector
DHS is designated as the sector-specific agency for the dams sector. The dams sector comprises dam projects, navigation locks, levees, hurricane barriers, mine tailings impoundments, and other similar water retention and/or control facilities.

Defense Industrial Base Sector
The defense industrial base sector is the worldwide industrial complex that enables research and development (R&D), as well as design, production, delivery, and maintenance of military weapons systems, subsystems, and components or parts, to meet U.S. military requirements.

Emergency Services Sector
DHS is designated as the sector-specific agency for the emergency services sector. A system of prevention, preparedness, response, and recovery elements, the emergency services sector represents the nation's first line of defense in the prevention and mitigation of risk from terrorist attacks, manmade incidents, and natural disasters.

Energy Sector
The U.S. energy infrastructure fuels the economy of the twenty-first century. The Department of Energy is the sector-specific agency for the energy sector.

Financial Services Sector
The Department of Treasury is designated as the sector-specific agency for the financial services sector.

Food and Agriculture Sector

The U.S. Department of Agriculture (USDA) and the Department of Health and Human Services (HHS) are designated as the co-sector-specific agencies for the food and agriculture sector.

Government Facilities Sector

DHS and the General Services Administration are designated as the co-sector-specific agencies for the government facilities sector.

Health Care and Public Health Sector

HHS is designated as the sector-specific agency for the health care and public health sector.

Information Technology Sector

DHS is designated as the sector-specific agency for the information technology sector.

Nuclear Reactors, Materials, and Waste Sector

DHS is designated as the sector-specific agency for the nuclear reactors, materials, and waste sector.

Transportation Systems Sector

DHS and the Department of Transportation are designated as the co-sector-specific agencies for the transportation systems sector.

Water and Wastewater Systems Sector

The Environmental Protection Agency (EPA) is designated as the sector-specific agency for the water and wastewater systems sector.

vulnerability assessments regarding which kinds of terrorist attacks or other intentional acts are the probable threats to

A. Substantially disrupt the ability of the system to provide a safe and reliable supply of drinking water; or
B. Otherwise present significant public health concerns.

As part of our critical infrastructure, they become more than water plants but targets for the terrorist. In response to the September 11, 2001 attacks, the EPA formed the Water Security Division (WSD) in the Office of Ground Water and Drinking Water. WSD oversees all drinking water and wastewater homeland security matters. The Office of Homeland Security (OHS) was created in the EPA Office of the Administrator to oversee all EPA matters related to homeland security (Figure 11.1).

The WSD tackled a host of issues relating to security and the water supply, and these tasks can be broken down into the following:

- Sector profile and goals
- Identifying assets, systems, networks, and functions

- The public drinking water systems regulated by EPA and delegated states and tribes provide drinking water to 90 percent of Americans.
- A public water system provides water for human consumption through pipes or other constructed conveyances to at least 15 service connections or serves an average of at least 25 people for at least 60 days a year.
- A public water system may be publicly or privately owned.
- There are approximately 155,000 public water systems in the United States.
- EPA classifies these water systems according to the number of people they serve, the source of their water, and whether they serve the same customers year-round or on an occasional basis.

EPA has defined three types of public water systems:

Community Water System (CWS): A public water system that supplies water to the same population year-round.

Non-Transient Non-Community Water System (NTNCWS): A public water system that regularly supplies water to at least 25 of the same people at least six months per year. Some examples are schools, factories, office buildings, and hospitals which have their own water systems.

Transient Non-Community Water System (TNCWS): A public water system that provides water in a place such as a gas station or campground where people do not remain for long periods of time.

FIGURE 11.1   Information about public water systems in the United States. From: EPA, Information about public water systems, http://www.epa.gov/dwreginfo/information-about-public-water-systems (accessed February 7, 2016).

- Assessing risks
- Prioritizing infrastructure
- Developing and implementing protective programs
- Measuring progress
- Protection R&D
- Managing and coordinating responsibilities

Here one witnesses an agency running full steam regarding the question of security and water. The infection of a water supply would be a major health risk and likely cause more casualties than any aircraft flying into a building.[4] The EPA views threat analysis broadly, encompassing natural events, criminal acts, insider threats, and foreign and domestic terrorism. Natural catastrophic events are typically addressed as part of emergency response and business continuity planning, yet the same skill sets necessary for the planning and mitigation of the terrorist attack on the water supply are needed.

To analyze and prepare for threats and attacks, the agency needs to think of the predictable methods the terrorist would employ. Assessment requires a certain amount of foresight. The oft-cited methodology regarding water facilities usually includes

- Chemical, biological, or radiological (CBR) contamination attacks on drinking water assets, especially distribution systems

- Vehicle-borne improvised explosive devices and improvised explosive device attacks on infrastructure, especially single points of failure and chemical storage sites
- Cyber attacks on industrial control systems
- Chemical attacks, which may include introduction of a combustible contaminant into a wastewater collection system, affecting infrastructure or the treatment process

Hence, it is risk assessment in all its glory that water facilities have to engage in. The homeland security professional needs to ask questions that anticipate the risk and corresponding plan. At most water facilities, the threats are encompassed in these queries:

- What are the most plausible threats, contaminants, and threat scenarios facing the drinking water industry?
- How does this information compare with intelligence information on possible threats?
- What types of biological and chemical contaminants could be introduced into water systems, and what are their physical, chemical, and biological properties?
- What are the potential health impacts of these contaminants?
- What are the most effective means to destroy contaminants in water?
- How can this information be combined with reporting, analysis, and decision-making to arrive at a reliable system?
- Can effective methods be developed to ensure that a sufficient number of qualified laboratories exist to perform rapid analysis of water contaminants in the event of an attack?
- If contaminants are introduced into a water system, where will they travel?
- How quickly will they travel?
- What will be their concentration at various points along their path?
- Can human exposures and the health impacts of these contaminants be effectively minimized?
- How can water that has been contaminated be effectively treated so that it can be released to wastewater systems or otherwise disposed of?
- Are alternative water supplies available in the event of an attack?
- How would water utilities or governments most effectively select a cost-effective early warning system?

Any meaningful security plan will anticipate these questions and will prompt the security professional to devise a plan that mitigates the damage and redirects the water facility to positive productivity after this event. Most water facilities need to rely on both internal and external constituencies to fully comprehend the dynamics of their location. The interplay between state and federal regulators alone gives some sense of this necessary interconnection (Figure 11.2).

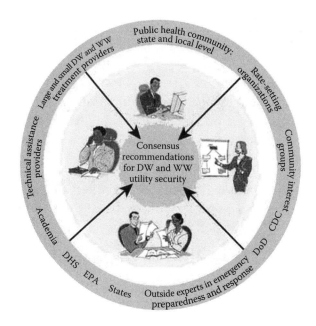

FIGURE 11.2   Recommendation for utility security. DW = drinking water; WW = wastewater.

Internet Exercise: Find out about the Water Information Sharing and Analysis Center (WaterISAC) professional association of water providers and the security tool made available by this group at http://www.dhs.gov/critical-infrastructure-sectors.

Most water facilities engage in a serious self-assessment program that looks to these 14 variables, as published by the EPA:

- Explicit commitment to security
- Promote security awareness
- Defined security roles and employee expectations
- Vulnerability assessment up to date
- Security resources and implementation priorities
- Contamination detection
- Threat-level-based protocols
- Emergency response plan (ERP) tested and up to date
- Utility-specific measures and self-assessment
- Intrusion detection and access control
- Information protection and continuity
- Design and construction standards
- Communications
- Partnerships

To ensure basic compliance with these criteria, the water facility should conduct its own vulnerability assessment. The EPA, as well as a host of software companies, makes available vulnerability assessment programs. The EPA publishes vulnerability guidelines, which are reproduced in the following section (Table 11.1).

TABLE 11.1 What Are Some Points to Consider in Vulnerability Assessments?

Basic Element	Points to Consider

1. Characterization of the water system, including its mission and objectives.
 	
(Answers to system-specific questions may be helpful in characterizing the water system.)
	• What are the important missions of the system to be assessed? Define the highest priority services provided by the utility. Identify the utility's customers:
	
	  • General public
	  • Government
	  • Military
	  • Industrial
	  • Critical care
	  • Retail operations
	  • Firefighting
	
	• What are the most important facilities, processes, and assets of the system for achieving the mission objectives and avoiding undesired consequences? Describe the:
	
	  • Utility facilities
	  • Operating procedures
	  • Management practices that are necessary to achieve the m mission objectives
	  • How the utility operates (e.g., water source including ground and surface water)
	  • Treatment processes
	  • Storage methods and capacity
	  • Chemical use and storage
	  • Distribution system
	
	In assessing those assets that are critical, consider critical customers, dependence on other infrastructures (e.g., electricity, transportation, other water utilities), contractual obligations, single points of failure (e.g., critical aqueducts, transmission systems, etc.), chemical hazards and other aspects of the utility's operations, or availability of other utility capabilities that may increase or decrease the criticality of specific facilities, processes and assets.

2. Identification and prioritization of adverse consequences to avoid.	• Take into account the impacts that could substantially disrupt the ability of the system to provide a safe and reliable supply of drinking water or otherwise present significant public health concerns to the surrounding community. Water systems should use the vulnerability assessment process to determine how to reduce risks associated with the consequences of significant concern.
	• Ranges of consequences or impacts for each of these events should be identified and defined. Factors to be considered in assessing the consequences may include:
	
	  • Magnitude of service disruption
	  • Economic impact (such as replacement and installation costs for damaged critical assets or loss of revenue due to service outage)
	  • Number of illnesses or deaths resulting from an event
	  • Impact on public confidence in the water supply
	  • Chronic problems arising from specific events
	  • Other indicators of the impact of each event as determined by the water utility. Risk reduction recommendations at the conclusion of the vulnerability assessment should strive to prevent or reduce each of these consequences.

(Continued)

TABLE 11.1 (Continued) What Are Some Points to Consider in Vulnerability Assessments?

Basic Element	Points to Consider

3. Determination of critical assets that might be subject to malevolent acts that could result in undesired consequences.	• What are the malevolent acts that could reasonably cause undesired consequences? Consider the operation of critical facilities, assets and/or processes and assess what an adversary could do to disrupt these operations. Such acts may include physical damage to or destruction of critical assets, contamination of water, intentional release of stored chemicals, interruption of electricity or other infrastructure interdependencies.
	• The "Public Health Security and Bioterrorism Preparedness and Response Act of 2002" (PL 107–188) states that a community water system which serves a population of greater than 3,300 people must review the vulnerability of its system to a terrorist attack or other intentional acts intended to substantially disrupt the ability of the system to provide a safe and reliable supply of drinking water. The vulnerability assessment shall include, but not be limited to, a review of:
	  • Pipes and constructed conveyances
	  • Physical barriers
	  • Water collection, pretreatment and treatment facilities
	  • Storage and distribution facilities
	  • Electronic, computer or other automated systems that are utilized by the public water system (e.g., Supervisory Control and Data Acquisition (SCADA))
	  • The use, storage, or handling of various chemicals
	  • The operation and maintenance of such systems

4. Assessment of the likelihood (qualitative probability) of such malevolent acts from adversaries (e.g., terrorists, vandals).	• Determine the possible modes of attack that might result in consequences of significant concern based on the critical assets of the water system. The objective of this step of the assessment is to move beyond what is merely possible and determine the likelihood of a particular attack scenario. This is a very difficult task as there is often insufficient information to determine the likelihood of a particular event with any degree of certainty. • The threats (the kind of adversary and the mode of attack) selected for consideration during a vulnerability assessment will dictate, to a great extent, the risk reduction measures that should be designed to counter the threat(s). Some vulnerability assessment methodologies refer to this as a "Design Basis Threat" (DBT) where the threat serves as the basis for the design of countermeasures, as well as the benchmark against which vulnerabilities are assessed. It should be noted that there is no single DBT or threat profile for all water systems in the United States.

Differences in geographic location, size of the utility, previous attacks in the local area and many other factors will influence the threat(s) that water systems should consider in their assessments. Water systems should consult with the local FBI and/or other law enforcement agencies, public officials, and others to determine the threats on which their risk reduction measures should be based. Water systems should also refer to EPA's "Baseline Threat Information for Vulnerability Assessments of Community Water Systems" to help assess the most likely threats to their system. This document is available to community water systems serving populations greater than 3,300 people. If your system has not yet received instructions on how to receive a copy of this document, then contact your Regional EPA Office immediately. You will be sent instructions on how to securely access the document via the Water Information Sharing and Analysis Center (ISAC) website or obtain a hardcopy that can be mailed directly to you. Water systems may also want to review their incident reports to better understand past breaches of security.

5. Evaluation of existing countermeasures. (Depending on countermeasures already in place, some critical assets may already be sufficiently protected. This step will aid in identification of the areas of greatest concern, and help to focus priorities for risk reduction.)

- *What capabilities does the system currently employ for detection, delay and response?*
  - Identify and evaluate current detection capabilities such as intrusion detection systems, water quality monitoring, operational alarms, guard post orders, and employee security awareness programs.
  - Identify current delay mechanisms such as locks and key control, fencing, structure integrity of critical assets and vehicle access checkpoints.
  - Identify existing policies and procedures for evaluation and response to intrusion and system malfunction alarms, adverse water quality indicators, and cyber-system intrusions.

  It is important to determine the performance characteristics. Poorly operated and maintained security technologies provide little or no protection.

  - *What cyber-protection system features does the utility have in place?* Assess what protective measures are in place for the SCADA and business-related computer information systems such as:
    - Firewalls
    - Modem access
    - Internet and other external connections, including wireless data and voice communications
    - Security policies and protocols

  It is important to identify whether vendors have access rights and/or "backdoors" to conduct system diagnostics remotely.

  - *What security policies and procedures exist, and what is the compliance record for them?* Identify existing policies and procedures concerning:
    - Personnel security
    - Physical security
    - Key and access badge control
    - Control of system configuration and operational data
    - Chemical and other vendor deliveries
    - Security training and exercise records

(Continued)

TABLE 11.1 (Continued) What Are Some Points to Consider in Vulnerability Assessments?

Basic Element	Points to Consider
6. Analysis of current risk and development of a prioritized plan for risk reduction.	• Information gathered on threat, critical assets, water utility operations, consequences, and existing countermeasures should be analyzed to determine the current level of risk. The utility should then determine whether current risks are acceptable or risk reduction measures should be pursued.
	• Recommended actions should measurably reduce risks by reducing vulnerabilities and/or consequences through improved deterrence, delay, detection, and/or response capabilities or by improving operational policies or procedures. Selection of specific risk reduction actions should be completed prior to considering the cost of the recommended action(s). Utilities should carefully consider both short- and long-term solutions. An analysis of the cost of short- and long-term risk reduction actions may impact which actions the utility chooses to achieve its security goals.
	• Utilities may also want to consider security improvements in light of other planned or needed improvements. Security and general infrastructure may provide significant multiple benefits. For example, improved treatment processes or system redundancies can both reduce vulnerabilities and enhance day-to-day operation.
	• Generally, strategies for reducing vulnerabilities fall into three broad categories:
	• Sound business practices: Affect policies, procedures, and training to improve the overall security-related culture at the drinking water facility. For example, it is important to ensure rapid communication capabilities exist between public health authorities and local law enforcement and emergency responders.
	• System upgrades: Include changes in operations, equipment, processes, or infrastructure itself that make the system fundamentally safer.
	• Security upgrades: Improve capabilities for detection, delay, or response.

Source: EPA, *Vulnerability Assessment Fact Sheet* (Washington, DC: U.S. Government Printing Office, 2002), EPA 816-F-02-025.

Note: Some points to consider related to the six basic elements are included in the following tables. The manner in which the vulnerability assessment is performed is determined by each individual water utility. It will be helpful to remember throughout the assessment process that the ultimate goal is twofold: to safeguard public health and safety, and to reduce the potential for disruption of a reliable supply of pressurized water.

Internet Exercise: Learn how to prepare for flooding's impact on the water supply at http://www.epa.gov/sites/production/files/2015-06/documents/flooding.pdf.

11.3 Agriculture and Food

Just as water contamination has enormous impacts on the public health of the nation, so too does the integrity of its food supply. Here again, the terrorist envisions a target that has widespread potential for harm to a significant portion of the population.[5] Agriculture and food systems are vulnerable to disease, pests, or poisonous agents that occur naturally, are unintentionally introduced, or are intentionally delivered by acts of terrorism. Food can be attacked on many fronts, including

- Biological and chemical agents
- Naturally occurring, antibiotic-resistant, and genetically engineered substances
- Deadly agents and those tending to cause gastrointestinal discomfort
- Highly infectious agents and those that are not communicable
- Substances readily available to any individual and those that are more difficult to acquire
- Agents that must be weaponized and those that are accessible in a usable form[6]

America's agriculture and food system is an extensive, open, interconnected, diverse, and complex structure, and, as a result, the perfect forum for the terrorist.

Responsibility for the food supply, from a security perspective, resides in three government agencies: the USDA, the Food and Drug Administration (FDA), and DHS. In a recent report, these agencies set out a vision statement on the food supply (Figure 11.3).[7]

Vision and Purpose of DHS: Food and Agricultural Section

The FA Sector comprises complex production, processing, and delivery systems. The mission of the FA Sector is to protect against a disruption in the food supply that would pose a serious threat to public health, safety, welfare, or to the national economy. These food and agriculture systems are almost entirely under private ownership, and they operate in highly competitive global markets, strive to operate in harmony with the environment, and provide economic opportunities and an improved quality of life for U.S. citizens and others worldwide.

Differences in commodity type, farm size, operator, and household characteristics complicate prevention and protection efforts for individual operations and, ultimately, the sector as a whole. In recent years, changes in the rules of trade, shifts in domestic policy, and new developments in technology have altered the competitive landscape of global agriculture and challenges facing American farmers.

Securing this sector presents unique challenges because food and agriculture systems in the United States are extensive, open, interconnected, and diverse, and they have complex structures. Food products move rapidly in commerce to consumers, but the time required for detection and identification of attacks and contaminations, such as animal or plant disease introduction or food contamination, can be lengthy and complex. Therefore, attacks and contaminations on the FA Sector could result in severe animal, plant, public health, and economic consequences (https://www.dhs.gov/food-and-agriculture-sector).

FIGURE 11.3   Vision statement for the food and agriculture sector. From: DHS, Food and Agriculture Sector-Specific Plan: An Annex to the National Infrastructure Protection Plan (2010).

FIGURE 11.4　A Midwestern farm.

As appropriate, the USDA takes the lead role in the protection of our food supply. As it notes, "The protection and integrity of America's agricultural production and food supply are essential to the health and welfare of both the domestic population and the global community"[8] (Figure 11.4).

Internet Exercise: The list of food recalls due to safety and health questions will be surprising. Visit http://www.fsis.usda.gov/FSIS_Recalls/Recall_Case_Archive/index.asp.

The impact of food and agriculture contamination is not lost on DHS. Its recommendations on the integrity of the food chain are incisive, asking those entrusted with its safety to truly consider the ramifications of contamination. DHS poses seven criteria for consideration when weighing the impact of food contamination.

Criticality: What will be the public health impacts and economic costs associated with the attack?

Accessibility: How easy will it be for a terrorist to gain access and egress from the location of the food and agricultural product?

Recuperability: How readily will the food supply system recover from an attack?

Vulnerability: How easy or difficult will the attack be?

Effect: What calculable losses will there be directly resulting from the attack?

Recognizability: Are targets easy to discover and identify?

Shock: In a cumulative sense, how significant are the health, economic, and psychological impacts that result from the attack? (https://www.dhs.gov/food-and-agriculture-sector)

In each of these categories, the ramifications of a food contamination event are obvious. As in the water supply, the far-reaching impacts of food contamination are almost impossible to measure. Yet those entrusted with production must be mindful of their product's safety and security as well. Whether it is grain or cattle, soybeans or chicken, the agricultural entrepreneur must tend to questions of security on a daily basis.

USDA mission area	Agency
Farm and foreign agriculture services	• Farm service agency (FSA) • Foreign agricultural service (FAS) • Risk management agency (RMA)
Food, nutrition, and consumer services	• Center for nutrition policy and promotion (CNPP) • Food and nutrition service (FNS)
Food safety	• Food safety and inspection service (FSIS)
Natural resources and environment	• Forest service (FS) • Natural resources conservation service (NRCS)

FIGURE 11.5 USDA's participation in homeland security. From: USDA, DHS, and FDA, *Critical Infrastructure and Key Resources for Sector Specific Plan as Input to the National Infrastructure Protection Plan* (Washington, DC: U.S. Government Printing Office, 2007), 15.

Determining exactly how to ensure security in the agricultural sphere is no simple undertaking. Aside from the broad range of products and services, there is the added dilemma of multiple agency responsibility. While the USDA may be at the forefront, its policymaking on food and its safety is influenced by myriad other agencies, such as the FDA and EPA, and its own internal history has protocols and programs that have historically dealt with food safety. In this area, it is clear that many adjustments and realignments have had to take place—some readily and others with the usual bureaucratic resistance. Figure 11.5 demonstrates the levels of participation already evident in the USDA prior to and after 9/11.

Meshing all of this historic practice into a unified and seamless vision of security in light of 9/11 is a challenging undertaking. What emerges from the USDA is an agency in full recognition of this challenge. It urges its constituency to conduct risk assessments, to realize that security questions are central to farm operation, and to accept some level of personal responsibility for the integrity of facility and product.

In fact, the USDA fully integrates the functions of homeland security into its very makeup, as evidenced by its organizational chart in Figure 11.6.

The USDA calls on all owners in the agricultural sector to view security in both general and specific product terms. In the more general arena, it recommends the following assessment protocol:

- Procedures are in place for notifying appropriate law enforcement when a security threat is received, or when evidence of actual product tampering is observed.
- Procedures are in place for heightened awareness (especially when the DHS terrorism threat level is elevated) for unusual activities around the farm and increased disease symptoms among animals or crops.
- A current local, state, and federal government Homeland Security contact is maintained.

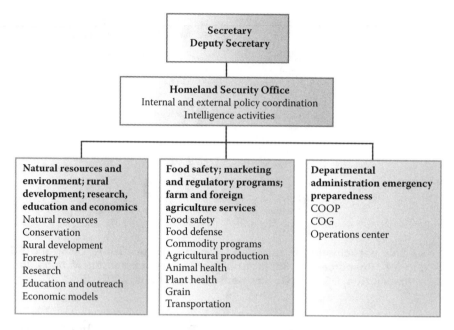

FIGURE 11.6 **USDA structure for homeland protection and food safety. From: USDA, DHS, and FDA, *Critical Infrastructure*, 36.**

- All employees are encouraged to report any sign of product tampering.
- Facility boundaries are secured to prevent unauthorized entry.
- "No Trespassing" and "Restricted Entry" signs are posted appropriately.
- Alarms, motion detection lights, cameras, and other appropriate security equipment are used in key areas, as needed.
- Facility perimeter is regularly monitored for signs of suspicious activity or unauthorized entry.
- Doors, windows, gates, roof openings, vent openings, trailer bodies, railcars, and bulk storage tanks are secured at all times.
- Outside lighting is sufficient to allow detection of unusual activities.
- Fire, smoke, and heat detection devices are operable throughout the farm.
- Storage tanks for hazardous materials and potable water supply are protected from, and monitored for, unauthorized access.
- Wells and other water supplies are secured and routine testing is performed.
- Truck deliveries are verified against a roster of scheduled deliveries.
- Unscheduled deliveries are held away from facility premises pending verification of shipper and cargo.
- Records are maintained for all vehicles and equipment: make, model, serial number, service date, and so on.
- Vehicles and equipment are secured or immobilized when not in use; keys are never left in unattended vehicles.

- Machinery is removed from fields and stored appropriately; valuable equipment and tools are locked in a secure building.
- Entry into facility is controlled by requiring positive identification (i.e., picture ID).
- New employees are screened and references are checked.
- Visitors and guests are restricted to nonproduction areas unless accompanied by a facility employee.
- Where required by biosecurity procedures, visitors wear clean boots or coveralls (disposable boots and coveralls are provided for visitors).
- Areas are designated for check-in and check-out for visitors/deliveries (with a sign-in sheet for name, address, phone number, reason for visit).
- An inspection for signs of tampering or unauthorized entry is performed for all storage facilities regularly.
- Hazardous materials are purchased only from licensed dealers.
- A current inventory of hazardous or flammable chemicals (including drugs, chemicals, pesticides, and fertilizers) or other products (including chemical trade names, product type, EPA numbers, quantity, and usage) is maintained, and discrepancies are investigated immediately.
- A current inventory of stored fuel (diesel, gasoline, fuel oil, propane, oxygen, acetylene, kerosene, etc.) is maintained.
- A disease surveillance plan is available.
- Risk management plans have been developed or updated and shared with employees, family, visitors, customers, and local law enforcement.
- Plans include awareness of animal and plant health, as well as signs of tampering with crops, livestock, supplies, vehicles, equipment, and facilities.
- Orientation/training on security procedures is given to all facility employees at least annually.
- Passwords for USDA systems and programs are protected to prevent unauthorized user entry.[9]

11.3.1 Strategic Partnership Program on Agroterrorism

Attacks against the agricultural system would be an effective and frightful way of inflicting a terrorist act, and law enforcement needs to anticipate the possibility. "Agroterrorism has been defined as the deliberate introduction of an animal or plant disease with the goal of generating fear, causing economic losses or undermining social stability."[10] Knowledge about food supply resides in a bevy of private and public entities and will require a major collaboration. Blending diverse agencies with distinct approaches to security has been a challenge for those protecting the food supply. Put another way, law enforcement officials, such as the FBI or Customs, will see the food problem through a prism of enforcement, while food safety specialists at the USDA or FDA may see things from a different perspective. The Strategic Partnership Program on Agroterrorism (SPPA) makes a noble effort to meld these various visions and to unify these diverse perspectives into one framework—that of food safety. Just as critically, the SPPA will enlist private industry concerns, from farmers to grain processors, from stockyard owners to fertilizer companies. The objectives of the SPPA are as follows:

- Validate or identify sector-wide vulnerabilities by conducting critical infrastructure/key resources (CI/KR) assessments in order to
  - Identify gaps.
  - Inform Centers of Excellence and Sector Specific Agencies (SSA) of identified research needs.
  - Catalog lessons learned.
- Identify indicators and warnings that could signify planning for an attack.
- Develop mitigation strategies to reduce the threat/prevent an attack. Strategies may include actions that either industry or government may take to reduce vulnerabilities.
- Validate assessments conducted by the United States Government (USG) for food and agriculture sectors.
- Gather information to enhance existing tools that both USG and industry employ.
- Provide the USG and the industry with comprehensive reports including warnings and indicators, key vulnerabilities, and potential mitigation strategies.
- Provide sub-sector reports for the USG that combines assessment results to determine national critical infrastructure vulnerability points to support the National Infrastructure Protection Plan (NIPP) and national preparedness goals.
- Establish and/or strengthen relationships between Federal, State, and local law enforcement and the food and agriculture industry along with the critical food/agriculture sites visited.[11]

SPPA relies on industry visitations to reach its conclusions about safety and security in the agricultural sector. This is why private industry—namely, farmers and food suppliers—is so integral to the SPPA process. SPPA assessments are conducted on a voluntary basis between one or more industry representatives for a particular product or commodity. As recommended by DHS and the USDA, industry production processes are evaluated in light of law enforcement officials. Together, they conduct a vulnerability assessment using the seven criteria noted previously: criticality, accessibility, recuperability, vulnerability, effect, recognizability, and shock.

As a result of each assessment, participants identify weaknesses in the production cycle as well as recommendations on protective measures and mitigation steps that may reduce the vulnerability. By 2008, the assessments shown in Table 11.2 had been conducted under the SPPA program.

Proposed future inspections, conducted by the USDA and the FDA, will tackle a host of foodstuffs and agricultural products including those shown in Table 11.3.

Internet Resource: For full instructions on how to devise a food safety program, see http://www.fsis.usda.gov/PDF/Food_Defense_Plan.pdf.

TABLE 11.2 Assessments Conducted

	SPPA Assessments, Trade Associations, and Subsectors					
Industry	Food/ Commodity Assessed	Date	States	Trade Associations	SSA	Subsector(s)
Yogurt	Yogurt	November 2005	TN, MN	International Dairy Foods Assn., National Yogurt Assn.	FDA	Processors/ manufacturers
Grain export elevator	Corn	December 2005	LA	National Grain and Feed Assn.	FDA/USDA	Producers/ plants
Bottled water	Bottled water	January 2006	NJ	International Bottled Water Assn.	FDA	Processors/ manufacturers
Baby food	Baby food (jarred)	February 2006	MI	Food Products Assn.	FDA	Processors/ manufacturers
School kitchens	Spaghetti sauce with meat	February 2006	NC	None	USDA	Restaurant/food service
Frozen food	Frozen pizza varieties	March 2006	WI, FL	American Frozen Food Institute	FDA/USDA	Processors/ manufacturers
Swine production	Swine	March 2006	IA	Multiple host farms	USDA	Producers/ animals
Apple juice	Apple juice	April 2006	NH	Food Products Assn.	FDA	Processors/ manufacturers
Fresh produce	Lettuce (bagged)	May 2006	CA	United Fresh Fruit and Vegetable Assn., Produce Marketing Assn., International Fresh-Cut Produce Assn., Western Growers Assn.	FDA	Processors/ manufacturers, producers/ plants
Infant formula	Infant formula (powdered)	June 2006	AZ	International Formula Council	FDA	Processors/ manufacturers
Ready-to-eat chicken products	Chicken strips	June 2006	AR	American Meat Institute	USDA	Processors/ manufacturers
Beef cattle feedlot	Cattle	July 2006	NE	National Cattlemen's Beef Assn.	USDA	Producers/ animals
Dairy processing	Milk	July 2006	NY	International Dairy Foods Assn.	FDA	Processors/ manufacturers
Ground beef	Ground beef	August 2006	KS	American Meat Institute	USDA	Processors/ manufacturers

(Continued)

TABLE 11.2 (Continued) Assessments Conducted

	SPPA Assessments, Trade Associations, and Subsectors					
Industry	Food/ Commodity Assessed	Date	States	Trade Associations	SSA	Subsector(s)
Livestock auction markets (cattle sale barn)	Cattle	August 2006	MO	Livestock Marketing Assn., Missouri Cattlemen's Assn., National Cattlemen's Beef Assn.	USDA	Producers/ animals
Dairy cattle farm	Dairy cattle	September 2006	ID	Idaho Dairymen's Assn., Idaho Department of Agriculture	USDA	Producers/ animals
Soybean farm	Soybean	October 2006	IL	Illinois Crop Improvement Assn., National Corn Growers Assn.	USDA	Producers/ plants
Corn/grain	Corn	November 2006	IL	National Corn Growers Assn.	USDA	Producers/ plants
Retail-fluid milk	Milk (1 gallon containers)	January 2007	TX	International Dairy Foods Assn.	FDA	Processors/ manufacturers, retail
Link sausage processing	Sausage	Mar 2007	WI	American Meat Institute	USDA	Processors/ manufacturers
Stadium retail food service	Hot dogs, ketchup	Mar 2007	KS	Kansas State University	FDA	Restaurant/food service
Correctional institution food processing	Ground beef patties	April 2007	OH	Ohio Department of Rehabilitation and Correction	USDA	Processors/ manufacturers
Egg products	Eggs (liquid)	April 2007	PA	United Egg Assn.	USDA	Processors/ manufacturers
Commercial feed mill	Animal feed	June 2007	IA	National Grain and Feed Assn.	FDA	Processors/ manufacturers
Hot dogs	Hot dogs	June 2007	PA	American Meat Institute	USDA	Processors/ manufacturers
Breakfast cereal	Frosted flakes	July 2007	MN	Grocery Manufacturers/ Food Products Assn.	FDA	Processors/ manufacturers
Domestic grain cooperative	Grain (all)	July 2007	NE, IA	National Grain and Feed Assn.	USDA	Producers/ plants
Grocery stores	Rotisserie chicken	August 2007	PA	Food Marketing Institute	FDA	Retail

(Continued)

TABLE 11.2 Assessments Conducted

SPPA Assessments, Trade Associations, and Subsectors						
Industry	Food/ Commodity Assessed	Date	States	Trade Associations	SSA	Subsector(s)
High fructose corn syrup	High fructose corn syrup	September 2007	AL	Corn Refiners Assn.	FDA	Processors/ manufacturers
USDA commodity warehouse	Beef trimmings	September 2007	MO	None	USDA	Warehousing and logistics
Distribution centers	Lettuce	November 2007	VA	International Foodservice Distributors Assn.	FDA/USDA	Warehousing and logistics
Import reinspection facility	Beef trimmings	November 2007	MD	International Assn. of Refrigerated Warehouses, Global Cold Chain Alliance	USDA	Warehousing and logistics
Poultry broilers	Poultry	November 2007	GA	Georgia Poultry Federation	USDA	Producers/ animals
Flour	Flour	February 2008	OK	North American Millers' Assn.	FDA	Processors/ manufacturers
Beet sugar	Beet sugar	Mar 2008	MN	U.S. Beet Sugar Assn.	USDA	Processors/ manufacturers
Transportation (livestock hauling)	Cattle	May 2008	CO	Agricultural and Food Transporters Conference— American Trucking Assn.	USDA	Producers/ animals, warehousing, and logistics

Source: U.S. Food and Drug Administration, *Strategic Partnership Program Agroterrorism (SPPA) Initiative: Final Summary Report September 2005–September 2008* (2008), Appendix A, http://www.fda.gov/downloads/Food/FoodDefense/UCM181069.pdf (accessed February 7, 2016).

The USDA's Food Safety and Inspection Service (FSIS) has developed a surveillance program to randomly screen and check food facilities as well as be stationed at ports of entry. Food safety officers are a sought-after career track due to the excellent working conditions and challenging work. FSIS continues to hire import surveillance liaison officers who are responsible for the agency's oversight of food defense issues relating to imported food products at ports of entry, at border entries, and in commerce around the country. In particular, they have expanded their liaison activities with DHS's Customs and Border Protection.

Internet Resource: To learn about jobs in food safety, see www.fsis.usda.gov/Factsheets/FSIS_Workforce_Introduction_of_CSO/index.asp.

TABLE 11.3 USDA and FDA Site Visits Initially Proposed

USDA Proposed Site Visits	FDA Proposed Site Visits
Production agriculture • Aquaculture production facility • Beef cattle feedlot • Cattle stockyard/auction barn • Citrus production facility • Corn farm • Dairy farm • Grain elevator and storage facility • Grain export handling facility • Poultry farm • Rice mill • Seed production facility • Soybean farm • Swine production facility • Veterinary biologics firm **Food processing and distribution** • Deli meats processing • Ground beef processing facility • Hot dog processing • Import reinspection facilities • Liquid eggs processing • Poultry processing • Retailers (further processing on site) • School food service central kitchens • Transportation companies • Warehouses	• Animal by-products • Animal foods/feeds • Baby food • Breaded food, frozen, raw • Canned food, low acid • Cereal, wholegrain, not heat treated • Deli salads • Dietary supplement, botanical, tablets • Entrees, fully cooked • Flour • Frozen packaged entrees • Fruit juice • Gum arabic (ingredient) • High-fructose corn syrup (ingredient) • Honey • Ice cream • Infant formula • Milk, fluid • Peanut butter • Produce, fresh-cut and modified atmosphere packaged • Retail setting • Seafood, cooked, refrigerated, ready to eat • Soft drink, carbonated • Spices • Vitamin/microingredient premixes/flavors • Vitamins, capsules • Water, bottled • Yogurt

Source: FDA, DHS, USDA, and FBI, *Strategic Partnership Program Agroterrorism (SPPA) Initiative: Second Year Status Report July 2006–September 2007*, http://www.fda.gov/Food/FoodDefense/FoodDefensePrograms/ucm08992.htm.

11.3.2 Infectious Animals

Animals can be efficient carriers of illness, catastrophic pathogens, and other threats to public health. Recent cases of mad cow disease heighten the impact of disease on public health integrity. Avian flu (AI), swine flu, and rabies are other examples of well-publicized cases. "Direct disease threats to livestock have been seen domestically and internationally. They come in the form of foot and mouth disease (FMD), bovine spongiform encephalopathy (BCE), various animal flues and parasites."[12] The USDA has long recognized the meaningful nature of these threats and correlates how they can relate to the problem of homeland security. Working hand in hand with DHS, the USDA, by and through its Agricultural Research Service (ARS), conducts extensive research on animal diseases and their potential

FIGURE 11.7   Plum Island Animal Disease Center.

for catastrophic consequences. The Plum Island Animal Disease Center is one of the major centers where this form of analysis is conducted (Figure 11.7).

The Plum Island facility conducts high-level animal research under the following mission:

- Development of sensitive and accurate methods of disease agent detection and identification
- Development of new strategies to control disease epidemics, including rDNA vaccines, antiviral drugs, and transgenic, disease-resistant animals
- Assessment of risks involved in importation of animals and animal products from countries where epidemic foreign animal diseases occur
- Diagnostic investigations of suspect cases of FAD outbreaks in U.S. livestock
- Testing of animals and animal products to be imported into the United States to make sure those imports are free of FAD agents
- Production and maintenance reagents used in diagnostic tests and vaccines
- Training of animal health professionals in the recognition and diagnosis of animal disease

In the northeast corner of the United States, ARS is conducting a myriad of research undertakings at the following facilities:

Washington, DC
- National Arboretum

Newark, DE
- Beneficial Insects Introduction Research

Boston, MA
- Jean Mayer Human Nutrition Research Center on Aging

Beltsville, MD
- Beltsville Human Nutrition Research Center
- Beltsville Agricultural Research Center

Fort Detrick, MD
- Foreign Disease-Weed Science Research

Orono, ME
- New England Plant, Soil and Water Research Laboratory
- National Cold Water Marine Aquaculture Center

Geneva, NY
- Plant Genetic Resources Research
- Grape Genetics Research

Ithaca, NY
- Robert W. Holley Center for Agriculture & Health

Orient Point, NY
- Plum Island Animal Disease Center

University Park, PA
- Pasture Systems & Watershed Management Research

Wyndmoor, PA
- Eastern Regional Research Center

Kearneysville, WV
- Appalachian Fruit Research Laboratory

Leetown, WV
- Cool and Cold Water Aquaculture Research[13]

Working in consort with these facilities is the Animal and Plant Health Inspection Service (APHIS) of the USDA. APHIS performs a host of functions to ensure the safety of animals and the containment of infectious diseases. At airport terminals, seaports, and border stations, officers inspect international conveyances and the baggage of passengers for plant and animal products that could harbor pests or disease organisms. At international airports, detector dogs in APHIS's Beagle Brigade help find prohibited agricultural materials. Officers also inspect ship and air cargoes, rail and truck freight, and package mail from foreign countries. At animal import centers, APHIS veterinarians check animals in quarantine. Overseas, APHIS operates preclearance programs to eliminate pests in some imported products right at the source (Figure 11.8).

For a list of some job opportunities at APHIS, review their careers Web page in Figure 11.9.

FIGURE 11.8   APHIS logo.

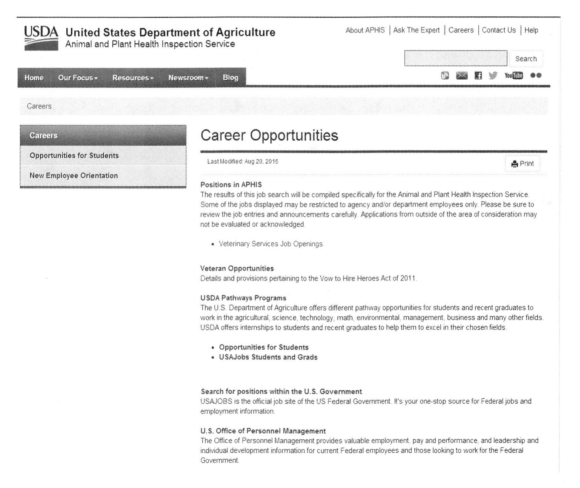

FIGURE 11.9   APHIS careers Web page. (From U.S. Department of Agriculture. Animal and Plant Health Inspection Service. Career opportunities. https://www.aphis.usda.gov/aphis/banner/careers.)

11.3.3 Infectious Diseases and Bioterrorism

The idea that disease can be an agent of the terrorist is not new.[14] In World War I, mustard gas and other virulent gases were used on the battlefield. In Saddam Hussein's Iraq, he thought so little of the Kurds that he used biological agents on them. Anthrax cases have been in the headlines in the last decade. The release of dangerous pathogens and disease-borne agents has allegedly occurred on the battlefield in certain nations, though we have yet to see a full-scale terrorist attack using these agents (Figure 11.10).[15]

The list of communicable diseases contains a full range of conditions that need reporting to local, state, and federal health authorities. DHS, HHS, and other agencies mandate the reporting of any case that makes the list of diseases (Table 11.4). The list of communicable diseases is regularly updated by both the Centers for Disease Control and Prevention (CDC) and various state health departments.

For those entrusted with security, the problem of disease generally comes in the form of biological agents used in terror attacks. Hence, the term *bioterrorism* has become part of the security vocabulary.[16] The CDC defines bioterrorism as an attack involving a

deliberate release of viruses, bacteria, or other germs (agents) used to cause illness or death in people, animals, or plants. These agents are typically found in nature, but it is possible that they could be changed to increase their ability to cause disease, make them resistant to current medicines, or to increase their ability to be spread into the environment. Biological

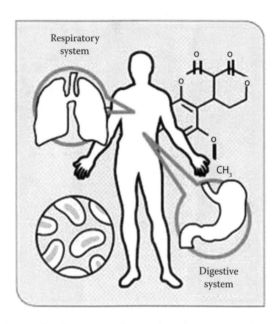

FIGURE 11.10 Biological attack effects on the major systems of the human body. A biological attack is the release of germs or other biological substances. Many agents must be inhaled, enter through a cut in the skin, or be eaten to make you sick. Some biological agents can cause contagious diseases; others do not.

TABLE 11.4 List of Reportable Communicable Diseases, 2016

Anthrax	Arboviral diseases, neuroinvasive and non-neuroinvasive	Babesiosis
Botulism/*Clostridium botulinum*	Brucellosis	Campylobacteriosis
Chancroid	*Chlamydia trachomatis* infection	Cholera
Congenital syphilis	Cryptosporidiosis	Coccidioidomycosis/valley fever
Cyclosporiasis	Dengue virus infections	Diphtheria
Ehrlichiosis and anaplasmosis	Giardiasis	Gonorrhea
Haemophilus influenzae, invasive disease	Hansen's disease/leprosy	Hantavirus infection, non-Hantavirus pulmonary syndrome
Hantavirus pulmonary syndrome (HPS)	Hemolytic uremic syndrome (HUS), postdiarrheal	Hepatitis A, acute
Hepatitis B, acute	Hepatitis B, chronic	Hepatitis B, perinatal infection
Hepatitis C, acute	Hepatitis C, chronic	HIV infection (AIDS has been reclassified as HIV Stage III) (AIDS/HIV)
Influenza-associated pediatric mortality	Invasive pneumococcal disease (IPD)/*Streptococcus pneumoniae*, invasive disease	Legionellosis/Legionnaires' disease or Pontiac fever
Leptospirosis	Listeriosis	Lyme disease
Malaria	Measles/rubeola	Meningococcal disease
Mumps	Novel influenza A virus infections	Pertussis/whooping cough
Plague	Poliomyelitis, paralytic	Poliovirus infection, nonparalytic
Psittacosis/ornithosis	Q fever	Rabies, animal
Rabies, human	Rubella/German measles	Rubella, congenital syndrome (CRS)
Salmonellosis	Severe acute respiratory syndrome, associated coronavirus disease (SARS)	Shiga toxin–producing *Escherichia coli* (STEC)
Shigellosis	Smallpox/variola	Spotted fever rickettsiosis
Streptococcal toxic shock syndrome (STSS)	Syphilis	Tetanus/*Clostridium tetani*
Toxic shock syndrome (other than streptococcal) (TSS)	Trichinellosis/trichinosis	Tuberculosis (TB)
Tularemia	Typhoid fever	Vancomycin-intermediate *Staphylococcus aureus* and vancomycin-resistant *S. aureus* (VISA/VRSA)
Varicella/chickenpox	Varicella deaths	Vibriosis
Viral hemorrhagic fever (VHF)	Yellow fever	Zika virus disease and Zika virus, congenital infection

Source: CDC, 2016 nationally notifiable infectious diseases, http://wwwn.cdc.gov/nndss/conditions/notifiable/2016/infectious-diseases (accessed August 25, 2016).

agents can be spread through the air, through water, or in food. Terrorists may use biological agents because they can be extremely difficult to detect and do not cause illness for several hours to several days. Some bioterrorism agents, like the smallpox virus, can be spread from person to person and some, like Anthrax, cannot.[17]

The CDC tracks and publishes data on the more pressing agents, such as anthrax (Figure 11.11).

Internet Resource: For the HHS-recommended protocol for countermeasures for bioterrorism, see http://emergency.cdc.gov/bioterrorism/prep.asp.

For DHS and HHS, and their collegial partners both governmental and private, the world of bioterrorism is front and center. At the DHS level, bioterrorism will involve three fronts:

- Infrastructure: Strengthen health systems, enhance medical communications, and maximize their contribution to the overall biodefense of the nation.
- Response: Improve specialized federal capabilities to respond in coordination with state and local governments.
- Science: Meet the medical needs of our bioterrorism response plans by developing specific new vaccines, medicines, and diagnostic tests (Figure 11.12). Develop an early warning system for bioterrorism.

In the area of infrastructure, both DHS and HHS stress the need for hospital facilities to be in a proactive and reactive capacity when bioterrorism strikes. HHS has devised the Hospital Preparedness Program (HPP), which seeks to elevate the capacity of hospitals to handle public health problems and to prepare for and respond to bioterrorism and other public health emergencies. Priority areas include interoperable communication systems, bed tracking, personnel management, fatality management planning, and hospital evacuation planning. During the last decade, HPP funds have also improved bed and personnel surge capacity, decontamination capabilities, isolation capacity, pharmaceutical supplies, training, education, and drills and exercises.

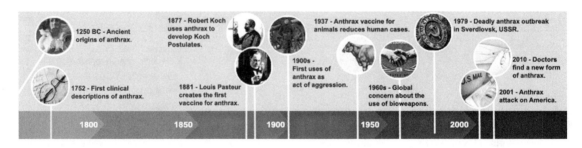

FIGURE 11.11 Anthrax timeline. From: CDC, Anthrax timeline, http://www.cdc.gov/anthrax/images/anthrax-timeline.jpg.

FIGURE 11.12 DHA chemist.

Internet Exercise: Find out about the 2015 grant funding programs targeted for Ebola at http://www.hhs.gov/about/news/2015/02/20/hhs-invests-in-enhancing-domestic-preparedness-efforts-for-ebola.html.

Hospitals, outpatient facilities, health centers, poison control centers, EMS, and other health-care partners work with the appropriate state or local health department to acquire funding and develop health-care system preparedness through this program. Most hospitals now have designated officers and offices that are responsible for homeland issues and the training of staff and administration in emergency response.

As for response capacity, hospitals and other medical facilities should have interoperable communications systems, task forces and advisory boards, and a steady stream of communication protocols that interconnect state, local, and federal authorities. Response also implies the capacity to react in the event of an attack. In biological and chemical situations, the medical facility needs adequate stockpiles of vaccine. Medical facilities need to be assured that suitable vendors and companies can supply basic medical goods.

Bioterrorism is primarily a study in science, and the countermeasures need to employ the highest and most sophisticated forms of scientific method. Hospitals should be engaged in serious research that relates to bioterrorism. The study of pathogens and corresponding antidotes should be central to that research, as well as analysis of compounds that will counter the effects of biological agents. Finally, scientific investment should include enhanced laboratory facilities. The Biomedical Advanced Research and Development Authority (BARDA) is one of the chief scientific authorities in R&D. BARDA manages Project BioShield, which includes the procurement and advanced development of medical countermeasures for CBR and nuclear agents, as well as the advanced development and procurement of medical countermeasures for pandemic influenza and other emerging infectious diseases.

11.3.3.1 Project BioShield

The Project BioShield Act[18] and the result, Project BioShield, was enacted in 2004.[19] The general aim of the project was to provide suitable vaccines and other medical supplies in the event of bioterrorism. The overall goals of the program were to

- Expedite the conduct of NIH R&D on medical countermeasures based on the most promising recent scientific discoveries.
- Give the FDA the ability to make promising treatments quickly available in emergency situations.
- Ensure that resources are available to pay for next-generation medical countermeasures (Project BioShield will allow the government to buy improved vaccines or drugs).

Project BioShield's rightful stress is on the pathogens that can cause global damage. Presently, the project has targeted biological threats that either have an antidote or are in need of serious research. In 2007, Project BioShield reported both threats and antidotes in its annual report (Table 11.5).

In 2013, Project BioShield reported the funding priorities that directly correlate to the finding of antitoxins and other remedial measures in the event of bioterrorism. BioShield divided up its resources into specific threats and the remedy thereto (Figure 11.13).

Looked at from another vantage point, BioShield spends the bulk of its research allocation on searching out vaccines for anthrax, smallpox, and botulism. The Project BioShield annual report to Congress (Table 11.6) charts this distribution of funds.[20]

11.3.3.2 Strategic National Stockpile

The CDC plays a major role in any bioterrorism event. Their most important task in the event of bioterrorism is the maintenance and oversight of the National Pharmaceutical Stockpile (NPS). The stockpile is a repository for lifesaving pharmaceuticals, antibiotics, chemical interventions, as well as medical, surgical, and patient support supplies, and equipment for prompt delivery to the site of a disaster, including a possible biological or chemical terrorist event anywhere in the United States. The NPS serves in a support role to local and state emergency, medical, and public health personnel.

A primary purpose of the NPS is to provide critical drugs and medical material that would otherwise be unavailable to local communities. The CDC prioritizes the stockpile based on the seriousness of the threat and the availability of both the agent and the antidote. The stockpile targets biological agents: smallpox, anthrax, pneumonic plague, tularemia, botulinum toxin, and viral hemorrhagic fevers (Figure 11.14).

Internet Exercise: Find out about the many activities of the stockpile at http://www.cdc.gov/phpr/stockpile/stockpile.htm#sns1.

TABLE 11.5 Projected Future Top-Priority Medical Countermeasure Programs

	Threat	Disease	Current Project BioShield Acquisition Programs	Projected Future Top-Priority Medical Countermeasure Programs		
				Threat-Specific Programs	Broad-Spectrum Antibiotic (B) Antiviral (V)	Diagnostic (D) Biodosimetry or Biosassay (B)
Chemical	Volatile nerve agents	Nerve agent toxicity		Enterprise CHEMPACKs Volatile nerve agent, single antidote		
Biological	Bacillus *anthracis* (bacteria), including multi-drug-resistant strains	Anthrax	Anthrax therapeutics (antitoxins) Anthrax vaccine (AVA, rPA)	Anthrax antitoxin(s) Anthrax vaccine(s) (next generation)	B	D
	Botulinum toxins (from *Clostridium botulinum* bacteria)	Botulism	Botulinum antitoxin			D
	Burkholderia mallei *Burkholderis pseudomallei* (bacteria)	Glanders, melioidosis			B	D
	Filoviruses Ebola and Marburg	Hemorrhagic fever		Filovirus medical countermeasures	V	D
	Francisella tularensis (bacteria)	Tularemia			B	

(Continued)

TABLE 11.5 (Continued) Projected Future Top-Priority Medical Countermeasure Programs

Threat	Disease	Current Project BioShield Acquisition Programs	Projected Future Top-Priority Medical Countermeasure Programs		
			Threat-Specific Programs	Broad-Spectrum Antibiotic (B) Antiviral (V)	Diagnostic (D) Biodosimetry or Biosassay (B)
Junin virus	Argentine hemorrhagic fever			V	
Rickettsia prowazekii (bacteria)	Typhus			B	D
Variola virus	Smallpox	MVA smallpox vaccine	Smallpox antiviral(s) Smallpox vaccine (next generation)	V	D
Yersinia pestis (bacteria)	Bubonic plague			B	D
Radiological/ nuclear	Radiological/ nuclear agents	Pediatric KI DTPA ARS medical countermeasures	Radionuclide-specific agents/decorporation agents ARS/DEARE medical countermeasures		B

Source: HHS, *Project BioShield: Annual Report to Congress: 2006–2007* (Washington, DC: U.S. Government Printing Office, 2007), 20, https://www.medicalcountermeasures.gov/barda/cbrn/project-bioshield-overview/project-bioshield-annual-report.aspx.

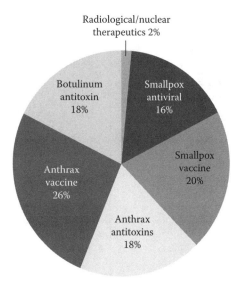

FIGURE 11.13 Project BioShield procurements, for fiscal years 2004–2012. From: Interview at Biomedical Advanced Research and Development Agency, November 2012.

11.3.3.3 National Select Agent Registry Program

The CDC net spreads into other territories involving dangerous substances. The National Select Agent Registry Program oversees the use and possession of biological agents and toxins that have the potential to pose a severe threat to public, animal, or plant health. The National Select Agent Registry Program currently requires registration of facilities, including government agencies, universities, research institutions, and commercial entities, that possess, use, or transfer biological agents and toxins that pose a significant threat to the public. Possession, as well as loss or theft of toxins and biological agents, needs to be reported to the CDC. A sample reporting form in the event of loss or theft is provided in Appendix V.

11.4 Pandemic Threats

The term *pandemic* connotes many things and generally conjures up images of fear and trepidation. Some pandemics are more serious than others. A flu outbreak, the nonlethal variety, is a pandemic of sorts. And then there are those outbreaks that are more serious and which cause death on a global scale, such as bird flu—the H1N1 virus where nearly 300 people died worldwide (Figure 11.15).

At other levels of potential destruction, the fears are well founded, for pandemic instances are global in scope and have the capacity to injure and kill on a widespread basis.[21] Ebola surely ranks up in the higher echelon of threats on the African continent. While the spread appears in check in 2015–2016, the re-emergence is very likely in the years ahead (Figure 11.16).

TABLE 11.6 Project BioShield Acquisition Activity

Countermeasure Area/Product	Date of Contract Award	Delivery to Strategic National Stockpile	Contract Recipient	Status at the Close of CY 2012	Total Funding (Millions)	Reason for Use of Authority
Anthrax Therapeutics						
Monoclonal antibody (Raxibacumab®, formerly Abthrax)	9/2005 (Base)	Completed (2008)	HGS	20,000 doses delivered; NDA filed with FDA (2008) and additional studies required by FDA (2009).	$174	Raxibacumab is an antitoxin used to treat anthrax and, along with vaccines and antibiotics, is part of a three-pronged approach taken by the USG to prepare for and respond to an anthrax attack. $8M was added to the contract to support studies required by the FDA. Cangene/Emergent submitted their BLA to the FDA in July 2014.
	7/2009 (Option)	Completed (2012)	HGS	45,000 doses delivered of 45,000 contracted.	$152 (2009) $8 (2011)	
Anthrax immune globulin (AIG®)	9/2005 (Base)	Completed (2011)	Cangene	10,000 doses delivered.	$144 (2005) $16.6 (2012)	AIG is an antitoxin used to treat anthrax and, along with vaccines and antibiotics, is part of a three-pronged approach taken by the USG to prepare for and respond to an anthrax attack.
Replenishment of anthrax antitoxins	9/2013	N/A	Elusys	N/A	$0.1	Base award only.
	9/2013	N/A	Emergent	Cell bank will be delivered to CIADMs in 2014.	$0.45	Procurement of cell bank used to manufacture monoclonal anthrax antitoxins as a risk mitigation strategy.
	9/2013	N/A	Pharm-Athene	Cell bank will be delivered to CIADMs in 2014.	$1.08	Procurement of cell bank used to manufacture monoclonal anthrax antitoxins as a risk mitigation strategy.
	9/2013	Ongoing	Glaxo-Smith-Kline	9,806 delivered of the 60,000 treatment courses. Cell bank will be delivered to CIADM in 2014 .	$196.8	60,000 treatment courses of Raxibacumab to maintain current preparedness to 2017 and procurement of cell bank.
	9/2013	Ongoing	Cangene	18,404 liters of plasma delivered.	$63.4	10,000 treatment course equivalents of plasma to be collected and stored as plasma to maintain preparedness to 2018.

	Date	Status	Company	Delivered	Price	Notes
	9/2014	TBD	Glaxo-Smith-Kline	0 delivered of the 32,704 treatment courses.	$105	Additional treatment courses of Raxibacumab will maintain preparedness levels through 2018 allowing for SNS to incorporate future procurements into their multiyear budget.
Anthrax Vaccines						
AVA (BioThrax®, anthrax vaccine absorbed)	5/2005	Completed (2006)	Emergent (formerly BioPort)	10 million doses delivered.	$243	BioThrax® is the U.S.-licensed vaccine for anthrax and, along with antitoxins and antibiotics, is part of a three-pronged approach taken by the USG to prepare for and respond to an anthrax attack. Emergent submitted their supplemental BLA for postexposure prophylaxis to the FDA in October 2014.
AVA (BioThrax®, anthrax vaccine absorbed)	9/2007	Completed (2008)	Emergent	18.75 million doses delivered.	$448 (2008) $8.7 (2012)	
rPA (recombinant protective antigen)	11/2004	N/A	VaxGen	Terminated 12/19/05.	$2	Contract terminated.

(Continued)

TABLE 11.6 (Continued) Project BioShield Acquisition Activity

Countermeasure Area/Product	Date of Contract Award	Delivery to Strategic National Stockpile	Contract Recipient	Status at the Close of CY 2012	Total Funding (Millions)	Reason for Use of Authority
Botulism Therapeutics						
Botulinum antitoxin (HBAT) therapeutic	9/2006	Ongoing	Cangene	148,702 doses delivered of 200,000 contracted. In addition, all plasma necessary to manufacture an additional 100,000 doses has been collected and is being maintained by BARDA as frozen plasma.	$415 (2006) $61 (2011)	Equine-derived polyclonal sera to multiple strains of (A-G) of *C. botulinum* used as a therapeutic for botulism. Re-evaluation of the requirement led to a decrease in the number of doses necessary in the SNS. Thus, HHS/BARDA has met the requirement. The contract was modified and $61 million in additional funds were added to maintain the horse herd, stockpile plasma, and continue stability testing of plasma and product in the SNS. This contract modification will ensure preparedness out to 2025.
Smallpox Vaccine						
Imvamune®, MVA (modified vaccinia Ankara) smallpox vaccine	6/2007 (Base)	Completed (2013)	Bavarian Nordic	20 million delivered of 20 million contracted.	$505 (2007) $37 (2013)	Imvamune is an attenuated smallpox vaccine designated for immunocompromised persons as part of the overall strategy of using vaccines and antiviral drugs for preparedness for and response to a smallpox attack.
Imvamune®, MVA (modified vaccinia Ankara) smallpox vaccine; option to deliver 4 million doses	3/2013 (Option)	Completed (2014)	Bavarian Nordic	4 million delivered of 4 million contracted.	$110 (2013)	

Imvamune®, MVA (modified vaccinia Ankara) smallpox vaccine; option to deliver 4 million doses	9/2014 (Option)	Completed (January 2015)	Bavarian Nordic	4 million delivered of 4 million contracted.	$118 (2014)	Imvamune is an attenuated smallpox vaccine designated for immunocompromised persons as part of the overall strategy using vaccines and antiviral drugs for preparedness for and response to a smallpox attack.
ST-246	5/2011	Ongoing	SIGA Tech. Inc.	1.2 million out of 1.7 million treatment courses.	$433 (2011)	The SNS formulary currently contains smallpox vaccine for the general population, smallpox vaccine for immunocompromised individuals and vaccinia immune globulin (VIG) to treat adverse reactions to the vaccine for the general population. ST-246 may be used to treat those individuals who are symptomatic with disease for which the vaccine has no efficacy. Late-stage development and procurement of this drug complements the HHS formulary of medical countermeasures to provide an appropriate response after a smallpox incident. In addition, this contract works toward the USG goal of developing two smallpox antivirals.

Medical Countermeasures for Radiological, Nuclear, and Chemical Threats

Potassium iodide (ThyroShield®)	3/2005	Complete	Fleming	4.8 million doses, deliveries complete.	$18	Provides capability for pediatric treatment. Note: the PHEMCE reduced this requirement and the SNS does not currently maintain this product.
IV calcium/zinc DTPA (diethylene triamine pentaacetic	12/2005	Complete	Akorn	473,710 doses, deliveries complete.	$22	Decorporation agent for radionuclear treatment.

(Continued)

TABLE 11.6 (Continued) Project BioShield Acquisition Activity

Countermeasure Area/Product	Date of Contract Award	Delivery to Strategic National Stockpile	Contract Recipient	Status at the Close of CY 2012	Total Funding (Millions)	Reason for Use of Authority
G-CSF cytokine for neutropenia, associated with exposure to ionizing radiation	9/2013	Completed product maintained under VMI	Amgen	0/35,203 treatment courses. Note: this product will be maintained as vendor-managed inventory (VMI).	$157.7	Neutropenia is one of the subsyndromes associated with exposure to ionizing radiation. Amgen's Neupogen® is approved by the FDA to treat neutropenia resulting from chemotherapy treatment and can be used under EUA for neutropenia associated with exposure to ionizing radiation.
GM-CSF cytokine for neutropenia, associated with exposure to ionizing radiation	9/2013	Completed product maintained under VMI	Sanofi-aventis	0/4,340 treatment courses. Note: this product will be maintained as vendor-managed inventory (VMI).	$36.8	Neutropenia is one of the subsyndromes associated with exposure to ionizing radiation. Sanofi-aventis' Leukine® is approved by the FDA to treat neutropenia resulting from chemotherapy treatment. Funding will provide late-stage development for additional nonclinical studies that may be necessary to use under an EUA. Sanofi-aventis will be pursuing approval for the ARS indication as well.
Midazolam to treat seizures associated with exposure to chemical nerve agents	9/2013	TBD	Meridian (Pfizer)	0/2.3 million treatment courses.	$60.8	Midazolam offers advantages over the current product in the SNS CHEMPACKs, diazepam. Midazolam is faster acting, longer acting, and can be administered intramuscularly as opposed to intravenous for diazepam. Midazolam will replace diazepam as it expires in the CHEMPACKs. Funding will also support approval for status epilepticus in adults and pediatrics and seizures resulting from exposure to chemical nerve agents in adults and pediatrics.

Source: HHS, Project BioShield annual report: January 2014–December 2014 (Washington, DC: HHS, 2015), https://www.medicalcountermeasures. gov/barda/cbrn/project-bioshield-overview/project-bioshield-annual-report.aspx.

FIGURE 11.14   CDC stockpiles.

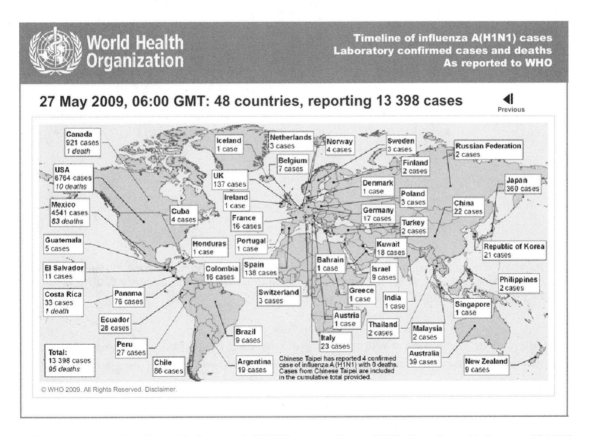

FIGURE 11.15   Timeline of influenza A (H1 N1) cases. From: WHO, Timeline of influenza A(H1N1) cases: Laboratory confirmed cases and deaths as reported to WHO, http://www.who.int/csr/disease/swineflu/history_map/InfluenzaAH1N1_maps.html.

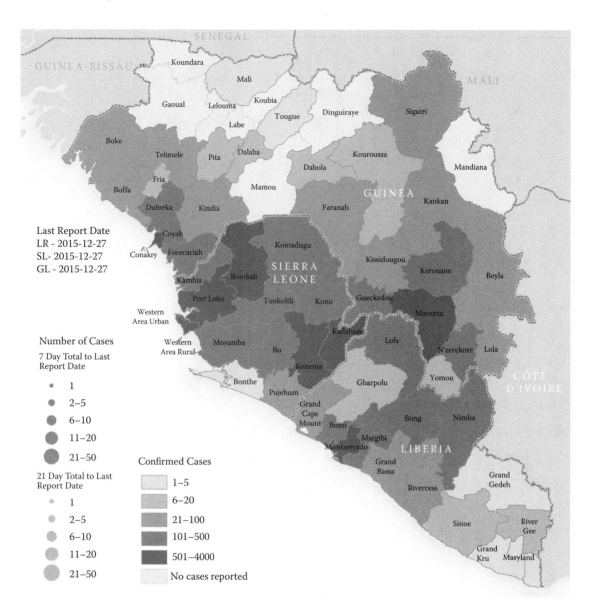

FIGURE 11.16   Geographical distribution of new and total confirmed Ebola cases in Guinea, Liberia, and Sierra Leone, January 6, 2016. From: WHO, *Ebola Situation Report*, January 6, 2016 (accessed February 7, 2016).

Pandemics are not a new phenomenon but have long been tracked globally. Pandemics fall into these basic categories:

- Bird flu is commonly used to refer to AI (see the following category). Bird flu viruses infect birds, including chickens, other poultry, and wild birds such as ducks.
- AI is caused by influenza viruses that occur naturally among wild birds. Low-pathogenic AI is common in birds and causes few problems. Highly pathogenic H5N1 is deadly to domestic fowl, can be transmitted from birds to humans, and

is deadly to humans. There is virtually no human immunity and human vaccine availability is very limited.

- Pandemic flu is virulent human flu that causes a global outbreak, or pandemic, of serious illness. Because there is little natural immunity, the disease can spread easily from person to person. Currently, there is no pandemic flu.
- Seasonal (or common) flu is a respiratory illness that can be transmitted person to person. Most people have some immunity, and a vaccine is available.[22]

To compare and contrast the pandemic form with other sorts of flu or influenza, see Figure 11.17. Pandemics are largely the by-product of influenzas (Figure 11.18). Influenza viruses have mutated and caused pandemics or global epidemics. In the United States, the most severe outbreaks occurred in 1918 (Figures 11.19 and 11.20).

Internet Resource: For a history of flu epidemics, visit http://www.flu.gov/pandemic/history/1918/index.html.

The very definition of pandemic implies a broad impact, a disease or infection with the capacity to cover a large swath of geography. A pandemic is a global disease outbreak. For example, a flu pandemic occurs when a new influenza virus emerges for which people have little or no immunity, and for which there is no vaccine. Or a disease may be spread in an airborne fashion, such as the avian influenza witnessed in China and other Asian locales. The World Health Organization (WHO) gauges the severity of influenza outbreak by phases—with the infection commencing in lower animal forms, progressing to various

Pandemic Flu	Seasonal Flu
Rarely happens (three times in the twentieth century).	Happens annually and usually peaks in January or February.
People have little or no immunity because they have no previous exposure to the virus.	Usually some immunity built up from previous exposure.
Healthy people may be at increased risk for serious complications.	Usually only people at high risk, not healthy adults, are at risk of serious complications.
Health-care providers and hospitals may be overwhelmed.	Health-care providers and hospitals can usually meet public and patient needs.
Vaccine probably would not be available in the early stages of a pandemic.	Vaccine available for annual flu season.
Effective antivirals may be in limited supply.	Adequate supplies of antivirals are usually available.
Number of deaths could be high. (The U.S. death toll during the 1918 pandemic was approximately 675,000.)	Seasonal flu-associated deaths in the United States over 30 years ending in 2007 have ranged from about 3,000 per season to about 49,000 per season.
Symptoms may be more severe.	Symptoms include fever, cough, runny nose, and muscle pain.
May cause major impact on the general public, such as widespread travel restrictions and school or business closings.	Usually causes minor impact on the general public, some schools may close and sick people are encouraged to stay home.
Potential for severe impact on domestic and world economy.	Manageable impact on domestic and world economy.

FIGURE 11.17 Seasonal flu vs. pandemic flu. Modified from: Flu.gov, About pandemics: Seasonal flu versus pandemic flu, www.pandemicflu.gov/individualfamily/about/pandemic/index.html.

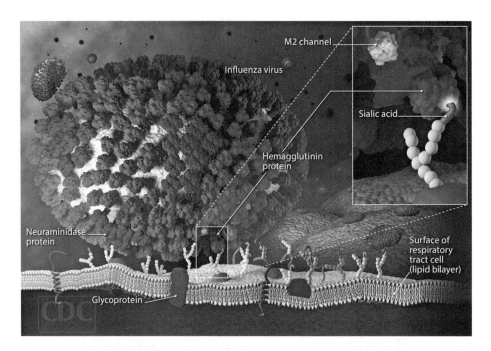

FIGURE 11.18 This image illustrates the very beginning stages of an influenza (flu) infection. Most experts think that influenza viruses spread mainly through small droplets containing influenza virus. These droplets are expelled into the air when people infected with the flu cough, sneeze, or talk. Once in the air, these small infectious droplets can land in the mouths or noses of people who are nearby. From: CDC, Influenza (flu), http://www.cdc.gov/flu/images.htm (accessed February 7, 2016).

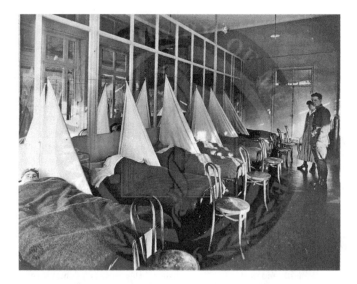

FIGURE 11.19 In July, an American soldier said that while influenza caused a heavy fever, it "usually only confines the patient to bed for a few days." The mutation of the virus changed all that (Credit: National Library of Medicine). From: HHS, The great pandemic: The United States in 1918–1919, http://www.flu.gov/pandemic/history/1918/the_pandemic/influenza/index.html.

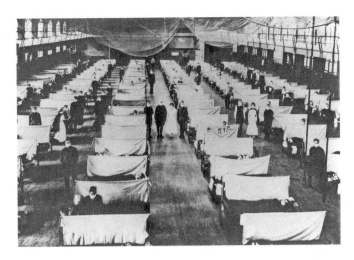

FIGURE 11.20   When it came to treating influenza patients, doctors, nurses, and druggists were at a loss (Credit: Office of the Public Health Service Historian). From: HHS, The great pandemic, http:// www.flu.gov/pandemic/history/1918/the_pandemic/iowa_flu2.jpg.

levels of human infection, to eventual reductions.[23] It is difficult to predict when the next influenza pandemic will occur or how severe it will be. Wherever and whenever a pandemic starts, everyone around the world is at risk. Countries might, through measures such as border closures and travel restrictions, delay the arrival of the virus, but they cannot stop it.

Health professionals are concerned that the continued spread of a highly pathogenic avian H5N1 virus across Eastern Asia and other areas represents a significant threat to human health. The H5N1 virus has raised concerns about a potential human pandemic because

- It is especially virulent.
- It is being spread by migratory birds.
- It can be transmitted from birds to mammals and, in some limited circumstances, to humans.
- Like other influenza viruses, it continues to evolve.

Pandemics have been witnessed throughout human history, with the twentieth century experiencing myriad events. The National Institute of Health tracks the past 100 years (Figure 11.21).

11.4.1 Planning, Preparedness, and Response

Recognizing both the epidemiological and terrorist implications of the pandemic, state, federal, and local governments need to prepare for and respond to this event.[24] Globally, the WHO has a system of alerts and notices as to potential or actual pandemics. Each day, the WHO publishes existing or developing threats, an example being Figure 11.22.

At the federal level, a prevention and response program has been formalized. The National Strategy for Pandemic Influenza guides the country's preparedness and response to an influenza pandemic, with the intent of (1) stopping, slowing, or otherwise limiting the

■ Major pandemic
◯ The appearance of a new influenza strain in the human population

1918
■ **Pandemic**
"Spanish flu" H1N1
The most devastating flu pandemic in recent history, killing more than 500,000 people in the United States, and 20 million to 50 million people worldwide.

1957–58
■ **Pandemic**
"Asian flu" H2N2
First identified in China, this virus caused roughly 70,000 deaths in the United States during the 1957–58 season. Because this strain has not circulated in humans since 1968, no one under 30 years old has immunity to this strain.

1968–69
■ **Pandemic**
"Hong Kong flu" H3N2
First detected in Hong Kong, this virus caused roughly 34,000 deaths in the United States during the 1968–69 season. H3N2 viruses still circulate today.

1976
Four soldiers in a US army base in New Jersey are infected with swine influenza, resulting in one death.

1977
◯ **Appearance of a new influenza strain in humans**
"Russian flu" H1N1
Isolated in northern China, this virus was similar to the virus that spread before 1957. For this reason, individuals born before 1957 were generally protected; however children and young adults born after that year were not because they had no prior immunity.

1997
◯ **Appearance of a new influenza strain in humans**
H5N1
The first time an influenza virus was found to be transmitted directly from birds to people, with infections linked to exposure to poultry markets. Eighteen people in Hong Kong were hospitalized, six of whom died.

1999
◯ **Appearance of a new influenza strain in humans**
H9N2
Appeared for the first time in humans. It caused illness in two children in Hong Kong, with poultry being the probable source.

2002
◯ **Appearance of a new influenza strain in humans**
H7N2
Evidence of infection is found in one person in Virginia following a poultry outbreak.

FIGURE 11.21   Timeline of human flu pandemics, including human cases of avian and swine influenza viruses. From National Institute of Allergy and Infectious Diseases, National Institute of Health, Timeline of human flu pandemics, http://www.niaid.nih.gov/topics/flu/research/pandemic/pages/timelinehumanpandemics.aspx.

2003

◉ **Appearance of a new influenza strain in humans**

H5N1

Caused two Hong Kong family members to be hospitalized after a visit to China, killing one of them, a 33-year-old man. (A third family member died while in China of an undiagnosed respiratory illness.)

H7N7

In the first reported cases of this strain in humans, 89 people in the Netherlands, most of whom were poultry workers, became ill with eye infections or flu-like symptoms. A veterinarian who visited one of the affected poultry farms died.

H7N2

Caused a person to be hospitalized in New York.

H9N2

Caused illness in one child in Hong Kong.

2004

◉ **Appearance of a new influenza strain in humans**

H5N1

Caused illness in 47 people in Thailand and Vietnam, 34 of whom died. Researchers are especially concerned because this flu strain, which is quite deadly, is becoming endemic in Asia.

H7N3

Is reported for the first time in humans. The strain caused illness in two poultry workers in Canada.

H10N7

Is reported for the first time in humans. It caused illness in two infants in Egypt. One child's father is a poultry merchant.

2005

H5N1

The first case of human infection with H5N1 arises in Cambodia in February. By May, WHO reports 4 Cambodian cases, all fatal. Indonesia reports its first case, which is fatal, in July. Over the next three months, 7 cases of laboratory-confirmed H5N1 infection in Indonesia, and 4 deaths, occur.

On December 30, WHO reports a cumulative total of 142 laboratory-confirmed cases of H5N1 infection worldwide, all in Asia, with 74 deaths. Asian countries in which human infection with H5N1 has been detected: Thailand, Vietnam, Cambodia, Indonesia and China.

2006

H5N1

In early January, two human cases of H5N1 infection, both fatal, are reported in rural areas of Eastern Turkey, while cases in China continues to spread. As of January 25, China reports a total of 10 cases, with 7 deaths. On January 30, Iraq reports its first case of human H5N1 infection, which was fatal, to the WHO.

In March, the WHO confirmed seven cases of human H5N1 infection, and five deaths, in Azerbaijan. In April, WHO confirmed four cases of human H5N1 infection, and two fatalities, in Egypt.

In May, the WHO confirmed a case of human H5N1 infection in the African nation of Djibouti. This was the first confirmed case in sub-Saharan Africa. Throughout 2006, 115 human cases of H5N1 infection occur, with 79 deaths.

2007

H5N1

In early January, two human cases of H5N1 are confirmed in Indonesia. By the end of 2007, 88 confirmed cases occur in Indonesia, Cambodia, China, Lao People's Democratic Republic, Myanmar, Nigeria, Pakistan and Vietnam, with 59 deaths.

FIGURE 11.21 (Continued)

H7N7

In May, four cases of H7N7 avian influenza were confirmed in the United Kingdom among individuals exposed to infected poultry.

2008
H5N1

On May 28, Bangladesh reports its first case of human H5N1 infection to the WHO. By the end of the year, 40 cases are confirmed in Bangladesh, Cambodia, China, Egypt, Indonesia and Vietnam.

2009
H5N1

On January 7, Indonesia confirmed a new case of human infection with H5N1 influenza. Since that time, new cases have been identified in Egypt, China, Indonesia and Vietnam.

⊙ **Appearance of a new influenza strain in humans**
H1N1

In April, human infection with a new strain of H1N1 influenza is confirmed in Mexico. Within weeks, human infections spread to the United States and cases begin occurring in other regions around the world.

FIGURE 11.21   (Continued)

spread of a pandemic to the United States; (2) limiting the domestic spread of a pandemic, and mitigating disease, suffering, and death; and (3) sustaining infrastructure and mitigating impact to the economy and the functioning of society.[25] The strategy charges HHS with leading the federal pandemic preparedness. Working with the WHO, federal officials seek to mitigate and contain as well as prevent future events from taking place (Figure 11.23).

The key elements in planning and response include the following:

1. In advance of an influenza pandemic, HHS will work with federal, state, and local government partners and the private sector to coordinate pandemic influenza preparedness activities and to achieve interoperable response capabilities.

2. In advance of an influenza pandemic, HHS will encourage all Americans to be active partners in preparing their states, local communities, workplaces, and homes for pandemic influenza and will emphasize that a pandemic will require Americans to make difficult choices. An informed and responsive public is essential to minimizing the health effects of a pandemic and the resulting consequences to society.

3. In advance of an influenza pandemic, HHS, in concert with federal partners, will work with the pharmaceutical industry to develop domestic vaccine production capacity sufficient to provide vaccines for the entire U.S. population as soon as possible after the onset of a pandemic and, during the pre-pandemic period, to produce up to 20 million courses of vaccine against each circulating influenza virus with pandemic potential and to expand seasonal influenza domestic vaccine production to cover all Americans for whom vaccine is recommended through normal commercial transactions.

4. In advance of an influenza pandemic, HHS, in concert with federal partners and in collaboration with the states, will procure sufficient quantities of antiviral drugs to treat 25% of the U.S. population and, in so doing, stimulate development of expanded

Zika virus infection – Panama

Disease Outbreak News
22 December 2015

On 14 December 2015, the National IHR Focal Point (NFP) of Panama notified PAHO/WHO of one (1) additional laboratory-confirmed case of Zika virus infection.

As of 17 December, 4 cases of Zika virus had been confirmed by reverse transcription polymerase chain reaction (RT-PCR). All laboratory-confirmed cases of Zika virus infection are female ranging in age between 25 and 59 years.

A total of 95 suspected cases, with symptoms compatible with Zika virus infection, have also been reported in the Ustupu and Ogobsugun islands, Guna Yala province. Of the 95 suspected cases, 4 tested positive for dengue virus by RT-PCR. The first case of dengue was confirmed approximately two weeks prior to the confirmation of Zika virus infection. This indicates co-circulation of the two viruses in the same community. Of the remaining 91 suspected cases, 30 were negative for both dengue and chikungunya. Suspected cases are distributed across all ages, with the highest number concentrated in the age group 25–34. Women account for the majority of cases (66%).

Public health response

Panamanian health authorities are implementing various public health measures:

- carrying out information, education and communication activities—e.g., leaflets in three languages (Guna, Spanish and English) have been developed and distributed;
- conducting vector control activities.

WHO advice

The proximity of mosquito vector breeding sites to human habitation is a significant risk factor for Zika virus infection. Prevention and control relies on reducing the breeding of mosquitoes through source reduction (removal and modification of breeding sites) and reducing contact between mosquitoes and people. This can be achieved by reducing the number of natural and artificial water-filled habitats that support mosquito larvae, reducing the adult mosquito populations around at-risk communities and by using barriers such as insect screens, closed doors and windows, long clothing and repellents. Since the Aedes mosquitoes (the primary vector for transmission) are day-biting mosquitoes, it is recommended that those who sleep during the daytime, particularly young children, the sick or elderly, should rest under mosquito nets (bed nets), treated with or without insecticide to provide protection. Mosquito coils or other insecticide vaporizers may also reduce the likelihood of being bitten.

During outbreaks, space spraying of insecticides may be carried out following the technical orientation provided by WHO to kill flying mosquitoes. Suitable insecticides (recommended by the WHO Pesticide Evaluation Scheme) may also be used as larvicides to treat relatively large water containers, when this is technically indicated.

Basic precautions for protection from mosquito bites should be taken by people traveling to high risk areas, especially pregnant women. These include use of repellents, wearing light colored, long sleeved shirts and pants and ensuring rooms are fitted with screens to prevent mosquitoes from entering.

WHO does not recommend any travel or trade restriction to Panama based on the current information available.

FIGURE 11.22 WHO emergency outbreak news on the Zika virus. From: WHO, Emergency preparedness, response: Zika virus infection—Panama, http://www.who.int/csr/don/22-december-2015-zika-panama/en (accessed February 7, 2016).

Phase 1	No animal influenza virus circulating among animals has been reported to cause infection in humans.
Phase 2	An animal influenza virus circulating in domesticated or wild animals is known to have caused infection in humans and is therefore considered a specific potential pandemic threat.
Phase 3	An animal or human-animal influenza reassortant virus has caused sporadic cases or small clusters of disease in people, but has not resulted in human-to-human transmission sufficient to sustain community-level outbreaks.
Phase 4	Human-to-human transmission (H2H) of an animal or human-animal influenza reassortant virus able to sustain community-level outbreaks has been verified.
Phase 5	The same identified virus has caused sustained community level outbreaks in two or more countries in one WHO region.
Phase 6	In addition to the criteria defined in Phase 5, the same virus has caused sustained community level outbreaks in at least one other country in another WHO region.
Post-peak period	Levels of pandemic influenza in most countries with adequate surveillance have dropped below peak levels.
Possible new wave	Level of pandemic influenza activity in most countries with adequate surveillance ns1ng again.
Post-pandemic period	Levels of influenza activity have returned to the levels seen for seasonal influenza in most countries with adequate surveillance.

FIGURE 11.23 Global pandemic phases and the stages for federal government response. From: FEMA, *Pandemic Influenza Continuity of Operations Annex Template Instructions*, 13, http://www.fema.gov/media-library-data/1396880633531-35405f61d483668155492a7cccd1600b/Pandemic+Influenza+Template.pdf.

domestic production capacity sufficient to accommodate subsequent needs through normal commercial transactions. HHS will stockpile antiviral medications in the Strategic National Stockpile, and states will create and maintain local stockpiles.

5. Sustained human-to-human transmission anywhere in the world will be the triggering event to initiate a pandemic response by the United States. Because we live in a global community, a human outbreak anywhere means risk everywhere.

6. The United States will attempt to prevent an influenza pandemic or delay its emergence by striving to arrest isolated outbreaks of a novel influenza wherever circumstances suggest that such an attempt might be successful, acting in concert with WHO and other nations as appropriate. At the core of this strategy will be basic public health measures to reduce person-to-person transmission.

7. At the onset of an influenza pandemic, HHS, in concert with federal partners, will work with the pharmaceutical industry to procure vaccine directed against the pandemic strain and to distribute vaccine to state and local public health departments for predetermined priority groups based on preapproved state plans.

8. At the onset of an influenza pandemic, HHS, in collaboration with the states, will begin to distribute and deliver antiviral drugs from public stockpiles to healthcare facilities and others with direct patient care responsibility for administration to pre-determined priority groups.[26]

Internet Exercise: Review the essential planning elements for a pandemic influenza outbreak as recommended by FEMA at http://www.fema.gov/media-library-data/1396880633531-35405f61d483668155492a7cccd1600b/Pandemic+Influenza+Template.pdf.

Pandemic planning also incorporates the resources of state and local law enforcement—agencies that are on the front lines throughout this public health threat (Figure 11.24).[27]

Every entity of government and the private sector should anticipate and prepare for the potential pandemic. As in all other areas of homeland security planning, the agency must be predictive yet reasonable in its approach and anticipate the required resource in the event of a pandemic.

Internet Resource: See data from the CDC on how influenza is tracked at www.cdc.gov/flu/weekly/index.htm.

Pandemic planning and preparedness need occur during periods of "calm," when strategic planning is clear and free from the intensity of the moment.[28]

Internet Resource: HHS has produced a bevy of materials that anticipate the prevention as well as impact of a pandemic. See http://www.flu.gov/planning-preparedness/index.html.

11.5 Conclusion

This chapter deals with the public health dimensions of the homeland security problem. Biotoxins and bioterrorism must weigh heavily on the minds of those entrusted with minimizing the effects of these and other threats. DHS fully understands the potential for massive public health risk and injury. Working closely with the EPA, HHS, the USDA, and the Department of the Interior, DHS looks for those actions that might cause extensive public harm in a health context. Hence, water, its facilities and corresponding security, and threat assessment plans receive significant attention.

Equally important will be potential threats against our agricultural and food supplies. That contamination of the food chain would be an extraordinary public health dilemma cannot be overemphasized. Farm installations must also dwell on secured practices to ensure integrity in the food chain. Diseased animals represent a threat too. Featured within the chapter is the infectious animal disease facility at Plum Island in the waters near Rhode Island and New York. The SPPA highlights and targets the most common threats to the agricultural marketplace and its providers. Just as crucial in the homeland defense of our agricultural infrastructure is the inspection plan of facilities by the USDA. Finally, the

LAW ENFORCEMENT PANDEMIC INFLUENZA PLANNING CHECKLIST

In the event of pandemic influenza, law enforcement agencies (e.g., State, local, and tribal Police Departments, Sheriff's Offices, Federal law enforcement officers, special jurisdiction police personnel) will play a critical role in maintaining the rule of law as well as protecting the health and safety of citizens in their respective jurisdictions. Planning for pandemic influenza is critical.

To assist you in your efforts, the Department of Health and Human Services (HHS) has developed the following checklist for law enforcement agencies. This checklist provides a general framework for developing a pandemic influenza plan. Each agency or organization will need to adapt this checklist according to its unique needs and circumstances. The key planning activities in this checklist are meant to complement and enhance your existing all-hazards emergency and operational continuity plans. Many of the activities identified in this checklist will also help you to prepare for other kinds of public health emergencies.

Information specific to public safety organizations and pandemic flu preparedness and response can be found at http://www.ojp.usdoj.gov/BJA/pandemic/resources.html. For further information on general emergency planning and continuity of operations, see www.ready.gov. Further information on pandemic influenza can be found at www.pandemicflu.gov.

Develop a pandemic influenza preparedness and response plan for your agency or organization.

Completed	In Progress	Not Started	
☐	☐	☐	Assign primary responsibility for coordinating law enforcement pandemic influenza preparedness planning to a single person (identify back-ups for that person as well) with appropriate training and authority (insert name, title, and contact information here).
☐	☐	☐	Form a multidisciplinary law enforcement/security planning committee to address pandemic influenza preparedness specifically. The planning team should include at a minimum: human resources, health and wellness, computer support personnel, legal system representatives, partner organizations, and local public health resources. Alternatively, pandemic influenza preparedness can be addressed by an existing committee with appropriate skills and knowledge and relevant mission (list committee members and contact information here). This Committee needs to have the plan approved by the Agency Head.
☐	☐	☐	Review Federal, State, and local public health and emergency management agencies' pandemic plans in areas where you operate or have jurisdictional responsibilities. Ensure that your plan is NIMS (National Incident Management System) compliant and align your plan with the local Incident Command System (ICS) and local pandemic influenza plans to achieve a unified approach to incident management. See "State and Local Governments," www.pandemicflu.gov/plan/states/index.html and http://www.fema.gov/emergency/nims/index.shtm.
☐	☐	☐	Verify Command and Control areas of responsibility and authority during a pandemic. Identify alternative individuals in case primary official becomes incapacitated.
☐	☐	☐	Set up chain of command and procedures to signal activation of the agency's response plan, altering operations (e.g., shutting down non-critical operations or operations in affected areas or concentrating resources on critical activities), as well as returning to normal operations.
☐	☐	☐	Determine the potential impact of a pandemic on the agency or organization by using multiple possible scenarios of varying severity relative to illness, absenteeism, supplies, availability of resources, access to legal system representatives, etc. Incorporate pandemic influenza into agency emergency management planning and exercise.
☐	☐	☐	Identify current activities (by location and function) that will be critical to maintain during a pandemic. These essential functions might include 911 systems in communities where law enforcement is responsible for this activity, other communications infrastructures, community policing, information systems, vehicle maintenance, etc. Identify critical resources and inputs (e.g., employees, supplies, subcontractor services/products, and logistics) that are necessary to support these crucial activities.

September 4, 2007
Version 1

CDC

FIGURE 11.24   Law enforcement pandemic influenza planning checklist from the CDC. From: HHS, Law enforcement pandemic influenza planning checklist, www.flu.gov/planning-preparedness/business/lawenforcement.pdf.

Develop a pandemic influenza preparedness and response plan for your agency or organization *(continued)*

Completed	In Progress	Not Started	
☐	☐	☐	Develop, review, and approve an official law enforcement/security pandemic influenza preparedness and response plan. This plan represents the output of many or all of the activities contained in this checklist. This plan can be an extension of your current emergency or business continuity plans with a special focus on pandemic influenza and should identify the organizational structure to be used to implement the plan. Include procedures to implement the plan in stages based upon appropriate triggering events.
☐	☐	☐	Develop a pandemic-specific emergency communications plan as part of the pandemic influenza preparedness and response plan, and revise it periodically. The communications plan should identify a communication point of contact, key contacts and back-ups, and chain of communications and clearance. Plan may also include potential collaboration with media representatives on the development of scripts based on likely scenarios guided by the public information officer(s). Coordinate with partners in emergency government and public health in advance.
☐	☐	☐	Designate an individual to monitor pandemic status and collect, organize, and integrate related information to update operations as necessary. Develop a plan for back-up if that person becomes ill during a pandemic. Develop a situational awareness capability that leadership can use to monitor the pandemic situation, support agency decisions, and facilitate monitoring of impact.
☐	☐	☐	Distribute pandemic plan throughout the agency or organization and develop means to document employees/staff received and read the plan.
☐	☐	☐	Allocate resources through the budgeting process as needed to support critical components of preparedness and response identified in your plan.
☐	☐	☐	Periodically test both the preparedness and response plan and the communications plan through drills and exercises; incorporate lessons learned into the plans.

Plan for the impact of a pandemic on your employees

Completed	In Progress	Not Started	
☐	☐	☐	Develop contingency plans for 30 – 40% employee absences. Keep in mind that absences may occur due to personal illness, family member illness, community mitigation measures, quarantines, school, childcare, or business closures, public transportation disruptions, or fear of exposure to ill individuals, as well as first responder, National Guard, or military reserve obligations.
☐	☐	☐	As necessary, plan for cross-training employees, use of auxiliary personnel and recent retirees, recruiting temporary personnel during a crisis, or establishing flexible worksite options (e.g., telecommuting) and flexible work hours (e.g. staggered shifts) when appropriate.
☐	☐	☐	Develop a reporting mechanism for employees to immediately report their own possible influenza illness during a pandemic (24/7).
☐	☐	☐	Establish compensation and leave policies that strongly encourage ill workers to stay home until they are no longer contagious. During a pandemic, employees with influenza-like symptoms (such as fever accompanied by sore throat, muscle aches and cough) should not enter the worksite to keep from infecting other workers. Employees who have been exposed to someone with influenza, particularly ill members of their household, may also be asked to stay home and monitor their symptoms.
☐	☐	☐	Employees who develop influenza-like symptoms while at the worksite should leave as soon as possible. Consult with State and local public health authorities regarding appropriate treatment for ill employees. Prepare policies that will address needed actions when an ill employee refuses to stay away from work. Federal agencies can consult guidance provided by the Office of Personnel Management (OPM) at www.opm.gov/pandemic.
☐	☐	☐	Identify employees who may need to stay home if schools dismiss students and childcare programs close for a prolonged period of time (up to 12 weeks) during a severe pandemic. Advise employees not to bring their children to the workplace if childcare cannot be arranged. Plan for alternative staffing or staffing schedules on the basis of your identification of employees who may need to stay home.
☐	☐	☐	Identify critical job functions and plan now for cross-training employees to cover those functions in case of prolonged absenteeism during a pandemic. Develop succession plans for each critical agency position to ensure the continued effective performance of your organization by identifying and training replacements for key people when necessary. These replacements should be integrated into employee development activities, and should include critical contracted services as well.
☐	☐	☐	Develop policies that focus on preventing the spread of respiratory infections in the workplace. This policy might include social distancing practices, the promotion of respiratory hygiene/cough etiquette, the creation of screening mechanisms for use during a pandemic to examine employees for fever or influenza symptoms, using the full range of available leave policies to facilitate staying home when ill or when a household member is ill, and appropriate attention to environmental hygiene and cleaning. (For more information see the www.pandemicflu.gov and http://www.pandemicflu.gov/plan/community/mitigation.html as well as OPM's guidance at www.opm.gov/pandemic.)

FIGURE 11.24   (Continued).

Plan for the impact of a pandemic on your employees *(continued)*

Completed	In Progress	Not Started	
☐	☐	☐	Provide educational programs and materials (language, culture, and reading-level appropriate) to personnel on: • pandemic fundamentals (e.g., signs and symptoms of influenza, modes of transmission, medical care), • personal and family protection and response strategies (e.g., hand hygiene, coughing/sneezing etiquette, etc.). Post instructional signs that illustrate correct infection control procedures in all appropriate locations, including offices, restrooms, waiting rooms, processing rooms, detention facilities, vehicles, etc. and, • community mitigation interventions (e.g., social distancing, etc.). See www.pandemicflu.gov, www.cdc.gov/flu/protect/stopgerms.htm, http://www.cdc.gov/flu/protect/covercough.htm, www.cdc.gov/flu/professionals/infectioncontrol/resphygiene.htm, and http://www.pandemicflu.gov/plan/community/mitigation.html.
☐	☐	☐	Provide training for law enforcement officers, office managers, medical or nursing personnel, and others as needed for performance of assigned emergency response roles. Identify a training coordinator and maintain training records. Ensure all staff are familiar with the local Incident Command System (ICS) and understand the roles and persons assigned within that structure. See http://www.fema.gov/emergency/nims/index.shtm for more information
☐	☐	☐	Stock recommended personal protective equipment (PPE) and environmental infection control supplies and make plans to distribute to employees, contractors, and others (including detainees) as needed. These supplies should include tissues, waste receptacles, single-use disinfection wipes, and alcohol-based hand cleaner (containing at least 60% alcohol). EPA registered disinfectants labeled for human influenza A virus may be used for cleaning offices, waiting rooms, bathrooms, examination rooms, and detention facilities. PPE may include gloves, surgical masks and respirators (disposable N95s or higher respirators or reusable respirators) eye protection, pocket masks (for respiratory resuscitation) and protective cover wear (e.g., impervious aprons). The specific uses for the above supplies will be advised by State and local health officials during a pandemic. Further information can be found at www.pandemicflu.gov. and at http://www.osha.gov/Publications/OSHA3327pandemic.pdf.
☐	☐	☐	Provide information to employees to help them and their families prepare and plan for a pandemic. See www.pandemicflu.gov/plan/individual/index.html.
☐	☐	☐	Work with State and/or local public health to develop a plan for distribution of pandemic influenza vaccine and antiviral medications to law enforcement personnel. See current HHS recommendations for pandemic influenza vaccine and antiviral use at http://www.hhs.gov/pandemicflu/plan/sup6.html and http://www.hhs.gov/pandemicflu/plan/sup7.html.
☐	☐	☐	Encourage and track seasonal influenza vaccination for employees every year. See www.cdc.gov/flu/protect/preventing.htm. Encourage all employees and their families to be up-to-date on all adult and child vaccinations recommended by the Advisory Committee on Immunization Practices. See www.cdc.gov/nip/recs/adult-schedule.htm and www.cdc.gov/nip/recs/child-schedule.htm.
☐	☐	☐	Evaluate employee access to and availability of health care, mental health, social services, community, and faith-based resources during a pandemic, and improve services as needed. See www.hhs.gov/pandemicflu/plan/sup11.html.

Plan for providing services to the public during a pandemic

Completed	In Progress	Not Started	
☐	☐	☐	Identify community–based scenarios and needs likely to occur in a pandemic emergency, and plan how to respond. These might include security of health care and/or vaccine distribution sites, sites that store antiviral medications or vaccines, first-responder activities, protection of critical infrastructure, management of panic and/or public fear, crowd/riot control, enforcement of public health orders, etc.
☐	☐	☐	Develop traffic flow plans to deal with standard traffic management and traffic flow around health-care delivery sites, including vaccine and antiviral distribution sites
☐	☐	☐	Anticipate community vulnerabilities (vulnerable populations, crimes of opportunity, fraudulent schemes, etc.) and specifically train employees to respond.
☐	☐	☐	Develop guidance for managing/assisting special populations (e.g., persons who are homeless, substance abusers, elderly, and individuals with disabilities, etc.) during a pandemic. This will require coordination with public health agencies, social services, correctional facilities, legal system representatives, and community-based organizations serving these populations.
☐	☐	☐	Work with local and/or State health departments or other relevant resources to ensure health protection and care for detainees or other individuals for whom the agency has responsibility.
☐	☐	☐	Establish policies on post-arrest management of an ill or exposed individual, including what to do should a care facility, precinct, and/or other law enforcement facility refuse entry to an ill or exposed individual.

FIGURE 11.24   (Continued).

Plan for coordination with external organizations and help your community

Completed	In Progress	Not Started	
☐	☐	☐	Review your pandemic influenza preparedness and response plan with key stakeholders inside and outside the agency, including employee representatives, and determine opportunities for collaboration, modification of the plan, and the development of complementary responsibilities.
☐	☐	☐	Share preparedness and response plans with other law enforcement agencies and law enforcement support agencies in your region or State (to include the National Guard) in order to share resources, identify collaboration strategies, and improve community response efforts. Develop, review, and modify local and State mutual aid agreements, if necessary. Mutual aid during an influenza pandemic can not be counted on as multiple jurisdictions in a given region may be affected simultaneously and have limited aid to offer. Availability of one State's National Guard to support another States plans under an existing compact (e.g., Emergency Management Assistance Compact) may be limited due to competing demands in their home State.
☐	☐	☐	Coordinate all requests for assistance with the next higher level governmental entity (e.g., local officials coordinate with State officials, State officials coordinate with Federal officials). Coordination is essential to ensure the assets: (1) can be provided in accordance with existing laws, (2) the requested resources are available. During a pandemic influenza, assistance from the next higher level of government may be limited due to competing higher priority demands and the effects of the influenza pandemic on these assets.
☐	☐	☐	Integrate planning with emergency service and criminal justice organizations such as courts, corrections, probation and parole, social services, multi-jurisdictional entities, public works, and other emergency management providers (fire, EMS, mutual aid, etc.).
☐	☐	☐	States should plan on utilizing their National Guard to perform law enforcement and security functions during a pandemic influenza. The National Guard under the command and control of the respective State's Governor is not subject to Posse Comitatus Act restrictions as are Federal military forces. Availability of one State's National Guard to support another States plans under an existing compact (e.g., Emergency Management Assistance Compact) may be limited due to competing demands in their home State.
☐	☐	☐	Security functions are essential during a pandemic influenza. Through your city or county attorney, corporation counsel or other appropriate authority, collaborate with the Office of the State Attorney General to clarify and review the authorities granted to law enforcement to include the National Guard. Suggest clarifications and work arounds as needed, and integrate into agency policy, training, and communications activities.
☐	☐	☐	Identify local or regional entities, such as health-care agencies, community organizations, businesses, or critical infrastructure sites, to determine potential collaboration opportunities. This collaboration might involve situational awareness, exercises or drills, or public safety training.
☐	☐	☐	Collaborate with local and/or State public health agencies to assist with the possible investigation of contacts within a suspected outbreak, the enforcement of public health orders, as well as the provision of security, protection, and possibly, critical supplies to quarantined persons. Each law enforcement agency will need to interact with local, State, county, and tribal public health officials to define the extent of the authorities provided from State legislation, develop procedures for the local initiation, implementation, and use of those authorities, as well as define protections from liability for law enforcement that may arise from quarantine and isolation enforcement. Operational planning must be flexible enough to address all scenarios in an all hazards environment, and in light of emerging infectious diseases.

CS113326

FIGURE 11.24 (Continued).

chapter introduces the health dimensions of biological agents as threats to public health, the role of medical facilities in terms of response, and the particular strategies for agents.

Keywords

Agroterrorism

Animal and Plant Health Inspection Service

Assessment protocol

Avian flu

Bioterrorism

Bird flu

Chemical agent

Communicable disease

Contamination

Department of Agriculture

Environmental Protection Agency

Epidemic

Food Safety and Inspection Service

Food safety officer

H5N1

Hospital Preparedness Program

Import surveillance liaison officer

Infectious disease

Influenza

Mad cow disease

National Select Agency Registry Program

Pandemic

Pandemic flu

Pathogen

Project BioShield

Seasonal flu

Strategic Partnership Program on Agroterrorism

Strategic National Stockpile

Swine flu

Virus

Water Security Division

World Health Organization

Discussion Questions

1. In what way do federal and state agencies deal with water and its protection?
2. What role do hospitals play in questions of homeland defense and public health?
3. Explain how the food chain can be compromised.
4. Explain how biotoxins can cause massive damage to the public health. Give specific examples.
5. Why does DHS rely so heavily on the USDA in public health planning?
6. Relate the purpose and aim of Project BioShield.
7. With the rise of medicine and clinical intervention, will a pandemic be more or less likely?

Practical Exercises

1. Visit the EPA's water security home at http://water.epa.gov/infrastructure/watersecurity/index.cfm. Click on and research their various water security tools.
2. Envision how the food production cycle affords the terrorist opportunity. How could this be so? Author a hypothetical fact pattern that shows how food production may oddly be a forum for the terrorist.

3. Animals and plants may also afford the terrorist threat and terror opportunities. Relate four potential scenarios where this might occur.

4. Contact your state homeland security agency. Find out about pandemic preparedness and recovery.

Notes

1. All of these activities conjure up devastation and fear in the populace. It will be crucial for government to address the magnitude of the potential harm while respecting the rule of law. See B. K. Collins and H. Morrow, Using shared technology in bioterrorism planning and response: Do privacy laws affect administrative judgments? *The Homeland Security Review*, 4, 2010: 43.

2. DHS, Critical infrastructure sectors, http://www.dhs.gov/critical-infrastructure-sectors (accessed February 7, 2016).

3. D. K. Stocker, P. Griffin, and C. Kocher, A functionalist's perspective on bioterrorism and global adversity, *The Homeland Security Review*, 4, 2010: 2.

4. EPA, Planning for an emergency drinking water supply (June 2011), http://www.epa.gov/sites/production/files/2015-03/documents/planning_for_an_emergency_drinking_water_supply.pdf (accessed February 7, 2016).

5. See Congressional Research Service (CRS), *The Federal Food Safety System: A Primer* (Washington, DC: Library of Congress, January 11, 2011), http://www.fas.org/sgp/crs/misc/RS22600.pdf.

6. FDA, Risk Assessment for Food Terrorism and Other Food Safety Concerns (Silver Spring, MD: FDA, 2003), http://seafood.oregonstate.edu/.pdf%20Links/Risk%20Assessment%20for%20Food%20Terrorism%20and%20Other%20Food%20Safety%20Concerns.pdf (accessed February 7, 2016).

7. USDA, DHS, and FDA, *Critical Infrastructure and Key Resources for Sector Specific Plan as Input to the National Infrastructure Protection Plan* (Washington, DC: U.S. Government Printing Office, 2007), 2.

8. USDA, *Pre-Harvest Security Guidelines and Checklist 2006* (Washington, DC: U.S. Government Printing Office, 2006), p. 3, http://www.usda.gov/documents/PreHarvestSecurity_final.pdf.

9. USDA, *Pre-Harvest Security Guidelines*, 10–11.

10. D. K. Stocker, P. M. Griffin, C.J. Kocher, and T. M. Raquet, Agroterrorism: Risk assessment and proactive responses, *The Homeland Security Review*, 5, 2011: 17. See also: K. Govern, Agroterrorism and ecoterrorism: A survey of Indo-American approaches under law and policy to prevent and defend against these potential threats ahead, *Florida Coastal Law Review*, 10, 2009: 223.

11. FDA, Strategic Partnership Program Agroterrorism (SPPA) initiative, http://www.fda.gov/Food/FoodDefense/FoodDefensePrograms/ucm080836.htm (accessed February 7, 2016).

12. Stocker, Griffin, Kocher, and Raquet, Agroterrorism, 17, 20.

13. USDA, Agricultural Research Service, "Northeast area research projects," http://www.ars.usda.gov/main/site_main.htm?modecode=80-00-00-00 (accessed February 7, 2016).

14. See CRS, *Federal Efforts to Address the Threat of Bioterrorism: Selected Issues and Options for Congress* (Washington, DC: Library of Congress, February 8, 2011), http://www.fas.org/sgp/crs/terror/R41123.pdf. For examples of experts who downplay the threat posed by bioterrorism, see M. Leitenberg, *Assessing the Biological Weapons and Bioterrorism Threat*, Strategic Studies Institute, U.S. Army War College; Scientists Working Group on Biological and Chemical Weapons, Center for Arms Control and Non-Proliferation, *Biological Threats: A Matter of Balance*, January 26, 2010; Scientists Working Group on Biological and Chemical Weapons, Biological threats: A matter of balance, *Bulletin of the Atomic Scientists*, February 2, 2010.

15. See CRS, *Federal Efforts*, 8–9.

16. See J. Tropper, C. Adamski, C. Vionion, and S. Sapkota, Tracking antimicrobials dispensed during an anthrax attack: A case study from the New Hampshire anthrax exercise, *Journal of Emergency Management*, 9, January/February 2011: 65.

17. CDC, Emergency preparedness and response: Bioterrorism overview, http://emergency.cdc.gov/bioterrorism/overview.asp.

18. Project BioShield Act of 2004, P.L. 108–276, *U.S. Statutes at Large*, 118, 2004: 835.

19. For an update on BioShield's many activities, see Robert Kadlec, Renewing the Project BioShield Act: What has it bought and wrought? (Policy brief) (Washington, DC: Center for a New American Security, 2013), http://www.cnas.org/files/documents/publications/CNAS_RenewingTheProjectBioShieldAct_Kadlec.pdf (accessed February 7, 2016); CRS, *Project BioShield: Authorities, Appropriations, Acquisitions, and Issues for Congress* (Washington, DC: CRS, May 27, 2011), http://www.fas.org/sgp/crs/terror/R41033.pdf (accessed February 7, 2016).

20. CRS, *Project BioShield*, 8.

21. There are even more legal issues and potential liabilities associated with pandemics when compared with other natural disasters. See B. Courtney, Five legal preparedness challenges for responding to future public health emergencies, *Journal of Law, Medicine & Ethics*, Spring 2011: 60.

22. HHS, PandemicFlu.gov, http://pandemicflu.gov/general/index.html (accessed February 27, 2009).

23. WHO, *Pandemic Influenza Preparedness and Response: A WHO Guidance Document* (Washington, DC: U.S. Government Printing Office, 2009).

24. For general advice on the preparedness model, see WHO, Pandemic influenza preparedness: Sharing of influenza viruses and access to vaccines and other benefits, 63rd World Health Assembly, Provisional agenda item 11.1 (April 2010), http://apps.who.int/gb/ebwha/pdf_files/WHA63/A63_4-en.pdf. See also WHO, Regional pandemic influenza preparedness and response plan, 2009–2010 (May 2009) http://www.afro.who.int/index.php?option=com_docman&task=doc_download&gid=3762; J. R. Langabeer II and J. L. DelliFraine, Incorporating strategic management into public health emergency preparedness, *Journal of Emergency Management*, 9, March/April 2011: 17.

25. DHS, *Pandemic Influenza: Preparedness, Response and Recovery Guide for Critical Infrastructure and Key Resources* (Washington, DC: DHS, 2006), http://www.flu.gov/planning-preparedness/business/cikrpandemicinfluenzaguide.pdf.

26. HHS, *HHS Pandemic Influenza Plan: Part 1; Strategic Plan* (Washington, DC: HHS), http://www.hhs.gov/pandemicflu/plan/part1.html (accessed May 28, 2012). See also: FEMA, *Continuity of Operations: An Overview of Continuing Planning for Pandemic Influenza* (Washington, DC: FEMA, 2011), http://www.fema.gov/pdf/about/org/ncp/pandemic_influenza.pdf.

27. G. Waight et al., The role of medical students in influenza pandemic response, *Journal of Emergency Management*, 9, March/April 2011: 60.

28. J. R. Langabeer II and J. L. DelliFraine, Incorporating strategic management into public health emergency preparedness, *Journal of Emergency Management*, 9, March/April 2011: 17, 25.

Chapter **12**

The Future of Homeland Security

12.1 Introduction

In the past 15 years, the Department of Homeland Security (DHS) has evolved in dramatic ways—in both a bureaucratic and a mission sense. The fact that this agency was born with such speed, and that it subsequently metamorphosed into a full-blown department, is testimony to its unique nature in the world of government. Nothing moves all that quickly in the worlds of bureaucracy and government entities. DHS travels at speeds never before charted in the annals of the political process.

However, viewed another way, it is valid to question whether there is consensus on exactly what *homeland security* even is. The fact that there are hundreds, even thousands, of initiatives in homeland defense proves very little about their universal relevance to what might be described as *core missions*. Shortly after 9/11, it seems improbable that livestock, corn, avian and swine flu, the Internet, and telecommunications would be the vernacular and purview of the homeland initiative. Prior to 9/11, the principles and practices of homeland defense were rather narrowly constructed.

Today there is the very real danger of mission creep. Some entities outside and within the government have convinced themselves that areas that seem far afield from homeland security have direct connections to the homeland security universe. Thinking broadly, just about every human activity could fall under the homeland security umbrella. In some cases this would be right; in other cases, this would be wrong and even counterproductive. Some of these "wrong" choices are often to the detriment of citizens' privacies and civil liberties granted in the Constitution. Security is clearly of prime importance, but we must tread lightly.

DHS as currently constructed and operated still has the capacity to jump on any new program initiative that it can invent or that someone can imagine. In short, DHS has never met a program it did not like (or could not rationalize). While the administrators and operatives within DHS may not intend this, the operational life-form of DHS plays and feeds on fear itself, to the tune of billions of taxpayer's dollars. Strategists and policymakers bandy about every imaginable solution, while fear of the unknown event, plot, or disaster hangs like a specter over every decision. DHS cannot protect every citizen in every quarter, in every situation. DHS cannot possibly design and divine policy for every facet of human life.

Today, there is equally the danger of mission confusion to the point of chaos. In multiple quarters of the dialogue there is a strong divergence of opinions on whom and why these terror acts exists and how to defend against them. On the one hand, President Obama has stated that climate change is the most serious challenge of our time. Yet other, more immediate tragedies take place that consume national attention and DHS resources. With the potential widespread and global environmental repercussions, does climate change outstrip the severity and devastation of nuclear bombs or weapons of mass destruction? At Fort Hood and at the San Bernadino shootings of November 2015, when the perpetrators exclaimed "Allahu Akbar" prior to their acts, are we to ignore any potential connection between radical Islamic fundamentalism and the events that occurred? There needs to be recognition that increasing self-radicalization throughout the world, including within the United States, is directly tied to Islamic extremist propoganda available online.

Even the employees of DHS, fully surveyed in 2015, manifest a current lack of confidence in both the leadership and direction of the agency.[1] In a phrase, both mission creep and mission confusion undermine employee morale and esprit de corps. When the DHS director, Jeh Johnson, indicated he is concerned with the privacy rights of foreign terrorists and, as a result, does not feel it proper to check their activities on social media, you have some questionable policy decision-making coming from the top.

Turning to the academic sector, even among colleges and universities there is a lack of consensus on what the homeland curriculum should be and what the homeland student should study. As Drs. William Pelfrey Sr. and Jr. cogently argue:

> Unfortunately, there is no clear roadmap to homeland security nor is there a consensus on appropriate curricula for homeland security programs. A review of federal publications on homeland security is dizzying. A myriad of Presidential Directives, Department of Homeland Security Publications, commission reports, and other publications leaves most academics and practitioners with their heads spinning.[2]

That debate is instructive on how so many constituencies in homeland security have acted since the early days after 9/11. As DHS talks about unification, efficiency, and universal mission, there should be concern about the notion of trying to be all things to all people.

DHS has placed itself in the tenuous position of being guarantor in all aspects of human activity and motion. As an example, one of the most difficult of man-made tragedies to thwart is active shooter scenarios. Lone-wolf shooting events such as the July 2012 Aurora, Colorado, movie theater shooting that killed 12; the August 2012 shooting at a Sikh temple in Oak Creek, Wisconsin, that killed six; and the unspeakable shooting of 26 innocent children, teachers, and school administrators at Sandy Hook Elementary School in Newtown, Connecticut, are only increasing in frequency.[3]

To be sure, our nation is beset by violent activities at every sector and locale imaginable, from wealthy suburbs to gang shootings in the streets in Chicago. Active shooters alone are arresting our attention from things that assure the safety and tranquility of our homeland. From 2000–2013 the array of active shooter events continued its upward and seemingly inevitable rise, as the FBI charts in Figure 12.1.

And the rise of this form of violence, sometimes jihadi driven, as the Fort Hood and San Bernardino cases demonstrate—at other times the product of mental health breakdowns in individuals and families—adds to the misunderstanding and real confusion in how to handle the challenges of homeland protection.

Indeed, our culture is now so plagued by political factions that we cannot even agree that terror is terror; radical Islamic fundamentalism is an undeniable issue for policymakers and there is in fact an ongoing war on terrorism. The lack of cohesion and sensibility as to purpose, terms, and outlook adds to the confused perceptions we have and other nations see from afar. The Fort Hood case cannot simply be written off as workplace violence given Major Hasan's deep ties to the jihadi movement. Nor can terms such as *misguided individuals* or *inappropriate gun violence* adequately or accurately describe the intense terror that the public experiences from attacks motivated wholly or in part by radical Islamic fundamentalist ideology. DHS has promised that food will be safe, that water will always be

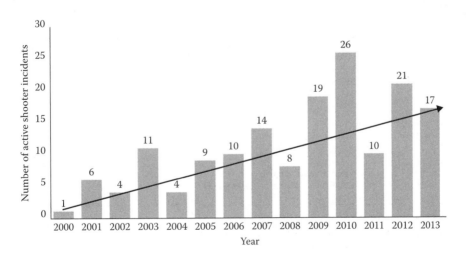

FIGURE 12.1 Active shooter incidents in the United States, 2000–2013. From: FBI, *A Study of Active Shooter Incidents in the United States between 2000 and 2013* (Washington, DC: Texas State University and FBI, 2013), 8, https://www.fbi.gov/about-us/office-of-partner-engagement/active-shooter-incidents/a-study-of-active-shooter-incidents-in-the-u.s.-2000-2013 (accessed February 8, 2016).

drinkable, that planes will never be hijacked, that trains will never be derailed by terrorists. And yet, we still hear new reports of plots to smuggle explosives onto planes, the extremely costly expense, delays, and inability to finish the virtual fence initiative on the U.S.–Mexico border, and an aging U.S. power and utilities infrastructure that is subject to supervisory control and data acquisition (SCADA) and cyber attacks. It is no wonder that the public is concerned about DHS's direction, mission, and focus.

DHS must recognize and know, on some level, that it cannot do all it seeks to accomplish. The Federal Emergency Management Agency (FEMA) seems to acknowledge this reality when it labels its current effort as *government centric*.

We fully recognize that a government-centric approach to emergency management is not enough to meet the challenges posed by a catastrophic incident. *Whole community* is an approach to emergency management that reinforces the fact that FEMA is only one part of our nation's emergency management team; that we must leverage all of the resources of our collective team in preparing for, protecting against, responding to, recovering from, and mitigating against all hazards; and that collectively we must meet the needs of the entire community in each of these areas.[4]

As DHS seeks to generate enthusiasm within the public, especially in publishing documents such as "One Team, One Mission, Securing the Homeland, 2008–2013,"[5] the contents of the report paint a somewhat disappointing picture of half successes. In "Goal 1: Protect Our Nation from Dangerous People," arguably the central reason for the mission of DHS, the results by and large are mixed to poor no matter how you look at it (Figure 12.2).

Select Reported Measures for Goal 1: Protect Our Nation from Dangerous People	
Measure	**FY 2013 Target**
Border miles under effective control (including certain coastal sectors).	*
Air passenger apprehension rate for major violations [Percent of the total number of individual passengers with major violations of customs and immigration laws and regulations that were apprehended based on statistical estimates of the total number of violations that came through our international airports]	43.5%
Land border apprehension rate for major violations. [Percent of the total number of vehicles travelers with major violations of customs and immigration laws and regulations that were apprehended based on statistical estimates of the total number of violations that came through the Points of Entry (POEs)]	37.5%
Percent of at-risk miles under strategic air surveillance.	95%
Percent of undocumented migrants who attempt to enter the U.S. via maritime routes that are interdicted [As estimated, based upon data obtained from the U.S. Coast Guard and U.S. Customs and Border Protection]	71.5%
Number of incursions into the U.S. exclusive economic zone (EEZ)	185
Percent of time that Coast Guard assets included in the Combatant Commander Operational Plans are ready at a Status of Resources and Training System (SORTS) rating of 2 or better.	100%
* The degree of effective control will be determined by the resources devoted to the task as developed in the Department's FY 2010–14 budget proposal and by funding provided by Congress.	

FIGURE 12.2 Goal 1 performance. (From: One Team, One Mission, Securing the Homeland, 2008–2013.)

FIGURE 12.3 Bering Sea: the Coast Guard cutter Healy breaks ice around the Russian-flagged tanker vessel Renda 250 miles south of Nome, Alaska, January 6, 2012. (From: U.S. Coast Guard photo by Petty Officer 1st Class Sara Francis.)

Less than half of the air passengers with major violations of customs and immigration laws and regulations are apprehended. Just over one-third of vehicle travelers with major violations of customs and immigration laws and regulations are apprehended. The only true success story among those listed is that of the Coast Guard—an agency that remains mission oriented and does what it does exceedingly well. As exhibited by its response in the Haiti earthquake of 2011 and the BP oil spill, and per the Coast Guard's own posture statement for 2011, it is rightfully characterized as an entity "biased for action," with an "ability to meet expanded mission requirements."[6] DHS as a whole could learn much from this key player in both emergency response and homeland defense roles (Figure 12.3).

At present, DHS seemingly continues down a path of agency building by looking for more fields of coverage and control. With a nation $19 trillion in debt and counting, and a military complex now facing severe and significant cuts, little—including DHS's massive budget—will be spared the budgetary realities of the decade to come.[7]

Internet Exercise: Visit the U.S. Debt Clock to get some sense of how staggering our national debt has become at http://www.usdebtclock.org.

12.2 Growth without Reason

From its inception, DHS was running on a different clock than its governmental counterparts. Aside from its origination, it could change like a chameleon. Today's threat was tomorrow's agenda item, only lower on the list. DHS could consume, like a ravenous beast, most of its competing agencies, even those with a historically different approach. Nothing is all that surprising about bureaucracies growing, self-perpetuating, and feeding on mission to develop other parts of the bureaucratic puzzle. Yet this journey is neither a trek nor a run, but a propulsion that simply knows no bounds. FEMA's inclusion in DHS is an excellent illustration of this phenomenon. In FEMA the natural disaster sets the tone—the hurricane, the earthquake, the fire, and so on. That is what FEMA was intended to direct its energies toward. Even so, FEMA would be subsumed into the DHS model. Some have wondered whether this tendency to simply swallow any event resembling a disaster has been good for DHS or FEMA. It is a question worth asking, and in the hubbub of growth and bureaucratic delirium, a pandemic of frenzy if there ever was one, one must stop and smell the roses. To grow and evolve is natural. To grow without much thought is mindless. Maybe FEMA's response to hurricane damage is not really the building blocks of DHS. Maybe earthquakes are flat out different and do not benefit from the DHS mentality. While not perfect, the generally positive signs in the planning in advance of and in response to Hurricane Sandy in the fall of 2012 indicate that FEMA may in fact be able to operate and function successfully within DHS. Certainly the leadership, response, and rebuilding efforts in the wake of Sandy show remarkable improvement over such efforts during, and in the wake of, Hurricane Katrina. Hopefully such improvement can be a repeatable trend across DHS.

As you read through the pages of this text, you have witnessed growth in both form and substance. You have witnessed the absorption of departments at a pace never seen before. You have gleaned that the term *infrastructure* means more than brick and mortar—that the FDA has a homeland plan just as the National Monuments Agency does. Everyone has a plan. Everyone combats terrorism. Page by page you have read about new plans, new stratagems, new policies, new mergers, and realignments. You can get dizzy reading about these changes. And one other thing—you can be sure that what is here likely will be different in a short time. I contend that more is not always more. Sometimes more is less. Fewer results, less efficiency, less coordination. Is it possible to take on too many agencies, too much responsibility, and thus lose the focus of what is truly important or necessary?

As an example, does the hiring of 60,000 new border agents—throwing sheer numbers at the problem—automatically guarantee a more secure border? Or is the border today any safer or more reassuring than 3 years ago? There is no definitive answer to such questions and while there has been progress in some areas, results are dubious at best in others.

Revisiting policy and enforcing current laws on the books would take care of many of the issues. We build fences to keep people out, but illegal immigration is still a consistent problem. While border security is necessary, a more holistic policy solution would include (1) increased border security in conjunction with encouraging legitimate immigration and naturalization and (2) a more consistent policy on illegal immigrants within the country. Establishing a reliable, efficient process for those individuals and families who are in the country now and want to become U.S. citizens would help alleviate some of the strain on the system, set the proper tone, and provide a clear and consistent path to obtaining citizenship. Current considerations around taking in foreign refugees, including those from the Syria conflict, cause serious and impassioned debate. Much of the disscussion surrounds the identification and vetting of individuals before taking them into our country. In addition, there is the overall perception of other countries to consider—about our willingness to help, or not, as a world power and leader in what is inarguably a human rights crisis. At present, it remains to be seen how all will play out.

Why do our agencies neglect targeting those that should be targeted and continue to search the 9-year-old child's Minecraft backpack or the coat of an 80-year-old grandmother? These are just singular, but simple and reflective examples of a department that does things in ways that belie notions of efficiency and targeted focus. A DHS that operates as the agency does at present will not last into the next century. It will not be nimble enough to last. Even DHS knows this reality. In 2010, DHS announced a threefold mission concerning how it will unfold in the decade to come: first, it will need to consolidate duplicitous operations; second, it will need to streamline these bulky and cumbersome systems; and lastly, it will need to be open to the world. Talk of change is in the air, and whether the nature and sheer size of DHS can adapt remains unclear. DHS is well meaning when it relays the following:

We have taken significant steps to create a unified and integrated Department that will enhance our performance by focusing on:

- Accountability
- Efficiency
- Transparency, and
- Leadership development (One Team, One Mission, Securing the Homeland, 2008–2013)

The future of homeland security can be prosperous and highly effective; it can help prevent attacks and thwart the terrorist who seeks to disrupt and destroy our way of life. Ultimately, it can provide levels of security and safety at costs more aligned with reality and the mission of government in general.

12.3 Curbing Expansionism in Mission

To have any chance at a prosperous future, DHS will have to simplify. There is too much under its roof, and much of what sits under its tent does not belong. DHS's new mission encompasses the following:

Three key concepts form the foundation of our national homeland security strategy designed to achieve this vision:

- Security
- Resilience
- Customs and Exchange

There are five homeland security missions:

1. Prevent terrorism and enhancing security
2. Secure and manage our borders
3. Enforce and administer our immigration laws
4. Safeguard and secure cyberspace
5. Ensure resilience to disasters

In addition, we must specifically focus on maturing and strengthening the homeland security enterprise itself.[8]

The simplicity of the mission—a safer America through secure borders and the deterrence and prevention of terrorism—causes one to pause on the expansionist mentality that has occurred with the growth of DHS. The agencies in Table 12.1 became part of DHS in 2003. The table lays out the first expansionist event in the history of DHS.

Just for the sake of argument, does the merger and consolidation make sense in all cases? Can the Secret Service not carry out its mission without being tethered to DHS? What about the Energy Security and Assurance Program? Does DHS have the expertise to handle the subject matter? And the Plum Island Animal Disease Center—would it not make better sense to leave Plum Island with the Department of Agriculture? Does it seem likely that a terrorist event would occur with livestock? Noted already was the suitability of the FEMA merger. Why would hurricane response assist in DHS's mission? It is the author's view that DHS is struggling with its own identity, from its initial manifestation to its subsequent transformations. Instead of being attentive to its basic mission of security and counterterrorism, it has wandered into peripheral territory, only partially touching on questions of security. The net effect of this expansionism has been the dilution of other services and functions in government. Some departments are underfunded budget-wise and are adapting to missions that are tangential to their overall purpose.[9] For DHS to survive into the future, it may require shedding functions that stand far afield from its ultimate end or purpose. William L. Waugh Jr. notes in "The Future of Homeland Security and Emergency Management":

> Mission problems were expected with the integration of non-terrorism programs into a department focused on the terrorist threat. FEMA, in particular, has responsibilities unrelated to dealing with terrorism, such as the National Flood Insurance Program and the National Earthquake Hazard Reduction Program. Other DHS components also have diverse non-terrorism responsibilities, not least of which are the U.S. Coast Guard's responsibilities related to oil spills, boating safety, and air-sea rescue.[10]

It is a legitimate critique, for why does DHS involve itself in flood insurance, geospatial maps, and computer security breaches? Are these activities consistent with mission or causing stress internally and externally? To be sure, the financial stress alone, the budgetary demands of new obligations, has either drained historic budgets or added to tightness in existing budgets.

By 2005, departmental changes were being referred to as *structural adjustments*. Change continued its unabated pace with new recommendations for the department. New offices, directors, realignments, and mergers continued without reservation. For example, a new director of operations coordination was implemented. The director's primary function was to improve coordination and efficiency of operations. By this time, DHS was tackling so many functions that it was feeling the pressure and stress of nonaligned functions. Why else would DHS need a director of operations coordination?

In general, DHS continues to realign itself and is trying to serve many masters. For the future health of the agency, DHS may need to adhere to a different model that sticks to the fundamentals of what the department can and should do. To that end, what the future holds remains to be seen.

TABLE 12.1 Departmental Movements in the History of DHS

Original Agency (Department)	Current Agency/Office
The U.S. Customs Service (Treasury)	U.S. Customs and Border Protection: Inspection, border and ports of entry responsibilities U.S. Immigration and Customs Enforcement: customs law enforcement responsibilities
The Immigration and Naturalization Service (Justice)	U.S. Customs and Border Protection: Inspection functions and the U.S. Border Patrol U.S. Immigration and Customs Enforcement: Immigration law enforcement; detention and removal, intelligence, and investigation U.S. Citizenship and Immigration Services: Adjudications and benefits programs
The Federal Protective Service	U.S. Immigration and Customs Enforcement
TSA (Transportation)	TSA
Federal Law Enforcement Training Center (Treasury)	Federal Law Enforcement Training Center
Animal and Plant Health Inspection Service (part) (Agriculture)	U.S. Customs and Border Protection: Agricultural imports and entry inspections
Office for Domestic Preparedness (Justice)	Responsibilities distributed within FEMA
FEMA	FEMA
Strategic National Stockpile and the National Disaster Medical System (HHS)	Returned to HHS, July 2004
Nuclear Incident Response Team (Energy)	Responsibilities distributed within FEMA
Domestic Emergency Support Teams (Justice)	Responsibilities distributed within FEMA
National Domestic Preparedness Office (FBI)	Responsibilities distributed within FEMA
Chemical, Biological, Radiological, and Nuclear Countermeasures Programs (Energy)	Science and Technology Directorate
Environmental Measurements Laboratory (Energy)	Science and Technology Directorate
National Biodefense Defense Analysis Center (Defense)	Science and Technology Directorate
Plum Island Animal Disease Center (Agriculture)	Science and Technology Directorate
Federal Computer Incident Response Center (GSA)	US-CERT, Office of Cyber Security and Communications in the National Programs and Preparedness Directorate
National Communications System (Defense)	Office of Cyber Security and Communications in the National Programs and Preparedness Directorate
National Infrastructure Protection Center (FBI)	Dispersed throughout the department, including the Office of Operations Coordination and the Office of Infrastructure Protection
Energy Security and Assurance Program (Energy)	Integrated into the Office of Infrastructure Protection
U.S. Coast Guard	U.S. Coast Guard
U.S. Secret Service	U.S. Secret Service

12.4 The Merits of Decentralization

While DHS touts the value of the decentralized model in much of its literature, it has erected centralized superstructures of operations. DHS is about as centralized a department as it gets. It is overly large and overly bureaucratic on a number of levels.

In August 2011, the traditionally conservative think tank the Heritage Foundation urged DHS to engage in the sort of decentralizing self-assessment that would cause culture shock. In short, get smaller by spinning off the responsibilities or return them to the place from which they were originally grabbed. By 2015, critics of DHS had become a far more common force in the appropriations process to continually fund it, and in the intellectual and think tank constituencies that critique its operations.[11] Give back to the states and localities, that know their populations, the task of homeland defense. One must coordinate, but not at the expense of statewide and local visions. Their recommendations:

- Establishing a framework for empowering state and local authorities to meet their responsibilities for disaster response and domestic counterterrorism operations, particularly for ensuring state and local input into national policies and promoting intelligence-led policing.
- Adopting a fair, honest, and realistic approach to immigration enforcement that recognizes state and local authorities as responsible partners and abjures an "amnesty first" strategy, which would simply encourage more illegal border crossings and unlawful presence. Sensible and functional border security, immigration, and workplace laws are vital to focusing scarce resources on the pressing security threat posed by transnational criminal cartels based in Mexico.
- Overhauling the process for declaring federal disasters and dispensing homeland security grants. Current policies and programs waste resources and do not promote resiliency or preparedness.
- Maintaining the use of key counterterrorism tools, such as those authorized under the USA PATRIOT Act, and establishing a national domestic counterterrorism and intelligence framework that clearly articulates how intelligence operations at all levels should function to combat terrorism.
- Rethinking the Transportation Security Administration (TSA) and restructuring its mission from providing airport security to making aviation security policy and regulations and devolving screening responsibility to the airport level under supervision of a federal security director.[12]

While any of these points can be, and have been, debated from multiple angles, this list does identify some of the key issues at the heart of homeland security and the future of DHS. Consensus opinion among many in and around government circles confirms that to change tack and move in a new direction will require a major cultural shift in how the respective agencies within DHS see and appreciate the responsibilities of homeland security. This will not happen overnight.

Despite this, there are positive signs of regional, state, and local cooperation. Advisory councils and committees exist to foster local influence. Partnerships abound with the federal DHS and states and localities. Although these are steps in the right direction, it is clear that federalism reigns supreme in the affairs of homeland security. In grants, in policymaking, in budgetary allotments, in federal appointments to staff positions, the federal system dominates the states and localities. This domination diminishes the role of local input and control in matters of homeland security.

To that end, Samuel Clovis Jr. proposes the following characteristics of collaborative federalism for homeland security:

- Homeland security is a national issue requiring national solutions. As such, the role of Congress and its executive agent DHS is that of facilitation and leadership, providing guidelines, milestones, and enough funding to make a difference.
- State and local governments have maximum flexibility in implementing homeland security programs to gain greater efficiency and better situational awareness.[13]

Collaboration signifies meaningful input and participation rather than a sometimes formulaic reaction to posted policy and funding mechanisms. Instead of implementing one-size-fits-all states and localities, DHS might be better served looking to the localities for their needs assessment and turning over more tasks and functions to localities.

12.5 The Rise of Technology

For too long, both prior to joining DHS and in their current structure, the many functions of homeland security have been performed manually by people, often at extraordinary cost. Mentioned already were the more than 100,000 employees in TSA and Border Patrol. To have any future, DHS will have to operate with leaner staffing and financial budgets. It cannot survive long term with high payrolls necessitated by huge staffing, nor should some of the rote functions of TSA employees be reserved for personnel. It appears that machines can do a comparable job, and we may be on our way to seeing more and more reliability in technologies to help security functions. DHS already knows that science and technology will lead the way in any future for DHS. Just a few examples of current initiatives are shown in Figure 12.4.

DHS's reliance on outside authority and analysis is one of its greatest recent accomplishments. DHS has aggressively developed partnerships with universities and colleges, as well as private associations, nonprofits, think tanks, and research centers, including its many designated "Centers for Excellence." Such partnerships include

- Center for Borders, Trade, and Immigration Research (CBTIR), led by the University of Houston, develops technology-based tools, techniques, and educational programs for border management, immigration, trade facilitation, and targeting and enforcement of transnational borders.
- Coastal Resilience Center of Excellence (CRC), led by the University of North Carolina at Chapel Hill, conducts research and education to enhance the Nation's ability to safeguard people, infrastructure, and economies from catastrophic coastal natural disasters such as floods and hurricanes.

The **Apex Air Entry/Exit Re-engineering** (AEER) program, developed in partnership with U.S. Customs and Border Protection (CBP), seeks ways to increase CBP's capacity to screen travelers entering the United States and to confirm the departure of non-U.S. citizens from U.S. airports. AEER determines how to use new technologies and processes to expedite screening by evaluating current commercial biometric technologies to support air entry and emerging exit applications.

The **Apex Border Situational Awareness** (BSA) program will enable the Homeland Security Enterprise to achieve increased border situational awareness, leading to increased border incursion detection, interdictions, and deterrence. CBP and partner law enforcement agencies (federal, state, local, tribal, international) need improved situational awareness to more effectively and efficiently deploy resources to the areas of highest risk, especially along the land border between the ports of entry on the U.S. southwest border. The goal of the Apex BSA program is to improve border situational awareness by establishing an enterprise capability to 1) access more data sources, 2) make available decision support tools to translate the available data into actionable information and intelligence, and 3) share that actionable information and intelligence with partner law enforcement agencies.

The **Apex Real-Time Biothreat Awareness program** aims to provide timely information to multiple authorities, enabling a collaborative, confident, and effective response that ultimately minimizes the impacts of a biological incident. DHS envisions a biosurveillance system that integrates and analyzes data from multiple sources and provides real-time, action-able information. Through this program, S&T will help authorities better prepare for incidents in which biological material is released. Authorities will be able to quickly gain situational awareness about the potential biological threat, the exposed population and the likelihood of infection to provide responders and decision makers with the data needed to make informed, confident decisions that will saves lives and money and restore normal operations quickly.

The **Flood Apex program** will create a decision support system of systems for community risk assessment and resilience planning to save lives, reduce property loss, and enhance resilience to disruptive events such as floods. With support from S&T, FEMA will be able to 1) leverage existing data sources to create multidimensional representations of community functions using an integrated, system-of-systems approach; 2) enhance collaboration around disaster risk reduction; 3) identify indicators of community resilience and opportunities to introduce advanced technologies; 4) empower commu-nities with a decision support tool to enable both pre-event, scenario-based risk planning and adaptive recovery in the postevent environment; and 5) enable faster decision-making. The RAPID Apex will culminate in development of the National Flood Decision Support Tool, which will be transitioned to FEMA to assist federal, state, local, tribal and territo-rial users in making investment decisions related to flood hazards.

The **Apex Next Generation Cyber Infrastructure program** addresses the challenges facing our nation's critical infra-structure sectors, enabling infrastructure to operate effectively, even in the face of sophisticated, targeted cyberattacks. The program seeks to provide technologies and tools to protect critical systems and networks. This includes the ability to 1) detect the presence of a cyberthreat without relying on a known cybersignature, 2) understand how the threat impacts operations, and 3) neutralize the threat in a manner that does not impact operations. This project will initially work in partnership with the financial sector but will be expanded later.

The **Screening at Speed program** seeks to create an almost invisible checkpoint by integrating imaging, trace detection, x-ray technologies, and software systems. S&T is working with the TSA, Department of Energy national laboratories, uni-versities, and industry on this program. The goal is to reduce invasiveness and inconvenience to passengers while increas-ing capability to respond to evolving threats.

The **Apex Next Generation First Responder** (NGFR) program seeks to develop a scalable and modular ensemble that includes an enhanced duty uniform, personal protective equipment, wearable computing and sensing technology, and robust voice and data communication networks. To do so, NGFR will harness the best existing and emerging technolo-gies and integrate them in a well-defined and standards-based open architecture. By providing core capabilities suitable for all jurisdictions and disciplines, as well as specialized technology more appropriate for metropolitan areas, NGFR's cutting-edge technologies will accelerate decision-making and improve response. With enhanced protection, communi-cation and situational awareness, first responders can better safeguard lives and property before, during, and after inci-dents. Additionally, as part of the NGFR, S&T launched the Responder Technology Alliance, bringing together responders, industry, federal agencies, research institutions, academia and other stakeholders to focus on the most difficult technology challenges along the road to identifying the "Responder of the Future."

The **Apex Border Enforcement Analytics Program** (BEAP), developed in partnership with U.S. Immigration and Customs Enforcement (ICE), seeks ways to address the staggering amount of operational and trade data received as part of ICE's export control mission. Using big data technologies, BEAP seeks ways to refine and provide relevant information to the appropriate investigation more efficiently.

FIGURE 12.4 DHS's Science and Technology Directorate Apex programs. From: DHS, Science & Technology, Apex programs, http://www.dhs.gov/science-and-technology/apex-programs (accessed February 9, 2016).

- Critical Infrastructure Resilience Institute (CIRI), led by the University of Illinois at Urbana-Champaign, conducts research and education to enhance the resilience of the Nation's critical infrastructure and its owners and operators.
- Arctic Domain Awareness Center of Excellence (ADAC), led by the University of Alaska Anchorage, develops and transitions technology solutions, innovative products, and educational programs to improve situational awareness and crisis response capabilities related to emerging maritime challenges posed by the dynamic Arctic environment.
- Center for Visualization and Data Analytics (CVADA), co-led by Purdue University (visualization sciences—VACCINE) and Rutgers University (data sciences—CCICADA), creates the scientific basis and enduring technologies needed to analyze large quantities of information to detect security threats to the nation.
- Center of Excellence for Awareness and Localization of Explosives-Related Threats (ALERT), led by Northeastern University, develops new means and methods to protect the nation from explosives-related threats.
- Center of Excellence for Zoonotic and Animal Disease Defense (ZADD), co-led by Texas A&M University and Kansas State University, protects the nation's agriculture and public health sectors against high-consequence foreign animal, emerging and zoonotic disease threats.
- Food Protection and Defense Institute (FPDI), led by the University of Minnesota, defends the safety and security of the food system by conducting research to protect vulnerabilities in the food supply chain. FPDI was formerly named the National Center for Food Protection and Defense (NCFPD).
- Maritime Security Center of Excellence (MSC), led by Stevens Institute of Technology, enhances Maritime Domain Awareness and develops strategies to support Marine Transportation System resilience and educational programs for current and aspiring homeland security practitioners.
- National Center for Risk and Economic Analysis of Terrorism Events (CREATE), led by the University of Southern California, develops advanced tools to evaluate the risks, costs and consequences of terrorism.
- National Consortium for the Study of Terrorism and Responses to Terrorism (START), led by the University of Maryland, provides policy makers and practitioners with empirically grounded findings on the human elements of the terrorist threat and informs decisions on how to disrupt terrorists and terrorist groups.
- Center for Maritime, Island and Remote and Extreme Environment Security (MIREES), co-led by the University of Hawaii and Stevens Institute of Technology, focuses on developing robust research and education programs addressing maritime domain awareness to safeguard populations and properties in geographical areas that present significant security challenges.
- Center for Advancing Microbial Risk Assessment (CAMRA), co-led by Michigan State University and Drexel University and established jointly with the U.S. Environmental Protection Agency, fills critical gaps in risk assessments for mitigating microbial hazards.

- Coastal Hazards Center of Excellence (CHC), co-led by the University of North Carolina at Chapel Hill and Jackson State University, performs research and develops education programs to enhance the nation's ability to safeguard populations, properties and economies from catastrophic natural disasters.
- National Center for Border Security and Immigration (NCBSI), co-led by the University of Arizona and the University of Texas at El Paso, develops novel technologies, tools and advanced methods to balance immigration and commerce with effective border security.
- National Center for the Study of Preparedness and Catastrophic Event Response (PACER), led by Johns Hopkins University, optimizes the nation's medical and public health preparedness, mitigation and recovery strategies in the event of a high-consequence natural or man-made disaster.
- National Transportation Security Center of Excellence (NTSCOE) was established in accordance with H.R.1, Implementing the Recommendations of the 9/11 Commission Act of 2007, in August 2007. NTSCOE is a seven-institution consortium focused on developing new technologies, tools and advanced methods to defend, protect and increase the resilience of the nation's multimodal transportation infrastructure.[14]

In the coming years, technology will replace the human person in carrying out the mission of DHS in many cases, hopefully for the better. While controversial in many circles, many plane and helicopter applications are poised be replaced with drones for use in border security, surveillance, law enforcement, and search and rescue operations, although drones have been challenged on both functional and constitutional fronts (Figure 12.5).[15]

TSA employees, who presently search bags and laptops, will continue to be aided by new and emerging technologies (Figure 12.6).

DHS and its Science and Technology Directorate know keenly where the winds are blowing—to science and the role of technology securing the country. DHS committed

FIGURE 12.5 Air force drone.

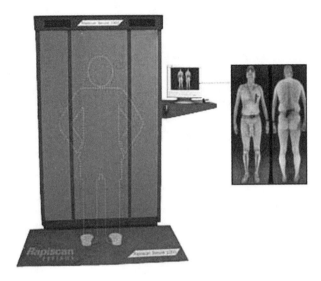

FIGURE 12.6   Millimeter wave.

substantial funding, though with a slight decrease to science and technology, in the 2015 cycle (Figure 12.7).[16]

This trend will continue into the long-term future. With new products and designs to track cargo, to sniff out explosives, to detect biological agents, and to prevent IED explosions, the role of technology will only increase in the years to come.

Other areas in need of innovation and creative upgrade are surveillance practice, sensor capacity, robotics in hazardous situations, and new methods and protocols in all aspects of information technology. On top of these challenges, the virtual reality all of us find ourselves entangled with—in commerce and social media, in finance and government benefits, in credit cards and check deposits—is the brave new world of cybersecurity.[17]

Reality and the virtual world are now natural, interconnected handmaidens rather than separate entities, for it is crucial that we learn how to fight in both theaters of war. As a result, the DHS of the future will rely on technology in a much more substantial way than today.

12.6 The Need for a New Way of Thinking: Jump Out of the Box

Much of what has and continues to take place in homeland security has taken place with limited to little objection. It is hard to argue that terrorism is a growing global and domestic threat and that it makes sense to take efforts to ensure the country's safety and security. However, it would be wise to take a step back, assess, and consider what we are doing and what needs to be done by way of homeland security. I mean this in three different senses.

Budget request
Dollars in thousands

	FY 2013 revised enacted		FY 2014 enacted		FY 2015 Pres. budget		FY 2015 +/− FY 2014	
	FTE	$000	FTE	$000	FTE	$000	FTE	$000
Management and administration	334	$126,519	337	$129,000	337	$130,147	—	$1,147
Acquisition and operations support	—	45,991	—	41,703	—	41,703	—	—
Laboratory facilities	128	158,083	130	547,785	130	435,180	—	(112,605)
Research, development, and innovation*	—	425,295[1]	—	462,000	—	433,788	—	(28,212)
University programs	—	38,339	—	39,724		31,000	—	(8,724)
Gross discretionary	462	$794,227	467	$1,220,212	467	$1,071,818	—	($148,394)
Emergency/ supplemental	—	3,087	—	—	—	—	—	—
Total budget authority	462	$797,314	467	$1,220,212	467	$1,071,818	—	($148,394)
Less prior year rescissions	—	(245)	—	(133)	—	—	—	133
Total	462	797,069	467	1,220,079	467	1,071,818	—	(148,261)

*This amount includes a reprogramming of $6.5 million from S and T to the U.S. secret service.

FIGURE 12.7 DHS budget allotments 2013–2015. From: DHS, *Budget-in-Brief: Fiscal Year 2015* (Washington, DC: DHS, 2015), 149, http://www.dhs.gov/sites/default/files/publications/FY15BIB.pdf (accessed February 9, 2016).* This amount includes a reprogramming of $6.5 million from S&T to the U.S. Secret Service.

First, why do we do what we do in so many cases? Is the threat real as described? If the threats were as real and meaningful as the experts indicate, would these events not occur with greater regularity? Is it really necessary to check passengers in airports as presently done? Is there some proof, if we chose not to frisk and search people, that terrorism would rise without resistance? More people die in suicide and car crashes each year, though no programs to deal with these tragedies have come around the bend. I do not make light of these things. I only point out that one wonders about assumptions. Do more procedures automatically translate to greater security? There has yet to be one event of terrorism involving aircraft since 9/11, though not for lack of trying (refer to the Christmas Day bomber mentioned in Chapter 2). Currently under investigation is whether the Russian en route from Egypt was the victim of terror bomb plants. ISIS has taken credit for the destruction. Russia is claiming a bomb brought down the Metrojet airbus, but the Egyptian government is still inconclusive on the matter.[18] A party could conclude that this lack of recent successful terror plots against aviation assets results from such a diligent and enlightened security program. Others might argue sheer coincidence or luck. Thus, the question remains whether the TSA investment, as it currently stands, is justified given the paucity of events. Or have we ever considered that our fears are disproportionate to the potential risk or harm? Why do we assume these fears are properly correlated?

Benjamin Freidman's *Managing Fear: The Politics of Homeland Security*,[19] forces this sort of examination—begging whether fear can be justified in its present form. He is particularly piercing when he engages the threat of bioterrorism.

Eight years later and counting, with plenty of conventional terrorism abroad and almost none in the United States, evidence is mounting that these trends are overstated or wrong—that September 11 was more an aberration than a harbinger of an age of deadlier terrorism. Terrorism using biological or nuclear weapons should still worry us, but the common claim that these sorts of attacks are virtually inevitable is an overstatement.[20]

Freidman goes on to further argue that our fears may be "inflated" and, given this reality, it is just the place for a bureaucrat to finds a comfy nest.[21]

Thinking outside any box is not an easy task, and thinking outside a governmental box is almost an impossibility. Yet, this is what must happen in order for DHS to thrive into the next century. It cannot use law enforcement techniques suitable for the twentieth century when, in some cases, technology can substitute. Homeland professionals of the future should not accept the status quo and need to look beyond the holiday and the personal day. Leap out of the box and do things differently than the traditional way of doing task and function. A few examples of this thinking might be to

- Target terrorists through behavioral profiling
- Have random rather than mandatory checkpoints at air and transportation facilities
- Allow frequent fliers to skip security systems; this has been done for registered fliers on an increasing basis
- Allow local police authorities to assume some homeland functions
- Insist on a grant program that is not universally applied but targeted to localities and their needs
- Disburse budgetary allotments at the local level
- Return non-DHS functions to previous agencies
- Halt the onerous license requirements for American citizens
- Decentralize more DHS operations to the states and localities

These are representative suggestions for how DHS and its staff might think outside the usual constraints.

In general, the future of DHS largely depends on the demand due to circumstance, incident, and event, and whether the functions of response remain local or national responsibilities. Regardless, we know with certainty that terrorism is not going away and, as such, there seems to be a long-term place and need for DHS in the future.

Notes

1. DHS, Statement by secretary Jeh C. Johnson on the 2015 federal employee viewpoint survey results (September 28, 2015), http://www.dhs.gov/news/2015/09/28/statement-secretary-jeh-c-johnson-2015-federal-employee-viewpoint-survey-results (accessed February 8, 2016).

2. W. V. Pelfrey, Sr. and W. V. Pelfrey, Jr., Sensemaking in a nascent field: A conceptual framework for understanding the emerging discipline of homeland security, *The Homeland Security Review*, 4, 2010: 161.

3. FBI, *A Study of Active Shooter Incidents in the United States between 2000 and 2013*, (Washington, DC: Texas State University and FBI, 2013), https://www.fbi.gov/about-us/office-of-partner-engagement/active-shooter-incidents/a-study-of-active-shooter-incidents-in-the-u.s.-2000-2013 (accessed February 8, 2016).

4. FEMA, *FEMA Strategic Plan: Fiscal Years 2011–2014*, FEMA P-806 (Washington, DC: DHS, February 2011), http://www.fema.gov/pdf/about/strategic_plan11.pdf.

5. DHS, *One Team, One Mission, Securing Our Homeland*.

6. U.S. Coast Guard, *United States Coast Guard 2011 Posture Statement, with 2012 Budget in Brief* (Washington, DC: USCG, February 2011).

7. E. Beidel, Homeland security market "vibrant" despite budgetary concerns, *National Defense*, September 2011, 34. For a full view of research and development funds for DHS, see: Congressional Research Service, Federal Research and Development Funding: FY2011 (Washington, DC: Library of Congress, March 25, 2011).

8. DHS, Our mission, http://www.dhs.gov/our-mission (accessed February 8, 2016); Homeland Security Act of 2002, P.L. 107–296, *U.S. Statutes at Large*, 116, 2002: §101(b).

9. D. M. West, A vision for homeland security in the year 2025, Governance Studies at Brookings, June 26, 2012, http://www.insidepolitics.org/brookingsreports/homeland_security.pdf (accessed February 8, 2016).

10. W. L. Waugh Jr., *Future of Homeland Security and Emergency Management* (Emmitsburg, MD: Emergency Management Institute, 2011).

11. D. Inserra, Reforming DHS through the appropriations process, Heritage Foundation Issue Brief #4230 on Homeland Security, http://www.heritage.org/research/reports/2014/05/reforming-dhs-through-the-appropriations-process (accessed February 9, 2016).

12. See M. Mayer, J. J. Carafano, and J. Zuckerman, Homeland security 4.0: Overcoming centralization, complacency, and politics, Heritage Foundation Special Report #97 (August 23, 2011), http://www.heritage.org/research/reports/2011/08/homeland-security-4-0-overcoming-centralization-complacency-and-politics.

13. S. H. Clovis Jr., Federalism, homeland security and national preparedness: A case study in the development of public policy, *Homeland Security Affairs*, 2, October 2006: 17 (accessed February 8, 2016).

14. DHS, Science and technology: Centers of excellence, http://www.dhs.gov/science-and-technology/centers-excellence (accessed February 9, 2016).

15. M. Peck, DHS's border drones prove ineffective, *Federal Times*, January 13, 2015, http://www.federaltimes.com/story/government/dhs/programs/2015/01/07/dhs-border-drone-cbp/21385613/ (accessed February 9, 2016); D. Sarkar, CBP's $260M investment in drone border security program shows little return, DHS IG tells panel, *Fierce Government*, July 16, 2015, http://www.fiercegovernmentit.com/story/cbps-360m-investment-drone-border-security-program-shows-little-return-dhs/2015-07-16 (accessed February 9, 2016); DHS, Office of Inspector General, U.S. customs and border protection's unmanned aircraft system program does not achieve intended results or recognize all costs of operations, OIG-15-17, December 24, 2014, https://www.oig.dhs.gov/assets/Mgmt/2015/OIG_15-17_Dec14.pdf (accessed February 9, 2016).

16. DHS, *Budget-in-Brief Fiscal Year 2015* (Washington, DC: DHS, 2015), 149, http://www.dhs.gov/sites/default/files/publications/FY15BIB.pdf (accessed February 9, 2016).

17. DHS, *Blueprint for a Secure Cyber Future* (Washington, DC: DHS, 2015), http://www.dhs.gov/blueprint-secure-cyber-future.

18. A. Aboulenein and L. Noueihed, Islamic State says "Schweppes bomb" used to bring down Russian plane, Reuters U.S. Online Edition (November 19, 2015), http://www.reuters.com/article/us-egypt-crash-islamicstate-photo-idUSKCN0T725Q20151119 (accessed February 9, 2016).

19. B. York, *Washington Examiner*, January 9, 2011, http://washingtonexaminer.com/politics/beltway-confidential/2011/01/journalists-urged-caution-after-ft-hood-now-race-blame-palin.

20. B. H. Friedman, Managing fear: The politics of homeland security, *Political Science Quarterly*, 126, 2011: 77, 80. See also M. Leitenberg, Assessing the threat of bioterrorism, in B. H. Friedman, J. Harper, and C. A. Preble, eds., *Terrorizing Ourselves: Why Counterterrorism is Failing and How to Fix It* (Washington, DC: Cato Institute, 2010), 162–163.

21. Friedman, Managing fear, 83.

Appendix I: United States Department of Homeland Security: Homeland Security Advisory Council

AI.1 Official Designation

Homeland Security Advisory Council (HSAC)

AI.2 Authority

This charter establishes HSAC under the authority of Title 6 United States Code, Section 451. This committee is established in accordance with and operates under the provisions of the *Federal Advisory Committee Act* (FACA), Title 5 United States Code, Appendix.

AI.3 Objectives and Scope of Activities

HSAC shall provide organizationally independent, strategic, timely, specific and actionable advice to the Secretary and senior leadership on matters related to homeland security. HSAC serves strictly as an advisory body with the purpose of providing advice upon the request of the Secretary. HSAC advice to the Secretary may encompass:

A. Strategy and policy: Recommendations for the development of strategies and policies that will further the Department's ability to prevent, protect against, respond to, and recover from terrorist attacks, major disasters, or other emergencies.
B. Leadership and coordination: Recommendations on improving the Department's leadership and coordination, internally across the Department, externally across

the Federal Government, and among state, local, tribal governments, first responders, the private and non-profit sectors, academia, and research communities.

C. Management and implementation: Recommendations on the development and implementation of specific programs or initiatives to prevent, protect against, respond to, and recover from terrorist attacks, major disasters, or other emergencies.

D. Evaluation and feedback: Recommendations on the efficiency and effectiveness of Department of Homeland Security (DHS) programs to prevent, protect against, respond to, and recover from terrorist attacks, major disasters, or other emergencies.

AI.4 Descriptions of Duties

The duties of the HSAC are solely advisory in nature.

AI.5 Official to Whom the Committee Reports

HSAC reports to the Secretary of Homeland Security.

AI.6 Agency Responsible for Providing Necessary Support

DHS is responsible for providing financial and administrative support to the HSAC. Within DHS, the Office of Policy provides this support.

AI.7 Estimated Cost, Compensation, and Staff Support

Estimated annual operating costs for the HSAC is $712,165.00 which includes travel and per diem, and other administrative expenses, and four Full-Time Equivalent to support the Council.

AI.8 Designated Federal Officer

A full-time or permanent part-time employee of DHS shall be appointed by the Secretary as the HSAC Designated Federal Officer (DFO). The DFO or the Alternate DFO shall approve or call HSAC meetings, approve meeting agendas, attend all committee, subcommittee, and task force meetings, adjourn any meeting when the DFO determines adjournment to be in the public interest, and chair meetings in the absence of the Chair or Vice Chair or as directed by the Secretary.

AI.9 Estimated Number and Frequency of Meetings

Meetings of the HSAC may be held with the approval of the DFO; it is expected that the HSAC will meet quarterly, or as frequently as the Secretary desires. Committee meetings are open to the public unless a determination is made by the appropriate DHS official in accordance with DHS policy and directives that the meeting should be closed in accordance with Title 5, United States Code, subsection (c) of Section 552b.

AI.10 Duration

Continuing.

AI.11 Termination

This charter is in effect for two years from the date it is filed with Congress unless sooner terminated. The charter may be renewed at the end of this two-year period in accordance with Section 14 of FACA.

AI.12 Member Composition

HSAC shall be composed of not more than 40 members who are appointed by and serve at the pleasure of the Secretary.

All members shall serve as Special Government Employees as defined in section 202(a) of Title 18 United States Code. Term length shall be up to three years and approximately one-third of the terms shall expire each year in order to promote membership continuity and currency of expertise. In the event the HSAC terminates, all appointments to the committee shall terminate.

In order for the Secretary to fully leverage broad-ranging experience and education, the HSAC must be professionally, technically, and culturally diverse. These members shall all be national leaders found within diverse and appropriate professions and communities from around the Nation. The membership shall be drawn from the following fields:

Police, fire, emergency medical services and public works;
Public health and hospital managers;
State, local, and tribal officials;
National policy makers;
Experts in academia and the research community;
Leaders from the private sector;
Owners and operators of critical industries, resources, and infrastructure.

AI.13 Officers

The Secretary shall designate a Chair and a Vice-Chair from among the appointed members of HSAC. The Vice-Chair will act as Chair in the absence or incapacity of the Chair or in the event of a vacancy in the office of the Chair.

AI.14 Subcommittees

The Secretary may establish subcommittees, task forces, or working groups for any purpose consistent with this charter. All subcommittee members shall be appointed by and serve at the pleasure of the Secretary. In the event the subcommittee or HSAC terminates, all appointments to the subcommittee shall terminate.

Subcommittees shall be composed of a number of HSAC and non-HSAC members to be determined by the DFO. The DFO, with the consultation of the HSAC Chair, shall designate a Chair and Vice Chair for each of the subcommittees from among the HSAC's members.

Subcommittees may not work independently of HSAC and must present their work to HSAC for full deliberation and discussion. Subcommittees have no authority to make decisions on behalf of the HSAC and may not report directly to the Federal Government or any other entity.

The HSAC currently has five active subcommittees: the Foreign Fighter Task Force, the DHS Employee Morale Task Force, the DHS Grant Review Task Force, the CBP Integrity Advisory Panel, and the Faith-Based Security and Communications Subcommittee.

AI.15 Recordkeeping

The records of HSAC, formally and informally established subcommittees or other subgroups of the committee, shall be handled in accordance with General Records Schedule 26, Item 2 or other approved agency records disposition schedule. These records shall be available for public inspection and copying, in accordance with the *Freedom of Information Act* (Title 5, United States Code, section 552).

AI.16 Filing Date

March 6, 2015: Agency Approval Date

February 25, 2015: GSA Consultation Date

March 11, 2015: Date Filed with Congress

Source: US Department of Homeland Security, Homeland Security Advisory Council, https://www.dhs.gov/sites/default/files/publications/HSAC%20Charter%20Final%20 3.6.15_0_0.pdf.

Appendix II: Glossary

absolute risk
Level of risk expressed with standard units of measurement that allows for independent interpretation without comparison to estimates of other risks.

absolute risk (unmitigated)
Level of risk that exists without risk controls.

acceptable risk
Level of risk at which, given costs and benefits associated with risk reduction measures, no action is deemed to be warranted at a given point in time.

accidental hazard
Source of harm or difficulty created by negligence, error, or unintended failure.

adaptive risk
Category of risk that includes threats intentionally caused by humans.

adversary
Individual, group, organization, or government that conducts or has the intent to conduct detrimental activities.

alternative futures analysis
Set of techniques used to explore different future states developed by varying a set of key trends, drivers, and/or conditions.

asset
Person, structure, facility, information, material, or process that has value.

attack method	Manner and means, including the weapon and delivery method, an adversary may use to cause harm on a target.
attack path	Steps that an adversary takes or may take to plan, prepare for, and execute an attack.
baseline risk	Current level of risk that takes into account existing risk mitigation measures.
Bayesian probability	The process of evaluating the probability of a hypothesis through (1) the specification of a prior probability and (2) modification of the prior probability by incorporation of observed information to create an updated posterior probability.
Bayesian probability (subjective probability)	See **subjective probability** (synonym).
break-even analysis	Variant of **cost–benefit analysis** that estimates the threshold value at which a policy alternative's costs equal its benefits.
capability	Means to accomplish a mission, function, or objective.
consequence	Effect of an event, incident, or occurrence.
consequence assessment	Product or process of identifying or evaluating the potential or actual effects of an event, incident, or occurrence.
cost-effectiveness analysis (CEA)	Analytic technique that compares the cost of two or more alternatives with the same outcome. Alternatively: analytic technique that evaluates an alternative by how much it delivers per unit cost, or how much has to be spent per unit benefit.
cost–benefit analysis (CBA)	Analytic technique used to compare alternatives according to the relative costs incurred and the relative benefits gained.
countermeasure	Action, measure, or device intended to reduce an identified risk.
criticality	Importance to a mission or function, or continuity of operations.
criticality assessment	Product or process of systematically identifying, evaluating, and prioritizing based on the importance of an impact to mission(s), function(s), or continuity of operations.
decision analysis	Techniques, body of knowledge, and professional practice used to provide analytical support for making decisions through a formalized structure.

deterrent	Measure that discourages, complicates, or delays an adversary's action or occurrence by instilling fear, doubt, or anxiety.
direct consequence	Effect that is an immediate result of an event, incident, or occurrence.
economic consequence	Effect of an incident, event, or occurrence on the value of property or on the production, trade, distribution, or use of income, wealth, or commodities.
enterprise risk management	Comprehensive approach to risk management that engages organizational systems and processes together to improve the quality of decision-making for managing risks that may hinder an organization's ability to achieve its objectives.
evaluation	Process of examining, measuring and/or judging how well an entity, procedure, or action has met or is meeting stated objectives. Evaluation is the step in the risk management cycle that measures the effectiveness of an implemented risk management option.
event tree	Graphical tool used to illustrate the range and probabilities of possible outcomes that arise from an initiating event. Event trees use forward logic; they begin with an initiating event and work forward in time to determine the possible outcomes. The probabilities used in event trees are conditional probabilities because they are based on the assumption that the initiating event has already occurred.
fault tree	Graphical tool used to illustrate the range, probability, and interaction of causal occurrences that lead to a final outcome. Fault trees use inductive (backwards) logic; they begin with a final occurrence and work backwards in time to determine the possible causes. A fault tree can be used to quantitatively estimate the probability of a program or system failure by visually displaying and evaluating failure paths.
frequency	Number of occurrences of an event per defined period of time or number of trials.
frequentist probability	Interpretation or estimate of probability as the long-run frequency of the occurrence of an event as estimated by historical observation or experimental trials.

function	Service, process, capability, or operation performed by an entity, asset, system, network, or geographic area.
game theory	Branch of applied mathematics that models interactions among agents, where an agent's choice and subsequent success depend on the choices of other agents that are simultaneously acting to maximize their own results or minimize their losses.
hazard	Natural or man-made source or cause of harm or difficulty.
horizon scanning	Process of identifying future trends, drivers, and/or conditions that may have an effect on future events, incidents, or occurrences.
human consequence (health)	Effect of an incident, event, or occurrence that results in injury, illness, or loss of life.
implementation	Act of putting a procedure or course of action into effect to support goals or achieve objectives.
incident	Occurrence, caused by either human action or natural phenomena, that may cause harm and that may require action.
indirect consequence	Effect that is not a direct consequence of an event, incident, or occurrence, but is caused by a direct consequence, subsequent cascading effects, and/or related decisions.
integrated risk management	Structured approach that enables the distribution and employment of shared risk information and analysis and the synchronization of independent yet complementary risk management strategies to unify efforts across the enterprise.
intent	A state of mind or desire to achieve an objective.
intentional hazard	Source of harm, duress, or difficulty created by a deliberate action or a planned course of action.
likelihood	Chance of something happening, whether defined, measured, or estimated objectively or subjectively, or in terms of general descriptors (such as rare, unlikely, likely, almost certain), frequencies, or probabilities.
likelihood (statistical)	Conditional probability of observing a particular event given the hypothesis under consideration is true. In statistical usage, there is a clear distinction between probability and likelihood: whereas probability allows us to predict unknown outcomes based on known parameters, likelihood allows us to estimate unknown parameters based on known outcomes.

marginal probability	See **probability**.
mission consequence	Effect of an incident, event, operation, or occurrence on the ability of an organization or group to meet a strategic objective or perform a function.
mitigation	Ongoing and sustained action to reduce the probability of, or lessen the impact of, an adverse incident.
model	Approximation, representation, or idealization of selected aspects of the structure, behavior, operation, or other characteristics of a real-world process, concept, or system.
natural hazard	Source of harm or difficulty created by a meteorological, environmental, or geological phenomenon or combination of phenomena.
net assessment	Multidisciplinary strategic assessment process used to provide a comparative evaluation of the balance of strengths and weaknesses.
network	Group of persons or components that share information or interact with each other in order to perform a function.
nonadaptive risk	Category of risk that includes threats caused by natural and technological hazards.
normalized risk	Measure of risk created by mathematically adjusting a value in order to permit comparisons.
operational risk	Risk that has the potential to impede the successful execution of operations.
primary consequence	See **direct consequence**.
probabilistic risk assessment	Type of quantitative risk assessment that considers possible combinations of occurrences with associated consequences, each with an associated probability or probability distribution.
probability	Numerical value between 0 and 1 assigned to a random event (which is a subset of the sample space) in such a way that the assigned number obeys three axioms: (1) the probability of the random event "A" must be equal to, or lie between, 0 and 1; (2) the probability that the outcome is within the sample space must equal 1; and (3) the probability that the random event "A" or "B" occurs must equal the probability of the random event "A" plus the probability of the random event "B" for any two mutually exclusive events. Probability can be roughly interpreted as the percent chance that something will occur. A probability of 0 indicates the occurrence is impossible; 1 indicates that the occurrence will definitely happen.

psychological consequence	Effect of an incident, event, or occurrence on the mental or emotional state of individuals or groups resulting in a change in perception and/or behavior.
qualitative risk assessment methodology	Set of methods, principles, or rules for assessing risk based on non-numerical categories or levels.
quantitative risk assessment methodology	Set of methods, principles, or rules for assessing risks based on the use of numbers where the meanings and proportionality of values are maintained inside and outside the context of the assessment.
redundancy	Additional or alternative systems, subsystems, assets, or processes that maintain a degree of overall functionality in case of loss or failure of another system, subsystem, asset, or process.
relative risk	Measure of risk that represents the ratio of risks when compared to each other or a control.
residual risk	Risk that remains after risk management measures have been implemented.
resilience	Ability to adapt to changing conditions and prepare for, withstand, and rapidly recover from disruption.
return on investment (risk)	Calculation of the value of risk reduction measures in the context of the cost of developing and implementing those measures.
risk	Potential for an unwanted outcome resulting from an incident, event, or occurrence, as determined by its likelihood and the associated consequences. Risk is defined as the potential for an unwanted outcome. This potential is often measured and used to compare different future situations. Risk may manifest at the strategic, operational, and tactical levels.
risk acceptance	Explicit or implicit decision not to take an action that would affect all or part of a particular risk.
risk analysis	Systematic examination of the components and characteristics of risk.
risk assessment	Product or process which collects information and assigns values to risks for the purpose of informing priorities, developing or comparing courses of action, and informing decision-making.
risk assessment methodology	Set of methods, principles, or rules used to identify and assess risks and to form priorities, develop courses of action, and inform decision-making.

risk assessment tool	Activity, item, or program that contributes to determining and evaluating risks.
risk avoidance	Strategies or measures taken that effectively remove exposure to a risk.
risk communication	Exchange of information with the goal of improving risk understanding, affecting risk perception, and/or equipping people or groups to act appropriately in response to an identified risk.
risk control	Deliberate action taken to reduce the potential for harm or maintain it at an acceptable level.
risk data	Information on key components of risk that are outputs of or inputs to risk assessments and risk analyses.
risk exposure	Contact of an entity, asset, system, network, or geographic area with a potential hazard.
risk governance	Actors, rules, practices, processes, and mechanisms concerned with how risk is analyzed, managed, and communicated.
risk identification	Process of finding, recognizing, and describing potential risks.
risk indicator	Measure that signals the potential for an unwanted outcome as determined by qualitative or quantitative analysis.
risk management	Process of identifying, analyzing, assessing, and communicating risk and accepting, avoiding, transferring, or controlling it to an acceptable level considering associated costs and benefits of any actions taken.
risk management alternatives development	Process of systematically examining risks to develop a range of options and their anticipated effects for decision makers.
risk management cycle	Sequence of steps that are systematically taken and revisited to manage risk.
risk management methodology	Set of methods, principles, or rules used to identify, analyze, assess, and communicate risk, and accept, avoid, transfer, or control it to an acceptable level considering associated costs and benefits of any actions taken.
risk management plan	Document that identifies risks and specifies the actions that have been chosen to manage those risks.
risk management strategy	Course of action or actions to be taken in order to manage risks.

risk matrix	Tool for ranking and displaying components of risk in an array.
risk mitigation	Application of measure or measures to reduce the likelihood of an unwanted occurrence and/or its consequences.
risk mitigation option	Measure, device, policy, or course of action taken with the intent of reducing risk.
risk perception	Subjective judgment about the characteristics and/or severity of risk.
risk profile	Description and/or depiction of risks to an entity, asset, system, network, or geographic area.
risk reduction	Decrease in risk through risk avoidance, risk control, or risk transfer.
risk score	Numerical result of a semiquantitative risk assessment methodology.
risk tolerance	Degree to which an entity, asset, system, network, or geographic area is willing to accept risk.
risk transfer	Action taken to manage risk that shifts some or all of the risk to another entity, asset, system, network, or geographic area.
risk-base decision-making	Determination of a course of action predicated primarily on the assessment of risk and the expected impact of that course of action on that risk.
risk-informed decision-making	Determination of a course of action predicated on the assessment of risk, the expected impact of that course of action on that risk, as well as other relevant factors.
	Sample usage: "While increased patrols lessened the likelihood of trespassers, residual risk remained due to the unlocked exterior doors."
scenario (risk)	Hypothetical situation comprised of a hazard, an entity impacted by that hazard, and associated conditions including consequences when appropriate.
secondary consequence	See **indirect consequence**.
semiquantitative risk assessment methodology	Set of methods, principles, or rules to assess risk that uses bins, scales, or representative numbers whose values and meanings are not maintained in other contexts.
sensitivity analysis	Process to determine how outputs of a methodology differ in response to variation of the inputs or conditions.

simulation	Model that behaves or operates like a given process, concept, or system when provided a set of controlled inputs.
social amplification of risk	Distortion of the seriousness of a risk caused by public concern about the risk and/or about an activity contributing to the risk.
strategic foresight	Range of activities associated with longer range planning and alternative futures analysis.
strategic risk	Risk that affects an entity's vital interests or execution of chosen strategy, whether imposed by external threats or arising from flawed or poorly implemented strategy.
subject matter expert	Individual with in-depth knowledge in a specific area or field.
subjective probability	Interpretation or estimate of probability as a personal judgment or "degree of belief" about how likely a particular event is to occur, based on the state of knowledge and available evidence.
system	Any combination of facilities, equipment, personnel, procedures, and communications integrated for a specific purpose.
target	Asset, network, system or geographic area chosen by an adversary to be impacted by an attack.
threat	Natural or man-made occurrence, individual, entity, or action that has or indicates the potential to harm life, information, operations, the environment, and/or property.
threat assessment	Product or process of identifying or evaluating entities, actions, or occurrences, whether natural or man-made, that have or indicate the potential to harm life, information, operations, and/or property.
threat shifting	Response of adversaries to perceived countermeasures or obstructions, in which the adversaries change some characteristic of their intent to do harm in order to avoid or overcome the countermeasure or obstacle.
unacceptable risk	Level of risk at which, given costs and benefits associated with further risk reduction measures, action is deemed to be warranted at a given point in time.
uncertainty	Degree to which a calculated, estimated, or observed value may deviate from the true value.

unmitigated risk	See **residual risk**.
value of statistical life (VSL)	Amount people are willing to pay to reduce risk so that on average one less person is expected to die from the risk.
vulnerability	Physical feature or operational attribute that renders an entity, asset, system, network, or geographic area open to exploitation or susceptible to a given hazard.
vulnerability assessment	Product or process of identifying physical features or operational attributes that render an entity, asset, system, network, or geographic area susceptible or exposed to hazards.
willingness to accept	Amount a person is willing to accept to forgo a benefit.
willingness to pay	Amount a person would be willing to pay, sacrifice, or exchange for a benefit.

Appendix III: FY 2010 NIMS Implementation Objectives and Metrics for Federal Departments and Agencies

Introduction

Homeland Security Presidential Directive 5 (HSPD-5) *Management of Domestic Incidents* called for the establishment of a single, comprehensive national incident management system. As a result, the U.S. Department of Homeland Security released the National Incident Management System (NIMS) in March 2004. NIMS provides a systematic, proactive approach guiding departments and agencies at all levels of government, the private sector, and nongovernmental organizations to work seamlessly to prepare for, prevent, respond to, recover from, and mitigate the effects of incidents, regardless of cause, size, location, or complexity, in order to reduce the loss of life, property, and harm to the environment. This consistency provides the foundation for implementation of the NIMS for all incidents, ranging from daily occurrences to incidents requiring a coordinated Federal response. The NIMS document, as revised in 2008, reflects contributions from stakeholders and lessons learned during recent incidents.

Federal departments and agencies play an important role in ensuring effective NIMS implementation; not only must they implement NIMS within their departments and agencies, they must also ensure that the systems and processes are in place to communicate and support NIMS compliance at all jurisdictional levels.

The long-term goal of NIMS is to provide a consistent template for all aspects of emergency management and incident response. This template should be sustainable, flexible, and scalable to meet changing incident needs and allow for integration of other resources from various partners through mutual aid agreements and/or assistance agreements.

Federal NIMS Implementation

In 2004, a memorandum to the departments and agencies from the Secretary of U.S. Department of Homeland Security recommended departments and agencies to adopt the NIMS and use it in their individual domestic incident management and emergency prevention, preparedness, response, recovery, and mitigation activities. Since that time, the FEMA National Integration Center (NIC) has engaged its Federal stakeholders to expand on this foundation and add additional activities—each developed to enhance the way that incidents are managed at all levels of government.

Specifically, this memorandum outlined the following important first-steps for the successful implementation of the NIMS:

1. Identify existing or anticipated FY 2005 Federal preparedness assistance programs
   HSPD-5 established ambitious deadlines for NIMS adoption and implementation, including the requirement that, beginning in Fiscal Year 2005, Federal departments and agencies make adoption of the NIMS a requirement, to the extent permitted by law, for providing Federal preparedness assistance through grants, contracts, or other activities. FY 2005 was a start-up year for NIMS implementation and full compliance with the NIMS was not required for grantees to receive FY 2005 grant funds. Grantees were encouraged to direct preparedness assistance (beginning in FY 2005) to implementing the NIMS (in accordance with the eligibility and allowable uses of the grants).

   Also, Federal departments and agencies were asked to identify any existing or anticipated programs that provide preparedness assistance (*grants or contracts that contribute to building preparedness and response capabilities*) to States and local entities along with a point of contact and contact information for each program.
2. Submit a plan for adopting and implementing the NIMS
   By December 31, 2004, the head of each Federal department and agency was required to submit a plan to adopt and implement the NIMS. The Assistant to the President for Homeland Security reviewed plans and advised the President on whether such plans effectively implement the NIMS. Federal department and agency plans must reflect full adoption and implementation of the NIMS by September 30, 2005.
3. Incorporate the NIMS into emergency operations plans
   All department and agencies were immediately to incorporate NIMS concepts, principles, and terminology into existing Emergency Operations Plan (EOP), Comprehensive Emergency Management Plan (CEMP), or other similar plans.

Federal NIMS Implementation in FY 2010

In FY 2010, there are 22 Implementation Objectives for Federal Departments and Agencies (reference Attachment 1). Beginning in FY 2010, Federal departments and agencies can measure progress of NIMS implementation through responses to performance-based "metrics." The NIC coordinated a Federal work group in 2006–2007, which crafted the NIMS

Implementation Metrics (reference Attachment 2). Additionally, NIC will expand its NIMS Compliance Assistance Support Tool (NIMSCAST) to incorporate both federal department users and accounts. As with State, territory, tribe, and local governments, the NIMSCAST provide Federal departments and agencies with a way to collect and report data relating to NIMS implementation. NIC will analyze this data to help shape the future of its NIMS implementation at the federal level.

The breakdown of NIMS Implementation Objectives and Metrics, by NIMS component, is as follows:

Summary		
NIMS Component	Objectives	Metrics
Adoption and infrastructure	1–6	1–15
Preparedness [planning, training, exercises]	7–12	16–25
Communication and information management	13–14	26–28
Resource management	15–17	29–31
Command and management [ICS/MACS/public information]	18–22	32–40

Attachment 1: NIMS Implementation Objectives

The 22 Implementation Objectives for Federal Departments and Agencies are below:

NIMS Implementation Objective

Adoption

1. Formally adopt NIMS within Federal department/agency and encourage formal NIMS adoption as appropriate by external partners (trade associations, private sector partners, contractors, grantees, and vendors) with incident management responsibilities.

2. Designate a single point of contact within the department/agency to serve as the principal coordinator for NIMS implementation.

3. Promote or encourage other external partners and stakeholders without formal or legal agreements to adopt NIMS formally.

4. Develop a phased NIMS Implementation Plan for each specific department/agency.

5. Annually verify department/agency progress on NIMS implementation.

6. To the extent permissible by Federal laws and regulations, incorporate measurement of NIMS implementation into existing department/agency audits and reviews of incident management preparedness funding (e.g., grants, future year contracts).

Preparedness

7. Revise and update department/agency incident management plans and standard operating procedures/standard operating guidelines to incorporate NIMS components, terminology, principles, and policies.

8. Promote the department/agency, non-governmental and private sector use of cooperative agreements (e.g., Mutual Aid Agreements, Memorandums of Understanding/Agreement, Letters of Agreement, and Interagency Agreements).

(Continued)

NIMS Implementation Objective
9. Implement NIMS training to include appropriate personnel (as identified in the *Five-Year NIMS Training Plan*, released February 2008) and in accordance with their incident management responsibilities.
10. Incorporate NIMS into all applicable department/agency incident management exercises and evaluation programs (e.g., the Homeland Security Exercise and Evaluation Program [HSEEP].)
11. Evaluate the implementation of NIMS in all department/agency incident management exercises to identify gaps in implementation.
12. Incorporate NIMS corrective actions into department/agency preparedness/response plans and procedures.

Communication and Information Management

13. As appropriate, apply standardized and consistent terminology, including the use of plain language, in all department/agency communication protocols and/or plans for incident management and planned events.
14. Develop systems, tools, and processes to ensure that incident managers at all levels share a common operating picture of an incident. (e.g., use of the Homeland Security Information Network.)

Resource Management

15. Develop a department/agency inventory of incident management assets and identify those assets that conform to NIMS Resource Type Definitions.
16. Utilize response asset inventory for mutual aid/assistance requests, exercises, incident management, and planned events.
17. To the extent permissible by Federal law, incorporate relevant national standards to achieve equipment, communication, and data interoperability into existing department/agency business practices and procedures.

Command and Management

18. Manage all interagency emergency incidents and planned events in accordance with Incident Command System (ICS) organizational structures, doctrine, and procedures defined in NIMS.
19. Use ICS in department/agency Incident Action Plans (IAPs) and common communications plans.
20. Coordinate and support emergency incident and event management through Multiagency Coordination Systems (MACS).
21. Establish a Public Information system within the department/agency to include Joint Information System and Joint Information Center.
22. Ensure department/agency can gather, verify, coordinate, and disseminate critical Public Affairs information during an incident.

Attachment 2: Implementation Metrics

Key assumptions regarding Federal NIMS implementation metrics aggregation are:

1. Each Department/Agency will assign a Principal NIMS Coordinator (PNC) (*Example: Principal NIMS Coordinator for the Department of Justice*).
2. Principal NIMS Coordinators will be responsible for:
   - Implementing the NIMS;

- Identifying components with incident management responsibilities;
- Distributing NIMS metrics questions to components with incident management responsibilities;
- Aggregating responses from Department/Agency and its components; and
- Reporting the status of Department/Agency NIMS implementation activities to FEMA's National Integration Center.

3. Each Department/Agency's components will assign a NIMS Coordinator (*Example: NIMS Coordinator for the ATF, DEA, FBI, or U.S. Marshals Service*)

4. Component NIMS Coordinator (CNC) will be responsible for:
- Implementing the NIMS;
- Identifying sub-components with incident management responsibilities;
- Distributing NIMS metrics questions to sub-components with incident management responsibilities;
- Aggregating responses from Department/Agency Component and its sub-components; and
- Reporting the status of Department/Agency Component NIMS implementation activities to the Department/Agency Principal NIMS Coordinator.

Each question is coded to indicate at what level the question should be answered.

- **(PNC)**: Question answered by Department/Agency Principal NIMS Coordinator on behalf of the Department/Agency
- **(CNC)**: Question answered by Department/Agency sub-component unit NIMS Coordinator(s) and compiled by Department/Agency Principal NIMS Coordinator

NIMS Adoption Metrics

IMPLEMENTATION OBJECTIVE #1

- **Formally adopt NIMS within Federal department/agency.**
- *Encourage formal NIMS adoption as appropriate by external partners (trade associations, private sector partners, contractors, grantees, and vendors) with incident management responsibilities.*

		Rationale for asking the question at the indicated level.
1. Has the department/agency formally adopted NIMS as its all-hazards, incident management system? **(PNC) (CNC)** [ ] Yes [ ] No ▪ If "Yes," what authority was used to adopt NIMS: [Check all that apply.] [ ] Executive Level Policy Statement [ ] Proclamation [ ] Resolution [ ] Other authority, explain: [ ] ▪ If "No," which of the following impedes adoption: [Check all that apply.] [ ] Plans [ ] Policy [ ] Personnel [ ] Funding [ ] Other, explain: [ ]		*The PNC should answer this question because NIMS is typically adopted department-wide.* *However, some CNCs should answer this question because they have a unique and/or independent status (e.g., U.S. Coast Guard).*
2. Has the department/agency issued a NIMS adoption policy for all internal stakeholders with incident management responsibilities? **(PNC) (CNC)** [ ] Yes [ ] No • If "Yes," explain: [ ] • If "No," explain: [ ]		*The PNC should answer this question because the NIMS adoption policy is typically top-down and department-wide.* *However, some Components should answer this question because they have a unique and/or independent status (e.g., U.S. Coast Guard).*

3. Has the department/agency notified external partners (trade associations, private sector partners, contractors, grantees, and vendors) with incident management responsibilities of the department/agency's NIMS adoption policy? **(CNC)**

[ ] Yes
[ ] No

- If "Yes," explain: [   ]
- If "No," explain: [   ]

The CNC should answer this question because this activity is typically carried out by Department/Agency Component and may not be an overall Department/Agency activity.

4. Have the department/agency external partners formally adopted NIMS as appropriate as their all-hazards, incident management system? **(CNC)**

	Yes	No	Not Applicable
Contractors	[ ]	[ ]	[ ]
If "No," explain: [ ]			
Grantees	[ ]	[ ]	[ ]
If "No," explain: [ ]			
Vendors	[ ]	[ ]	[ ]
If "No," explain: [ ]			
Other, identify: [ ]	[ ]	[ ]	[ ]
If "No," explain: [ ]			

The CNC should answer this question because this activity is typically carried out by a Department/Agency Component(s) and may not be an overall Department/Agency activity.

- Which of the following impedes adoption: [Check all that apply.]

[ ] Plans
[ ] Policy
[ ] Personnel
[ ] Funding

[ ] Other, explain: [   ]

5. To what extent does the department/agency monitor external partners with incident management response duties to ensure that they have adopted NIMS: [Select current level of effort.] **(CNC)**

[ ] No effort has been made towards monitoring external stakeholders

[ ] Monitoring procedures have been developed, but external stakeholders have NOT been monitored

[ ] External stakeholders have been monitored, and monitoring is ongoing

The CNC should answer this question because this activity is typically carried out by a Department/Agency Component(s) and may not be an overall Department/Agency activity.

	Rationale for asking the question at the indicated level.
IMPLEMENTATION OBJECTIVE #2: **Designate a single point of contact within the department/agency to serve as the principal coordinator for NIMS implementation.**	

6. Has the department/agency designated a single point of contact as the principal coordinator for NIMS implementation? **(CNC)**
 	
[ ] Yes
[ ] No
 	
   ▪ If "Yes," who has been designated? _____ (Name, Title, Email Address, Phone Number, and Mailing Address)
 	
     ● What was the date of appointment? _____ (MM/DD/YYYY)
 	
   ▪ If "No," when will the department/agency designate a single point of contact for NIMS implementation? _____ (MM/DD/YYYY)
 	
     ● Which of the following impedes designating a single point of contact for NIMS implementation: [Check all that apply.]
 	
       [ ] Plans
       [ ] Policy
       [ ] Personnel
       [ ] Funding
       [ ] Training
       [ ] Education
       [ ] Other, explain: [   ]
	The CNC should answer this question because this activity is typically carried out by a Department/Agency Component(s) and may not be an overall Department/Agency activity.

	Rationale for asking the question at the indicated level.

IMPLEMENTATION OBJECTIVE #3:
 	
To the extent possible, promote and encourage formal adoption of NIMS to appropriate external partners and stakeholders without formal or legal agreements to formally adopt NIMS.
 	
7. Has the department/agency promoted and encouraged NIMS adoption? **(CNC)**
 	
    [ ] Yes
 	
    [ ] No
 	
  ■ If "Yes," identify the methods used to promote and encourage NIMS adoption: [Check all that apply.]
 	
      [ ] Press Release
      [ ] Email
      [ ] Website
      [ ] Mailings (e.g., newsletters, letters, etc.)
      [ ] Meetings (e.g., committees, conferences, working groups, etc.)
      [ ] Exercises (e.g., drills, tabletop, full-scale)
      [ ] Newsletter
      [ ] Article
      [ ] Other, explain: [   ]
 	
  ■ If "No," identify which of the following impedes promoting and encouraging NIMS adoption: [Check all that apply.]
 	
      [ ] Plans
      [ ] Policy
      [ ] Personnel
      [ ] Funding
      [ ] Exercises
      [ ] Education
      [ ] Other, explain: [   ]
	The CNC should answer this question because this activity is typically carried out by a Department/Agency Component(s) and may not be an overall Department/Agency activity.

	Rationale for asking the question at the indicated level.
IMPLEMENTATION OBJECTIVE #4: **Develop a phased NIMS Implementation Plan:** • **Communicate NIMS implementation activities to internal and external stakeholders;** • **Monitor NIMS implementation by department/agency;** • **Measure NIMS implementation by department/agency;** • **Report department/agency NIMS implementation status on an annual basis to the FEMA National Integration Center; and** • **Update implementation plans as needed.** 8. Has the department/agency developed a NIMS Implementation Plan that communicates NIMS implementation activities to *internal* stakeholders? **(PNC)** [ ] Yes [ ] No ▪ If "Yes," which method is or will be used to communicate NIMS implementation activities to *internal* stakeholders: [Check all that apply.] [ ] Meetings (e.g., committees, conferences) [ ] Mailings (e.g., newsletters, letters) [ ] Exercise [ ] Education [ ] Email or other electronic means (e.g., websites) [ ] Other methods used to communicate NIMS implementation activities, explain: [ ] ▪ If "No," which of the following impedes the communication of NIMS implementation activities to *internal* stakeholders: [Check all that apply.] [ ] Plans [ ] Policy [ ] Personnel [ ] Funding [ ] Exercise [ ] Education [ ] Other, explain: [ ]	*The PNC should answer this question because this activity is typically carried out by overall Department/Agency activity.*

9. Has the department/agency developed a NIMS Implementation Plan that communicates NIMS Implementation Objectives to *external* stakeholders? **(CNC)** [ ] Yes [ ] No ■ If "Yes," which method is or will be used to communicate NIMS implementation activities to *external* stakeholders: [Check all that apply.] [ ] Meetings (e.g., committees, conferences) [ ] Mailings (e.g., newsletters, letters) [ ] Email or other electronic means (e.g., websites) [ ] Other methods used to communicate NIMS implementation activities, explain: [ ] ■ If "No," which of the following impedes the communication of NIMS implementation activities to *external* stakeholders: [Check all that apply.] [ ] Plans [ ] Policy [ ] Personnel [ ] Funding [ ] Exercise [ ] Education [ ] Other, explain: [ ]	*The CNC should answer this question because this activity is typically carried out by a Department/Agency Component(s) and may not be an overall Department/Agency activity.*
10. Has the department/agency developed a NIMS Implementation Plan that monitors internal NIMS implementation activities? **(PNC)** [ ] Yes [ ] No ■ If "Yes," explain the method that is or will be used by the department/agency to monitor internal NIMS implementation: [Narrative.] ■ If "No," which of the following impedes the department/agency from monitoring internal NIMS implementation activities: [Check all that apply.] [ ] Plans [ ] Policy [ ] Personnel [ ] Funding [ ] Exercise [ ] Education [ ] Other, explain: [ ]	*The PNC should answer this question because monitoring the NIMS implementation activities is typically a top-down effort.*

11. Has the department/agency developed a NIMS Implementation Plan that measures NIMS implementation activities by internal stakeholders? **(PNC)**
 	
    [ ] Yes
    [ ] No
 	
    ● If "Yes," explain the method that is or will be used by the department/agency to measure NIMS implementation by internal stakeholders: [Narrative.]
 	
    ● If "No," which of the following impedes measuring NIMS implementation activities by internal stakeholders: [Check all that apply.]
 	
        [ ] Plans
        [ ] Policy
        [ ] Personnel
        [ ] Funding
        [ ] Training
        [ ] Education
        [ ] Other, explain: [   ]
	The PNC should answer this question because monitoring the NIMS implementation activities is typically a top-down effort.

12. Has the department/agency maintained the currency of its NIMS Implementation Plan? **(PNC)**
 	
    [ ] Yes
    [ ] No
	The PNC should answer this question because updating the department/agency's NIMS implementation status is typically a top-down effort.

13. Has the department/agency reported its department/agency's implementation status to the FEMA's National Integration Center? **(PNC)**
 	
    [ ] Yes
    [ ] No
 	
    ■ If "Yes," which method is or will be used to report the department/agency's implementation status: [Check all that apply.]
 	
        [ ] Common Network Drive
        [ ] Courier
        [ ] Email
        [ ] NIMS Compliance Assistance Support Tool (NIMSCAST)
        [ ] Secure Portal
        [ ] Other, explain: [   ]
	The PNC should answer this question because reporting to the NIC on NIMS implementation status is typically a top-down effort.

- If "No," which of the following impedes the annual reporting of the department/agency's NIMS implementation status: [Check all that apply.]

  [ ] Plans
  [ ] Policy
  [ ] Personnel
  [ ] Funding
  [ ] Exercise
  [ ] Education
  [ ] Other, explain: [   ]

	Rationale for asking the question at the indicated level.
IMPLEMENTATION OBJECTIVE #5: **Annually verify department/agency progress on FY 2005 NIMS implementation activities:** • **Identify existing FY 2005 Federal Preparedness Awards programs.** • **Submit a plan for adopting and implementing the NIMS to the NIC.** • **Identify and incorporate the NIMS into Emergency Operations Plans (EOPs) and all incident management plans.**	
14. Has the department/agency verified the status of FY 2005 NIMS implementation activities, including: **(CNC)** 		Yes	No
---	---	---
Identifying existing or anticipated preparedness assistance programs	[ ]	[ ]
If "No," explain: [ ]		
Submitting a plan for adopting and implementing the NIMS to the NIC	[ ]	[ ]
If "No," explain: [ ]		
Updating Emergency Operations Plans (EOPs) to incorporate NIMS	[ ]	[ ]
If "No," explain: [ ]				*The CNC should answer this question because this activity is typically carried out by a Department/Agency Component(s) and may not be an overall Department/Agency activity.*

IMPLEMENTATION OBJECTIVE #6:

To the extent permissible by Federal laws and regulations, incorporate measurement of NIMS implementation into existing department/agency audits and reviews of incident management preparedness awards (e.g., grants, contracts).

15. Has the department/agency: **(CNC)**

	Yes	No	No Preparedness Awards
Verified NIMS compliance as a condition for distribution of preparedness funding	[ ]	[ ]	[ ]
If "No," explain: [ ]			
Evaluated NIMS implementation and compliance during grant-related audit and review processes	[ ]	[ ]	[ ]
If "No," explain: [ ]			

Rationale for asking the question at the indicated level.

The CNC should answer this question because this activity is typically carried out by a Department/Agency Component(s) and may not be an overall Department/Agency activity.

Preparedness Metrics

IMPLEMENTATION OBJECTIVE #7:

Revise and update department/agency incident management plans and Standard Operating Procedures/Standard Operating Guidelines (SOP/SOGs) to incorporate NIMS components, terminology, principles, and policies, to address the following activities:

- Planning;
- Training;
- Resource Management;
- Response;
- Exercises;
- Equipment;
- Evaluations; and
- Corrective actions.

Rationale for asking the question at the indicated level.

16. Have the following incident management elements been revised and updated to incorporate NIMS components, terminology, principles, and policies: **(CNC)**

	Yes	No
Planning	[ ]	[ ]
Training	[ ]	[ ]
Response Activities	[ ]	[ ]
Exercises	[ ]	[ ]
Equipment Acquisition	[ ]	[ ]
Evaluations	[ ]	[ ]
Corrective Actions	[ ]	[ ]

The CNC should answer this question because this activity is typically carried out by a Department/Agency Component(s) and may not be an overall Department/Agency activity.

17. To what extent have the following NIMS components, terminology, principles and policies been incorporated into incident management plans and SOPs/SOGs: **(CNC)**

	Not Incorporated	Partially Incorporated	Fully Incorporated
Flexibility	[ ]	[ ]	[ ]
Scalability	[ ]	[ ]	[ ]
Standardization	[ ]	[ ]	[ ]
Interoperability & Compatibility	[ ]	[ ]	[ ]

The CNC should answer this question because this activity is typically carried out by a Department/Agency Component(s) and may not be an overall Department/Agency activity.

IMPLEMENTATION OBJECTIVE 8:

Promote the department/agency, non-governmental and private sector use of cooperative agreements (e.g. Mutual Aid Agreements, Memorandums of Understanding/Agreement, Letters of Agreement, and Interagency Agreements).

18. What actions have been taken to determine the level of participation by the department/agency in mutual aid: [Check all that apply.] **(CNC)**

	Yes	No	No Cooperative Agreement
Identified existing agreements within the department/agency	[ ]	[ ]	[ ]
If "No," explain: [ ]			
Identified existing agreements with other departments/agencies	[ ]	[ ]	[ ]
If "No," explain: [ ]			
Identified existing agreements between the department/agency and external stakeholders (contractors, grantees, and vendors)	[ ]	[ ]	[ ]
If "No," explain: [ ]			
Performed a gap analysis to determine areas of deficiency related to all cooperative agreements	[ ]	[ ]	[ ]
If "No," explain: [ ]			
Established a dialogue with stakeholders to reduce the gaps in cooperative agreements	[ ]	[ ]	[ ]
If "No," explain: [ ]			

Rationale for asking the question at the indicated level.

The CNC should answer this question because this activity is typically carried out by a Department/Agency Component(s) and may not be an overall Department/Agency activity.

- Which of the following impedes the department/agency's participation in cooperative agreements: [Check all that apply.]

  [ ] Plans
  [ ] Policy
  [ ] Training
  [ ] Organization
  [ ] Personnel
  [ ] Funding
  [ ] Other, explain: [   ]

IMPLEMENTATION OBJECTIVE 9:

Implement the following NIMS training to include appropriate personnel (as identified in the *Five-Year NIMS Training Plan*, released February 2008) and in accordance with their incident management responsibilities:

- **IS-700a *National Incident Management Systems, An Introduction***
- **IS-800b *National Response Framework, An Introduction***
- **ICS-100: *Introduction to the Incident Command System (ICS)***
- **ICS-200: *ICS for Single Resources and Initial Action Incidents***
- **ICS-300: *Intermediate ICS For Expanding Incidents***
- **ICS-400: *Advanced ICS***
- **ICS-402: *ICS for Executives and Senior Officials***

| | Rationale for asking the question at the indicated level. |

19. Does the department/agency coordinate its incident management training with the *NIMS Five-Year Training Plan?* **(CNC)**

    [ ] Yes
    [ ] No
- If "No," which of the following impedes coordination of the department/agency's incident management training with the NIMS National Standard Curriculum: [Check all that apply.]

    [ ] Plans
    [ ] Policy
    [ ] Training
    [ ] Organization
    [ ] Personnel
    [ ] Funding
    [ ] Other, explain: [   ]

The CNC should answer this question because this activity is typically carried out by a Department/Agency Component(s) and may not be an overall Department/Agency activity.

20. In the table below, indicate the number of department/agency personnel that have completed the following courses (out of the total number of people identified): [Gray boxes are not applicable.] **(CNC)**

	Entry-level personnel	First-line supervisors	Middle management	Executives	Personnel trained as ICS trainers
IS-700	[/]	[/]	[/]	[/]	[/]
IS-800	[/]	[/]	[/]	[/]	[/]
ICS-100	[/]	[/]	[/]	[/]	[/]
ICS-200	[/]	[/]	[/]	[/]	[/]
ICS-300	[/]	[/]	[/]	[/]	[/]
ICS-400	[/]	[/]	[/]	[/]	[/]
ICS-402				[/]	

The CNC should answer this question because this activity is typically carried out by a Department/Agency Component(s) and may not be an overall Department/Agency activity.

21. List and describe resources (e.g., Federal Training Facilities, Internet Training, Classroom Training) currently being used to provide NIMS training: **(CNC)**

- Which of the following impedes the use of resources to provide NIMS training: [Check all that apply.]

  [ ] Plans
  [ ] Policy
  [ ] Training
  [ ] Organization
  [ ] Personnel
  [ ] Funding
  [ ] Other, explain: [   ]

The CNC should answer this question because this activity is typically carried out by a Department/Agency Component(s) and may not be an overall Department/Agency activity.

	Rationale for asking the question at the indicated level.

IMPLEMENTATION OBJECTIVE 10:
 	
Incorporate NIMS into all applicable department/agency incident management exercises and evaluation programs (e.g., the Homeland Security Exercise and Evaluation Program (HSEEP).
 	
22. Does the department/agency incorporate NIMS in an exercise and evaluation program (e.g., the Homeland Security Exercise and Evaluation Program (HSEEP))? **(CNC)**
 	
    [ ] Yes
    [ ] No
 	
▪ If "No," which of the following impedes the use of NIMS in an exercise and evaluation program (e.g., the Homeland Security Exercise and Evaluation Program (HSEEP)): [Check all that apply.]
 	
    [ ] Plans
    [ ] Policy
    [ ] Personnel
    [ ] Funding
    [ ] Exercise
    [ ] Training
    [ ] Education
    [ ] Other, explain: [   ]
	The CNC should answer this question because this activity is typically carried out by a Department/Agency Component(s) and may not be an overall Department/Agency activity.

23. Which of the following types of applicable incident management exercises have incorporated NIMS/ICS: [Check all that apply.] **(CNC)**

Drills	Tabletop Exercises	Functional Exercises	Full-Scale Exercises	Other
[ ]	[ ]	[ ]	[ ]	[ ]

The CNC should answer this question because this activity is typically carried out by a Department/Agency Component(s) and may not be an overall Department/Agency activity.

- Which of the following impedes incorporating NIMS/ICS into all applicable incident management exercises: [Check all that apply.]

  [ ] Plans
  [ ] Policy
  [ ] Equipment
  [ ] Funding
  [ ] Training
  [ ] Education
  [ ] Other, explain: [   ]

IMPLEMENTATION OBJECTIVE 11: **Evaluate the implementation of NIMS in all department/agency incident management exercises to identify gaps in implementation.**	**Rationale for asking the question at the indicated level.**

24. Does the department/agency evaluate the implementation of NIMS in all incident management exercises? **(CNC)**
 	
[ ] Yes
[ ] No
 	
▪ If "No," explain: [   ]
 	
● Which of the following impedes the evaluation of NIMS implementation in all incident management exercises: [Check all that apply.]
 	
    [ ] Plans
    [ ] Policy
    [ ] Personnel
    [ ] Funding
    [ ] Education
    [ ] Training
    [ ] Other, explain: [   ]
	The CNC should answer this question because this activity is typically carried out by a Department/Agency Component(s) and may not be an overall Department/Agency activity.

IMPLEMENTATION OBJECTIVE 12: **Incorporate corrective actions into department/agency preparedness/response plans and procedures.**	Rationale for asking the question at the indicated level.

25. Does the department/agency incorporate corrective actions (e.g., after action reports, and/or lessons learned) in the following areas: [Check all that apply.] **(CNC)**
 	
[ ] Preparedness plans
[ ] Response plans
[ ] Response procedures
[ ] Recovery plans and procedures
[ ] None, explain: [   ]
 	
▪ Which of the following impedes incorporating corrective actions in preparedness/response plans and procedures: [Check all that apply.]
 	
  [ ] Plans
  [ ] Policy
  [ ] Personnel
  [ ] Funding
  [ ] Education
  [ ] Training
  [ ] Other, explain: [   ]
	The CNC should answer this question because this activity is typically carried out by a Department/Agency Component(s) and may not be an overall Department/Agency activity.

Communication and Information Management Metrics

	Rationale for asking the question at the indicated level.
IMPLEMENTATION OBJECTIVE #13: **Apply standardized and consistent terminology, including the use of plain language, in all department/agency communication protocols and/or plans for incident management and planned events.**	

26. Does the department/agency apply standardized and consistent terminology in all communication protocols and/or plans for incident management and planned events? **(CNC)**
 	
[ ] Yes
[ ] No
 	
• If "No," which of the following impedes the application of standardized and consistent terminology in all communication protocols and/or plans for incident management and pre-planned (recurring/special) events: [Check all that apply.]
 	
  [ ] Plans
  [ ] Policy
  [ ] Personnel
  [ ] Funding
  [ ] Training
  [ ] Exercise
  [ ] Education
  [ ] Other, explain: [   ]
	The CNC should answer this question because this activity is typically carried out by a Department/Agency Component(s) and may not be an overall Department/Agency activity.

27. Does the department/agency use plain language in all department/agency incident management communications for:

	Yes	No
Exercises	[ ]	[ ]
▪ If "No," explain: [	]	
Incidents	[ ]	[ ]
▪ If "No," explain: [	]	
Daily Operations	[ ]	[ ]
▪ If "No," explain: [	]	

The CNC should answer this question because this activity is typically carried out by a Department/Agency Component(s) and may not be an overall Department/Agency activity.

IMPLEMENTATION OBJECTIVE #14: **Develop systems, tools, and processes to ensure that incident managers at all levels share a common operating picture of an incident. (e.g. use of the Homeland Security Information Network.)**	Rationale for asking the question at the indicated level.
28. Does the department/agency have a system, tool, and/or process to share a common operating picture: **(CNC)**	*The CNC should answer this question because this activity is typically carried out by a Department/Agency Component(s) and may not be an overall Department/Agency activity.*

	Yes	No
System	[ ]	[ ]
▪ If "Yes," identify the system: [ ] ▪ If "No," explain: [ ]		
Tool	[ ]	[ ]
▪ If "Yes," identify the tool: [ ] ▪ If "No," explain: [ ]		
Process	[ ]	[ ]
▪ If "Yes," identify the process: [ ] ▪ If "No," explain: [ ]		

Resource Management Metrics

IMPLEMENTATION OBJECTIVE #15: **Develop a department/agency inventory of incident management assets and identify those assets that conform to NIMS Resource Typing definitions (maintained by National Integration Center).**	Rationale for asking the question at the indicated level.

29. Has the department/agency developed an inventory of its incident management assets? **(CNC)**
 	
   [ ] Yes
   [ ] No
 	
  ■ If "Yes," does the inventory of incident management assets conform to NIMS Resource Typing definitions maintained by FEMA's National Integration Center?
 	
     [ ] Yes
     [ ] No
 	
    ● If "No," explain: [   ]
 	
  ■ Which of the following impedes developing an incident management inventory that conforms to NIMS Resource Typing definitions: [Check all that apply.]
 	
     [ ] Plans
     [ ] Policy
     [ ] Personnel
     [ ] Equipment
     [ ] Training
     [ ] Funding
     [ ] Education
     [ ] Other, explain: [   ]
	The CNC should answer this question because this activity is typically carried out by a Department/Agency Component(s) and may not be an overall Department/Agency activity.

IMPLEMENTATION OBJECTIVE #16: **Utilize the response asset inventory for exercises, incident management, and planned events.**	Rationale for asking the question at the indicated level.
30. Does the department/agency utilize the response asset inventory for:	*The CNC should answer this question because this activity is typically carried out by a Department/Agency Component(s) and may not be an overall Department/Agency activity.*

	Yes	No
Exercises	[ ]	[ ]
▪ If "Yes," how?: [ ]		
▪ If "No," explain: [ ]		
Mutual Aid/ Assistance Requests	[ ]	[ ]
▪ If "Yes," how?: [ ]		
▪ If "No," explain: [ ]		
Planned Events	[ ]	[ ]
▪ If "Yes," how?: [ ]		
▪ If "No," explain: [ ]		

	Rationale for asking the question at the indicated level.
IMPLEMENTATION OBJECTIVE #17: **To the extent permissible by Federal law, ensure that relevant national standards to achieve equipment, communication, and data interoperability are incorporated into existing department/agency business practices and procedures.**	
31. To what extent are national standards incorporated into department/agency business practices and procedures for: **(CNC)** 		Not Incorporated	Partially Incorporated	Fully Incorporated
Equipment	[ ]	[ ]	[ ]
Communications	[ ]	[ ]	[ ]
Data	[ ]	[ ]	[ ] | - Which of the following impedes incorporating national standards into business practices and procedures: [Check all that apply.] [ ] Plans [ ] Policy [ ] Personnel [ ] Equipment [ ] Training [ ] Exercise [ ] Funding [ ] Education [ ] Other, explain: [ ]	*The CNC should answer this question because this activity is typically carried out by a Department/Agency Component(s) and may not be an overall Department/Agency activity.*

Command and Management Metrics

IMPLEMENTATION OBJECTIVE #18:

Manage all interagency emergency incidents and planned events in accordance with Incident Command System (ICS) organizational structures, doctrine, and procedures, as defined in the NIMS.

32. Does the department/agency manage all task-level, interagency emergency incidents and preplanned (recurring/special) events in accordance with ICS organizational structures, doctrine and procedures, as defined in the NIMS? **(CNC)**

[ ] Yes
[ ] No
[ ] Not Applicable

- If "No," which of the following impedes the management of all task-level, interagency emergency incidents and preplanned (recurring/special) events in accordance with ICS organizational structures, doctrine and procedures, as defined in the NIMS: [Check all that apply.]

  [ ] Plans
  [ ] Personnel
  [ ] Funding
  [ ] Education
  [ ] Training
  [ ] Exercise
  [ ] Other, explain: [   ]

Rationale for asking the question at the indicated level.
*The **CNC** should answer this question because this activity is typically carried out by a Department/Agency Component(s) and may not be an overall Department/Agency activity.*

	Rationale for asking the question at the indicated level.
IMPLEMENTATION OBJECTIVE #19: **Use ICS in department/agency Incident Action Plans (IAPs) and common communications plans.**	
33. Does the department/agency use IAPs, as prescribed in NIMS, during incident management? **(CNC)** [ ] Yes [ ] No [ ] Not Applicable ■ If "No," which of the following impedes the use of IAPs by the department/agency during incident management activities: [Check all that apply.] [ ] Plans [ ] Personnel [ ] Funding [ ] Education [ ] Training [ ] Exercise [ ] Other, explain: [ ]	*The CNC should answer this question because this activity is typically carried out by a Department/Agency Component(s) and may not be an overall Department/Agency activity.*
34. Does the department/agency use common communication plans, as prescribed in NIMS, during incident management? **(CNC)** [ ] Yes [ ] No [ ] Not Applicable ■ If "No," which of the following impedes the use of common communication plans by the department/agency during incident management activities: [Check all that apply.] [ ] Plans [ ] Personnel [ ] Funding [ ] Education [ ] Training [ ] Exercise [ ] Other, explain: [ ]	*The CNC should answer this question because this activity is typically carried out by a Department/Agency Component(s) and may not be an overall Department/Agency activity.*

35. Do the IAPs used by the department/agency incorporate the following ICS concepts: **(CNC)**

	Yes	No	
Designation of measurable objectives	[ ]	[ ]	*The CNC should answer this question because this activity is typically carried out by a Department/Agency Component(s) and may not be an overall Department/Agency activity.*
▪ If "No," explain: [ ]			
Designation of command staff positions	[ ]	[ ]	
▪ If "No," explain: [ ]			
Manageable span of control	[ ]	[ ]	
▪ If "No," explain: [ ]			
Clear chain of command	[ ]	[ ]	
▪ If "No," explain: [ ]			
Use of plain language	[ ]	[ ]	
▪ If "No," explain: [ ]			

36. Do the common communications plans used by the department/agency incorporate the following NIMS concepts: **(CNC)**

	Yes	No	
Use of communications equipment and facilities assigned to the incident	[ ]	[ ]	*The CNC should answer this question because this activity is typically carried out by a Department/Agency Component(s) and may not be an overall Department/Agency activity.*
▪ If "No," explain: [ ]			
Installation of and testing of all communications equipment	[ ]	[ ]	
▪ If "No," explain: [ ]			
Supervision and operation of the incident communications	[ ]	[ ]	
▪ If "No," explain: [ ]			
Distribution and recovery of communications equipment assigned to incident personnel	[ ]	[ ]	
▪ If "No," explain: [ ]			
Maintenance and repair of communications equipment on site	[ ]	[ ]	
▪ If "No," explain: [ ]			

IMPLEMENTATION OBJECTIVE #20: **Coordinate and support emergency incident and event management through Multiagency Coordination Systems (MACS).**			Rationale for asking the question at the indicated level.
37. Does the department/agency use Multiagency Coordination Systems for: **(CNC)**			
	Yes	No	
Preplanned (Recurring/Special) Events	[ ]	[ ]	
▪ If "Yes," explain how a MACS has been successfully used to manage preplanned events: [ ]			
Incident-specific Hazards	[ ]	[ ]	
▪ If "Yes," explain how a MACS has been successfully used to manage incident-specific hazards: [ ]			*The CNC should answer this question because this activity is typically carried out by a Department/Agency Component(s) and may not be an overall Department/Agency activity.*
No-notice Events	[ ]	[ ]	
▪ If "Yes," explain how a MACS has been successfully used to manage no-notice events: [ ]			
Specific Events	[ ]	[ ]	
▪ If "Yes," explain how a MACS has been successfully used to specific events: [ ]			
Coordinating with State/Territorial Emergency Operations Centers (EOCs)			
▪ If "Yes," explain how a MACS has been successfully used to communicate with State/Territorial Emergency Operations Centers (EOCs): [ ]			
Coordinating with Multiagency Coordination Entities			
▪ If "Yes," explain how a MACS has been successfully used to communicate with Multiagency Coordination Entities: [ ]			

- Which of the following impedes the department/agency from establishing a MACS: [Check all that apply.]

  [ ] Plans
  [ ] Policy
  [ ] Training
  [ ] Organization
  [ ] Personnel
  [ ] Funding
  [ ] Other impediments, explain: [   ]

38. Which of the following functions is coordinated by the department/agency's MACS: [Check all that apply.] **(CNC)** [ ] Situation assessment [ ] Critical resource acquisition and allocation [ ] Tribal/local, state/territory, and Federal disaster coordination [ ] Coordination with elected and appointed officials [ ] Coordination of summary information [ ] Incident priority determination [ ] Other functions coordinated by the department/agency's MACS, explain: [ ]	*The CNC should answer this question because this activity is typically carried out by a Department/Agency Component(s) and may not be an overall Department/Agency activity.*

	Rationale for asking the question at the indicated level.

IMPLEMENTATION OBJECTIVE #21:

Establish a Public Information system within the department/agency to include Joint Information System (JIS) and a Joint Information Center (JIC).

39. Has the department/agency's established Public Information to include a Joint Information System (JIS) and a Joint Information Center (JIC) as incidents dictate? **(CNC)**
 	
  [ ] Yes
  [ ] No
 	
  ▪ If "Yes," how many individuals are trained in using Publication Information [   ] out of a total of [   ]?
 	
  ▪ If "No," explain: [   ]
 	
    ▪ Which of the following impedes the establishment of Public Information to include a Joint Information System (JIS) and a Joint Information Center (JIC) as incidents dictate: [Check all that apply.]
 	
        [ ] Plans
        [ ] Personnel
        [ ] Funding
        [ ] Education
        [ ] Training
        [ ] Exercise
        [ ] Other, explain: [   ]
	The CNC should answer this question because this activity is typically carried out by a Department/Agency Component(s) and may not be an overall Department/Agency activity.

IMPLEMENTATION OBJECTIVE #22:

Ensure Public Information system can gather, verify, coordinate, and disseminate critical public affairs information during an incident.

		Rationale for asking the question at the indicated level.
40. During an incident/planned event can the department/agency public information system:		*The CNC should answer this question because this activity is typically carried out by a Department/Agency Component(s) and may not be an overall Department/Agency activity.*
	Yes No	
Gather information	[ ] [ ]	
Verify information	[ ] [ ]	
Coordinate information	[ ] [ ]	
Disseminate information	[ ] [ ]	

Appendix IV: Biological Incident Annex

Coordinating Agency	Cooperating Agencies
Department of Health and Human Services	Department of Agriculture
	Department of Commerce
	Department of Defense
	Department of Energy
	Department of Homeland Security
	Department of the Interior
	Department of Justice
	Department of Labor
	Department of State
	Department of Transportation
	Department of Veterans Affairs
	Environmental Protection Agency
	General Services Administration
	U.S. Agency for International Development
	U.S. Postal Service
	American Red Cross

Introduction

Purpose

The purpose of the Biological Incident Annex is to outline the actions, roles, and responsibilities associated with response to a human disease outbreak of known or unknown origin requiring Federal assistance. In this document, a biological incident includes naturally occurring biological diseases (communicable and noncommunicable) in humans as well as terrorist events. This definition also includes those biological agents found in the environment, or diagnosed in animals, that have the potential for transmission to humans (zoonosis). Incidents that are restricted to animal, plant, or food health or safety are reviewed in other annexes. Actions described in this annex take place with or without a Presidential Stafford Act declaration or a public health emergency declaration by the Secretary of Health and Human Services (HHS). This annex outlines biological incident response actions including threat assessment notification procedures, laboratory testing, joint investigative/ response procedures, and activities related to recovery.

Scope

The objectives of the Federal Government's response to a biological terrorism event or to a naturally occurring disease outbreak with a known or novel pathogen are to:

- Detect the event through disease surveillance and environmental monitoring.
- Identify and protect the population(s) at risk.
- Determine the source of the disease.
- Assess the public health, law enforcement, and international implications.
- Control and contain any possible epidemic (including providing guidance to State, tribal, territorial, and local public health authorities).
- Augment and surge public health and medical services.
- Identify the cause and prevent the recurrence of any potential resurgence, additional outbreaks, or further spread of disease.
- Assess the extent of residual biological contamination and conduct response, restoration, and recovery actions as necessary.
  - The unique attributes of this response require separate planning considerations that are tailored to specific health concerns and effects of the disease (e.g., terrorism versus natural outbreaks, communicable versus noncommunicable, etc.).
  - Specific operational guidelines, developed by respective organizations to address the unique aspects of a particular biological agent or planning consideration, will supplement this annex and are intended as guidance to assist Federal, State, tribal, territorial, and local public health and medical planners.

Special Considerations

Detection of a bioterrorism act against the civilian population may occur in several different ways and involve several different modalities:

An attack may be surreptitious, in which case the first evidence of dissemination of an agent may be the presentation of disease in humans or animals. This could manifest either in clinical case reports to domestic or international public health authorities or in unusual patterns of symptoms or encounters within domestic or international health surveillance systems.

A terrorist-induced infectious disease outbreak initially may be indistinguishable from a naturally occurring outbreak; moreover, depending upon the particular agent and associated symptoms, several days could pass before public health and medical authorities even suspect that terrorism may be the cause. In such a case, criminal intent may not be apparent until some time after illnesses are recognized.

Environmental surveillance systems, such as the BioWatch system, may detect the presence of a biological agent in the environment and trigger directed environmental sampling and intensified clinical surveillance to rule out or confirm an incident. If confirmed, the utilization of environmental surveillance systems may allow for mobilization of a public health, medical, and law enforcement response in advance of the appearance of the first clinical cases or a rapid response after the first clinical cases are identified.

Other cooperating departments and agencies listed in this annex may detect acts of bioterrorism or biological incidents through their normal operations and surveillance efforts. Should this occur, notifications should be made according to approved interagency response protocols, consistent with the health and law enforcement assessment process described in this annex.

Policies

This annex supports policies and procedures outlined in the *National Response Framework*, Emergency Support Function (ESF) #8—Public Health and Medical Services Annex, ESF #10 – Oil and Hazardous Materials Response Annex, ESF #11—Agriculture and Natural Resources Annex, ESF #15—External Affairs Annex, the Terrorism Incident Law Enforcement and Investigation Annex, and the International Coordination Support Annex.

HHS serves as the Federal Government's primary agency for the public health and medical preparation and planning for and response to a biological terrorism attack or naturally occurring outbreak that results from either a known or novel pathogen, including an emerging infectious disease.

The Department of Agriculture (USDA) serves as the Government's primary agency for outbreaks and/or attacks that may occur in animals used in the commercial production of food. USDA may also serve as the Government's primary agency for attacks on food processing/slaughtering facilities under its regulatory purview. In the event of a food or animal event, HHS may provide additional public health and veterinary epidemiological assistance to USDA. Wildlife events will be placed under the purview of the Department of the Interior (DOI), while those involving marine animals will be managed and monitored by the Department of Commerce.

The Secretary of Homeland Security is the principal Federal official for domestic incident management. Pursuant to the Homeland Security Act of 2002, the Secretary is responsible for coordinating Federal operations within the United States to prepare for, respond to, and recover from terrorist attacks, major disasters, and other emergencies, including biological incidents.

State, tribal, territorial, and local governments are primarily responsible for detecting and responding to disease outbreaks and implementing measures to minimize the health, social, and economic consequences of such an outbreak.

The Attorney General has lead responsibility for criminal investigations of terrorist acts or terrorist threats by individuals or groups inside the United States, or directed at U.S. citizens or institutions abroad. Generally acting through the Federal Bureau of Investigation (FBI), the Attorney General, in cooperation with other Federal departments and agencies engaged in activities to protect our national security, shall also coordinate the activities of the other members of the law enforcement community to detect, prevent, preempt, and disrupt terrorist attacks against the United States. If any agency or government entity becomes aware of an overt threat involving biological agents or indications that instances of disease may not be the result of natural causes, the Department of Justice (DOJ) must be notified through the FBI's Weapons of Mass Destruction Operations Unit (WMDOU).

If the threat is deemed credible by the FBI in coordination with HHS or USDA, the FBI, in turn, immediately notifies the National Operations Center (NOC) and the National Counterterrorism Center (NCTC). The Laboratory Response Network (LRN) is used to test samples for the presence of biological threat agents. Any agency or organization that identifies an unusual or suspicious test result should contact the FBI to ensure coordination of appropriate testing at an LRN laboratory. Decisions on where to perform additional tests on samples are made by the FBI, in coordination with HHS or USDA. All relevant threat and public health assessments should be provided to the NOC. Test results on human samples from non-LRN facilities are considered a "first pass" or "screening" test.

Once notified of a credible threat or disease outbreak, HHS convenes a meeting of ESF #8 partners to assess the situation and determine appropriate public health and medical actions. The Department of Homeland Security (DHS) coordinates overall nonmedical support and response actions across all Federal departments and agencies. HHS leads public health and medical emergency response efforts across all Federal departments and agencies.

The FBI coordinates the investigation of criminal activities if such activities are suspected.

HHS provides guidance to State, tribal, territorial, and local authorities and collaborates closely with the FBI in the proper handling of any materials that may have evidentiary implications (e.g., LRN samples, etc.) associated with disease outbreaks suspected of being terrorist or criminal in nature. If evidentiary materials are shared with or procured from foreign governments, HHS and the FBI will coordinate and share information with the Department of State (DOS) as appropriate.

HHS will be supported by other Federal agencies as appropriate during the various states of a biological incident response in the preparation, planning, and/or response processes and will perform the roles described in this annex in coordination with DHS and State partners. If the incident response progresses such that it requires multiagency participation, DHS will serve as the Incident Coordinator. HHS will serve as the coordinating agency for public health issues as will other agencies for their area of technical expertise.

If there is potential for environmental contamination, HHS collaborates with the Environmental Protection Agency (EPA) in developing and implementing sampling strategies and sharing results.

In the event of an outbreak of an agriculturally significant zoonotic disease or human foodborne pathogen, HHS collaborates with USDA during the preparation, planning, and/or response processes.

Given the dynamic nature of a biological incident, HHS, in collaboration with other departments and agencies, determines the thresholds for a comprehensive Federal Government public health and medical response. These thresholds are based on specific event information rather than predetermined risk levels.

Federal public announcements, statements, or press releases related to a threat or actual bioterrorism event will be coordinated with the DHS Office of Public Affairs consistent with ESF #15, if activated.

Planning Assumptions

In a biological incident, Federal, State, tribal, territorial, and local officials require a highly coordinated response to public health and medical emergencies. The biological incident also may affect other countries, or be of international concern, and therefore involve extensive coordination with DOS and the international health community (e.g., notification to the World Health Organization (WHO) and other international health organizations under the International Health Regulations (IHR)).

Disease transmission may occur from direct contact with an infected individual or animal, an environmental reservoir (includes contaminated surface or atmospheric dispersion), an insect vector, or contaminated food and water. Indirect contact transmission may also occur, where contaminated inanimate objects (fomites) serve as the vehicle for transmission of the agent. Hands may also play a role in indirect transmission.

A biological incident may be distributed across multiple jurisdictions simultaneously. This could require the simultaneous management of multiple "incident sites" from national and regional headquarters locations in coordination with multiple State, tribal, territorial, and local jurisdictions.

A response to contagious and noncontagious public health emergencies may require different planning assumptions or factors.

The introduction of biological agents, both natural and deliberate, is often first detected through clinical or hospital presentation. However, there are other methods of detection, including environmental surveillance technologies such as BioWatch, and medical and syndromic surveillance systems. Early detection of biological agents offers an opportunity to take proactive measures to mitigate the consequences of disease outbreak. Routine fish and wildlife health and disease surveillance, including investigation of wildlife mortality events conducted on public lands and in public laboratories, provides the opportunity for early detection of biological agents and acts of bioterrorism. Animal health surveillance in the agriculture sector provides similar opportunities.

No single entity possesses the authority, expertise, and resources to act unilaterally on the many complex issues that may arise in response to a nonroutine disease outbreak and loss of containment affecting a multijurisdictional area. The national response requires close coordination between numerous agencies at all levels of government and with the private sector.

The Federal Government supports affected State, tribal, territorial, and local health jurisdictions as requested or required. The response by HHS and other Federal agencies is flexible and adapts as necessary as the outbreak evolves.

The LRN provides analytical support to inform public health assessment of the potential for human illness associated with exposure and the scope of this kind of risk. The LRN also provides for definitive testing of both environmental and clinical samples, as well as limited supporting analysis of food samples that may be implicated as part of epidemiological investigations associated with incident response to cases of human illness. Early HHS, FBI, USDA, EPA, and DHS coordination enhances the likelihood of successful preventive and investigative activities necessary to neutralize threats and attribute the source of the outbreak. (The Food Emergency Response Network (FERN) is a complementary system that integrates the Nation's food-testing laboratories at the local, State, and Federal levels into a network that is able to respond to emergencies involving biological, chemical, or radiological contamination of food. The FERN structure is organized to ensure Federal and State interagency participation and cooperation in the formation, development, and operation of the network.)

Response to disease outbreaks suspected of being deliberate in origin requires consideration of special law enforcement and homeland security requirements as well as international legal obligations and requirements.

An investigation into intentional biological threats or incidents will likely require the initiation of a joint criminal and epidemiological investigation. The FBI would coordinate criminal investigative activities with appropriate State/local and Federal partner agencies, such as DHS, HHS, and USDA.

Concept of Operations

Biological Agent Response

The key elements of an effective biological response include (in nonsequential order):

- Rapid detection of the outbreak or introduction of a biological agent into the environment.
- Rapid dissemination of key safety information, appropriate personal protective equipment, and necessary medical precautions.
- Swift agent identification and confirmation.
- Identification of the population at risk (to include animals, marine life, and plants).
- Determination of how the agent is transmitted, including an assessment of the efficiency of transmission.
- Determination of susceptibility to prophylaxis and treatment.
- Definition of the public health and medical services, human services, and mental health implications.
- Control and containment of the epidemic when possible, and use of mitigation strategies when containment is not possible (e.g., in the event of an influenza pandemic).
- Identification of the law enforcement implications/assessment of the threat.
- Augmentation and surging of local health and medical resources.
- Protection of the population through appropriate public health and medical actions.
- Dissemination of information to enlist public support and provide risk communication assistance to responsible authorities.

- Assessment of environmental contamination and cleanup/decontamination/proper disposal of bioagents that persist in the environment, and provision of consultation on the safety of drinking water and food products that may be derived from directly or environmentally exposed animals, crops, plants and trees, or marine life.
- Tracking and preventing secondary or additional disease outbreak.
- Administration of countermeasures when appropriate.

Primary Federal functions include supporting State, tribal, territorial, and local public health and medical capacities according to the policies and procedures detailed in the *National Response Framework* and its annexes (e.g., ESF #8).

Outbreak Detection

Determination of a Disease Outbreak

The initial indication of a biological incident may be the recognition by public health and medical authorities that a significantly increased number of people are becoming ill and presenting to local healthcare providers.

One tool to support this process is the National Biosurveillance Integration System (NBIS). NBIS leverages the individual capabilities of multiple surveillance systems by integrating and analyzing domestic and international surveillance and monitoring data collected from human health, animal health, plant health, and food and water monitoring systems. This integrated cross-domain analysis allows for enhanced situational awareness and potentially reduced detection time, thus enabling more rapid and effective biological incident response decisionmaking.

As a result of the nature in which a disease outbreak may be recognized, critical decision-making support requires integrated surveillance information, identification of the causative biological agent, a determination of whether the observations are related to a naturally occurring or deliberate outbreak, and identification of the population(s) at risk.

Laboratory Confirmation

During the evaluation of a suspected disease outbreak, laboratory samples are distributed to appropriate laboratories. During a suspected terrorist incident, sample information is provided to the FBI for investigative use and to public health and emergency response authorities for epidemiological use and agent characterization to facilitate and ensure timely public health and medical interventions, as well as environmental cleanup. If the incident begins as an epidemic of unknown origin detected through Federal, State, tribal, territorial, or local health surveillance systems or networks, laboratory analysis is initiated through the routine public health or animal health laboratory systems.

Identification (Analysis and Confirmation)

The samples collected and the analyses conducted must be sufficient to characterize the causative agent of the outbreak. LRN and FERN laboratories fulfill the Federal responsibility for rapid analysis of biological agents. In a suspected terrorism incident, sample collection activities and testing are coordinated with the FBI and LRN member(s).

Suspicious Substances

Since there is no definitive/reliable field test for biological agents of concern, all potential bioterrorism samples are transported to an LRN laboratory, where expert analysis is conducted using established Federal protocols/reagents. A major component of this process is to establish and maintain the law enforcement chain of custody and arrange for transport.

The following actions occur if a positive result is obtained by an LRN on an environmental sample submitted by the FBI or other designated law enforcement personnel:

- The LRN immediately notifies the local FBI of the positive test result and informs the appropriate public health officials.
- The local FBI Field Office makes local notifications and contacts the FBI Headquarters WMDOU.
- FBI Headquarters convenes an initial threat assessment conference call with the local FBI, HHS, and appropriate Federal, State, tribal, territorial, and local response officials to review the results, assess the preliminary information and test results, and arrange for additional testing.
- FBI Headquarters immediately notifies DHS of the situation. Situational updates will be provided, as appropriate.
- Original samples may be sent to HHS/Centers for Disease Control and Prevention for confirmation of LRN analyses. As appropriate, the FBI will direct additional forensic examination of biological materials and/or evidence.
- HHS provides guidance on protective measures such as prophylaxis, treatment, continued facility operation, and use of personal protective equipment.
- HHS, EPA, and cooperating agencies support the determination of the contaminated area. EPA will provide data to support the determination of the contaminated area and to assist with decisions regarding whether to shelter-in-place. EPA will also play a role in the decontamination of facilities and outdoor areas.

Notification

Any disease outbreak suspected or identified by an agency within HHS or through a Federal, State, tribal, territorial, or local public health partner as having public health implications is brought to the immediate attention of HHS (as detailed in the ESF #8 Annex), in addition to the notification requirements contained in the *National Response Framework*.

Any potentially significant biological agent, disease outbreak, or suspected bioterrorism act affecting or involving animals, plant health, or wildlife should involve notifications to USDA (animals and plant health) and DOI (wildlife).

Following these initial notifications, the procedures detailed in the ESF #8 Annex are followed. Instances of disease that raise the "index of suspicion" of terrorist or criminal involvement, as determined by HHS or USDA (for animal and plant diseases), are reported to FBI Headquarters. In these instances, FBI Headquarters, in conjunction with HHS and/or USDA, examines available law enforcement and intelligence information, as well as the technical characteristics and epidemiology of the disease, to determine if there is a possibility of criminal intent. If the FBI, in conjunction with HHS or USDA, determines that the information represents a potential credible terrorist threat, the FBI communicates the situation immediately to the NCTC and NOC, which notifies the White House, as appropriate. If warranted, the FBI, HHS, and/or USDA and respective State, tribal, territorial, and/or local health officials will conduct a joint law enforcement and epidemiological investigation to determine the causative agent of the disease outbreak, the extent of the threat to public health and public safety, and the individual(s) responsible.

In the event of an environmental detection of a biological threat agent above established agency-specific thresholds, the responsible agency should contact HHS, the FBI, and the NOC within 2 hours of laboratory confirmation. The FBI and HHS, in conjunction with DHS, will convene an initial threat assessment conference call with appropriate Federal, State, tribal, territorial, and local officials to examine the potential threat and public health risk posed by the detection. Coordination of assessment and response activities will involve officials from the impacted State, tribal, territorial, and local jurisdiction(s).

Activation

Once notified of a threat or disease outbreak that requires or potentially requires significant Federal public health and medical assistance, HHS requests activation of ESF #8 from FEMA and convenes a meeting of its internal components and the ESF #8 partner organizations to assess the situation and determine the appropriate public health and medical actions. DHS coordinates all nonmedical support, discussions, and response actions.

The immediate task following any notification is to identify the affected and vulnerable population and the geographic scope of the incident. The initial public health and medical response includes some or all of the following actions:

- Targeted epidemiological investigation (e.g., contact tracing).
- Dissemination of key safety information and necessary medical precautions.
- Intensified surveillance within healthcare settings for patients with certain clinical signs and symptoms.
- Intensified collection and review of potentially related information (e.g., contacts with nurse call lines, laboratory test orders, school absences, over-the-counter pharmacy sales, unusual increase in sick animals, wildlife deaths, decreased commercial fish yields).
- Organization and potential deployment of Federal public health and medical response assets (in conjunction with State, tribal, territorial, and local officials) to include personnel, medical and veterinary supplies, and materiel (e.g., the Strategic National Stockpile (SNS) and the National Veterinary Stockpile (NVS)).

If there is suspicion that the outbreak may be deliberate, the FBI may establish a Joint Operations Center (JOC), which may be integrated into the Joint Field Office structure, if established, to coordinate investigative and intelligence activities among Federal, State, tribal, territorial, and local authorities. Within the JOC structure locally, and the FBI's Strategic Information and Operations Center in Washington, DC, responsible public health officials would be integrated into the established structures to coordinate the interaction between law enforcement and public health investigations.

Actions

Controlling the Epidemic

The following steps are required to contain and control an epidemic affecting large populations:

HHS assists State, tribal, territorial, and local public health and medical authorities with epidemic surveillance and coordination.

HHS assesses the need for increased surveillance in State, tribal, territorial, and local entities not initially involved in the outbreak and notifies the appropriate State, tribal, territorial, and local public health officials with surveillance recommendations should increased surveillance in these localities be needed.

DHS coordinates with HHS and State, tribal, territorial, and local officials on the messages released to the public to ensure that communications are timely, consistent, accurate, and actionable. Messages should address anxieties, alleviate any unwarranted concerns or distress, and enlist cooperation with necessary control measures. Public health and medical messages to the public should be communicated by a recognized health authority (e.g., the U.S. Surgeon General). (See the Public Affairs Support Annex.)

Consistent with the IHR, if the outbreak first arises within the United States, HHS, in coordination with DOS, immediately notifies and coordinates with appropriate international health agencies. Given the nature of many disease outbreaks, this notification and coordination may have occurred earlier in the process according to internal operating procedures. HHS advises the NOC when notifications are made to international health agencies.

The public health system, starting at the local level, is required to initiate appropriate protective and responsive measures for the affected population, including first responders and other workers engaged in incident-related activities. These measures may include mass vaccination or prophylaxis for populations at risk and populations not already exposed, but who are at risk of exposure from secondary transmission or the environment.

HHS evaluates the incident with its partner organizations and makes recommendations to the appropriate public health and medical authorities regarding the need for isolation, quarantine, or shelter-in-place to prevent the spread of disease.

The Governor of an affected State or territory implements isolation and/or social-distancing requirements using State/local legal authorities. The tribal leader of a recognized tribe may also order a curfew, isolation, social distancing, and quarantine under tribal legal authorities. In order to prevent the import or interstate spread of disease, HHS may take appropriate Federal actions using the authorities granted by title 42 of the U.S. Code, 42 CFR parts 70 and 71, and 21 CFR part 1240. These measures may include State, tribal, territorial, and local assistance with the implementation and enforcement of isolation and/or quarantine actions if Federal authorities are invoked.

Where the source of the disease outbreak has been identified as originating outside the United States, whether the result of terrorism or a natural outbreak, HHS works in a coordinated effort with DHS and other supporting agencies to identify and isolate persons, cargo, mail, or conveyances entering the United States that may be contaminated.

The scope of the disease outbreak may require mass isolation or quarantine of affected or potentially affected persons. Depending on the type of event, food, animals, and other agricultural products may need to be quarantined to prevent further spread of disease. In addition, livestock or poultry may need to be vaccinated or depopulated, and the movement of animals and equipment on and off affected premises may be restricted. In this instance HHS and USDA will work with State, tribal, territorial, and local health and legal authorities to recommend the most feasible, effective, and legally enforceable methods of isolation and quarantine. If interstate travel restrictions, including restrictions on arriving international travelers, are determined to be necessary, HHS will work closely with DOS, DHS, the Department of Transportation, and State, tribal, territorial, and local authorities to implement any recommended measures. In the event that foreign nationals are subject to isolation and/or quarantine, HHS will work through DOS to notify affected foreign governments.

Decontamination

For certain types of biological incidents (e.g., anthrax), it may be necessary to assess the extent of contamination and decontaminate victims, responders, animals, equipment, transportation conveyances, buildings, critical infrastructure, and large outdoor areas. Such decontamination and related activities take place consistent with the roles and responsibilities, resources and capabilities, and procedures contained in the ESF #8, ESF #10, ESF #11, and ESF #14 Long-Term Community Recovery Annexes, the Terrorism Incident Law Enforcement and Investigation Annex, and the Catastrophic Incident Annex. (Note: Chemicals used for biological decontamination (e.g., for inactivating highly infectious biological agents such as *Bacillus anthracis* spores) must be registered for that purpose by EPA under the Federal Insecticide, Fungicide, and Rodenticide Act. If, during an emergency, a response entity wants to use a chemical that has not been registered for inactivating the specific biological agent(s) of concern, a request for an emergency exemption from registration must be submitted to and granted by EPA.)

Special Issues
International Notification/Implications

A biological incident may involve internationally prescribed reportable diseases. In addition to case reporting, biological incidents with global public health significance must also be reported to international public health authorities. A biological incident may also have implications under the Biological Weapons Convention if it can be attributed to actions of a foreign party; DOS would manage the diplomatic aspects of any such case.

Per the IHR, once a positive determination is made of a biological incident determined to be of sufficient concern and to be a "public health event of international consequence," HHS, working with DOS and DHS, notifies WHO through the appropriate regional office, the Pan American Health Organization. HHS, in coordination with DOS, notifies other international health agencies as appropriate.

Allocation and Rationing

If critical resources for protecting human life are insufficient to meet all domestic needs, the Secretary of Health and Human Services makes recommendations to the Secretary of Homeland Security regarding the allocation of scarce Federal public health and medical resources.

Responsibilities

The procedures in this annex are built on the core coordinating structures of the *National Response Framework*. The specific responsibilities of each department and agency are described in the respective ESF and Incident Annexes.

Source: Federal Emergency Management Agency, National Response Framework, https://www.fema.gov/pdf/emergency/nrf/nrf_BiologicalIncidentAnnex.pdf.

Appendix V: CDC Reporting Form for Loss, Release, or Theft of Agents or Toxins

INCIDENT FORM TO REPORT POTENTIAL THEFT, LOSS, RELEASE, OR OCCUPATIONAL EXPOSURE (APHIS/CDC FORM 3)

FORM APPROVED
OMB NO.0579-0213
OMB NO. 0920-0576
EXP DATE 12/31/2018

INSTRUCTIONS

Detailed instructions are available at http://www.selectagents.gov/form3.html. **Answer all items completely and type or print in ink. This report must be signed and submitted to either APHIS or CDC:**

Animal and Plant Health Inspection Service
Agriculture Select Agent Services
4700 River Road Unit 2, Mailstop 22, Cubicle 1A07
Riverdale, MD 20737
FAX: (301) 734-3652
E-mail: AgSAS@aphis.usda.gov

Centers for Disease Control and Prevention
Division of Select Agents and Toxins
1600 Clifton Road NE, Mailstop A-46
Atlanta, GA 30329
FAX: (404) 471-8375
E-mail: form3@cdc.gov

Accession Number:

(For Program Use ONLY)

Submit completed form only once by either e-mail, fax, or mail

SECTION 1 – TO BE COMPLETED BY ALL ENTITIES		
1. Date of Incident:	2. Date of Immediate Notification:	3. Type of Immediate Notification: ☐ E-mail ☐ Fax ☐ Telephone
4. Name of Entity (entities registered with CDC or APHIS) or Name of Hospital or Laboratory (non-registered entities):		5. Entity Registration Number (For select agent registered entities only):
6. Physical Address:	7. City:	8. State: 9. Zip Code:
10. Responsible Official (registered) or Name of Laboratory Supervisor (non-registered):		
11. Telephone #:	12. Fax #:	13. E-mail address:

14a: Type of Incident:

☐ Theft ☐ Loss ☐ Release

☐ Unintended Animal Infection ☐ Unintended Plant Agent Release

☐ Other

14b: Transfer:

☐ Transfer incident (complete Sections 1 and 2 and Appendix B)

15. Did the release result in a potential exposure?

☐ No ☐ Yes ☐ N/A (If Yes, explain in Blocks 28 or 30)

Did the release result in a laboratory-acquired infection?

☐ No ☐ Yes ☐ N/A (If Yes, explain in Blocks 28 or 30)

If yes, has medical surveillance been initiated?

☐ No ☐ Yes ☐ N/A (If Yes, explain in Blocks 28 or 30)

16. Time incident occurred:	17. Location of incident (building and room #):	18. Location of incident within room (e.g., freezer, incubator, centrifuge):
19. Biosafety level: ☐ BSL2 ☐ BSL3 ☐ BSL4 ☐ ABSL2 ☐ ABSL3 ☐ ABSL4 ☐ PPQ Agent ☐ BSL3Ag	20. Date of last inventory (for reporting loss only):	21. Name of Principal Investigator:

SECTION 2 – TO BE COMPLETED BY ALL ENTITIES		
22. Name of Select Agent or Toxin	23. Characterization of Agent (e. g., strain, ATCC #)	24. Quantity / Amount
A		
B		
C		

25. Provide a detailed summary of events including a timeline of what occurred. Whenever possible, conduct a risk assessment of the event and determine if the root cause can be identified. State specifically what personal protective equipment was worn and what, if any, medical surveillance was provided or planned. If incident involves a non-human primate, please state species. For discovery of select agents and toxins in unregistered locations, include your entity's plan of action to assure no future discoveries, how discovered agents were found and disposition of the discovered agents, inventory reconciliation and assurance that the discovered material was safeguarded against unauthorized access, theft, loss, or release.

Block 25. Continued: (Use Appendix A for continuation, if necessary)

SECTION 3 – TO BE COMPLETED BY ALL ENTITIES ONLY FOR RELEASE OF
SELECT AGENTS AND TOXINS OR OCCUPATIONAL EXPOSURE

26. An internal review of laboratory procedures and policies has been initiated to lessen the likelihood of recurrences of theft, loss or release of select agents and toxins at this entity.

☐ No   ☐ Yes   If yes, please provide additional details.

27. What were the hazards posed to humans by the extent of the release or occupational exposure?

28. What is the estimated extent of the release or exposure in relation to the proximity of susceptible humans, animals, and plants?

29. Provide a brief summary of how the laboratory and work surfaces were decontaminated after the release.

30. In select agents and toxins posing a risk to humans, please state how many laboratorians were potentially exposed and provide a brief summary of the medical surveillance provided (do not provide names or confidential information).

Certification: I hereby certify that the information contained on this form is true and correct to the best of my knowledge. I understand that if I knowingly provide a false statement on any part of this form, or its attachments, I may be subject to criminal fines and/or imprisonment. I further understand that violations of the select agent regulations may result in civil or criminal penalties, including imprisonment. 7 CFR 331, 9 CFR 121, 42 CFR 73.

Signature of Respondent: _____   Title: _____

Typed or printed name of Respondent: _____   Date: _____

APPENDIX A
ADDITIONAL SHEET FOR CONTINUATION OF INFORMATION

Continue Form 3 comments here. State which block from the Form 3 the continuation is from.
(Example: The following statement is a continuation of block 25:):

☐ Continue on next page

APPENDIX A
ADDITIONAL SHEET FOR CONTINUATION OF INFORMATION

APPENDIX B	
IF THE INCIDENT OCCURRED DURING TRANSFER, COMPLETE SECTIONS 1 AND 2 OF FORM 3 AND PROVIDE THE FOLLOWING INFORMATION (INCLUDE A COPY OF THE RELEVANT APHIS/CDC FORM 2)	
1. Transfer authorization number from APHIS/CDC Form 2:	2. Date Shipped:
3. Name of Carrier:	4. Airway bill number, bill of lading number, tracking number:

5. Package Description (size, shape, description of packaging including number and type of inner packages; attach additional sheets as necessary):

6. Package with select agents and toxins received by requestor: ☐ No ☐ Yes If yes, date of receipt:	7. Package with select agents and toxins appears to have been opened: ☐ No ☐ Yes If yes, include explanation in box 5 above.
8. Sender was contacted regarding incident: ☐ No ☐ Yes	9. Carrier/courier was contacted regarding incident: ☐ No ☐ Yes

Certification: I hereby certify that the information contained on this form is true and correct to the best of my knowledge. I understand that if I knowingly provide a false statement on any part of this form, or its attachments, I may be subject to criminal fines and/or imprisonment. I further understand that violations of the select agent regulations may result in civil or criminal penalties, including imprisonment. 7 CFR 331, 9 CFR 121, 42 CFR 73.

Signature of Respondent: _____   Title: _____

Typed or printed name of Respondent: _____   Date: _____

Public reporting burden: Public reporting burden of providing this information is estimated to average 1 hour per response, including the time for reviewing instructions, searching existing data sources, gathering and maintaining the data needed, and completing and reviewing the collection of information. An agency may not conduct or sponsor, and a person is not required to respond to a collection of information unless it displays a currently valid OMB control number. Send comments regarding this burden estimate or any other aspect of this collection of information, including suggestions for reducing this burden to CDC/ATSDR Reports Clearance Officer; 1600 Clifton Road NE, MS D74, Atlanta, Georgia 30329; ATTN: PRA (0920-0576).

Index